Ludovic Piette: *Jour de fête à Pontoise/Conseil Général du Val d'Oise*

"... a village that affected him as a thing of whiteness, blueness and crookedness, set in coppery green, and that had the river flowing behind or before it - one couldn't say which ... Such a river sets one afloat almost before one can take up oars ... "

Henry James
The Ambassadors (1903)

Travel Publications

38 Clarendon Road – WATFORD Herts WD1 1 SX - U.K.
☎ (01923) 415 000
www.michelin-travel.com
TheGreenGuide-uk@uk.michelin.com

Manufacture française des pneumatiques Michelin
Société en commandite par actions au capital de 2 000 000 000 de francs
Place des Carmes-Déchaux – 63 Clermont-Ferrand (France)
R.C.S. Clermont-Fd B 855 200 507

No part of this publication may be reproduced in any form
without the prior permission of the publisher.

© Michelin et Cie, Propriétaires-éditeurs, 2001

Dépôt légal mai 2001 – ISBN 2-06-000227-3 – ISSN 0763-1383
Printed in France 04-01/4.1

Typesetting: NORD COMPO, Villeneuve d'Ascq
Printing and binding: I.F.C., Saint-Germain-du-Puy

Cover design: Carré Noir, Paris 17ᵉ arr.

THE GREEN GUIDE:
The Spirit of Discovery

*The exhilaration of new horizons,
the fun of seeing the world,
the excitement of discovery: this is
what we seek to share with you.
To help you make the most of your
travel experience, we offer first-hand
knowledge and turn a discerning eye
on places to visit.
This wealth of information gives
you the expertise to plan your own
enriching adventure. With THE
GREEN GUIDE showing you the way,
you can explore new destinations
with confidence or rediscover old
ones.
Leisure time spent with THE GREEN
GUIDE is also a time for refreshing
your spirit, enjoying yourself, and
taking advantage of our selection
of fine restaurants, hotels and other
places for relaxing.
So turn the page and open a window
on the world. Join THE GREEN
GUIDE in the spirit of discovery.*

Contents

Nave of the Basilica, St-Denis

R. Mazin/DIAF

Carillon bells, Douai

P. Cheuva/DIAF

4

Maps and plans

Wedding dish

H. Gyssels/DIAF

Temple of Love in the gardens of Versailles

R. Mazin/DIAF

Michelin maps

Michelin products are complementary: for each of the sites listed in The Green Guide, map references are indicated which help you find your location on our range of maps. The image below shows the maps to use for each geographic area covered in this guide. To travel the roads in this region, you may use any of the following:

● the **regional maps** on a scale of 1:200 000 nos 236, 237 and 241, which cover the main roads and secondary roads, and include indications for finding tourist attractions.

● the **detailed maps** are based on the regional map data, but with a reduced format (about half a region), which makes them easier to consult and fold. For the Île-de-France, Flandre, Picardie and Artois, use maps 51, 52, 53, 55, 56, 60 and 61.

● the **departmental maps** (on a scale of 1:150 000, an enlargement of the 1:200 000 maps) are very easy to read, and make it easy to travel on all of the roads in the following departments: Nord (4059), Oise (4060) and Pas-de-Calais (6062).They come with a complete index of place names and include a plan of the towns which serve as administrative seats (préfectures).

● the **local maps** which are useful in the Paris region include maps 101 and 106 (Île de France) and the maps of suburban Paris, 18, 20, 22 and 24.

And remember to travel with the latest edition of the **map of France no 989** (1:1 000 000), which gives an overall view of the region of Normandy, and the main access roads which connect it to the rest of France. Also available in atlas format: spiral bound, hard back, and the new mini-atlas – perfect for your glove compartment.

Michelin is pleased to offer a route-planning service on the Internet: **www.michelin-travel.com**. Choose the shortest route, a route without tolls, or the Michelin recommended route to your destination; information from The Red Guide and The Green Guide. *Bon voyage!*

Using
this guide

- The **summary maps** on the following pages are designed to assist you in planning your trip: the **Map of principal sights** identifies major sights and attractions, the **Map of regional driving** tours defines selected itineraries.

- We recommend that you read the **Introduction** before setting out on your trip. The background information it contains on history, the arts and traditional culture will prove most instructive and make your visit more meaningful.

- The main towns and attractions are presented in alphabetical order in the **Sights** section. In order to ensure quick, easy identification, original place names have been used throughout the guide. The clock symbol ⊙, placed after monuments or other sights, refers to the **Admission times and charges** section at the end of the guide.

- The **Practical information** section offers useful addresses for planning your trip, seeking accommodation, enjoying outdoor activities and more. Consult this section for the opening hours and admission prices for monuments, museums and other tourist attractions; festival and carnival dates; suggestions for thematic tours on scenic railways and through nature reserves etc.

- We have selected **hotels and restaurants**, and other places for **entertainment** in many of the towns in this guide. Turn to the pages bordered in blue.

- The **Index** lists attractions, famous people and events, and other subjects covered in the guide.

Let us hear from you. We are interested in your reaction to our guide, in any ideas you have to offer or good addresses you would like to share. Send your comments to Michelin Travel Publications, 38 Clarendon Road, Watford, Herts WD 1 1SX, U.K. or by e-mail to TheGreenGuide-uk@uk.michelin.com.

Versailles gardens

B. Kaufmann/MICHELIN

Key

Selected monuments and sights

⊚ ⇒   Tour - Departure point

🏛 ⚲   Catholic church

🏛 ⚲   Protestant church, other temple

✡ ✉ 🕌   Synagogue - Mosque

▰   Building

■   Statue, small building

⚲   Calvary, wayside cross

◎   Fountain

●━━■►   Rampart - Tower - Gate

⋈   Château, castle, historic house

∴   Ruins

⌣   Dam

✿   Factory, power plant

☆   Fort

⋒   Cave

⛏   Prehistoric site

▼   Viewing table

⥁   Viewpoint

▲   Other place of interest

Sports and recreation

🏇   Racecourse

⛸   Skating rink

≋ ≋   Outdoor, indoor swimming pool

⛵   Marina, sailing centre

⌂   Trail refuge hut

□━■━■━□   Cable cars, gondolas

□┼┼┼┼┼□   Funicular, rack railway

🚂   Tourist train

◇   Recreation area, park

🎢   Theme, amusement park

🦌   Wildlife park, zoo

⊛   Gardens, park, arboretum

⊛   Bird sanctuary, aviary

🚶   Walking tour, footpath

☺   Of special interest to children

Abbreviations

A   Agricultural office (Chambre d'agriculture)

C   Chamber of Commerce (Chambre de commerce)

H   Town hall (Hôtel de ville)

J   Law courts (Palais de justice)

M   Museum (Musée)

P   Local authority offices (Préfecture, sous-préfecture)

POL.   Police station (Police)

⛨   Police station (Gendarmerie)

T   Theatre (Théatre)

U   University (Université)

	Sight	Seaside resort	Winter sports resort	Spa
Highly recommended ★★★		�кос☆☆☆	✳✳✳	⚚⚚⚚
Recommended ★★		☆☆	✳✳	⚚⚚
Interesting ★		☆	✳	⚚

Additional symbols

🛈	Tourist information
═══ ═══	Motorway or other primary route
❶ ❶	Junction: complete, limited
↔ ══	Pedestrian street
ⅈ═════ⅈ	Unsuitable for traffic, street subject to restrictions
⊓⊓⊓⊓ ----	Steps - Footpath
🚆 🚉	Train station - Auto-train station
🚌 🚏	Coach (bus) station
—•—	Tram
⊜	Metro, underground
P/R	Park-and-Ride
♿	Access for the disabled
⊗	Post office
☎	Telephone
⊠	Covered market
•⤬•	Barracks
△	Drawbridge
∪	Quarry
✕	Mine
B F	Car ferry (river or lake)
⛴	Ferry service: cars and passengers
⇀	Foot passengers only
③	Access route number common to Michelin maps and town plans
Bert (R.)...	Main shopping street
AZ B	Map co-ordinates

hotels and restaurants

20 rooms: *250/375F*	Number of rooms: price for one person/ double room
half-board or *full board: 280F*	Price per person, based on double occupancy
⊐ 45F	Price of breakfast; when not given, it is included in the price of the room (i.e., for bed-and-breakfast)
up to 5 pers: *week 2400F*	Maximum capacity of lodging Price per week
3 "gîtes" : *2/7 pers* *week* *2300/6000F*	Number of lodgings Capacity smallest/largest unit Weekly rate for smallest/largest unit
100 apt: *2/7 pers:* *week* *2000/5000*	Number of apartments (residential hotel or holiday camp) mini/maxi capacity of apartments, mini/maxi rate per week
100 beds: *50F*	Number of beds and price per person (hostel)
120 sites: *80F*	Number of camp sites and cost for 2 people with a car
110/250	Restaurant mini/maxi price fixed menu (lunch and dinner) or à la carte
rest. *110/250F*	Lodging where meals are served mini/maxi price fixed menu or à la carte
food service	Light meals and snacks available
meal 85F	"Family style" meal
reserv	Reservation recommended
⇎	No credit cards accepted
P	Reserved parking for hotel patrons

The prices correspond to the higher rates of the tourist season

Principal sights

★★★ Highly recommended

★★ Recommended

★ Interesting

Sight described in this guide

COMPIÈGNE ★★★

Arras ★★

Douai ★

Ermenonville

Spas ‡ and seaside resorts ⚲ are classified according to the quality and range of facilities offered

Itinerary described in this guide: look up one of the sites in the index at the back of the guide to find the page where the tour is described

Driving tours

See the pages following for a description of each tour

1	The Avenois countryside
2	The Artois region
3	Castles and Cathedrals
4	The Opal Coast
5	Belfries in Flanders
6	The valleys of Picardy
7	Royal Palaces of Ile-de-France
8	From Versailles to Chartres through Rambouillet Forest

METZ

CHÂLONS-EN-CHAMPAGNE

Roman ruins
Religious building
Château, castle or historic house
Tourist train
Fortifications
Garden, park
Battle site or other historic site
Sports and recreation area
Megalithic monument
Museum, art gallery
Viewpoint
Wildlife park, zoo
Amusement park
Bird sanctuary, aviary
Boat trips
Outstanding natural site
Old town
Picturesque village

CHÂLONS-EN-CHAMPAGNE
ST-DIZIER
Provins
TROYES

AUXERRE

Meaux
Disneyland Paris
Vaux-le-Vicomte
Fontainebleau
Barbizon
Milly-la-Forêt
Fleury-en-Bière
Courances
Melun
NEVERS

Écouen
Versailles
Abbé de Port-
Royal-des-Champs
Breteuil
Rambouillet
Étampes
LOIRET

Forêt de
l'Isle Adam

St-Germain-en-Laye
Dampierre
Thoiry
Montfort-l'Amaury
ORLÉANS

Maintenon
Chartres
CHARTRES

EURE-ET-LOIR

7

8

la Roche-Guyon
Mantes-la-Jolie
Vétheuil
Évreux
CAEN
ALENÇON
LE MANS
Châteaudun

Driving Tours

1 The Avenois countryside

This drive takes you through the region known as L'Avenois, named for the main town, Avesnes-sur-Helpe. In fact, there are two rivers named Helpe, the Majeure and the Mineure, which flow through the Regional Nature Park. Since the Middle Ages, the landscape has been marked by small villages settled around the mills and forges, which sprung up beside powerful abbeys. There are plenty of opportunities to stop along this part of the itinerary and enjoy the amenities of the park. The southern section of the drive crosses a more open landscape, dotted with historic monuments and old-fashioned villages.

2 The Artois region

After visiting Lille and Villeneuve-d'Ascq, and taking a spin through the Belgian region of Tournaisis, follow this road to the regions of Hainaut and Cambraisis, where you may wish to take advantage of the natural benefits of the spring water at Saint-Amand. Continue on to the capital of the Artois region, Arras. Along the way, you will discover reminders of the wars which wracked the region: sturdy belfries standing square against the skyline; fortified gateways; remarkable buildings in the Flemish Gothic style. You may stop at any time to enjoy a moment in a traditional brasserie, listen to the chiming of a carillon, or discover a museum of modern art. If you happen to visit at carnival time, you may even see jolly giants roaming the streets, and be carried away by the festivities!

3 Castles and Cathedrals

This tour, starting from Amiens, meanders through the countryside of Picardy to the Oise and Beauvaisis regions. After Beauvais, you enter into the distinctive landscape of the Bray, where groves and meadows alternate. The village of Gerberoy is one of the most beautiful in all of France. As you contemplate the many marvellous Gothic churches, don't forget to stop and enjoy the regional cuisine of Picardy, which includes many vegetable-based dishes such as hearty soups.

4 The Opal Coast

Catch the fresh sea breezes as you drive along the cliff-top roads or stop to clamber in the dunes and play on the beaches of the Côte d'Opale. Many travellers enjoy a tour of the busy harbours at Boulogne and Calais; there are also traditional craftsmen at work in the region – for example, a stop-over in Desvres is a chance to see the unique ceramics made there. Inland, the Boulonnais countryside is a patchwork of fields, trees and hedgerows; the Audomarois wetlands are a protected area where you may visit the Regional Nature Park's exhibit areas and participate in nature discovery walks. If you are feeling hot and tired, why not take a boat ride on the watergangs, canals running between the fields which are home to many species of waterfowl. Seafood-lovers will find what they crave here, and the fresh local produce is a lovely complement to regional specialities.

5 Belfries in Flanders

Leave the busy city of Lille behind and head out to the hills and dales of Flanders. This little region has a style of its own, as you will soon see by observing the architecture of the fortified villages, the belfries, churches and mills, and inside the charming little eateries and watering holes known locally as *estaminets*. Local brewers contribute to the festivities when traditional popular festivities are held. This corner of France is a favourite with those who love good beer!

6 The valleys of Picardy

This is a good tour to make when all the family is along for the ride, as there is something for everyone. Start by following the lazy path of the River Somme from Amiens. Make a stop to visit the Samara Prehistoric Park or the Marquenterre nature reserve, where you can observe many species of birds. Time for water play, or time for a snooze on the warm sand at Berck-sur-Mer or Le Touquet-Paris-Plage. The Abbey and gardens at Valloire are likely to be less crowed than the beach, and offer a lovely and restful setting for sunburnt travellers. Follow the Canche valley as far as Naours, where an amazing network of underground passageways is big enough to shelter 3000 people.

7 Royal Palaces of Île de France

This large circle, with the city of Paris at the centre, encompasses some of the most impressive royal residences of France. Vaux-le-Vicomte is a wonderment of symmetry and landscape design, and visitors are moved by the sad fate of the man who built it. Fontainebleau, on the edge of the large forest of the same name, evokes the imperial grandeur of Napoleon as well as echoes of his downfall. Bretueil and Dampierre are in beautiful natural settings, which make them good places for an excursion if you feel like spending some time outdoors as well as in. Versailles, of course, is legendary for its splendour as well as its role in history. Just on the outskirts of Paris, the Château of St-Germain-en-Laye is especially interesting for the prehistoric art collection. Écouen is home to the national museum of the Renaissance.

8 From Versailles to Chartres through Rambouillet Forest

The forest of Rambouillet has a prestigious past as the favoured hunting ground of kings and, later Republican presidents of France. Many parts are open to the public and the establishment of the Haute Vallée de la Chevreuse Regional Nature Park has preserved typical local villages and churches. On the way to Chartres, the forest gives way to a great plain, and from a great distance, you will see the cathedral spires rise up on the horizon. It is not difficult to imagine how pilgrims of past centuries felt as they neared this magnificent manifestation of religious faith. After admiring the famous stained-glass windows, it is worth strolling around the old streets of town, which have managed to keep their authenticity despite the many tourists who come to visit the monument every year.

St-Valery-sur-Somme

Pratt. Pub...

Introduction

Landscapes

Picardy, Artois, Île-de-France (the region around Paris) and Paris itself all lie within the vast geological area known as the Paris Basin which borders on Flanders and the great plain of Northern Europe beyond. The Paris Basin is linked by the Burgundy sill to the Rhône Basin (southeast) and by the Poitou sill to the Aquitaine Basin (west). The landscape of the Paris Basin comprises forests, lush alluvial valleys with slow-flowing rivers and limestone plateaus providing arable land, dotted with sandy patches. The climate tends towards stormy summers and temperate winters with damp springs and autumns. Under Clovis, Île-de-France was part of the Frankish kingdom, the first French territory with its two capitals Soissons and Compiègne. Clovis' descendants were deposed in 751 by Pépin the Short, whose son Charlemagne was consecrated King of the Franks by the Pope in Rome in 774. In 843 Charlemagne's kingdom was carved up and the land lying west of the provinces bordering the Meuse, Saône and Rhône rivers was designated France. The former territory of the Franks was reduced to the Duchy of France and the two counties of Orléans and Étampes. It was only four centuries later that this duchy was called Île-de-France (the 'island of France' because of its position between the Seine, Aisne, Oise and Marne rivers). During the Norman invasion, the Duc de France valiantly defended Paris and one of the members of this House – Hugh Capet – was elected King of France at Senlis in 987. Hugh Capet's descendants governed France until 1848, except during the Revolution and the First Empire (1793-1814).

NORTHERN FRANCE

Picardy – This area northwest of Paris and Île-de-France is a land of plateaux and valleys but it also has a long coastline.

Plateaux – The wide and virtually flat plateaux of this former province are covered with a thick layer of silt, making them very fertile and well-suited to the cultivation of sugar-beets and cereals, fields of which stretch without interruption as far as the eye can see. To the east, the **Santerre** (*Sana terra*: good earth) and **Vermandois** regions are characterised by large farms, often complemented by a sugar refinery or a distillery. St-Quentin, the administrative and industrial centre of the Aisne *département*, is the principal town. To the east and south, the **Laonnois**, **Noyonnais** and **Soissonnais** regions mark the transition with Île-de-France, in particular the prestigious Valois region with its mantle of forests. Western Picardy is divided by wide valleys. Where the silt on the plateau was swept away the soil is poorer, as in the **Ponthieu** region where the villages have long, daubed walls devoid of windows. In the **Vimeu** region, where the chalk has decomposed into flinty clay, the cold, damp ground has created a mixed landscape of farmland crisscrossed by hedges and trees, cider-apple orchards and small, scattered villages. Near Beauvais the chalky, silt-covered plateau suddenly reveals a verdant hollow: the **Pays de Bray**, a wooded area interspersed with meadows where stock-farming is the main activity.

Valleys – The verdant wide-mouthed valleys are bisected by the Somme, Authie and Canche rivers. These waters flow so slowly they have difficulty in making their way, losing themselves in ponds and marshes full of fish and waterfowl. The floors of the valleys are a mix of old peat bogs, rows of poplars, stock-farming fields and, on the outskirts of towns (Abbeville, Amiens, Péronne, Montdidier), vegetable gardens *(hortillonnages)* surrounded by canals.

Towns have developed along the valleys: Montreuil on the Canche; Doullens on the Authie; Péronne, Amiens and Abbeville on the Somme.

The capital of this region is Amiens, a great industrial centre with factories producing tyres, electronics, video games, domestic appliances car parts and chemical products.

Coast – To the south, near Ault, the Picardy plateau meets the sea, ending in a sharp cliff of white chalk banded with flint. North of the Somme Bay a maritime plain called the **Marquenterre** area has been created by debris torn from the Normandy coast and carried northward by the currents, gradually forming an offshore bar. Only the Somme, Authie and Canche rivers have carved a passage to the sea; there are therefore few large ports but several seaside resorts, the largest of them, Le Touquet, seated beside the dunes.

The coastal plain lies between the dunes and the old coastal bar, which is marked by a noticeable cliff. The drained and dried plain is now used for fields of wheat and oats, and for raising salt-pasture lambs on the grassy shores known as *mollières*.

In the past St-Valery-sur-Somme, Le Crotoy and Étaples were important ports; today they harbour only fishing boats and yachts.

Y Tierny/MICHELIN

The Opal Coast at the Site des deux Caps

Artois – The former province of Artois, which lies on an extension of the Picardy plateaux, is a rise of land running northwest to southeast. It ends in an escarpment of about 100m (Vimy Ridge, Notre-Dame de Lorette Hill) which divides the Paris Basin from the Anglo-Belgian Basin. The great plain of Flanders begins at the foot of this escarpment. The Artois hills overlook the Boulonnais region to the northwest and the Lens plain and Arras' agricultural plain, fed by the River Scarpe, to the southwest. The well-watered hills of Artois are however bare to the southeast, in the **Ternois** region where there are outcrops of chalk; to the northwest, the chalky top layer of soil has decomposed into flinty clay resulting in lush, damp countryside which includes Hesdin Forest and mixed agricultural and meadow land.

Montreuil-sur-Mer – Rue du Clape-en-Bas

The **Boulonnais** region forms an enclave in the chalk layer, revealing outcrops of harder, older rocks. This "buttonhole" ends below the Channel.

The landscape of the Boulonnais is very different from neighbouring areas. In the north, where Artois rises again, the Upper Boulonnais forms a chalky plateau which in places reaches over 200m/650ft in altitude.

In the area where the land forms a hollow, the Lower Boulonnais, the wooded countryside is dotted with whitewashed farms. The clay has created meadows that are used for rearing the dappled-grey "Boulonnais draughthorses" and for other stock-breeding. The soil also supports the Desvres and Boulogne forests, while Hardelot Forest grows in sandier soil.

Boulogne, France's foremost fishing port, stands at the mouth of the River Liane. To the north, the edge of the calcareous plateau forms the cliffs of the Opal Coast *(see La CÔTE D'OPALE)*.

Hainault and Cambrésis – Hainault (capital: Valenciennes) and Cambrésis (capital: Cambrai) are extensions of the chalky plateaux of Artois and Picardy. They are also covered with a thick layer of silt that is ideal for growing sugar beets and wheat, with excellent per-acre harvests. The plateaux are divided by wide river valleys such as those of the Scarpe, Sambre, Selle and Escaut (Scheldt). Meadows of fodder crops and pasture give them the look of farming country. The forests of St-Amand and Mormal appear where there is flinty clay, the result of decomposition of the chalk.

Thiérache and Avesnois – These two relatively hilly regions form the tail of the Ardennes uplands, covered at the western end by marl and chalk mixed with marl. The **Thiérache** is a damp region, part forest and part pasture. When carefully drained the cold, non-porous ground provides pasture for cows. The dairies produce butter, cheese and condensed milk. The **Avesnois** is crossed by the River Helpe Majeure and River Helpe Mineure, tributaries of the River Sambre. This region resembles the Thiérache, but is marked by summits rising to over 250m/820ft in places. It is also an area of pastureland famous for its dairy cows and cheeses, especially Maroilles.

Flanders – The Flemish plain, which continues into Belgium, is bounded to the south by the hills of Artois and to the east by the plateaux of Hainault and Cambrésis.

Coastal Flanders – The wet and windy *Blooteland* (bare land protected by dunes separating the area from the sea) has been gradually reclaimed from the sea since the Middle Ages. The engineers, including the famous **Coebergher**, who came mostly from the Low Countries, drained the land gradually using great dams, canals and pumps, thus creating the marshes *(Moëres)*. Today it is a low-lying region where the grey clay yields crops of sugar-beets, cereals, flax and chicory, and the nearby pastures are grazed by sheep, pigs, horses and cattle. The flat countryside, scattered with great isolated farms built around square court-yards, is dominated by belfries, bell-towers, windmills and, on the coast, the factory chimneys and harbour cranes of Dunkirk and Calais.

Inland Flanders – Known as *Houtland* (wooded land) in contrast to the bare coastal area, the "Flemish lowlands" consist of lush countryside divided by rows of poplars, willows or elms. The *censes*, white-walled Flemish farms with red roofs, stand out against this green background.

A series of summits extends into Belgium, comprising the **Monts des Flandres** range. In addition to providing beautiful meadows where cows, horses and pigs thrive, the rich soil is also used for growing various crops such as cereals, fruit and vegetables in gardens among the St-Omer canals, and plants for industrial processing (hops near Bailleul, flax in the Lys Valley, chicory, sugar beets).

However, two small areas between Lille and Douai are different: the bare plateaux of the **Mélantois** and the **Pévèle** regions. The coal fields *(see Economy)* stretching from Béthune to Valenciennes have given rise to a "black country" marked by slag-heaps, brick mining towns and mine-shaft frames.

Between the Lys Valley and the River Escaut (Scheldt) lies the industrial conurbation of Lille-Roubaix-Tourcoing-Armentières. Once a major textile centre *(see LILLE)*, it is currently undergoing extensive urban renewal.

ÎLE-DE-FRANCE

Pays de France – This arable plateau extending between St-Denis, Luzarches and the Dammartin-en-Goële ridge was in the heart of royal territory. The layer of marl covering the subsoil has made the area extremely fertile, and the huge fields are planted with wheat and beetroot.

Parisis – Parisis lies between the River Oise and River Seine and the Pays de France. The area was once occupied by the Gauls, who gave it its name and christened the French capital. Parisis is an alluvial plain with few rivers that slopes towards the Seine. It is dominated by limestone hillocks covered in sand and grit.

Beyond the industrial suburbs of Paris, market gardens and orchards spread along the limestone slopes of the plain, while the sandy stretches are forested.

Senlisis – Geographers and historians have often grouped this region with Valois, but in fact it was part of the Crown territory, the central core of Île-de-France. Senlisis, which is bordered by the Oise, the Dammartin-en-Goële ridge and the Valois itself, is one of the most picturesque regions near the capital. Arable land is found on the silty soils, while the sandy areas have favoured the development of forestry.

Valois – Valois is surrounded by Senlisis and the Oise, Automne and Ourcq rivers. It acquired strategic importance as early as Roman times and has remained one of the most important regions in French history. First a county, then a duchy, Valois was twice given to one of the king's brothers. On two occasions the descendants of this royal line, known as the Princes de Valois, acceded to the throne.

Multien – Multien is an area of rolling landscapes and ploughed fields bounded by the River Marne, the Valois and the Goële ridge. It was the scene of fierce combat in September 1914.

French Vexin – Three rivers border this limestone platform: the Oise, the Epte and the Seine. West of the River Epte is the Normandy Vexin. The loess covering is an extremely fertile topsoil which favours cereal cultivation, especially wheat, and vegetable crops. Cattle rearing is concentrated in the valleys planted with poplar trees. The Buttes de Rosne, a series of outliers stretching from Monneville to Vallangoujard, are covered in woods. They include the strip of land running north of the Seine.

Mantois – Mantois is an enormous plateau situated between the River Eure and River Oise. It consists of forests to the east and arable land to the west. The small towns dotting its many valleys are well worth a visit.

Hurepoix – Bounded by Mantois, Beauce, Fontainebleau Forest and the Seine, the Hurepoix region has suffered from recent urbanisation. However, by avoiding major roads and referring to map no 106, you will enjoy exploring its varied landscapes.

Gâtinais – The Gâtinais is defined by the River Seine and the Hurepoix, Beauce and Champagne regions. The French Gâtinais, a clay plateau, lies east of the River Loing while the Orléanais Gâtinais (to the west) is an area of sand and sandstone. This second area is covered by Fontainebleau Forest, popular because of its splendid groves and sandstone boulders. The lush valley of the Loing, which attracted a number of well-known artists to the area (Corot, Millet), is dotted with charming small towns.

French Brie – French Brie is located between the River Seine and River Grand Morin and has Champagne Brie as its northern border. Historically, the former belonged to the king of France, while the latter was the property of the Comte de Champagne. The area is watered by four meandering rivers – Seine, Marne, Petit Morin and Grand Morin – and has many large farms specialising in large-scale wheat, sugar-beet and vegetable cultivation. French Brie contains sites as varied as the Chateau de Vaux-le-Vicomte and Disneyland Paris.

FORESTS

Île-de-France has some magnificent forests, including Rambouillet, Compiègne and Fontainebleau which feature among the finest in the country. The forests form a "green ring" around Paris that is a delight for weekend hikers, bikers and horseback riders among others.

Woods and forests have a timeless appeal: lush greenery in springtime, shaded groves in summer, the deep russet tones of autumn or the crisp frosts of winter. Forests also provide a multitude of fauna and flora to study or flowers, fruit, nuts and mushrooms to harvest in season. Many also have charming picnic areas. Those who take time to understand the life cycle of a forest also understand its infinite variety.

State forests and private forests – Three types of forest exist in France: state, private and local. The most interesting for hikers are the state forests, as they have an extensive network of roads, paths and lanes; and their magnificent groves form a picturesque setting. The aim of the forest ranges is to preserve the natural habitat. The most beautiful French forests used to feature protected forest zones known as "artistic reserves" in which unusually striking trees were left untouched by the axe, even when they died. This practice was given up in favour of "biological reserves". Forests on private estates are not open to the public, apart from the roads that run through them.

Trees – Like all living things, trees breathe, reproduce and need nourishment. Mineral nutrients are drawn from the earth by the roots and distributed to all parts of the tree via the sap running through the trunk and leaves.

Different trees require different kinds of soil. Chestnut trees, for instance, cannot survive on limestone sites, whereas oaks will flourish on a variety of soils.

Trees, like other plants, breathe through their leaves and reproduce through their flowers. Flowers will bear fruit if they are fertilised by pollen of their own species. Very few trees have hermaphrodite flowers – presenting both male and female characteristics – like roses, acacias etc. Consequently the pollen is usually carried from the male flower to the female flower by insects, or sometimes by the wind. Trees may also reproduce by their shoots; thus, when a youngish tree trunk is razed to the ground, a number of stool shoots will emerge from the stump. Conifers do not produce offshoots.

The trees of Île-de-France fall into two categories: deciduous and coniferous.

Deciduous – These trees shed their leaves every autumn and grow them again in the spring. Beeches, oaks, hornbeams, birches and chestnut trees belong to this category.

Coniferous – In place of leaves, coniferous species have needles which they shed regularly throughout the year. The needles are renewed every four to five years. Their sap contains resin – they are also known as resinous trees – and the fruit is generally cone-shaped. Pines, cypresses, cedars and fir trees are all conifers, as is the larch, which loses its needles every year.

Trees of the Île-de-France forests – Most species of deciduous trees can be found around Paris. The most common are listed below.

Oak – One of the most esteemed forest trees, the oaks' hard but beautiful wood is used for both carpentry and ornamental woodwork. In former times oak bark was much sought after by local tanners. Some of the oaks tower 40m/132ft high with trunks over 1m/3ft in diameter. Trees can be felled up to the age of 250 years.

M. Viard/JACANA

M. Viard/JACANA

Oak

Beech

Beech – Although it resembles the oak in its habit, beech is slightly more elegant. The wood is mainly used for everyday furniture and railway sleepers but it is also popular as fuel. The trunk is cylindrical, the bark smooth and shiny; young shoots have a crooked, gnarled appearance. Beeches grow as tall as oaks but are no longer commercially viable beyond 120 years.

Hornbeam – A remarkably tough species, the hornbeam resembles the beech; it also lives to the same age, but is shorter and its bark features numerous grooves.

Chestnut – This tree can grow to great heights and can live for several hundred years, but is generally felled much younger as very old chestnut trees become hollow and prone to disease. Its wood was traditionally used by the cooperage industry for making staves, posts and stakes; nowadays it is used in the production of chipboard. Chestnut trees will grow only on siliceous soil.

Birch – Even when it reaches 25m/82ft in height the birch retains a graceful, slim trunk of white bark – which peels off in fine layers – and shimmering leaves. Damp, sandy soil is an excellent terrain for all varieties of birch. Although it is excellent firewood, it is mainly used in making wood pulp for the paper industry.

Scots Pine – This species, the most commonly found conifer in Île-de-France, is ideal for reafforestation, particularly in sandy terrain. Since the mid-19C it has been planted in plots of land where there is meagre or non-existent vegetation. Scots pines have short needles (4-6cm/1.5-2.5in) which grow in pairs, smallish cones (3-5cm/1-2in) and reddish-ochre bark.

Foresters often plant Scots pines alongside exotic or Mediterranean (maritime pine) resinous species. A great favourite is the Corsican pine, a tall, handsome tree with a perfectly straight trunk. It can grow to 50m/165ft, but old trees develop large grey patches on their bark.

The science of forestry – If a forest is not tended, it will invariably deteriorate. In order to develop fully and reach their proper size, trees must be given breathing space and be placed in an environment which meets their specific requirements. The first step in a reafforestation campaign is to plant fir trees, which have few needs and produce wood in a very short time. Their roots retain the earth, otherwise washed away by surface water, and the needles build up thick layers on the ground. Next, hornbeams, birches and beeches are planted to increase the fertility of the soil, and finally oaks. Many of the beech groves are left as this species is considered to be commercially profitable.

Rotations – The prime concern of foresters is always to have trees ready for felling. Consequently, when trees are felled foresters ensure they are immediately replaced with seedlings. For example, a forest may be divided into 10 units, and every five years the unit with the oldest trees is cleared and then replanted. Thus, within 50 years the forest is entirely renewed while remaining commercially viable – a technique known as rotation.

Forest managers try to avoid exposing a large sector of the forest, as leafy plants such as hazel and mulberry trees can set in and choke the young shoots. Two, three or four groups within each sector are formed according to the trees' approximate age, and a programme of successive felling is planned. This ensures that only limited areas are deforested at any one time.

Whatever the rotation for a given forest, its appearance is bound to change depending on the thickness of the vegetation and the forestry techniques applied.

There are three types of plantation in Île-de-France:

Groves – After the land has been sown, the weaker shoots are choked by the stronger ones in a process of natural selection. The trees – planted fairly close to one another – spread vertically. After some time the land is cleared around the finer species to encourage them to develop, and eventually these are the only ones that remain. This grove, where the widely spaced trees are all the same age, is called a *futaie pleine*; the rotation is rather long, 50 or even 80 years for very tall trees. *Futaie jardinée* is another type of grove, in which the trees are planted and cut at different times, so that the sector features a variety of "age groups"; older trees are always felled first.

A fully matured grove is a truly impressive sight, with its powerful trunks and its rich canopy of foliage producing subtle effects of light and shade.

Copses – The trees are younger. Rotation ranges from 5 to 30 years, depending on whether pit props, logs for heating or firewood is wanted. A copse is a sector of forest where a group of mature trees are razed to the ground once they have been cut. The shoots growing around the stump develop into a multitude of young bushy, leafy trees.

Copses with Standards – If, when cutting a copse, the finest trees are left standing, these will dominate the new shoots. If they survive a series of fellings, they will grow to be extremely strong. The utilisation of copses with standards produces both fuel wood (from the copses) and timber for industrial purposes (from the older species).

Fauna and flora – Forests contain not only trees but also countless varieties of plants and animals. Hunts are still organised in certain forests.

Nature lovers will find forests fascinating as the rich, damp soil is remarkably fertile, sustaining moss, lichen, mushrooms, grasses, flowers, shrubs and ferns.

Flowers – April is the season of laburnum, hyacinths and daffodils. May brings hawthorn, lily-of-the-valley, columbine and the delightful catkins of the hazel tree. In June there is broom, heather, campanula, scabious and wild pinks. During the autumn, russet and gold leaves are as attractive as the forest flowers.

Fruit – Wild strawberries and succulent raspberries ripen during July and August, while blackberries can be harvested in August and September together with the new crop of hazelnuts. October is the time for sloes and sweet chestnuts.

Mushrooms – Some varieties of mushrooms – *Russula virescens, chanterelle comestible* and *mousseron* – are always edible. Other species are difficult to identify and may be dangerous. If in doubt, mushroom pickers should consult a professional mycologist or the local chemist *(pharmacien)*.

GARDENS IN ÎLE-DE-FRANCE

Three successive trends defined the official canons of ornamental gardening in Île-de-France, the home of many royal residences.

16C – During the 16C gardens were not considered as an essential part of an estate, but merely in the same category as outbuildings. They were generally of geometric shape and resembled a chessboard, where each of the squares contained carefully trimmed spindle and box forming arabesques and other elaborate patterns. These motifs were called *broderies*. Gardens were enclosed within a sort of cloister made with stonework or greenery, from which visitors could enjoy a good view of the garden. Paths featuring fragments of marble, pottery and brick cut through the grounds. Though water did not play any significant part in the general appearance of the gardens, there were basins and fountains encircled by balustrades or tall plants. They were there to be observed in their own right and for people to admire the ornamental statues and water displays.

Most of them have now disappeared, at least in Île-de-France. There is, however, an outstanding example in Villandry in the Loire Valley *(see The Green Guide, Châteaux of the Loire)*.

17C-early 18C: The Formal Garden – Although **André le Nôtre** cannot be credited with "inventing" the **formal French garden**, he was undoubtedly the one person who raised this art form to absolute perfection. Its purpose was twofold: to enhance the beauty of the château it surrounded and to provide a superb view from within. The garden's main features were fountains, trees, statues, terraces and a sweeping perspective.

The château was fronted by a "Turkish carpet" of parterres with flowers and evergreen shrubs forming arabesques and intricate patterns. These were symmetrically flanked by basins with fountains, usually adorned with statues. Fountains were also placed on the terrace bearing the château and the upper lawns, which was the starting-point of the central perspective along a canal or a green carpet of lawn *(tapis vert)* lined with elegant groves of tall trees.

The groups of trees planted along the perspective were designed to be perfectly symmetrical. They were crossed by a network of paths, with clearings at the intersections offering splendid vistas extending into the far distance. Hedges lined the paths, concealing the massive tree trunks and providing a backdrop for marble statues. As hedges were fragile and expensive to maintain, however, most were later removed or greatly reduced in height from their original 6-8m/20-26ft. Each grove of trees featured a "curiosity": perhaps a fountain with elaborate waterworks, a colonnade or a group of sculpted figures.

The enormous variety of designs and styles used for the parterres and surrounding trees, bushes and hedges ensured that these formal gardens were never monotonous. They were conceived as an intellectual pursuit, giving pleasure through their stately proportions and perspectives, the skilful design and the sheer beauty of each detail.

Late 18C-19C: The Landscape Garden – In the 18C, manipulating the landscape into rigid geometric patterns was no longer fashionable. The tendency instead was to imitate nature. The landscape garden – also called the Anglo-Chinese garden – consisted of lush, rolling grounds dotted with great trees and rocks, pleasantly refreshed by streams and tiny cascades. A rustic bridge might cross a river flowing into a pond or lake covered with water-lilies and surrounded by willow trees, and a mill or dairy might add the final touch to this Arcadian scene. The 18C fascination for philosophy, characteristic of the Age of Enlightenment, was also reflected in contemporary gardening, which saw the introduction of symbolic or exotic monuments or **"fabriques"** (a technical term originally referring to architectural works depicted in paintings). These follies were dotted throughout the grounds to enhance the landscape.

Antique temples and medieval ruins were particular favourites, while tombs and mausoleums became popular just before the Revolution. Chinese and Turkish sculptures were also fashionable. An unfinished temple, for instance, would remind visitors of the limits of science, while an oriental pagoda standing beside a crumbling tower symbolised the fragility of human achievements.

Sentimentality, romance and melodrama were popular features of many art forms. Such trends also affected landscape gardens, giving rise to a number of new sights including the secret lovers' grotto, the bench of the tired mother, the grave of the rejected suitor etc.

Most of these estates were ravaged during the Revolution, and few of their fragile monuments survived. Efforts are now being made to restore what was left. The most outstanding example of an 18C folly in the region is the Cassan Pagoda at L'Isle-Adam *(see illustration p. 216)*.

Particularly fine gardens may still be found at Versailles, Vaux-le-Vicomte, Chantilly, Courances, St.-Cloud, Sceaux, Champs, Fontainebleau, Rambouillet and Ferrières.

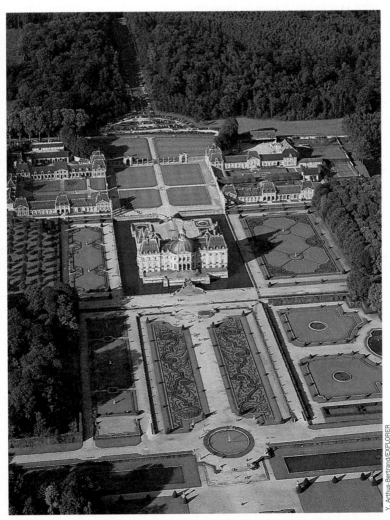

Y. Arthus-Bertrand/EXPLORER

Aerial view of Vaux-le-Vicomte

Economy

NORD – PAS-DE-CALAIS

The Nord-Pas-de-Calais area has had a high population density since the Middle Ages due to its landscapes, geographical location, temperate climate and agricultural resources. It has always been a major trading area, whose towns acquired wealth from textiles and trade very early on in their history and enjoyed a great deal of autonomy, symbolised by their belfries.

The region also has a coastal belt that includes Boulogne, France's leading fishing port. The Pas-de-Calais, the busiest maritime area in the world, constitutes the French side of the Straits of Dover, the narrowest stretch of water between the continent and Great Britain and the main trade route to Northern Europe.

The industrial infrastructure in the Nord-Pas-de-Calais region is still the second largest in France. Although industrial employment is decreasing overall, the area's small and medium-size enterprises are implementing modernisation strategies aimed at expansion, especially in the export market. In doing so, they are taking full advantage of the proximity of vast European markets and the ease of access afforded by the Nord-Europe high-speed train, the Channel Tunnel and the dense network of roads. This situation has attracted a great deal of foreign investment (it is the leading region in France for international investors, including Coca-Cola, MacCain, IBM, Rank Xerox, 3M etc).

Metallurgy – The discovery and extraction of coal in the 19C attracted heavy industries (mining, iron and steelmaking) to the area. Mining ceased in 1990, leaving deep scars. Reconversion is currently underway.

The iron and steel industry has been through many crises over the past few decades. Formerly, the main criteria leading to the opening of a works was proximity to raw materials. Since the 1960s, economies have acquired a global dimension which, in addition to a reduction in transport costs, has led to the importing of raw materials with higher mineral contents. The foundries and steelworks then moved towards ports, and numerous traditional industrial sites closed down. Meanwhile, Dunkirk acquired one of the most efficient steelworks in Europe and Gravelines was selected as the site for an ultra-modern aluminium works (Pechiney).

French rail equipment (especially the VAL, the driverless subway first built in Lille in 1983 and now exported worldwide) is produced mainly in the Valenciennes and Douai areas. The automobile industry has plants in Douai (Renault), Maubeuge (MCA, a Renault subsidiary), Douvrain (Française des Mécaniques) and Hourdain (Peugeot-Fiat).

The chemicals industry (9 000 jobs) has developed in the field of organic chemistry using tar and other coal by-products.

Textiles and Glassware – The textile and clothing industries, which had been traditional employers since the Middle Ages, have been seriously affected by international competition (especially from Third-World countries where wages are low). This has led to a need for huge increases in productivity in a market subject to the uncertainties of fashion. The enormous efforts made to achieve technical and commercial modernisation and train workers are unable to stem the constant flow of layoffs. Despite these difficulties, the Nord-Pas-de-Calais area still supplies the entire national production of linen (Lys Valley), 95 % of worsteds, 22 % of woollen fabrics, 38 % of thread and 20 % of cottons, not to mention the famous Calais and Caudry lace.

The glassware and crystal industries include the PPG works in Boussois, Sicover in Aniche and, best-known of all, the Arques glass and crystal works which has achieved an outstanding increase in turnover and now exports to 160 countries.

Food-processing – The food-processing industry is now the region's leading sector. Regional produce supplies flour mills and biscuit factories in the Lille area, starch works, breweries etc. Chicory refineries enjoy a worldwide reputation. Beets have engendered a whole industrial sector with crushing mills, sugar and other refineries, and distilleries. All of these buildings have given the plain its own particular landscape near Cambrai and Thumeries. Canning factories produce 30 % of the total national production of tinned vegetables and ready prepared meals and 50 % of fish (Boulogne).

New Sectors – The region's geographical situation is ideal for the expansion of several different services (accounting for 62 % of total jobs) including logistics, distribution, tourism, business services etc. Mail order is also an important sector of employment. With a steadily increasing work force of 18 000, it provides regional companies with a wide range of business opportunities. Of the 10 largest French companies in this sector, five operate from this area. The top two are La Redoute and Trois Suisses.

Coal Fields – Coal extraction in the coal fields of the Nord-Pas-de-Calais area dates from the 18C. The deposit in this region lies at the western end of a large coal depression which extends into Belgium (Borinage at Mons, Charleroi coal fields) and Germany (Ruhr coal fields).

After 270 years of extraction, all the mines have now closed.

The deposit – The coal fields extend eastward from the hills of the Artois region for about 120km/75mi to the Belgian border; the deposit is 4-12km/2.5-7.5mi wide and was mined to a depth of 1 200m/3 937ft. However, the irregularity of the seams, their small openings (sometimes less than 0.80m/3ft) and the presence of numerous geological flaws made extraction progressively harder and led to an increasing deficit.

Closure of the mines – The pits employed up to 220 000 people in 1947, but a decline in the yield from these mines started to appear in the late 1950s. In 1959, when productivity still reached 29 million tonnes, a plan of progressive shutdown was implemented which led to the closure of the last pit on 21 December 1990.

Coal extraction

J. Dupont/EXPLORER

Industrial Recycling – A range of different industries developed around the working of the mines: production of oval coal briquettes, foundry and special coke; the manufacture of facing bricks; the sale of mine gas; the production of electricity in power stations which run largely on fuel products gathered from the slag heaps; the use of shale, also from slag heaps, for road foundations and as ballast for railway lines. Over 329 either flat or conical slag heaps remain today, about 70 of which are still commercially exploitable. With the prospect of imminent closure, the mining companies formed subsidiaries to take over from them; these make up the regional industrial group Filianor.

PICARDY

Despite being a rural area, Picardy nonetheless sustains lively industrial activities. Traditionally the region's industry was textiles, but this has largely been replaced by metal-based industries (agricultural and car equipment, mopeds etc). Chemical products include glass (St-Gobain) and rubber (tyres in Amiens) in particular.

Linked to agriculture, the sugar refineries, food-manufacturing plants and especially the canning factories – based in the Santerre area at Estrée, Rosières and Péronne – all play an important part in the region.

ÎLE-DE-FRANCE

A high population density – Although Île-de-France covers only 2.2 % of the surface area of France, over 18 % of the French population resides in the province. This huge concentration of over 10 million inhabitants has gradually focused around the natural junctions of the Seine, Marne and Oise river basins. These large, slow rivers separate vast plateaux bearing rich countryside including the Brie and Beauce regions, and the large forests of Fontainebleau, Halatte, Rambouillet, Marly and St-Germain.

Today the development of the Paris region tends to respect these natural tracts and instead focuses urban and economic growth around the new towns: Cergy-Pontoise, Évry, St-Quentin-en-Yvelines, Marne-la-Vallée and Melun-Sénart.

The foremost industrial region in France – The Paris region employs over 15 % of the national labour force. Alongside the various industries (metallurgy, mechanical engineering, electrical and electronics manufacturing, chemicals, clothing and fashion), highly specialised and ultra-modern businesses have also developed.

The Paris and Île-de-France region is the foremost business market in France.

Historical table and notes

Celts and Romans

BC	
Circa 300	The north of Gaul taken by a Celto-Germanic tribe, the Belgae.
57	Belgian Gaul conquered by Caesar. Bavay, Boulogne and Amiens became important Roman centres.
AD 1C-3C	Roman peace. Northern France becomes part of the province of Second Belgium (capital at Reims).
406	Frankish invasion.

Merovingians and Carolingians

486	Territory from the Somme to the Loire rivers occupied by Clovis following the defeat of the Roman army at Soissons: his kingdom was called Francia in Latin.
561	The kingdom of France divided into three parts: northern France incorporated into Neustria.
6C and 7C	Creation of bishoprics and founding of many abbeys.
768	Charlemagne crowned King of Neustria in Noyon.
800	Charlemagne proclaimed Emperor of the western world.
9C and 10C	Norman and Hungarian invasions. Withdrawal of the abbeys into the towns.
911	The Duchy of Normandy created after the Treaty of St Clair-sur-Epte, ending Normans' ambitions in Île-de-France.
987	Hugh Capet, duke and suzerain of the land extending from the Somme to the Loire rivers, elected King of France in Senlis.

RMN

Battle of Bouvines, Horace Vernat

The Middle Ages

11C and 12C	Period of prosperity. Development of the clothmaking industry in Flanders, Artois and Picardy.
	Towns obtain charters and build belfries.
1180-1223	The Valois, Clermont, Meulan, Artois and Vermandois regions and the region around Amiens and Lille annexed to the royal kingdom by Philippe Auguste.
1214	Battle of Bouvines: victory for Philippe Auguste over the Count of Flanders and his allies King John of England, the Holy Roman Emperor Otto IV and the counts of Boulogne and Hainault.

1272	Ponthieu under the authority of the kings of England.
1314	Flanders annexed by Philip the Fair.
1337	Beginning of the Hundred Years War. The death of Philip the Fair and his three sons ("the accursed kings") result in a problem of succession: Philip the Fair's nephew, Philip de Valois, preferred by the French barons over his grandson, Edward III, King of England. The following century marked by battles between the French and the English who lay claim to the French Crown, as well as between the Armagnacs, supporters of the family of Orléans, and the Burgundians, supporters of the dukes of Burgundy.
1346	Battle of Crécy: victory for Edward III of England.
1347	Calais surrendered to the English with the famous episode of the Burghers of Calais.
1369	Marriage of Philip the Bold, Duke of Burgundy, with Marguerite, daughter of the Count of Flanders: Flanders under Burgundian authority.
1415	Battle of Agincourt: victory for Henry V of England.
1420	The Treaty of Troyes signed by Isabeau of Bavaria, wife of the mad king Charles VI, depriving the Dauphin of his rights of succession and designating her son-in-law, Henry V of England, heir to the French throne.
1422	Death of Charles VI. France divided between the English, the Burgundians and the Armagnacs. Charles VII, the legitimate heir, resident in Bourges.
1430	Joan of Arc taken prisoner at Compiègne.
1435	Picardy and the Boulonnais region yielded to the Duchy of Burgundy in the Treaty of Arras.
1441	English supremacy over Île-de-France ends with the liberation of Pontoise.
1477	Invasion of Picardy, Artois, Boulonnais and Hainault by Louis XI following the death of Charles the Bold; only Picardy subsequently held.
	Marriage of Marie of Burgundy, daughter of Charles the Bold, to Maximilian of Austria: Flanders brought under Habsburg control.

From the Bourbons to the Revolution

16C	Through the House of Habsburg, Flanders included in the empire of Charles V of Spain.
1520	Meeting between Henry VIII of England and François I at the Field of the Cloth of Gold, Guînes.
1529	Peace of Dames signed at Cambrai: claims to Artois and Flanders renounced by François I.
1557	St-Quentin taken by the Spanish.
1558	Calais taken from the English by the Duke of Guise.
1562	Beginning of the Wars of Religion.
1585	Philip II of Spain allied with the Catholic League (Treaty of Joinville).
1593	Henry of Navarre converts to Catholicism after capturing most of Île-de-France; crowned King Henri IV of France.
1598	Edict of Nantes.
1659	Following the Treaty of the Pyrenees, marriage agreed between Louis XIV and Maria-Theresa of Spain; Artois brought under French sovereignty.
1661	The construction of a huge palace at Versailles commissioned by Louis XIV.
1663	Marriage of Louis XIV with Maria-Theresa, who according to local custom was to inherit all of the Brabant region from her mother. When the inheritance passes to another heir, Louis XIV declares the war of "Devolution" on the Spanish Low Countries.

RMN

Duke of Guise

1668	Walloon Flanders given to Louis XIV by the Treaty of Aix-la-Chapelle.
1678	Louis XIV allowed to annexe the other northern towns by the Treaty of Nimegen.
1713	The borders of northern France established definitively (Treaty of Utrecht).
1789	French Revolution.

From the First to the Second Empire

1802	Treaty of Amiens.
1803	Napoleon's army mustered at the Boulogne Camp for a possible invasion of England.
1804	Napoleon crowned Emperor of France.
1812	Russia invaded by Napoleon's troops.
1814	France invaded. Unconditional abdication by Napoleon at Fontainebleau. Louis XVIII, returned from exile in England, is enthroned in 1815.
1840	Attempted uprising against King Louis-Philippe organised by Louis-Napoleon in Boulogne.
1848	Louis-Napoleon elected President of the Republic; crowned Emperor (Napoleon III) in 1852.
1870-71	Franco-Prussian War. End of the Second Empire signalled by the defeat at Sedan: the Third Republic proclaimed. Paris besieged by Prussians: Alsace and part of Lorraine given up under the Treaty of Frankfurt.

Les Adieux de Fontainebleau, Horace Vernet

20C

1914	Outbreak of the First World War. France attacked by German armies through neutral Belgium; four years of bloody trench warfare follow.
1915 to 1918	Battles throughout northern France and Flanders: in Artois (Neuville-St-Vaast, Vimy), in Picardy (Somme Valley, Chemin des Dames in the Aisne Valley, St Quentin) and in Île-de-France (Ourcq Valley, Battle of the Marne).
	11 November: armistice signed in Compiègne Forest.
1919	End of the war with the Treaty of Versailles.
1939	Outbreak of the Second World War. In June 1940 France overrun by the German army; occupation of much of the country. The "French State", established at Vichy, collaborates closely with the Germans. The north of France cut off from the rest of the country by a boundary. France's honour saved by General de Gaulle's Free French forces and by the courage of the men and women of the Resistance.
	By 1942 all France occupied; the French fleet scuttled at Toulon. Allied landing in Normandy in June 1944, and in the south of France in August; Paris liberated. The "Dunkirk pocket" retaken by the Allies. The German surrender signed at Reims on 7 May 1945.
1976	Creation of the "Île-de-France" administrative region.
1987	Start of building works for the Channel Tunnel linking France and England.
1994	6 May: official opening of the Channel Tunnel.
1996	Inauguration of Evry Cathedral.
1998	Inauguration of the Stade de France in St-Denis for the World Cup, won by the French team.

Architecture and Art

ABC OF ARCHITECTURE

Religious architecture

MANTES-LA-JOLIE – Ground plan of Notre-Dame (12C-14C)

Basilical plan without transept: the sacristy was added in the 13C, the radiating chapels and the Chapelle de Navarre in the 14C.

Ambulatory: an extension of the aisles round the chancel allowing the faithful to file past the relics.

Sacristy

Side aisles

Nave

Chancel

Axial chapel: in churches which are not dedicated to the Virgin, this chapel is often consecrated to her (Lady chapel)

Bay: transverse sections of the nave between two pillars

Porch

Side chapel (chapelle de Navarre)

Radiating chapels

CHARTRES – Notre-Dame Cathedral

Cross-section of the cathedral (11C) before the fire of 1194

Cross-section of the present edifice (13C)

Timber roofing

Flying buttress

Pier of a flying buttress

Blind triforium: a series of simulated openings

Upper gallery where small groups can convene

Pointed vault

Buttress supporting the base of the wall

Barrel vault: semi-circular vault

Crypt: an underground church or chapel intended to house relics; the crypt of Chartres Cathedral is the largest in France (about 220m/240yd long)

Capital

RAMPILLON – Main doorway of the church (13C)

Tympanum

Carved **lintel** depicting the rising of the dead

Pointed archivolt

Trefoil arch

Recessed arches spanning an opening and forming the **archivolt**

Embrasure embellished with statues of the apostles

Carved cornerpiece between an arch and its frame

Upright post to which St Eliphe's statue is bonded

Historiated base

R. Corbel/MICHELIN

33

AMIENS – West front of the cathedral (13C)

The vast cathedral is the edifice which best reflects the blossoming of Rayonnant Gothic architecture.

Kings' gallery decorating the west front of many cathedrals: it includes 22 statues representing Christ's royal lineage

Finial: a flower-shaped ornament finishing off a pinnacle

Gargoyle: a rainwater spout

Great rose-window

Openwork **gallery** consisting of **trefoil arches** surmounted by quatrefoil openings

Tympanum made of four **historiated** bands

Gable: a steeply pitched ornamental pediment surmounting doorways and windows, here decorated with **crockets.**

Band: a carved ornamental strip

Canopy: a richly decorated baldaquin surmounting a statue

Recessed arches spanning an opening and forming the **archivolt**

Upright post to which a statue is generally bonded (here the "Beau Dieu")

Door leaf

Jambs: uprights supporting the archivolt

Embrasure embellished with statues carved in the **round**

R. Corbel/MICHELIN

BEAUVAIS – East end of the cathedral (13C)

In spite of the missing spire (which collapsed in 1573) and nave (never built owing to lack of funds), the cathedral has a magnificent chancel representing the apogee of Gothic building techniques with vaulting soaring to a height of 48m/157ft.

Pinnacle

Gargoyle

Pier of a flying buttress

"Chartraine" window formed by two lancet windows surmounted by a rose-window

Tracery: stone openwork in the upper part of a window

Double-span flying buttress

Quatrefoil openwork railing

Buttress

Dripstone

Radiating or apsidal chapel

Base

SENLIS – Notre-Dame Cathedral (12C-13C)

Cell or quarter: a segment of vaulting defined by intersecting ribs

Intersecting ribs

Lunette: part of the ribbed vaulting which does not extend to the keystone

Pendant keystone

Transverse arch: a reinforcing arch under a vault

Tierceron: an intermediate rib

Tracery: delicate stone openwork in the upper part of a window

Clerestory window

Equilateral arch: a pointed arch whose radii are equal to its span

Gallery

Openwork railing

Composite pillar formed by several bonded columns

Pointed main arcade

R. Corbel/MICHELIN

AIRE-SUR-LA-LYS – Organ of the collegiate church (1653)

This richly carved organ comes from the former Cistercian abbey of Clairmarais near Aire-sur-la-Lys.

Flame vase crowning the recess

Recess

Great organ case: the wooden frame enclosing the pipes

Little organ case

Organ loft

Baldaquin surmounted by a lantern

Clock

Front: a set of large pipes at the front of the organ

Stop: a set of pipes

Set of vertical pipes which can be grouped to form polygonal or cylindrical columns

Massive **base** supporting the weight of the pipes

QUAËDYPRE – High altar and altarpiece of the church (late 17C)

In the 17C and 18C, altarpieces were architectural compositions towering above the altar and intended to channel the congregation's religious fervour.

Scrolled ornament

Statue in a recess, representing the secondary theme

Apex

Entablature

Predella: the bottom part of the altarpiece, divided into small panels

Tabernacle: a small container intended to receive the consecrated bread and wine

Altar

Medallion

Rounded pediment

Crowning piece

Curved pediment

Altar picture: it depicts the main theme of the altarpiece and consists of a painting, a statue or a carved group

Twin columns

Rotating recess making it possible to display a monstrance above the tabernacle

Steps leading to the altar

R. Corbel/MICHELIN

36

Château de COURANCES (16C-17C)

Chimney stack: a masonry structure in which several chimneys are grouped

Sandstone bond

Curved pediment

Slightly projecting wing

Triangular pediment

Brick panels

Segment-arched window

Oculus

Ties: some of the stones are recessed to reinforce the construction

Central block

Horse-shoe staircase (as in Fontainebleau)

String-course

Pavilion standing in front of the main building

Balustrade: a railing consisting of a flat top supported by balusters

Château de CHANTILLY stables – Dome (1721-1740)

Fame: an allegorical figure (winged woman blowing a trumpet)

Break line

Air-vent

Fleur-de-lis escutcheon

Mansard: a four-sided hipped roof

Dome

Lower slope of a hipped roof

Tympanum

Semi-circular pediment

Ionic pilaster surmounted by a scrolled capital

High-relief sculpture

Agrafe: an ornament placed on the keystone of an opening

Console: S-shaped ornamental bracket supporting the cornice

Fanlight: the upper part of a window or door

Boss: projection left on a stone after it has been cut

Door leaf

R. Corbel/MICHELIN

37

RUE – Belfry (15C)

Symbolising the power of the city, the belfry was used as a watchtower as well as the aldermen's meeting place.

Watchman's **platform**

Polygonal roof

Bartizan

Cornice: a horizontal projection crowning a wall

Reveal: the side of a dormer window

Dormer window

Pinnacle

Clock

Louvre

Watchpath

Corbel

Buttress

Trefoil openwork **railing**

ARRAS – Façades overlooking the Grand'Place (15c-17C)

Left is the Hôtel des Trois Luppars (1467), the oldest house lining the square, right is a house dating from 1684.

Bartizan

Corbie-stepped gable

Gable, decorated with mouldings

Scroll

Large **Gothic-arched opening**

Ogee arch

Cornice

Mullioned window: a mullion is the vertical element of a tracery window

Broken-barrel arch

Ties: every other stone is recessed to reinforce the construction

Semi-circular arch

Arcading

Foliated **capital**

Sandstone **monolithic column**

R. Corbel/MICHELIN

38

CHATOU – 19C pavilion

This type of pavilion, built of course-grained limestone, is characteristic of suburban domestic architecture.

Porous **coarse-grained limestone**

Modillion: a small console supporting a cornice

Pinnacle

Crown: an ornament crowning an edifice or part of an edifice

White-limestone **bond**

Entablature: the projecting part at the top of a façade, meant to support the timberwork

Metope: a space between modillions in a cornice, here decorated with ceramics

Corner stonework

Balustrade

Wrought-iron balcony

Military architecture

LE QUESNOY – Fortifications (12C and 17C-19C)

These well-preserved fortifications, remodelled by Vauban from 1667 onwards, are set in green surroundings.

Bastion: polygonal defence work projecting from the outer wall of a fortification

Bastion surmounted by a **cavalier**

Gun embrasure

Parade ground

Barracks

Gate

Ravelin with inside ditch

Face: one of the sides of a work forming a salient angle and facing the enemy.

Underground barracks

Curtain wall: a section of wall between two bastions

Flank of a work forming an angle with one of the faces

Orillion: a masonry work forming part of the defence of a bastion

Ravelin: a projecting outerwork forming a salient angle

Ditch

V-shaped **outerwork** built in front of a bastion or ravelin

R. Corbel/MICHELIN

39

LIVING LIKE KINGS

After the 15C, medieval castles were converted from fortresses into residential châteaux. Windows were enlarged, doors and openings were richly adorned. Towers, once strategic elements of the defensive structure, became decorative features, along with crenellated battlements and moats. By the second half of the 16C, such characteristics had become superfluous. Façades were embellished with statues and rows of superimposed columns. Roofs were high and presented a single slope.

The Château d'Écouen *(see p 189)* is a fine example of the French Renaissance style, as is the Richelieu Pavillon of the Louvre (1546-1654), in Paris. The style, which succeeded Gothic as the style dominant in Europe after the mid-16C, first developed in Italy. The name describes the «rebirth» of interest in Roman and Greek art and learning. By the early 17C, the Classical style of architecture had emerged, as expressed in the magnificence of royal palaces.

François I (reigned 1515-47)

The early phase of the French Renaissance culminated in the François I style *(see FONTAINEBLEAU, p 193)*. The decorative aspects mingle Gothic embellishments with elements inspired by Italian art, and the design features round arches and symmetrical composition. Many of the elegant buildings erected by the monarch bear his distinctive emblem: a crowned salamander.

Henri IV (r. 1589-1610) – Louis XIII (r. 1610-43)

Louis XIII was strongly influenced by the Henri IV style (Place des Vosges, Paris), which marked the beginnings of the Classical period of French architecture. The principal characteristics of this style, which prevailed during the first half of the 17C, are the exact symmetry of the main building and the use of brick panels set into white stonework. Carved ornamentation is limited and sober. Most often, the design is a central block flanked by two end pavilions *(see Château de COURANCES p 255)*. Louis XIII built the first palace in Versailles *(see p 368)* in this style, in brick, stone and slate.

Louis XIV (reigned 1643-1715)

Under the skilful hand of François Mansart, civil architecture gave up its straightforward character and acquired a less domestic, nobler appearance. The early period shows columns and pilasters that stand the height of a single floor of the château. Triangular and arched pediments top doorways and windows. Numerous chimneys sprout from the high roofs *(see Château de MAISONS-LAFITTE p 242)*.

Châteaux built during the second period are characterised by a high ground floor, a very high first floor and a relatively low second floor. A balustrade conceals the roof. The horizontal lines of the building are broken by rows of sturdy columns and tall windows. Ornamental sculpture is limited to the rooftop and the summit of the front pavilions, and inspired by classical models. Versailles *(see p 368)* represents the culmination of the high Classical period.

Louis XV (reigned 1715-74)

After 1700, the Louis XIV style and its harsh angles were mellowed by soft, rounded contours. Under Louis XV, oval spaces and curved surfaces were favoured. Windows and pediments display intricate ornamentation, while the rest of the façade remains austere, without columns; the roof is formed by two sloping planes *(see the stables at CHANTILLY p 37, 137)*. Over time, Classical yielded more and more to Rococo (also known as Baroque classicism in France), which is distinguished by profuse, often semi-abstract ornamentation, and lightness of colour and weight.

Louis XVI (reigned 1774-92)

The influence of the elegant Louis XV style is still apparent in works of this period, but over-abundant curves are replaced by right angles. Columns make a conspicuous comeback, placed on unadorned façades. This phase is known as classicist, for many of the decorative motifs are inspired by Antiquity, a trend that introduced the so-called Pompeian and the Empire styles that followed *(see VERSAILLES: Petit Trianon p 393)*. The French Revolution brought an abrupt end to building in this style.

Fontainebleau – Galerie François I, fresco by Primaticcio

Renaissance: First Fontainebleau School – Ornate decoration in a free interpretation of the Italian masters. The frescoes framed by stuccowork are above the wainscoting. Coffered ceilings and rafters.

Gros-Bois – Dining room

Louis XIII style – The decorative features are more restrained. Above the wainscoting are huge tapestries or frescoes. The ceiling rafters are visible but in most instances the coffering has disappeared.

Versailles – Salon de Vénus

Louis XIV style – The decoration is luxurious in the materials used but understated in design. Marble panels decorate the walls. The ceiling is divided into painted compartments separated by gilded stuccowork.

Champs – Mme de Pompadour's bedchamber

Louis XV style – Right angles have been banished. Curves, scrolls and arabesques soften straight lines. Light-coloured wainscoting has replaced the marble panels. Mouldings with plant and floral motifs, volutes, cartouches and shells.

Versailles – Louis XVI's gaming room

Louis XVI style – The decoration is still elegant and light in colour, but straight lines have come back into fashion. The severity of the rectangular panels is relieved by reeds and ribbons or garlands.

Compiègne – Napoleon's bedchamber

Empire style – Antique green or crimson-red hangings have replaced the wainscoting. Straight lines and semicircular arches predominate. Heavy mouldings and motifs stand out against the dark woodwork.

RELIGIOUS ARCHITECTURE

Île-de-France and the regions north of Paris offer a rich variety of architectural styles: Gallo-Roman at Bavay; Romanesque at Morienval, Rhuis and Chartres; Gothic architecture throughout Île-de-France where it was born, and the later Flamboyant Gothic mainly in Picardy; Renaissance influence at Amiens and Cassel; Classical architecture in and around Paris; and Baroque in Flanders.

Many of the earliest buildings of note were constructed for religious purposes, and the development of architectural styles is best understood through them. A church consisted basically of a chancel reserved for members of the clergy, where the high altar and the reliquaries were located, and of a nave for the congregation. This simple layout characterised the early churches, built on a basilical plan. During the Romanesque period the plan of the church developed into the shape of a cross. The narthex at the entrance received those who had not been baptised, and the nave was enlarged with aisles. In places of pilgrimage, an ambulatory and side aisles were added to the chancel to facilitate processions. Architects followed this layout as it was convenient for celebrating Mass and easy to build.

Romanesque (11C-12C)

Architects in Romanesque times knew how to build huge, lofty churches; but, as the heavy stone vaulting often caused the walls to settle or cave in, they made the windows as small as possible and added aisles surmounted by galleries to support the sombre nave.

One of the main types of roofing in Romanesque churches is groined vaulting, in which two identical barrels meet at right angles. The barrel in line with the nave is supported by the transverse arch, while the one set at a right angle is supported by the main arch or by a recess in the wall. Rhuis and Morienval churches and the Royal Doorway of Chartres Cathedral are splendid examples of Romanesque art.

Gothic (12C-15C)

The transition from Romanesque to Gothic architecture – which originated in Île-de-France – was a slow, natural process that developed in response to the demand for wider, higher and lighter churches. Gothic art, typified by quadripartite vaulting and the use of pointed arches, evolved from sombre 12C Romanesque sanctuaries into light 13C churches and the extravagantly ornate buildings of the 15C. It is rare to find a church with entirely unified features reflecting a given period in history. Building a church was a costly and lengthy operation subject to changes in public taste and building methods as the work progressed. Towards the late 13C famous personalities and guilds were granted the privilege of having a chapel built in their honour in one of the side aisles. In exchange they were expected to make a generous contribution towards the building or its maintenance.

Architects – The names of the architects of great religious edifices are known to us only from the Gothic period onwards, through texts or through inscriptions carved around the "labyrinths" outlined on cathedral floors. That is how Robert de Luzarches was revealed as responsible for the plans of Amiens Cathedral.

The most outstanding master builder in the north of France, however, was undoubtedly **Villard de Honnecourt**, born near Cambrai. The towers of Laon Cathedral, Vaucelles Abbey *(south of Cambrai)*, and the chancels at St-Quentin and Cambrai *(no longer extant)* have all been attributed to him.

West fronts – Most main façades were set facing west. Nave and aisles had their own doorway flanked by buttresses that were bare in the 12C and 13C, ornate in the 15C. The tympanum featured ornamentation, and in the 14C its gable was elaborately carved, with crockets adorning the ramps. 13C rose windows were fairly small; in the 14C they were enlarged across the west front to provide light for the nave. As windows grew larger, façades became more delicate. A gallery was built at the base of the towers to break the rigid vertical perspective created by the buttresses and bell-towers; in the 15C this was reduced to a balustrade and the gables further embellished.

Ideally, west fronts were to be richly decorated with stone carvings, but in many cases they were the last part to be completed. Architects were often obliged to forego ornamentation, and even towers, owing to insufficient funds. In other cases, even the transepts were given remarkable façades *(see Chartres)*.

Spires – After lightening the façades of Gothic churches, architects turned to the spires. By the Flamboyant period the open-work masonry was markedly ornate. In the 19C many bell-towers in the region were given a spire by followers of Viollet-le-Duc.

Flying buttresses – In Early Gothic churches the pillars in the nave were supported by masonry concealed in the galleries. During the 12C these walls were reduced to arches *(see below)* supported by sturdy piers. Soon afterwards the galleries themselves were replaced with a row of flying buttresses outside. A number of high openings could therefore be incorporated into the church interior, producing a far more luminous nave.

From then on, tall churches can be schematically described as stone frames consisting of columns supporting diagonal arches and resting on two or three levels of flying buttresses. The buttresses were in turn supported by a series of tall pillars bearing pinnacles.

Diagonal arches – Towards the end of the 11C groined vaulting was extremely common; but, as it was difficult to build and liable to crack, a group of architects from England, Milan and Île-de-France decided to reinforce the groins.

They found that by building the diagonal arches first and by consolidating them with a small amount of rubble, vaulting that was both sturdy and light was achieved.

By supporting this vaulting on a series of arches, so that the weight of the masonry would have to be borne at the springing, the architects could dispense with the walls in between the arches and replace them with stained-glass windows; this in turn greatly enhanced the luminosity of the interiors.

This significant development heralded the age of quadripartite vaulting.

Vaulting – Quadripartite vaulting, in which the thrust is supported by four main arches, is easy to install in a square-shaped bay. In the 12C bays were enlarged and it was no longer possible to build them square, as the pillars propping up the walls would have been too far apart. The problem was initially resolved by covering the bays two by two, thus forming a square again. An extra transverse arch was then added and made to rest on slim pillars alternating with stout piers.

This type of vaulting – upheld by three diagonal arches – is known as sexpartite vaulting because of the number of its divisions.

When more sophisticated diagonal arches were made to support the vaulting above rectangular bays, the intermediary resting points were eventually discarded.

After the 15C, Flamboyant architects put in additional, decorative ribbing of complex design that formed liernes and tiercerons, and subsequently stars and intricate networks. The main supporting arches were flanked by ornamental arches of no practical use. The keystones – usually pendant – grew thinner and longer.

Elevations *(see illustrations opposite)* – Gothic elevations reflect the continual search for higher and lighter buildings.

Transitional Gothic (A) – The term Transitional Gothic covers the birth and early stages of Gothic architecture, from about 1125 to 1190. The first use of diagonal vaulting in France appeared over the ambulatory in the Romanesque abbey church at Morienval *(see p 264)*.

Though some Romanesque details – such as semicircular arches – can still be observed in Early Gothic buildings, there were several significant changes. The new interiors presented four-storey elevations consisting of high clerestory windows at the top lighting the nave directly, a triforium (a narrow, arcaded passageway below the clerestory), a gallery – instrumental in supporting the walls as high up as possible – and arcading at ground level. There were often openings behind the gallery but never behind the triforium.

The pillars of the main arches initially consisted of a thick column; this was later replaced by twinned columns supporting the arches and the colonnettes above. Laon Cathedral is a good example of Early Gothic architecture. Semicircular transept endings like the famous south arm at Soissons Cathedral were also a feature.

Early Gothic (B) – This great period (c 1180-1250), when Gothic architecture was in its ascendancy, produced some of France's finest masterpieces, among them Chartres Cathedral *(see illustration p 139)*.

| Transitional (12C) | Early Gothic (early 13C) | High Gothic (late 13C-early 14C) | Flamboyant (15C and 16C) |

Characteristics include arches and windows pointed and shaped like a lancet; clerestory windows surmounted by a round opening; the gallery replaced by external flying buttresses. The numerous colonnettes originating from the vaulting rested on the shaft that bore the weight of all the main arches. This pier was generally a large round column flanked by four colonnettes.

High Gothic (C) – This was the golden age of the great cathedrals in France, lasting from about 1250 and the reign of St Louis to around 1375 when the Hundred Years War blocked the progress made by medieval architects.

At this time High Gothic, known as Rayonnant in French, reached its peak: the three-storey elevation (large arcades, triforium – the wall at the back now pierced with stained-glass – and tall clerestory windows) lightened the nave and formed one huge single stained-glass window in the chancels of churches with no ambulatory; the wall area was reduced to a minimum and the springers supporting the vaulting were doubled by another series of arches. In many cases the colonnettes started from the ground, at the point where they surround the pillar of the main arches. Two slight mouldings – level with the main arches and the springers – were the only features to break the vertiginous ascent. Beauvais Cathedral is the most outstanding example of High Gothic *(see illustration p 99)*.

Flamboyant Gothic (D) – This last stage in Gothic architecture, which could develop no further, succumbed to ornamental excess, aided by the fine, easily worked Picardy stone.

The style owes its name to the flame shapes in the tracery of the bays and rose windows, and to the exuberant carved and sculpted decoration which tended to obscure the structural lines of the buildings: doorways were crowned with open-work gables, balustrades were surmounted by pinnacles, vaulting featured complex designs with purely decorative arches (called liernes and tiercerons) converging on ornately worked keystones. The triforium disappeared, replaced by larger clerestory windows. Arches came to rest on columns or were continued by ribbing level with the pillars. The latter were no longer flanked by colonnettes. In some churches, the ribs formed a spiral around the column.

Flemish civil architecture – From the late 13C the particular nature of Flemish Gothic architecture manifested itself in the civic buildings, belfries and town halls erected by the cities that had obtained charters.

Belfries – Symbol of the town's power, the belfry was either an isolated building (Bergues, Béthune) or part of the town hall (Douai, Arras, Calais). It was built like a keep with watchtowers and machicolations. The rooms above the foundations – which housed the prison – had various functions, such as guard-room. At the top, the bell-room enclosed the **chimes**. Originally these consisted of only four bells. Today they often number at least 30 bells which play every hour, half-hour and quarter-hour. The bell-room is surrounded by watchtowers from which the sentry looked out for enemies and fires. At the very top is a weather vane symbolising the city: thus the lion of Flanders stands at Arras, Bergues and Douai.

Town halls – Town halls are often imposing with striking, richly embellished façades: niches, statues, gables and pinnacles might adorn the exterior.

Inside, the large council chamber or function room had walls decorated with frescoes illustrating the history of the town.

The most beautiful town halls (Douai, Arras, St-Quentin, Hondschoote, Compiègne) were built in the 15C and 16C. Many suffered damage and modification over the centuries and some were completely rebuilt in their original style, as at Arras.

Renaissance (16C)

Renaissance architecture, under the influence of Italian culture, favoured a return to classical themes: columns with capitals imitating the Ionic and Corinthian orders; façades decorated with niches, statues and roundels; pilasters flanking the windows. Quadripartite vaulting was replaced by coffered ceilings and barrel vaulting. Architects introduced basket-handled arches and semicircular or rectangular openings. Inverted brackets replaced flying buttresses. West fronts, and sometimes the north and south façades too, kept their heavy ornamentation. Spires were replaced by small domes and lantern towers.

Isolated examples of Renaissance art – not widely adopted in the north of France – are the Maison du Sagittaire in Amiens and the Hôtel de la Noble Cour in Cassel.

Baroque and Classical (17C-18C)

Architecture – Through the 17C and 18C, architecture presented two different faces. One was Baroque, dominated by irregular contours, an abundance of exuberant shapes, generous carving and much ornamentation. The other was Classical, a model of stateliness and restraint, adhering strictly to the rules of Antiquity with rows of Greek columns (Doric, Ionic and Corinthian), pedimented doorways, imposing domes and scrolled architraves. The Baroque style flourished in Flanders, Hainault and Artois which fell under Spanish influence, while the Classical style found favour in Picardy and Île-de-France.

Moret-sur-Loing – Maison de François I

Ouzounoff/DIAC

The Baroque Chapelle du Grand Séminaire in Cambrai is one of many religious buildings erected in the 17C following the influence of the Counter Reformation and its main engineers, the Jesuits. Civil buildings include the House of Gilles de la Boé in Lille and the Mont-de-Piété in Bergues. The Mint in Lille, with its bosses and richly carved ornamentation, exemplifies **Flemish Baroque**.

The Petit Trianon at Versailles is a famous example of Classical architecture.

In Arras, Baroque and Classical elements were combined for the town's splendid main squares framed by houses with arcades and volutes. Combined elements can also be seen at the abbeys in Valloires and Prémontré and at the Château de Long.

Sculpture – The finely grained and easily worked chalky stone found in Picardy was used for much decorative work. By the 13C the "picture carvers" in Amiens and Arras were already displaying the specific Picardy traits discernible throughout later centuries: lively, finely detailed figures going about their everyday life. The calendar at Amiens is a good example of this engaging art.

In the late 15C and early 16C the Picardy wood carvers *(huchiers)* became renowned through their work on the stalls in Amiens Cathedral; the door panels in St Wulfram's in Abbeville; the finely worked frames of the "Puy-Notre-Dame" paintings.

Baroque art favoured abundant decorative sculpture. Buildings were covered with a profusion of ornamental fruit, flowers, cornucopias, *putti*, niches, statues, vases etc.

Monasteries in Île-de-France

A considerable number of priory, convent and abbey ruins are to be found in Île-de-France, and numerous districts and street names recall the many religious communities that have not survived.

Abbeys in the history of Île-de-France – Abbeys wouldn't exist if people didn't feel a strong calling to take up ecclesiastical duties. At the same time, there would be no abbeys if the clergy had not been given any land. After the 5C, when the victorious Franks divided up the Gallo-Roman territory, it would have been impossible for any religious community to survive without the help of donations. There were many aspiring monks in France up to the 18C, and the different communities were almost entirely dependent on the generosity of benefactors. As the suzerain of Île-de-France was none other than the supreme ruler of France, the king, this region was graced with an abundance of local monasteries.

In the early days of Christianity, during the late 4C, Île-de-France was covered with forests; but the land was also fertile and the area attracted monks who wanted to live in peace and escape the terrible famine ravaging the country. Soon afterwards the Merovingian monarchs, who had been strongly backed by the clergy, encouraged the creation of religious foundations, to which they made considerable contributions. The wealthy Carolingians continued to endow these abbeys, and the practice was kept up by the Capetians and their vassals for over 800 years (Chaalis and Royaumont). French kings favoured monasteries because the monks used to reclaim uncultivated land and because the monasteries were constantly praying for their patrons. Religious faith was strong from the 10C to the 17C, and kings made donations to abbeys for a variety of reasons: to thank God for a victory, to seek expiation for an offence committed against the Church, to express his own personal belief or to offer a dowry to dowager queens or royal princesses about to take the veil.

Religious Orders – The term abbey does not apply to just any Christian community whose members lead a frugal, secluded life. In fact it designates a group of men or women, placed under the authority of an abbot or an abbess, who live according to a rule approved by the Pope. The monks' day is usually divided into chores related to community life, and spiritual and liturgical duties, which are the main purpose of the association.

All abbeys have an abbot or abbess, who generally enjoys the same rank as a bishop. He or she is elected by fellow companions and incarnates the spiritual and temporal leader of the abbey. After the 16C, the Pope gave the king of France the right to appoint abbots and abbesses. These prelates were called commendatory abbots and usually lived in the king's entourage.

Sometimes, to administer new domains or to fulfil the wish of a patron who wanted to receive monks on his land, the abbots would build a priory. This small community was supervised by a prior who was answerable to the abbey. The Cistercians set up many granges, farming colonies run by lay brothers.

Monastic Rules – The Benedictine Order – created by St Benedict in the 6C – was undoubtedly the order which flourished the most in France. Its members founded over 1 000 abbeys throughout the country. The Benedictine rule was subsequently reformed, leading to the creation of two additional orders.

The first originated in the late 10C from Cluny in Burgundy, but unfortunately all the Cluniac houses died out during the Revolution. The second – the Cistercian Order – was, and still is, extremely powerful. It was St Bernard of Cîteaux, also a native of Burgundy, who founded the order in the 11C. He was a firm believer in asceticism and introduced a number of new rules: he condemned elaborate ceremonies and the decoration of churches; monks could no longer be paid tithes, nor could they receive or acquire land; strict rules were laid down on diet, rest was limited to seven hours and monks had to sleep in their clothes in a common dormitory.

They shared their time between liturgical worship – 6-7hr a day – manual labour, study and contemplation. In the 17C, Abbot de Rancé added further austerities to the Cistercian rule (silence, diet). This new rule was named after La Trappe, the monastery near Perseigne where it originated. It is presently enforced in abbeys of strict observance.

The other two main orders that founded abbeys in France were the Augustinian friars and the Premonstratensian canons, both dating from the 12C.

Other communities include the Carmelite Order, the Order of St Francis (Franciscans and Capuchins), the Order of Preachers and the Society of Jesus (Jesuits). They do not follow monastic rules, nor do they found abbeys. Their activities (missionary work, caring for the sick) bring them into contact with the lay world. They live in convents or houses under the authority of the prior, the Mother Superior etc.

A collegiate church is occupied by a community of canons accountable to their bishop.

Monastic buildings – The cloister is the centre of an abbey; its four galleries allow the nuns and monks to take their walks under cover. One of the cloister walls adjoins the abbey church, while another gives onto the chapter-house where monks meet to discuss community problems under the chairmanship of the abbot. The third gallery opens onto the refectory and the fourth onto the calefactory, the only room with heating where the monks study or do manual labour.

The dormitory is generally placed above the chapter-house. It communicates with the church by means of a direct staircase so that the monks could readily attend early morning and night Mass.

Lay brothers – These are believers who cannot or will not take holy orders and therefore have a different status. They spend most of their time in the fields and the workshops, and have their own dormitory and refectory. They may not enter the chapter-house or the chancel of the church. Since the Vatican II Council (1962-65) lay brothers have become more and more involved in the life of the community.

Visitors are not allowed to enter the "enclosure" and are lodged in the guest-house. The poor are housed in the almshouse.

Monasteries also include an infirmary, a noviciate, sometimes a school, and the buildings needed to run the abbey: barns, cellars, winepress, stables and cowsheds.

R. César/TOP

Cloister, Abbaye de Royaumont

RURAL HOUSING IN THE NORTH

The Coast, Inland Flanders and Artois – Whether in Picardy, Artois or Flanders, the same type of houses can be found along the coast: long and low to form a defence against the west winds which often bring rain. They are capped by high-pitched roofs covered with Flemish S-shaped tiles called *pannes*. Their whitewashed walls are cheered by brightly coloured doors and shutters; the bases of the buildings are tarred against the damp.

Behind this apparent uniformity lie very different construction techniques.

In Picardy the walls consist of daubing on wood laths; in certain areas the surface is left plain, as in Ponthieu, but it is more usually whitewashed, giving a spruce look in summer to the flower-bedecked villages along the River Canche and River Authie.

In Flanders the usual building material is more generally brick, sandy coloured in maritime areas and ranging from red to purplish or brown further inland. The great Lille and Artois regional farms, known as **"censes"**, are built around a courtyard with access through a carriage gateway often surmounted by a dovecote.

Some large, partly stone-built farms in the Boulonnais hills are actually old seignorial homes with a turret or fortifications, giving the impression of a manor house.

Hainaut, Avesnois, Thiérache and Soissonnais – In the Hainaut and Avesnois regions houses are massively built, usually consisting of one-storey brick buildings with facings and foundations in regional blue stone.

Their slate roofs are reminiscent of the nearby Ardennes region.

Construction in the Thiérache region, the land of clay and wood, consists of daubing and brick with slate roofs. There are many old dovecotes in the region, either over carriage gates or free-standing in courtyards. Villages in close proximity to one another huddle around their fortified churches *(see La THIÉRACHE)*.

The houses in the Soissonnais region are similar to those of Île-de-France. Beautiful white freestone is used for walls and crow-stepped gables, contrasting with flat, red roof tiles which take on a patina with the years.

Windmills – In the early 19C there were nearly 3 000 windmills in northern France. Today no more than a few dozen still exist, registered, protected and restored by the Association Régionale des Amis des Moulins du Nord-Pas-de-Calais (ARAM).

Post mills – Built of wood, these mills are the most common in Flanders. The main body of the structure and the sails turn around a vertical post. On the exterior – the side opposite the sails – a beam known as the "tail" is linked to a wheel which is turned to position the entire mill according to the wind direction. Some 14 of this type remain in northern France, including those at Boeschepe, Cassel, Hondschoote, Steenvoorde, Villeneuve d'Ascq and St-Maxent.

On a **tower mill** (or smock mill when made of wood) only the roof, to which the sails are attached, turns. This type of mill is more massive and is usually built of brick or stone; the Steenmeulen at Terdeghem near Steenvoorde is the only one still in working order, but there are other fine specimens at Templeuve and Watten (Nord) as well as Achicourt, Beuvry, Guemps (Pas-de-Calais), and Louvencourt (Somme).

Water mills – Water mills can also be seen throughout the region, particularly in the Avesnois, Ternois, Thiérache and Valenciennes areas. The shape and size of the wheel, which is the essential part of the mill, depends on the rate of flow of the river and on the specific features of the site. Some of these mills are open to the public: Felleries, Sars-Poteries, Marly (Nord), Esquerdes, Maintenay, Wimille and Wissant (Pas-de-Calais).

MILITARY ARCHITECTURE

Of the defensive systems in the north of France, relatively few date from the Middle Ages: the town walls of Boulogne and Laon, and the castles at Coucy, Rambures, Picquigny, Lucheux, Septmonts and Pierrefonds. In contrast, numerous 17C star fortifications along the northeastern border have been preserved, some in their entirety, as at Bergues and Le Quesnoy, others only partially: Avesnes, Maubeuge, Cambrai, Douai, St-Omer, Péronne.

Before Vauban – It was under the last of the Valois kings that the military engineers, who had studied Italian examples, adopted a system of curtain walls defended at the corners by bastions. Bastions in the shape of an ace of spades with projections were introduced to protect the men defending the curtain wall. This feature can be seen at Le Quesnoy. Bastions and curtain walls, usually with stone bonding, were crowned with platforms bearing cannon. Raised towers allowed the moats or ditches and surrounding area to be watched. In the 17C Henri IV employed an engineer, **Jean Errard** (1554-1610) nicknamed the Father of French Fortification, who specialised in castrametation. In the north Errard fortified Ham and Montreuil and built the citadels at Calais, Laon, Doullens and Amiens which still stand today. In 1600 he published an authoritative *Treatise on Fortification* which served until Vauban's time.

Halluin

St-Vaast-en-Cambrésis

Maintenay

J. Bruggeman/ARAM

Villeneuve-d'Ascq

Wormhout

49

The Age of Vauban – Inspired by his predecessors, **Sébastien le Prestre de Vauban** (1633-1707) established a system of his own characterised by bastions with half-moons surrounded by deep moats. Making the most of the natural obstacles and using local materials (brick in the north), he also tried to give an aesthetic quality to his works by adorning them with carved monumental stone gateways (Bergues, Lille, Maubeuge).

On the coast and along the border of Flanders and Hainaut, Vauban established a long line of double defences, known as the **"pré carré"**. These two close lines of fortresses and citadels were designed to prevent the enemy's passage and to ensure mutual back-up in case of attack.

The first line consists of 15 sites from Dunkirk and Bergues to Maubeuge, Philippeville and Dinant. The second runs a little way behind and includes 13 towns extending from Gravelines and St-Omer to Avesnes, Marienbourg, Rocroi and Mézières. Some of these strongpoints were Vauban's own creations such as the citadel at Lille, which he himself called the queen of citadels; others existed already and were remodelled.

For over a century this group of fortifications succeeded in defending the north of France, until the invasions of 1814 and 1815.

During the French campaign in 1940 Le Quesnoy, Lille, Bergues, Dunkirk, Gravelines and Calais all formed solid strongholds protecting the retreat of the Franco-British armies.

Atlantic Wall – The concrete bunkers of the Atlantic Wall that stretch along the coast-line were erected by the **Todt Organisation**, which from 1940 used prisoners of war for the task. The Nord-Pas-de-Calais region was considered a war zone against England, and in 1944 about 10 000 constructions were counted on the French coast. In the deep forests of Eperlecques and Clairmarais enormous concrete installations were built for launching the V1 and V2 rockets on London. The Eperlecques Bunker *(see p 329)*, today designated a historic monument, is one of the most impressive examples of this type of monumental concrete architecture, along with the fort at Mimoyecques *(see p 211)*.

Art

FAIENCE AND PORCELAIN IN ÎLE-DE-FRANCE

Faience – This is the term commonly applied to any ceramics made of porous clay and glazed with waterproof enamel. The enamel was initially transparent but, in the 9C, it became opaque thanks to the discovery in the Middle East of tin glaze. The Arabic influence throughout the Mediterranean Basin led to the development of faience in Moorish Spain and Italy from the 15C onwards. The Spanish island of Majorca gave its name to "majolicaware", the term describing Italian Renaissance ceramics. The name "faience" probably derives from Faenza, the Italian town renowned for its majolica.

Faience developed in France in the 16C and 17C with leading pottery centres such as Nevers and Rouen. The latter influenced the early producers of faience in Île-de-France such as Pierre Chicaneau who settled in St-Cloud in 1674. In the 18C as porcelain became more popular, the number of potteries increased in the region and the first pieces of porcelain were produced. The famous ceramist Jacques Chapelle set up the works in **Sceaux** in 1748 and circumvented the Vincennes-Sèvres monopoly on faience by creating "Japanese-style faience". The Rococo style, vivid colours, and original decorations, many of them in relief, brought success to Sceaux until the end of the 18C. This period was marked by the discovery in England of "fine faience" or white lead-glazed earthenware. Its reasonable cost and elegance, along with the exceptionally liberal conditions laid down in the Treaty of Vergennes (1786), ensured its popularity and it was massively imported into France. This know-how was gradually taken over in Île-de-France by the works in **Montereau**, **Creil** and **Choisy-le-Roi**. However, the end of the 19C confirmed the preference for porcelain, and faience went into a decline.

Porcelain – Porcelain was discovered in China in the 12C. It is a thin, white ceramic ware that is slightly translucent. Body and glaze are fired together. In the 16C, the popularity of porcelain from the Far East led to numerous experiments in Europe to try and achieve a product that would rival it. The high level of imports by the French East India Company is indicative of European interest in this mysterious technique. Craftsmen did not know the exact nature of the paste used by the Chinese and they progressed by trial and error, using processes similar to the ones used for faience. A very fine marl used on its own was vitrified by the introduction of a sort of glass called frit. The resulting ceramic was "soft-paste" porcelain that could be scratched by steel.

In the early 18C, the basic ingredient of porcelain, white china clay, was discovered in Saxony. The secrets of the production process were jealously kept in Meissen near Dresden. In France, it was not until 1769 that the output from a white china clay quarry near St-Yriex in the Limousin area enabled craftsmen to produce "hard-paste" porcelain. Sèvres produced porcelain exclusively from the beginning of the 19C onwards. This new product, in which body and glaze were fired together at a very high temperature (1 400°C/2 500°F), was remarkably strong but more difficult to decorate.

Only five colours are suitable for high-temperature firing – blue, green, yellow, purplish brown and reddish orange. The introduction of low-firing techniques revolutionised the production of faience and porcelain. The enamel was fired in succession at low temperatures, enabling the use of a wide range of fresh, vivid colours. The porcelain works in **St-Cloud** (1697-1766) were the first to master the techniques required to produce "soft-paste" porcelain. It was famous for its "white" ware and applied gilding that differed greatly from the technique used by Sèvres. Numerous porcelain works opened in quick succession in the 18C, with the backing of princes or the royal family. The works in **Chantilly** (1725-1800), for example, were set up by Cirquaire Cirou with the support of Louis-Henri de Bourbon, Prince de Condé. In **Mennecy**, it was the Duke de Villeroy who provided the necessary patronage in the face of ever-increasing privileges granted to some of the works. The one with the highest level of support was in **Vincennes**. Madame de Pompadour and Louis XV both took a keen interest in the company that set up works in **Sèvres** in 1756. The earliest designs were "natural" flowers and the works gradually specialised in the production of dinner services, statuettes and even veritable pictures in porcelain. Because of the processes used, the decoration and enamel combined perfectly, giving an incomparable blending. In its early days, the Sèvres porcelain works enjoyed exclusive rights to the use of gold on all its products. Even now, unless there is some technical reason against it, all its products must include some gold. "Biscuit-ware", another of the specialities of these works, is the term used to describe a production method in which the body of the paste is left unglazed so that the gracefulness of the statuettes is not altered.

STAINED GLASS

Notre-Dame-de-la-Belle-Verrière
Detail of 12C-13C stained glass, Chartres Cathedral

Since the early Middle Ages, church windows have been adorned with coloured glass. Unfortunately, none of these very early works have survived.

During the Gothic period, master glassmakers played an important role in the completion and ornamentation of churches. Thanks to them, both the clergy and the congregation could appreciate the shimmering light that came streaming through the roundels. Stained glass is not purely decorative, however. To the Church it is an invaluable teaching aid, permanently communicating catechism, sacred history and the lives of the saints.

The art of making stained glass – Stained-glass windows consist of juxtaposed pieces of coloured glass held together by strips of lead. The window is divided into panels to ensure perfect solidity. When the various coloured pieces have been selected and cut to shape, the glassmaker completes the shading and details of the figures with touches of *grisaille*, a brownish pigment containing silica that is painted on and blends with the glass in the melt. The glass panels are then reassembled and fixed in place in the window. Patches of lichen may develop on stained-glass windows: it starts to attack the lead after 100 years and has been known to break through the glass after 300 to 400 years. However, it is man rather than erosion who is to blame for the disappearance of numerous early stained-glass windows: in the 18C many were dismantled and replaced by plain glass, which afforded a better view of the aisles.

The development of stained glass – Technical developments in glass-making were prompted by artistic trends but also by the search for greater economy and the wish to produce lighter tones.

12C – Stained-glass windows were small, with fairly heavy borders. The ornamentation around the main figures was extremely limited.

13C – To ensure perfect cohesion between the panels and the leading, the iron armatures were fastened to the walls.

The clerestory windows presented tall, isolated figures. The lower windows, which could be observed more closely, had medallions depicting scenes from the lives of the saints. This genre is known as historiated stained glass. Panels included architectural features and embellishments. Borders were heavy and the scenes show a marked attempt at realism. Historiated roundels were set in a *grisaille* framework enhanced by brightly painted rose-windows. The daily lives of craftsmen were evoked in lively anecdotal scenes. The lower windows were generally divided into panels composing geometric motifs (stars, diamonds, clover-leaves).

14C – The loss of wealth led to a considerable increase in window space. For reasons of economy, more and more *grisaille* was produced, its starkness softened by delicate shading and graceful foliage motifs. Angels and rosy cherubs adorned the barer parts of the windows. Borders became smaller and lettering made an appearance. In the second half of the 14C glassmakers discovered that silver staining could be used to accentuate a variety of bright colours: yellow on a white background, light green on blue, amber on red etc.

15C – The leading was no longer produced using a plane, but instead stretched on a wire-drawing bench: the lead strips were thinner, therefore more flexible and able to hold together larger and thinner panes of glass than previously. Glassmakers worked with a lighter type of glass, and the colours used in the decoration were less vivid. In some churches, two thirds of the window was taken up by *grisaille*. These panels featured Gothic canopies with high gables and openwork pinnacles. The craftsmanship was of a remarkable quality, and master glassmakers began to sign their own work, introducing original themes.

P. Tétrel/EXPLORER

Soft-paste porcelain figure (St-Cloud)

Porcelain water pitcher (Chantilly, 18C)

Porcelain sauceboat (Vincennes, 18C)

"Bachelier" vase (Sèvres, 18C)

Porcelain jardiniere (Mennecy, 18C)

Faience plate (Montereau, 19C)

Faience plate (Choisy-la-Roi, 19C)

RMN

16C – Stained glass drew inspiration from the works of the great painters and from contemporary engravings. Glassmakers had become masters at cutting glass from large sheets – using a diamond and no longer a red-hot iron – and they also excelled at painting with enamels. Stained-glass windows developed into large, transparent paintings in which minute attention was given to detail, perspective and design. In some buildings religious themes were replaced by classical scenes taken from Antiquity.

17C and 18C – The use of coloured glass decreased. Stained glass was painted and decorated with enamels.

LANDSCAPE PAINTING

Although many painters were employed in the internal decoration of châteaux and abbeys around Paris, it was not until the 19C that painters began to show an interest in the surrounding landscapes.

Until the 18C, French masters had used landscapes merely as a background to their work, either as a decorative element or to enhance the atmosphere through composition and colour. It was so poorly regarded that often a major artist painting a portrait or other subject would leave the background landscape to be painted by a studio assistant. The two most celebrated French landscape painters were the 17C classicists Nicolas Poussin and Claude Lorrain. Poussin gave his views the heroic qualities of his subject and Lorrain painted scenes of a lost, idyllic Antiquity.

Camille Corot (1796-1875) – Corot was the pioneer of contemporary landscape painting in France. He lived in Barbizon from 1830 to 1835 and worked outdoors in Fontainebleau Forest and all over Île-de-France, studying the contrasts and soft hues of light in the undergrowth, along shaded paths and on the edge of the plain. He later took up painting lakes in a search for more delicate variations; the ponds at Ville-d'Avray (south of St-Cloud), with their subtle reflections, were his favourites.

Painters of the Oise – The group was founded in 1845 by two of Corot's followers, Charles-François Daubigny and Jules Dupré. Daubigny (1817-78) liked to paint the rippling waters of the River Oise and the greenery and blossoms of the orchards and groves. He led a peaceful life: his work paid well and received universal acclaim. He could often be found working on the Île de Vaux near Auvers, or in a small rowing boat he had converted into a studio. Jules Dupré (1811-89), a close friend of Théodore Rousseau, used darker colours and belonged to the Barbizon School. He seldom left his house in L'Isle-Adam.

In 1865 the lithographer and satirical cartoonist Honoré Daumier (1808-79) moved from the capital to Valmondois in Île-de-France, when he met with serious financial difficulties.

In 1866 **Camille Pissarro** (1830-1903) initially settled in Pontoise for two years. Uninterested in the nearby streams and rivers, he concentrated on meadows, grassy slopes, country villages and street scenes featuring peasant women, which he portrayed in a deliberately poetic manner. His gift for expressing light, his qualities as a teacher and his kindliness made him the father figure of the Impressionist movement.

The Barbizon School – Its representatives drew inspiration from the landscapes of Fontainebleau Forest and the nearby Bière plain. The founder of the movement was **Théodore Rousseau** (1812-67) who settled in a modest country cottage in 1847 and stayed there until his death. Diaz and Charles Jacque were among his close friends. They remained cheerful and humorous despite the lack of success of their paintings and their consequent penury. It was only towards the end of the Second Empire that

Moret bridge by Alfred Sisley (1893)

H. Lewandowski/RMN

Musée d'Orsay /RMN

Gare St-Lazare by Claude Monet (Musée d'Orsay)

their talent was acknowledged. Troyon (1810-65) specialised in rural scenes repre-senting cattle. Barye, the highly respected animal sculptor, also took up landscape painting because of his love of nature. The charms and hardships of country life were portrayed particularly well in the work of **Jean-François Millet** (1814-75), who lived in Barbizon from 1849 until his death.

The artists of this school generally favoured the dark colours of tree bark and under-growth, and their preferred subjects included dusk, soft lighting and stormy skies. These sombre tones were criticised by their detractors, who claimed they painted with "prune juice".

Around 1865 a new group of artists fell under the spell of these magical woodlands and Pierre-Auguste Renoir, Alfred Sisley and Claude Monet settled in Chailly. Though they did not associate themselves with the Barbizon community, they did accept advice from their elders. Diaz encouraged the young Renoir to work with lighter tones. Here too the seeds of Impressionism were being sown.

Impressionism – The second-generation artists wanted their work to capture the essence of light itself and to reflect the vibrant quality of colour. The term "Impressionist" was actually coined by a sarcastic journalist in 1874, but was adopted by the group as they felt it conveyed the double revolution they had brought about in the field of painting.

The Impressionist Revolution – The Impressionist movement revolutionised artistic con-ventions on two counts: it paid little attention to form and it invented a new technique. Until then, the representation of reality was fundamentally important and no artist would have dared to neglect the lines and shapes of his subject, whether a portrait, still-life painting or landscape. Painters showed little concern for light and its effects, considered a minor component, and priority was given to subject matter. For the Impressionists, light and the analysis of its effects became the principal subject; all the rest – contours, scenes, people – was simply an excuse to paint light.

Religious and historical works, as well as family portraits and everyday scenes, were no longer interesting in themselves. The Impressionists' favourite subjects were those that played with light: water, snow, fabrics, flesh, flowers, leaves, or fruit.

They wished to capture the infinite depths of the skies, the shimmering of light on water, a dress or a human face. When depicting the undergrowth, they wanted to show how the russet tones glitter in sunlight, how bright colours sparkle...

Such fleeting and indefinite concepts were no longer attainable using traditional tech-niques. As priority was given to the vibration of light around the edges of objects, the process that applied paint along contours was banished. Traditionally, the layers of paint were applied slowly and acquired their definite colour after the oil had solidi-fied. They were then coated with varnish to produce a transparent effect and to give depth to the colours. Naturally this technique was far too lengthy to capture the ephemeral quality of light. As a consequence, the Impressionists developed a tech-nique more suited to their purpose that involved very little oil and dispensed with varnish. Their art consisted in applying quick, small dabs of colour. The exact shade was conveyed by the juxtaposition of touches of pure colour, the final effect being assessed by the eye of the viewer.

The Impressionists were harshly criticised, even insulted at times, and it was only after a 20-year struggle that their work was fully acknowledged. Île-de-France – with its rivers, lakes, gardens, orchards, showers of rain, mists, elegant ladies and regattas – provided them with countless sources of inspiration.

The Painters – The Impressionist School was founded in Honfleur where **Claude Monet** (1840-1926), a painter from Le Havre, was encouraged by the seascape specialist Eugène Boudin to paint landscapes. **Boudin** (1824-98), a friend of Corot's, was also a precursor of Impressionism: his paintings are full of air and light. Following his example, Monet and later the Dutch artist Jongkind worked on the luminosity of the landscapes around the Seine estuary. They were joined by Bazille and **Sisley**, whom they had befriended in Gleyre's studio, and began to paint around Fontainebleau Forest too, though they remained separate from the Barbizon School. Pissarro, Cézanne and Guillaumin, who met at the Swiss Academy, were called "The Famous Three" (Le Groupe des Trois).

The painters were strongly supported by **Édouard Manet** (1832-83), one of their elders who was upsetting artistic conventions and scandalising the public with his bold colours and compositions. It was Manet who encouraged the Impressionists to pursue their efforts at painting light. In 1863, following clashes between the artists and the official salons that refused to show these new works, a now-famous independent exhibition of the rejected works (Salon des Refusés) was set up on the orders of Napoleon III. It gave birth to, and led to the naming of, the Impressionist movement. In 1871 small groups of amateur painters, pupils and friends, including **Paul Cézanne**, joined Pissarro at Pontoise and Docteur Gachet in Auvers. Another group based in Argenteuil and Louveciennes included **Renoir**, Monet, Sisley and Edgar Degas, who had originally studied under Ingres. Monet's innovative technique put him at the head of the movement and inspired both Manet and later Berthe Morisot.

In the 1880s, Renoir moved to Chatou just west of Paris, where he frequented the Maison Tomaise, a restaurant first opened in 1815 and now restored. After 1880 the group broke up but its members remained faithful to painting with light colours. Sisley moved to Moret, drawn to the River Loing, while Monet settled in Giverny on the banks of the Epte (see The Green Guide Normandy). For practical reasons, Pissarro left the Oise Valley to live in Eragny, near Gisors.

Georges Seurat (1859-91) remained in Paris but concentrated on the landscapes around the capital and along the Channel coast. His technique amounted to breaking down the subject matter into small dabs of colour, each consisting of a series of dots (points). Maximilien Luce (1858-1941) also experimented with this method – known as Pointillism or Divisionism – in the vicinity of Mantes.

Cézanne later returned to Aix-en-Provence where, through the use of colour, tone and accentuated outlines, he developed stylised masses that laid the foundations for the Cubist movement.

Renoir travelled to Algeria and Venice, inspiring him to paint some of his finest works. Degas and Toulouse-Lautrec (1846-1901) lived in Paris. They were fascinated by circuses and theatres where swirling dancers and performers were bathed in complex illuminations created by artificial lighting.

The Dawn of the 20C – The followers of the **Nabis** and **Fauve** movements, which preceded Cubism and the new art forms born in the wake of the First World War, also set up their easels – and sometimes even their studios – in the picturesque outskirts of Paris. On his return from a stay in Pont-Aven, where Paul Gauguin had shown him the magic of composing in flat, bold colours, Paul Sérusier converted his friends from the Académie Julian to the same style and formed the Nabis movement (a Hebrew word meaning prophet). **Maurice Denis** (1870-1943) became the leader of the group, which included Bonnard, Rouss el, Vuillard, Maillol, Vallotton and others.

The early Fauves (meaning "wild beasts") included extremely diverse artists – Matisse, Dufy, Braque, Derain, Vlaminck, Rouault, Marquet. Their paintings of bright, even violent colour created an uproar when they were first shown. The painters, never a coherent group, were influenced by the paintings of **Van Gogh** who had died in 1890 leaving a collection of brilliant canvases composed of strong, vigorous brushstrokes of pure colour.

The coasts and countryside of the north of France and the region around Paris continue to attract many artists.

Folklore and traditions of the North

For dates of festivals and other events see the Calendar of Events at the end of the guide.

The people of Picardy and the north of France belong to the "Picardy nation" that used to spread from Beauvais to Lille and from Calais to Laon, extending as far as Tournai and Mons. The common language of this "nation" formed a bond between its inhabitants, who are known for being hard workers with a taste for good food and lively merrymaking. Even now, the slightest excuse is found to celebrate or get together in an *estaminet* (the Walloon word for a café) for a beer or two. Natives of Flanders, Artois, Lille and Picardy all have this same fondness for gatherings which is reflected in their many group activities: carnivals, celebrations, patron saint's days, village fairs and associations (each village has its own band).

The Ducasse or Kermesse – The words *ducasse* (from *dédicace*, meaning a Catholic holiday) and *kermesse* ("church fair" in Flemish) now both designate a town or village patron saint's day. This holiday has preserved aspects of its religious origins (Mass and procession) but today also includes stalls, competitions, traditional games, jumble sales etc.

Carnivals – Carnival time is an occasion to dress up in costume and watch parades of floats and giant figures. It traditionally takes place on Shrove Tuesday *(Mardi Gras)* – as in Dunkirk, where it lasts for three days – but in reality carnival parades take place throughout the year in the North.

Famous Giants – Giants originate from various myths, legends and stories and include:
– legendary founders, such as Lydéric and Phinaert in Lille;
– famous warriors like the Reuzes from Dunkirk and Cassel, said to originate from Scandinavia;
– historic figures, such as Jeanne Maillotte in Lille, the inn-keeper who fought off the "Howlers"; the beautiful Roze in Ardres, who saved the town from dragonnades; the Elector of Bergues, portraying Lamartine; Roland in Hazebrouck, one of Baudouin of Flanders' Crusaders, who distinguished himself at the taking of Constantinople;
– famous couples, like Martin and Martine, the two jack o' the clocks of Cambrai; Colas and Jacqueline, the gardeners of Arras; Arlequin and Colombine in Bruay; Manon and Des Grieux in Hesdin;
– popular figures, like Gédéon, the bell-ringer of Bourbourg, who saved the belfry chimes from being stolen; the pedlar Tisje Tasje of Hazebrouck, symbol of the Flemish spirit, with his wife Toria and his daughter Babe Tisje; Pierrot Bimberlot in Le Quesnoy; and Ko Pierre, a drum major, in Aniche;
– legendary heroes: Gargantua in Bailleul; Gambrinus, the king of beer, in Armentières; Yan den Houtkapper, the woodcutter who made a pair of wooden boots for Charlemagne, in Steenvoorde; Gayant of Douai, said to have delivered the town from brigands;
– representatives of trades, like the vegetable gardener Baptistin in St-Omer; the miner Cafougnette in Denain; and the fisherman Batisse in Boulogne;
– or simply a child, like the famous Binbin in Valenciennes.
Giants are often accompanied by their families – as they do marry and are given large families – and are surrounded by skirted horses, devils, bodyguards and wheels of fortune. Sometimes they have their own hymn, such as the Reuzelieds in Dunkirk and Cassel.

Materials – Traditionally the giants' bodies are made from a willow frame on which a painted *papier mâché* head is placed. Once dressed in their costumes, the giants are then carried by one or more people who make them dance in the procession.
The tallest is Gayant in Douai, who is 8.40m/28ft tall.
As giants are often now made of heavier materials (steel tubing, cane, plastic), they are frequently pulled along in carts or on wheels rather than carried.

Town Chimes – Chimes in town belfries, which regularly sound out their melodic tunes, lend a rhythm to life in northern French towns. Since the Middle Ages, when four bells were tapped by hand with a hammer, there have been many additions: a mechanism, a manual keyboard, pedals, all of which have made it possible to increase the number of bells (62 in Douai) and to increase the variety of their sounds.
Carillon concerts are held in Douai, St-Amand-les-Eaux and Maubeuge (east of Valenciennes).

Traditional Games and Sports – Traditional entertainments remain popular: marionettes, ball games, real tennis, ninepins, darts, lacrosse (an ancestor of golf), archery (which is also a traditional sport of the Valois area), cock-fighting, pigeon-breeding etc. A popular bar game is the *billard Nicolas*, where players squeeze a bulb to blow a marble across a round playing area.

Billard Nicolas

Archery – In the Middle Ages archers were already the pride of the counts of Flanders, who would have the archers accompany them on all their expeditions. As soon as individual towns were founded the archers formed associations or guilds. They appeared at all public ceremonies, dressed in brightly coloured costumes, brandishing the great standard of their association.

Today archery is practised in several ways. A method particular to the North is vertical or "perch" shooting, which consists in firing arrows upward to hit dummy birds attached to gratings suspended from a pole. At the top of this pole, about 30m/98ft off the ground, is the hardest target of all, the **"poppinjay"** *(papegai)*. Archers must hit this bird with a long, ball-tipped arrow and the winner is proclaimed "King of the perch".

In winter the sport is practised indoors: arrows are shot horizontally at a slightly tilted grating.

Still grouped in brotherhoods, the archers gather every year to honour their patron, St Sebastian.

Crossbow – The art of the crossbow, which also dates from the Middle Ages, has its own circle of enthusiasts organised in brotherhoods. Their gatherings, colourful events featuring these curious weapons from another time, are often given evocative names such as the King's Crossbow Shoot.

Javelin – This feathered arrow measuring 50-60cm/20-24in is thrown into a tightly tied bundle of straw which serves as a target. It is the same principle as for the game of darts, which is played in many cafés.

The Game of "Billons" – A *billon* is a tapering wooden club about 1m/3ft long, weighing about 2-3kg/4-7lb. Two teams throw their *billons* in turn towards a post 9m/30ft away. The aim is to land the narrower end of the club nearest to the post and this may be achieved by dislodging the *billons* of the opposing team.

Bouchon – Teams face each other in cafés, and knock down the cork and wood "targets" with their metal paddles. The best players participate in competitions at local festivals.

Cock-Fighting – Cock-breeders and anxious gamblers watch bloody and vicious fights to the death between roosters.

Pigeon-Breeding – Pigeon fanciers *(coulonneux)* raise their birds to fly back to the nest as quickly as possible. For pigeon-racing competitions, which are very popular, the birds are carried in special baskets to a distance of up to 500km/310mi and must then return to their dovecote at record speed. A pigeon can fly over 100km/60mi per hour on average.

Singing Finch Competitions – Finches have also become part of the folklore in the north of France, where they participate in trilling contests. Some can trill as many as 800 times an hour.

Ratting Dogs – Cruel ratting competitions have always had a certain popularity in this region. Three rats are put in a cage, then a dog. Spectators time how long it takes the dog to kill its adversaries. The fastest dog is the victor.

Northern Giants

Yan den Houtkapper *Steenvoorde*

Martin and Martine *Cambrai*

Gayant and his wife *Douai*

The Sailor's wife *Grand-Fort Philippe*

Mother Reuze *Cassel*

Illustrations: R. Corbel/MICHELIN

Food and drink

The Cuisine of Picardy – Soups are the great local specialities, in particular those made from tripe *(tripe)*, pumpkin *(potiron)* or frogs *(grenouille)*, as well as the famous vegetable soup *(soupe des hortillons)*. The people of Picardy and Artois love their vegetables: beans from Soissons, Laon artichokes, St Valery carrots, peas from the Vermandois and leeks which are used in a delicious pie, the *tarte aux porions*.

Starters include duck pâté in a pastry case *(pâté de canard en croûte)* – prepared in Amiens since the 17C – snipe pâté *(pâté de bécassines)* from Abbeville and Montreuil, eel pâté *(pâté d'anguilles)* from Péronne. The *ficelle picarde* is a ham pancake in a creamy mushroom sauce.

Duck, snipe and plover, eel, carp and pike from the River Somme are often on the menu. Seafood (shrimps known as *sauterelles*, cockles called *hemons*) is common, as well as sole, turbot, fresh herring and cod, often cooked with cream.

Flemish Cuisine – Flemish cooking, washed down with beer and often followed by a glass of gin or a *bistouille* (coffee with a dash of alcohol), contains several typical dishes:

– rabbit with prunes or raisins and pigeon with cherries;
– home-made potted meat made from veal, bacon, rabbit and sometimes chicken *(potjevleesch)*;
– mixed stew of veal, mutton, pork offals, bacon and vegetables *(hochepot)*;
– braised beef in a beer sauce flavoured with onions and spices *(carbonade)*;
– eel sautéed in butter and stewed in a wine sauce with herbs *(anguille au vert)*;
– small smoked herrings, a speciality of Dunkirk *(craquelots)*;

Among the other specialities of the north of France are chitterling sausages *(andouillettes)* from Arras and Cambrai, trout from the River Canche and River Course, and cauliflowers from St-Omer.

Cheeses of the North – Local cheeses, except for the one from **Mont des Cats**, are strong. Most come from the Thiérache and Avesnois regions rich in pastureland. The best is **Maroilles**, created in the 10C by monks from Maroilles Abbey: it has a soft centre with a crust soaked in beer, similar to cheese from Munster. The other cheeses in the region are derived from it: **Vieux Lille**, also called Maroilles Gris (grey Maroilles); **Dauphin** (Maroilles with herbs and spices); **Cœur d'Avesnes** or Rollot; and the delicious **Boulette d'Avesnes** (Maroilles with spices, rolled in paprika). **Flamiche au Maroilles**, a creamy, highly flavoured quiche, is one of the most famous dishes from the northern region of France.

Brie – The Brie region in Île-de-France is famous for its soft cow's milk cheeses with surface mould. There are two types, Brie and double or triple-cream cheeses (**Lucullus**, **Grand Vatel**, **Gratte-Paille** etc) often made from the fat left over from the production of Brie, a legendary cheese that already enjoyed a reputation for excellence in the 13C. Brie was as popular with the commoners of Paris as with royalty, and it was the outright winner of a competition organised during the Congress of Vienna in 1815 bringing together all the best cheeses from throughout Europe. There are certain characteristics common to all Brie cheeses. They are made from partially skimmed raw cow's

A tempting selection ...

J. P. Bonhomet/SCOPE

milk, the rind is white with reddish marks, the cheese is soft in texture and pale yellow in colour, the fat content is approximately 45 %, and the maturing period does not exceed seven weeks. Setting these features aside, several varieties of Brie have developed and they differ depending on the area of production. The best-known are Brie de Meaux and Brie de Melun.

Cakes – The local pancakes *(crêpes)*, waffles and sweet breads *(tartines* and *brioches)* can make entire meals in themselves; the brioches with bulging middles are called *coquilles.*
Tarts, such as the delicious *tartes au sucre* sprinkled with brown sugar, are often served for dessert. Sweets are accompanied by the light, chicory coffee which people from the region drink at any time of the day.

F. Jalain/EXPLORER

Brewers in Lille

Brown Sugar Tart Recipe – Mix 375g/13oz flour, 90g/3oz sugar, 20g/0.7oz yeast blended with warm water, with 1 egg yolk and 60g/2oz butter. Knead and leave the dough to rise until it has doubled in size. Put into a greased sponge tin and leave the dough to rise again for 30min. Add 100g/3.5oz brown sugar and dot with knobs of butter. Bake for 30min in a hot oven (220°C – Thermostat 7).

Beer – Gambrinus, the king of beer, is greatly revered in the north of France as is St Arnould, the patron saint of brewers. Beer *(la bière)* was already known in Antiquity. In Gaul it was called *cervoise*. During the Middle Ages brewing beer was a privilege of the monasteries. It spread enormously in Flanders under John the Fearless, Duke of Burgundy and Count of Flanders, who developed the use of hops.

The Brewing Process – Beer is obtained by the mashing and fermentation of a mixture of water and malt, flavoured with hops. Barley grains are soaked in water (malting) until they germinate. The malted barley, dried and roasted in a kiln, becomes **malt**. This is powdered and then mixed with pure water and hops and cooked, according to each manufacturer's secret procedure. This operation, called brewing, transforms the starch in the malt into sugar and makes it possible to obtain the **wort**. With the addition of a raising agent, the wort begins to ferment.
Beer brewing was formerly undertaken simply by a brewer, with his boy handling a sort of pointed shovel *(fourquet)*, but is now a large and sophisticated industry.
Much French beer and lager (paler, "aged" beer containing more bubbles and often less alcohol) is produced in the Pas-de-Calais region, which is rich in water, barley and hops. The hops grown in Flanders have a particularly strong flavour. The largest breweries are in the areas around Lille-Roubaix and Armentières, and the Scarpe and Escaut (Scheldt) river valleys. On the eve of the First World War, the region had 2 600 reweries. Today, there are only 17 left. However, many small breweries are now operating locally.
Different beers have their own characteristics: the traditional, slightly bitter lager *(bière blonde)* of the north; the relatively sweet and fruity regional dark beer *(bière brune)* or the richly flavoured, amber-red beer *(bière rousse)*.
Consumption has decreased over the past dozen years or so and is now at the level of 39.3l/86 pints per person a year.

Gin – Gin is made from wheat, oats, malted barley and rye turned into meal. After cooking, the action of the yeast causes them to ferment.
The resultant "cereal wine" is distilled with juniper berries and the drink begins to produce its characteristic aroma.
Gin is still produced in the Nord-Pas-de-Calais region, in Houlle, Wambrechies and Loos. Another drink produced in Loos is an aperitif called *chuche-mourette*, consisting of *crème de cassis* and gin.

The Hall of Mirrors, Château de Versailles

RMN

Sights

ABBEVILLE

Population 23 787
Michelin map 52 folds 6, 7 or 236 fold 22

Abbeville (pronounced Abb'ville) is the capital of the Ponthieu region and stands on the edge of the River Somme, about 20km/12mi from the sea. In the 19C artists flocked to its medieval streets overlooked by the towers of the Collégiale St-Vulfran; since the Second World War it has taken on a more modern aspect.

HISTORICAL NOTES

Medieval conflicts – The town derives its name from the Latin *Abbatis Villa* meaning abbot's villa, and originally developed around the country house of the abbot of St-Riquier. From the 13C to the 15C Abbeville became the property of the English, the Burgundians and the French, depending on the outcome of the struggles for possession of the Somme Valley. Abbeville finally became French under Louis XI in the 15C.

In 1514 the young and attractive Mary of England (Henry VIII's sister) was married here to King Louis XII – then aged 52 – who died of consumption the following year.

Enlightened Capitalists: the Van Robais – This Dutch family settled in Abbeville as a result of Colbert's wish to free the national economy from its dependence on foreign imports by manufacturing products in France.

Josse Van Robais arrived in Abbeville in 1665 to establish a factory making fine cloth, aided by various privileges, not least of which was a guaranteed monopoly. Van Robais brought with him his family, his Protestant chaplain, about 50 workers and his weaving looms, which he installed in Faubourg Hocquet.

Thus the Royal Tenter Works (Manufacture Royale des Rames) was founded, one of the first "integrated" businesses, dealing not only with all aspects of spinning and weaving but also with the finishing (dressing, fulling, dyeing etc).

The firm's success was consolidated by Josse's grandson, Abraham Van Robais (1698-1779): during the 18C about 2 500 people were employed, 250 of whom were weavers. All that remains of the factory built between 1709 and 1713 at 264 chaussée d'Hocquet are the main entrance and a dovecote (1712).

The Father of Prehistory: Boucher de Perthes (1788-1868) – Jacques Boucher de Perthes was a handsome and intelligent man, the multi-talented author of a minor master-piece called "Portraits" written in the style of La Bruyère. In 1825 after a wild and worldly youth he succeeded his father as Head of Customs in Abbeville, which at the time was a busy seaport.

He became passionately interested in prehistory, scanning the alluvial layers of the Somme – exposed by dredgers widening the canal – in search of the sharpened flints which, he believed, should accompany the bones of prehistoric peoples. From 1830 he was assisted by the doctor, **Casimir Picard**. Following Picard's death in 1841, Boucher de Perthes struggled on, continuing to explore the woodland peat of La Portelette – close to what is now Abbeville station – and the quarries of St-Acheul, near Amiens. From the study of his finds he gathered material for a work on "Celtic and Antediluvian Antiquities" in which he asserted his belief in the existence of Paleolithic man, contemporary with the large extinct pachyderms.

His discoveries were met with scepticism. Boucher de Perthes would pay 10 centimes for an oddly shaped rock or stone, and one of his cousins recalled how, on meeting a peasant breaking rocks, she asked what he was doing: "Making prehistoric axes for Mr Boucher de Perthes" was the reply.

The tragic days of May-June 1940 – After the German breakthrough at Sedan and the Panzer drive to the sea, Abbeville became a nerve centre of the French Resistance. From 20 May intense bombing by Stukas struck the town centre, almost all of which burned, destroying 2 000 houses and leaving hundreds of people dead or wounded. At night, the Germans entered the town and established a large bridgehead on the south bank of the Somme, extending as far as Huppy and Bray-lès-Mareuil, with the well-fortified Caubert Heights (Monts de Caubert) as a strong point. A fierce counter-attack by the French 4th Armoured Division under **Colonel de Gaulle** and by the Scots reduced the German pocket but did not succeed in breaching the Caubert Heights' defences.

SIGHTS *2hr*

Collégiale St-Vulfran ⊙ – St Wulfram's Collegiate Church, which looks like a cathedral, was begun in 1488; the west front was built first, but construction of the nave was interrupted in 1539 owing to lack of money, and it was not until the 17C that the chancel was finished in neo-Gothic style.

★**West Front** – The Flamboyant west front shows how late-15C architecture had become merely a vehicle for sculpture. Flanked by small watch-turrets, the towers rise to 55m/180ft; they were immortalised by 19C Romantic paintings and by Victor Hugo.

Central Doorway – The door has preserved its Renaissance panels, given by Jehan Mourette, the head of a brotherhood of poets (Confrérie du Puy Notre-Dame d'Abbeville). In the centre, the figures of the Evangelists are framed by St Peter *(left)* and St Paul *(right)*. Scenes from the life of the Virgin can be seen above a frieze of horsemen.

Interior – Note the abstract stained-glass windows in the chancel which were designed by William Epstein.

Old House – *29 rue des Capucins, on the corner of rue des Teinturiers.*
This corbelled house is an example of 15C-16C domestic architecture.

St-Vulfran church

S. Sauvignier/MICHELIN

Église du St-Sépulcre ⊘ – Only the bell-tower, the piers and archivolts of the nave, the two side aisles and the Chapel of the Holy Sepulchre remain from the original 15C building, which was altered substantially in the late 19C into Flamboyant Gothic style. The contemporary **stained-glass windows★★** by Alfred Manessier represent the Passion and the Resurrection of Christ.

★**Musée Boucher de Perthes** ⊘ – Facing the square, which is graced by the statue of the local sailor, Admiral Courbet (1827-85), stand the museum buildings: a 13C belfry, a small 15C edifice (formerly the Mint) and a new building to the rear. The museum houses medieval sculpture, ceramics and tapestries, paintings from the 16C to the 18C and 17C furniture from Picardy. Note, in particular, a work by Camille Claudel and a superb silver Virgin and Child (1568) as well as the Boucher de Perthes prehistoric collections and a mammoth tooth discovered on Ault beach.

EXCURSIONS

★**Château de Bagatelle** ⊘ – *Southeast of the town, at 133 route de Paris.*
Abraham Van Robais had Bagatelle built c 1740 as his villa in the country, where he could relax and receive his business clients. It originally consisted of only the ground floor to which was added, 15 years later, an attic storey with bull's-eye windows to provide living accommodation; the mansard roof dates from about 1790. In spite of subsequent additions this is a charming residence, characterised by a harmony and unity of style.

Interior – Reception rooms: Rococo decoration, 18C furniture, delicately painted panelling. A graceful double staircase with a wrought-iron balustrade was ingeniously adapted to fit the hall, to give access to the low-ceilinged first-floor rooms.

Grounds – The formal French garden is adorned with statues and the botanical park contains a large and varied collection of plants, including some rare species.

Eating out

MID-RANGE

L'Escale en Picardie – *15 rue des Teinturiers* – ☎ *03 22 24 21 51* – *closed Feb school holidays, 20 Aug-8 Sept, Sun evening, Mon and public holidays* – *125/285F*. An address that will undoubtedly delight fish and seafood lovers! All the produce is freshly caught, lovingly prepared and served with a beaming smile. Enjoy a delicious meal by the fireplace before setting out on your travels...

Where to stay

MID-RANGE

Hôtel de France – *19 place du Pilori* – ☎ *03 22 24 00 42* – ▫ – *69 rooms 280/700F – : 50F – restaurant 98F.* This modern, recently renovated hotel in the town centre with functional, soundproofed rooms caters essentially to businessmen and passing trade. Modern decoration with all necessary amenities. The restaurant offers several menus including one for children.

S. Sauvignier/MICHELIN

Château de Bagatelle

Monts de Caubert – *5km/3mi west of Abbeville.*
At the first sharp bend before a road junction, turn left onto the narrow road running along the crest of the rise. Some 1.5km/1mi further on is a wayside cross from which there is a good view over the Somme Valley, Abbeville and the plains of Ponthieu beyond.

The Vimeu Region – The Vimeu region of Picardy, between the River Somme and River Bresle gets its name from a tributary of the latter. It seems like an isolated plateau, grooved by green valleys with hedged meadows full of apple trees. This farming country also contains many châteaux and villages hidden among the trees. Locksmithing and wrought-iron making have been the traditional occupations of the area since the 17C.

Friville-Escarbotin – *15km/9mi southwest of St-Valéry-sur-Somme.*
The **Musée des Industries du Vimeu** ⓥ traces the history of small-scale metalwork: locksmithery, taps and fittings, ironmongery, ship chandlery etc. The ground floor displays 19C machines (pedal-worked drill) and reconstructed workshops: locksmith's shop, keymaker's workshop, local foundry. Among the collections of locks, bars and bolts, note the display of 135 padlocks, the smallest of which is made from a gold coin.
The first floor displays modern objects (audio-visual presentation).

Huppy – *10km/6mi southwest of Abbeville.*
This village boasts a 15C and 16C **church** ⓥ (Renaissance stained glass) and a 17C **château** *(private)*, where Colonel de Gaulle established his headquarters on 29 May 1940 *(plaque)*; he was promoted to General on 1 June. The local art museum is housed in the bell-tower: sacred art and presentation of the village; General de Gaulle's stay in Huppy is also recalled.

St-Maxent Windmill – *13km/8mi southwest of Abbeville.*
This timber windmill, which was in use until 1941, retains its post, its counterbalancing "tail", its roof of chestnut shingles, its three storeys for sifting, and its mechanism and millstones.

ALBERT

Population 10 010
Michelin map 52 fold 9 or 236 fold 25

The town, which was originally called Ancre, from the river which flows through it, was the seat of a marquess; the title was acquired in 1610 by Marie de Medici's favourite, Concino Concini. Following his tragic death in 1617, which heralded the queen mother's disgrace, Louis XIII offered Ancre to Charles d'Albert, Duc de Luynes, who gave it his name.
Albert was almost totally destroyed during the Battle of the Somme in 1916 and the Battle of Picardy in 1918 *(see Introduction: Historical notes)* and is today a well-planned, modern town. Méaulte, a large suburb to the south, is the home of aircraft factories founded by Potez but now run by the Aérospatiale.

SIGHTS

Basilique Notre-Dame-de-Brébières – The basilica is a popular place of pilgrimage *(see Calendar of events)*. The tower (70m/230ft high) is surmounted by a poignant statue of the Virgin and Child by Albert Roze. A shell hit the dome during the First World War, causing the statue to lean to one side; fortunately, it has now found its balance again! Inside, the 11C Miraculous Virgin is venerated.

Musée des Abris – Somme 1916 ⓥ – An underground air-raid shelter (1939) houses an exhibition illustrating the daily life of *Poilus* (soldiers) during the First World War.

BATTLEFIELDS *Round trip of 34km/21mi – 45min.*

A circuit east and north of Albert commemorates the British and South African soldiers under Douglas Haig who fell during the Allied attack in summer 1916 (Battle of the Somme).

Take D 929 northeast towards Bapaume.

On the right lies a British cemetery.

La Boisselle – Traces of explosions still suggest some of the violence of the fighting which occurred in this village.

Take D 20 on the right. Cross Bazentin and Longueval, then turn left.

Mémorial sud-africain et musée commémoratif du bois de Delville ☉ – The memorial and the museum, housed in a small-scale replica of Capetown Castle, commemorate the many South African soldiers who lost their lives during both World Wars.

Return to D 20 and turn right onto D 107 then left onto D 929.

THE SALTED PIG TAVERN

La Taverne du Cochon Salé – *Rue Albert, 80300 Authuille – 6km/3.7mi north of Albert by D 50 then D 151 – ☎ 03 22 75 46 14 – closed 1-15 Jan, Sun evening and Mon – 110/145F.* The owner of this restaurant used to be a pork butcher and his motto is to enjoy life to the full... Naturally, cold cuts and pork meat are an important part of the menu but you should also try his speciality, a loaf made with foie gras.

Pozières – This British cemetery is encircled by columns. The names of 14 690 men who went missing in action are engraved on the memorial.

Turn right onto D 73.

Mémorial britannique de Thiepval – The brick-built triumphal arch overlooking the Ancre Valley bears the names of 73 367 British soldiers.

Continue on D 73.

The **Tour d'Ulster** *(right)*, a replica of a tower near Belfast, was erected in memory of the dead of the 36th Irish Division.

The road then runs through the Ancre Valley.

★**Parc-mémorial de Beaumont-Hamel** – This wind-swept plateau was the site of a battle fought by the Newfoundland Division in July 1916 on the opening day of the Battle of the Somme. The monument, topped by a Newfoundland Caribou, includes a viewing platform: view of the battlefield.

Return to the Ancre Valley and turn right onto D 50 to Albert.

AMIENS★★★

Conurbation 156 120
Michelin map 52 fold 8 or 236 fold 24

Amiens, the capital of Picardy, is an important communications centre and the setting for a beautiful cathedral. Devastated during the two World Wars, it is now essentially a modern town, sheltering the precious remains of its past in picturesque areas. The delicious gastronomic specialities include chocolate wafers, macaroons, pancakes filled with ham and mushrooms with a white sauce *(ficelles picardes)* and the famous duck pâtés in pastry *(pâtés de canard en croûte)*.

"Amiens in 2000, an ideal town" stated Jules Verne. Was he right? Well, it's up to you to decide!

HISTORICAL NOTES

St Martin's Cloak – In Gallo-Roman times Amiens was the capital of a Belgian tribe, the Ambiani; in the 4C the town was converted to Christianity by Firmin and his companions. At that time, **St Martin**, a horseman in the Roman legion stationed here, met a beggar shivering in the north wind; he sliced his cloak in two with his sword and gave half to the poor man. This episode is recalled in a low-relief sculpture by J Samson (1830) on the north wall of the law courts (Palais de Justice), place d'Aguesseau.

Eating out

MID-RANGE

Marissons – *Pont de la Dodane* – ☎ *03 22 92 96 66* – *closed 24 Dec-5 Jan, Sat lunchtime and Sun* – *120/265F*. A former shipping workshop has been converted into this restaurant in a tiny flower garden used as a terrace in summer. In winter, settle at one of the round tables in a dining area enhanced by its exposed beams and sloping framework.

L'Aubergade – *78 route Nationale, 80480 Dury* – *6km/4mi south of Amiens by N 1 heading towards Beauvais* – ☎ *03 22 89 51 41* – *closed Feb school holidays, 3-17 Aug, Sun evening and Mon* – *115/400F*. Diners come from afar to have the pleasure of sampling the cuisine here. The restaurant occupies a white-stone house lying on the outskirts of Amiens. The dining room is decorated in pastel hues and features furniture made with white-leaded wood.

Where to stay

MID-RANGE

Hôtel Carlton – *42 rue Noyon* – ☎ *03 22 97 72 22* – *23 rooms 500-740F* – ⌂ *65F* – *restaurant 89/105F*. The 19C façade of this imposing mansion conceals a modern hotel boasting the latest creature comforts. All the rooms are furnished with waxed furniture and adorned with mural paintings. The restaurant Le Bistrot, decorated more modestly, mainly serves grilled meat.

Chambre d'Hôte M. et Mme Saguez – *2 rue Grimaux, 80480 Dury* – *6km/3.7mi south of Amiens by N 1 heading towards Beauvais* – ☎ *03 22 95 29 52* – ⌂ – *4 rooms 260/320F*. The comfortable, non-smoking rooms have been set up in an annex to the huge 19C main building. Only 10min from Amiens town centre, you can discover the joys of the countryside, such as a ride in an old-fashioned carriage...

On the town

Café Bissap – *50 rue St-Leu* – ☎ *03 22 92 36 41* – *daily 11am-3am*. This Afro-West Indian bar is a highly popular meeting place. The superb decoration consisting of frescoes and African material is barely visible through the crowds of customers. Good humour is the prevailing mood here. Try one of the rum cocktails or other specialities from tropical climes.

L'Auberge du Vert Galant – *57 rue du Halage* – ☎ *03 22 91 31 66* – *daily 10am-1am, in winter Sat-Sun only*. This café and its huge leafy terrace enjoy a privileged location at the water's edge, nestling at the heart of 300ha of marshes used for growing vegetables. Boat rentals and dances can be arranged. A charming place at any time of day.

Le Squale – *18 rue de la Dodane* – ☎ *03 22 72 20 46* – *Mon-Sat 6pm-3am*. Superb Australian bar laid out on two levels and embellished by Aboriginal frescoes, surfboards and an old petrol pump. The 600sq yd back garden dotted with heated tents is the perfect place to sip one of the owner's home-made cocktails. Theme evenings.

Texas Café – *13 rue des Francs-Mûriers* – ☎ *03 22 72 19 79* – *Mon-Sat 9pm-3am*. Join in the wild ambience in this vast karaoke room set against a wood and brick backdrop. If you don't feel like singing, you can always dance, play billiards, darts or cards, or else share a conversation over a beer or a cocktail.

Vents et Marées – *48 rue du Don* – ☎ *03 22 92 37 78* – *open Mon-Sat 5pm-3am*. The iron staircase will take you down into a strange world indeed. Designed as a barge resting on the water's surface and adorned by a standing exhibition of strip-cartoon plates, this congenial café exudes a warm, friendly atmosphere that will go straight to your heart!

Showtime

Comédie de Picardie – *62 rue des Jacobins* – ☎ *03 22 22 20 20* – *Mon-Fri 1-7pm, Sat 1-6pm*. This venue, where local, national and international productions are performed on stage every year, has a seating capacity of 400.

La Lune des Pirates – *17 quai Bélu* – ☎ *03 22 97 88 01* – *www.lalune.net* – *consult the calendar of events*. Formerly one of Amiens' most popular cafés, La Lune des Pirates has now branched out into the performing arts. It stages a variety of modern plays and shows reflecting a broad spectrum of styles and cultures, complemented by exhibitions and other artistic events.

Maison de la Culture d'Amiens (Amiens Arts Centre) – *Place Léon-Gontier –* ☎ *03 22 97 79 77 – film showings Mon-Sat at 6.30pm and 9pm, Sun at 5.30pm.* With two traditional cinemas (1 070 and 300 seats), a cinema for avant-garde films and two exhibition galleries, this arts centre, open to foreign influences, offers a highly eclectic and challenging selection of events. Programmes available from the reception area.

Théâtre de Marionnettes – **Chés Cabotans d'Amiens** – *31 rue Édouard-David –* ☎ *03 22 22 30 90 – www.ches-cabotans-damiens.com – consult the of events – reception area open daily 9am-noon, 2-6pm except Sun mornings – closed in Sept.* Tribute is paid to the art of puppetry, with a fascinating show performed in a miniature, beautifully designed theatre. The puppets displayed in the ground floor exhibition are extremely moving: each has its own expression, history and language (a combination of French and Picardy dialect).

Shopping

Atelier de Jean-Pierre Facquier – *67 rue du Don –* ☎ *03 22 93 40 01/ 03 22 92 49 52 – Tues-Fri 2-6.30pm, Sat 10am-noon, 2-6pm – closed one week in summer.* The legendary or fictitious wooden characters created by Jean-Pierre Facquier are all masterpieces of craftsmanship. Each figurine is unique and clad in sumptuous fabrics carefully chosen by his wife.

Caveau St-Loupien – *55 rue du Hocquet –* ☎ *03 22 72 40 40 – www.caveau-saint-loupien.com – Mon 2.30-7.30pm, Tues-Sun 10.30am-12.30am, 2.30-7.30pm.* Dubbed an expert in Picardy gastronomy, the owner of this boutique proposes around 50 different types of home-made mustard, conserve of goose or duck laced with beer or wine, jam made with milk, Picardy cider and the famous Amiens macaroons.

Schaetjens – *21 rue des Trois-Cailloux –* ☎ *03 22 91 32 73 – daily except Tues 8.30am-7.30pm – closed 3 weeks in Aug.* Both sweet and savoury fare can be purchased in this shop, specialised in the making of cakes, chocolate and delicatessen dishes, such as duck pâté wrapped in a pastry case, a recipe dating back to 1643.

Science, Technique, Tradition

Galerie du Vitrail – *40 rue Victor-Hugo –* ☎ *03 22 91 81 18 – guided tours daily except Sun at 3pm – closed public holidays.* A master glassworker, who can be seen plying his trade, presents his private collection of stained glass pieces, one of which dates back to the 13C.

The "head of John the Baptist" – In 1218 the Romanesque church on the site was destroyed by fire. Bishop Evrard de Fouilloy and the people of Amiens immediately decided to build a replacement, something exceptional, worthy of sheltering the "head of John the Baptist", the precious relic brought back in 1206 from the fourth crusade by Wallon de Sarton, canon of Picquigny.

Birth of an Industry: Textiles – Affiliated to the Hanse of London (a merchants' guild), Amiens was very prosperous in the Middle Ages. The cloth business and wine trade, the port, and the influx of pilgrims who came to worship the relic said to be the head of John the Baptist, all contributed to the bustling atmosphere. **Woad**, a precious tinctural plant found locally and in the Santerre area, was treated here where it was known as *waide*; when milled the plant produces a beautiful blue, which was exported to England. The late 15C saw the production of a woollen serge mixed with silk *(sayette)* which gave the products of Amiens *(Articles d'Amiens)* a far-reaching reputation. The famous **"Amiens Velvets"** were introduced during Louis XIV's reign.

Steely Assaults – The valleys of the River Somme and River Aisne are major obstacles to invaders from the north, and being the bridgehead, Amiens has suffered many attacks. In 1918, during the Battle of Picardy, the town was attacked by Ludendorff and bombarded with 12 000 shells. It was set ablaze in 1940 during the Battle of the Somme. In 1944 its prison was the target of a dangerous aerial attack aimed at helping the imprisoned Resistance members to escape (Operation Jericho).

Local Heroes – Amiens was the birthplace of several writers including **Choderlos de Laclos** (1741-1803), famous for *Les Liaisons Dangereuses*, Paul Bourget (1852-1925) and **Roland Dorgelès** (1885-1973), author of *Les Croix de Bois*, as well as the physician **Édouard Branly** (1844-1940) who invented the coherer, a device for detecting radio waves.
In place René-Goblet a monument commemorates another local hero: **Marshal Leclerc de Hauteclocque** who distinguished himself during the Second World War.

★★★ CATHÉDRALE NOTRE-DAME ⏱

Amiens Cathedral is the largest Gothic building in France (145m/475ft long with vaults 42.5m/139ft high).

The plans of the church were entrusted to **Robert de Luzarches** who was succeeded by Thomas de Cormont and then his son Renaud. The cathedral was begun in 1220 and the speed with which it was built explains the remarkable unity of style, though the towers remained uncrowned until the beginning of the 15C. The cathedral was later restored by Viollet-le-Duc. It miraculously escaped damage in 1940.

Exterior

The west front *(see illustration in Architecture and Art)* of Amiens Cathedral has a horizontal emphasis, consisting of several bands: the three doorways; the two galleries including the Kings' Gallery *(galerie des rois)* with its enormous figures; the great Flamboyant rose-window (renewed in the 16C) framed by twinned open bays; and the small bell-ringers' gallery *(galerie des sonneurs)* topped by light arcading between the towers. Elegant sculptures – some damaged by pollution – further enhance the ensemble. The **central doorway** is framed by the Wise and Foolish Virgins who, together with the Apostles and the Prophets on the piers, escort from a respectable distance the famous **Beau Dieu**, a noble and serene Christ standing on lavender and basil. He is the focal point of this enormous carved Bible. The tympanum portrays the Last Judgment presided over by a more archaic and severe God. The **left doorway** is dedicated to **St Firmin** the evangelist of Amiens and to the Picardy region. The quatrefoils on the base enclose lively representations of a **Calendar** symbolised by the signs of the Zodiac and the corresponding Labours of the Months. The **right doorway** is dedicated to the **Mother of God.**

Walk along impasse Voron.

On the north side, note the statue of Charles V (**4**) on the 14th buttress supporting the tower.

Go round the cathedral to the right, passing a giant St Christopher (**1**), an Annunciation (**2**), and, between the 3rd and 4th chapels, a pair of woad merchants with their sack (**3**).

Follow rue Cormont to place St-Michel.

From here there is a fine view of the **east end** with its pierced flying buttresses, and the soaring lead-covered chestnut **spire** (112.70m/370ft high).

Retrace your steps and enter the cathedral through the south doorway.

The **south doorway**, known as the Golden Virgin Doorway because of the statue which used to adorn the pier, is dedicated to St Honoré who was bishop of Amiens. Visitors can mount the 307 steps of the towers, for a close up view of the spires and statuary atop the cathedral, and a wide-angle view of the city below.

Interior

The sheer size and the amount of light inside the cathedral are striking.

The **nave** is the highest in France, reaching 42.50m/139ft. Its elevation consists of large and exceptionally high arcades surmounted by a band of finely detailed foliage, a blind triforium and a clerestory; 13C recumbent bronze effigies of the cathedral's founding

"Beau Dieu", the central doorway of the cathedral

bishops lie in the third bay: Evrard de Fouilloy (**5**) and Geoffroy d'Eu (**6**); the latter faces towards St-Saulve Chapel which contains a figure of Christ in a long gold robe.

On the flagging, renewed in the 19C, the meandering lines of the labyrinth (**7**) have been restored. In the past the faithful would follow the lines on their knees, as a Way of the Cross. At the centre, the names of those responsible for the cathedral are inscribed: Robert de Luzarches, Thomas and Renaud de Cormont (the original stone is in the Picardy Museum).

The **north transept** is adorned with a 14C rose-window with star-shaped central tracery. The font (**8**), to the left of the door, dates from 1180 and was originally used to wash the dead. On the west wall a painted sculpture in four parts

represents Christ and the money lenders in the Temple (**9**) (1520).

The **south transept**, which is illuminated through a Flamboyant rose-window, bears on its west wall four scenes in relief (**10**) portraying the conversion of the magician Hermogene by St James the Great (1511).

The perspective back down the nave reveals its elegance and the boldness of the organ loft supporting the **great organ** (**11**) (1442) with its delicate golden arabesques, crowned by the majestic rose-window at the west end.

The **chancel** is enclosed within a beautiful 18C choir screen, wrought by Jean Veyren. The 110 Flamboyant oak **stalls★★★** were created between 1508 and 1519 by the master cabinet-makers Arnould Boulin, Antoine Avernier and Alexandre Huet. They are arranged in two rows and surmounted by wooden tracery, and are presided over by two master-stalls destined for the king and the dean of the chapter. Over 4 000 figures on the misericords, stall ends, canopies, pendentives and brackets realistically and spiritedly evoke Genesis and Exodus, the life of the Virgin Mary, and scenes of 16C life in Amiens. One worker carved himself holding his mallet (**12**) and inscribed his name: Jehan Turpin.

In the **ambulatory** on the right, on the choir screen above two recumbent effigies, eight remarkable carved and coloured stone groups (1488) under delicate Gothic canopies evoke the **life of St Firmin** (**13**), his martyrdom and his exhumation by St Saul three centuries later. The highly expressive figures are wearing 15C dress: the nobles in sumptuous attire, the humble poorly dressed and the executioner in curious breeches. Behind the main altar, facing the central chapel containing a 19C gilded statue of the Virgin Mary, are the tomb of Cardinal de la Grange (1402) and the much larger tomb of Canon Guislan Lucas, famous for its **Weeping Angel** (**14**) carved by Nicolas Blasset (1628). In the apsidal chapels vestiges of the 13C stained-glass windows remain.

The choir screen north of the chancel bears scenes from the **life of St John** (**15**) (1531) – read from right to left.

Trésor – The collection, put together in the 19C and 20C, is housed in the cloisters and a room next to the sacristy. The old treasure disappeared during the Revolution apart from the "face of John the Baptist", displayed on a silver gilt platter.

Among the other treasures, note the three pieces from the Abbaye du Paraclet near Amiens: the cross decorated with filigree work and engraved stones (13C), the votive crown and the reliquary vase (14C), as well as St Firmin's reliquary, beautiful 13C Mosan work.

TOWN WALK

Park the car close to the cathedral. Shopping enthusiasts will particularly enjoy rue du Hocquet and place du Don. Walk across the River Somme to explore the narrow streets of Quartier St-Leu.

★**Quartier St-Leu** – Several arms of the Somme flow through this district, which has undergone widescale renovation in an effort to preserve its special charm. Craft and antique shops, cafés and restaurants now occupy the spaces where tanners, millers, weavers and dyers once worked.
From the bridge known as **Pont de la Dodane**, there is a fine **view** of the cathedral. A stroll through the streets (rue Bélu, rue des Majots, rue Motte, rue d'Engoulvent) lined with small colourful half-timbered houses gives a feel of the area's discreet charm.

Église St-Leu, a 15C hall-church with three aisles, has a 16C Flamboyant Gothic bell-tower.

The **Théâtre des Marionnettes** ⏲ is nearby.

Return to place Notre-Dame and walk along the south side of the cathedral which is best viewed from the pedestrian street leading to place Aguesseau.

On the corner of the law courts, a low-relief sculpture by J Samson (1830) depicts the story of St Martin's Cloak.

Logis du Roi et Maison du Sagittaire – The King's Lodging (1565), featuring a pointed-arch door decorated with a Virgin with a Rose, is the seat of the **Rosati** of Picardy, a society with the motto "Tradition, Art and Literature". The adjacent building is the **Sagittarius House** (1593) with its Renaissance front, which owes its name to the sign of the Zodiac embellishing its two arches.

Old Theatre – The Louis XVI façade was the work of Rousseau in 1780; the building now houses a bank. Three large windows are framed by elegant low-relief sculptures depicting garlands, medallions, muses and lyres.

Bailliage – The restored front is all that remains of the bailiff's residence built under François I in 1541, presenting mullioned windows, Flamboyant gables and Renaissance medallions. On the right, note the "fool" wearing a hood with bells.

Bell-tower – The enormous bell-tower in place au Fil consists of a square 15C base and an 18C belfry surmounted by a dome. Looking down rue Chapeau-des-Violettes, you will see the **Église St-Germain**, built in Flamboyant Gothic style in the 15C; its tower leans slightly. On your way back to the cathedral, stop by the statue of Marie without a shirt, a half-naked little nymph symbolising spring, carved by Albert Roze in the pompous style in fashion at the turn of the last century.

Hortillonnages ⏲ – These small vegetable gardens known as **aires** have been worked since the Middle Ages by market gardeners or hortillons (from the Latin hortus meaning garden) who supplied the local population with fruit and vegetables. The gardens stretch over an area of 300ha/740 acres amid a network of canals or **rieux** fed by the many arms of the River Somme and River Arve.

Puppets

Famous for its string puppets dating back to about 1785, Amiens now boasts its own puppet theatre. Known in the Picardy dialect as **cabotans**, puppets are about 50cm/19in in height, carved out of wood and operated from above. The king of St-Leu (the district existed in medieval times) is **Lafleur**. He is the leader of the *cabotans* and is undoubtedly the most expressive embodiment of the spirit and character of the Picardy people. Since the 19C, but arguably from an earlier date, this mythical, truculent, bold, irreverent, and brave character with a fiery temper has expressed plain common sense and described the nobility and pride of the province in the language of his ancestors. Wherever he is, wherever he comes from, and however far away he is, he is always recognisable for his impressive height, his characteristic gait, and most of all, his 18C valet's livery of beautiful red Amiens velvet. He is often accompanied by his wife Sandrine and his friend Tchot Blaise. His motto is "Drink, eat and do nothing".

Office Cultural, Amiens

Lafleur and Sandrine

At present, fruit trees and flowers are tending to replace vegetables and the gardeners' huts are becoming weekend holiday homes.

The **"market-on-the-water"** to which the market gardeners come to sell their produce is held every year on the third Sunday in June. In September, the town holds a riverside festival.

The towpath is also a pleasant place for a walk.

ADDITIONAL SIGHTS

★★ Musée de Picardie ⊘ – The building housing the Picardy Museum was constructed between 1855 and 1867 for the Picardy Society of Antiquaries and is an imposing example of Napoleon III architecture.

In the rotunda, the American artist Sol LeWitt created a mural using Indian ink wash.

Archeology – This department is housed in the basement. In addition to the Egyptian antiquities (serpentine statuette of Imenhotep) and Ancient Greek exhibits (head of Kuros) the collection includes items uncovered during digs in the region.

Remains of the ancient town of **Samarobriva**, which extended over 200ha/ 494 acres and had a population of 20 000 in the 2C, include sections of its baths, forum, amphitheatre and miscellaneous utilitarian objects such as glassware and ceramics.

Sculpture – On the ground floor. There are many objects representing **medieval art**. The sculptures formerly adorned the cathedral or various churches and abbeys in the region that have been destroyed over the years. In addition to the works by local sculptors Albert Roze *(Head of an Old Woman from Picardy)* and Nicolas Blasset *(Ecce Homo)*, sculpture is represented by 19C Romantic and Realist works.

Painting – The Grand Salon contains huge historical paintings (18C-19C) by Van Loo and Vernet.

Enormous murals by Puvis de Chavannes adorn the main stairway and first-floor rooms. The Notre-Dame du Puy gallery and part of the following room house the works of art of the Confrérie du Puy Notre-Dame d'Amiens.

Some of these paintings on wood have retained their sumptuous frames, fashioned by those who carved

> ### Confrérie du Puy Notre-Dame
>
> This literary and religious society devoted to the glorification of the Virgin Mary was founded in Amiens in 1389. The master of the brotherhood was elected on an annual basis and used to recite his "royal hymn" from a podium or *puy*. The refrain or *palinode* was unusual in that it was a play on words based on the name of the donor who from 1450 onwards, was required to offer to the cathedral a votive painting referring to the theme of the *palinode*.

the cathedral stalls. François I is recognisable in the panel with a Renaissance canopy (1518) entitled *Au juste pois, véritable balance* ("True scales, just weight"); Henri IV appears under the Gothic canopy bearing the poem entitled *Terre d'où prit la vérité naissance* ("Land where Truth was born") (1601). The remarkable Virgin with Palm Tree (1520) in its high openwork wood frame shows the Virgin Mary surrounded by saints and the donors and their family, with Amiens Cathedral in the background. The Nieuwerkerke gallery presents 17C paintings from the Spanish School (Ribera and El Greco), the Dutch School (Frans Hals) and the French School (Simon Vouet). Subsequent rooms exhibit 18C French painting including works by Oudry, Chardin, Fragonard and Quentin de La Tour, as well as the nine *Chasses en pays étrangers* (Hunts in Foreign Lands) by Parrocel, Pater, Boucher, Lancret, Van Loo and De Troy for Louis XV's small apartments at Versailles. Italian masters (Guardi, Tiepolo) express the charm of Venetian painting.

The Charles-Dufour gallery is dedicated to 19C French landscape painters and in particular to the Barbizon School (Millet, Isabey, Corot, Rousseau).

Modern art is represented by Balthus, Masson, Fautrier, Dubuffet and Picabia.

Musée d'Art local et d'Histoire régionale ⊘ – The **Hôtel de Berny★** was built in 1634 to accommodate the meetings of the treasurers of France, and is a good example of the Louis XIII style with its pink brick bonding and stone trimmings. It derives its name from the last owner, Gérard de Berny (1880-1957), who dedicated himself to creating the refined interior on view today and then bequeathed the building to Amiens as a museum of local art.

The furniture and woodwork come from other residences in the region. The dining room features an immense fireplace attributed to Jean Goujon and elegant 18C panelling which used to adorn the entrance hall of the Château de Grange-Bléneau owned by the Marquis de La Fayette. On the first floor, note the Louis XVI gilded room and the panelling from the library of the old abbey at Corbie.

Paintings show Amiens as it used to be, while several portraits present local celebrities: Mr and Mme Choderlos de Laclos, Jules Verne, Branly and Parmentier, the "inventor" of the potato in France.

AMIENS

0   300 m

75

Quartier St-Leu

Centre de documentation Jules-Verne ⊘ – Jules Verne (1828-1905) was born in Nantes but he spent much of his life in Amiens where he wrote *Voyages extraordinaires*. He played an active part in local life and was a town councillor. His home, the so-called "house with a tower" provides a vast amount of information (more than 20 000 documents) about the writer and his works. It also contains a reconstruction of his study, a number of personal effects, a model of the *Nautilus*, and his portrait in the form of a hologram.

Jardin archéologique de St-Acheul ⊘ – St-Acheul, one of the suburbs of Amiens, has, since 1872, given its name to a Paleolithic period, the **Acheulian**. Numerous bifacial tools were discovered on this site. The garden of St Acheul extends across a former gravel quarry in a pleasant rural setting which has not altered the character of the original site. A footbridge leads to an observation tower (19m/62ft) which offers a panoramic view of the site, the Somme Valley and Amiens. Cross sections and diagrams show the successive stages which led to the formation of the valley.

A long alleyway dotted with panels, known as the **fil du temps** (passing time), lists the most important dates in Man's evolution: it takes you on a journey back in time and space to 450 000 BC and leads to the entrance of the garden where a **geological cross section** shows the successive layers of sediment accumulated since that time. Descriptive panels, a viewing table and a key of the cross section explain the history of the area.

EXCURSIONS

Sains-en-Amiénois – *9km/5.6mi south along D 7.* The **church** contains a 13C **tomb** and recumbent effigies of St Fuscien and his companions, Victoric and Gentien, who were martyred in the 4C; below, a bas-relief portrays their decapitation.

Boves – *11km/6.8mi by* ③ *on the town plan.* The **ruins** of the 12C castle overlook this small town, which from 1630 was the seat of a marquess. Road D 167 leads to the grassy courtyard, and from there to the motte bearing two imposing sections of wall from the keep.

From the top there is an extensive **view:** south over the lakes of Fouencamps, north to Amiens.

Conty – *22km/14mi south by D 210 then right onto D 920.*

Église St-Antoine is a 15C and 16C church in a unified Flamboyant style; its right side offers a curious row of projecting gargoyles. The tower is crowned with a pyramid-shaped roof, like the collegiate church in Picquigny, and bears traces of cannon-balls dating from the 1589 siege of Conty by the Catholic League; in the corner, a statue of St Anthony the hermit. On the left of the west front, steps lead down to St Anthony's fountain.

ARRAS★★

Conurbation 79 607
Michelin map 53 fold 2 or 236 fold 15

Arras, the capital of the Artois region, hides its little-known artistic beauties, the 18C Grand-Place and place des Héros, behind a serious, reserved appearance. The city, a religious, military and administrative centre, is surrounded by boulevards that replaced the old Vauban-like fortifications. Chitterling sausages *(andouillettes)* and chocolate hearts are the local gastronomic specialities.

HISTORICAL NOTES

Influence in the Middle Ages – The Roman town of Nemetacum, capital of the Atrebates, was founded on the slopes of Baudimont hill, which is still known as La Cité today. In the Middle Ages the town developed around the Benedictine abbey of St Vaast, forming the district known as La Ville. From that time on, Arras grew from being a grain market and the centre of woollen cloth manufacture to being a cradle of art, patronised by bankers and rich Arras burghers.

In terms of literature, the town is famous for its troubadours *(trouvères)* such as Gautier d'Arras, **Jean Bodel**, author of *Le Jeu de saint Nicolas*, and above all the 13C **Adam de la Halle** who brought dramatic art to Arras with his play *Le Jeu de la Feuillée*. From 1384 the manufacture of high-warp tapestries, under the patronage of the dukes of Burgundy, brought Arras widespread fame – and the word *arras* passed into English to indicate a tapestry wall-hanging. After the Renaissance, this activity decreased as Beauvais and Antwerp took over.

Youth of "The Incorruptible" – **Maximilien de Robespierre**, whose father was an Artois Council barrister, was born in Arras in 1758. Orphaned at an early age, the young man became the *protégé* of the bishop and received a scholarship to attend the Louis-le-Grand School in Paris. Robespierre became a barrister on his return to Arras and was not only accepted by the Arras Academy but also affiliated with the **Rosati** (an anagram of "Artois") poetic society. During this period the pale young man, later the spirited leader of the Revolution, courted young ladies for whom he wrote verse.

In Arras, Robespierre knew **Joseph Lebon** (1765-95), a member of the Oratorian order who was mayor of the town during the Reign of Terror. During this time the former priest presided over the destruction of many churches and regularly sent aristocrats and rich farmers to the guillotine set up in place du Théâtre. Lebon himself was later to perish under the blade in Amiens.

Arras and the Battles of Artois – During the First World War, the front was until 1917 constantly near Arras which suffered heavy shelling as a result. The most violent conflicts took place in the strategically important hills north of the town. After the Battle of the Marne the retreating Germans fought to hold on to them, their backs to the rich coal basin, clinging to Vimy Ridge and the slopes of Notre-Dame-de-Lorette Hill. In the autumn of 1914 they emerged to attack Arras, but were stopped after battles at Ablain-St-Nazaire, Carency and La Targette.

In May and June 1915 General **Foch**, in command of the French forces in the north, attempted to pierce the German ranks; his troops took Neuville St-Vaast and Notre-Dame-de-Lorette. The attack failed at Vimy however, which was won only in 1917, by the Canadians.

⬛ MAIN SQUARES *1hr*

★★★ **Grand'Place and place des Héros** – The two main squares in Arras, the spectacular Grand'Place and place des Héros, which are joined by the short rue de la Taillerie, are extremely impressive. They existed as early as the 11C but have undergone many transformations through the centuries. Today's magnificent façades are remarkable examples of 17C and 18C Flemish architecture. The local council of the period was careful to control the town's development, permitting citizens to construct only "in stone or brick, with no projecting architectural elements". The façades – formerly embellished with carved shop signs, a few of which remain – rest on monolith-columned arcades which protected market stallholders and customers alike from inclement weather.

As evening comes the squares take on a different charm when the gables, discreetly floodlit, stand out against the night sky.

The oldest house round the **Grand'Place**, dating from the 15C *(no 49, north side)*, has three Gothic arches surmounted by a great corbie-stepped gable *(see illustration in ABC of architecture)*.

The smaller and livelier of the two squares, **place des Héros**, is surrounded by shops and overlooked by the belfry.

Stand facing the town hall and take rue D.-Delansorne which starts in the left-hand corner of place des Héros and leads to rue Paul-Doumer.

On the corner of rue Doumer stands the **Palais de Justice** (Law Courts), the former seat of the Artois government (1701), embellished with Corinthian pilasters and its side entrance (1724) decorated with Regency shells.

From rue Doumer, follow the second or third side street on the left.

Eating out

MODERATE

La Taverne de l'Écu – *18-20 rue Wacquez-Glasson* – ☎ *03 21 51 42 05* – *80/180F.* You can choose between a brasserie-style menu and regional specialities in this charmingly appointed tavern situated in a pedestrian precinct. Try the *écuflette*, a variation on the better-known *flammenküche*, a baked gateau garnished with onions and bacon bits.

Aux Grandes Arcades – *8-12 Grand'place* – ☎ *03 21 23 30 89* – *www.ville-arras.fr/resto/arcades* – *89/205F.* Two formulas are available to you at this restaurant situated on the imposing Grand'place, a brasserie-type menu and a more elaborate choice of dishes for a proper meal. Wine samplings are held in the superb 15C vaulted cellar. There are also a few rooms for those wishing to stay on.

MID-RANGE

Le Régent – *Rue Anatole-France in St-Nicolas – north of Arras by rue Michelet* – ☎ *03 21 71 51 09 – closed Sat lunchtime, Sun and public holidays (evenings)* – *135/290F.* A wealthy 18C residence that seems immune to the passing of time. Attractive old-fashioned decor and garden running along the banks of the Scarpe, a charming asset in the summer season. Ask to see the impressive wine list. A few rooms are available to visitors.

La Faisanderie – *45 Grand'place* – ☎ *03 21 48 20 76 – closed 4-10 Jan, Feb school holidays, 1-21 Aug, Sun evening and Mon* – *145/315F.* Meals are served in the splendid vaulted cellar of this 17C manor house. Authentic brick setting boasting a wonderful array of red hues. Regional dishes and several menus including one for children.

Where to stay

MODERATE

Chambre d'Hôte Château de Saulty – *82 rue de la Gare, 62158 Saulty* – *19km/12mi southwest of Arras heading towards Doullens by N 25* – ☎ *03 21 48 24 76 – closed Jan –* 🛏 *– 5 rooms 190/290F.* At the entrance to the village proudly stands a 1835 château, surrounded by a 15ha/37-acre park. After a restful night in a large, comfortable and elegant room, tuck into a scrumptious breakfast including home-made jam and fresh fruit juice and take a stroll in the orchard.

MID-RANGE

Hôtel Diamant – *5 place des Héros* – ☎ *03 21 71 23 23* – 🅿 *– 12 rooms 290/310F –* 🍽 *38F.* Strategically located at the foot of the church tower in the town centre, this hotel offers excellent service and a warm welcome. Smallish rooms.

Hôtel Univers – *3 place de la Croix-Rouge* – ☎ *03 21 71 34 01* – 🅿 *– 37 rooms 370/620F –* 🍽 *55F – restaurant 120/260F.* The only remaining feature of this former monastery at the heart of the city is its austere façade. Inside, comfort and cosiness reign supreme, with a decoration blending antique furniture with regional brick masonry. Large bedrooms and radiant dining room.

On the town

Irish Pub – *7 place des Héros* – ☎ *03 21 71 46 08 – Mon-Fri 11am-1am, Sat-Sun 11am-2am.* A French variation on the Irish pub, only lighter and larger. The wooden tables and worn parquet flooring lend an undeniably French touch to the place. At night, when the bustling crowds have left, it is pleasant to sit out on the terrace.

L'Océan Vert – *2 rue des Augustines* – ☎ *03 21 50 26 50 – Mon-Thur 2pm-1am, Fri-Sat 3pm-2am, Sun 3pm-1am (access for the disabled) – closed 15 July-15 Aug.* The younger generation love to congregate in this pub, whose lofty premises accommodate 22 billiard tables. The special evenings organised here (karaoke, striptease, Belgian DJs) are always a huge success.

Le Louisiane – *12 rue de la Taillerie – half-way between the two squares* – ☎ *03 21 23 18 00 – louisiarr@caramail.com – Tues-Sat noon-1am, Sun-Mon 3pm-1am.* The name of the club suggests you are entering jazzland, a fact confirmed by the smiling figure of the Black trumpet player standing at the entrance. Soberness and discretion are the dominant notes in this cosy establishment, where regulars enjoy meeting up for a friendly chat.

Showtime

Théâtre d'Arras (Missionné) – *7 place du Théâtre* – ☎ *03 21 71 66 16 – the-atredarras@nordnet.fr – consult the of events – reception area open Tues-Sat 2-7.15pm.* Closed July-Aug. A small Italianate theatre with a seating capacity of

400 listed as a historic building. The programming is highly eclectic, with performances ranging from concerts to plays to songs etc. Major cultural events are held at the Casino (1 100 seats).

Shopping

Caudron – *11-15 place de la Vacquerie* – ☎ *03 21 71 14 23* – *Mon 2-7pm, Tues-Sat 9am-noon, 2.30-7pm – closed 14 July-31 Aug.* Although this craftsman works with imported porcelain (the Arras factory closed down in 1790), his kiln allows him to fire the pieces at a very high temperature. Thanks to this technique, the colour can spread evenly on the porcelain surface, recreating the legendary blue glazing that won the city of Arras international acclaim. You can admire some splendid examples of pottery inspired by traditional themes such as the Korean Tree of Life or a delicate flower motif known as *barbeau*.

Pâtisserie Yannick-Delestrez – *50 place des Héros* – ☎ *03 21 71 53 20* – *daily 8am-8pm.* This tempting cake shop serves a wonderful array of pastries and sweetmeats, including two of the town's most long-standing specialities *les petits rats*, layered praline chocolates, and *le cœur d'Arras à l'ancienne*, a shortbread biscuit shaped as a heart that was first baked three centuries ago.

Sport

Stade d'Eau Vive – Base Nautique Robert-Pecqueur – *Rue Laurent-Gers, 62223 St-Laurent-Blangy – 2km/1mi northeast of Arras* – ☎ *03 21 73 74 93 – Mon-Fri 8am-noon, 2-5pm – booking essential Sat-Sun.* Designed for the 2004 Olympic Games, this artificial stream 300m/985ft long and 12m/40ft wide was made by digging a channel between the River Scarpe and one of its arms. Kayaks, rafts and canoes can be rented at very reasonable prices.

Place du Théâtre – It was in this lively square that the guillotine stood during the darkest hours of the Revolution. The **theatre** dates from 1784 (though its façade is restored), and was built where the fish market once stood; it faces the **Ostel des Poissonniers** (1710), a narrow Baroque house carved with sea gods and mermaids. In rue des Jongleurs, note the majestic 18C **Hôtel de Guines**; at no 9 rue Robespierre the former residence of the famous revolutionary is to be seen.

Place du Wetz-d'Amain – The square is graced by a pretty Renaissance house, to which a Classical stone porch was added later. It served as refuge to the monks of Mont St-Éloi.

Turn back, follow rue du Gén.-Barbot which crosses rue St-Aubert; turn left on tur A.-Briand; Église Notre-Dame-des-Ardents is on your left. One of the streets on the right leads to place V.-Hugo and the lower town.

Église Notre-Dame-des-Ardents – Fragments of the Holy Taper a miraculous candle entrusted by the Virgin Mary to two minstrels to cure ergotic poisoning in the 12C, are safeguarded. The silver reliquary is to the left of the high altar, in a latticed recess *(lighting below, to the right)*.

Basse-ville – This district lies between the town and the citadel. It is arranged regularly around the lovely, octagonal **place Victor-Hugo**, built in 1756, where the cattle market used to take place.

Grand'Place

B. Kaufmann/MICHELIN

ARRAS

Follow rue des Promenades towards the Jardins du Gouverneur and Jardin des Allées: a **stele** erected in honour of the Rosati depicts a marquess and a 20C man watching a procession of muses.

Nearby stands the **British memorial** dedicated to the many British soldiers lost in the Battles of Artois (1914-18).

From place V.-Hugo, walk to the Cité district via rue Victor-Hugo then cours de Verdun on the right; cross place du 33ᵉ and continue along rue de Châteaudun leading to rue d'Amiens.

Cité – **Place de la Préfecture** was the heart of medieval Arras. Today the *préfecture* (county council) occupies the former bishop's palace, finished in 1780. Opposite, the **Église St-Nicolas-en-Cité** (1839) rises on the site of Notre-Dame-de-la-Cité Cathedral, which was destroyed between 1798 and 1804. It houses a triptych depicting *The Climb to Calvary*, painted in 1577 by P Claessens of Bruges.

Follow rue Baudimont on the right for 135m/150yd to reach **place du Pont-de-Cité**. The name recalls the bridge on the River Crinchon (now flowing underground), which linked the Cité to the town when each had its own fortifications.

From the square, follow rue de Turenne which skirts the Jardin Minelle (on the left) and leads to quai du Rivage.

Ancien hospice St-Éloi ....**AZ D**	Église Notre-Dame-	Mémorial britannique ....**AZ**
Ancienne abbaye	des-Ardents.....................**BZ**	Mur des Fusillés ....**AZ**
St-Vaast ....**BY**	Église	Palais
Cathédrale ....**BY**	St-Nicolas-en-Cité ....**AY**	de justice ....**BZ J**
Citadelle ....**AZ**	Hôtel de Guines ....**BY F**	Jardins du Gouverneur
Demeure	Hôtel de ville et beffroi .....**BY H**	et des Allées....................**AZ**
de Roberspierre..............**BY E**	Jardin Minelle ....**AZ**	Théâtre ....**BZ T**

The **Jardin Minelle**, which replaced the town's fortifications, is a haven of peace. **Place de l'Ancien-Rivage** is situated at the back of the pleasant **quai du Rivage**. The square-turreted house was the former St-Éloi hospice, founded in 1635 by one of the town's goldsmiths. Until the 19C, this square formed a dock linked to the old harbour.

Return to the Grand'Place along rue du Mont-de-Piété, place G.-Mollet and rue Ste-Croix

ADDITIONAL SIGHTS

★**Hôtel de ville and belfry** ⊘ – The town hall was destroyed in 1914 and rebuilt in the Flamboyant style. The beautiful front, with its uneven arches, stands on the western side of place des Héros and the graceful 75m/246ft belfry, with its 40-bell peal, rises over the more severe-looking Renaissance wings.

Downstairs, an audio-visual presentation on the history of Arras is an excellent introduction to the town. The **Circuit des souterrains** (tour of the underground passages) ⊘ starts here. The 10C galleries, cut into the limestone bank on which the town stands, served as a refuge in times of trouble (during the First World War the British set up a field hospital here) and above all as an enormous wine cellar, as the famous **caves** *(boves)* are at the ideal temperature for storing wine.

★ANCIENNE ABBAYE ST-VAAST ⊘ (BY) *1hr*

The old abbey was founded in the 7C by St Aubert on the hill overlooking a tributary of the River Scarpe, and was entrusted with the relics of the first bishop of Arras, St Vaast. **Cardinal de Rohan**, commendatory abbot, began reconstructing the abbey buildings in 1746 in a style combining balance and elegance to produce an austere sense of beauty; they were deconsecrated during the Revolution, then restored after 1918.

★**Musée des Beaux-Arts** ⊘ – Nouveau texte d'introduction. The museum offers a splendid account of the town's history: archeological finds, medieval sculpture, 15C tapestries, the cathedral treasury, 17C procelain and paintings (French and Dutch schools, large religious works) and pre-Impressionist paintings.

14C funerary mask – Musée des Beaux-Arts

Musée des Beaux-Arts

The **Italian Room** (**1**) decorated with the original lion from the belfry (1554) in Arras is used as a reception area. The tour begins in a series of small rooms on the left (**2** and **3**) containing the Gallo-Roman archaeology collection. The porphyry statue of Attis from a 2C-3C sanctuary in honour of Attis and Cybele bears witness to the influence of Near Eastern religions carried abroad by the army and merchants.

The **galleries around the small cloister** (**4**), known as the Cour du Puits, contain some fine medieval sculptures and paintings: Virgin and Child by Pépin de Huy, tapestries made in Arras (legend of St Vaast), statues. The 16C is illustrated by triptychs by **Bellegambe** (Adoration of the Christ Child) and an Entombment by Vermeyen.

Refectory – A tapestry bearing the arms of Cardinal de Rohan hangs above the great marble fireplace.

Grand cloître – The spacious main cloister, which used to lead through a peristyle into the minster, contains capitals carved with garlands and rosettes.

The **staircase** is decorated with a fine series of paintings by Giovanni Baglioni (1571-1644).

The **first floor** is given over to paintings from the 16C to 18C by the French School (Vignon, Nicolas de Largillière, Boullongne, Vien, Bouliar, Doncre...) and the Dutch School (Brueghel the Younger, Adriaen Van Utrecht, Barent Fabritius, a student of Rembrandt, and Rubens). 17C and 18C sculpture.

In the **gallery** on the south side of the small cloister are the *Fruit Seller* by P Van Boucle, a painting from the studio of Pieter Brueghel the Younger (the original is in Brussels) showing *The Numbering at Bethlehem*. In the gallery on the south side of the small cloister are the *Fruit Seller* by P Van Boucle; *Parrot, Jay, Bullfinch and Chaffinch* by Adriaen Van Utrecht; *The Three Angels at Abraham's House* by Barent Fabritius, who studied with Rembrandt, as is evident in the use of the same bronze tones; and *St Francis of Assisi* shown receiving the stigmata, an early work by Rubens.

A new section (on the landing) devoted to 17C painting is housed in the east gallery contains 17C and 18C sculptures.

It leads into the recently opened **Salle des Mays de Notre-Dame**, a room which owes its name to the works that were given to Notre-Dame Church in Paris every springtime between 1603 and 1707 by the guild of gold and silversmiths. It contains huge works by La Hyre, Sébastien Bourdon, Louis de Boullongne, Philippe de Champaigne, Joseph Barrocel and Jouvenet.

On the **2nd floor**, the rooms on the front of the building contain the ceramics collections from the 16C to the 19C: Italian earthenware, glazed earthenware, Arras and Tournai porcelain decorated with light, delicate motifs (note the **"Buffon bird dinner service"** commissioned by the Duc d'Orléans in 1787).

Around the small cloister are works by various schools of early-19C French landscape artists (Barbizon, Lyon and Arras), including Corot and Dutilleux. One spacious room is given over to large 19C works (**Delacroix, Chassériau**). Next to this room is the Salle Louise-Weiss containing 19C small paintings by Monticelli, Ribot and Ravier.

Cathédrale ⊘ – *Entrance in rue des Teinturiers. Open every afternoon.*
The old abbey church of St Vaast was built according to plans prepared by Contant d'Ivry in the 18C. It was finished in 1833 and elevated to a cathedral, to replace Notre-Dame-de-la-Cité.

ANCIENNE ABBAYE
ST-VAAST

The Classical façade is graced by a monumental flight of steps; the luminous interior presents an Antique splendour. A line of lofty columns bearing Corinthian capitals flanks the nave, transept and chancel. Enormous 19C statues of saints, from the Pantheon in Paris, adorn the side aisles.

The right transept is decorated with large frescoes, in which St Vaast may be seen taming a bear. To each side of the altar is a Nativity and a Resurrection by Desvallières.

Parc ASTÉRIX★★

Michelin map 106 fold 9 or 237 fold 18

Access from Paris: *By car: A 1 motorway, exit "Parc Astérix". By train: RER line B to Roissy-Charles-de-Gaulle, then by shuttle bus to the park.*

Asterix the Gaul, hero of the famous cartoon strip by Goscinny and Uderzo known throughout the world and translated into several languages, provides the theme for this 50ha/123 acre fun park; it is a fantasy world for all ages which offers a journey into the past. The park opened on 30 April 1989. The Gauls, and in particular Asterix's friends, the mighty Obélix who follows him everywhere, Panoramix who prepares magic potions, Assurancetourix the bard and Abraracourcix the chief of the tribe are the heroes, but beware the Romans are never very far away!

TOUR ⓥ *allow a whole day*

The park presents carefully reconstructed "historical" sections, various attractions, shows and audio-visual displays and offers a choice of snacks and meals.

Via Antiqua – Situated at the entrance to the park, this "street" is lined with houses symbolising, through their architecture, Asterix' various journeys across Europe (Germany, Helvetica, Hispania etc). It leads to a huge rock from which the popular hero greets visitors.

Where to stay

LUXURY

Les Trois Hiboux – *Parc Astérix, 60128 Plailly* – ☎ *03 44 62 68 00* – *www.par-casterix.fr* – *closed 15 Nov-15 Jan* – *100 rooms from 860F* – ☕ *69F* – *restaurant 95/145F*. According to local legend, the three forests surrounding this theme park were once frequented by three owls, who would scour the grounds in search of their prey... Although this was a long time ago, you may still hear their lonely screeching if you choose to stay at this cosy hotel nestling among the woods. Sleep tight!

PARC ASTÉRIX

0   100 m

N

GOUDURIX ★★

Halte de Chevalie

Escadrille des As

Mini Carrousel

Petites Chaises Volantes

Petits Drakkars

Pl. du Moyen-

Galère

TONNERRE DE ZEUS ★★

GRAND   LAC

Arcimbold

Menhir

GRÈCE   **ANTIQUE**   Théât de Panora

Rivière d'Elis

THÉÂTRE DE POSÉIDON ★

Colonnade du Temple de Zeu

Hydre de Lerne

Labyrinthe de Dédale

VOL D'ICARE

Palais de Minos   **Cheval de Troie**   Arcades d'Olympie   **CITÉ**

★ **DESCENTE DU ST**

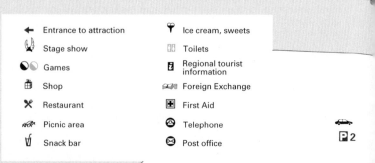

←	Entrance to attraction	♟	Ice cream, sweets
🕴	Stage show	⬚⬚	Toilets
◖◗	Games	🛈	Regional tourist information
🎁	Shop	💱	Foreign Exchange
✕	Restaurant	✚	First Aid
🐾	Picnic area	☏	Telephone
🥤	Snack bar	✉	Post office

🚗

P 2

MAIN BASSE SUR
LA JOCONDE ★★

L'OXYGÉNARIUM

Le Restaurant
du Cirque

Chaises Volantes

Chevaux du Roy

Animal
Studio

Les
Galapagos

a Cour
Miracles

AVENUE   DE   PARIS ★★

Les Chaudrons

Théâtre de la Fontaine

Relais Gaulois

Théâtre du
Barde

Nationale 7

Petite tempête

Huttes Gauloises

VILLAGE   D'ASTÉRIX ★

MENHIR EXPRESS ★★

Petits
Capitaines

DOMAINE   LACUSTRE

Mini
Village

Trans' Arverne

Petits Chars
Tamponneurs

FORÊT DES

Camp de
Petibonum

DRUIDES

BALADE
D'ASTÉRIX

Espions
de César ★

Petit
Train

GRAND SPLATCH ★

cades
Pompéi

Flotille
de Néron

ARENES

ROMAINE

ux Fastes
e Rome

Carrousel
de César

Bataille d'Alésia

Caius
Cepadérefus

VIA

ANTIQUA

Visitor
information

Maison de l'Oise

Tickets

P 3-4-5-6

HOTEL

P1

Descente du Styx

Gaule Antique – The very heart of this area is the Village d'Astérix, a veritable Gallic village consisting of huts, where visitors can meet such well-known figures as Obélix with his menhirs, Panoramix and Assurancetourix the bard in his hut perched in the treetops. Here and there are fights, festivities or hunting scenes. The **Balade d'Astérix** reveals a few strange scenes and a tour of the **Forêt des Druides** attracts young and not so young visitors alike. Nearby, the atmosphere is much damper at the **Grand Splatch**.

However, the most popular site is a Stone Age village built on piles, which gets its wealth from the production of menhirs. An ingenious delivery system called **Menhir Express★★** takes anybody who dares on a trip through a network of canals bristling with surprises!

Grèce Antique – The entrance to this part of the park is marked by the colonnade from the Temple of Zeus. The **Vol d'Icare** (Icarus' flight) takes visitors out of Daedalus' labyrinth but you still have to defeat the terrible **Hydre de Lerne** and if you're really brave, you can incur the wrath of the gods by taking a ride on the impressive **Tonnerre de Zeus★★** (top speed 80kph/50mph).

Empire Romain – In the arena are terrible fights between gladiators and some amazing circus acts performed by the **Stars de l'Empire**. If you wish to know what is afoot in the Gallic village, join the **Espions de César★** (Caesar's spies) who have devised a very efficient surveillance system (5m/16ft above ground level). And why not brave Hell itself by trying the **Descente du Styx★**.

Moyen Âge – A long journey in time takes place along **Avenue de Paris★★**. Ten centuries of history are illustrated here, each period represented by people in costume, typical shops and its own special atmosphere. The Middle Ages come alive thanks to street entertainers, glassmakers and potters living and working in dark, mysterious streets. There are interesting demonstrations of ancient crafts and a strange carnival regularly livens up the medieval square.

17C – To illustrate this colourful period, the king's **musketeers** confront the Cardinal's musketeers in a seemingly endless series of pitiless duels. Artistic and literary life is remembered, too, through **La Fontaine's fables**.

Temps Modernes – Going on holiday has not always been plain sailing as you can see from the numerous adventures to be encountered along the **Nationale 7** main road to the south of France. However, it may not be necessary to leave for the country as the **Oxygénarium** has been specially designed to offer city dwellers the combined benefits of water and fresh mountain air: guaranteed thrills! More excitement is round the corner with **Goudurix★**, a gigantic roller coaster taking visitors through a succession of vertiginous drops, swooping round corners, and going into spins and loops, all at breathtaking speed.

This trip through time ends in 1930, in **Main basse sur la Joconde★**, a splendid enactment of a historical detective story during which a gang of thieves attempts to steal the Mona Lisa.

AUVERS-SUR-OISE ★

Population 6 154

Michelin map 101 folds 3, 4, 106 fold 6 or 237 fold 17

This village stretches over 7km/4.5mi from the River Oise to the escarpment edging the Vexin plateau. The old path, now a series of narrow streets winding their way from Valhermeil to Cordeville, still carries the memory of the artists who brought it fame. Here and there, panels indicate the scenes portrayed by Impressionist painters. It is the district around the church, however, which constitutes the favourite "place of pilgrimage" for art lovers.

Doctor **Paul Gachet** (1828-1909) moved to Auvers in 1872. An enthusiastic painter and engraver, with an unquenchable thirst for novelty he was the centre of attraction for a new generation of painters, known as the "Impressionists" *(see p 87)* who came to stay and paint locally.

The Impressionists have left many reminders of their stay in Auvers. Spend a day here to have a look at the home of Dr Gachet and the Maison du Pendu immortalised by Cézanne. The surrounding area is full of scenic beauty, thanks to the vast fields of corn that so inspired the artists.

IN VAN GOGH'S FOOTSTEPS

Use the map in the "brochure-pass" issued at the Maison Van Gogh to locate the various sites with ease.

Church – The best view of the church is from the back of the terrace, near the east end. The well-proportioned chancel and 12C bell-tower were depicted by Van Gogh in one of his expressive paintings, now in the Orsay Museum in Paris.

A bust portraying the painter Charles-François Daubigny stands at the foot of the church.

Monument de Van Gogh – In the Van Gogh Park located in rue du Général-de-Gaulle stands Van Gogh's statue, a work by sculptor Ossip Zadkine.

Van Gogh's grave – The famous Dutch painter is buried in the cemetery that lies on the plateau *(follow the road behind the church)*. His tomb stands against the left-hand wall.

Church at Auvers by Van Gogh (Musée d'Orsay, Paris)

His brother Theo, who gave him moral support all his life and who died soon after him, rests by his side. **View** of Auvers' bell-tower.

★**Maison de Van Gogh** ⊘ – This is actually the **Auberge Ravoux**, an inn made famous by the celebrated artist who stayed there several months before his tragic death. Feeling terribly guilty towards his brother Theo, on whom he was entirely dependent, Van Gogh shot himself in the chest while he was out in a field; he died on 29 July 1890 in the room he occupied in the Auberge Ravoux.

The inn has been carefully restored and has retained its interior decoration and its sector of activity *(local cuisine and wines)*. Outside are panels describing the artist's eventful life. The small garret he occupied has remained unchanged and, despite the absence of furniture, gives some insight into the ascetic conditions under which he lived *(tours restricted to five visitors at a time because of the lack of space)*. The tour ends with a moving audio-visual presentation illustrating Van Gogh's stay in Auvers.

ADDITIONAL SIGHTS

Musée de l'Absinthe ⊘ – The famous green liqueur reached the peak of its popularity in the cafés of the 19C. It was often described as the **"green muse"** and was closely linked to the life of the artists of the day who spent a great deal of time in cafés. The documents, posters and objects displayed in the museum bring back to life the history of a drink which had a profound social influence until it was banned in 1915.

Eating Out

MID-RANGE

Auberge Ravoux – *Facing the town hall (Mairie)* – ☎ *01 30 36 60 60 – closed Sun, Mon, Tues and Wed evenings in low season – booking essential – 195F.* This former artists' café, enhanced by a charming turn-of-the-century decor, was Van Gogh's last place of residence. History lovers will enjoy its highly evocative atmosphere. Superb counter and imposing, crudely carved wooden tables. Sample the tasty traditional cuisine and lively local wines.

LUXURY

Hostellerie du Nord – *Rue du Général-de-Gaulle* – ☎ *01 30 36 70 74 – closed 4-14 Apr, 15 Aug-4 Sept, Sat lunchtime, Sun evening and Mon – 270/370F.* A stone's throw from the famous church that was to inspire Van Gogh, this restaurant was patronised by a great many artists, namely Daubigny and Cézanne. Its glorious past is reflected by the objects and paintings displayed in the hallway, which has been laid out in the manner of an art gallery.

Maison-Atelier de Daubigny ⊘ – **Charles-François Daubigny** (1817-78), a landscape painter, settled in Auvers on the advice of his friend Camille Corot. He had a studio-house built in 1860 and asked his family and friends to take part in the interior decoration. Charles, his son Karl and his daughter Cécile as well as Corot and Daumier left a mark of their artistic inspiration on the walls and doors. Charles Daubigny decorated his daughter's childhood bedroom with panels depicting some of Perrault's tales *(Tom Thumb* and *Little Red Riding Hood)*, which express his deep love for her. Daubigny loved to paint on the River Oise, aboard a small specially designed boat. Later on, Monet followed his example (note the boat in the garden). In 1890, Van Gogh painted Daubigny's garden and, in his last letter to his brother Theo, he gives details about the colours he chose for the painting and asks his advice.

Château d'Auvers ⊘ – This 17C château, which has been restored and laid out with extensive use of audio-visual presentations, offers visitors a chance to enjoy a **Journey Back to the Days of the Impressionists★** ⊘ and gain some insight into the wonderful adventure that was Art in the 19C. Using reconstructions of interiors and the projection of some 500 works, it brings to life the Paris of the time, a city undergoing immense change thanks to the work of Baron Haussmann, and a city where the wealthy middle classes led a bustling, frivolous life with little appreciation of the new style of painting.

Although some of the artists fed on the capital's atmosphere for their works (Degas, Toulouse-Lautrec), most of them preferred to travel on the brand-new railway from Paris to the seaside in search of new sources of inspiration. They found it in the open-air bars *(guinguettes)* in Asnières and Chatou, along the banks of the Seine and the Oise (Argenteuil, Vétheuil, Auvers-sur-Oise etc.), in the lush countryside of the Paris basin (haystacks by Monet and Thornley), in the sea, the harbours (Le Havre), the cliffs (Étretat) and the beaches.

AVESNES-SUR-HELPE

Population 5 108
Michelin map 53 folds 6, 7 or 236 fold 29

The quiet town, which stands on the south bank of the River Helpe-Majeure, has preserved some of its Vauban-like fortifications. It is the ideal starting point of drives through the Avesnois region, its patchwork of hedged-in meadows and slate-roofed hamlets.

In the 17C, a Protestant from Avesnes, Jessé de Forest, left his home town to go and live in America. He settled in Long Island where the district of Forest Hill was later named after him.

TOWN WALK

Grand'Place – The town's narrow main square is surrounded by old houses with high slate roofs.

Église St-Nicolas ⊘ – A graceful onion dome tops the 60m/197ft belfry-porch of this hall-church (1534). Inside, there are two monumental Louis XV altarpieces with paintings by Louis Watteau.

Hôtel de ville – A double staircase with wrought-iron balustrades fronts the 18C Classical town hall in blue Tournai stone.

Walk round the church and follow rue d'Albert.

Square de la Madeleine – Located on top of one of the bastions, it provides a bird's-eye view of the Helpe Valley.

EXCURSIONS

Cartignies – *6km/3.7mi southwest along D 424.* The village boasts some 40 **bluestone oratories**.

Pont-de-Sains – *10km/6.2mi southeast along D 951.* Picturesque setting. The castle once belonged to Talleyrand then to his niece, the Duchess of Dino.

Maroilles – *12km/7.5mi west along D 962.* This place is famous for its cheeses, Maroilles and Dauphin, which used to be the speciality of the former Benedictine abbey (a few 17C buildings can still be seen). Lovely watermill.

★★THE AVESNOIS REGION

The Avesnois region, which lies south of Maubeuge and extends along the Belgian border, is known for its undulating countryside of orchards, woodlands and pastures, through which meander the River Helpe-Majeure and River Helpe-Mineure, and for its pretty villages of brick, slate and stone. Of the many small bandstands, built on village squares by the foundries of the Sambre Valley, only about 20 have survived. The finest are in Beugnies, Floursies, Marbraix, Solre-le-Château, Avesnes, Cartignies, Dourlers and Trélon.

The vast forests and the cluster of lakes around Liessies and Trélon are traces of a period when the great abbeys – Maroilles, Liessies and St-Michel – dominated the region, constructing mills and forges on every river. Some of the local churches contain works of art from these abbeys.

Many small industries developed in the 18C and 19C: glassmaking at Sars-Poteries, Trélon and Anor, wood turning at Felleries, spinning at Fourmies, marble quarrying at Cousoire etc.

Today the museums at Sars-Poteries, Felleries, Trélon and Fourmies recall the time when the region was highly populated and active.

Round tour

Leave Avesnes by D 133 (east) towards Liessies.

Just outside Avesnes there is a good view *(right)* of the town's beautiful surroundings and its ramparts.

Ramousies – The 16C **church** ⊘ contains two beautiful Renaissance altarpieces, from Antwerp workshops, which once belonged to Liessies Abbey. One depicts the life of St Sulpice; the other represents the Passion.
The 13C crucifix is from the oldest calvary in northern France.

Continue along D 80 to Felleries.

Felleries – Since the 17C the town's inhabitants have specialised in *bois-joli:* turned wood and cooperage. These workshops developed at the same time as the textile industry, the former making bobbins and spindles for the latter.

In Avesnes...

DINING

La Crémaillère – *26 place du Général-Leclerc* – ☎ *03 27 61 02 30* – *closed 2-14 Jan, evenings except Wed, Fri and Sat* – *110/250F.* Its discreet façade, red brick framed by dark wood, harmoniously blends in with the other buildings laid out around the church square. Inside the dining room, the visible beams stand out against the bright yellow walls. You will appreciate the chef's imaginative approach and unusual combinations of flavours.

BED AND BREAKFAST

Chambre d'Hôte La Villa Mariani – *5 Grand'place, 59740 Solre-le-Château* – ☎ *03 27 61 65 30* – ⌷ – *3 rooms 220/290F.* Relax in a luxuriant setting, a true haven of peace, and succumb to the charm of this 19C time-honoured mansion set up on the village square. Temporary art exhibitions are regularly held on the premises.

Chambre d'Hôte Les Prés de la Fagne – *2 rue Principale, 59132 Baives* – *1km/0.6mi east of Wallers-Trelon* – ☎ *03 27 57 02 69* – ⌷ – *5 rooms 240/340F* – *meal 100F.* This tastefully restored 17C barn is a successful association of old and new. In some of the rooms, guests may even find a bathtub at the foot of their bed! Horse rides can be arranged for experienced riders.

The **Moulin des Bois-Jolis Museum,** ⊘ housed in a 16C watermill, brings together a wide variety of treen (wooden) items made in Felleries: butter moulds, salt boxes, spindles, tops etc.

Sars-Poteries – Since the 15C the earth around Sars has been used by potters, and many small pottery workshops exist locally while the larger factories specialising in pipes, ducts etc have all closed. In the 19C, two glassworks were set up specialising in dinner services and bottles. In 1900, they employed a work force of 800 but by 1938 the economic slump forced them to close.

DINING INSARS

Auberge Fleurie – *67 rue du Général-de-Gaulle* – ☎ *03 27 61 62 48 – closed 3-20 Jan and 18-25 Aug – booking essential – 150/340F.* A pretty brick façade painted white and window boxes bursting with flowers in summer... Besides this lovely sight, the Auberge Fleurie offers a tasty, carefully studied menu that will not fail to tempt you. The restaurant opens onto a garden-terrace that is much appreciated in high season. A few rooms have recently been made available to guests.

★**Musée-Atelier du Verre** ⊘ – Housed in the former home of the glassworks manager, this museum boasts an unusual collection of popular glassware made by the workers for their own use. The pieces were nicknamed

bousillés (meaning "made after working hours") and they enabled the workers to make full use of their talent, artistry and imagination.

There are highly ornate engraved lamps, large dishes, "revenge inkwells" (so named because the glass workers did not know how to write but they had the most beautiful inkwells), strange "Passion bottles" containing representations of the instruments of Christ's Passion (these bottles were taken on pilgrimages to Notre-Dame de Liesse) and a range of miscellaneous objects. As a result of local digs, the museum has built up a collection of grey-sandstone objects with glazed cobalt-blue decoration (17C and 18C).

In association with the glass workshop, the museum welcomes international artists and, by doing so, extends its contemporary glass collection.

The menhir, known as the **Pierre de Dessus-Bise**, stands 90m/100yd from the church, on place du Vieux Marché. According to tradition, sterile women who sit on it are then able to bear children.

The **watermill** ⊘ north of the village was built in 1780 and still contains its great wheel and workings.

Take D 962 east, then turn left 3km/1.9mi further on.

Lez-Fontaine – In the 15C **church** the wooden vaults are decorated with paintings dating from 1531.

Follow D 27 to Solre-le-Château.

Solre-le-Château – The seigneurial château no longer exists but there are still many 17C and 18C houses. The sober Renaissance **town hall** (late 16C) has an austere bell-tower. A covered market was held on the ground floor; note the Gothic writing on the keystones.

Walk through the archway leading to place Verte.

The lovely 16C Gothic **church** is made of local blue stone. The powerful **belfry** was part of the fortifications; its base forms a most unusual porch, open on three sides. The mauve spire (1612) is crowned by a large bulb with openings where the watchman stood. Inside there is a double transept, wooden barrel-vaulting with carved tie-beams in the nave and diagonal vaulting in the chancel. The church also contains an 18C organ, 16C stained glass and Renaissance woodwork. The square is surrounded by fine 17C and 18C houses.

Take D 963 south towards Liessies.

Liessies – The village originated with an 8C Benedictine abbey which had exclusive use of the surrounding woods. The abbey prospered and by the 17C the abbots were powerful lords, but the Revolution led to the break up of the 13C abbey church and the monastic buildings.

The **Église St-Jean-et-Ste-Hiltrude** stands near the site of the old abbey. It contains beautiful 15C to 18C statues and remnants of the abbey, including a precious **Romanesque cross** of gilded copper decorated with chased enamelwork and gemstones, as well as some 17C paintings (life of St Hiltrude).

The **abbey park**, situated near the church, is open to the public. Several trails enable visitors to discover the local fauna and flora as well as former monastic buildings. Summer exhibitions are organised in the church and in the Bûcher aux Moines (inside the park).

The village is the starting point of an excursion to the 18C **Château de la Motte**, built of red brick and to **Bois l'Abbé Forest**.

The 18C **Calvaire de la Croix-Trélon** stands to the east of the intersection of the Trélon road (D 963) and the Château de la Motte access road. View of the Helpe Valley.

From Liessies follow D 133 along the Helpe Valley.

The road becomes more winding, the slopes are increasingly covered with thick woods.

★**Parc départemental du Val-Joly** – The construction of the dam at Eppe-Sauvage on the Helpe-Majeure created a magnificent reservoir surrounded by the wooded banks of the River Helpe and its tributary, the Voyon. The park has many leisure facilities including swimming, tennis, sailing, fishing, riding, hiking and mountain biking, archery, and boating or pedalo. There is also an aquarium (22 tanks). The park includes a camp site with bungalows for hire as well as shopping and catering facilities.

Eppe-Sauvage – This village, close to the Belgian border, nestles in a pretty location in the hollow of a basin formed where the River Helpe and River Eau d'Eppe meet. In the **Église St-Ursmar**, with its 16C chancel and transept, there are two remarkable 16C painted wood triptychs.

After Eppe-Sauvage, the valley opens out and becomes less wooded; marshes, called *fagnes*, are frequent along its floor. A beautiful manor farm may be seen.

Moustier-en-Fagne – This small village derives its name from a 16C priory, or *moustier*. Olivetan Benedictines, who devote themselves to painting icons, live in the monks' quarters. They are near the **church** dedicated to St Dodon, the hermit invoked for back ailments, who was originally from this village. A handsome **manor house** with crow-stepped gables, built in 1520, is visible *(left)* on entering Moustier-en-Fagne.

Continue south and, 2km/1mi beyond Moustier, fork left onto D 283, then turn right.

The top of a knoll (225m/738ft high) affords a clear **view** of **Trélon Forest**.

Chapelle des Monts – *15min on foot over wild heath.*

This 18C chapel is surrounded by a grassy terrace and age-old lime trees. The quarries and lime kiln date from the 19C.

Wallers-Trélon – Built entirely in blue stone, this beautiful village owes its unique appearance to the numerous quarries nearby.

Nature trails allow visitors to discover the unusual flora of the **Monts de Baive**, which flourishes owing to the chalky soil.

Take D 83 south; turn right onto D 951 to Trélon.

> ### Blue-stone oratories
>
> Blue-stone oratories have been built in the Avesnois and Thiérache regions since 1550; they are located in various places, mostly on the roadside, but also in fields, along ancient footpaths and even in woods or set in walls. These characteristic constructions consist of a narrow shaft surmounted by a fine recess, closed off by wire mesh as in Le Favril or Dimont, and a larger crowning piece. Each recess was intended to hold one or several polychrome statues carved by the clog makers of Mormal Forest. The oratories were erected for various reasons: in thanksgiving for a cure (as in Bérelles), to ask for a favour, to assert a certain social status, to abide by a family tradition. The Avesnois region is said to possess more than 700 blue-stone oratories including some 40 of them in the village of Cartignies alone.

Trélon – Formerly known for its glass industry, Trélon is today the location of the **Atelier-musée du verre** ☉, a branch of the Fourmies-Trélon Folk Museum. In the heart of the old hall of the 19C glassworks, which still contains two kilns from 1850 and 1920 together with their equipment, glassworkers demonstrate the blowing and shaping of glass.

South beyond Olhain the route follows the Helpe Mineure Valley, and is bordered by a sprinkling of ponds.

Fourmies – *See Fourmies.*

Sains-du-Nord – The **Maison du Bocage** ☉, a branch of the Fourmies-Trélon Folk Museum, has been established in a 19C farm. Exhibitions present life and work in the woodlands and pastures of the Avesnois (stock farming, cheese-making etc).

AZINCOURT

AGINCOURT – Population 250

Michelin map 51 fold 13 or 236 fold 13 – 12km/7.5mi northeast of Hesdin

Musée d'Azincourt

Crossbowman stringing
his crossbow

Situated in the middle of the hills of Artois, this flower-decked village recalls one of the most famous battles in the Hundred Years War.

The **Battle of Agincourt**, which was fought on 25 October 1415, was one of the bloodiest defeats ever suffered by the French aristocracy which lost 10 000 men and saw 1 500 men taken prisoner, including the poet Charles d'Orléans. The site chosen as the battlefield left little space for the knights to manoeuvre and the land was water-logged; the horses were quickly bogged down. Moreover, the knights were hindered by the medieval concept of warfare and were obliged to fight on foot in their heavy armour. Despite superiority of numbers, they were massacred by the English archers concealed behind a fence and by the English footsoldiers armed with axes and leaded clubs. The victory gave greater weight to Henry V's claims to the throne of France.

Up to 1734 this fateful spot was known locally as Carrion (La Carogne).

A **calvary** erected in 1963 recalls this historic episode, as does, at the junction of D 104 and the road to Maisoncelle, an inscription at the foot of the pine-encircled menhir.

Musée de Traditions populaires et d'Histoire locale ☉ – Documents, photographs, copies of arms and armour, and small models depict the weaponry of the time. The events of the battle are evoked in a video presentation. A model shows the battlefield. Some of the 14C paving found on the site of the old castle are also on show in a display case.

A round trip *(map provided)* leaving from the museum leads to the battlefield where a viewing table and various maps are displayed.

AL FRESCO, ANYONE?

Le Charles VI – *12 rue Charles-VI – ☎ 03 21 41 53 00 – closed 2 weeks in Jan, Mon evening from mid-Nov to mid-Apr and Sun evening – 82/130F.* After walking round the famous battlefield, pay a visit to this pretty restaurant, where you will soon discover that culinary tradition, fresh produce and reasonable prices are not always mutually exclusive! Terrace for the summer season.

BAILLEUL

Population 13 847

Michelin map 51 fold 5 or 236 fold 5

Situated in the hilly area known as Monts de Flandre, the town of Bailleul was damaged in 1918 during the last German onslaught in this region. It was rebuilt in authentic Flemish style. The Shrove Tuesday Carnival, headed by the giant Gargantua, offers Doctor Picolissimo the opportunity of throwing tripe to the crowd. The drive through the Monts de Flandre, described below, shows that Flanders is not as flat as some people say. A strange event takes place in July every year, the Fête des Épouvantails (the festival of scarecrows): at the end of the procession, the scarecrows are burnt and the popular ball can begin.

SIGHTS

Grand-Place – In spite of having been destroyed eight times, Bailleul and its Grand-Place have always regained their typically Flemish atmosphere. Before settling down in a local tavern with a glass of "3 Monts" beer, have a closer look at the town hall and its belfry in neo-Flemish style. The brick façades decorated with corner stones features a proclamation balcony.

Église St-Vaast – The Romano-byzantine edifice, situated behind the town hall, is decorated with a fine set of stained-glass windows.

Rue du Musée – The street is lined with fine houses, in particular no 3, the town's cultural centre with its Marguerite-Yourcenar hall.

Présidial – This harmonious edifice (1776), the oldest in Bailleul, used to house the law courts.

Beffroi ⊘ – The belfry towering over the town hall housed the cloth market in medieval times. There is a 13C Gothic room at ground level and from the watch-path at the top, the vast **panorama**★ includes the plain and Monts de Flandre to the north and the slag heaps of the mining area to the south. When the weather is clear, the city of Lille is visible. The peal of bells chimes well-known Flemish tunes.

Musée Benoît-De-Puydt ⊘ – Founded in 1859, this elegant museum displays glazed earthenware from Delft and Northern France, porcelain from China and Japan, 16C to 18C furniture and carved wood as well as paintings from the Flemish, French and Dutch schools. Note in particular a breast-feeding Virgin by Gérard David and an Adoration of the Magi by Pieter Brueghel. In addition, a large tapestry from Flanders (18C) and 19C portraits hang in the museum.

Maison de la dentelle ⊘ – The school occupies a Flemish-style house; the pediment is decorated with a lace-maker and her spinning wheel. Every year some 100 students learn the technique of bobbin lace-making.

> ### Lace-making in 2001
>
> In the 17C, lace-making was already a local tradition but it reached its heyday during the 19C, when there were as many as 800 lace-makers in the area. The first school was founded in 1664. Lace-making declined from 1900 onwards, owing to the introduction of machines. Today the tradition lives on. The International Lace-making Weekend takes place every third year (third weekend in July, next one in 2001) with the participation of lace-makers worldwide.

ROUND TOUR

Northern heights *allow half a day*

This itinerary will take you through the Flemish countryside into Belgium. On the way, you will see hills, mills, typical local taverns and taste "special" beer and soft cheese...

Follow D 23 then turn left on D 223.

On your right (on the Belgian side) is Mont Kemmel crowned by a hotel. On the same side but closer is Mont Rouge (Rodeberg).

Turn left again on D 318.

Mont Noir – Straddling the border between France and Belgium, Mont Noir (Black Hill), so-called owing to its dark wooded slopes, is part of the Monts de Flandres range. The hill (altitude 131m/429ft) offers views of Ypres, Mont Rouge and Mont des Cats, surmounted by its monastery. Mont Noir has been immortalized in *Archives du Nord (How Many Years)*, the autobiographical work of writer and French Academy member **Marguerite Yourcenar** (1903-87) who spent many of her childhood years here.

Within the Parc départemental du Mont Noir, the **Villa Mont-Noir★**, dating from the 1920s, is a cultural and literary centre which welcomes resident European writers. In the English-style park, a marked trail, *In the footsteps of Marguerite Yourcenar*, recalls her childhood.

Mont des Cats – Also known as Catsberg (altitude 158m/514ft), this hill is part of the Monts de Flandres range. It lies in pleasant undulating countryside where fields of hops, poplar trees, and red roofs form the "humanised landscape" defined by geographer Brunhes.
Gourmets know this area for its wonderful cheeses which are similar to Port Salut. On top of the hill are the neo-Gothic buildings of a Trappist **monastery** ☉ founded in 1826 and restored since that time.

Église paroissiale St-Bernard – In the parish church *(to the right of the monastery entrance)* are some interesting stained-glass windows by Michel Gigon (1965) representing Fire and Darkness, Death and Resurrection.

Centre d'accueil C. Grimminck ☉ – The centre consists of an exhibition hall, a shop selling products from the monastery and a room where the monks' daily life is the subject of an audio-visual presentation.
Turn back and follow D 10 to Boeschepe.

Moulin de Boeschepe ☉ – The village of Boeschepe at the foot of Mont des Cats has a restored windmill, the **Ondankmeulen** (the mill of ungratefulness) ☉, next to a delightful bar *(estaminet)*, which sells some 50 different kinds of beer.
Follow D 139 past the Belgian border and continue to Poperingue.

Poperingue – The inhabitants are known as *Keikoppen*, "tough heads". On the Grand'Place, a stone weighing 1 650kg/3 638lb testifies to this reputation. The Cathédrale St-Bertinus, a Flemish hall-church, is a fine example of the transition from the Romanesque style to the Gothic style.

Leave Poperingue via N 308 towards Dunkerque and turn left to Watou, also in Belgium.

Watou – This village is ideal for anyone wishing to sample the authentic atmosphere of an *estaminet* (a bar), where the locals drink beer while playing various games.
Return to Bailleul along D 10.

BARBIZON★★

Population 1 407
Michelin map 106 fold 45 or 237 fold 30
10km/6mi northwest of Fontainebleau – Local map see Forêt de FONTAINEBLEAU

Lying on the edge of the Fontainebleau Forest, the village of Barbizon, which was part of Chailly until 1903, was a popular spot with landscape painters *(see Introduction: Landscape Painting)* and still carries memories of the artists who made it famous. The Bas-Bréau coppices nearby are reminders of a time when, according to the Goncourt brothers, "every tree was like an artist's model surrounded by a circle of paint-boxes".

The Barbizon Group – Breaking the rules of studio work and official art, the Barbizon artists were landscape painters who perfected the technique of working directly from nature after two great masters: Théodore Rousseau (1812-67) and Jean-François Millet (1814-75). The local people were happy to welcome these nature-loving artists who rose at dawn and whose genius and mischievous nature enlivened local weddings and banquets. Next came the writers, seduced by the beauty of the forest and the congenial atmosphere of this small, international community: George Sand, Henri Murger, the Goncourt brothers, Taine etc. Thereafter, Barbizon remained a fashionable spot.
Millet, a patriarch with nine children, died after a life of hard work, his eyes forever riveted on the landscapes of the Bière plain. Like Rousseau, he was buried at **Chailly Cemetery** *(plan of graveyard at entrance)*.

LA GRANDE RUE *1hr – From the junction of D 64 to the forest.*

Barbizon is a long high street (Grande Rue) lined with hotels, restaurants and villas. Many of these buildings bear commemorative plaques of the artists who stayed there.

★Auberge du Père Ganne ☉ – This was a popular meeting-place for artists, many of whom had rooms here. The inn has now become the **Musée de l'École de Barbizon**. A lively educational audio-visual display describes "Ganne's painters" who revolutionised art and brought life and laughter to the inn by their tricks. The "Officers'" dining room on the ground floor is representative of their habit of decorating all

The Gleaners by Millet (Musée d'Orsay, Paris)

the wood panelling in the inn as a means of paying for their keep. They decorated cupboards, doors, the sideboard, the fireplace, in fact any flat surface, all of them ideal as supports for the talents of the artists. On the first floor the museum has numerous paintings indicating the influence of Barbizon on Impressionists through the "Back to Nature" theme. The lack of popular enthusiasm for this school was probably due to the dark colours which were soon to be replaced by the brilliant hues of the Impressionists.

Maison-atelier de Théodore Rousseau – Behind the war memorial is the small house that is now an annex of the Barbizon School Museum. It is used for temporary exhibitions and contains a collection of old photographs of Fontainebleau Forest during the days of the "Colourists".

Monument de Millet et de Rousseau – A bronze medal embedded in the rock is the work of Henri Chapu. Behind this monument, a plaque set into another rock commemorates the centenary of the setting up of the first artistic reserve in 1853 at the instigation of Rousseau.

Eating Out

MID-RANGE

Le Relais de Barbizon – *2 avenue du Général-de-Gaulle* – ☎ *01 60 66 40 28* – *closed 16-25 Aug, 11-27 Dec, Tues evening and Wed* – *105/205F*. A modest, unassuming inn at the entrance to the village. Clean, cosy dining room with an area set aside for family gatherings. Delicious cuisine made with fresh local produce. Wide choice of menus.

L'Ermitage St-Antoine – *51 Grande-rue* – ☎ *01 64 81 96 96* – *closed 24 Dec-2 Jan, Mon evening and Tues* – *140/180F*. This 19C farmhouse converted into a café exudes great charm with its sturdy beams, tiled floor and painted wooden panels adorning the walls. Meat eaters will relish its delicious entrecôtes, but you can also choose one of the daily specials chalked up on a slate.

Where to stay

MODERATE

Chambre d'Hôte La Ferme des Vosves – *155 rue de Boissise, 77190 Village de Vosves* – *10km/6.2mi north of Barbizon by N 7, N 372, D 142, then N 472 and rue de la Gare* – ☎ *01 64 39 22 28* – ✉ – *3 rooms 250/300F*. Take time to stroll through the pretty gardens surrounding this former farmhouse overlooking the River Seine. The sparsely furnished rooms are wonderfully quiet and you will be won over by the hosts' generous hospitality as well as the reasonable prices he charges.

LUXURY

Auberge Les Alouettes – *4 rue Antoine-Barye* – ☎ *01 60 66 41 98* – 🅿 – *22 rooms 280/390F* – 🍽 *40F* – *restaurant 170/200F*. This modest establishment makes a point of charging highly affordable prices, a rare occurrence in these parts. We warmly recommend this charming hotel with its small garden, old-fashioned painted doors, unpretentious rooms and intimate dining area, perfect for a romantic encounter in the winter months.

On the town

Bizon's Club – *1 rue Grande* – ☎ *01 60 66 40 01* – *Wed-Sun 11pm-dawn*. This is the main nightclub in the vicinity of Fontainebleau Forest, where a trendy yet select clientele comes to soak up the warm, friendly atmosphere. A huge dance floor with techno music caters for the younger generation, whereas the small club downstairs pays tribute to the songs of the 1980s.

Art

Auberge du Père-Ganne – *92 Grande-rue* – ☎ *01 60 66 22 27* – *Apr-Sept, daily except Tues 10am-12.30pm, 2-6pm, Sat, Sun and public holidays 10am-6pm* – *closed 25 Dec.* The Auberge du Père Ganne, an inn where many painters used to take up residence, has now become the **Musée de l'École de Barbizon**. An audiovisual presentation evokes the lives of these artists, who were to dramatically redefine the art of landscape painting and whose lively, mischievous presence soon became a hallmark of the inn. The pictures and painted furniture executed by these artists in residence clearly demonstrate that the Barbizon School exerted a strong influence over Impressionism.

BAVAY★

Population 3 751

Michelin map 53 fold 5 or 236 folds 18, 19

Bavay was originally the capital of the old Belgian tribe the Nervii; today it is a small town with low houses, known for its confectionery called "Chiques de Bavay".

Bagacum during the Roman Occupation – At the time of Caesar Augustus, Bagacum was an important town in Roman Belgium. It was a judicial and administrative centre, the seat of a curia, a military post and a supply centre situated at the junction of seven roads that led to Utrecht, Boulogne, Cambrai, Soissons, Reims, Trier and Cologne, this last being the busiest. The routes, still recognisable in the present road network, were furrowed by carts which dug ruts, traces of which can be found in the forum. Ravaged at the end of the 3C, Bagacum never regained its former splendour.

SIGHTS

Grande Place – The brickwork of the 17C belfry contrasts with the 18C town hall, built of granite, next to it. A fluted column in the square supports a statue of Brunhilda, Queen of Austrasia, who took a great interest in road networks.

Remains of the Roman City – In 1942 Canon Bièvelet began searching on a site cleared in the bombing of 17 May 1940, during which Bavay had been badly damaged. Excavations revealed the remains of a large group of monumental buildings: a civil basilica, a forum, a portico above a horseshoe-shaped underground gallery *(cryptoporticus)* and a room over a deep cellar stand along an east-west axis. A few houses have also been found south of the walls built after the invasions of the second half of the 3C.

Musée archéologique ⊘ – Housed in a large modern building, the archeological museum exhibits various objects found during excavations. An audio-visual show presents daily life, trade, religious life and craft activities at the time of Bagacum. The numerous pots, dishes and vases with busts of divinities on them are a reminder that Bavay was an important pottery production centre. Delightful bronze figurines are among the treasures from a bronze-founder's hoard.

EXCURSION

Bellignies – *3km/2mi north of Bavay on D 24.*
In the 19C Bellignies-les-Rocs, in the middle of the Hogneau Valley, developed a marble industry: men were employed for cutting and women for polishing. It was an important business right up to the Second World War.

Musée du Marbre et de la Pierre bleue ⊘ – The tools traditionally used to cut and polish marble are displayed in the museum, together with typical examples of the workshops' output.

BEAUVAIS★★

Conurbation 57 704
Michelin map 55 folds, 9, 10 or 236 fold 33

This attractive city, which is the capital of the Oise region and the hometown of talented people such as the fashion designer Givenchy and the plane manufacturer Marcel Dassault, has retained its striking cathedral, an architectural masterpiece almost defying the laws of gravity.

Bishops and Burghers – Beauvais, the capital of the Belgian tribe the Bellovaci, became a Gallo-Roman city enclosed within walls during the 3C. From the 11C the city had as its lord a bishop, who was often in conflict with the town's wealthy merchants and jealous of their franchises. One of the bishops, Pierre Cauchon, has a dubious claim to fame: while the town wanted to surrender to Charles VII, Cauchon rallied to the English. Chased out of Beauvais in 1429 by the burghers, he took refuge in Rouen where, on 30 May 1431, he sent Joan of Arc to the stake.

Jeanne Hachette – On 27 June 1472 Beauvais was besieged by Charles the Bold, Duke of Burgundy, who was marching on Paris with 80 000 men. The town had no troops so men and women ran to the ramparts and watched in horror as ladders were laid against the fortifications. Jeanne Laîné, the daughter of a humble craftsman, saw an assailant appear at the top of the wall, a standard in hand. She threw herself on him, tore away his banner and struck him with a hatchet, sending him flying into the moat below. This example fired the courage of the others; the resistance gained momentum, giving time for reinforcements to arrive. Charles lifted the siege on 22 July.
Each year, at the end of June, Beauvais honours Jeanne "Hachette".

Tapestries – In 1664 Colbert founded the Manufacture Royale de Tapisserie. The artisans worked on horizontal looms producing low-warp tapestries in wool and silk which are noted for being extremely fine; they were usually used as upholstery. The Manufacture Royale changed its name to Manufacture Nationale in 1804. The workshops, which were evacuated to Aubusson in 1939, were unable to return to Beauvais after the buildings were destroyed in 1940. The looms were relocated to the Gobelins Works in Paris and remained there until Beauvais could welcome them back in 1989.

Ceramics and stained glass – Pottery making has been going on in the area since Gallo-Roman times. Glazed earthenware and stoneware, manufactured locally since the 15C, have made the Beauvais region one of the great ceramic centres of France. Around 1850, pottery workshops were replaced by ceramic and tile factories which in turn attracted fine pottery workshops in their vicinity. Beauvais' 16C stained glass is also famous, particularly that by the Leprince family.

AROUND THE FORMER BISHOP'S PALACE *about 45min*
Park the car in the town centre (place J.-Hachette, place des Halles...).

Place Jeanne-Hachette – There is a fine statue of the local heroine opposite the town hall with its beautifully restored 18C façade.
Take the short rue de la Frette, turn right on rue Beauregard then left on rue Saint-Pierre.

Eating out

MID-RANGE

Petite France – *7 route de Gisors, 60112 Crillon – 15km/9.3mi northwest of Beauvais by D 149, D 901 then D 133 – ☏ 03 44 81 01 13 – closed 13 Aug-5 Sept, Sun and Mon evenings and Tues – 135/170F.* Stop by this welcoming inn on the road to Gisors. The small, cosy dining room behind the bar with its crowded tables, visible beams and rustic furniture, creates an intimate atmosphere. Excellent value for money.

Where to stay

MODERATE

Chambre d'Hôte La Ferme du Colombier – *14 rue du Four-Jean-Legros, 60650 Savignies – 10km/6.2mi northwest of Beauvais heading towards Rouen by D 1 – ☏ 03 44 82 18 49 – ✍ – 4 rooms 190/240F – meal 80F.* Tired of the city? Then come and spend a few days down on the farm! Your closest neighbours here will be the sheep reared by your hosts. The large, comfortable rooms have been set up in a nearby annex. Cooking facilities available. Enquire about the rambling and cycling tours organised by your hosts.

On the town

Au Bureau – *8 rue des Jacobins – ☏ 03 44 45 04 42 – daily 11am-1am.* This smart green and gold pub is one of a chain set up throughout northern France. The appealing decor consists of an imposing counter carved in black wood, velvet wall seats and lavish carpets. Classy establishment with a good sense of design.

Les P'Tits Trucs – *6 rue Philippe-de-Dreux – ☏ 03 44 48 31 31 – Mon-Sat noon-10pm.* This tiny tea room is housed in a curious-looking building whose walls are covered with mirrors and curtains of white or pink beads. The dining room has an old-fashioned lace lampshade and a host of potted plants. Lovely garden for sitting out when the weather warms up.

Showtime

Théâtre de Beauvais – *Place Georges-Brassens – ☏ 03 44 06 08 20 – www.theatre-beauvais.com – consult the of events – reception area open Mon-Sat 1-7pm – closed July-Aug.* The theatre stages a wide range of live performances and cultural events classical and experimental stage, dance and ballet, music, comedy, acting, entertainment, exhibitions etc.

Sport

Plan d'Eau du Canada – *Rue de la Mie au Roy – ☏ 03 44 45 33 93 – daily 10am-7pm – closed 3 Sept-2 July.* This 30ha/75-acre artificial lake next to the beach is a popular weekend destination among local residents. This water sports complex offers facilities for renting canoes, kayaks, sailing dinghies, sailboards, pedal-boats...

Ruins – On the corner, you will see traces of the Collégiale St-Barthélémy and, opposite, behind the Galerie Nationale de la Tapisserie, the ruins of Gallo-Roman town walls.

From rue St-Pierre which runs alongside the cathedral, turn right on rue du Musée then on rue de l'Abbé-Gellée.

Ancien palais épiscopal – The former bishop's palace is a fine architectural ensemble restored in 2000. The 14C fortified doorway is flanked by two large towers with pepper-pot roofs. It was built by Bishop Simon de Clermont de Nesle with 8 000 *livres* of fines that the town had to pay after the riot of 1306 during which the bishopric was pillaged. At the far end of the courtyard stands the main body of the palace; set ablaze in 1472 by the Burgundians, it was rebuilt around 1500 and retains an elegant Renaissance façade. The buildings house the Musée départemental de l'Oise.

Old houses – The town's oldest house, known as the **Maison François I** (15C) was taken from its original site along rue Oudry and rebuilt in rue de l'Abbé-Gelée.

Follow rue J.-Racine on the right then turn right on rue Carnot leading to the pedestrian area close to place J.-Hachette.

SIGHTS

***Cathédrale St-Pierre** ○ – The history of the cathedral has been tumultuous. Its unique appearance is due to the great technical drama of its construction and the desperate efforts of the bishops and chapters to raise the necessary funds: an exhausting struggle which was prolonged over four centuries but finally abandoned before the enormous project was completed.

During the Carolingian period a small cathedral, Notre-Dame, was erected; known as the **Basse-Œuvre**, now only three of the nave's bays remain complete, adjoining the newer building.

In 949 another cathedral was begun, but it was destroyed by two fires.

Subsequently, in 1225, the bishop and chapter decided to erect the biggest church of its day, a New Work **(Nouvel-Œuvre)** dedicated to St Peter.

While building a grandiose cathedral might seem a reasonable ambition in the Gothic period, in this case aspiration overcame sense. When the construction of the chancel was started in 1238, the clergy and the master builders wanted to better both past and future architects: the height to the vault's keystone was to be slightly above 48m/158ft, making the roof (68m/223ft high) about the height of the towers of Notre-Dame in Paris.

It took 25 years to achieve this feat but for once the medieval architects had over-estimated their ability. The pillars were too widely spaced and the buttresses on the piers too weak. In 1284 the chancel collapsed: 40 more years of work and an enormous amount of money went into saving it. The three large arches of the chancel's right bays were reinforced by the addition of intermediary piers, the flying buttresses multiplied, the abutments strengthened.

No sooner had this task been finished than the Hundred Years War prevented any continuation. The cathedral still only consisted of a chancel and its dependent parts. In 1500 the bishop decided to resume work and entrusted the construction of the transept to Martin Chambiges, assisted by Jean Vast; funds were mainly obtained through the sale of exemptions and, in 1550 the transept was finally completed. Unfortunately, instead of building the nave next, it was decided to erect an open-work tower over the transept crossing, surmounted by a spire. The cross at the top of the spire was positioned in 1569, at a height of 153m/502ft (Strasbourg's is 142m/466ft). As there was however no nave to counterbalance the thrusts, the piers gave way, on Ascension Day in 1573, just as the procession had left the church. After that, despite tremendous efforts and sacrifices, the clergy and people of Beauvais were able to restore only the chancel and the transept: the unfinished cathedral would never again have a spire, and would never have a nave.

***Chevet** – *See illustration in the Introduction: ABC of architecture.* The chancel dates from the 13C. Like the Flamboyant transept arms, it is shored up by flying buttresses with high piers which rise up to the roof. The transept arms were to have been very long and framed by towers.

Beauvais – The cathedral

B. Kaufmann/MICHELIN

South transept façade – The façade is richly decorated and bears two high turrets flanking the **Portail de St-Pierre** (St Peter's Doorway), the embrasures, tympanum and arching of which are adorned with niches beneath openwork canopies. The doorway is surmounted by a large rose-window with delicate tracery.

Interior – The dizzying height of the vaults (almost 48m/157ft high) is immediately apparent. The generous transept is almost 58m/190ft long, and the chancel is extremely elegant. There is an open triforium and the clerestory is 18m/59ft high. Seven chapels open off the ambulatory.

★★**Stained-glass windows** – The transept features most of the 16C compositions. The south rose-window features the Eternal Father in the central medallion. Underneath, 10 Prophets and 10 Apostles or Doctors stand in two rows. Opposite, in the north transept, there are 10 Sibyls counterbalancing the Prophets (1537).

★**Astronomic Clock** ⊘ – This monumental clock was made by the engineer Louis-Auguste Vérité from 1865 to 1868. It comprises 90 000 parts and has been reassembled several times. The lower part resembles a fortress with numerous windows. In the glazed openings 52 dials show the length of the days and nights, the seasons etc.

To the right of the astronomical clock is an old 14C clock with chimes that play psalms corresponding to the different periods of the year.

Basse-Œuvre – Traces remain of the old 10C cathedral built from salvaged Gallo-Roman quarry stones known as *pastoureaux*. It served as the parish church until the 1789 Revolution.

★**Église St-Étienne** – The nave and the transept of the church dedicated to St Stephen are Romanesque. Their restraint, softened by the "Beauvais-style" bracketed cornices, contrasts with the architectural richness of the chancel, rebuilt a little after 1500 in a refined Flamboyant style. The chancel, which is higher than the nave, is encircled by chapels. The tower flanking the west front served as the town belfry.

The left aisle gives on to a Romanesque doorway with a finely carved tympanum and arching. From this side a good view is offered of the north transept's lovely Wheel of Fortune, symbolising the frailty of earthly things.

★★**Stained-glass windows** – The chancel's Renaissance stained-glass windows, by Engrand, are most beautiful; among them is the extraordinary **Tree of Jesse**★★★ with its stunning design, colours and translucency.

★**Musée départemental de l'Oise** ⊘ – The collections are displayed on four levels.

The **towers at the entrance** to the museum contain the medieval collections: woodcarvings from churches and abbeys, sculpted fragments from some of Beauvais' timber-framed houses and frescoes.

Beauvais, Église St-Etienne –
Detail from the Tree of Jesse

The **cellars** (12C and 16C) are devoted to regional archeology. Note the Gallic warrior from St-Maur, the 1C AD metal statuette and the stele carved with a bearded Mercury (3C).

The upper floors house the fine arts collections (mainly paintings) from the 16C to the 20C: 16C French School, 17C and 18C Italian and French Schools, French landscape artists of the 19C including **Corot** *(The Fountain from the French Academy in Rome* and *The Old St-Michel Bridge, Paris)* and **Huet**, Art Nouveau furniture, Beauvais tapestry work, France at the turn of the last century and during the Roaring Twenties. Ceramics from the Pays de Bray (19C and early 20C) are displayed under the imposing 16C roof.

Galerie nationale de la Tapisserie ○ – Housed in a low-roofed building beyond the cathedral's east end, the gallery stages exhibitions giving an overview of French tapestry from the 15C to the present day.

Manufacture nationale de la tapisserie ○ – The national tapestry works have, since 1989, been housed in the former slaughterhouses. Today the factory contains about a dozen looms. The weavers work under natural light and follow the artist's cartoon, weaving on the reverse side and monitoring their work with a mirror. The entire production is reserved for the State.

Église de Marissel ○ – *1.5km/1mi east along rue de Clermont and rue de Marissel which branches off to the right.*
The village is now almost a suburb of Beauvais and its restored church rises on a terrace from where the cathedral's huge mass is visible, 2km/1.25mi away. A painting by Corot from 1866, now in the Louvre, made the church famous.
The 16C west front with its Flamboyant doorway was inspired by the cathedral. The east end has a Romanesque chapel wedged between the Gothic transept and chancel.

EXCURSIONS

Château de Troissereux ○ – *8km/5mi northwest of Beauvais.*
The stone and brick castle, standing near the River Thérain, was built in the Renaissance style, in the late 16C or early 17C. The interior decoration and the furniture date from the 18C.
A pavilion overlooking the main courtyard contains a very old clockwork.
The English-style park, adorned with ornamental ponds and a "grand canal", shelters a great variety of birds including rare species.

★★**Gerberoy** – *21km/13mi northwest of Beauvais by D 901. After Lachapelle-sous-Gerberoy, turn left.*
This fortified town perched on a knoll was forgotten from the 17C until the painter Le Sidaner (1862-1939) fell under its charm and settled here. Since then numerous figures from the world of arts and letters have come to live in the old, timber-framed houses *(restored)* which line the cobbled streets. On the first floor of the town hall, a small **museum** ○ devoted to local history contains some of Le Sidaner's paintings. Note the terraced gardens laid out by the artist on the site of the old fortress. The gateway which gave access to the castle leads to the modest 15C **collegiate church**. A shaded walk now follows the line of the old ditches.

Eating out

MID-RANGE

Hostellerie du Vieux Logis – *25 rue du Logis-du-Roy* – ☎ *03 44 82 71 66* – *closed 20 Dec-3 Jan, Feb school holidays, Mon and Thur evenings from Nov to Mar, Sun and Tues evenings and Wed* – *122/255F.* This half-timbered house blends in nicely with the picturesque village of Gerberoy. The dining hall features wooden framework and an impressive brick fireplace. We recommend the "sweet menu" and the "medieval barbecue". Terrace for the summer months, where tea is served in the afternoon.

Where to stay

MODERATE

Chambre d'Hôte M. et Mme Bruandet – *13 Hameau de Bellefontaine, 60650 Hannaches* – *5km/3mi southwest of Gerberoy by D 930 then D 104 heading towards Bellefontaine* – ☎ *03 44 82 46 63* – *http://bellefontaine.free.fr* – *closed Jan* – ⊡ – *3 rooms 200/250F* – *meal 85F.* The most striking feature of this Picardy farmhouse is the resolutely modern style of the furniture adorning the rooms and the sculptures in the square courtyard. The imaginative and talented designs were conceived by the owner himself, who is a sculptor by profession. Enquire about local hiking tours.

BERGUES★

Population 4 163
Michelin map 51 fold 4 or 236 fold 4

Bergues is now a wealthy little Flemish town leading a peaceful life within ramparts which overlook a region famous for its pastures, butter and cheese. It grew rich on the wool trade and rivalled Dunkirk (Dunkerque).

The warm tones of the buildings' yellow-ochre bricks are reflected in the waters of the moat and canals which partly surround the town. Despite having been badly damaged in 1940, Bergues has retained its old character through the austere but harmonious rebuilding of the bombed districts. The winding streets, the large squares and the silent quays along the edge of the River Colme are reminiscent of Bruges. On the façade of the town hall, a bust of **Lamartine** recalls that the writer, brother-in-law to Mr de Coppens d'Hondschoote, was elected to represent Bergues in the French *chambre des députés* 1833, after a first, unsuccessful attempt two years earlier.

Eating out

MID-RANGE

Taverne le Bruegel – *1 rue du Marché-aux-Fromages* – ☎ *03 28 68 19 19* – *closed 20-30 Dec* – *115/145F*. An old building dating back to 1597 houses this congenial tavern where carbonade and other Flemish specialities are served to customers in a cosy ambience, enhanced by a brick decor and wooden furniture. The warm welcome and delicious cuisine has earned it an excellent reputation locally.

Le Cornet d'Or – *26 rue de l'Espagnole* – ☎ *03 28 68 66 27* – *closed Sun evening and Mon except public holidays* – *168/335F*. The somewhat austere façade of this restaurant may be forbidding but step inside and you will not regret it! You will discover a rustic-style dining room with flowered tablecloths and a cosy, intimate atmosphere. The cuisine relies heavily on tradition while drawing inspiration from modern gastronomic trends. Much appreciated by local gourmets.

Where to stay

MODERATE

Hôtel Au Tonnelier – *Near the church* – ☎ *03 28 68 70 05* – *closed 10-30 Aug and 21 Dec-10 Jan* – *11 rooms 200/350F* – ☑ *36F* – *restaurant 130/160F*. This house close to the village church features pretty windows bursting with flowers in spring and summer. The former café with its wooden counter serves as an entrance to the prettily appointed dining room. Sparsely furnished rooms available for weary travellers.

WALLED TOWN *6km/3.5mi, about 2hr30min*

The walls, pierced by four gateways and surrounded by a deep moat, date partly from the Middle Ages (Bierne Gate, Beckerstor, curtain wall east of Cassel Gate) and partly from the 17C, when the defences were developed by Vauban after the Treaty of Aix-la-Chapelle (1668), which gave Bergues to France (eastern hornwork, Cassel Gate, Hondschoote Crown). These fortifications were used by the French troops during the 1940 defence of Dunkirk, and the Germans had to use Stukas and flame-throwers to breach the walls.

◨ *Start from the Belfry, place de la République.*

Belfry ⊙ – Erected during the 14C, remodelled in the 16C and dynamited by the Germans in 1944, the belfry (54m/177ft high) was rebuilt by Paul Gélis who sought to preserve the main structure of the former edifice while simplifying the exterior decoration. It is made of yellow bricks known as "sand bricks" and is surmounted by the lion of Flanders; the **carillon** ⊙ comprises 50 bells. From the top there is a good view over the Flemish plain.

Follow rue M.-Cornette to the Porte de Cassel.

Porte de Cassel – This gateway was built in the 17C with a **drawbridge**; its triangular pediment features a carved sun, Louis XIV's emblem. From the outside, there is a view to the right over the **medieval curtain wall** towards the towers of St Winnoc.

Walk along the western rampart.

Rempart Ouest – The western rampart was erected in 1635. Beyond the **Poudrière du Moulin** (the Mill Powder Magazine) stands the **Tour Nekestor**, dating from the time of the dukes of Burgundy. The wall continues towards the **Porte de Bierne** (16C) with its drawbridge, offering views of the **ruins of a medieval tower** and some **ancient locks**.

Climb on top of the northern rampart via the steps to the right of the quayside gate.

Rempart Nord – The northern rampart links the **Porte de Dunkerque**, which overlooks the beginning of the inner canal, the **Tour Guy-de-Dampierre** (1286), named after the 22nd Count of Flanders and the first **Porte d'Hondschoote**.

Leave the walled area via the Porte d'Hondschoote and avenue Vauban.

★**Couronne d'Hondschoote** – On the north side of the walls, Vauban used the branches of the River Colme to build an extensive system of bastions and ravelins completely surrounded by large moats filled with carp, pike-perch and tench which is used as a bird sanctuary; viewed from above, this defensive system forms a sort of crown, hence its name.

Retrace your steps and climb back onto the rampart.

Belfry

Couronne and abbaye de St-Winoc – The Couronne de St-Vinoc was designed to protect the abbey of the same name. It comprises three mighty **bastions** (1672-92): the St-Vinoc bastion, the King's bastion and the St-Pierre bastion. The **abbey** is accessible from the Couronne across avenue du Général-de-Gaulle. Only ruins remain of this famous Benedictine establishment. Most of the buildings were destroyed during the Revolution; all that survives is the 18C marble front door, the Tour Pointue (rebuilt in 1815) which marks the site of the abbey's façade and the 12C-13C square tower of the transept crossing, supported by reinforced buttresses.

Continue along the ramparts from the third bastion (St-Pierre) of the Couronne de St-Vinoc.

Rempart Sud – Follow the southern rampart past three small 13C round towers followed by the Faux-Monnayeurs and Couleuvriniers towers to return to the Porte de Cassel.

Walk up rue M.-Cornette and turn left along rue Carnot which leads to rue Faidherbe.

Rues Carnot and Faidherbe – These streets are lined with lovely 18C buildings including several mansions such as the **Hôtel de Hau de Staplande**, along rue Carnot.

From rue Faidherbe, turn right on rue du Mont-de-Piété.

Mont-de-piété – This elegant building with a Baroque gable is constructed of brick and white stone, and includes an ingenious combination of decorative elements: pilasters, niches, cartouches, pediments. It was designed by **Wenceslas Coebergher** (1561-1634), an extraordinary character who was painter, architect, economist and engineer; in the Flanders region he occupied himself with the draining of the Moëres, the marshes near Hondschoote, and introduced the first pawnshops *(monts-de-piété)*. This pawnshop was inaugurated in 1633 and continued in business until 1848. The town museum has been housed inside since 1953.

Musée municipal ⊘ – The most outstanding of all the paintings in the municipal museum is undoubtedly the *Hurdy-Gurdy Player*, a vast canvas by Georges de la Tour (1593-1652) exhibited on the first floor. There are also works by several 16C-17C Flemish artists including a sketch by Rubens, portraits by Van Dyck, Cossiers and Simon de Vox.

The natural history section on the second floor includes a particularly extensive collection of birds and butterflies. The collection of 16C to 19C drawings is displayed on a rotating basis (Poussin, Lebrun, Tiepolo etc).

To return to the belfry, walk round the church situated opposite the Mont-de-Piété and follow rue de la Gare.

EXCURSIONS

Quaëdypre – *5km/3mi southeast along D 916 and D 37.* This village, located on a small hill, has a **hall-church** ⊘ with three equal aisles and an interior decorated with 17C carved woodwork: high altar *(see Introduction: ABC of architecture)* with a painting by Goubau, an artist from Aubverp who was Largillière's tutor; communion table, pulpit and confessional from the Dominican church in Bergues; organ loft and stalls formerly in St Winoc's Abbey, Bergues.

West-Cappel – *10km/6mi southeast along D 110 then D 4.* This is a peaceful village on a rise. **Église St-Sylvestre** ⊘, rebuilt in the 16C of "sand bricks", boasts a mighty porch-belfry, three aisles and a taller chancel.

Den Leeuw Windmill ⊘ – *8km/5mi south via D 916 then turn right onto D 110.* On the outskirts of **Pitgam** stands a recently restored wooden post mill dating from 1776.

BLÉRANCOURT

Population 1 268
Michelin map 56 fold 3 or 236 folds 36, 37

Only a few sections survive from the former château of the dukes of Gesvres, built in the 17C by Salomon de Brosse and abandoned during the Revolution. In 1917 a group of American women led by Miss Ann Morgan moved into the remaining parts. They came to give help to areas devastated by the war.

Musée national de la coopération franco-américaine (**National Museum of Franco American Cooperation**) ⊘ – Two monumental entrances lead into the main courtyard surrounded by a moat. Pavilions frame the second doorway: the right one contains the library, documents and archives, the left one is filled with memorabilia concerning Miss Morgan. The two wings of the museum itself partly recreate the château's ground floor: souvenirs of the American War of Independence, paintings and sculptures executed between 1800 and 1945 by French artists in the United

States and by American artists in France (1926 portrait of *Peggy Guggenheim* by Alfred Courmes and *Still Life* by JF Peto painted around 1900), presentation of America's humanitarian help during the Great War. Finish the tour with a stroll through the garden planted with American trees and the arboretum.

Maison de Saint-Just ⊘ – **Louis-Antoine de Saint-Just** arrived in Blérancourt in 1776 and lived in this house with his family. He only subsequently left the village to fulfil his duties as a member of the Convention assembly to which he was elected in 1792. During the Revolution, he joined the Montagnards, a group founded by Robespierre and took a stand in favour of the execution of Louis XVI. As a member of the Comité de Salut Public in 1793, he was in charge of laying down the principles of the Terror and was guillotined in 1794. The restored house contains a permanent exhibition illustrating his life.

18C engraving depicting the "Independence" coiffure

BOULOGNE-SUR-MER★★

Conurbation 95 930
Michelin map 51 folds 1, 2 or 236 folds 1, 2

Boulogne, once a Roman city, is situated where the Liane Valley opens up after running between steep hills. The town, which has a rough but appealing look and busy streets, is today the largest European centre of the fish trade and the home of an international industrial fish-processing complex (freezing, canning, smoking and salting). Boulogne's illustrious citizens include the literary historian **St Beuve**, (1804-69), the engineer **Frédéric Sauvage** (1786-1857), the inventor of the propeller used in steam navigation and **Auguste Mariette** (1821-81).

The local speciality is the **craquelin de Boulogne**, a rich pastry traditionally enjoyed after the Christmas midnight mass with a cup of *roustintin* (chocolate flavoured with kirsch).

The Miracle of Our Lady – In 636 during Dagobert's reign a boat with neither crew nor sails came aground on the shore at Boulogne, carrying a statue of the Virgin Mary. At the same time, the congregation praying in the chapel (which stood on the site of the present basilica) were notified of the event by an apparition of the Virgin. This miracle led to the establishment of a famous **pilgrimage** which was undertaken by 14 kings of France and five kings of England.

The prestige of the statue of Notre-Dame de Boulogne was sometimes used for political ends. Louis XI, for example, appropriated the county that belonged to the dukes of Burgundy by declaring that the Madonna which was held in such great esteem in Boulogne was the real "Lady" of the town, that as king he was her vassal on Earth and that he was therefore taking charge of the town's interests.

"Imperial" Boulogne – Boulogne is linked to Bonaparte because from 1803 to 1805 he kept his troops mustered at the **Boulogne Camp** *(camp de Boulogne)* for a possible invasion of England. On 26 August 1805 Napoleon I, crowned a year earlier, finally abandoned his project in order to set his Grande Armée against the Austrians.

In August 1840 the future Napoleon III tried to raise the town against Louis-Philippe, but the attempt floundered and he was imprisoned in Ham Fort.

Mariette, the founder of Egyptology – The young man from Boulogne, who was working at the Louvre Museum in Paris, left for Cairo in 1850, entrusted with the task of finding Coptic manuscripts. Instead he discovered Memphis, the ancient capital of the Pharaohs. During the following 30 years, he travelled throughout Egypt and was responsible for numerous excavation projects. He also founded the Boulaq Museum, which later became Cairo's Egyptian Museum, and set up the department of Egyptian Antiquities. In 1879 he was promoted to the rank of pasha by the Egyptian authorities.

Eating out

MODERATE

Ferme-Auberge du Blaisel – *Chemin de la Lombarderie, 62240 Wirwignes – 12km/7.5mi southeast of Boulogne by D 341 heading towards Desvres – ☎ 03 21 32 91 98 – closed 23 Dec-5 Jan and Wed – booking essential Sat-Sun – 90/130F*. Lunch or dinner at the Ferme Blaisel is an excellent opportunity to rediscover the true flavours of fresh local produce. And if you begin to feel sleepy at the end of the meal, check into one of the bed and breakfast rooms available on the premises.

MID-RANGE

Restaurant de Nausicaa – *Boulevard Ste-Beuve – ☎ 03 21 33 24 24 – 105/172F*. This split-level restaurant set up inside the Centre National de la Mer commands panoramic views of the beach and harbour entrance. Naturally, a large part of the menu is taken up by dishes centring around fish, seafood or shellfish!

Where to stay

MODERATE

Chambre d'Hôte Le Clos d'Esch – *126 rue de l'Église, 62360 Echinghen – 4km/2.5mi from Boulogne by D 940 heading towards St-Léonard then D 234 heading towards Echinghen – ☎ 03 21 91 14 34 – closed 23 Dec-3 Jan – ⊟ – 4 rooms 200/250F*. If you want to get away from the noise and stress of the city, this is definitely the place for you. A recently restored farmhouse in a hamlet will provide a restful break in a charmingly rural setting. The upstairs rooms are especially nice.

MID-RANGE

Hôtel Métropole – *51 rue Thiers – ☎ 03 21 31 54 30 – closed 22 Dec-2 Jan – ▣ – 25 rooms 360/480F – ☕ 46F*. Conveniently situated in the town centre, this hotel has a lovely little garden giving onto a prettily appointed breakfast parlour. As for the bedrooms, they are all comfortable and soundproofed and some are fitted with air conditioning. The decoration is either modern or a touch more conventional.

Hôtel de la Ferme du Vert – *62720 Wierre-Effroy – 10km/6.2mi northeast of Boulogne by N 42 then D 234 – ☎ 03 21 87 67 00 – closed 15 Dec-15 Jan – ▣ – 16 rooms 320/680F – ☕ 52F – restaurant 130/230F*. Everything here is conducive to rest and tranquillity! Although the rooms are all different, they do have three things in common: simplicity, good taste and excellent design. Gourmets will enjoy visiting the restaurant, not to mention the organic cheese dairy set up on the premises, whose home-made products are also served in the dining room... Cheeses for sale.

Hôtel Cléry – *In the village, 62360 Hesdin-l'Abbé – 9km/5.6mi southeast of Boulogne by N 1 – ☎ 03 21 83 19 83 – closed 15 Dec-27 Jan – ▣ – 22 rooms 453/847F – ☕ 60F – restaurant 145/210F*. A soothing park dotted with century old trees is the backcloth to this impressive 18C mansion. The rooms are appointed with flowery fabric and antique furniture bought from flea markets over the years. Evening meals are served to residents in a small dining room.

On the town

Irish Pub Shamrock – *6-10 rue du Doyen – ☎ 03 21 83 61 61 – Mon-Sat noon-1am in winter, noon-2am in summer, Sun 5pm-2am*. Standing behind his marble counter lit up by a series of small lamps, the owner of this beautiful ban carved in red wood bears a striking resemblance to the French singer Georges Brassens. A former English teacher and tourist guide, he remains a dedicated lover of music. He and his wife lend a cultural touch to their cosy establishment, which boasts velvet wall seats, visible stonework and a superb selection of stained glass. Soft music and warm welcome guaranteed.

L'Out-Back – *10 rue Monsigny – ☎ 03 21 30 25 82 – loutback@yahoo.com – Mon-Thur 11am-1am, Fri-Sat 11am-2am*. A light wood decor typifies this huge Australian bar adjoining a pretty terrace with lush vegetation. The imposing pirogue hanging above the entrance and the crocodile at the bar were both brought back from the antipodes, as were the other curiosities adorning the room.

Showtime

Cabaret Sam – *24 rue Alexander-Fleming – ☎ 03 21 87 32 69 – consult the of events – performances start at 8pm*. The owners' objective was to make culture accessible to all and they have definitely got the message across! Every evening people from all walks of life flock to this small venue (200 seats). The programme is extremely varied and strives to reveal new, undiscovered talent.

BOULOGNE-SUR-MER

Sport

Club de la Côte d'Opale – *272 boulevard Ste-Beuve* – ☎ *03 21 83 25 48* – *daily 8.30am-noon, 2-6pm.* Facilities for renting sand-yachts and speed-sails for all ages (lessons for 6-year-olds and over).

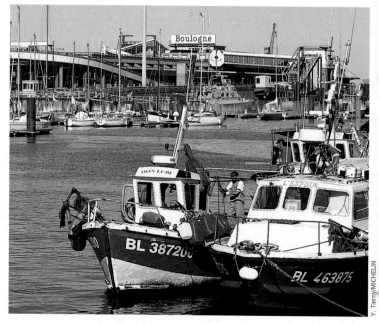

Boulogne-sur-Mer – The fishing port

LA VILLE BASSE

Harbour installations – The **outer harbour** is protected by two jetties, one of which, the Digue Carnot is 3 250m/over 2mi long.
The **inner harbour** consists of a tidal dock reserved for ferries, small trawlers and yachts and the Napoleon and Loubet docks for the big fishing boats.
At night the sorting of the trawled fish takes place in the refrigerated markets alongside Loubet dock.

Quai Gambetta, overlooked by tall buildings, is busiest when the trawlers unload their catch, some of which is sold on the spot.
Already quite well known in the 18C, the fine, white-sand **beach** became very fashionable from the mid 19C onwards. An equestrian statue of San Martin stands on the promenade. The general spent the last few months of his life in Boulogne. Completely destroyed during the war, the harbour installations have since been reconstructed and enlarged, and now extend beyond Boulogne to Le Portel where the **commercial port** is located.

Fish trade centre

Industrial trawlers unload their catch around midnight; coastal-fishing boats come back in the early hours of the morning. The catch is offered for sale and refrigerated during the fish auction *(la criée)* which starts between 6 and 7am. The batches are then sent round to factories for processing. This is completed by 11am and the parcels end up at the harbour station (112 unloading bays, 24 refrigerated-transport companies) to be dispatched to various destinations: Paris/Rungis, Strasbourg, Lyon, Marseille, Bordeaux... and abroad, where they arrive the same day or the next morning at the latest.

★★LA VILLE HAUTE *3hr*

The upper town, enclosed by ramparts, stands on the site of the old Roman *castrum* or fortified town. It is overlooked by the enormous dome of Notre-Dame basilica and is popular with tourists in summer, offering pleasant strolls along the ramparts or through the streets and past the historic buildings of the walled town.

Ramparts – The fortifications were built in the early 13C by Philippe le Hurepel, Count of Boulogne and son of Philippe-Auguste, on the foundations of the Gallo-Roman walls and were strengthened in the 16C to 17C. The ramparts form a rectangle (325_410m/1 066_1 345ft) reinforced by the **castle** to the east, and are pierced by four gates – Gayole, Dunes, Calais and **Degrés** which is pedestrian only – flanked by two towers. The parapet walkway is accessible from each gateway and offers lovely **views**★ of the town and the port.

At the western corner the **tour Gayette**, a former jail, was the site of the take-off for the balloon flight in 1785 by **Pilâtre de Rozier** and Romain who were attempting to cross the Channel; they crashed near Wimille, just north of Boulogne.

A pyramid-shaped monument surmounted by a statue stands in the garden between Boulevard Auguste-Mariette and the ramparts: it is dedicated to **Mariette** the Egyptologist, whom the statue shows in Egyptian costume.

Stroll through the Upper Town

🔳 *Enter the ramparts through the western Porte des Dunes into place de la Résistance and place Godefroy-de-Bouillon.*

The **library** is located in the old Annonciades Convent. The 17C buildings and the cloisters house study and exhibition rooms, while the main reading room occupies the 18C chapel with its superb coffered ceiling, visible through the windows from the square.

The **law courts** dating from 1852, have a neo-Classical façade, with statues of Charlemagne and Napoleon in two niches.

The 13C Gothic **belfry** ⊘ *(access from the Hôtel de Ville)*, has a 12C base (the former keep from the castle of the counts of Boulogne) and an 18C octagonal section at the top. It houses Gallo-Roman statues and regional antique furniture as well as a beautiful stained-glass window portraying Godefroy de Bouillon.

The top of the belfry *(183 steps)* offers an extensive **view**★ of Boulogne and its surroundings.

Place de la Résistance leads into place Godefroy-de-Bouillon, located at the junction of the four main streets.

The square owes its name to the leader of the first crusade, who was a member of the House of Boulogne.

The 18C façade of the **Hôtel de Ville** of red brick with stone dressings, contrasts sharply with the primitive Gothic belfry.

Opposite the town hall stands the Louis XVI **Hôtel Desandrouin**; Napoleon stayed here several times from 1803 to 1811.

Follow rue de Puits-d'Amour alongside Hôtel Desandrouin and turn right.

Rue Guyale – The merchants' guildhall used to stand on this street, which has been restored and reveals the back of the Annonciades Convent and the rough-stone façades of the old houses, one of which is occupied by the Tourism Development Office.

From place Godefroy-de-Bouillon take rue de Lille.

At no 58 is the oldest **house** in Boulogne (12C). The Basilique Notre-Dame stands on the left. Rue du Château on the right leads to the former residence of the counts of Boulogne.

Basilique Notre-Dame ⊘ – *Access via the south transept in rue de Lille.*

The basilica was built from 1827 to 1866 on the site of the old cathedral (destroyed after the Revolution) and has preserved the Romanesque crypt. It is a popular place of pilgrimage. Inside, a powerful Corinthian colonnade supports the building. The superb, soaring **dome**★ with its circle of large statues rises behind the chancel; beyond it, in the central chapel, stands the wooden statuette of Our Lady of Boulogne (Notre-Dame de Boulogne), crowned with precious stones. Every year the statuette is carried in a procession during which the traditional sun-shaped headdresses, bonnets and Indian shawls of the region are worn.

★**Crypt and Treasury** ⊘ – Under the basilica, a labyrinth of underground passages links 14 chambers. One of them houses the Treasury which contains religious statues and objects (chalices, reliquaries) from various churches in the region, and the relic of the Holy Blood offered by Philip the Fair to Our Lady of Boulogne.

Continue through several rooms to the **crypt of the painted pillars** dating from the 11C, discovered during the construction of the new basilica.

Take rue du Château opposite.

★**Château-musée** ⊘ – Formerly the residence of the counts of Boulogne, this powerful-looking polygonal building was the first in western Europe to abandon the traditional keep. Flanked by round towers, it protected the most vulnerable part of the ramparts facing the plateau; in the 16C a horseshoe bastion was added on one side. The castle is separated from the ramparts by a moat, which was spanned by a drawbridge.

The varied collections are displayed in rooms throughout the four floors of the castle.

The archeology of the Mediterranean is represented by an Egyptian section (sarcophagi and numerous funerary objects, the gift of Mariette the Egyptologist) and also by a beautiful group of **Greek vases**★★, among them a black-figure jug portraying the suicide of Ajax.

Boulogne-sur-Mer – Château-musée

Beyond this are rooms containing ceramics and earthenware from the main French and foreign manufacturers and remarkable pieces of porcelain. The Boulogne Camp and Napoleon are evoked on the stairway and landing of the third level. In the next room, works by painters of the Opal coast reveal the artistic talent that flourished around Boulogne in the 19C.

Among the ethnographic collections, the **Eskimo and Aleutian masks★★** brought back from a voyage to North America by the anthropologist Pinart, and the objects from the South Sea Islands including a Maori battle canoe from New Zealand, are particularly interesting. Three rooms are devoted to 17C, 18C and especially 19C painting: Corot, Boudin and Fantin-Latour, together with sculptures by Rodin, Pompon and Carpeaux.

The enormous guard-room displays collections from the Middle Ages and the Renaissance: copper and brassware, wood and stone sculptures, Gothic furniture and woodwork, an exceptional glazed earthenware finial, paintings, and coins. The archeological collections are exhibited in the underground rooms.

SIGHTS IN THE LOWER TOWN

★★★**Nausicaa** ⊘ – *Allow 3hr 30min.* Designed by architect Jacques Rougerie, who specialises in buildings with a maritime theme, and Christian Le Conte, a specialist in museography, the **Centre National de la Mer**, is the largest sea life centre in Europe; it aims to provide information about fauna in warm and cold ocean environments, the rational management of marine resources and the trades linked to them. It strives to increase public awareness of problems of pollution and excessive exploitation of the sea's resources, two problems which are threatening this vast communal reserve.

Visitors are invited to undertake a voyage to the centre of the sea, in a building dappled with bluish light and filled with aquatic music. There are 36 aquariums with more than 10 000 marine animals from the world's seas. Nausicaa is also a scientific research centre with a 40m/130ft long test basin designed by the Institut Français pour la Recherche et l'Exploitation de la Mer (IFREMER). It is used to simulate the working of hydrodynamic fishing boats.

Journey through the World's Seas – Visitors step into the world of plankton. The circular aquarium contains jellyfish.

Plankton

This generic name refers to organisms that cannot withstand maritime currents. They vary in size from the microscopic phytoplankton (plant plankton), to zooplankton no bigger than the head of a pin, and to several tens of metres for certain jellyfish extended by their filaments. Plankton is of vital importance. It forms the basis of all marine life, producing organic matter from mineral salts and the energy afforded by sources of light. It generates much of the planet's oxygen.

After being informed about the reproduction cycle of species from tropical seas and the Mediterranean, visitors are able to discover some magnificent specimens and observe their habits: mimicry, grouping together in shoals, occupation and defence of a hunting ground. Video terminals provide information about the senses of fish in general.

Next comes the Espace Diamant des Thons, a strange aquarium shaped like a reverse pyramid and containing a shoal of *sérioles* (of the tuna family).

Man and the sea – A long circular corridor illustrates the relationship between man and the sea going back thousands of years. A **celestial dome** forms the setting of the area devoted to resources from the sea and to the dangers which threaten the coastline.

Tropical Lagoon Village – Visitors then arrive on the beach of a paradisiacal island surrounded by the greenish-blue waters of a **lagoon**. From the pontoon, they can observe the lagoon full of colourful fish on one side, and the open sea with characteristic shoals of fish on the other. Steps lead beneath the surface to a vast panoramic window which reveals a stunning landscape with tropical fish darting among coral formations.

Control of marine resources – An audio-visual show (use special glasses to get the 3-D effect) is devoted to the various uses of marine resources.

Underwater observatory – Visitors then aim for the underwater observatory to be confronted with Californian sea-lions diving and swimming through the waves. The **aerial observatory** shows the same sea-lions stretched out on the rocks in a typical Californian setting of cliffs and log cabins.

An escalator leads to the **hands-on basin**, full of cod, pollack and turbot, where children can stroke the friendly thorn-back rays.

The tour takes visitors to a reduced-scale fish farm where the new fish-farming techniques are described. The adjacent area is devoted to various fishing techniques and a film shows night work aboard a trawler in the North Sea.

The visit ends with the spectacular **Anneau des sélaciens**, a panoramic circular tank filled with sharks.

Off the foyer are a cinema (130 seats), a multimedia library, souvenir shops, a restaurant, bar and cafeteria.

Église St-Nicolas – The church, standing in place Dalton where the market is held *(Wednesdays and Saturdays)*, is the oldest in Boulogne despite its Classical façade. It was built from 1220 to 1250, and underwent many alterations in the 16C (apse, transept, chancel vaults, chapels) and in the 18C when the nave was rebuilt. The 17C high altar features spiral columns and a fine painting of *The Flagellation* by Lehmann, a pupil of Ingres.

Musée San Martin ⊘ – From 1848 to 1850 this house was inhabited by the Argentinian general San Martin who, in 1816, freed his country from Spanish rule and then also liberated Chile (1817) and Peru (1821). He died in a room on the second floor, in 1850: mementoes of the illustrious soldier.

Musée d'Histoire naturelle ⊘ – The museum has a collection devoted to the study of paleontolgy, including life-size models of dinosaurs in their natural environment, as well as various species of reptiles and fish from the Jurassic Era. Four rooms are devoted to comparative anatomy and zoology, with two dioramas illustrating the ecology of the forests and the coastal cliffs. Many mineral samples and sea shells are on display.

EXCURSIONS

Calvaire des marins – *From Nausicaa, access by rue de la Baraque-de-l'Empereur and rue de la Tour-d'Odre.*
The calvary stands on the plateau where once stood the tour Odre, a Roman lighthouse collapsed in the 17C, owing to the crumbling of the cliff. The calvary and the sailors' chapel also collapsed recently; fortunately, the calvary was saved and now stands near a new chapel (1996) shaped like a ship. From the calvary's surroundings and the platform of the neighbouring wartime bunker there is a plunging **view**★ over the beach, Nausicaa, the channel entrance, the harbour

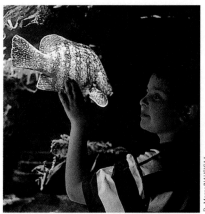
Face to face with fish at Nausicaa

P. Mores/NAUSICAA

111

area and the English coast when the weather is clear. Not far from here, following the cliff, a marker indicates the site of the hut from which the Emperor stood watching the coast of England as well as the Napoleonic powder magazine.

★**Colonne de la Grande Armée** ⏱ – *3km/2mi north by N 1 and turn left on a small road.*

Designed by the architect **Eloi Labarre** (1764-1833) to commemorate the Boulogne Camp, the column was started in 1804 but only finished under Louis-Philippe. The column is of marble from nearby Marquise, rises 54m/177ft high and is 4m/13ft in diameter. On its base, a bronze low-relief sculpture portrays Field Marshal Soult offering the plans of the column to the Emperor. A staircase *(263 steps)* leads to the square platform (190m/623ft above sea level) from where the **panorama**★★ extends over the lush countryside of the Boulogne region and, on a clear day, across the Channel as far as the white cliffs of Dover. Other sights include Cap Gris-Nez *(north)*, the jetties of Boulogne's port, the rocks of Le Portel, Alprech Point lighthouse, the Upper Town *(west and south)* and the triumphal avenue which leads to the column *(east)*.

Monument de la légion d'honneur – *2km/1.25mi north by D 940 and a path to the right.*

This obelisk marks the site of the throne on which Napoleon I sat on 16 August 1804, for the second distribution of the Legion of Honour decorations (the first took place on 14 July 1804 at the Invalides in Paris). The troops were deployed in a huge semicircle on the slopes of Terlincthun Valley; 2 000 men received their crosses, arranged for this ceremony in the shields and helmets of the ancient military heroes Du Guesclin and Bayard.

Château de Pont de Briques – *5km/3mi south on N 1.*

This modest 18C château *(private)* became famous because Napoleon stayed there when he came to visit the troops at the Boulogne Camp (1803-05); his apartments were in the right wing. The Emperor dictated his plan of campaign against Austria – which ended with his victory at Austerlitz in December 1805 – in the salon here.

Viewpoint of St-Étienne-au-Mont – *5km/3mi along D 52 then right up a steep hill (13 %).*

From the cemetery adjacent to the isolated hilltop church (alt 124m/407ft), there is a fine **view**★ of the Liane Valley; Boulogne, over which towers the dome of Notre-Dame basilica, can be seen downstream whereas, the inland scenery is dominated by the dark Boulogne Forest.

Le Portel – *5km/3mi southwest.*

The town has a sandy **beach** dotted with rocks and bordered by a raised promenade, facing the small isle on which stands **fort de l'Heurt,** built by Napoleon in 1804. A statue of Our Lady of Boulogne watches over the Epi jetty.

Alprech Point lighthouse perches on the cliff, to the south.

Eating out in Hardelot

MID-RANGE

Brasserie L'Océan – *100 boulevard de la Mer* – ☎ *03 21 83 17 98* – *140/180F.* Who could ever tire of the blissful sight of the sea stretching before your eyes... In high season, sit out on the terrace to feel the ocean breeze brush against your cheek... Decent cooking, with understandable emphasis on seafood.

Where to stay in Hardelot

MID-RANGE

Chambre d'Hôte La Colo – *131 avenue de la Princesse-Louise* – ☎ *03 21 83 88 54* – ✉ – *4 rooms 300/350F.* A former holiday camp for children, this bed and breakfast housed in a 1940 villa has now been equipped with all the latest amenities. Pretty rooms decorated with bright Provençal colours. A restful stopping place in the middle of a pine forest.

LUXURY

Hôtel du Parc – *111 avenue Francois-1ᵉʳ* – ☎ *03 21 33 22 11* – *closed mid-Dec to mid-Jan* – 🅿 – *82 rooms from 580F* – ☕ *59F* – *restaurant 140F.* A modern hotel tucked away among the trees... This idyllic setting is enhanced by outdoor pools, tennis courts and a health farm, providing everything you could possibly wish for. The large rooms, appointed with painted wooden furniture and embellished with discreet fabrics, look onto the surrounding countryside.

Typical landscape of the Boulonnais region

Y. Tierny/MICHELIN

⚓⚓ **Hardelot-Plage** – *15km/9mi south by D 940 and D 113^E.*
This elegant seaside and sporting resort features a magnificent, gently sloping beach of fine sand. Leisure facilities include paths for walking, riding and cycling; golf; sailing; a country club with tennis courts and a swimming pool.
The **château** north of the village, by the Lac des Miroirs, retains some of its 13C fortifications. In the 19C it was bought by an Englishman who had the château rebuilt in the style of Windsor Castle with crenellations and turrets.

Forêt de Boulogne – *10km/6mi east by N 42 and D 341.*
The road climbs the slopes of **Mont Lambert** (189m/620ft); a television aerial rises from the top.
The forest covers 2 000ha/4 940 acres and contains forest roads, bridle paths, parking facilities and picnic areas. The lush Liane Valley borders the forest to the south and east; the village of **Questrecques** nestles in delightful surroundings.

ROUND TRIP

Le Boulonnais *75km/46mi – about 3hr*

The Boulonnais is a region of lush countryside around Boulogne. Its complex relief is due to the juxtaposition of differing geological formations: marble in Marquise, sandstone in Outreau and chalk in Desvres and Neufchâtel, where it lies under a layer of clay. In some places, outcrops rise over 200m/656ft in altitude.
The plateau between Guînes and the River Aa is intermittently bare or dotted with copses and affords an unrestricted view in all directions; here and there great farms surrounded by thickets and pastures grow cereals and sugar beet.
The Wimereux, Liane, Hem and Slack valleys are deep and narrow, providing fertile ground for orchards (cider apples) and meadows. A local breed of cow grazes peacefully here, in addition to the Northern Blue and the Flemish Red cows; sheep are put out to pasture with Boulonnais draughthorses, which are powerful grey animals capable of pulling as much as a ton in weight.
The modest villages with their low, white-washed stone houses are devoted to stock farming; they are scattered around the manor houses, which were Royalist dens during the Revolution.
The Boulonnais forms part of the nature park known as the Parc naturel régional Nord-Pas-de-Calais.
Leave Boulogne eastwards along N 42; 3km/2mi on, beyond the roundabout, turn onto D 232.

This picturesque road, edged with beeches and old elms, descends sharply into the freshness of the **Wimereux Valley** which is carpeted with meadows and scattered with copses.

Souverain-Moulin – The château and its outbuildings look very attractive in their leafy setting.
Take D 233 (east) to Belle, then turn left onto D 238 and right onto D 251. Turn right again onto D 127.

Le Wast – Many local people take walks which end at this charming village. The **church** ⊘ features a Romanesque portal with Eastern-looking festoons, and rounded arches supported by capitals decorated with acanthus leaves which curve to form scrolls. St Ide, the mother of Godefroy de Bouillon and the founder of the priory, was buried here in the 12C.

113

The **Maison du Parc national régional du Nord-Pas-de-Calais, zone du Boulonnais** is situated in the **manoir du Huisbois** ⓘ a beautiful 17C house of local grey stone. The information centre provides documentation, a library, a video centre and exhibitions all relating to the Boulonnais. A trail starting here leads through typical countryside: farmland crisscrossed by hedges and trees.

From N 42 to Saint-Omer, turn left on D 224 to Licques.

Licques – All that remain of the Premonstratensian abbey founded in the 12C and rebuilt in the 18C, are the abbey church's tall nave (late 18C) and a few buildings from the same period, now occupied by the presbytery, the town hall and the school. Some 2km/1.25mi along D 224 north towards Ardres, the road offers a good **view** over Licques and the River Hem basin.

Licques is famous for its turkeys introduced in the area in the 17C by the monks of the local abbey and celebrated today on the third Sunday in December.

From Licques, follow D 191 west through Sanghem and Hermelinghen.

Beyond Le Ventu the road begins to climb, overlooking the entire region. There are beautiful **views**★ over the verdant, undulating Boulonnais countryside.

At Hardinghen, take D 127 southwest and D 127ᴱ to Réty.

Rety – The small Flamboyant **church** (late 15C; 12C tower) has decorative stonework which creates a chequered effect. Inside, note the chancel's carved keystone in the centre of a stone crown. The cemetery has been turned into an attractive garden.

Turn left beyond Rety onto D 232. After crossing D 127E, turn right to Hydrequent.

Hydrequent – The **Maison du marbre et de la géologie** ⓘ is a centre concentrating on the formation of marble and coal in the Boulonnais. The marble, which is actually limestone formed during the Carboniferous Era or the later, Jurassic period, is rich in fossils as can be seen on the various display panels. Some 26 different types of marble exist. During the Primary Era this region was covered by a lush forest (model showing the animals and giant plants whose decomposition eventually formed coal). The **Marquise quarry** yields a type of "marble" which has been used for many buildings, among them Canterbury Cathedral in England; granules of the rock were used more recently for the vaults of the Channel Tunnel. The plaster cast of a dinosaur skeleton found locally (during the building of the motorway in 1991) and an audio-visual presentation of the quarryman's trade may also be viewed.

Return to D 232.

Almost immediately, a pretty mill beside the River Slack comes into view *(left)*.

In Wierre-Effroy take D 234 to Conteville-lès-Boulogne, then take D 233 along the banks of the River Wimereux.

Wimille – The graves of the aeronauts Pilâtre de Rozier and Romain are in the old cemetery.

Return to Boulogne.

Musée de l'Air et de l'Espace du BOURGET★★

LE BOURGET AIR AND SPACE MUSEUM
Michelin map 20, 101 folds 7, 17, 106 fold 20 and 237 fold 18

Access: *Leave Paris by motorway A 1 then follow signs.*

Le Bourget airfield was created in 1914 and rapidly became an important airport and military air base. It was from here that Nungesser and Coli set off in their *White Bird* on 8 May 1927 in a doomed attempt to reach the American coast. Thirteen days later, in the early hours of 22 May, Lindbergh successfully landed his *Spirit of St Louis* in Paris, after achieving the first non-stop solo flight across the Atlantic in the history of aviation. Costes and Bellonte were the first to accomplish this feat in the opposite direction when *Question Mark* landed on 1 September 1930.

Since the Charles-de-Gaulle airport at Roissy became operational, Le Bourget has been used mainly for private aircraft and business flights.

Every two years, Le Bourget hosts the International Air and Space Show *(see Calendar of events)*.

Visit of the museum ⓘ – The museum has been laid out in the former terminal building at Le Bourget and it boasts some extraordinary collections retelling the history of the conquest of the skies. The adventure began with **hot air balloons**★ after the experiment carried out by Rozier and Arlandes in 1783 and a 1.6:3 model of their balloon can be seen in the museum, to recall the event. This first success resulted in the rapid expansion of ballooning. The decisive step came with the crossing of the English Channel. It cost the lives of Rozier and Romain in their balloon in 1785 but was a triumph for JP Blanchard the same year. A veritable fashion for hot air balloons then took over the interior design sector. The museum has more than 400 objects reflecting this enthusiasm including knickknacks, wall fabrics, engravings, ceramics, and furniture (note the copy of G Tissandier's desk). Later, balloons were to prove very useful in military operations or as a means of transport (postal services, means of escape for statesman Gambetta) during the Franco-Prussian war of 1870. The system was perfected and the balloons could then be steered. They provided inspiration for a great painter and photographer, Nadar. Meanwhile, Jules Verne was forecasting the days of machines "heavier than air" in his novel *Robur le Conquérant*.

Note the basket of an enormous Zeppelin and the "squadron's bar" reconstructed in an Adrian-type prefab where the drabness is lightened by the songs of Maurice Chevalier.

The **Grande Galerie**★★ traces the early years of aviation and has the largest collection in the world dealing with this period. The first prototypes were gliders, like the one flown by Massa-Biot (1879). Some of the aircraft were inspired by bionics, among them Clément Ader's strange *Éole*, which was designed after observation of a bat. The pioneers had boundless imagination and the lightness of the aircraft structures is astounding. Among the earliest aircraft, note Farman's *Voisin* (first round 1km/0.6mi trip, in Issy-les-Moulineaux, 1907), the elegant and popular *Levasseur Antoinette* (1908), the *Blériot-XI* which succeeded in flying across the Channel etc. With the outbreak of the First World War, aviation underwent rapid progress. Aircraft structures and power were increased and the skies became the setting for the first aerial battles. This period is well represented with Guynemer's *Spad-VII* and the *Spad-XIII* painted in the colours of flying ace René Fonck (75 victories).

After the war, aeronautics continued to develop and records were made or broken. **Hall A** contains the famous *Potez-53* (it achieved average speeds of 322kph/200mph over a distance of 2000km/1243mi in 1933), the very powerful *Caudron 714R* (900hp), the *Breguet XIX* "Nungesser-Coli" in which Costes and Le Brix made the first successful crossing of the South Atlantic in 1927. The Second World War is represented in **Hall B** by some fearsome fighters such as the *Spitfire MK-16* used by the Free French Airforce, the *YAK-3* painted in the colours of the Normandie-Niemen squadron, or the enormous *P-47 Thunderbolt* (a 2000hp fighter bomber). The first jet-engined planes appeared at the end of the war. **Hall C** has an exhibition of amazing prototypes with thermopropulsion such as the *Leduc-010* and the *Nord-1500 Griffon*. The **other three halls** cover the French Air Force since 1945 (*Mystère-IV, Super Sabre*), aerial sports (*Stampe et Vertongen* bi-plane from Belgium and the first autogiros), and the conquest of space (*Diamant* launcher, reproduction of the famous *Sputnik* space capsule). Outside are examples of French technology at its best with a gigantic model of *Ariane-V*, 45m/146ft high, and a Concorde in its new shed.

Musée de l'Air et de l'Espace – Concorde

Musée de l'Air et de l'Espace

Château de BRETEUIL★★

Michelin map 101 fold 32, 106 fold 29 and 237 fold 28

Access from Paris: *Pont de Sèvres and N 118 towards the motorway to Chartres (A 10). Take the Saclay exit and follow the signs to Chevreuse (N 306 then D 906). From Chevreuse, the château is signposted.*

Known for many years as Bévilliers or Buvilliers, Breteuil is one of the most charming châteaux in the Île-de-France region. It offers a fascinating insight into the illustrious Le Tonnelier de Breteuil family who have been living in the castle since 1712. The estate has several attractive features: its architecture, fine furniture, souvenirs of a family of famous diplomats, a pleasant park with varied scenery and, as a special treat for children, well-known fairy-tale characters.

Tour ⊘ – The château is built in the Louis XIII style in brick and stone. It consists of a main building flanked by two low wings. The tour begins with an introduction to the most famous members of the family, including Gabrielle-Émilie de Breteuil, a brilliant scientist who was known for her long love affair with Voltaire, and Louis-Auguste de Breteuil, ambassador and government minister during the reign of Louis XVI.

On the first floor, the family memorabilia takes on quite another dimension thanks to the waxwork figures which bring back to life a few historical events. Louis XVI is shown with Louis-Auguste de Breteuil and Marie-Antoinette, signing the arrest warrant for the Cardinal de Rohan who was implicated in the mysterious affair of the Queen's necklace. Note the Dauphine's spinning wheel and the portrait of the Dauphin (the future Louis XVII) by Koucharsky. Further on is Louis XVIII, sitting in the actual wheelchair used by him and thought to have been made by Jacob. He is talking business with Duc Decazes and Charles de Breteuil. The lacquer bedchamber which accommodated so many illustrious guests provides the setting for a tableau with Proust while in the smoking room the figures represent Henri de Breteuil, Gambetta and the future Edward VII laying down in 1881 the bases of the Entente Cordiale.

The château's most outstanding exhibit remains the **Teschen table★★**, a table inlaid with stones, gems and petrified wood. The play of light across its surface shows it off to its full advantage. This superb piece of craftsmanship was given to Louis-Auguste de Breteuil (1730-1807) by Empress Maria Teresa of Austria. He had been the successful mediator during discussions leading to the Treaty of Teschen (1779) which put an end to a serious regional conflict between the Empire and Prussia. The Breteuil family's international importance is also illustrated by its links with the British royal family, an example of which was Edward VII's visit to the château on 3 May 1905. The sumptuous meal served to him is remembered in the dining room where the table has been laid and in the kitchens reconstructed as they were at that time.

Perrault's Fairy Tales	1 Little Red Riding Hood	3 Puss in Boots	5 Wild Ass's Skin
	2 Sleeping Beauty	4 Tom Thumb	6 Bluebeard

★★The park – Lying on the edge of a plateau overlooking the upper Chevreuse Valley, the 75ha/185 acre park provides some beautiful views and diverse landscapes. Near the château are the **formal French gardens** created by the Duchênes in accordance with Le Nôtre's principles. They include a lake, a 16C dovecote, statues and topiaried yews and boxwood. The **Princes' Garden** is vividly and variously coloured with flowering cherries, roses and some outstanding peonies. A box **maze** occupies one of the terraces of the orangery. Two ponds lower down form an ideal setting for a romantic stroll.

The harmonious setting is completed by waxwork tableaux in the outbuildings representing several of **Perrault's Fairy Tales**. Play areas have also been laid out for younger visitors. At the bottom of the slope are two lakes in romantic, untamed surroundings, an ideal place for a stroll.

CALAIS

Conurbation 101 768
Michelin map 51 fold 2 or 236 fold 2

Calais is divided into two distinct districts: the administrative and industrial centre, Calais-Sud, and the maritime centre, Calais-Nord, which was rebuilt after the last war. Calais is the leading passenger port in France and the second in the world with a traffic totalling 20 million passengers a year. The town gave its name to the Pas-de-Calais, the strait known on the north side of the Channel as the Straits of Dover. The history of the town has been considerably influenced by its proximity to the English coast, only 38km/23.5mi away, and on a clear day the white cliffs of Dover are visible from the promenade and the vast sandy beach west of Calais harbour's entrance. Calais is the ideal starting point for excursions along the Opal Coast to Le Touquet.

The Channel Tunnel – The "Chunnel" is the realisation of more than two centuries of dreams and unfinished projects.

From utopia to reality – Over the past 250 years there have been 27 proposals, the oldest of which was made in 1750 by M Desmarets, who wanted to rejoin Britain to the mainland by a bridge, a tunnel or a causeway. From 1834 onwards, Aimé Thomé de Gamond, who is known as the "Father of the Tunnel", put forward several different propositions, all of them technically viable.

First attempts – In 1880, 1 840m/over 1mi of galleries were dug out on the site called the "Puits des Anciens". 2 000m/1.25mi were tunnelled out on the English side before the work was stopped. A fresh approach was tried in 1922 with the Whitaker machine. The technical progress of the 1960s gave the project a boost but a 400m/433yd gallery was abandoned once again.

Birth of Eurotunnel – During a Franco-British summit conference in September 1981, the idea of building a fixed link was again mooted by British Prime Minister Margaret Thatcher and French President François Mitterrand. In October 1985, after an international competition, four projects were shortlisted and it was the Eurotunnel project which was finally selected, on 20 January 1986. A Franco-British treaty was signed on 12 February 1986 in Canterbury Cathedral with a view to the construction of the tunnel. The first link between France and England was esstablished on 1 December 1990 (service tunnel). The official opening of the tunnel and of the Shuttle service took place on 6 May 1994.

Facts and figures – Most of the tunnel lies at a depth of 40m/130ft below the seabed, in a layer of blue chalk. Enormous tunnel-digging machines bored their way through the rock at a rate of 800 to 1 000m/867 to 1 083yd a month.

The **trans-Channel link** consists, in fact, of two railway tunnels 7.60m/25ft in diameter connected every 375m/406yd to a central service gallery 4.80m/16ft in diameter built for the purposes of ventilation, security, and system maintenance. The tunnels contain a single track and the trains run in one direction only, taking passengers and freight. The tunnels have a total length of 50km/31mi of which 40km/24mi are beneath the Channel.

Y. Tierny/MICHELIN

Le Shuttle – *Folkestone to Calais*. The green and blue shuttle is 775m/0.5mi long. Passenger shuttles have one two-storey train for cars and one single-storey train for coaches and caravans. There are special shuttles for TGV's. A *rame* consists of 147 coaches, including one for embarkation and another for disembarkation.

The Shuttle operates round the clock throughout the year. Departures vary depending on the volume of traffic (2 to 4 services every hour during the day, one per hour at night). The crossing lasts 35min, including 28min in the tunnel.

Eurostar – High-speed trains operated by the French, Belgian and British railway companies run a daily service between Paris, Brussels and London. It takes approximately 3hr to travel from Paris-Gare du Nord to London-Waterloo. There are also several trains per day between Lille and London.

The Burghers of Calais – After his success at Crécy **Edward III** of England needed to create a powerful base in France. He began the siege of Calais on 3 September 1346 but eight months later had still not been able to breach the valiant defence led by the town governor, Jean de Vienne; in fact, it was famine that forced the inhabitants to capitulate in the end.

Six burghers, led by **Eustache de Saint-Pierre**, prepared to sacrifice themselves in order that the other citizens of Calais would be spared the sword. In thin robes, "barefoot, bareheaded, halters about their necks and the keys to the town in their hands", they presented themselves before the king to be delivered to the executioner. They were saved by the intercession of Queen Philippa of Hainault.

Calais was in the hands of the English for over two centuries and was liberated only in 1558, by the Duke of Guise. This was a mortal blow to **Mary Tudor**, Queen of England, who said: "If my heart were laid open, the word "Calais" would be engraved on it."

Lace – Together with Caudry-en-Cambrésis, Calais is the main centre of machine-made lace, employing about 2 000 workers using over 350 looms. Englishmen from Nottingham introduced the industry at the beginning of the 19C; quality was improved around 1830 when the first Jacquard looms were introduced.

Three quarters of Calais' lace is exported, to 140 different countries; 80 % of it is used for lingerie, 20 % for dresses (wedding gowns, cocktail and evening dresses, off-the-peg and designer clothing). Traditional lace made with the Leavers machine is entitled to a quality label created in 1991, representing a peacock.

TOWN WALK

🔲 *Start from the theatre. Walk along boulevard Jacquard, a lively shopping street, as far as place du Soldat-Inconnu, between the town hall and the Parc St-Pierre.*

★★ Monument des Bourgeois de Calais (Monument to the Burghers of Calais) – This famous work by Rodin is located in between the Hôtel de Ville and Parc St-Pierre. It dates from 1895 and exemplifies the sculptor's brilliance: the bronze group is simultaneously full of vitality and pathos. Each of the six life-size figures should be admired separately: their veins and muscles exaggerated, their forms tense and haughty. They express the heroic nobility of the men obliged to humiliate themselves before the king of England. *In 2001, the statue was removed temporarily to Italy for restoration and exhibition.*

The Burghers of Calais by Rodin

Eating out

MODERATE

La Boudinière – *2691 route de Waldam, 62215 Oye-Plage – 14km/8.7mi east of Calais by D 119 – ☎ 03 21 85 93 14 – closed 29 Jan-11 Feb and Wed from Oct to Mar – 76/190F.* This small restaurant nestled in the Calais countryside offers traditional fare of excellent quality. The meat is particularly succulent as the owner chooses the cuts himself. Smiling welcome and quiet dining room.

MID-RANGE

Aquar'aile – *255 rue Jean-Moulin – ☎ 03 21 34 00 00 – closed 15-29 Feb, 16-31 Aug, Sun evening and Mon – 130/230F.* At your feet lie the sea, the beach, the port and the ferries dancing on the water's surface. Such is the lovely view from Aquar'aile, a panoramic restaurant. While you dine, you can admire the shimmering reflections cast by the blue ceiling above your head. There are menus for all types of budget and the nearby harbour guarantees fresh fish and seafood every day.

Le 1900 – *4 rue Royale – ☎ 03 21 97 58 41 – closed Mon evening – 160/240F.* Settle on a red velvet wall seat in this turn-of-the-century brasserie and entrust your order to one of the waiters clad in a long white apron. The appetisers brought to your table will whet your appetite while you wait for your first course!

Where to stay

MODERATE

Métropol Hôtel – *43 quai du Rhin – ☎ 03 21 97 54 00 – closed 16 Dec-1 Jan – ▣ – 40 rooms 250/380F – ☲ 49F.* Conveniently located near the train station, the shopping centre and Rodin's famous sculpture The Burghers of Calais. English-style saloon-bar. The rooms, appointed with light wooden furniture, are remarkably soundproofed.

MID-RANGE

Chambre d'Hôte Le Manoir du Meldick – *2528 avenue du Général-de-Gaulle, Le Fort Vert, 62730 Marck – 6km/3.7mi east of Calais by D 119 – ☎ 03 21 85 74 34 – ☒ – 5 rooms 265/315F.* Only a few minutes away from Calais harbour and yet blissfully quiet, this bed and breakfast offers a subtle combination of elegance and sophistication. Large, comfortable rooms and charming welcome.

On the town

Fahrenheit – *59 place d'Armes – ☎ 03 21 96 86 88 – daily 10am-1am.* With its fake attic, its cosy, padded wall seats, its terrace and its pretty garden, this newly opened establishment has already earned a well-deserved reputation in the area.

Shopping

Le Bar à Vins – *52 place d'Armes – ☎ 03 21 96 96 31 – daily except Wed 9am-7.30pm, Sun 9.30am-4.30pm.* This wine bar boasts an exceptional cellar containing both rare vintages and cheaper bottles purchased locally by the owner, whose motto is, "Read beyond the label!" The congenial, talkative wine buff has made friends with most of his clients...

Hôtel de ville – The beautiful and graceful town hall is built of brick and stone in the 15C Flemish style yet dates only from the turn of the last century. The belfry (75m/246ft) can be seen for miles in all directions; the sound of its bell is very appealing. Inside, a **stained-glass window** which recalls the departure of the English diffuses the sunlight over the grand staircase.

Rejoin the boulevard. After the bridge, continue in the same direction. Boulevard Clemenceau runs past the tourist office and Parc Richelieu where you have to turn right.

Église Notre-Dame – Construction of the church started at the end of the 13C, when the nave was built. The building was finished during the English occupation at the end of the 14C, which explains the surprising look of the tower, chancel and transept: despite being in France, they recall the English perpendicular Gothic style. In 1691 Vauban had a large cistern built on the north side. The wedding of Captain Charles de Gaulle with a young Calais woman was celebrated here in 1921.

Follow rue de la Paix. On the right stands the former Tour du Guet and place d'Armes.

Place d'Armes – Before the devastation of the war, this was the heart of medieval Calais. Only the 13C **watchtower** has survived. The belfry and the town hall beside it are popular subjects for artists.

Follow boulevard Clemenceau and rue Royale. Cross the H.-Hénon bridges and continue straight ahead until you reach to beach.

To the left is the Bassin Ouest, to the right is the Bassin du Paradis and the rear harbour used as a marina.

Beach and West Pier – A promenade pier runs alongside the fine-sand beach. From the west pier, there are fine views of the harbour. Traffic is as dense as before the opening of the Channel Tunnel. In the distance you can see Cap Blanc-Nez (on the right) and the English cliffs.

From the pier, a watch-path skirting the dock and running round Fort Risban leads to the rear harbour.

Built in the 16C, on the site of a former English tower, Fort Risban used to defend the entrance to the harbour.

Walk back across the H.-Hénon bridges, turn left and walk along quai de la Colonne-Louis-XVIII then continue towards the Courgain district.

Rear harbour – Along quai de la Colonne-Louis-XVIII, which recalls the king's landing in 1814, a monument (Monument des Sauveteurs) is dedicated to the heroic action of Calais rescue teams.

The Courgain district *(further forward)*, which was rebuilt after the war, is where many sailors live. The lighthouse is located behind this area.

Le phare ⊘ – The lighthouse (53m/174ft tall; *271 steps*) was built in 1848 to replace the watchtower beacon. From the top there is a surprisingly wide and splendid panoramic **view★★** over Calais, the harbour, the basins, the town's stadium, place d'Armes and the unexpectedly large Church of Our Lady.

SIGHTS

★ Musée des Beaux-Arts et de la Dentelle ⊘ – The fine arts and lace museum gives an insight into changes in sculpture over the 19C and 20C and styles of painting between the 17C and 20C.

Musée des Beaux-Arts et de la Dentelle, Calais

Calais lace depicting the Blériot-XI crossing the Channel

19C sculpture is centred on the works of Rodin and the studies he made for *The Burghers of Calais*. The concept of modern sculpture is made quite clear through the works of Rodin's predecessors, including Carrière-Belleuse, Carpeaux, Barye, and of some of his students, Bourdelle and Maillol.

Paintings from the 17C to the 19C by the Flemish and North-European schools.

There are also works by modern and contemporary artists such as Jean Dubuffet *(Landscape around Calais)*, Félix Del Marle *(Construction-Colour)*, Picasso *(The Old Man, Womain's Face)*, Fautrier, Lipchitz, Arp....

The **lace section**, located in a former tulle-making factory, deals with machine-made Calais lace and with hand-made lace. The history of lace is illustrated by production techniques, haute-couture dresses, pieces of lace and lingerie from the 17C to the present day (the museum owns more than 400 000 samples of machine-made lace)

Musée de la Guerre ⊘ – Opposite the town hall, in the middle of Parc St Pierre, there is a large bunker that was used as a telephone exchange by the Germans during the Second World War. Posters, tracts, memorabilia and letters in some of the rooms evoke the Resistance, the occupation of Calais and the Battle of Britain. The documents and the museum's simplicity make this a moving visit.

CALAIS

CAMBRAI★

Population 33 092
Michelin map 53 folds 3, 4 or 236 fold 27

Cambrai stands in the centre of a rich cereal and sugar beet region, on the east bank of the River Escaut (or Scheldt). Traditionally, cambric linen was made here, bleached in the sunny meadows then used to make handkerchiefs and fine lingerie. In gourmet terms, Cambrai is known for its small chitterling sausages *(andouillettes)*, its tripe and its mint-flavoured sweets *(bêtises de Cambrai)*. The town's heroes are the giants Martin and Martine who are said to have killed the local tyrant.

The town is built of white limestone and is overlooked by the three towers of the belfry, the cathedral and St Gery's Church. Once military and archiepiscopal, Cambrai today looks peaceful, a ring of boulevards having replaced the ramparts.

The "Swan of Cambrai" – In 1695 François de Salignac de La Mothe-Fénelon (1651-1715), a great lord, man of the Church and famous writer, was made archbishop of Cambrai. **Fénelon** was venerated by his flock for his gentleness and charity, and learned while in Cambrai that Rome had condemned his Maximes des Saints; this work defended quietism, a doctrine made fashionable by Mme Guyon, which exalted the "Pure Love of God". In response the former tutor of the Duke of Burgundy first climbed into the pulpit to preach obedience to the Church's decisions and then wrote a pastoral letter to the same effect, thus showing an admirable humility.

The charity of the "Swan of Cambrai" was often called upon during the War of Spanish Succession; starving peasants from the surrounding Cambrai region poured into the archdiocese, where Fénelon welcomed them. On one occasion a cow was lost on the way to the archbishop, who immediately set out on foot with a servant to find the animal; he found the cow and was able to return it to its poor owner. Fénelon died at Cambrai after a carriage accident.

Bêtises de Cambrai

These oblong mint-flavoured sweets, with a yellow stripe on the side are, according to legend, the result of the fortunate mistake of a 19C confectioner's apprentice. His mother complained that he had once again blundered and made a mistake (bêtise), hence the name given to the mint humbugs which were nevertheless appreciated for their digestive and refreshing qualities. Another old legend tells how men who went to an important market held on the 24th day of every month would behave irresponsibly and waste their money on sweets made in front of them!

◪ OLD TOWN *allow 2hr*

Porte de Paris – This town gate, a vestige of the medieval fortifications, is flanked by two round towers dating from 1390.

Follow avenue de la Victoire towards the town hall, visible at the end of the street. Place du St-Sépulcre appears shortly on the left.

Cathédrale Notre-Dame ⊘ – Originally dedicated to the Holy Sepulchre, the abbey church was elevated to the rank of cathedral after the Revolution. It was built in the 18C and has been altered several times since; the tower dates from 1876. An 18C convent building stands to the right.

The rounded chapels terminating the transept arms are decorated with large *trompe-l'œil grisailles*, painted in 1760 by the Antwerp artist Martin Geeraerts. They represent the Virgin Mary *(south)* and Christ *(north)*. Fénelon's tomb, sculpted by David d'Angers in 1826, is in the apsidal chapel. The prelate raises himself, looking heavenward in a Romantic burst of emotion; his hands are particularly fine.

A statue of Fénelon by Auricoste stands to the left of the cathedral.

Chapelle du Grand Séminaire – The chapel is set back from the square. It was completed in 1692 and formerly belonged to the Jesuit school; its lively and theatrical Baroque façade nevertheless retains a symmetry through the regular arrangement of windows, pilasters, scrolls and firepots.

Among the richly carved decor, note the high-relief sculpture of the Assumption, which was added in the 19C during restoration.

Maison espagnole – *Tourist office.* This wooden house, its gables sheathed in slate, dates from the late 16C. You can see the medieval cellars and, on the first floor, the oak carvings which once adorned the façade.

Note the 17C and 18C private residences along rue du Grand-Séminaire, rue de l'Epée and rue de Vaucelette. One of these, carefully restored, houses the fine arts museum. As you walk across place Jean-Moulin, note the rounded east end of the chapel of the former St-Julien hospital.

Place Fénelon – The square is located on the site of the old cathedral, a splendid Gothic structure demolished after the Revolution. The 17C entrance porch still remains from Fénelon's **archiepiscopal palace.**

Église St-Géry ⊘ – Overlooked by a tower (76m/249ft tall), the old church of St Aubert's Abbey rises on the site once occupied by a temple believed to have been dedicated to Jupiter Capitolinus. Construction of this austere Classical building lasted from 1698 to 1745. The ambitious plans called for a chancel with an ambulatory and radiating chapels, preceded by a monumental canopy resting on four colossal Baroque columns.
The beautiful **rood screen** (1632), which formerly closed off the chancel entrance, was moved to the

Église St-Géry – *The Entombment* by Rubens

west end of the nave. It is a good example of the Baroque style with its contrasting red and black marble and its carved decoration by Gaspard Marsy, creating an impression of movement or even agitation: *putti* on the wing, alabaster statues and high-relief carvings relating the miracles of Christ. The monumental pulpit, installed in 1850, was the work of Cambrai craftsmen. The chancel contains 18C furniture: an altar and, in particular, the wood panels with medallions depicting the lives of St Augustine and St Aubert.
The north transept houses Rubens' enormous dramatic painting, **The Entombment**★★. The 14C **statue** in the south transept was discovered in 1982 during excavations in the crypt and represents a bishop.
Cross place du 9-Octobre to reach place Aristide-Briand.

Eating out

MODERATE

Le Crabe Tambour – *52 rue Cantimpré* – ☎ *03 27 83 10 18* – *closed 2-5 Jan, 1-22 Aug, Mon, Sun evening and public holiday evenings* – *98/160F.* The owner of this restaurant, which is slightly out of the way, has decided to centre his menu around fish and seafood. You can even sample a bouillabaisse. There are two dining rooms; one is appointed with rustic-style furniture and decorated with bright colours.

Where to stay

MID-RANGE

Château de la Motte Fénelon – *Square du Château – north of Cambrai by allée St-Roch* – ☎ *03 27 83 61 38* – **P** – *40 rooms 320/1150F* – ☲ *55F* – *restaurant 145/240F.* The two salons in this outstanding 19C château surrounded by a park will take you back to the days of court life... The rooms housed in the separate bungalows are less luxurious. The vaulted red-brick cellar serves as a backdrop to the restaurant Les Douves.

LUXURY

Château de Ligny – *59191 Ligny-en-Cambrésis – 17km/10.6mi southeast of Cambrai by D 940 then D 15* – ☎ *03 27 85 25 84* – *closed Feb school holidays* – **P** – *13 rooms from 650F* – ☲ *80F* – *restaurant 240/420F.* A park in the village centre is the setting for this 13C and 17C château with an imposing tower and sturdy walls. The lofty bedrooms each have their own style. One of the dining halls features a medieval decor complete with stained glass, visible stonework and beams; the other one, embellished with wainscoting and parquet flooring, exudes a cosy atmosphere.

L. Lecat/Musée de Cambrai

Cambrai – Musée des Beaux-Arts: Fragment of a 14C Annunciation

Place Aristide-Briand – The square was entirely rebuilt after the First World War and is dominated by the cold and majestic lines of the **hôtel de ville** which was rebuilt at the end of the 19C but was set ablaze during the First World War. Its reconstruction in the 1920s, together with that of the square itself, respected the old façade and its Louis XVI peristyle; this was largely due to the commitment of the Parisian architect, Antoine. The hall is surmounted by a columned bell-tower, flanked by the town's two jack-o'-the-clocks, Martin and Martine. According to legend these two individuals, who appear in parades as giants, were 14C blacksmiths who dealt with the lord ravaging the region by felling him with hammer blows. The bronze figures (2m/6.5ft tall), dressed as turbaned Moors, date from 1512; they strike the town bell with their hammers to sound the hour.

The southwest corner of the square marks the beginning of a long avenue, Mail St-Martin, which offers a good view of the 15C-18C **belfry** (70m/230ft tall), which is all that remains of St Martin's Church.

Porte Notre-Dame – This piece of the old fortifications was built at the beginning of the 17C; it owes its name to the statue of the Virgin Mary which adorns the outer face. The gate is unusual for its diamond-shaped stones and its grooved columns. The sun representing Louis XIV was added to the pediment after the town was captured from the Spanish by the French.

ADDITIONAL SIGHTS

Musée des Beaux-Arts ⊘ – The town museum is housed in a mansion built for the Comte de Francqueville c 1720. It has been restored and substantially extended, with the addition of two new buildings.

The **archeology** department occupies the vaulted 18C cellars. Three themes recall the Gallo-Roman period: ceramics, housing and funerals. Exhibits from the Merovingian period include funerary artefacts from sites near Cambrai, Les Rues-des-Vignes (pairs of gilded silver fibulae) and Busigny, all of which were explored in 1986. The section devoted to osteo-archeology gives a clearer insight into man during the Dark Ages (age of the deceased, traces of disease or illness etc).

An audio-visual presentation based on a relief map of the town serves as an introduction to a tour of the department devoted to **Cambrai and its heritage**.

The many sculptures come from religious buildings that have been demolished. The set from the Abbaye St-Géry in Les Monts-des-Boeufs (12C) consists of three statue-columns representing the seasons, a capital and small tympana, one of which illustrates the legend of Pyramus and Thisbe. Alabaster statues come from the former cathedral church. A painting by Van der Meulen is a graphic description of the capture of Cambrai by Louis XIV in 1677.

The **Fine Arts** section gives a panoramic overview of Dutch painting in the late 16C and 17C. The collection includes still-life paintings by Nicolas Van Veerendael and *The Card Players* by Rombouts.

The 18C French School is represented by Berthelemy *(Esther Fainting)*, de Lajoue *(Astronomy)*, and Wille *(The Dying Moments of a Beloved Wife)*. From the 19C and 20C are portraits, religious subjects and landscapes by Durand, Boudin, Utrillo, Marquet, Friesz etc.

The museum also has a sculpture collection, with works by Rodin, Camille Claudel, Bourdelle, Zadkine (*Il penseroso*, 1951) and the contemporary artist Georges Jeanclos (he carved the doorway for St-Ayoul Church in Provins).

Beguine convents

Beguine convents consisted of small terraced houses forming an enclosure for single women or widows wishing to lead a life of devotion and charity. There were 11 of them in Cambrai. The Béguinage St-Vaast, which dates from 1354, was transferred to rue des Anglaises in 1545. This is the last such enclosure still existing in France.

CAMBRAI

CASSEL★

Population 2 177

Michelin map 51 fold 4 or 236 fold 4

Cassel is a small town that is Flemish in both its customs and appearance: an enormous cobbled main square (Grand' Place), narrow, winding streets and low whitewashed houses. It stands at the top of Cassel Hill, the green slopes of which, formerly dotted with windmills, overlook the flat Flanders region.

Local traditions are still celebrated: the religious fête with its mass, parades, traditional games and competitions; archery; the carnival; the procession of the Reuze giants.

"Cassel Hill" – The highest point of the region (176m/577ft high) and a link in the Flemish hill-range, the hill looks surprisingly large rising up in the middle of the Flemish plain; although about 30km/18mi from the coast, it is used as a landmark by sailors. Its peak is made up of a very hard ferruginous layer.

To the east, **Mont des Récollets** (159m/521ft high) owes its name to a convent of Recollect nuns which existed there from 1615 to 1870.

Two World Wars – From October 1914 to June 1915 **General Foch** had his head-quarters at Cassel. From here he followed the progress of the battle of Flanders which was raging on the banks of the Yser. He stayed at the Hôtel de Schoebecque at no 32 of what is now rue du Maréchal-Foch.

In May 1940 members of the British expeditionary corps retreating towards Yser and Dunkirk fought a fierce rearguard action at Cassel, which resulted in 2 000 dead and 1 000 prisoners on the battlefield.

SIGHTS ////

Public Gardens – The gardens at the top of the hill occupy the site of a medieval castle which once incorporated a collegiate church, the crypt of which remains. An equestrian statue of General Foch stands in the garden's centre, together with an 18C wooden **windmill** ⊘ from Arneke which was re-erected here to replace the castle's original windmill.

A tour of the terrace offers an excellent **panorama**★★ *(viewing platforms)* over the picturesque jumble of Cassel's old rooftops, and beyond to the hills of Flanders and the plain, as far as the North Sea and the belfry of Bruges. A local saying maintains that "from Cassel you can see five kingdoms: France, Belgium, Holland, England and, above the clouds, the Kingdom of Heaven".

Grand' Place – The main square, irregularly shaped and cobbled, extends along the hillside near the church. It still has an attractive group of 16C, 17C and 18C houses on its south side, among them the Hôtel de la Noble Cour.

Hôtel de la Noble Cour – Under the Ancien Régime this 16C-17C house was the seat of the court in which the local lord dispensed justice. A high roof dotted with blind dormer windows crowns the façade, which is entirely of stone – unusual in the North – pierced by large windows with alternately triangular and curvilinear ped-iments; the elegant Renaissance doorway, flanked by grey marble columns, is decorated with Fames in the spandrels and with Sirens and foliate scrolls on the frieze.

The **museum** ⊘ includes the Archive Room with its Louis XV woodwork, the Grande Salle (Flemish furniture and 17C and 18C objects), the Court Room (collection of faiences and northern French porcelain), the Salon de la Châtellenie (Louis XV woodwork, Louis XVI furniture), and Foch's office, preserved as it was in 1915. The ground floor houses reconstructions of a Flemish interior and a bar.

Collégiale Notre-Dame – This is a Gothic Flemish church with three gables, three aisles, three apses and a square tower over the transept crossing. Foch often came here to pray and meditate.

Ancienne chapelle des Jésuites – Pleasant 17C brick and stone façade.

EXCURSIONS

Steenvoorde – *8km/5mi by D 948*. This typical small Flemish town with painted houses under red-tiled roofs was once famous for its sheets; today it is the home of one of the largest dairies in the area.

Eating out in Cassel

MODERATE

La Taverne Flamande – *34 Grand'place –* ☎ *03 28 42 42 59 – closed Feb school holidays, 21-26 Aug, 17-26 Oct, Tues evening and Wed – booking recommended – 68/150F*. This tavern situated on the Grand'place pays a vibrant homage to the local hero Reuze Papa, as does the menu and its many Flemish specialities. If you decide to settle on the summer terrace giving onto the valley, do not forget to take a look at the splendid counter inside.

T Kasteelhof – *8 rue St-Nicolas –* ☎ *03 28 40 59 29 – closed over Christmas, 1 Jan and Mon-Thur except in June and during school holidays – booking rec-ommended Sat-Sun – 100/150F*. This is believed to be the highest tavern in French Flanders! It serves delicious regional fare and you can even buy local pro-duce from the adjoining shop.

Au Roi du Potje Vleesch – *31 rue du Mont-des-Cats, 59270 Godewaersvelde – 12km/7.5mi east of Cassel by D 948 then D 18 –* ☎ *03 28 42 52 56 – closed Jan and Mon – booking essential Sat-Sun – 92/120F*. The charcuterie soon gives way to a former slaughterhouse, currently converted into a tavern. In a rustic-style decor of Flemish inspiration, sample some typical regional dishes such as *potjevleesc* and Henri le Douanier beer. Before leaving, remember to fill up your shopping bag.

The town celebrates the legend of its giant, Yan den Houtkapper, a wood-cutter who made a pair of everlasting boots for Charlemagne, in return he was given a suit of armour, which he still wears for the processions in which he is the hero.

Windmills ⊘ – Three well-preserved windmills can be seen near the town. The first, the **Steenmeulen** at Ter-deghem *(on D 947 south)*, is a truncated brick mill; the other two, the **Drievemeulen** *(on D 948 west)* and the **Noordmeulen** *(on D 18 northwest)*, are wooden postmills.

Wormhout – *10km/6mi north via D 218 and D 916.*

Moulin Deschodt ⊘ – This wooden post mill is the last of 11 windmills which stood in the town in 1780.

Musée Jeanne-Devos ⊘ – This charming Flemish house, flanked by a dove-cote and set within lovely gardens at the end of a cul-de-sac, is the old Wormhout presbytery (18C). It was

Wormhout – Moulin Deschodt

inhabited by Jeanne Devos who collected, until her death in 1989, a multitude of objects from daily life. A photographer by profession, she left thousands of photographs portraying the ordinary and extraordinary lives of the villagers nearby.

Abbaye de CHAALIS★

Michelin map 106 fold 9 and 237 fold 19

The estate lies on the edge of Ermenonville Forest near the Mer de Sable theme park *(see Excursions)* and, during the 19C, it evoked the gentle, romantic charm suggested by religious contemplation. Later, and up to 1912, Chaalis inspired its last owners to collect works of art and to entertain some of the most notable personalities of their time.

A prosperous abbey – Chaalis was a Cistercian abbey *(see Introduction: Monasteries in Île-de-France)*, built on the site of a former priory in 1136 by Louis the Fat. The monks led a pious and modest country life, husbanding the land, cultivating vines, keeping bees and fishing in the lakes.

St Louis paid frequent visits to the abbey: he took part in the monks' prayers and duties, even waited on them, cared for the sick and watched over the dying.

Decline – During the 16C the abbey was held *in commendam* and the abbots were appointed by the king. The first was Cardinal Ippolito d'Este, son of Alfonso d'Este and Lucrezia Borgia, a distant cousin of François I (the Cardinal's brother, Ercole II d'Este, married Renée of France, the second daughter of Louis XII). Better known as Cardinal of Ferrara, this enthusiastic art lover had his private chapel decorated with murals and commissioned fine gardens but he nevertheless preferred his Tivoli residence, the Villa d'Este, where he died in 1572.

In the 18C the ninth abbot, one of the Great Condé's grandsons, attempted a costly operation to restore the abbey to plans by Jean Aubert, the architect who designed the Great Stables at Chantilly. It was a disaster; after only one side of the building had been completed (1739, currently the Château-Museum) work stopped owing to lack of funds. This financial crisis prompted Louis XVI to close down the abbey in 1785. During the upheaval of the French Revolution, Chaalis was badly pillaged and the greater part of the building destroyed.

Restoration – The estate frequently changed hands. Romantic painters and poets appreciated the melancholy charm of the old walls and their lush, verdant setting. In 1850 the highly distinguished Mme De Vatry bought the abbey ruins; she converted the 18C building into a château, had the park refurbished and entertained lavishly.

These efforts were continued by Mme De Vatry's heirs and by the last owner, Nélie Jacquemart-André, the widow of banker Édouard André who founded the Paris museum which bears her name. She died in 1912 and bequeathed the estate to the Institute of France.

Abbaye de Chaalis

★FORMER ABBEY *1hr*

★**Church ruins** – Ready for consecration in 1219, Chaalis Abbey was the first Cistercian church built in the Gothic style. Of the original buildings there remain a staircase turret, the northern transept arm surrounded by radiating chapels – an unusual feature – and a section of wall from the north aisle with blind arcades reminiscent of the old cloister.

★**Chapelle de l'abbé** – Built around 1250, the chapel is a fine example of Gothic splendour from the time of the Sainte-Chapelle in Paris. On the right, a bronze bust portraying Mme Jacquemart-André marks the site of her grave. Beyond the chapel a strange 16C crenellated wall with asymmetrical merlons sets the boundaries of the rose garden. Above the heavy archway, the coat of arms of Cardinal Louis d'Este, nephew of Cardinal of Ferrara, is displayed.

From north of the château there is a fine perspective of the park with its flower beds and dazzling lake, restored in the 19C.

★★**Château-Musée** ⊘ – The personality and taste of Mme André are revealed as soon as one enters the **Salle des Moines** which houses Italian 15C Gothic furniture, small paintings, two panels from an altarpiece painted by Jean de Bellegambe, many religious statues (14C-16C French) and above all the famous **panels painted by Giotto★★**, depicting St John the Evangelist and St Lawrence.

This mixture of styles is apparent in the ground-floor gallery, containing various busts, chests and glass-cabinets and leading successively to the **dining room** (hunting scenes by Oudry and Desportes), the **library**, the **Medici hall** (Renaissance tapestries and furniture bearing the arms of the Medici family), the **billiard room** (*The Capture of Namur* and *The Capture of Valenciennes* by Martin des Batailles), the strange **Indian drawing room** (chests, altars, arms...) and the **large drawing room** (portraits by Nicolas de Largillière and Van Loo).

Ph. Gajic/MICHELIN

St Lawrence, by Giotto

The main staircase gives access to the **private apartments of Mme André**: the Eagles' Room decorated in Empire style, preceding the bedroom in two parts separated by a pair of imposing columns (huge gilt-wood tester bed dating from the Louis XV period); next come the water-green and gold bathroom and the boudoir with its tapestry, *The Country Ball*, after a design by Boucher.

The first-floor gallery is decorated with Renaissance paintings and furniture. The former cells have been turned into guestrooms fitted with bathrooms. The **Galerie Jean-Jacques Rousseau** (collection donated to the Institut de France by the last Marquis de Girardin in 1923) includes manuscript music scores, documents, memorabilia and personal objects...

> **Patrons of the arts**
>
> Of humble origin, Nélie Jacquemart (1841-1912) stayed for long periods, during her childhood, at Madame Vatry's who considered her almost as her daughter. She became acquainted with members of the aristocracy and the upper middle-class who were very useful to her in the pursuit of her career as a fashionable portrait painter, having studied with Léon Cogniet. In 1872, Édouard André, the heir to one of the largest fortunes in banking, commissioned a portrait from her; which still hangs in the private apartments of his Parisian mansion, and they met for the first time on this occasion. In 1881 they got married and their union was a happy one. Having no children, the couple devoted their efforts to collecting beautiful things, mainly from Italy, in the sumptuous mansion on boulevard Haussmann. Nélie André completed this collection after the death of her husband. In 1902, she realised one of her dreams: going to India; however she gave up the idea of a world tour when she learned that the Chaalis estate was for sale. She acquired it and devoted the last years of her life to it.

EXCURSIONS

Ermenonville – *3km/1mi south on N 330*. In May 1778 **Jean-Jacques Rousseau** was invited to stay at the Château d'Ermenonville *(private)* by the Marquis de Girardin, who had acquired the estate in 1763, and it is here that Rousseau rekindled his passion for nature; he walked, daydreamed in the park and taught music to his host's children, until his sudden death on 2 July from a stroke.

The **Parc Jean-Jacques Rousseau**★ ⊘, which the marquess had transformed from sandy, swampy land into a superb landscaped garden in the French style with shaded paths, graceful vistas, elegant rockeries and charming brooks, still contains some strategically sited monuments.

Mer de Sable ⊘ – *0.5km/0.25mi south on N 330*. The sand deposits date from the Tertiary Era and at the end of the Ice Age this region was probably one vast sandy moor covered with wild heather.

The landscape has been developed into a themed park evoking China, the Wild West or Morocco through characteristic scenery. Various scenes – of Indians attacking trains, fights beside a ranch, or displays of horsemanship – animate the different areas. The small train tour of the desert and the shows are complemented by various thrilling attractions (white-water rides, head-first slides etc) and more peaceful games. A glass-blower demonstrates his skill and sells his production on the site.

Forêt d'Ermenonville – The Ermenonville Forest (3 300ha/8 151 acres) forms, with the nearby forests of Chantilly and Harlatte, part of the second green belt of Paris. After 1840 the clearings in the vast heather-covered moor were planted with maritime and Scots pines, and country lanes have now been marked out as suitable for walks. Cars are not allowed on the forest roads except along the "Longue Route" leading to the crossroads and on the section linking Baraque de Chaalis to the commemorative monument marking the crash of the Turkish Airlines DC 10 on 3 March 1974, in which 346 people died.

The southwest of the forest, which enchanted Corot and Gérard de Nerval, is not accessible though the road from Mortefontaine to Thiers offers views of the lake and the wilder landscape.

Eating out

MID-RANGE

Rabelais – *3 place de l'Église, 60950 Ver-sur-Laurette – 3km/2mi south of Ermenonville by D 84 –* ☎ *03 44 54 01 70 – closed Sun evening and Wed – 150/300F*. On the church square, in the heart of a small village stands this charming inn, easily recognisable by its thatched canopy. The drawing room, decorated in pastel hues, is enhanced by a splendid fireplace. Traditional cuisine.

Where to stay

MID-RANGE

Château d'Ermenonville – ☎ *03 44 54 00 26 –* ▯ *– 49 rooms 390/1200F –* ☲ *80F – restaurant 195/450F*. This château, surrounded by a moat and a vast park, will take you back to the Age of Enlightenment. Lovely little salons and boudoirs. Big rooms with pretty wall hangings and antique furniture.

Château de CHAMPS★★

Access from Paris: *RER line A 4.*

Champs, built with the funds of two unfortunate financiers at the end of Louis XIV's reign, is characteristic of 18C architecture and decoration. In 1989, it was chosen as the setting of the film *Dangerous Liaisons* with Glenn Close and John Malkovich.

TOUR *about 1hr 30min*

★**Château** ⊘ – When the construction of Champs was completed by JB Bullet in 1708, his contemporaries were struck by the many changes made in the name of comfort. The rooms no longer communicated, the corridors were improved, each bedroom had its own closet and boudoir and a proper dining room was designed (until then the tables were laid in an antechamber). Mezzanines connecting with the ground floor by means of hidden staircases were built at the end of each wing: they provided accommodation for the guests' domestics.

Ph. Gajic/MICHELIN

Armchair - Salon chinois

On the ground floor, visitors are shown round the great salon, the dining room and the smoking room, with its portrait of Louis XV by a representative of the Van Loo School. The **Salon chinois**★★ is decorated with ornamental chinoiserie panels painted by Huet. The armchairs are upholstered with Beauvais tapestry depicting scenes from the *Fables* of La Fontaine: one of the collections executed after the cartoons of Oudry, director of the National Tapestry Works at Beauvais.

The boudoir is decorated with attractive Chinese pastoral scenes.

On the first floor, the Music Room offers a superb view of the park. Mme De Pompadour's bedroom may be visited – the marquess rented the château in 1757 – and the corner drawing room, embellished by superb rococo **wainscoting**★ and a portrait by Drouais of Mme De Pompadour dressed for gardening.

★★**Park** ⊘ – The park, which was unfortunately partly devastated by violent storms in December 1999, is a masterpiece of French gardening. Originally created by Claude Desgots, one of Le Nôtre's nephews, it was redesigned by Duchêne in the early 20C and features a sweeping perspective with elaborate boxwood patterns, fountains and groves.

Château de CHANTILLY★★★

Access from Paris: *SNCF rail link from Gare du Nord.*

The name Chantilly brings to mind a château, a forest, a racecourse and the world of horse racing in general. Because of its remarkable setting, its park and the treasures in its museum, the Château de Chantilly is considered one of the major sights in France. Chantilly is also rapidly becoming an important cultural centre thanks to the activities of the Centre des Fontaines with its library boasting 600 000 titles (philosophy, art, religion etc).

HISTORICAL NOTES

From Cantilius to the Montmorency – Over the past 2 000 years, five castles have occupied this part of the Nonette Valley. Above the ponds and marshes of the area rose a rocky island where **Cantilius**, a native of Roman Gaul, built the first fortified dwelling. His name and achievement gave birth to Chantilly. In the Middle Ages the building became a fortress belonging to the Bouteiller, named after the hereditary duties he carried out at the court of the Capetians; originally in charge of the royal cellars, the Bouteiller de France was one of the king's close advisers.

In 1386 the land was bought by the chancellor, Mr d'Orgemont, who had the castle rebuilt. The feudal foundations bore the three subsequent constructions. In 1450 the last descendant of the Orgemont married one of the Barons of Montmorency and Chantilly became the property of this illustrious family. It remained in their possession for 200 years.

Constable Anne, Duc de Montmorency – Anne de Montmorency was a devoted servant to a succession of six French kings from Louis XII to Charles IX. This formidable character gained a reputation as warrior, statesman, diplomat and patron of the arts.

Château de Chantilly

For 40 years, apart from a few brief periods, he remained the leading noble of the land, second to the king. Childhood friend and companion-in-arms to François I, close adviser to Henri II, he even had some influence over Catherine de' Medici, who looked favourably upon the man who had advised her on cures for her infertility.

Constable Anne owned 600 fiefs, over 130 castles and estates, four mansions in Paris and numerous posts and offices. He was immensely wealthy. When he went to court he was escorted by 300 guards on horseback. Through his five sons and the husbands of his seven daughters he controlled most of the country's highest positions and had connections with Henri II, as well as with all the other most distinguished French families.

In 1528 the feudal castle of the Orgemont was demolished and the architect Pierre Chambiges replaced it with a palace built in the French Renaissance style. On a nearby island Jean Bullant erected the charming château which still stands today; the Petit Château. It was separated from the Grand Château by a moat – now filled in – which was spanned by two superimposed bridges. An aviary was set up in the tiny garden on the island. Constable Anne ordered great loads of earth and built the terrace which bears his statue.

Plans were made for new gardens and the best artists in town were hired to decorate the two palaces. Chantilly had become one of the most celebrated estates in France and even Emperor Charles V expressed his admiration when he was shown round it.

In 1567 Montmorency, aged 75, engaged in hostilities against the Protestants and perished in the Battle of St-Denis. It was no easy task to kill this energetic soldier: five strokes of the sword cut his face to ribbons, two blows of the bludgeon smashed his head and an arquebus caused his spine to snap. Before collapsing, Constable Anne broke his opponent's jaw with the pommel of his sword.

The last love of Henri IV – Henri IV often stayed at Chantilly, with his companion-in-arms Henri I de Montmorency, the son of Constable Anne. At the age of 54 the king fell in love with his host's ravishing daughter Charlotte, aged only 15. He arranged for her to marry Henri II de Bourbon-Condé, a shy and gauche young man, whom the king hoped would prove an accommodating husband. The day after the wedding, however, Condé left the capital with his wife. Henri IV ordered them to return to Paris.

The young couple fled to Brussels, where they stayed under the protection of the king of Spain. Henri IV raged, implored, threatened and even went as far as to ask the Pope to intervene. Only when Henri was murdered by Ravaillac did the two fugitives return to France.

Henri de Montmorency – Encouraged by Louis XIII's brother, the scheming Gaston d'Orléans,

Henri IV

131

Henri II de Montmorency plotted against Richelieu. He was defeated at Castelnaudary near Toulouse and made a prisoner after receiving 18 wounds, including five by bullets. By way of an apology, he bequeathed to Cardinal Richelieu the two *Slave* statues by Michelangelo, now in the Louvre; those at Chantilly and Écouen are replicas.

The Great Condé – Charlotte de Montmorency and her husband the Prince of Condé the couple persecuted by Henri IV - inherited Chantilly in 1643 and the Château remained family property until 1830. Descendants of Charles de Bourbon, like Henri IV, the Princes of Condé were of royal blood and the heir apparent to the title was called the Duke of Enghien

The Great Condé was the son of Charlotte and Henri II. He applied himself to renovating the Château de Chantilly with the same energy and efficiency he had shown in military operations. In 1662 he commissioned Le Nôtre to redesign the park and the forest. The fountains at Chantilly were considered the most elegant in France and Louis XIV made a point of outclassing them at Versailles. The work lasted 20 years and the result was a splendid achievement, part of which still stands today.

The last of the Condés – The Prince of Condé died at Fontainebleau in 1686, to the king's great dismay. During the religious ceremony preceding the burial, Bossuet delivered a funeral oration which became famous.

The great-grandson of the Great Condé, Louis-Henri de Bourbon, alias "Monsieur le Duc", was an artist with a taste for splendour, who gave Chantilly a new lease of life. He asked Jean Aubert to build the Grandes Écuries, a masterpiece of the 18C, and set up a porcelain factory which closed down in 1870.

The Château d'Enghien was built on the estate by Louis-Joseph de Condé in 1769. His grandson the Duke of Enghien, who had just been born, was its first occupant. The father of the newly born baby was 16, his grandfather 36. The young prince died tragically in 1804; he was seized by the French police in the margravate of Baden and shot outside the fortress of Vincennes on the orders of Bonaparte.

During the French Revolution the main building was razed to the ground though the smaller château was spared. Louis-Joseph was 78 when he returned from exile. His son accompanied him back to Chantilly and the two of them were dismayed: their beloved château was in ruins and the park was in a shambles. They decided to renovate the estate. They bought back the plots of their former land, restored the Petit Château, redesigned and refurbished the grounds. The prince died in 1818 but the duke continued the work. He was an enthusiastic hunter and at the age of 70 he hunted daily. Thanks to his efforts, Chantilly became the lively, fashionable place it had been in the years preceding the Revolution. As in former times, the receptions and hunting parties attracted crowds of elegant visitors. The renovation and restoration work was a source of income for the local population.

The duke was worried by the Revolution of 1830, which raised his cousin Louis-Philippe to the throne, and considered returning to England. A few days later, he was found hanging from a window at his castle in St-Leu. He was the last descendant of the Condé.

The Duke of Aumale – The Duke of Bourbon had left Chantilly to his great-nephew and godson the Duke of Aumale, the fourth son of Louis-Philippe. This prince gained recognition in Africa when he captured Abd el-Kader and his numerous relations. The Revolution of 1848 forced him to go into exile and he returned only in 1870; in 1873 he presided over the court martial which sentenced Marshal Bazaine.

From 1875 to 1881 the duke commissioned Daumet to build the Grand Château in the Renaissance style. This castle, the fifth, still stands today. Back in exile between 1883 and 1889, he died in 1897 and the Institute of France inherited his estate at Chantilly, together with the superb collections that constitute the Condé Museum.

★★★THE CHÂTEAU

Several roads lead to the château. From Chapelle-en-Serval, crossing Chantilly Forest, the château suddenly rises into view from the carrefour des Lions; it appears to be floating on the water in a superb setting of rocks, ponds, lawns and stately trees.

From Paris, take N 16; do not drive through the town but turn right after the lower road and into the shady Route de l'Aigle which skirts the racecourse.

The road from Senlis through Vineuil offers a good view of the château and its park; leaving Vineuil, turn left at each junction.

Try to picture the Château de Chantilly at the time of the Condé when the two main buildings were still divided by an arm of water: the 16C Petit Château (or barbican) and the Grand Château, for which Daumet used the foundations of the former stronghold.

Cross the constable's terrace, which bears the equestrian statue of Anne de Montmorency, and enter the main courtyard through the main gateway (Grille d'Honneur), flanked by the two copies of Michelangelo's *Slaves*.

The Duke of Aumale did not intend to establish a **museum**★★ ⊙ for didactical purposes; he merely wanted to build up a fine art collection. He therefore hung them

Eating out

MID-RANGE

Le Verbois – *60740 St-Maximin* – *3.5km/2.3mi north of Chantilly by N 16* – ☎ *03 44 24 06 22* – *closed 15-30 Jan, 16-31 Aug, Sun evening and Mon* – *150/295F*. On the edge of the forest stands this elegant hunting pavilion built in freestone and overgrown with Virginia creeper. The cosy dining room boasts a lovely fireplace with a carved mantelpiece presenting hunting trophies. Renowned for its game and fish dishes. Large flower-filled garden.

Where to stay

MODERATE

La Calèche – *3 avenue du Maréchal-Joffre, 60500 Chantilly* – ☎ *03 44 57 02 55* – *closed 15 Aug-7 Sept and Mon* – 🅿 – *14 rooms 240F* – ☎ *25F* – *meal 59/130F*. This small, unpretentious hotel in the heart of Chantilly is the perfect address for those with a tight budget. The decently sized rooms offer all the necessary amenities. If you are pressed for time, the brasserie serves simple fare in an informal setting. Friendly welcome.

LUXURY

Château de la Tour – *60270 Gouvieux* – *3.5km/2.3mi west of Chantilly by D 909* – ☎ *03 44 62 38 38* – 🅿 – *41 rooms from 590F* – ☎ *70F* – *restaurant 210/290F*. This 20C mansion, which once belonged to a famous banker, overlooks a vast park that can be admired from the terrace. Depending on your mood, you may choose between the rooms appointed with antique furniture and those designed in a more contemporary style. The extremely elegant dining halls are furnished in the Louis XIII tradition.

Le Relais d'Aumale – *60560 Montgésin* – *5km/3.1mi southeast of Chantilly by D 924a* – ☎ *03 44 54 61 31* – 🅿 – *24 rooms from 680F* – ☎ *60F* – *restaurant 220/240F*. This former hunting lodge lying close to the forest is the ideal resting place for those in search of peace and quiet. The decoration of the bedrooms, varnished wooden furniture with a minimalist touch, was entrusted to a Swedish designer. The dining room streaming with light gives out onto a terrace. Traditional cuisine.

in chronological order of purchase though favourite works were sometimes placed in a separate room. The curators have respected his layout.

According to the terms of the duke's legacy, the Institute must agree "to make no changes to the interior and exterior architecture of the château". Moreover, it is not allowed to lend any of the exhibits.

The reception hall is the starting point for guided tours of the chapel and the various apartments – if a group has already formed, it is best to join it – as well as for unaccompanied tours of the collections. It is advisable to interrupt a visit to the collections if the custodians announce a guided tour of the apartments.

★**Appartements des Princes** ⊘ – Situated in the **Petit Château**, this suite, occupied by the Great Condé and his descendants, was embellished with Regency and Rococo **wainscoting★★**, especially in the 18C thanks to the Duke of Bourbon. It was not occupied by the Duke of Aumale who had taken up residence on the ground floor.

The antechamber and part of the library, the work of the Duke of Aumale, are located on the site of the old moat.

★**Cabinet des Livres** (Library) (**1**) – It contains a splendid collection of manuscripts, including **The Rich Hours of the Duke of Berry** *(Les Très Riches Heures du duc de Berry)* with 15C illuminations by the Limbourg brothers. This extremely fragile document is not permanently exhibited but visitors may see a facsimile by Faksimile Verlag of Luzern.

Another interesting reproduction is the psalter of Queen Ingeburge of Denmark. Among the ornamental motifs feature the monogram of the Duke of Aumale (H O for Henri d'Orléans) and the Condé coat of arms (France's "broken" coat of arms with a diagonal line symbolising the younger branch of the family).

Chambre de Monsieur le Prince (**2**) – This title referred to the reigning Condé Prince, in this case the Duke of Bourbon (1692-1740), who had a wainscot installed at the far end of the room, into which were embedded panels painted by C Huet in 1735. The famous Louis XVI commode was designed by Riesener and made by Hervieu.

Salon des Singes (**3**) – A collection of monkey scenes *(singeries)* dating from the early 18C is a masterpiece by an anonymous draughtsman; note the fire screen depicting the monkeys' reading lesson.

Galerie de Monsieur le Prince (**4**) – The Great Condé had ordered his own battle gallery, which he never saw completed (1692). The sequence was interrupted from 1652

Chantilly – Cabinet des Livres

to 1659 during his years of rebellion. A painting conceived by the hero's son portrays him stopping a Fame from publishing a list of his treacherous deeds and asking another Fame to issue a formal apology.

Chapelle – An **altar★** attributed to Jean Goujon and 16C wainscot and stained-glass windows from the chapel at Écouen were brought here by the Duke of Aumale. The apse contains the **mausoleum** of Henri II de Condé *(see above)* (bronze statues by J Sarrazin taken from the Jesuit Church of St-Paul-St-Louis in Paris) and the stone urn which received the hearts of the Condé princes. Up to the Revolution, the Condé necropolis was at Vallery in Burgundy, where another sepulchral monument celebrating Henri II still stands.

★★The collections (Grand Château) – Cross the **Galerie des Cerfs** (**A**) with its hunting theme; note the 17C Gobelins tapestries.

Galerie de Peinture (**B**) – The variety of paintings here reflects the eclectic tastes of the Duke of Aumale. Military events are illustrated on huge canvases (*Battle on the Railway Line* by Neuville, Meissonnier's *The Cuirassiers of 1805*). Orientalism is well represented with Gros' work, *The Plague Victims of Jaffa*, H Vernet's *Arab Sheikhs holding Council*, and *The Falcon Hunt* by Fromentin. Note, too, the famous portrait of *Gabrielle d'Estrées in her Bath* (16C French school), the portraits of Cardinals Richelieu and Mazarin by Philippe de Champaigne, and *The Massacre of the Holy Innocents* by Poussin.

Rotonde (**C**) – The *Loreto Madonna* by **Raphael**, **Piero di Cosimo**'s portrait of the ravishing Simonetta Vespucci, who is believed to have been Botticelli's model for his *Birth of Venus*, and Chapu's kneeling statue of Joan of Arc listening to voices are exhibited here.

Salle de la Smalah et Rotonde de la Minerve (**D**) – Family portraits of the Orléans (17C, 18C and 19C) and of Louis-Philippe's relations in particular: Bonnat's picture of the Duke of Aumale at the age of 68.

Cabinet de Giotto (**E**) – A room devoted to Italian Primitives: *Angels Dancing in the Sun* (Italian School, 15C).

Salle Isabelle (**F**) – Numerous 19C paintings including *Moroccan Guards* by Delacroix, *Horse Leaving the Stables* by Géricault, and *Françoise de Rimini* by Ingres.

Salle d'Orléans (**G**) – The glass cabinets contain **soft-paste Chantilly porcelain** manufactured in the workshops founded in 1725 by the Duke de Bourbon (armorial service bearing the Condé coat of arms or the Duke of Orléans' monogram).

Salle Caroline (**H**) – 18C painting has pride of place here, with portraits by Largillière and Greuze, *Young Woman Playing with Children* by Van Loo, *The Worried Lover* and *The Serenade Player* by Watteau, or *Snowstorm by* Everdingen.

Cabinet des Clouet (**K**) – A precious collection of small and extremely rare **paintings**★★ executed by the **Clouets**, Corneille de Lyon etc portraying François I, Marguerite of Navarre (stroking a little dog) and Henri II as a child etc.

Galerie de Psyché (**L**) – The 44 **stained-glass windows** (16C) that tell the story of the loves of Psyche and Cupid came from Constable Anne's other family home, Château d'Écouen.

★★★**Santuario** (**N**) – It houses the museum's most precious exhibits: Raphael's *Orléans Madonna*, named after the noble family, *The Three Ages of Womanhood*, also known as *The Three Graces*, by the same artist; *Esther and Ahasuerus*, the panel of a wedding chest painted by Filippino Lippi and 40 miniature works by Jean Fouquet, cut out of Estienne Chevalier's book of hours, a splendid example of French 15C art.

Cabinet des Gemmes (**P**) – It contains jewels of stunning beauty. The Pink Diamond, alias the Great Condé (a copy of which is permanently on show), was stolen in 1926 and subsequently found in an apple where the thieves had hidden it. The room also boasts an outstanding collection of enamels and miniatures.

Tribune (**R**) – Above the cornice of this polygonal room are painted panels representing episodes from the life of the Duke of Aumale and the house of Orléans. The paintings include *Autumn* by **Botticelli**, *Love Disarmed* and *Pastoral Pleasures* by **Watteau**, a portrait of Molière by **Mignard**, and on the "Ecouen Wall", three superb works by **Ingres**: a self-portrait, *Madame Devaucay* and *Venus*.

★**Petits Appartements** ○ – *Access by the stairway off the reception hall.* The Duke of Aumale had these private apartments designed and decorated by painter Eugène Lami specially for his marriage in 1844.

★★ PARK ○ *about 1hr*

Follow the route indicated on the plan and walk past the pond (Étang de Sylvie).

Jardin anglais ○ – The landscaped English-style garden was laid out on the surviving relics of Le Nôtre's park in 1820. Its charm derives from the pleasant groves (plane trees, swamp cypresses, weeping willows) rather than from the symbolic monuments: remains of a Temple of Venus and of Love (Île d'Amour).

Maison de Sylvie – *Private.* This is a small garden pavilion where Marie-Félicie enjoyed meeting her close friends.

Chapelle St-Jean – The chapel was erected on the estate by Constable Anne in 1538, with six other chapels, in memory of the seven churches of Rome he had visited in order to gain the indulgences granted to those who undertook this pilgrimage. He obtained from the Pope the same privileges for the chapels at Chantilly. Two other chapels still stand on the estate: St Paul's, located behind the Château d'Enghien, and Ste-Croix, on the lawns of the racecourse.

Take allée Blanche along the banks of the Canal des Morfondus.

MUSEUM
GROUND FLOOR
0   20 m

La Chute – These tiered waterfalls mark the start of the Grand Canal.
Return along allée Blanche; cross the Canal des Morfondus at the footbridge.

Le Hameau – Dating from 1775, it was built before the more famous Trianon at Versailles *(see p 395)*. Under the influence of Jean-Jacques Rousseau, French princes used to seek new horizons by creating miniature villages.
The mill and a few half-timbered buildings may be seen. These used to accommodate a kitchen, a dining room and a billiard room. The barn provided a drawing room that was restored by the Duke of Aumale. All the big parties included supper in this charming spot in the park.
Skirt the brook by the small village.

Les Hydrophiles – Electric boats glide along the Grand Canal, offering unusual vistas of the castle and the park.

Parterres – The parterres are framed by two avenues of young lime trees, called "The Philosophers' Path" because the great writers who visited Chantilly used to pace up and down the shaded avenue, exchanging their views and ideas.
Le Nôtre diverted the course of the River Nonette to make the Grand Canal and La Manche.
The circular Vertugadin lawns lie along the line of La Manche, flanked by delightful stretches of water. Between La Manche and the round basin (Bassin de la Gerbe) stands Coysevox's statue of the Great Condé, framed by the effigies of La Bruyère and Bossuet (statues of Molière and Le Nôtre, seated, may be seen in the near distance). A monumental stairway (Grand Degré) leads from the parterres up to the terrace; on either side of these imposing steps are grottoes, their carved decoration representing rivers.

THE HORSES' KINGDOM

The first races – The first official race meeting was held in Chantilly on 15 May 1834 at the instigation of the members of the Société d'Encouragement, an association founded in 1833. The patronage of both the Duke of Orléans and the Duke of Nemours, and the fashionable trends introduced by the Jockey Club dandies, appreciative of the soft grassy track, combined to make these races a major social event (*Prix du Jockey-Club* in 1836, *Prix de Diane* in 1843); before the opening of Longchamp in 1857, Parisian races used to be run on the hard ground of the Champ-de-Mars. The hunting parties, concerts, firework displays and aquatic entertainments at Chantilly delighted racegoers and socialites.

THE PARK

VINEUIL

Hameau
★Aérophile
la Chute
Morfondus
Blanche ★St-Jean
du
Pont
du
Roi
Parc de Sylvie
GR 11

SENLIS

By the end of the 19C the races had attracted huge crowds of visitors and the Northern France Railways set up a transport system whose efficiency has never been matched. In 1908 it became necessary to introduce 40 to 50 special trains composed of 16 carriages. A group of trains taking passengers back to Paris (leaving every 3min) were even permitted to run on the wrong side of the track between Chantilly and St-Denis, a rare breach of regulations indeed.

The riding capital – With a total of over 3 000 horses trained on the tracks in and around Chantilly, the Condés' town may be considered the capital of French thoroughbreds.

Jobs for 1 000 stable lads and a number of related occupations employ 10 % of the farming population of the Oise *département*. Each stable lad rides three horses every morning.

The racecourses – *Private*. One hundred trainers attend to their respective charges from sunrise to noon, either on the sandy or grassy tracks of the four courses, or along the sand-covered paths of the forest (in particular the "Route du Connétable" also known as the "Piste des Lions"). Numerous race meetings take place during the racing season in June *(see Calendar of events)*.

★★**Grandes écures (stables)** – Jean Aubert's masterpiece constitutes the most stunning piece of 18C architecture in Chantilly. The St-Denis Gateway - built astride the road leading to town - marks the site of an uncompleted pavilion. The most attractive façade of the stables overlooks the racecourse.

At the time of the Condé, this architectural complex housed a total of 240 horses, 500 dogs and around 100 employees (grooms, drivers, whips etc).

★★**Musée Vivant du Cheval et du Poney** ⊘ – This museum is brought to life by the 28 saddle and draught animals – 18 horses and 10 ponies – bred in France or in the Iberian peninsula which occupy the stalls and boxes built in the days of the Duke of Aumale.

In the central rotunda, 28m/92ft high, admire the water playing in the **fountain**, the basin of which was once used as a trough.

The exhibition in the east gallery focuses, through paintings and models, on the harness, the rider's costume and the general atmosphere of the competition in 30 equestrian events throughout the world.

Thirty-one rooms set up in the former sheds present the art of horse riding and a number of related professions: the blacksmith's trade, a veterinary's operating theatre etc. The last room illustrates France's betting system, the "PMU".

The tour ends with a demonstration of **dressage★** *(about 30min)*. The excellent acoustics, the rider's smart costume and the comments on the various exercises make it a delightful experience. Equestrian entertainments on the theme "Riding and the Arts" take place in the kennels' quarry at night.

J. Guillard/SCOPE

Musée Vivant du Cheval et du Poney

137

FORÊT DE CHANTILLY

The vast wooded area covers about 6 300ha/15 500 acres and has been reshaped by hunting enthusiasts over 500 years. Tree species which are sparse in some places because of the poor soil and abundance of game include oaks, hornbeams, lime trees and Scots pines in copses and groves, with additions of oak and beech seedlings since 1973.

The network of paths through the forest is suitable for country walks, and the light soil favours riding activities; training sessions take place at carrefour du Petit Couvert every morning. The forests of Coye, Orry and Pontarmé are reserved for walkers.

7.5km/4.5mi round tour – about 30min – not advisable at weekends. Leave Coye-la-Forêt northwards along route des Étangs, which follows the River Thève.

The road reaches the first of the Commelles ponds, Étang de la Loge, next to the Château de la Reine Blanche.

Château de la Reine Blanche – In 1825 this old mill was restored in the troubadour style by the last of the Condés, the Duke of Bourbon, who used it as a hunting pavilion.

It stands on the site of a legendary château believed to have been built by Queen Blanche of Navarre, wife of Philippe VI of Valois, after her husband's death around 1350. Part of the lodge is now occupied by a pancake house.

An avenue of age-old beeches completes this delightful **site**★.

Étangs de Commelles – They were used as fishponds by the monks from Chaalis Abbey. The road provides access to the car parks and to the causeways that crisscross the water, which makes it possible to explore the area around the ponds on foot.

Turn right, cross the third causeway and follow the forest road from La Fosse to Rohan, known as "rocade sud" (south ring road).

About 1km/0.6mi further on, there is a clearing on the right which is used as a leisure area.

The road rejoins the Thève Valley downstream from the Château de la Reine Blanche. Return to Coye.

CHARTRES★★★

Population 39 595
Michelin map 106 folds 37, 38 or 237 folds 26, 27

Access from Paris: *SNCF rail link from Paris Gare Montparnasse.*

Chartres is the capital of Beauce, France's famous corn belt, but for tourists the town is known mainly for the Cathedral of Our Lady, a magnificent edifice now on UNESCO's World Heritage list, which reigns supreme over a picturesque setting of monuments and old streets.

HISTORICAL NOTES

A town with a destiny – Since ancient times Chartres has always had a strong influence over religious matters. It is believed that a Gallo-Roman well, located on the Chartres plateau, was the object of a pagan cult and that in the 4C this was transformed into a Christian cult by the first evangelists. Adventius, the first known bishop of Chartres, lived during the middle of the 4C. A document from the 7C mentions a bishop Béthaire kneeling in front of Notre-Dame, which points to the existence of a Marian cult.

In 876 the chemise said to belong to the Virgin Mary was given to the cathedral by Charles the Bald, confirming that Chartres was already a place of pilgrimage. Up to the 14C the town of Chartres continued to flourish. Three representations of the Virgin are the subject of a special cult which has survived through the ages: Notre-Dame-de-Sous-Terre, Notre-Dame-du-Pilier and Notre-Dame-de-la-Belle-Verrière, but the cathedral features altogether 175 different illustrations portraying Mary.

Note that neither the cathedral nor the crypt contains any tombs; Chartres is a temple devoted exclusively to the Virgin, who remains protected from corruption.

The Pilgrimage – Chartres Cathedral was consecrated to the Assumption of the Virgin Mary in 1260; in the Middle Ages it attracted huge crowds of pilgrims.

In 1912 and 1913 the writer and poet **Charles Péguy** made the pilgrimage to Chartres. The strong influence it had on his work inspired a small group of enthusiasts after the First World War to follow suit and led later, in 1935, to the establishment of the "Students' Pilgrimage" *(see Calendar of events).*

Cathedral , Chartres

B. Kaufmann/MICHELIN

An exceptional man – In the **Église St-Jean-Baptiste** in the Rechèvres district to the north of the town lies the body of the abbot **Franz Stock**, whose tomb is still a place of pilgrimage.

This German priest, chaplain to the prisons of Paris from 1940 to 1944, refused to retreat with the Wehrmacht and was taken prisoner. At the Morancez prison camp near Chartres he founded a seminary for the prisoners of war and was the Superior there for two years. He died in February 1948 at the age of 43.

A bird's-eye view – For a view of the cathedral rising up above the Eure Valley, stand behind the Monument aux Aviateurs Militaires, a memorial to the French Air Force high above the east bank of the river. The **view★** is impressive. A few typical gable ends are visible in the old town and the roofs of two churches, St-Aignan and St-Pierre, can also be seen.

★★★CATHEDRAL ⊘ 1hr 30min

The 4 000 carved figures and the 5 000 characters portrayed by the stained-glass windows demanded a lifelong commitment from the specialists who studied them. The most famous expert is probably Étienne Houvet, a custodian who died in 1949; he photographed the building in minute detail and built up a supremely interesting collection.

A neat, swift construction – The building rests upon the Romanesque cathedral erected by Bishop Fulbert in the 11C and 12C: there remain the crypt, the towers and the foundations of the west front, including the Royal Doorway, and fragments of the Notre-Dame-de-la-Belle-Verrière stained-glass window. The remaining sections of the cathedral were built in the wake of the Great Fire of 1194; princes and dignitaries contributed generously to the work, while the poor offered their labour.

These efforts made it possible to complete the cathedral in 25 years, and to add on the north and south porches 20 years later, with the result that the architecture and decoration of Notre-Dame form a harmonious composition almost unparalleled in the history of Gothic art. By some miracle, the Wars of Religion, the French Revolution and the two World Wars spared the famous basilica, which Rodin referred to as "the Acropolis of France" on account of its aesthetic and spiritual value. Only the cathedral's "forest" – the superb roof timbers – were destroyed by flames in 1836, and subsequently replaced by a metal framework. Beneath the cathedral close, where it is planned to build an international medieval centre, archeological excavations covering an area of some 1 200m²/12 912sq ft are currently in progress. The remains of two 13C houses have been uncovered.

Exterior

West front – The two tall spires and the Royal Doorway form one of the most perfect compositions encountered in French religious art. The New Bell-Tower on the left was in fact built first; the lower part dates back to 1134. Its present name dates from the 16C, when Jehan de Beauce erected a stone spire (115m/377ft

Chartres — The Royal Doorway

high) to replace the wooden steeple which had burned down in 1506. The Old Bell-Tower (c 1145-64), rising 106m/384ft, is a masterpiece of Romanesque art, forming a stark contrast to the ornate Gothic construction. The Royal Doorway and the three large windows above date from the 12C. Everything above this ensemble was built at a later date: the rose-window (13C), the 14C gable and the king's gallery featuring the kings of Judah, the ancestors of the Virgin Mary. On the gable, the Virgin Mary is depicted presenting her son to the Beauce area.

The **Royal Doorway★★★** (Portail Royal), a splendid example of Late Romanesque architecture (1145-70), represents the life and triumph of the Saviour. The Christ in Majesty on the central tympanum and the statue-columns are famous throughout the world. The elongated features of the biblical kings and queens, prophets, priests and patriarchs study the visitors from the embrasures. While the faces are animated, the bodies remain rigid, in deliberate contrast to the figures adorning the arches and the capitals. The statues were primarily designed to be columns, not human beings

North porch and doorway – Leave the west front on your left and walk round the cathedral, stepping back to get a clear view of its lines. The nave is extremely high and unusually wide. The problem of how to support it was brilliantly resolved with the construction of three-tiered flying buttresses; the lower two arcs were joined together by colonnettes. The elegant Pavillon de l'Horloge near the New Bell-Tower is the work of Jehan de Beauce (1520).

The ornamentation of the north porch is similar to that of the doorway, executed at an earlier date. The characters - treated more freely than those on the Royal Doorway – are elegant and extremely lively, illustrating a new, more realistic approach to religious art. The statue of St Modesta, a local martyr who is pictured gazing up at the New Bell-Tower, is extremely graceful.

Once again, the decoration of the three doors refers to the Old Testament. The right door pays tribute to the biblical heroes who exercised the virtues recommended in the teachings of Christ. The central panel shows the Virgin Mary and the Prophets who foretold the coming of the Messiah. The door on the left presents the Annunciation, Visitation and Nativity, together with the Vices and Virtues. In the bishopric's garden, the raised terrace commands a view of the town below lying on the banks of the lower River Eure. Before reaching the garden gate, look left and note the archway straddling a narrow street. It used to open in the walls of the Notre-Dame cloister.

East end – The complexity of the double-course flying buttresses - reinforced here with an intermediate pier as they cross over the chapels - and the succession of radiating chapels, chancel and arms of the transept are stunning. The 14C St Piat Chapel, originally separate, was joined to Notre-Dame by a stately staircase.

South porch and doorway – Here, the upper stonework is concealed by a constellation of colonnettes. The perspective of these planes, stretching from the arches of the porch to the gables, confers to this arm of the transept a sense of unity that is lacking in the north transept.

The theme is the Church of Christ and the Last Judgment. In the Middle Ages, these scenes would usually be reserved for the west portal but in this case the Royal Doorway already featured ornamentation. Consequently, the scenes portraying the Coming of a New World, prepared by the martyrs, were destined for the left-door embrasures, while those of the Confessors (witnesses of Christ who have not yet been made martyrs) adorn the right door.

Christ reigns supreme on the central tympanum. He is also present on the pier, framed by the double row of the 12 Apostles with their lean, ascetic faces, draped in long, gently folded robes.

Among the martyrs, note the statues standing in the foreground: St George and St Theodore, both admirable 13C representations of knights in armour. These figures are quite separate from the columns - the feet are flat and no longer slanted - and are there for purely decorative purposes.

The most delightful feature of the sculpted porch is the display of medallions, grouped in sets of six and placed on the recessed arches of the three doorways: the lives of the martyrs, the Vices and Virtues etc.

Returning to the west front, note the Old Bell-Tower and its ironical statue of a donkey playing the fiddle, symbolising man's desire to share in celestial music. At the corner of the building, stop to admire the tall figure of the sundial Angel.

★ **Access to the New Bell-Tower** ⊙ – The tour *(195 steps)* leads round the north side and up to the lower platform of the New Bell-Tower. Seen from a height of 70m/230ft, the buttresses, flying buttresses, statues, gargoyles and Old Bell-Tower are most impressive. It is still possible to recognise the former Notre-Dame Cloister thanks to the old pointed roof. Enclosed by a wall right up to the 19C, this area was frequented by clerics - especially canons.

Interior

Enter the cathedral by the north doorway. The nave (16m/52ft) is wider than any other in France (Notre-Dame in Paris 40ft, Notre-Dame in Amiens 46ft), though it has single aisles. The vaulting reaches a height of 37m/121ft and the interior is 130m/427ft long. This nave is 13C, built in the style known as early or lancet Gothic. there is no gallery; instead, there is a blind triforium *(illustration, see Introduction: Religious Architecture).*

In a place of pilgrimage of this importance, the chancel and the transept had to accommodate large-scale ceremonies; they were therefore wider than the nave. In Chartres, the chancel, its double ambulatory and the transept form an ensemble 64m/210ft wide between the north and south doorways.

Note the gentle slope of the floor, rising slightly towards the chancel; this made it easier to wash down the church when the pilgrims had stayed overnight.

The striking state of semi-darkness in the nave creates an element of mystery which was not intentional: it is due to the gradual dimming of the stained glass over the centuries.

★★★ **Stained-glass windows** – The 12C and 13C stained-glass windows of Notre-Dame constitute, together with those of Bourges, the largest collection in France. The Virgin and Child and the Annunciation and Visitation scenes in the clerestory at the far end of the chancel produce a striking impression.

West front - These three 12C windows used to throw light on Fulbert's Romanesque cathedral and the dark, low nave that stood behind, which explains why they are so long.

The scenes *(bottom to top)* illustrate the fulfilment of the prophecies: *(right)* the Tree of Jesse, *(centre)* the childhood and life of Our Lord (Incarnation cycle) and *(left)* Passion and Resurrection (Redemption cycle).

Visitors may feast their eyes on the famous 12C "Chartres blue", with its clear, deep tones which are enhanced by reddish tinges, especially radiant in the rays of the setting sun. For many years, people believed that this particular shade

Chartres Cathedral — Central window of the west front: Detail of the Redemption cycle

H. Champollion/MICHELIN

of blue was a long-lost trade secret. Modern laboratories have now established that the sodium compounds and silica in the glass made it more resistant to dirt and corrosion than the panes made with other materials and in other times. The large 13C rose-window on the west front depicts the Last Judgement.

Transept – This ensemble consists of two 13C rose-windows, to which were added a number of lancet windows featuring tall figures. The themes are the same as those on the corresponding carved doorway: Old Testament (north), the End of the World (south).

The north rose (rose de France) was a present from Blanche of Castille, mother of St Louis and Regent of France, and portrays a Virgin and Child. It is characterised by the fleur-de-lis motif on the shield under the central lancet and by the alternating Castile towers and fleurs-de-lis pictured on the small corner lancets. The larger lancets depict St Anne holding the infant Virgin Mary, framed by four kings or high priests: Melchizedek and David stand on the left, Solomon and Aaron on the right.

The centre roundel of the south rose shows the risen Christ, surrounded by the Old Men of the Apocalypse, forming two rings of 12 medallions. The yellow and blue chequered quatrefoils represent the coat of arms of the benefactors, the Comte de Dreux Pierre Mauclerc and his wife, who are also featured at the bottom of the lancets.

The lancets on either side of the Virgin and Child depict four striking figures – the Great Prophets Isaiah, Jeremiah, Ezekiel and Daniel – with the four Evangelists seated on their shoulders.

The morality of the scene is simple: although they are weak and lacking dignity, the Evangelists can see further than the giants of the Old Testament thanks to the Holy Spirit.

★ **Notre-Dame-de-la-Belle-Verrière** (**1**) – *Illustration, see Introduction: Stained Glass.* This is a very famous stained-glass window. The Virgin and Child, a fragment of the window spared by the fire of 1194, has been mounted in 13C stained glass. Admire the superb range of blues.

Other stained-glass windows – The aisles of the nave and the chapels around the ambulatory are lit by a number of celebrated stained-glass windows from the 13C verging on the sombre side. On the east side, the arms of the transept have received two works of recent making, in perfect harmony with the early fenestration: St Fulbert's window (south crossing (**2**), donated by the American Association of Architects (from the François Lorin workshop - 1954), and the window of Peace (north crossing (**3**), a present from a group of German admirers (1971).

The Vendôme Chapel (**4**) features a particularly radiant 15C stained-glass window. It illustrates the development of this art, which eventually led to the lighter panes of the 17C and 18C.

★★ **Parclose** – The screen was started by Jehan de Beauce in 1514 and finished in the 18C. This fine work consists of 41 sculpted compositions depicting the lives of Christ and the Virgin Mary. These Renaissance medallions, evoking biblical history, local history and mythology, contrast sharply with the Gothic statues of the doorways.

Chancel – The marble facing, the Assumption group above the high altar and the low-relief carvings separating the columns were added in the 18C.

Organ (**5**) – The case dates from the 16C.

Vierge du Pilier (**6**) – This wooden statue (c 1510) stood against the rood screen, now sadly disappeared. The richly clothed Virgin is the object of a procession celebrated annually *(see Calendar of events)*.

Treasury ⊘ – Chapelle St-Piat has been built to house the cathedral treasury. It is linked to the east end of the cathedral by a Renaissance staircase. Inside are some superb items of church plate.

Chapelle des Martyrs – This chapel has been refurbished and now contains the **Virgin Mary's Veil**, laid out in a beautiful glass-fronted reliquary. Pilgrims used to pray to this veil, calling it a tunic or "Holy Chemise".

★ **Crypt** ⊘ – *Entrance outside the cathedral, on the south side (see plan above).* This is France's longest crypt (220m/722ft long). It dates largely from the 11C and features Romanesque groined vaulting. It is a curious shape: the two long galleries joined by the ambulatory pass under the chancel and the aisles and give onto seven chapels. The central area, which has been filled in, remains unexplored. Of the seven radiating chapels, only three are Romanesque. The other four were added by the master architect of the Gothic cathedral to serve as foundations for the chancel and the apse of the future building.

St Martin's Chapel (**7**), by the south gallery, houses the originals of the statues on the Royal Doorway: the sundial Angel etc.

A staircase, starting from the ambulatory, leads down to a lower crypt.

Gallo-Roman | **11C-12C**
9C | **13C**

Chapelle St-Piat-14C (Treasury)
Chapelle des Martyrs
Ambulatory
Sacristy
CHANCEL
Parclose ★★
Crypt
North Doorway
North arm of transept TRANSEPT South arm of transept
South Doorway
Access to Clocher Neuf
NAVE
Pavillon de l'Horloge 16C
Clocher Neuf
Clocher Vieux
Portail Royal ★★★

CATHEDRALE

8
9
10
11
7
Hearting

CRYPT

Crypte St-Lubin (**8**) – This crypt served as the foundations of the 9C church. A thick, circular column with a visible base backs onto a Gallo-Roman wall (**9**), its bond easily recognisable by the alternating bricks and mortar. The crypt was a safe place that protected the cathedral treasures in times of social unrest or natural disaster. Thus, the chemise of the Virgin survived the Great Fire of 1194.

Puits des Saints-Forts (**10**) – The lower part of this 33m/108ft deep shaft has a square section characteristic of Gallo-Roman wells. The coping is contemporary. The name dates back to 858; it is believed that several Christian martyrs from Chartres were murdered during a Norman attack, and their bodies thrown down the well.

Chapelle Notre-Dame-de-Sous-Terre (**11**) – A sacred retreat where pilgrims indulge in fervent praying. Since the 17C the chapel, together with the north gallery of the crypt, has played the part of a miniature church. It originally consisted of a small alcove where the faithful came to venerate the Virgin. The interior of the chapel and its decoration were refurbished in 1976. On this occasion, the 19C statue of the Virgin was replaced by a more hieratic figure, based on the Romanesque model, enhanced by a Gobelins tapestry.

ADDITIONAL SIGHTS

★**Old Town (Quartier St-André and banks of the Eure)** – *Follow the route indicated on the plan below.* This pleasant walk leads past the picturesque hilly site, the banks of the River Eure, an ancient district recently restored and the cathedral which is visible from every street corner. In the summer season, a small **tourist train** ⊙ tours the old town.

Église St-André ⊙ – This Romanesque church *(deconsecrated)* was the place of worship of one of the most active and densely populated districts in town. Most of the trades were closely related to the river: millers, dyers, curriers, cobblers, tanners, drapers, fullers, tawers, serge makers etc. The church was enlarged in the 13C, and in the 16C and 17C it received a chancel and an axial chapel resting on arches that straddled the River Eure and rue du Massacre. Unfortunately, both these structures disappeared in 1827 leaving a much less picturesque church.

Cross the Eure by a metal footbridge; there is a good **view**★ of the old humpback bridges. At the foot of the shortened nave of St Andrew's lie the remains of the arch that once supported the chancel. Wander upstream; the wash-houses and races of former mills have been prettily restored. Rue aux Juifs leads through an ancient district which has recently been renovated, featuring cobbled streets bordered by gable-ended houses and old-fashioned street lamps.

Eating out

MODERATE

Dix de Pythagore – *2 rue de la Porte-Cendreuse* – ☎ *02 37 36 02 38* – *closed 15 July-1 Aug, Mon and Tues - 92/300F*. A small, local establishment where you can interrupt your tour of the old city to have a quick meal. The dining room has been set up in a cellar. Family cooking in the regional tradition. Good value for money.

MID-RANGE

Le Café Serpente – *2 rue du Cloître-Notre-Dame* – ☎ *02 37 21 68 81* – *booking essential in winter* – *130/190F*. A bicycle hanging from the ceiling, posters adorning the walls and enamel plaques laid out all along the staircase: such is the decor of this charming, old-fashioned café opposite the cathedral. The food too is worthy of note: scrumptious salads, tasty daily specials and good country cooking available round the clock. An address to remember.

Moulin de Ponceau – *21 rue Tannerie* – ☎ *02 37 35 30 05* – *closed Sat lunchtime and Sun evening* – *145/250F*. This former mill off the banks of the River Eure is situated near the cathedral. The terrace-veranda affords lovely views of old Chartres and the ducks gliding along the river. The rooms feature pretty half-timbering and the meals are made with fresh regional produce.

Where to stay

MODERATE

Chambre d'Hôte La Ferme du Château – *In Léveville, 28300 Bailleau-l'Évêque* – *8km/5mi north of Chartres by N 154 then D 134* – ☎ *02 37 22 97 02* – ✍ – *3 rooms 250/350F* – *meal 100F*. This stately Beauce farmhouse located next to a small château offers pretty, comfortable and tastefully decorated rooms. Moreover, it is blissfully quiet and the friendly, elegant owners are a paragon of discretion!

MID-RANGE

Ibis Centre – *14 place Drouaise* – ☎ *02 37 36 06 36* – ▣ – *79 rooms 330/360F* – ⊆ *35F - restaurant 95F*. Built on the edge of the old city in accordance with regional tradition, this Ibis hotel lies close to the River Eure. The functional rooms have been renovated in a contemporary spirit. The dining hall with its terrace is especially popular during the summer season.

Le Grand Monarque – *22 place des Épars* – ☎ *02 37 21 00 72* – ▣ – *48 rooms 485/740F* – ⊆ *60F – restaurant 170/295F*. A 16C post house in the heart of the city. Comfortable, personalised rooms ranging from simple to extravagant with flowery fabric and four-poster beds. The dining hall features sturdy traditional furniture, wainscoting and a collection of paintings.

On the town

Brûlerie Les Rois Mages – *6 rue des Changes* – ☎ *02 37 36 50 52* – *Tues-Sat 9.15am-12.15pm, 1.30-7.30pm*. This quaint coffee-roasting shop with an old-fashioned touch, featuring brasserie-style tables and chairs, has an adjoining tea room. Sit down to enjoy a cup made with freshly roasted Moka Sidamo coffee beans or try one of the several dozen varieties of tea. Takeaway service available.

Rue des Écuyers – This is one of the most successful restoration schemes of the old town. At nos 17 and 19 the houses have 17C doorways with rusticated surrounds, surmounted by a bull's-eye window. Stroll along the street to rue aux Cois. The corner building is a delightful half-timbered villa, with an overhang in the shape of a prow. Opposite stands Queen Bertha's stair turret, a 16C structure, also half-timbered.

Central district

Place du Cygne – The street has been widened into a little square planted with trees and shrubs *(flower market on Tuesdays, Thursdays and Saturdays)* and is at present an oasis of calm in this lively shopping district in the town centre.

At the end of rue du Cygne, on place Marceau, a monument celebrates the memory of the young local general who died at Altenkirchen (1796) at the age of 27. His ashes have been shared among Chartres (funeral urn under the statue on place des Épars), the Panthéon and the Dome Church of the Invalides in Paris.

La Bodega – *20-22 place des Halles* – ☎ *02 37 36 90 07* – *Patrick-Pallion@ wanadoo.fr* – *Mon-Fri noon-1pm, Sat 3pm-2am*. The prude city of Chartres has now opened up to the steamy strains of Cuban music, as is clearly evidenced by this bar, where everything evokes the native island of Compay Secundo: the soundtrack, the setting and the tequila-based cocktails... Because of the many events organised at weekends (live concerts, karaoke evenings, dances etc), it has become one of the town's trendiest meeting places.

Shopping

Charcuterie des Épars – *6 rue Delacroix* – ☎ *02 37 21 03 05* – *Tues-Sat 8am-1pm, 3-7.30pm, Sun 9.30am-1pm – closed 3 weeks in July*. Master *charcutier* Michel Darreau offers his famous home-made speciality, *pâté de Chartres* (as a pie or a *terrine*). It was first made back in 1763, when a certain Philippe, master baker in Chartres, spent time perfecting the recipe. Originally, the pâté was made with the flesh of the *guignard*, a small migratory wader whose species has since died out. Today, pork butchers use duck or partridge instead.

Galerie de Chartres – *1 bis place du Général-de-Gaulle* – ☎ *02 37 84 04 33*. Auction sales are advertised in the two official publications La Gazette de l'Hôtel Drouot and Le Moniteur des Ventes. Set up in the former 16C Église Sainte-Foy, this auction house organises sales intended for an international clientele every weekend (ceramics, weapons, stamps, silverware, collectors' cameras and photographs). The gallery is among the few that specialise in toys and dolls for collectors.

La Galerie du Vitrail – *17 Cloître Notre-Dame* – ☎ *02 37 36 10 03* – *www.galerie-du-vitrail.com* – *15 Apr-31 Oct, Tues-Sat 9.45am-7pm, Sun and public holidays 10.30am-7pm; early Nov to mid-Apr, Tues-Sat 10.30am-1pm, 2-6.30pm*. This gallery pays tribute to the art of stained glass and its many forms. Visit the exhibition rooms displaying both early and recent stained-glass windows and the shop, where this technique has been applied to household items such as lamps, mirrors and mobiles. The owner Madame Loire is the only antique dealer in France who is an authority on stained glass. There is also a specialised bookstore.

Vegetable and poultry market – *Place Billard – Sat morning*. Every week a covered market houses a great many stalls groaning with fresh produce from the Beauce region. This lively, colourful market exuding delicious smells is one of the most popular in the area.

Migeon – *2 bis rue du Soleil d'Or* – ☎ *02 37 21 41 14* – *Tues-Fri 8.30am-12.30pm, 2.30-7.30pm, Sat 8am-1pm, 2-7.30pm, Sun 8.30am-1pm, 2.30-6pm*. This shop, specialised in the making of pastries, chocolate and ice cream, is renowned for its home-made local speciality: the *mentchikoff*, a praline sweet coated with meringue originally made in 1895 to celebrate the Franco-Russian alliance.

Atelier Loire – *16 rue d'Ouarville, 28300 Léves* – *in the Chartres area, driving north towards Dreux, 2km/1.2mi from the cathedral* – ☎ *02 37 21 20 71* – *Mon-Fri, free guided tours Fri at 2..30pm – closed Aug and public holidays*. A stately manor house dating from the early 20C, nestled in a pretty park embellished with stained-glass exhibits, is the setting for this workshop founded in 1946 by Gabriel Loire and currently run by his grandson. The art of stained glass and its different techniques are explained to visitors step by step, starting with the drawing up of plans by the artist, namely Adami, Miro or Fernand Léger, and ending with the execution of the piece by master glassworkers. The visit to the Atelier Loire is truly a magic experience enhanced by a kaleidoscope of shimmering colours.

★**Église St-Pierre** – This 12C and 13C Gothic church used to belong to the Benedictine abbey of St-Père-en-Vallée. The belfry-porch dates from pre-Romanesque times. The Gothic **stained-glass windows**★ can be traced back to the late 13C and early 14C, before the widespread introduction of yellow staining.

The oldest stained glass is that in the south bays of the chancel, portraying tall, hieratic figures from the Old Testament.

The windows in the semicircle of the chancel, with the most vivid tones, were mounted around 1300. Here the characters have been treated more freely.

The last windows to be installed were those in the nave (c 1305-15). They feature an alternation of medallions and religious figures (Apostles, bishops, abbots).

Monument de Jean Moulin – Jean Moulin was *préfet* (chief administrator) of Chartres during the German invasion; on 17 June 1940, despite having been tortured, he resisted the enemy and refused to sign a document claiming that the French troops had committed a series of atrocities. As he was afraid of being unable to withstand further torture, he attempted to commit suicide.

Moulin was dismissed by the Vichy government in November 1940 and, from then on, he planned and coordinated underground resistance, working in close collaboration with General de Gaulle.

Arrested in Lyon on 21 June 1943, he did not survive the harsh treatment he received from the Gestapo. In December 1964 he was honoured in the Panthéon.

Grenier de Loëns – From the 12C onwards, this half-timbered barn with treble gables in the courtyard of the old chapter house was used to store the wine and cereals offered to the clergy as a tithe. Renovated to house the **Centre international du Vitrail** Ⓤ which organises stained-glass exhibitions, the building now features a large hall with beautifully restored roof timbering and a magnificent 12C cellar with three aisles.

Musée des Beaux-Arts Ⓥ – The museum is housed in the old bishop's palace and occupies the first terrace of the bishopric's gardens. The large, handsome edifice which was built over four centuries consists of a 15C section arranged around an interior courtyard, a 17C and 18C façade, and an early-18C wing overlooking the garden.

On the ground floor, note the foyer with its horseshoe-shaped staircase and the chapel used for temporary exhibitions. The drawing rooms contain the 18C collections with paintings by Boucher, Fragonard, Watteau, Chardin etc as well as faience, pewter and a fine collection of old musical instruments.

The upper floor contains collections of works from Primitive painting to the 19C: *Fire in Chartres Cathedral in 1836* by FA Pernot, *Horses at Rest* by Corot and *Crucifixion* by Q Massys. Two of the rooms contain wooden statues, many of them painted, dating from the 16C to 19C.

The old sacristy, close to the chapel, houses 12 unusually large **enamels★** representing the Apostles, by Léonard Limousin. They were commissioned by François I in 1545 and offered by Henri II to Diana of Poitiers, for her residence at Anet. In the basement are sculptures, medieval religious artefacts (enamels, superb processional Cross) and archeological exhibits discovered locally (cruciform fibulae). The museum's new rooms house the permanent modern art collections as well as temporary exhibitions. There are several works by Vlaminck *(The House in Auvers, Red Bouquet with Anemones)* and J Guérin *(Flower Woman with the Poplar)*. The South Sea Island collection and works by master glass painter Navarre are also on show.

★Le COMPA: Conservatoire du Machinisme et des Pratiques Agricoles Ⓥ – *West of the town by D 24* . The museum is located in a strikingly converted, semicircular former railway shed. The spacious, modern-looking building, encircled by neat lawns offering a good view of Chartres and the cathedral, contains splendid, gleaming old machines and tools of copper, wrought iron or wood.

An **audio-visual display** depicts changes in farming practices in a voyage through time and space.

Tools and machines – At the museum's core stands an assortment of machines grouped according to function: seeders, binder-harvesters, combine-harvesters... Note the American MOLINE tractor, from 1910.

Land, men and methods – A comparison of two farming concerns in different regions of France, in 1860 and today, provides a better understanding of rural life. Ploughs from around the world illustrate the diversity in methods used by workers on the land.

Galerie des inventeurs et des inventions – The 80m/262ft long gallery introduces the figures responsible for major agricultural developments over the centuries.

The ideas and innovations of Pliny the Elder, Olivier de Serres, Henri de Vilmorin and, more recently, Ferguson and the national agricultural research centre (INRA) are explained through information panels and fascinating interactive displays.

Various types of cereals are also displayed. Visitors can even consult and print off a regional recipe.

Salle des tracteurs – The tour ends with an exhibition of tractors, the oldest dating from 1816, the most recent from 1954.

Musée de l'École Ⓥ – A classroom, belonging to the old teachers' training college, houses teaching aids and furniture evoking the schools of yesteryear: abacuses, magic lanterns using paraffin, books advocating humanist ethics, a collective money-bank with a separate compartment for each pupil etc.

Ph. Gajic/MICHELIN

COMPA, MOLINE tractor (1910)

LE VIEUX CHARTRES

Maison Picassiette ⊙ – *East of the town, 22 rue du Repas*. Built and decorated by Raymond Isidore (1900-64), this house offers an amazing medley of naive art. A number of monuments and numerous religious scenes are suggested by mosaic compositions made with extremely diverse materials: pieces of crockery, fragments of tinted glass, dollops of cement etc. Visitors are given a complete tour of the house, including the "chapel", the Black Courtyard ("tomb" crowned by a replica of Chartres Cathedral), the summer house (frescoes) and the garden which is dotted with statues and features a large-scale mosaic depicting Jerusalem.

Le CHEMIN DES DAMES

Michelin map 56 folds 4, 5 or 236 folds 37, 38, 39

Chemin des Dames, which means Ladies' Way, follows a ridge separating the Aisne Valley from the Ailette Valley. It derives its name from the daughters of Louis XV, known as *"Mesdames"*, who followed this route to get to the Château de la Bove, home of their friend the Duchess of Narbonne. The site still bears the marks of the bitter fighting which took place during the First World War.

Nivelle Offensive – In 1914, after the Battle of the Marne, the retreating Germans stopped here, having realised that the location was an excellent defensive spot which they fortified by making use of the quarries (boves or creuttes), hollowed out of the ridge.

General Nivelle, commander of the French armies from December 1916, searched for a way of penetrating their defence along Chemin des Dames. In spite of the difficult terrain, riddled with machine gun nests, on 16 April 1917 he sent an army under Mangin to attack the German positions. The French troops occupied the ridges following the first assault but the Germans clung onto the slopes of the Ailette Valley: the terrible French losses that ensued, together with the failure of the venture, caused a crisis of morale which provoked mutinies in parts of the French army.

General Nivelle and General Mangin were dismissed; **Marshall Pétain** took over and suppressed the rebellion. There are people today who think the mutineers should have been pardoned because they were only driven to despair by the horrors of war.

FROM SOISSONS TO CORBENY
52km/32mi – about 3hr 30min

★**Soissons** – *See Soissons.*

Drive northeast out of Soissons and take N 2 towards Laon.

Carrefour du Moulin de Laffaux – On this hill (169m/549ft), which marks the western extremity of the Chemin des Dames, stands the Monument aux Morts des Crapouillots, a memorial to those killed by trench mortar shells *(behind the restaurant)*. Laffaux windmill used to stand here.

Eating out

MODERATE

L'Auberge du Moulin Bertrand – *02860 Martigny-Courpierre – 4km/2.5mi from Cerny-en-Laonnois by D 967 then D 88 – ☎ 03 23 24 71 73 – closed Feb, Sun evening and Mon – booking essential – 90/240F.* Fresh market produce contribute to making the meals served here an epitome of gastronomic pleasure. After coffee, why not be tempted by a stroll along the banks of the lake or even a fishing expedition... In winter, you can curl up in front of the fireplace.

Where to stay

MODERATE

Chambre d'Hôte Le Clos – *02860 Chérêt – 8km/5mi south of Laon by D 967 – ☎ 03 23 24 80 64 – closed 15 Oct-15 Mar – ▱ – 5 rooms 200/280F – meal 100F.* A peaceful hotel exuding old-fashioned charm. The largish rooms are decorated with fine antique furniture. Pay a visit to the small museum on the premises.

A few miles further on, turn right onto D 18 (Chemin des Dames).

Signs along the route indicate the eight historic sites (equipped with parking and rest areas) where informative panels explain the stakes at play:
1 Fort de la Malmaison: fortifications date from the early 20C
2 Royère viewpoint: colonial troops
3 Cerny-en-Laonnois: necropolis and memorial
4 Caverne du Dragon: museum
5 Monument des Basques: Fighting France
6 Plateau de Californie: daily life in the trenches
7 Craonne Arboretum and village: mutineers
8 National assault vehicle monument, Berry-au-Bac: armoured vehicles

Fort de la Malmaison – This fort was taken by the colonial troops of the 38th Regiment from the Prussian guard in 1917. Malmaison Cemetery: German graves (1939-45).

Cerny-en-Laonnois – Near to the crossroads with D 967 stand the Chemin des Dames memorial, a chapel, and a French military cemetery (5 500 graves) which is neighbour to a cemetery for the German soldiers who died here too.

Caverne du Dragon ⊘ – The galleries dug out in the middle for the extraction of stone used to build Vauclair Abbey were baptised "Dragon's Cave" by the Germans. In 1915, they used it as a barracks (command post, dormitory, chapel, cemetery). Now a museum of remembrance, it serves to illustrate the daily life of soldiers through displays and videos. The sculptures, graffiti and carvings made by soldiers are moving reminders of their lives. A film and an animated model, "Theatre of Operations", demonstrate significant episodes of the conflict and explain the strategic importance of the site. From the entrance building *(shop, cafeteria)*, there is a view over the Aisne Valley.

D 18 follows the top of the ridge known as Hurtebise's Isthmus, which extends to the northeast on the Craonne plateau formed by the Vauclair and Californie plateaux.

Monument des Marie-Louise – In March 1814 the Hurtebise farm was fought over in the **Battle of Craonne** in which Napoleon, newly arrived from Corbeny, was victorious over Blücher. A hundred years later in September 1914 the same farm was the object of fierce fighting in which the Basques of the 36th Division excelled themselves. Memorial to both battles.

Turn left onto D 886 which descends into the Ailette Valley.

Abbaye de Vauclair ⊙ – The ruins of this Cistercian monastery, founded in 1134 by St Bernard, were uncovered in 1966. The best-preserved parts of the abbey are the undercroft, the refectory, the chapter-house and the calefactory. The foundations of the abbey church and the guesthouse are also visible. A herb garden with medicinal plants has existed since 1976 and an exhibition gallery stands nearby. All around, the ancient monastic forest of Vauclair covers 1 000ha/2 471 acres.

Return to Chemin des Dames and follow D 18 for another 2km/1mi.

Monument des Basques – The Hurtebise farm was again the centre of conflict in 1914, during which Basque soldiers from the 36th Division distinguished themselves. A monument commemorates their heroism.

Turn back and take D 895 to the right.

To the right, stands the observation point from which Napoleon directed the Battle of Craonne in 1814 (now his statue stands there).

▣ Plateau de Californie – From the car park, a path running along the edge of the forest is dotted with panels depicting the daily life of soldiers. An amazing sculpture illustrates the fierce fighting with soldiers' faces entangled in barbed wire. Fine view of the valley.

Arboretum – Where the path leads back to D 18, an arboretum has been erected on the site of the old village of Craonne. A new village has been built farther down the hill. It is possible to follow this itinerary to the tanks monuments in Berry-au-Bac.

Corbeny – Kings came to Corbeny Abbey the day after their coronation, in order to pray to the relics of St Marcou who had the power to cure the king's evil (scrofula).

COMPIÈGNE★★★

Conurbation 67 057
Michelin map 56 fold 2, 106 fold 10 inset or 236 fold 35

Compiègne, which was a royal residence long before it hosted the brilliant parties and receptions of the Second Empire, is bordered by one of the most beautiful forests in France, where the armistice of 11 November 1918 was signed and which is today a hiker's paradise with deer roaming freely.

HISTORICAL NOTES

Origins – Charles the Bald had a palace built to resemble the one in Aix-la-Chapelle (Aachen) built for Charlemagne and ceded to Charles' brother, Louis, in 843 when the Treaty of Verdun divided up the Carolingian Empire. He also founded an abbey which from the 10C preserved the relics of St Cornelius. The town developed around this royal abbey of St Cornelius (today only the 14C cloister remains), which preceded St Denis as the royal necropolis and centre of culture. Ramparts were built around Compiègne in the 13C; Charles V reinforced them and in 1374 added a castle that was the foundation for the palace.

Joan of Arc Imprisoned – In May 1430 the Burgundians and the English were camping beneath Compiègne's town walls, on the north side of the River Oise. **Joan of Arc** came to examine the enemy position and returned on the 23rd after a few days' absence, entering the town from the south. That same evening she attempted an assault, crossing the river and chasing the Burgundian vanguard from their Margny encampment. However, reinforcements came to the aid of the Burgundians from Clairoix and Coudun, while the English came from Venette, stealing along the Oise to attack from the rear; the French had no choice but to give ground. The Maid of Orléans covered the retreat with a handful of men. She reached the moat just as the commanding officer in Compiègne gave the order to raise the drawbridge, fearing the enemy would slip inside with the last of the French soldiers. A short skirmish ensued. A Picardy archer toppled Joan of Arc from her horse and she was immediately taken prisoner. The place of capture is located near place du 54ème-Régiment-d'Infanterie, where Frémiet's equestrian statue of the Maid of Orléans stands.

The Palace of Louis XV – All the kings of France enjoyed staying in Compiègne which they often visited. Yet, with four main buildings haphazardly arranged around a central courtyard, the château was not an obvious royal residence. Louis XIV said, "At Versailles, I am lodged like a king; at Fontainebleau, like a prince; and at Compiègne,

Palace, Compiègne

like a peasant." He had new apartments built facing the forest. His 75 visits here were marked by sumptuous feasts and, in particular, great military camps. The largest of these was in 1698, the last time the King stayed at Compiègne.

When Louis XV ordered the complete reconstruction of the palace in 1738 he was less interested in outdoing his predecessor, who had built so much, than in having a place where he could reside with his court and ministers. The architect Jacques Gabriel and his successor **Jacques-Ange Gabriel** were limited by the town and its ramparts, which obliged them to rebuild on the old foundations. As a further inconvenience, they could not destroy an old building until a new one had been completed, as the King refused to cease his visits to Compiègne during the rebuilding work.

Louis XV's master plan of 1751 was brought to a halt by the Seven Years War. Louis XVI continued the project and achieved a great deal but left it unfinished. In fact, it was not until 1785 that he was finally able to occupy the royal apartments, which would later accommodate Napoleon I. The south wing was finished that same year. Marie-Antoinette had personally overseen its arrangement, decor and furnishing but never actually stayed here herself. A great terrace was built in front of the palace's façade, which looked out onto a park. This terrace was connected to the gardens by a monumental central flight of steps, replacing the moat that had formerly been part of Charles V's fortifications.

From 1789 to 1791 the work continued, though at a slower pace, as the King hoped to withdraw to Compiègne. In 1795, in the aftermath of the Revolution, the furnishings were completely dispersed through auctions which lasted five months.

After the Revolution the palace served first as a military school, then as an engineering college. In 1806 it became an Imperial residence and Napoleon I had the palace entirely restored by the architect Berthaut, the painter Girodet and the decorators Redouté and the Dubois brothers.

Wedding Palace – It was in Compiègne Forest that, on 14 May 1770, the future Louis XVI was introduced to Marie-Antoinette of Austria for the first time; the young Dauphin was paralysed with shyness.

On 27 March 1810 the great-niece of Marie-Antoinette, Marie-Louise of Austria, was to arrive in Compiègne. She had married Napoleon I by proxy and this time the groom was impatient. Despite torrential rain, the Emperor ran to meet the princess and threw himself soaking wet into her carriage, smothering the terrified Marie-Louise with demonstrations of affection. The dinner planned in Soissons was cancelled and instead the Emperor and his bride had supper at Compiègne. Some days later the wedding ceremonies were celebrated at St-Cloud, serving only as the consecration of a union imposed at Vienna and willingly accepted at Compiègne.

In 1832, Louis-Philippe, who transformed the real tennis court into a theatre, married his daughter Louise-Marie to the first king of Belgium, Leopold of Saxe-Coburg.

The Second Empire "Series" – Compiègne was the favourite residence of Napoleon III and Empress Eugénie. They came every autumn for four to six weeks to enjoy the hunting season, receiving the kings and princes of Europe. They also received the celebrities of the time, arranged in five "series" of about 80 people, grouped by "affinities". Lodging the guests often posed great difficulties and many distinguished individuals had to content themselves with rooms under the eaves.

The hunts, theatrical evenings, charades and balls left the guests with little free time. Romantic and political intrigue mixed freely. One rainy afternoon, to amuse the Imperial couple and their guests, the writer Mérimée composed his famous dictation, comprising the words with the greatest spelling difficulties in the French language. The Empress made the highest number of mistakes, 62; Pauline Sandoz, Metternich's daughter-in-law, had the least with three. The luxuries and endless frivolities intoxicated the courtiers, who delighted in waltzes and long forest outings. The events of 1870 interrupted this joyous life and the work on the new theatre. During the Emperor's long periods of residence at Compiègne most of the First Empire furniture was replaced.

The World Wars – From 1917 to 1918 the palace was the general headquarters of generals Nivelle and then Pétain. In 1919 a fire damaged most of the royal apartments. The armistices of 11 November 1918 and 22 June 1940 *(see Forêt de COMPIÈGNE: Clairière de l'Armistice)* were signed in the forest. Compiègne suffered heavy bombing during the Second World War. **Royallieu**, a district south of the town, served from 1941 to 1944 as a centre from which prisoners were sent to various Nazi concentration camps (a memorial stands at the entrance to the military camp as well as in Compiègne railway station).

★★★ PALACE ⏱ 2hr

Viewed from the square the palace is paradoxically "a Louis XV château built almost entirely from 1751 to 1789".
This austerely Classical château covers a vast triangular area (3ha/7.5 acres); indeed, the regularity of its arrangement is even rather monotonous. The decoration inside and the collection of 18C and First Empire tapestries and furnishings is, however, exceptional. Among the many details unifying the various apartments are fine *trompe-l'œil* paintings by Sauvage (1744-1818) over the doors.

PALAIS DE COMPIÈGNE
1st FLOOR

0 _____ 40 m

A, B, C : Ground floor entrances

Historic Appartments

Rue du Four

★★ MUSÉE DE LA VOITURE

Petit Théâtre

Cour de l'Orangerie

APPARTEMENT DE L'IMPÉRATRICE

Petit Parc

Théâtre Impérial

Rue d'Ulm

Grand Hall

★★ APPARTEMENTS HISTORIQUES

Rue Othenin

Galerie Natoire

B

Rue

Salle Coypel

Cour de la Régie

APPARTEMENT DU ROI ET DES EMPEREURS

MUSÉE DU SECOND EMPIRE ★★

Musée de l'Impératrice

Cour d'Honneur

Escalier d'Apollon

Appartement du roi de Rome

C

Appartement double de Prince

A

Place du Général de Gaulle

Petit Parc

COMPIÈGNE

The Second Empire Museum and the Transport Museum are also in the palace. The new theatre, on which work began in 1867 during the reign of Napoleon III, was never completed because of the Franco-Prussian War in 1870. An association was set up in 1987 to rehabilitate it and organise productions there. As a result, the **Théâtre Impérial**, in which the interior layout is reminiscent of the opera house in Versailles, has become popular as a venue for concerts and operettas.

★★Historic Apartments (Appartements historiques) ⊙

The Historic Apartments of the palace begin with rooms devoted to its history; beyond them rises the Queen's Grand Staircase, or Apollo Staircase, which led directly to the Queen's apartments; further still is the entrance hall or Gallery of Columns which precedes the Grand Staircase (**1**). Climb the staircase with its beautiful 18C wrought-iron balustrade to the landing where a great Gallo-Roman sarcophagus lies; it served as the font in the vanished abbey church of St Cornelius and is a relic of very early Compiègne. The first-floor Guard-room (1785) (**2**) leads into the antechamber or Ushers' Salon (**3**), which gave access to both the King's apartment *(left)* and the Queen's *(right)*.

Appartement du Roi et des Empereurs (King's and Emperors' Apartment)

This apartment houses exceptional groups of objects, works and memorabilia.

Salle à manger de l'Empereur (**4**) – The decor and furnishings in the dining room are First Empire (early 19C). Pilasters and doors, surmounted by *grisaille* paintings by Sauvage, stand out against the fake rose-pink onyx. One of Sauvage's paintings is an extraordinary *trompe-l'œil* representing Anacreon. It was here that on 1 May 1814 Louis XVIII entertained Czar Alexander, who was still hesitating about returning the Bourbons to the throne of France. During the Second Empire a private theatre was established here, with those close to the empress taking part in charades and revues.

Salon des cartes (**5**) – First designated as the Nobles' Antechamber under Louis XVI, then as the Senior Officers' Salon under Napoleon I, this room ended up as the Aide-de-Camp Salon or the Card Salon under Napoleon III. The furnishings comprise elements from the First Empire (chairs covered in Beauvais tapestry) and from the Second Empire. Note the games: quoits and a pin table.

Salon de famille (**6**) – This room was once Louis XVI's bedchamber (large mirrors hide the alcove). The **view**★ onto the park extends the length of the avenue to the Beaux Monts.
The furnishings recall Empress Eugénie's taste for mixing styles: Louis XV armchairs, unusual little seats for two (*confidents*) or for three (indiscrets) etc.

Salle du Conseil (**7**) – Unfortunately only the original table has been returned; the rest of the furniture from the council chamber has been lost. Together with Versailles and Fontainebleau, Compiègne was one of the three châteaux where the king held counsel. Representatives of the Republics of Genoa and of the Kingdom of France signed two successive treaties here (1756 and 1764) which accorded France the right to garrison troops in the maritime citadels of Corsica. An immense tapestry illustrates *The Crossing of the Rhine by Louis XIV.*

Chambre de l'Empereur (**8**) – The Emperor's bedchamber has been restored to its appearance during the First Empire, with Jacob-Desmalter furnishings and friezes representing eagles.

Ph. Gajic/MICHELIN

Emperor's bedchamber

Bibliothèque de l'Empereur (**9**) – Formerly the King's Great Cabinet, this room was used as a library during the First Empire. The bookcase and the furnishings are by Jacob-Desmalter; the painted ceiling is the work of Girodet.

Appartement de l'Impératrice (Empress'Apartment)

These rooms comprised the queen's principal apartments, the only ones in which Marie-Antoinette ever stayed; later, they were particularly favoured by Empresses Marie-Louise and Eugénie.

Salon du Déjeuner (**10**) – The delightful breakfast room, with pale blue and yellow silk hangings, was prepared for Marie-Louise in 1809.

1st FLOOR

0 20 m

★★ **MUSÉE DE LA VOITURE**

Cour de l'Orangerie

15
14
16
13
12
17
11
10
9
8
7
6

Galerie des chasses de Louis XV

← **APPARTEMENT DE L'IMPÉRATRICE**

Grand Hall

Galerie

Galerie Natoire

du

Cour de la Chapelle

← **APPARTEMENT DU ROI ET DES EMPEREURS**

Bal
Chapelle

1
2
5
3
4

MUSÉE DU SECOND EMPIRE ★★

Cour d'Honneur

Escalier d'Apollon

Appartement "double" de Prince ↘

18

← **Appartement du roi de Rome**

HISTORIC APPARTMENTS

Salon de musique (11) – This was one of Empress Eugénie's favourite rooms; she furnished it herself. The Louis XVI pieces, from the apartment of Marie-Antoinette at St-Cloud, recall that the last sovereign consort of France kept the memory of the unfortunate queen alive.

Chambre de l'Impératrice (12) – The majestic tester bed is enclosed by white silk curtains and gold-embroidered muslin. Paintings by Girodet represent the seasons and the Morning Star appears in the centre of the ceiling. The round boudoir leading to the bedchamber, also built for Marie-Louise, served as a dressing-room and for taking baths.

The last three of these interconnecting rooms form a decorative First Empire ensemble. Seats are arranged formally around a couch in the **Grand Salon (13)**; the **Salon des Fleurs (14)** owes its name to the eight panels painted with lily like flowers, after Redoute; the **Salon Bleu (15)** strikingly contrasts blue walls and seats with a red marble fireplace and console tables. These rooms belonged to the imperial prince at the end of the Second Empire.

Salle à manger de l'Impératrice (16) – The walls of this modestly sized room are lined with stucco-marble, of a caramel colour more elegantly known as "antique yellow". It was here that the Archduchess Marie-Louise dined with the Emperor for the first time.

Galerie des chasses de Louis XV – The room is hung with Gobelins tapestries, which were woven as early as 1735 in accordance with sketches by Oudry. One represents a hunt along the River Oise and includes the silhouettes of Compiègne and the old Royallieu Abbey. The series continues in the **Galerie des Cerfs (17)**, formerly the Queen's Guard-room, then the Empress' Guard-room.

153

Galerie du Bal – The room (39_13m/128_43ft) was constructed within a few months for Marie-Louise's arrival, by gutting two floors of small apartments. The ceiling paintings glorify the Emperor's victories; the mythological scenes at the end of the room are by Girodet. Throughout the Second Empire the gallery served as a dining room at the time of the "series", the sovereigns presiding from the centre of an immense table set up for the occasion.

Galerie Natoire and Salle Coypel – They were built by Napoleon III to lead to the **Grand Théâtre** (never finished). Their decoration illustrates *The Story of Don Quixote*.

Chapel – The First Empire chapel is surprisingly small for such a vast château, as the great chapel planned by Gabriel was never built. It was here on 9 August 1832 that the marriage took place between Princess Louise-Marie, eldest daughter of Louis-Philippe, and Leopold I, King of Belgium. Princess Marie of Orléans, the French king's second daughter, designed the stained-glass window.

Appartement double de Prince, appartement du roi de Rome

Appartement double de Prince – Napoleon I had this apartment arranged to receive a foreign sovereign and his or her consort. This excellent group of Empire rooms comprises a dining room, four salons and a great bedchamber (original wallpaper, silk hangings, furniture).

Appartement du roi de Rome – The apartment has been restored to its appearance in 1811, when Napoleon I's son (five months old at the time) stayed in it for one month. All the original furnishings adorn the salon-boudoir, bathroom, boudoir, bedchamber and main drawing room. In the middle of the apartment a room (**18**) has been restored to appear as it did at the end of the 18C (Queen Marie-Antoinette's games room).

★★ MUSÉE DU SECOND EMPIRE ⊙

The museum is located in a series of small, quiet drawing rooms and presents life at Court and in the outside world, and the arts, during the Second Empire.

Beyond the first room, displaying Daumier's humorous drawings, a space is devoted to the "beauties" of the period. Princess Mathilde (1820-1904), one of the reign's great figures, has pride of place here. She was for a brief time the fiancée of Louis-Napoleon, her close cousin. After her Spanish marriage she devoted herself entirely to her salon in rue de Courcelles, which was much frequented by the important writers and artists of the day, and to her château in St-Gratien.

The museum owns the famous painting, *The Empress with her Ladies-in-Waiting* by Winterhalter (1855).

Among the many sculptures by Carpeaux in the last rooms, note the bust of Napoleon, aged by the fall of the Empire, and the statue of the Imperial Prince with his dog.

Musée de l'Impératrice – This collection was bequeathed by Mr and Mme F Ferrand and includes memorabilia of official life and life in exile, as well as popular objects associated with Empress Eugénie. Among the more moving items are those evoking the Empress and her son, the Imperial Prince, who was massacred by the Zulus.

Kitchens and Outbuildings – The evolution of the two-wheeler, starting with the heavy ancestors of the bicycle, hobbies (1817) which the rider set in motion by pushing off, can be seen in the former pantries. Pedals appeared with the 1863

Ph. Gajic/MICHELIN

The Empress with her Ladies-in-Waiting by Winterhalter

Michaux velocipede. The penny-farthing, built out of iron tubing, had an unusually large front wheel to increase its speed. Developments such as the invention of the chain belt, which first appeared on the English tricycle, rendered wheels of disproportionate size unnecessary. The true bicycle became possible in about 1890. The army took advantage of the idea by developing a folding velocipede just before the First World War.

First Floor – These rooms are devoted to foreign vehicles and their accessories: Dutch and Italian cabriolets, a Sicilian cart, palanquin, sleighs, coachmen's clothes etc.

The motorcar's "first steps"

The Panhard No 2, the first car equipped with a four-stroke Daimler engine, the 1895 vis-à-vis by Bollée & Son which was one of the entrants in the race from Paris to Marseille-en-Beauvaisis (north of Beauvais), the De Dion-Bouton series, the large 1897 break belonging to the Duchess of Uzès, the first woman driver, the 1899 "Never-satisfied" on Michelin tyres, which was the first car to attain speeds of 100kph/62mph, the 1900 4-CV Renault, the first saloon car. Steam, combustion and electric motors are also exhibited, showing the various ideas of the researchers and creators of the automobile industry.

★★ MUSÉE DE LA VOITURE ⊘

The museum was created in 1927 on the initiative of the Touring Club of France. None of the authentic royal carriages has been preserved in France. The collection of antique carriages features berlin coaches for travelling or ceremonial use in particular; these carriages were mounted on a base with two shafts, safer than a single shaft, to which the horses were harnessed.

Grand Hall – About 50 carriages are on display in what was formerly the kitchen courtyard, now covered over: the oldest, a travelling berlin coach which belonged to the kings of Spain, dating from c 1740; the berlin coach used by the Pope in Bologna, and the one in which Bonaparte made his entrance to the town in 1796; 18C and 19C travelling carriages, a mail-coach, charabancs, a Madeleine-Bastille omnibus and Orsay broughams are also on show.
The De Dion and Trépardoux's steam car and the 1924 Citroën from the Croisière Noire (the first trans-African car expedition) are among the finest exhibits.

ADDITIONAL SIGHTS

Hôtel de ville – This remarkable building was constructed under Louis XII in the late-Gothic style. It was restored during the last century and the façade statues date from this period. They represent, from left to right around the central equestrian statue of Louis XII: St Denis, St Louis, Charles the Bald, Joan of Arc, Cardinal Pierre d'Ailly who was born in Compiègne, and Charlemagne.

The belfry consists of two floors and a slate-covered spire, flanked by four pinnacled turrets. At the base of the spire, three figures, called *picantins* and dressed as Swiss foot-soldiers from the period of François I, ring the hours and the quarter-hours.

★ Musée de la Figurine historique ⊘ – *In the Hôtel de la Cloche, to the right of the Hôtel de Ville.*
The museum houses over

Compiègne – Hôtel de ville

100 000 model figures in tin, lead, wood, plastic, paper and cardboard; they are sculpted wholly or partly in the round, or are flat. A visit here offers an interesting retrospective of the development of dress, along with an evocation of historical events throughout the ages. Note in particular *The Review of French Troops at Betheny* in 1901 in front of the Czar of Russia and President Loubet (12 000 figures made by A Silhol, who participated in the parade himself); *The Battle of Waterloo* created by Charles Laurent from 1905 to 1923, which is completed by an audio-visual presentation; and *The Return of the Emperor's Ashes* with the veterans of the Napoleonic Wars.

Eating out

MODERATE

La Ciboulette – *87 rue de Paris* – ☎ *03 44 20 29 03 – closed 15 July-13 Aug, Sun evening and Mon – 98/195F.* A congenial, family atmosphere, a summer terrace, and a discreet location away from the town centre are the hallmarks of this small restaurant, which has succeeded in attracting a steady crowd of regulars. Booking recommended.

MID-RANGE

Le Bistrot des Arts – *35 cours Guynemer* – ☎ 03 44 20 10 10 – closed Sat lunchtime, Sun and public holidays – 115/130F. On the ground floor of the Hôtel des Beaux-Arts, this appealing brasserie is decorated with engravings and miscellaneous objects. The cuisine is delightfully fresh while at the same time drawing on culinary tradition.

À La Bonne Idée – *3 rue des Meuniers, 60350 St-Jean-aux-Bois – 8km/5mi southeast of Compiègne by D 332 then D 185* – ☎ *03 44 42 84 09 – www.a-la-bonne-idee.fr -closed 8 Jan-9 Feb – booking essential Sat-Sun – 130/380F.* A long walk in the country has made you hungry, so why not try your luck at this curious forest inn, which also doubles as a hotel?

Auberge du Buissonnet – *825 rue Vineux, 60750 Choisy-au-Bac – 5km/3mi northeast of Compiègne by N 31 then D 66* – ☎ *03 44 40 17 41 – closed Sun and Tues evenings and Mon – 149/220F.* Beyond the inn lies a pond where ducks and swans can be seen gliding together on the water, before engaging in play in the garden. It is advisable to choose a table near the window in the dining room or out on the terrace in summer.

Where to stay

MODERATE

Camping Municipal de Batigny – *60350 Pierrefonds – 15km/9.3mi southeast of Compiègne by D 973* – ☎ *03 44 42 80 83 – closed Nov-Mar – ✗ – booking recommended – 60 plots 34F.* The smallish, well-tended plots of land in this camp site, just off the road to Compiègne, are separated by leafy hedges with bursts of blossom. Clean and pleasant.

MID-RANGE

Hôtel des Beaux Arts – *33 cours Guynemer* – ☎ *03 44 92 26 26* – ▣ – *37 rooms 350/460F* – ⌁ *55F.* Stretching along the banks of the River Oise, the Hôtel des Beaux-Arts is a modern construction. The rooms are appointed with teak furniture and are efficiently soundproofed. The bigger bedrooms include a kitchenette.

LUXURY

Château de Bellinglise – *60157 Élincourt-Ste-Marguerite – 15km/9.3mi north of Compiègne by D 142* – ☎ *03 44 96 00 33* – ▣ – *35 rooms from 1 045F* – ⌁ *95F – restaurant 195/395F.* A gorgeous 16C château with red-brick walls and mullioned windows, and personalised rooms with their marble bathroom: this dream will come true if you spend a day or two at the Château de Bellinglise... The huge bay windows in the dining hall adorned with wainscoting open onto the wooded park surrounding the property.

On the town

Le Bouchon – *5 rue St-Martin* – ☎ *03 44 40 05 32 – daily noon-2pm, 7.30pm-1am.* The generous, extravagant man who runs this bar built with wood is a former rugby player. Wine and sport are therefore the two centres of attention here: the former is consumed on the tables while the latter is illustrated by photographs pinned up on the walls

Sweet Home Pub – *49 rue St-Corneille* – ☎ *03 44 86 51 00 – Mon 6pm-1am, Tues-Sat 11.30-1am.* Probably the most likeable pub in the whole of Compiègne, fronted by a fine wooden façade. The owners devote themselves to organising highly entertaining evenings folk or French rock concerts, stage productions, literary readings etc. The only grumpy characters are the garden gnomes...

Shopping

Au Relais du Château – *24 rue d'Ulm – place du Château* – ☎ *03 44 40 03 45 – Fri-Sun 8.30am-6pm in winter, daily in summer – closed over Christmas, the New Year, and one week in Feb.* Au Relais du Château is a beautiful shop providing a wide range of services: restaurant, tea room, delicatessen, bicycle and picnic hamper rental, tour operator etc. You are bound to find something that will tickle your fancy! Before leaving, take a look at the mouth-watering display of local produce...

Boat trips

Le Coche d'Eau – *Cours Guynemer* – ☎ *03 44 40 01 00 – Wed, Sat, Sun at 2.30pm and 5.30pm – closed Dec-Feb.* Three times a week, afternoon trips are organised along the River Oise and River Aisne, passing through the lock gates. Apply to the tourist office for details.

Église St-Jacques – The church features a 15C tower, the highest in the town, at one of the corners of its west front. This was the parish church of the king and the court, hence funds provided for the chancel to be reworked in marble in the 18C and for the addition of carved-wood panels at the base of the nave's pillars. The harmony of the Gothic style at the time of St Louis is particularly evident in the chancel with its narrow, clerestory lit triforium and the 13C transept. An ambulatory was added in the 16C.

The 13C stone Virgin and Child in the north transept, known as "Our Lady of the Silver Feet" *(Notre-Dame aux pieds d'argent)*, is the subject of much veneration. A chapel in the north aisle houses three 15C painted wooden statues.

From place St-Jacques, cross rue Magenta to reach rue des Lombards. Lovely houses including a timber-framed one dating from the 15C: **Vieille Cassine**, where the masters of the bridge once lived.

Tour de Beauregard – This former royal keep or "Governor's Tower", now in ruins, is located on the site of Charles the Bald's palace. The tower is all that remains from the time when Joan of Arc *(see above)* made her last, fatal military assault, which she began by leaving the town via the old St Louis bridge on 23 May 1430.

Musée Vivenel ⊘ – Compiègne's municipal museum is located in the Hôtel de Songeons; it is a pleasant building dating from the early 19C, the garden of which is now a public park.

Antiquity: Greek and Roman marbles and bronzes; Antique ceramics including a remarkable group of **Greek vases**★★ discovered in Etruria and Southern Italy *(Magna Graecia)*; successive civilizations, from prehistory to the end of the Gallo-Roman period, are evoked through the tools, weapons and various objects found at excavation sites; note the three bronze helmets dating from c 600 BC.

The first-floor rooms have preserved their Directoire wainscoting. The painting collections are displayed here (large altarpiece representing the Passion by Wolgemut, Dürer's teacher), together with ceramics (pitchers in "Flemish stoneware", Italian majolicas), ivories, Limousin enamels etc.

Park – The gardens are known as the Petit Parc; the main entrance gate is to the left, when facing away from the town. The Grand Parc surrounds it and is part of the forest.

Petit Parc – The Emperor's guiding idea was "to link the château as soon as possible to the forest, which is the true garden and the real beauty of this residence". The enclosing wall which blocked the view of the woods was taken down and replaced by iron railings. Beyond, the openness of avenue des Beaux-Monts creates a magnificent linear perspective (4km/6mi long), which was originally to have been closed with a monumental gateway to remind the Emperor's young bride of Schönbrunn.

Impatient to reach the forest without having to go through the town, Napoleon had a central ramp built for carriages between the terrace and the park; this was unfortunately at the expense of the glorious flight of steps by Gabriel. From then on the Petit Parc was replanted as a formal English garden and lost its importance. The present layout dates from the Second Empire.

FORÊT DE COMPIÈGNE

🔲 The State forest of Compiègne (14 500ha/35 800 acres) is a remnant of the immense Cuise Forest which extended from the edge of the Île-de-France to the Ardennes. It embraces delightful beech groves, magnificent avenues, valleys, ponds and villages.

The forest occupies a sort of hollow with the valleys of the River Oise and River Aisne on two sides. A series of hills and promontories sketches a sharply defined crescent to the north, east and south. These peaks rise on average 80m/262ft above the sandy base of the hollow, which is grooved with numerous rivulets. The largest of these, the Ru de Berne, links a series of ponds.

The forest is crisscrossed by 1 500km/930mi of roads and footpaths. François I first cut great rides through the trees, with Louis XIV and Louis XV later contributing to extend this network in order to create an ideal place for hunting.
The grounds, once the lands of Frankish kings, are today used by three different hunts.

Types of trees – The most common species in the forest are beech (40%), oak (30%) and yoke-elm (15%). Beech in particular occupies the southern plateau and its slopes, and the area immediately surrounding the town. Oak, which was planted long ago, thrives in the better-drained clay soil, as well as on the Beaux Monts. Since 1830 Norway pine and other conifers have grown in the poor, sandy soil where oaks would find it difficult to thrive.

A paved cycle path runs between Compiègne (east from carrefour Royal along route Tournante) and Pierrefonds.

Fishing regulations – A board in front of the forest warden's house at Étangs de St-Pierre lists the clubs and organisations which issue permits and licences.

★★Les Beaux Monts

1 Tour starting from Compiègne *18km/11mi - about 1hr*

Leave Compiègne by avenue Royale. At carrefour Royal, turn left onto route Tournante; the road crosses the long perspective of avenue des Beaux-Monts in two bends. At carrefour du Renard turn right onto route Eugénie.

Carrefour d'Eugénie – Some of the forest's oldest **oak trees★★** stand around this junction. The most ancient ones date from the time of François I.

Take the winding road on the left which climbs to Les Beaux Monts.

★★ **Les Beaux Monts** – Stop at the summit, near the Beaux Monts viewpoint *(point de vue)*; from here the **view★** stretches along the straight line of the avenue through the forest all the way to the palace, barely visible 4km/2.5mi away.

Continue to the junction and the Point de vue du Précipice.

Point de vue du Précipice (Precipice Viewpoint) – Here the extensive **view**★ overlooks the woody stretches of the valley of the River Berne and Mont St-Marc.

Return to the junction and take the road on the right down from Les Beaux Monts.

The road runs through a magnificent grove of oaks and beeches and reaches a straight road.

Turn right, cross route Eugénie and take the first road on the right.

Chapelle St-Corneille-aux-Bois – The secluded chapel was founded in 1164; it later passed to the abbey of St-Corneille in Compiègne. François I added a hunting lodge but its appearance today dates only from the time of Viollet-le-Duc (19C); the Gothic construction of the 13C chapel, however, has remained intact. The wardens of Compiègne Forest came here before the French Revolution to hear Sunday mass.

Continue to D 14; turn right to return to Compiègne (Vieux-Moulin-Compiègne).

★★Clairière de l'Armistice

② Direct road to the historic site *6km/3.5mi northeast – 1hr*

Leave Compiègne by N 31. Go straight across carrefour d'Aumont and continue to carrefour du Francport where you will see the monument to the liberators of Alsace and Lorraine and the car park.

A site where a network of tracks existed for heavy artillery installations was cleared to make room for the private train of the allied forces' commander-in-chief, Field-Marshal Foch, and for that of the German plenipotentiaries. The tracks were linked to the Compiègne-Soissons line at Rethondes station.

Today, rails and flagstones, marking the site of the railway carriages, surround a memorial commemorating the date.

On 7 November 1918 Maréchal Foch's private train arrived.

On 8 November, during the first few hours of daylight, the train arrived from Tergnier with the German negotiators. At 9am, they entered Foch's carriage-office. The Germans sat down at the conference table; General Weygand went to fetch the Maréchal who greeted the Germans in the following terms:

"Whom do I have the honour of addressing?"

"The plenipotentiaries sent by the German government," replied Erzberger, the group's leader. He handed the Commander-in-Chief the delegation's letters of credit and Foch withdrew to study them. When he had done so, he came back and, without sitting down, asked,

"What is the purpose of your visit?"

"We have come to hear the proposals of the Allied forces with a view to achieving an armistice on land, sea and in the air," replied Erzberger.

"I have no such proposals," answered Foch.

Oberndorff, the diplomat, broke in, "If you prefer, Sir, we could say that we have come to ask under what conditions the Allies would agree to an armistice".

"I have no conditions!" Erzberger then read out the note from President Wilson stating that Maréchal Foch was authorised to indicate the armistice conditions.

"Are you asking for an armistice?" asked the Maréchal. "If you are, I can tell you the conditions under which it could be achieved."

Oberndorff and Erzberger declared that they were indeed seeking an armistice. Weygand then read out the conditions and it took him one hour to do so (the document had to be translated). Everybody listened in silence. Three days were then granted to the Germans to study the proposals.

General von Winterfeldt, the only army officer in the German delegation, asked for a suspension of hostilities during the period allowed for consideration of the draft armistice. Foch refused. On the evening of 10 November, a radio message from Germany authorised the plenipotentiaries to sign the armistice. At about 2am, the Germans returned to the Maréchal's carriage and, at 5.15am, the agreement was signed. It came into effect on the same day, at 11am. During the morning, Maréchal Foch travelled in person to Paris to announce the good news to Raymond Poincaré, the President of the Republic, and to Clémenceau, the French Prime Minister.

On 14 June 1940, 22 years later, during the Second World War, the German Army entered Paris; on 21 June, at 3.30pm the French armistice delegation was received by Hitler and government dignitaries in the same car of the same private train, then located in its 1918 position. The leaders withdrew together and the representatives of the German high command gave their interlocutors the detailed document listing the victors' terms for an armistice.

It was signed on the evening of 22 June.

The clearing and its historic monuments were then ransacked by the occupation forces. Only the statue of Foch was spared.

Wagon du maréchal Foch ⊘ – The original, historic dining-car, which was converted into an office for Field Marshal Foch, was exhibited in the courtyard of the Invalides in Paris from 1921 to 1927 then returned to the forest clearing and placed in a shelter built for the purpose. Transported to Berlin as a trophy in 1940, it was destroyed in the Thuringia Forest in April 1945. In 1950 it was replaced by another carriage from a similar series. The places occupied by the delegates are indicated and the actual objects they used in 1918, put aside safely at the time, are now back inside the carriage.

The shelter also houses a large room devoted to the two armistices (11 November 1918 and 22 June 1940); the display includes contemporary newspapers, original documents, photographs, dummies in military uniform and remains of the original carriage.

★Le Mont St-Marc and the ponds

③ From Compiègne to Pierrefonds

26km/16mi - about 1hr 30min
Leave Compiègne by N 31.

Pont de Berne – It was here that the Dauphin, the future Louis XVI, met Marie-Antoinette for the first time; the future queen had just arrived from Vienna.

Turn right towards Pierrefonds. At Vivier-Frère-Robert turn left onto route du Geai.

★**Mont St-Marc** – The slopes of this long rise are covered with beeches. On reaching the plateau, turn left onto the forest road which follows the edge; there are good views of the valleys of the River Berne and River Aisne, Rethondes and Laigue Forest.

The road follows the northern promontory of the hill. Some 2.5km/1.5mi further along, **Carrefour Lambin** offers a particularly fine **view** of the Aisne Valley.

Return by the same road and fork left onto the first road suitable for vehicles; Drive down Route du Geai and continue towards Pierrefonds. Turn right and continue along the main street in Vieux-Moulin.

Vieux-Moulin – This former woodcutters' village later became a wealthy community of holiday homes. The little church, with a belfry resembling a Chinese hat, was rebuilt in 1860 at Napoleon III's expense.

Turn left at the junction with the war memorial and take route Eugénie (on the south bank) to Étang de l'Étot.

Étangs de St-Pierre – These ponds were created to stock fish; they were dug by members of the Celestine community from the priory of Mont-St-Pierre, to the west.

Empress Eugénie's former chalet is now a forest warden's house with exhibitions on the forest.

About 1km/0.5mi beyond the last pond, at a fork near the edge of the forest, take the small road left that climbs up to the hilltop districts of Pierrefonds.

★Les Grands Monts

④ From Pierrefonds to Compiègne

27km/17mi – about 1hr 30min

★★**Château de Pierrefonds** – *See PIERREFONDS.*
Leave Pierrefonds by D 85, heading west.

The road first rises to a wooded plateau, where the beautiful beech groves were largely destroyed during storms in 1984; it then descends into St-Jean-aux-Bois.

St-Jean-aux-Bois – This charming village was appropriately renamed "Solitude" in 1794. The 12C monastic buildings which were at the heart of the village can be seen along one side of it, marked by a moat filled with water. The Benedictine nuns left their abbey for Royallieu (on the outskirts of Compiègne) in 1634 as the forest was no longer safe; for a while Augustine canons took their place but in 1761 St-Jean was abandoned by its religious inhabitants.

The old fortified gate leads to the esplanade and the last vestiges of the abbey: the church, the chapter-house and the doorway to the "Small Courtyard" (formerly farm buildings). The architectural purity of the 13C **church**★ is remarkable. Inside, the sober harmony of the transept and chancel create an impression of grandeur. The slenderness of the columns separating each transept arm into two bays empha-

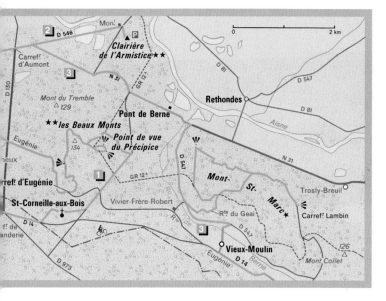

sises the church's height. The arrangement here - which was common later, in the 16C - is the only example in the region from that period. The *grisailles* recall the luminous atmosphere of the nave in the 13C.

The **chapter-house** *(salle capitulaire)* is located on the south side of the church; dating from c 1150, it is the oldest part of the structure. It serves today as a chapel annex and is generally open only for worship.

Ste-Périne – The pond surrounded by plane trees and poplars, and the woodland house in an old priory form an attractive sight.

The nuns of Ste-Périne (a linguistic contraction of Pétronille) occupied this hermitage from 1285 to 1626. Fear for their safety forced them to move first to Compiègne, then to Paris, then La Villette, Chaillot and finally Auteuil, where a retirement home still bears their name.

Turn round; turn right onto the main road to Crépy-en-Valois and at Vaudrampont turn right onto D 116.

At Étoile de la Reine roundabout turn sharp right onto route des Éluas and first left onto an unpaved road; park at carrefour Callisto.

★Les Grands Monts – This southern part of the forest is divided into the plateau and the swamps. The short trip described below *(30min on foot there and back)*, along an overhanging path shaded by beech groves, introduces some of the area's characteristics. Walk down route des Princesses; immediately after the barrier turn left onto the well-maintained path marked with yellow indicators which goes around the promontory. Turn back when the path becomes less accessible and reaches the bottom of the gully.

Turn round; continue along route des Éluas which runs downhill and round a hairpin bend.

Return to Compiègne by following the long route du Moulin.

A further itinerary **5** might take in the **village of Rethondes** ○, the church at **St-Crépin-aux-Bois**, and the 16C ruins of the beautiful priory church of the old **Prieuré Ste-Croix-d'Offémont**. The route des Princesses is a popular starting point for rambles.

CORBIE

Population 6 152
Michelin map 52 fold 9 or 236 fold 24

Corbie is a small town between the River Somme and River Ancre; it developed around the Benedictine abbey, where the powerful abbots held the title of Count and were allowed to mint coinage.

A Cradle for Saints – The monastery was founded in 657 by **St Bathild**, wife of the Frankish king Clovis II, and in Carolingian times became a centre of Christian civilization under the direction of **St Adalard**, Charlemagne's cousin. More than 300 monks took part day and night in the constant worship of the Lord; St Paschase Radbert wrote the first theological treatise on the Eucharist; apostolic activity developed. The

Somme valley, Corbie

abbey spread to Corvey in Westphalia, which was to become the main centre of evangelism in northern Europe under the impetus of St Anschaire (or Oscar), who was born in Corbie in 801. In the 11C **St Gerard**, a monk from Corbie, retreated to the area between the Garonne and the Dordogne, founding the Monastery known as La Sauve Majeure. **St Colette** (1381-1447), the daughter of a local carpenter, lived as a recluse and was favoured with several visions. She came out of seclusion to establish several convents of Poor Clares.

SIGHTS

Museum ⊘ – It is essentially devoted to the history of the abbey and contains Carolingian pottery, 16C coins, copies of manuscripts from the former library and a relief map of the siege of Corbie in 1636.

From the vast place de la République go through the 18C **monumental gateway** to the abbey; the cloister and convent buildings were razed during the Revolution.

Église St-Pierre ⊘ – The construction of the former abbey church lasted from the 16C to the 18C but in 1815

> **SIMPLE PLEASURES**
>
> **L'Abbatiale** – *Place Jean-Catelas* – ☎ *03 22 48 40 48 – closed Sun – 60/80F.* This unpretentious family establishment facing the church will greet you with warmth and genuine simplicity. Two menus are available to diners a brasserie-type formula or traditional restaurant fare. You can also stay the night. Highly affordable prices.

the transept and chancel were knocked down, since they were by then in a state of collapse.

The stylistic unity of the remaining buildings is due to the architects' continued use of the Gothic style throughout the Renaissance and Classical periods: this accounts for the ribbed vaults in the three aisles, the rose-window, the twin towers pierced by twin bays, and the west front featuring three doorways with broken arches, all following the style of Gothic cathedrals. Part of the decoration borrows from the Classical repertory, notably the cartouches on the porch coving.

The **interior** is now only about 36m/118ft long, as opposed to 117m/384ft originally (see the model of the church before the Revolution). The Treasury at one time contained 113 reliquaries which were often venerated by the French king and some of which have been preserved. The works of art include:
- the 15C statue of Our Lady of the Door *(south aisle, last pillar)*;
- St Bathild, an example of majestic 14C statuary *(end of south aisle, right of altar)*;
- a head of St Peter (13C) *(a pillar of north aisle)*;
- the 15C tomb of Abbot Raoul de Roye, the tutor of St Colette *(north aisle)*.

Chapelle Ste-Colette – The chapel was built in 1959 on the site of the house in which St Colette was born and contains a 16C statue of the saint kneeling.

EXCURSIONS

La Neuville – *2km/1mi northwest, on right bank of the River Ancre.*
Above the doorway of the early-16C church is a large, interesting **bas-relief** showing Christ's entry into Jerusalem on Palm Sunday. The relief is remarkable for its clarity and wealth of detail: spectators perched in the trees, in the background a miller wearing a cotton bonnet at the window of his mill etc.

Mysterious blue springs

In the Corbie area, in particular in Daours, Pont-Noyelles and Fréchencourt, there are mysterious fresh-water springs where water gushing out of the ground has hollowed out craters from which a strange blue light appears to emanate. The phenomenon has given rise to supernatural legends, but it is most likely related to specific characteristics of the surface of the water in such pools, which seems to absorb the wavelength of blue light.

Australian Memorial – *3km/2mi south. Leave Corbie by D 1 (towards Amiens) and in Fouilloy turn left onto D 23 towards Villers-Bretonneux.*
In spring 1918 the hills around **Villers-Bretonneux** were fiercely fought over by the Germans and the Australians, following the German offensive on Picardy; more than 10 000 Australian men lost their lives. A memorial and a cemetery recall their sacrifice. Extended **view** towards the River Somme and Amiens.

La CÔTE D'OPALE★
The OPAL COAST
Michelin map 51 folds 1, 2 or 236 folds 1, 2

The **Côte d'Opale** extends from Baie de Somme all the way round to the Belgian border; its name is derived from the creamy colour of the waves washing against the coast. The name was first used in 1911 by a local painter, Édouard Lévêque, but the landscapes had long been a source of inspiration for painters and writers including Corot and Victor Hugo.
The most spectacular part of the coastline is between Boulogne and Calais, where the cliffs skirt the Boulonnais hills. Between the sea and the sky there is only the Opal Coast bluff, characterized by promontories separating the small, dry valleys **(crans)**. A strong north-south current wears away the base of the cliffs, sometimes causing large parts to collapse. Research has shown that the cliff is eroded by about 25m/27yd every 100 years.
This part of the coast has been declared a major national site and named **Site des deux Caps** ⊙; it offers enjoyable rambles and nature trails.

FROM BOULOGNE TO CALAIS *49km/30mi – about 2hr 30min*

★**Boulogne-sur-Mer** – *See BOULOGNE-SUR-MER.*
Leave Boulogne by D 940.

D 940 is a winding coastal road offering glimpses of the sea, the ports and the beaches, leading across hill crests which are intermittently bare or covered with closely cropped meadows.
To the north the road comes to the Escalles *cran*, resembling a mountain pass but at an altitude of less than 100m/328ft. Car parks flank the road, allowing access to the sea or to walks among the dunes.

Wimereux – The opening to the Wimereux Valley *(see Le BOULONNAIS)* is the site of a large and popular seaside resort for families. A walk on the promenade built along the sand and pebble beach affords views of the Straits of Dover, the Grande Armée Column and Boulogne. The promenade narrows to a path leading to **Pointe aux Oies**, where on 6 August 1840 the future Napoleon III landed prior to his attempt to win over the garrison stationed at Boulogne.
Between Wimereux and Ambleteuse the road runs beside tall dunes.

Ambleteuse – This picturesque village stands on a hillside above the mouth of the River Slack, where boats can to beached. Ambleteuse was formerly a naval base protected by **Fort d'Ambleteuse** ⊙, built by Vauban between 1685 and 1690. Napoleon based part of his flotilla here at the time of the Boulogne Camp *(see BOULOGNE-SUR-MER)*. Today it is a beach among the coastal dunes, from which Boulogne's harbour entrance and, in clear weather, the white cliffs of the English coast, are visible.
The **Musée historique de la Seconde Guerre mondiale** ⊙ on the outskirts of Ambleteuse retraces the full story of this conflict, from the conquest of Poland in 1939 to the Liberation. About 100 different uniforms are exhibited, together with equipment worn or used by the armies involved in the war.

On a beach with lifeguards in attendance, pay attention to the colour of the flag flying near the lifeguard station:

Green: Lifeguards in attendance. Swimming authorised and not considered dangerous.

Orange: Lifeguards in attendance. Swimming considered dangerous.

Red: Swimming prohibited.

Eating out

MID-RANGE

La Sirène – *62179 Audinghen* – ☎ *03 21 32 95 97 – closed 21 Dec-31 Jan, evenings except Sat from Sept to Easter, Sun evening and Mon – 113/205F*. This fish restaurant commands superb views of the coastline, in particular the beach around Cap Gris-Nez. The chef's speciality is grilled lobster, served in one of the two dining rooms giving onto large bay windows.

Restaurant Liégeoise and Atlantic Hôtel – *The Pier, 62930 Wimereux* – ☎ *03 21 32 41 01 – closed Feb and Sun evening – 130/230F*. Seafood and shellfish lovers will be overwhelmed by the choice of freshly caught produce here. You may settle at the imposing bar, on the seaside promenade or in the panoramic dining room on the first floor. It is advisable to choose a room with a view of the sea.

Where to stay

MODERATE

Chambre d'Hôte La Grand'Maison – *Hamlet of La Haute-Escalles, 62179 Escalles – 2km/1mi east of Cap-Blanc-Nez by D 243* – ☎ *03 21 85 27 75 – ✉ – 6 rooms 200/300F*. Half-way between the two headlands, facing the British Isles, an 18C farmhouse overgrown with flowers will greet you with open arms. The perfect compromise between land and sea. Whether you like hiking, riding or windsurfing, you will appreciate the high standard of these comfortable rooms equipped with all modern amenities including television. Three gîtes (self-catering accommodation) are also available to tourists.

MID-RANGE

Hôtel Les Mauves – *62179 Audinghen – 3km/2mi southeast of Cap-Gris-Nez by D 191* – ☎ *03 21 32 96 06 – closed 16 Nov-31 Mar – ▣ – 16 rooms 320/520F – ☕ 46F – restaurant 120/235F*. A few hundred yards from the beach, a pretty brick cottage run by two sisters proposes simple but pleasant, carefully kept rooms (the renovated ones are slightly more comfortable). Delightful dining room with wooden flooring, rustic chairs and a fine collection of plates.

3km/2mi after Audresselles, turn left onto D 191.

★★**Cap Gris-Nez** – This "grey-nose cape" looks out to the English coast less than 30km/19mi away. The gently sloping cliffs rise to 45m/148ft. The lighthouse (28m/92ft tall) with beams visible 45km/28mi away, was rebuilt after the war. It stands at the tip of a bare, windswept peninsula dotted with the remains of ruined German pillboxes. The Gris-Nez branch of CROSS (Centre Régional d'Opération de Secours et de Sauvetage) is located underground; the organisation is responsible for watching over these waters, where maritime traffic is the heaviest in the world, and provides aid of any kind when needed. The crumbling debris from the cliffs mingles with the rocky reef known as "the Whales" (*Les Épaulards*) because, seen from a distance, it looks humpbacked and throws up spray.

Straight ahead, the **view**★ extends to the English cliffs which appear white next to the blue of the sky, and on the French side, the folds of the coastline, including the characteristic dry valleys between the cliffs, are visible. Cap Blanc-Nez (*right*) and Boulogne (*left*) may also be seen.

A memorial recalls that on 25 May 1940 the naval officer Ducuing and his sailors died here, defending the signal station against Guderian's armoured tanks.

"Flobarts" from Wissant

These fishing boats, whose origin goes back to the 17C, were used all along the Opal Coast for fishing herring, mackerel, cod and sole. Built of wood in the shape of half a walnut shell, they measured 5m/16ft in length and 2m/6.5ft in width and could land on a beach or any other place where there was no harbour. In addition, owing to their flat bottom and reduced draught, they hardly felt the impact of the waves. In the 1950s, engines replaced the traditional sails and the boats were launched with the help of tractors. Most of them have now been replaced by more efficient vessels; however, a few *flobarts* are still used as pleasure sailing boats. A *flobart* festival takes place every year during the last weekend in August.

The **Musée du Mur de l'Atlantique** ⊘ is in the Todt battery, a Second World War pillbox which served as a German missile launching base; missiles 2m/6ft long were fired on England from here. There are collections of arms and uniforms inside the museum. Note, in particular, the naval gun on rails (280 bore, made by Krupp in 1943), which is 35m/115ft long, could fire 15 times per hour and had a range of 62-86km/38.5-53.4mi.

⌂ **Wissant** – This splendid beach of fine, firm sand is well sheltered from the eastern winds and currents. It forms a vast curve between Cap Gris-Nez and Cap Blanc-Nez. Villas stand among the dunes overlooking the shore.

The **Musée du Moulin** ⊘ is housed in a flour mill driven by hydraulic power. It is well preserved and features pinewood parts, cast-iron waterwheels and a conveyor belt to lift the goods.

★★**Cap Blanc-Nez** – The "white-nose cape" is a vertical mass of chalk cliffs rising 134m/440ft above the waves, offering extensive **views**★ over the English cliffs and the French coast from Calais to Cap Gris-Nez.

The **Musée National du Transmanche** ⊘, located on Mont d'Hubert, faces Cap Blanc-Nez; it retraces the turbulent history of the strait, which scientists and scholars have always used to promote their ideas. The story began in 1751 with Nicolas Desmarets, who was the first to think of linking France to England. Later, Aimé Thomé de Gamond suggested a variety of options: a tunnel constructed of metal tubes, a concrete undersea vault, a pontoon, an artificial isthmus, a mobile bridge and a viaduct-bridge. He even dived to the bottom of the strait several times to collect numerous geological samples. Channel crossings were eventually achieved by balloon (Blanchard), plane (Blériot), steamboat (the first regular line was established in 1816), raft, on skis etc.

Lower down, near D 940, stands the monument to **Latham** (1883-1912), the pilot who attempted, unsuccessfully, to cross the Channel at the same time as Blériot. Between **Sangatte** and Blériot-Plage, the chalets are built directly on the sea-washed dunes. It is here that the Channel Tunnel emerges.

Blériot-Plage – The beautiful beach extends along to Cap Blanc-Nez. At Baraques (500m/550yd west of the resort), near D 940, a monument commemorates the first aerial crossing of the Channel, by **Louis Blériot** (1872-1936). On 25 July 1909 he landed his airplane in a valley on the Dover cliffs, after a flight of approximately half an hour.

Calais – *See CALAIS.*

Cap Gris-Nez

Y. Tierry/MICHELIN

COUCY-LE-CHÂTEAU-AUFFRIQUE★

Population 1 058
Michelin map 56 fold 4 or 236 fold 37

Coucy extends along a promontory overlooking the Ailette Valley on an impressive defensive **site★**, further sheltered by its medieval walls which used to incorporate 28 towers. Unfortunately, during the First World War the proud town suffered greatly from being in the front line of battle and in 1917 the Germans blew up the castle keep.

The Lord of Coucy – "I am not a king, nor a prince, a duke or a count either. I am the Lord (Sire) of Coucy" was the proud boast of the castle's owner, Enguerrand II (1192-1242) who, after fighting loyally and valiantly at Bouvines, sought to take possession of the French throne during Blanche of Castille regency.

SIGHTS

Château ⊘ – A bailey is entered before the castle proper. To the right of the bailey's entrance the Guard-room (Salle des Gardes) contains a model and documents relating to Coucy. The foundations of a Romanesque chapel are visible on the approach to the castle, which stands as an irregular quadrilateral at the end of the promontory. The great round towers, built with hoardings, which used to surround it were over 30m/98ft high and were even stronger than the royal keeps destroyed by the Germans in 1917.

The dwellings had been rebuilt by Enguerrand VII at the end of the 14C, then finished at the end of the 15C by Louis of Orléans, Charles VI's brother, who had bought Coucy from Enguerrand VII's daughter. Remains of two large chambers (Salle des Preuses and Salle des Preux) exist, with a cellar underneath. From the west tower there is a good view over the valleys of the River Ailette and River Oise.

> **ROOM WITH A VIEW**
>
> **Le Belle Vue** – *Ville Haute, 02380 Coucy-le-Château* – ☎ *03 23 52 69 70 – closed 24-27 Dec and 2 weeks in Jan* – 🅿 – *7 rooms 180/215F* – 🖙 *30F – restaurant 100/180F.* A sober decoration and a privileged location in the upper town are the two main assets of this hotel. The rooms on the second floor afford breathtaking views of the city gates and the plain extending beyond.

Porte de Soissons – This gate, which was built in the 13C, is reinforced by the Coucy tower and now houses the history museum.

Musée historique ⊘ – A model of the town and the castle are among the exhibits, together with engravings and old photographs, and figures dressed in period costumes. From the platform there is a good view over the Ailette Valley.

Église St-Sauveur ⊘ – This church nestles at the edge of the ramparts. Apart from the Romanesque west front (12C) and the 14C Gothic aisles, the building was almost totally rebuilt after the First World War.

Porte de Laon – This entrance dates from the 13C and played a major defensive role at the promontory's base; it is the only entrance with easy access and is therefore guarded by two huge round towers, with walls 8m/26ft thick at their base.

Domaine de la Grangère – This garden belonged to the Governor's House where in 1594 César, Duke of Vendôme, was born, the bastard son of Henri IV and Gabrielle d'Estrées, Duchesse de Beaufort. The lip of the well is made from a keystone from the castle keep.

BASSE FORÊT DE COUCY

Leave Coucy by Porte de Chauny; at the junction at the foot of the promontory, take D 934 towards Noyon, through Montoir.

Bois du Montoir – A 380mm mortar was concealed in this stretch of woodland. On several occasions in 1915, it fired on Compiègne which is 40km/25mi away, leaving enormous shell holes.

Folembray – The kennels of the Rallye-Nomade Hunt are located here. The hounds are used for deer hunting. François I enjoyed staying in the château with his favourite Françoise de Châteaubriand.
Nearby is the Folembray racing circuit run by Henri Pescarolo, a veteran racing driver.

CRÉCY-EN-PONTHIEU

Population 1 491
Michelin map 52 fold 7 or 236 fold 12

The name of Crécy conjures up pictures of the defeat of King Philippe VI of France at the hands of Edward III of England on 26 August 1346, at the beginning of the Hundred Years War.
Crécy is today a peaceful little town on the edge of a farmed basin at the source of the River Maye, facing the plateau on which Crécy Forest stands.

The Battle of Crécy – Crécy was the site of the bitter defeat inflicted on Philippe VI of France by Edward III of England at the beginning of the Hundred Years War. **Edward III** had landed in Normandy with 3 900 knights, 11 000 longbow men and 5 000 Welshmen armed with cutlasses; they rampaged through Normandy as far as Poissy and took up a defensive position at Crécy. Philip VI advanced with 1 200 knights, 6 000 Genoese archers and 20 000 men-at-arms. An attack was then launched by the French cavalry, in a spirited but ill-planned move. The assault disintegrated under the hail from the English archers, backed up for the first time in European history by bombardments; in the resulting carnage, 11 princes, 1 542 knights and 10 000 soldiers fell on the battlefield.

Church – The interior houses four large canvases from the Poussin School presenting the story of Moses. The paintings came from the now-ruined Dommartin Abbey *(near Tortefontaine on D 119, north of Crécy)*.

"Croix du Bourg" – Erected in the lower part of the town around the 12C, it remains a mystery. The top part is certainly post 1600.

Moulin Edouard III – *1km/0.5mi north on D 111.*
Beside the road *(right)* stands a hillock on the site of the windmill from where the King of England directed the battle. From the top there is a good **view** over the undulating plain *(viewing table)*.

"Croix de Bohême" – *On D 56 southeast of Crécy.* Philip's ally John the Blind, the old king of Bohemia, was killed while being carried to his badly wounded son at the heart of the battle; the spot where he fell is marked with the Cross of Bohemia (Croix de Bohême).

FORÊT DE CRÉCY *29km/18mi round trip – about 1hr*

The forest, which covers an area of 4 300ha/10 625 acres, has been laid out for tourism with lay-bys and picnic areas, signposted footpaths and bridlepaths, and the "Circuit des vieux chênes" or "Old Oak Trail" which can be followed by car or bike. The forest lies on the plateau to the south of the River Maye and is the natural habitat of deer, wild boar and pheasants. It is carpeted with lily-of-the-valley in springtime. Viewing tables have been set out on the edge of the forest in Forest-Montiers and Forest-l'Abbaye.

From Crécy, take the Forest-l'Abbaye road (D 111) to the crossroads at Le Monument then turn right onto the Forest-Montiers road through the woodland.
The Forest-Montiers road runs past some superb beech and oak copses.

Continue to Le Poteau de Nouvion then turn right onto the forest road called Le Chevreuil, to the crossroads at Les Grands-Hêtres hunting hide.

Hutte des Grands-Hêtres – This part of the forest, crossed by a footpath called Sentier des deux Huttes, is absolutely outstanding.

Return to Poteau de Nouvion and turn right towards N 1 and Forest-Montiers.

Forest-Montiers – It was here that St Riquier founded a hermitage, later to become a monastery (*moutier* in French). It was also here that François I's son, Charles, died of plague at the age of 23.

Take N 1 in a northerly direction.

Bernay-en-Ponthieu – See Bernay-en-Ponthieu.
The River Maye forms a myriad of lakes and ponds in the area around Bernay-en-Ponthieu.

Turn right onto D 938 and return to Crécy-en-Ponthieu.

The road overlooks the wide **Maye Valley** with its alternating fields of crops, meadows and thickets. The southern slopes are topped by the Crécy Forest.

CRÉPY-EN-VALOIS

Population 13 222
Michelin map 56 folds 12,13 or 237 fold 7

Crépy is in the heavily forested Valois, one of the oldest regions in France. The upper part of the town is strategically placed on a plateau between two streams.

The Valois dynasty – In 1328, the death of Charles IV, last son of Philip IV the Fair, marked the extinction of the direct line of Capetians, giving way to the House of Valois through Philip VI of Valois, the first cousin of Charles IV, who was chosen by the nobility and the clergy in preference to Edward III of England, Philip the Fair's own grandson by his mother. Edward decided not to accept his eviction and in 1346 he landed in Normandy, thus starting the Hundred Years War. The House of Valois prospered nevertheless and in turn founded the dynasty of the dukes of Burgundy. The grandson of Philip VI, Charles V, was a wise monarch who strengthened the State and recovered the major part of the territories lost to the English thanks to his constable, Du Guesclin. The last representatives of this dynasty which lasted until 1589, Charles VIII, François I, Henri II and III, contributed to the development of Italian – therefore Renaissance – art in France, while giving kingship a new, authoritarian stamp.

WHEN A HOTEL IS A CASTLE ...

Château de Geresme – *1 avenue de l'Europe* – ☎ *03 44 39 63 04* – ☐ *– 11 rooms 360/1200F* – ☐ *45F – restaurant 120/200F.* Some visitors may find the interior decoration of this modest 17C château a trifle ornate but they will certainly appreciate the quiet, comfortable rooms. Before retiring for the night, why not tuck into a good meal, have a refreshing drink at the bar or try your hand at French billiards?

Capital of the Valois – The counts and subsequently the dukes of Valois made Crépy their new capital. A 10C castle, as well as several monasteries and churches, testify to the importance Crépy had acquired between the 11C and the 14C. It was only after Henri II's reign that the princes showed a preference for Villers-Cotterêts. In 1790 the reorganisation of the French *départements* split the old Valois territory between Oise and Aisne. Crépy's golden age was over.

★**OLD TOWN** *1hr 30min*

Place Gambetta - This square has retained its quaint medieval charm. Among the 18C buildings, the **Maison des Quatre Saisons** (no 15) features four Rococo grotesque masks representing the four seasons. There are a number of fine house fronts dating from the 13C, 16C and 17C.

Follow rue des Ursulines, then turn right onto rue du Lion.

At no 5, note the 14C mansion **Hôtel du Lion** with its crow-stepped gables.

Église St-Denis – The majestic 16C transept consists of two bays. The nave was built in the 12C, the aisles in the 15C. The south aisle presents several small stone slabs celebrating the memory of the Ursuline nuns *(see below)*.

Abbaye St-Arnoul ⊘ – The ruins of this abbey - the necropolis of the counts of Valois - are at their most impressive when seen from the edge of the walls they dominate. On the opposite side stand the remains of a Gothic church. Excavations have uncovered a series of 11C colonnettes with their capitals, belonging to a former crypt.
Take the opposite direction to St-Denis and return to the town centre along a cobbled street; after a bend it leads to the **Maison de l'Intendant des Ursulines**, a superb 18C building and further along, to the entrance of the Ursuline convent. This was a teaching order present in Crépy from 1623 to 1791.

Return to place Gambetta.

Église St-Thomas – *Entrance in rue St-Lazare*. These distinguished ruins are the remains of a Gothic church built outside the ramparts in 1182 in memory of Thomas à Becket, Archbishop of Canterbury, 12 years after he was murdered in his own cathedral. The ruins include the west front, the first bay of the nave, the truncated tower and its 15C spire. The rest of the grounds is now a garden.

J.-M. Guinot/Musée de l'Archerie

18C statuette
of St Sebastian,
patron saint of archers

Musée de l'Archerie et du Valois ⓥ – The museum's charming collections are housed in the old castle. Archery is a traditional sport in the Valois area. Groups originated from part-civilian, part-military associations set up in the Middle Ages to train the militia in peacetime.

Wary of the strong religious and loyalist views of the archers, the members of the 1789 Constituent Assembly incorporated them into the National Guard. Archers' associations reappeared in the 19C, for social and sporting purposes.

The exhibitions in the museum's low-ceilinged chambers illustrate the history and folklore behind this sport. The display cases show the history of the bow and crossbow, from "primitive" weapons to present-day competition bows.

The room dealing with representations of St Sebastian, patron saint of archers, forms a happy transition between the museum and the upper chapel and large guard-room where, beneath magnificent 16C rafters, there is an exhibition of **sacred art**★ consisting mainly of statues from local rural churches (15C and 16C statues of the Virgin Mary).

Château de DAMPIERRE★★

Michelin map 101 fold 31, 106 fold 29 or 237 fold 28

Dampierre, situated in the narrow upper part of the Chevreuse Valley, is closely associated with two distinguished families, the Luynes and the Chevreuse. The château still belongs to the latter.

From 1675 to 1683 Jules Hardouin-Mansart rebuilt the Château de Dampierre for Colbert's son-in-law the Duke of Chevreuse, a former student at Port-Royal and the mentor of the Duke of Burgundy.

The castle and its park laid out by Le Nôtre form one of the rare estates close to Paris to have been so well preserved.

TOUR ⓥ

The main body of the château, surrounded by a moat, opens onto a courtyard flanked by stables and outbuildings. In front of it are two buildings with arcades. The pinkish tones of the brick harmonise with the sober stone string courses and columns, contrasting sharply with the darker hues of the park.

On the ground floor, visitors may admire Cavelier's statue of Penelope in the hall leading to the drawing rooms embellished with Louis XV wainscot, the suite occupied by Marie Leszczynska, and an imposing dining room decorated with Louis XIV panelling.

The first floor houses the Royal Suite, which accommodated Louis XIV, Louis XV and Louis XVI. The splendid 17C and 18C furnishings are beautifully preserved and reminiscent of the King's suite at Versailles. Note the furniture, portraits, wainscot, medallions and overdoor panels by old masters.

Château de Dampierre

C. Valentin/HOA QUI

169

Eating out

MODERATE

Country Road – *20 Grande-rue, 78720 Dampierre-en-Yvelines* – ☎ *01 30 52 52 07 – closed 24 Dec-5 Jan, Mon, Tues, Wed and evenings – 70/110F*. This charming house in the heart of the village prides itself on its typically British atmosphere. Order brunch, a mixed salad, a pastry or the chef's special in an Anglo-Saxon setting reflected in the choice of tablecloths, chinaware and hand-painted furniture.

MID-RANGE

Auberge du Château "Table des Blot" – *1 Grande-rue, opposite the château, 78720 Dampierre-en-Yvelines* – ☎ *01 30 47 56 56 – closed 20 Aug-2 Sept, 18-29 Dec, Feb school holidays, Sun evening, Tues lunchtime and Mon – 180/250F*. This family business known throughout the area is housed in a charming half-timbered building. A glass extension has been added to the fine dining hall with its pristine walls. Delicious food at affordable prices. The rooms are unpretentious and well kept.

The most amazing achievement stands at the top of the great staircase. The Salle de la Minerve is a formal reception room by Duban from the Restoration period. Ingres was commissioned to paint a fresco representing the Golden Age; it was never completed. The Duc Honoré de Luynes, who conceived the whole project, ordered a colourful 3m/10ft statue of Minerva, a miniature replica of the legendary gold and ivory Minerva of the Parthenon executed by Phidias in the 5C BC.

★ **Park** ⊙ – A walk round the castle starting from the right will lead you to a large ornamental pond, the favourite spot of many anglers. Water is omnipresent in this vast romantic park: canals, fountains and waterfalls embellish this green open space at the heart of the forest, in the centre of the picturesque Chevreuse Valley. The park and the castle form one of the rare protected estates near the capital.

EXCURSION

Vaux de Cernay – *4km/2.5mi south by D 91, 30min to 2hr walk*. The road *(D 91)* weaves up the wooded narrow valley, past a restaurant and across a brook by a mill, Moulin des Roches.

Park near the Chalet des Cascades.

The slopes surrounding the oaks and beeches are dotted with sandstone boulders, little falls and whirlpools.

Étang de Cernay – The pond was created by the monks of the local abbey to stock fish. A memorial to the 19C landscape painter Léon-Germain Pelouse stands at the top of the embankment, near a stately oak tree.

The walk may be continued for another 30min or 1hr by following the wide path which veers right and leads straight up to the wooded plateau. From the edge of the plateau turn back, bear right and return along the cliff path that skirts the promontory.

★ **Abbaye des Vaux-de-Cernay** ⊙ – The abbey was founded in the early 12C. It came under Cistercian rule and reached its heyday in the 13C but in the 14C it suffered from epidemics of plague and successive wars and started to decline. In 1791 it was abandoned by its last 12 monks and sold. The Rothschild family who bought the abbey in 1873 restored and preserved it until the Second World War. It has now been converted into a hotel.

In the **grounds**, the ruins of the abbey church may be seen (late-12C façade with rose-window), and the monk's building, now a concert hall.

Where to stay

MID-RANGE

Abbaye des Vaux de Cernay – *78720 Cernay-la-Ville – 2.5km/1.6mi west of Cernay by D 24 –* ☎ *01 34 85 23 00 –* 🅿 *– 117 rooms 410/1900F –* ☲ *80F – restaurant 265/415F*. It is a real privilege to sleep in this lovely Cistercian abbey and enjoy the peaceful atmosphere that permeates its beautiful park. The fine, lofty rooms are a pleasing combination of old-fashioned textures and modern comfort. Restaurant and tea room.

DISNEYLAND PARIS★★★

Michelin map 106 fold 22

Standing on the Brie plain about 30km/18mi east of Paris is a unique development in Europe: Disneyland Paris. Relive your childhood dreams in the space of a visit to the **Disneyland Paris theme park**. This theme park, like those in the United States (Disneyland in California opened in 1955 and Magic Kingdom in Florida opened in 1971) and Japan (Tokyo Disneyland, 1983), is a realisation of Walt Disney's dream of creating "a small, enchanted park where children and adults can enjoy themselves together". Not far from the hotels, the main entertainment centre, **Disney Village**, recreates the American way of life with shops, restaurants and a variety of entertainment. At a short distance from the complex lies **Golf Disneyland Paris** with its 27 hole course.

A magician called Walt Disney - Walt Disney's name is linked to innumerable cartoon strips and animated cartoons which have entertained children throughout the world, and the heroes of his creations - Mickey Mouse, Minnie, Donald, Pluto, Pinocchio, Snow White etc - no one can forget. He was born Walter Elias Disney in Chicago in 1901, the fourth child of Flora and Elias Disney. Walt soon showed great ability at drawing. After the First World War, in which he served as an ambulance driver in France, he

> ### How old is Mickey?
>
> The famous young mouse has not got a single wrinkle, yet he was born in 1928 thanks to Disney and the cartoonist of Dutch origin, Ub Iwerks. Mickey first appeared in a small film entitled *Plane Crazy*, based on the Charles Lindbergh's achievement. However, it was on 18 November of the same year that he made his debut as a star, together with the delightful Minnie, in the first silent cartoon film entitled *Steamboat Willie*. One small detail, age has caused Mickey to lose... not his hair but his tail!

returned to the United States where, in Kansas City, he met a young Dutchman called Ub Iwerks, who was also passionate about drawing. In 1923 the pair produced in Hollywood a series of short films called *Alice Comedies*. In 1928 Mickey Mouse, the future international star, was created. There next followed the era of the Oscar-winning, full-length animated cartoon films: *The Three Little Pigs* (1933), *Snow White and the Seven Dwarfs* (1937), *Dumbo* (1941). Disney productions also developed to include films starring real people, such as *Treasure Island* (1950) and *20 000 Leagues Under the Sea* (1954), and some mixing the two, for instance *Mary Poppins* (1964) which won six Oscars. On 15 December 1966 the man who had spent his life trying to bring dreams to life died; the Walt Disney Studios continued to make films, however, remaining faithful to Walt's ideas: *Aladdin* (1993), *The Lion King* (1994), *Pocahontas* (1995), *The Hunchback of Notre-Dame* (1996), *Hercules* (1997), *Mulan, a Chinese legend* (1998) and *Tarzan* (1999).

★★★DISNEYLAND PARIS THEME PARK ⊘

The large Disneyland Paris site (over 55ha/135 acres) comprises five territories or "lands", each with a different theme. As well as the spectacular shows featuring amazing automatons in particularly detailed settings, each region has shops, ice cream vendors, restaurants and self service restaurants.

The Newport Bay Club

Eating out

INSIDE THE THEME PARK

Whether you want to have a snack or an elaborate three-course meal, there are a great many restaurants to choose from. Here is a short list:

MODERATE

For a quick, inexpensive meal, go to the **Bella Notte** for a quick trip to Italy, settle at the terrace of **Colonel Hathi's** at the foot of a charming waterfall or opt for the buffet formula at the Victorian-style **Plaza Gardens**.

MID-RANGE

If you are not in a hurry, take time to stop at one of the following restaurants which offer both tasty cuisine and an unusual decor. Remember to book by calling 01 64 74 28 82 or by telling the City Hall, on the left when you enter the theme park.

Silver Spur Steakhouse – *Frontierland – closed Mon and Tues – 125/150F*. You can leave your horse at the entrance to this saloon bar typical of the Far West. You might not run into any cowboys or wealthy cattle breeders but you will be served delicious steaks grilled in front of you, just like those they eat down at the ranch. Note the imposing lamps decorated with silver stirrups.

Blue Lagoon Restaurant – *Adventureland – 150F*. Creole cuisine in a decidedly tropical ambience. In this luxuriant setting, be adventurous and try exotic dishes such as *accras de morue* (spicy fritter of cod), *boudins antillais* (polony made of pig's blood with bread onion, milk, garlic, chives and pepper) and *rougail de poissons...* (fish simmered with tomatoes and onions enhanced with Caribbean seasoning) as well as other seafood specialities from the French West Indies. Sit down at a table near the river near the "Pirates of the Caribbean".

Walt's Restaurant – *Main Street – closed Wed and Thur – 169F*. After climbing the sweeping staircase of this handsome Victorian mansion on Main Street and admiring the photographs of Walt Disney adorning the walls, choose a seat in one of the cosy salons of this comfortable restaurant. Our favourite dining areas were Discoveryland and the Library....

Auberge de Cendrillon – *Fantasyland – 175F*. Once upon a time there was a charming inn nestled at the foot of a lovely castle... Legend has it that a fair maiden in glass slippers would turn up in a carriage to settle in front of the huge fireplace or on the flower-filled terrace in summer and order a delicious meal...

OUTSIDE THE THEME PARK

Disney Village is a gastronomic melting-pot where all the different styles of American cuisine can be sampled. Before visiting the park itself, make a stop at Disney Village for lunch or dinner and prepare for a complete change of scenery...

MODERATE

Annette's Diner – *Disney Village* – ☎ *01 60 45 70 37 – 90/130F*. If you are suffering pangs of nostalgia for the 1950s, then this is the place for you. Treat yourself to an extravaganza of hamburgers, milkshakes and hot-dogs! The waiters occasionally interrupt their service to give you a free demonstration of their dancing skills... and encourage you to follow suit!

MID-RANGE

Rainforest Café – *Disney Village* – ☎ *01 60 43 65 65 – www.rainforestcafe.com – 120/220F*. Here you will need to walk through a boutique and not wade through the ocean waters to reach the shores of the Amazonian Forest. Gorillas, elephants and other tropical beasts will keep you company while you enjoy the mildly spicy dishes served in a sensational decor.

Los Angeles – *Disney Village* – ☎ *01 60 45 71 14 – 155F*. Fancy a trip to California? Then come here and tuck into pizzas, pasta dishes and mixed salads against a background dominated by low-key, pastel hues. In summer, eat out on the terrace affording pretty views of the lake.

The Steakhouse – *Disney Village* – ☎ *01 60 45 70 45 – closed Sat lunchtime – 170/250F*. This restaurant is paradise for wine buffs and meat eaters! Not only is the food excellent but the Chicago-inspired decoration recalling the Prohibition of the 1920s is a feast for the eyes. On Sundays, children will enjoy having brunch with some of the legendary Disney characters.

A FEW MILES FROM THE THEME PARK

Barely a stone's throw from Disneyland, an open-air café that holds country dances will transport visitors to the turn of the last century...

MID-RANGE

L'Ermitage – *Allée Jean-de-la Fontaine, Ecluse de Chalifert, 77144 Chalifert – 6km/3.7mi north of Disneyland by N 34 then D 45* – ☎ *01 60 43 41 43 – open Fri and Sat evenings and Sun – closed 6-23 Aug – booking essential – 160/295F.* The oldest guinguette set up along the banks of the Marne in 1860 continues to attract large crowds at weekends. People of all ages flock here to indulge in their favourite pastime and rediscover the festive ambience of days gone by... while at the same time sharing tea or dinner.

Where to stay

To make your stay a resounding success, you may choose to spend the night at one of the hotels located inside the theme park. They are all run by Disney and each decor suggests one American region. We have chosen two of them as well as two camp sites that offer bungalow accommodation. However, if you prefer to try your luck further away, a bed and breakfast or a camp site will provide cheaper accommodation in a more natural setting.

MODERATE

Chambre d'Hôte Bellevue – *77610 Neufmoutiers-en-Brie – 10km/6.2mi south of Disney by A 4, D 231 then D 96* – ☎ *01 64 07 11 05 – www.club-inter-net.fr/perso/ipgalpin –* ✉ *– 7 rooms 235/395F – meal 95F.* Located in a residential suburb, this simple yet elegant house with its lovely garden is the ideal destination for tourists. Half-way between Paris and Disneyland, it is an enchanting spot at the heart of Brie country.

Camping Base de Loisirs de Jablines-Annet – *77450 Jablines – 6km/3.7mi north of Disney by N 34 then D 45* – ☎ *01 60 26 09 37 – open 30 Mar-1 Oct – booking recommended Apr-Sept – 150 plots 125F.* Here it is possible to practise almost any sport and the longest beach in the Île-de-France area awaits you, only a few miles from Disneyland-Paris. The plots are separated by wide aisles with tiling offering lovely views of the surrounding landscape.

MID-RANGE

Camping Davy Crockett Ranch – *In Disneyland* – ☎ *01 60 45 69 00 – booking recommended in summer – 97 plots for up to 8 people 400F – eating facilities.* At the heart of Citry Forest, the land of trappers, this picturesque village of bungalows has a tropical swimming pool that will delight children and adults alike. The camp site, which can accommodate tents and caravans, organises many shows, for which it sometime charges.

LUXURY

Hôtel Santa Fé – *In Disneyland* – ☎ *01 60 45 78 00 –* 🅿 *– 1 000 rooms from 850F – restaurant 130F.* Check in here and you will suddenly find yourself in New Mexico. The reception office proudly sports a poster depicting the actor Clint Eastwood against a backdrop of Mexican pampas. The fans hanging from the ceiling are yet another reminder that we are in former Aztec land, as are the rooms with their solid, heavy furniture. The musical accompaniment with mariachi groups illustrates the same theme. Naturally, the cuisine could only be ... Tex-Mex!.

Hôtel Cheyenne – *In Disneyland* – ☎ *01 60 45 62 00 –* 🅿 *– 1 000 rooms from 990F – restaurant 130F.* Come and play Cowboys and Indians at this hotel, where the Far West epic has been faithfully reconstituted. Note the uniformed staff. Ideal for family holidays. Simple but comfortable rooms with rustic wooden furniture. Self-service restaurant.

Hôtel Séquoia Lodge – *In Disneyland* – ☎ *01 60 45 51 00 –* 🅿 *– 1 001 rooms from 1 195F – restaurant 115/150F.* If you are looking for escapism, rush towards the Rocky Mountains, whose majestic setting inspired the decoration here. You will be greeted by forest wardens and taken to your comfortable room. Two mountain-style restaurants with buffet formula. Swimming-pool and gym club.

Hôtel New-York – *In Disneyland* – ☎ *01 60 45 73 00 –* 🅿 *– 536 rooms from 1 550F – restaurant 115/195F.* The atmosphere in this hotel is heavily suggestive of Manhattan during the 1930s, a period that set the tone for the interior decoration of the fair-sized bedrooms. Two restaurants with terraces in high season. Indoor and outdoor pool.

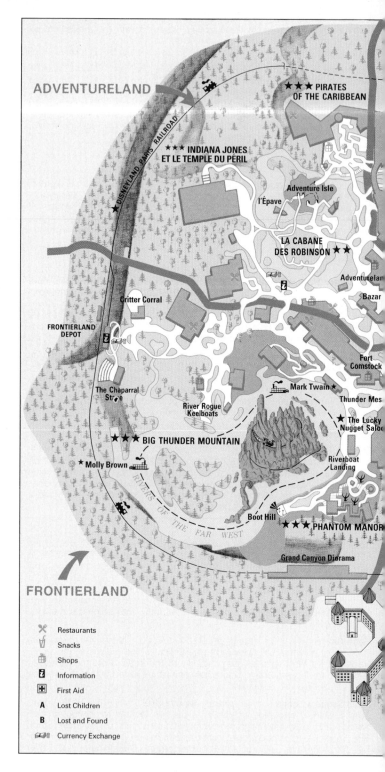

ADVENTURELAND

★★★ PIRATES
OF THE CARIBBEAN

★★★ INDIANA JONES
ET LE TEMPLE DU PÉRIL

Adventure Isle

l'Épave

LA CABANE
DES ROBINSON ★★

Adventurelan
Bazar

Critter Corral

FRONTIERLAND
DEPOT

Fort
Comstock

The Chaparral
St..e

Mark Twain ★

Thunder Mes

River Rogue
Keelboats

★ The Lucky
Nugget Salo

★★★ BIG THUNDER MOUNTAIN

★ Molly Brown

Riverboat
Landing

RIVERS OF THE FAR WEST

Boot Hill

★★★ PHANTOM MANOR

Grand Canyon Diorama

FRONTIERLAND

✕	Restaurants
∀	Snacks
🏬	Shops
ℹ	Information
⊞	First Aid
A	Lost Children
B	Lost and Found
💱	Currency Exchange

Every day, the **Disney Parade**★★, a procession of floats carrying all the favourite Disney cartoon characters, takes place. On some evenings and throughout the summer the **Main Street Electrical Parade**★★ adds extra illuminations to the fairytale setting. The fireworks display spectacularly rounds off an eventful day.

FANTASYLAND

Casey Jr.
le petit train du cirque

NTASYLAND
STATION

le Pays
des Contes de Fées

les Pirouettes du Vieux Moulin

★ ALICE'S
CURIOUS LABYRINTH

IT'S A SMALL WORLD ★ ★

ER PAN'S
GHT ★ ★

Mad Hatter's
Tea Cups

bo the
g Elephant

Voyages
inocchio ★

le Carrousel
de Lancelot ★

nche-Neige
les
t Nains ★

LE CHÂTEAU DE LA BELLE
AU BOIS DORMANT ★ ★

DISCOVERYLAND
STATION

STAR TOURS
★ ★ ★

VIDEOPOLIS

a Tanière
du Dragon

le Théâtre
du Château

LE VISIONARIUM ★ ★

"HONEY I SHRUNK
THE AUDIENCE" ★ ★

Central Plaza →

Orbitron
Machines volantes

SPACE
MOUNTAIN
★ ★ ★

Horse-Drawn
Streetcars

Street

A

les Mystères du
Nautilus ★

AUTOPIA

Liberty
Arcade

Main Street Motors

Main

Discovery
Arcade

Town Square

Main Street
Vehicles

City Hall

DISCOVERYLAND

MAIN STREET STATION

MAIN STREET, U.S.A.

DISNEYLAND HOTEL

0   100 m
0   300 ft

DISNEY VILLAGE
RESORT HOTELS   T.G.V.

Main Street USA

The main street of an American town at the turn of the 20C, lined with shops and restaurants with Victorian-style fronts, is brought to life as though by magic. Horse-drawn street cars, limousines, fire engines and Black Marias transport visitors from Town Square to Central Plaza (the hub of the park) while colourful musicians play favourite ragtime, jazz and Dixieland tunes. On each side of the road are **Discovery Arcade** and **Liberty Arcade** (exhibition and diorama on the famous Statue of Liberty at the entrance to New York harbour).

From Main Street station a small steam train, the **Disneyland Railroad★**, travels across the park and through the **Grand Canyon Diorama**, stopping at the station in each land.

Frontierland

The conquest of the West, the gold rush and the Wild West with its legends and folklore are brought together in Thunder Mesa, a typical western town, and Big Thunder Mountain a strange, arid wall of rock like the mountains of Mounument Valley (Arizona, Utah). It rises on an island washed by the Rivers of the Far West. The waters here are plied by two handsome **steamboats★**, the *Mark Twain* and the *Molly Brown*.

★★★**Big Thunder Mountain** - In the mountain, there's an old gold mine... On the banks of the lake, in the buildings belonging to a mining company, are crowds of travellers patiently waiting to board the **Mine Train**. The trip in the hurtling carriages racing down the track at top speed includes explosions and risks of rock falls. A thrilling ride for those who enjoy heart-pounding excitement.

★★★**Phantom Manor** - A dilapidated manor house stands high above the Rivers of the Far West. It used to be the home of people who had struck it lucky during the gold rush. Inside, strange things happen. The walls stretch and shrink. The tour through the rooms and basement continues in small black cars that take you to the ghost town of Thunder Mesa. When you leave, take a stroll to the **Boot Hill** cemetery and have a look at the strange tombstones.

★**The Lucky Nugget Saloon** - This horseshoe-shaped saloon - every western town had its saloon - is richly decorated. Dinner show: **Lilly's Follies** starring bright, sparkling dancers.

Adventureland

From Central Plaza, go through Adventureland Bazaar, a sort of desert fortress containing several exotically foreign shops. Adventureland conjures up pictures of exotic adventures, travel to far-distant lands, treasure island, and pirates.

Pirates or corsairs?

Pirates were adventurers without any scruples who roamed the seas, boarding and plundering merchant ships for their own profit. Corsairs, on the other hand, were commissioned by their government to track down merchant ships from enemy countries. The most famous corsairs were Jean Bart, Duguay-Trouin and Surcouf.

★★★**Pirates of the Caribbean** -
This fortress is easy to spot - the skull and crossbones fly at the top of its walls. Cross the underground passages which reserve a few surprises then go on board a small boat and watch the attack and ransacking of a Spanish harbour town by pirates. There are several different scenes, all with superb decors and lots of action.

★★★**Indiana Jones et le Temple du Péril** - In the jungle lies a ruined temple; courageous archeologists in wagons enter it and defy the laws of gravity. This is not for the faint-hearted.

★★**La Cabane des Robinson** - The Swiss Family Robinson survived a shipwreck and were able to salvage a few objects and building materials that enabled them to build a tree house in a giant banyan tree (an Indian fig). A staircase leads up to the various rooms with their wonderful furniture.

Fantasyland

The land of legends and fairy tales is indicated by Sleeping Beauty's castle. It is a village in which the houses symbolise various European countries. Strolling around it are such well-known figures as Mickey Mouse, Donald Duck, Pinocchio, Captain Hook, Chip 'n Dale, to name but a few. They will all be delighted to pose for a photograph.

Famous fairy-tale writers

Charles Perrault (1628-1703): *Sleeping Beauty*; Charles Lutwidge Dodgson, better known as Lewis Carroll (1832-98): *Alice in Wonderland*; the Grimm Brothers: *Snow-White and the Seven Dwarves*; anthology of German fairy tales; Carlo Collodi: *Pinocchio*; Hans Christian Andersen (1805-1875): *The Little Mermaid*; James Matthew Barrie (1860-1937): *Peter Pan*.

★★ Le Château de la Belle au Bois Dormant (Sleeping Beauty's Castle) - On the upper floor, stained-glass windows and Aubusson tapestries recount episodes from this famous fairy story. Below, in the depths of the castle, a huge scaly dragon appears to be sleeping...
From the ramparts, there is a magnificent view of Fantasyland.

★★ It's a Small World - A "cruise" that takes visitors past dolls dressed in national costume, singing and dancing in sets that represent their home countries. A hymn in praise of the gentleness and liveliness of children all over the world.

★ Alice's Curious Labyrinth - An episode from *Alice in Wonderland* in which the path to the Queen of Heart's castle is full of surprises.

★★ Peter Pan's Flight - Like Peter Pan, the boy who never grew up, the trip takes visitors over the rooftops of London and the Never-Never Land, and past episodes from the story of Peter Pan... all in small boats.

★ Les voyages de Pinocchio - The misadventures of Pinocchio drawn from the story by Carlo Collodi. Meet Gepetto, Jiminy Cricket, Stromboli, and Monstro the Whale.

★ Blanche-Neige et les Sept Nains (Snow White and the Seven Dwarfs) - In the mysterious forest crossed by small wagons is the wicked witch who cast a spell on Snow White.

★ Le Carrousel de Lancelot - This is an enchanting merry-go-round of brightly painted horses.

Discoveryland

This is the world of past discoveries and dreams of the future with the great visionaries such as Leonardo da Vinci, Jules Verne and HG Wells and their wonderful inventions.

★★★ Space Mountain - This superb attraction, which is unique to Disney, was inspired by Jules Verne's novel *From the Earth to the Moon*. A huge copper and bronze mountain encompassing a gigantic cannon pointing skywards awaits the most audacious visitors. After being catapulted towards the cosmos, they experience a mind-bending, and highly acrobatic, intergalactic trip.

★★★ Star Tours - A breathtaking trip on a spaceship. Based on George Lucas' famous film, *Star Wars*.
A stopover at the **Astroport Services Interstellaires** is highly recommended. Use the **Photomorph** to change your looks (peals of laughter guaranteed) and have your photo taken.

Visionaries

Leonardo da Vinci (1452-1512): as early as the 15C, he had conceived the parachute and the helicopter. Jules Verne (1828-1905) used to state: "Everything a man can imagine other men can realise". His science-fiction novels show how right he was. Herbert George Wells (1866-1946): this master of fantasy shook the Americans with his novel entitled *War of the Worlds*, which Orson Welles interpreted on radio in 1938.

Space Mountain

Disney

★★ "Chérie, j'ai rétréci le public" (Darling I have shrunk the audience) - An extraordinary experience awaits you in the hall of the Imagination Institute: the famous professor Wayne Szalinski is giving a public demonstration of his shrinking machine. Are you volunteering? If so, hang on... the settings may not be spot on!

★★ Le Visionarium - Ever dreamt of travelling back in time? This is your chance, in an amazing machine which offers a "voyage through time". Using the surround-vision process, the audience travels right across Europe and meets a number of famous people.

★DISNEY VILLAGE

Next to the theme park and Lake Disney, Disney Village can be seen from afar, with its tall steel columns reaching for the sky. At night the whole area is flooded with light. The main street of this American town offers continuous entertainment and a con-vivial atmosphere. On summer evenings, it is particularly lively once the theme park is closed for the night. Shops, restaurants and bars are crowded out. In the street, games of skill take place while tightrope walkers, acrobats on stilts, jugglers and musicians arouse the crowd's enthusiasm. Night-owls can then go on to the dis-cotheque **Hurricanes**. The quality of the shows, the increasing number of cinemas in the **Multiplexe Gaumont**, the reputation of establishments such as **Planet Hollywood**, have insured the success of this "village" which attracts a growing number of vis-itors from the Île-de-France region.

★★ Buffalo Bill's Wild West Show - The famous adventures of pioneer William Frederick Cody (1846-1917), alias Buffalo Bill, inspired this dinner-show which, complete with horses, bison, cowboys and Indians, evokes the epic days of the Wild West. The Texas-style meal, is served on tin plates. There is non-stop action with unexpected turns, special effects and plenty of laughs.

Billy Bob's Country Western saloon - This saloon is the ideal place to go to after the show: it is the favourite haunt of cowboys with beer flowing freely and country music creating a convivial atmosphere.

Crescend'O - Conceived by Muriel Hermine, this show combines circus acts on the ground, in the water and above ground into a dazzling production with colourful costumes.

Why Buffalo Bill?

Having taken part in the conquest of the Wild West, the Civil War, the war against the Cheyennes and the Sioux, William Cody became famous for his skill as a marksman and for hunting buffaloes during the building of the Kansas Pacific Railroad. A journalist, who later wrote about his achieve-ments, gave him the nickname of Buffalo Bill. As for our hero, he travelled through the United States and then Europe, staging his adventures in a par-ticularly lively show entitled *Buffalo Bill's Wild West Show*.

DOUAI★

Conurbation 199 562
Michelin map 51 fold 16 or 236 fold 16, 17

Douai stands on either side of the River Scarpe, which flows through its centre. The town has preserved the 18C layout and buildings that gave it the aristocratic look Balzac evoked in his *Recherche de l'Absolu*. The peaceful embankments of the Scarpe and the steep paved streets of the old town are ideal for a stroll.

Douai is proud of its two peals of bells, one in the belfry and the other a peripatetic peal of 50 bells which travels the length and breadth of France. A French bell-ringing school was founded in Douai by Jacques Lannoy, who still runs it today.

Every year in early July, five giant figures of the Gayant family are paraded through the town in medieval costume, accompanied by folklore groups.

Industrial, legal and intellectual centre – Large industrial firms, comprising metal-lurgy, chemicals and food, a national printing works and an important river freight trade all contribute to the town's economic prosperity. In addition, Douai is a major legal centre, with a Court of Appeal, a relic of the Flanders Parliament which sat here from 1713 to the Revolution.

The town also enjoys a distinguished reputation for intellectual activity, which began with the elegiac poetess **Marceline Desbordes-Valmore** (1786-1859) who was born here, and is maintained by the many educational institutions which have taken the place of the university, founded in the 16C but transferred to Lille in 1887.

Gayant's town – On 16 June 1479, Douai narrowly escaped falling into French hands. A procession was organised to thank the patron saint of the town and when peace with France was signed 60 years later, this annual event became more colourful with each corporation supplying a float decorated with symbolic characters. The wicker-workers' guild provided a gayant (giant in Picard dialect); a year later the fruiterers supplied him with a wife... the children soon followed.

Gayant's misfortunes – In 1770, the bishop of Arras forbade the procession, which celebrated a French defeat, and replaced it with another one on 6 July, intended to celebrate the arrival of French troops in Douai in 1667. The giants were given another lease of life in 1778 only to be wiped out again by the Revolution. They reappeared in 1801 and were given their present costumes 20 years later. Destroyed in 1918 and 1944, they were rebuilt each time with the same care.

Jean Bellegambe (1470-1534)

This artist, who seems to have spent his entire life in Douai, was a likeable character with wide-ranging artistic talent.

He mastered the transition from the Gothic tradition (religious subjects treated with realistic detail and harmonious colours) to the Italian influence of the Renaissance (works decorated with columns, pilasters, shells and garlands) which he linked with the objective, intimate realism of the Flemish School and the intellectualism of the French School. The latter is marked by a choice of subjects which are sometimes difficult to understand.

Bellegambe worked a great deal for the abbeys of the Scarpe Valley, and Douai's landscape and buildings can often be recognised in his works: the belfry and town gates, the towers of the abbey church of Anchin, Flines woods and the watery landscapes of the River Scarpe and River Sensée.

BELFRY AND SURROUNDING AREA *1hr*

Start from place d'Armes, a part-pedestrian zone with pavement cafés and fountains. The **Hôtel du Dauphin** is the only remaining 18C house here; its façade is adorned with trophies. It now houses the tourist office.

Walk along rue de la Mairie.

★**Belfry** ⊘ – Douai's belfry is one of the best known in northern France and has been made famous not only by the description given by Victor Hugo who stopped briefly in the town in 1837 but also by Corot's fine painting, now in the Louvre. It is an imposing square Gothic tower, sombre and grim, and was built from 1387 to 1410; it stands 64m/210ft tall (40m/131ft from the ground to the platform). The top of the belfry bristles with turrets, dormer windows, pinnacles and weathervanes, and is crowned with a Flemish lion.

The current **peal** of 62 bells is on the fourth floor. The bells replaced the famous ones which were destroyed by the Germans in 1917. They play the tune of the Scottish Puritans on the hour; on the half-hour, a boating song; at quarter past and quarter to the hour, a few notes of Gayant's tune.

From the top of the tower *(192 steps)*, Douai and its industrial suburb may be seen through the louvre-boarding.

Inside the **town hall** *(hôtel de ville)* the Gothic Council Chamber (15C), the old chapel (now the main hall), the White Salon with 18C wood panelling and the state room are open to visitors.

Follow the vaulted passageway and cross the courtyard of the town hall to rue de l'Université.

This street passes beside the old 17C **pawnshop** *(mont-de-piété)*, now a food and agriculture research laboratory; it then leads to the 18C **theatre** with its Louis XVI façade.

In rue de la Comédie to the right stands the **Hôtel d'Aoust**, a beautiful example of Louis XV architecture. Note the Rococo door and the allegorical statues representing the four seasons decorating the façade overlooking the courtyard. It used to be the headquarters of the Northern Collieries Board (Direction des Houillères du Nord).

Continue along rue de la Comédie and turn right onto rue des Foulons.

Along the left-hand side of rue des Foulons, literally "Fullers' Street", a reminder of the linen-drapers of the Middle Ages, are a few 18C houses. At no 132, note the **Hôtel de la Tramerie** (**K**) built in the Louis XIII style.

Follow rue de la Mairie on the right to return to the town hall.

Eating out

MID-RANGE

Le Storez – *116 rue Storez* – ✆ *03 27 98 88 80 – closed Aug, Sat lunchtime and Sun - 139F.* Opposite the Porte d'Arras, the remaining gateway belonging to the town's former ramparts, this brick house has been set up as a restaurant since 1896. The menu focuses on fish and seafood and the decor is decidedly "nostalgic".

Le Chat Botté – *Château de Bernicourt, 59286 Roost-Warendin – 10km/6.2mi northeast of Douai by D 917 and D 8 –* ✆ *03 27 80 24 44 - closed 1-15 Aug, Sun evening and Mon except public holidays – 160/390F.* A haven of peace in the middle of a shaded park. The restaurant is set up in one of the outbuildings. Painted rattan chairs and canvases signed by one of the family provide the dining room's decoration.

Where to stay

MID-RANGE

Hôtel de la Terrasse – *36 terrasse St-Pierre* – ✆ *03 27 88 70 04 –* 🅿 *– 26 rooms 295/600F –* ☕ *45F – restaurant 135/395F.* The perfect starting-point for a leisurely stroll along the nearby banks of the Scarpe. The functional, sound-proofed rooms are housed in three separate buildings. One of the dining rooms is adorned with paintings coming from the owner's private collection.

On the town

Aux Grès – *2 place St-Amé* – ✆ *03 27 88 61 08 – Tues-Thur 5pm-1am, Fri 5pm-2am, Sat 10am-2pm, 5pm-3am, Sun 5pm-1am.* The owner, an Englishman who fell in love with this pub ten years ago, has succeeded in perpetuating its charm: a brick and black oak decor, pretty paving, a tile awning above the bar, a fireplace and tree stumps used as tables. A homely haunt where convivial games of darts and chess are played out until the early hours.

La Miroiterie – *66 bis rue de Lens* – ✆ *03 27 99 30 30 – Mon-Fri 11.45am-2.30pm, 5.30pm-midnight, Sat 5.30pm-midnight.* Housed in a former mirror factory, this vast pub and its striking decor are laid out over three levels. The bar, magnified by the glare of airport spotlights, is dominated by a splendid pedimented dresser from Scotland. Do not miss the many theme evenings that are regularly organised on the premises, in particular the fashion parades that use the counter as a catwalk...

Le Minck - *61 place du Marché-aux-Poissons* – ✆ *03 27 97 77 91 – Mon-Thur 10am-1pm, Fri 10am-2pm, Sat 4pm-3am, Sun 5pm-1am.* Large, radiant café broken up into small, cosy areas. The owner is a jazz musician who holds concerts on Sundays but the jazzy atmosphere he has created permeates his establishment at all times. The walls are covered with paintings executed by local artists.

Showtime

L'Hippodrome – *Place du Barlet* – ✆ *03 27 99 66 60 – hippo@etnet.fr – consult the of events – booking available Mon 1-7pm, Tues-Sat 3-7pm – closed school holidays.* This state-funded theatre has a dodecagonal stage that can be remodelled depending on the type of performance. The programming here is renowned for being both eclectic and audacious, ranging from classical plays to techno nights... The venue is also used for the screening of experimental films.

Shopping

Aux Délices – *68 rue de la Mairie* – ✆ *03 27 88 69 19 – Mon 2-7.30pm, Tues-Sat 9am-12.30am, 2-7.30pm – closed 1-20 Aug.* Those who love caramel will be in paradise in this confectioner's shop, which sells one of Douai's oldest specialities, known as *gayantines*. This delicious sweetmeat has a caramel paste core flavoured with vanilla butter or chicory and coated with creamy fudge.

MUSÉE DE LA CHARTREUSE ⏱ *1hr*

The museum is installed in an interesting group of 16C, 17C and 18C buildings, which were once the old charter house. On the left is the Hôtel d'Abancourt; on the right, beneath a huge square tower, is the building in the Flemish Renaissance style constructed for the Montmorency family. This is where the first Carthusian monks settled in the 17C. They built the small cloister, the refectory, the chapterhouse and the church, which was completed in 1722. The great cloister and the monks' cells were destroyed in the 19C.

The museum is in two parts: the Fine Arts Section, and Archeology and Naturel History Section.

Fine Arts Section – The collections consist principally of fine early paintings.

Rooms 1 to 3 – Early Flemish, Dutch (the Master of Manne, the Master of Flemalle) and Italian paintings. Large 16C altarpieces from other abbeys are on display here. Especially noteworthy are **Anchin Polyptych★** by Bellegambe (room 2) portraying the Adoration of the Cross or the Adoration of the Holy Trinity, depending on whether the leaves are open or closed, and the Marchiennes Polyptych by Van Scorel (Utrecht School, 16C), dedicated to St James and St Stephen. Two masterpieces of the Italian Renaissance: Veronese's *Portrait of a Venetian Woman* and Carracci's *Scourging of Christ*, a work of rare intensity, are on display in room 3. The bronze *Venus of Castello* recalls the work of the famous sculptor and architect Giambologna. Although he conducted most of his career in Italy - Rome and particularly Florence - he was born in Douai in 1529 and trained in Flanders.

Rooms 4 to 10 - Relief map of Douai in 1709. 16C Flemish and Dutch Mannerism is exhibited: works by Roland Savery, the Antwerp artists Jean Matsys, son of Quentin, and Frans Floris, the Dutchmen Van Hemessen, Van Reymerswaele, Goltzius, Cornelis Van Haarlem etc.

Take the staircase in room 4 to the first floor.

Works by Rubens (Céres and Pan) and Jordaens (Study of a head); landscapes by Momper and Govaerts; a witchcraft scene by David Teniers. Interesting series of lesser 17C Dutch masters.

Rooms 11-12 – The French School (17C-19C) is well represented here by portrait painters: Le Brun *(Louis XIV on Horseback)*, Vivien, Largillière, Boilly, David *(Mme Tallien)* etc.

Works by Impressionist painters are also on show: Renoir, Sisley and Pissaro and Post-Impressionists.

Return to the ground floor.

Cloister – The cloister vaults are pointed despite having been built in 1663, in the middle of the Classical period. The red brickwork contrasts pleasantly with the white stone of the ribs and the framing, carved with Baroque designs.

Chapter-house – The chapter-house was built in the same year as the cloister (1663) and in the same style; it now holds temporary exhibitions.

Archeology and Natural History Section – *Turn left on leaving the Charter house and left again onto rue St-Albin.*

The evolution of man is traced from the Paleolithic Age to AD 400 through the findings of excavations in the north of France (first floor). The collection includes a cast of Biache Man's skull, discovered at Biache-St-Vaast, about 13km/8mi from Douai; the man is thought to have lived c 250000 BC. The Gallo-Roman period is illustrated through material found at Bavay (statuettes) and at Lewarde (busts). There are some interesting models of the Merovingian village of Brebières and the necropolis at Hordain.

This section also includes an **aquarium** and collections of exotic butterflies and stuffed birds.

MUSÉE DE LA CHARTREUSE
GROUND FLOOR
0   20 m

Chapter House

Temporary Exhibitions

★Anchin Polyptych

2

Refectory

CLOISTER

CHAPEL

N

1st floor

Passage

Reception

5 4   3   1

6

Rue   des   Chartreux

ARCHEOLOGY AND NATURAL HISTORY SECTION

ADDITIONAL SIGHTS

Palais de Justice ⊘ – The courts date from the early 16C but were almost entirely rebuilt in the 18C; they were once the refuge of Marchiennes Abbey and then became the seat of the Flanders Parliament. The main front, rebuilt under Louis XVI by the architect Lillois Lequeux, has a severe-looking central porch.

The first-floor courtroom, called the **grande salle du parlement** (1762), is furnished with a vast marble fireplace, carved Louis XV woodwork, a portrait of Louis XIV and allegorical paintings by Nicolas Brenet (1769).

The brick façade overlooking the River Scarpe bears traces of the original Gothic arching.

The old prison, from which a famous 18C French adventurer escaped, has been turned into an **exhibition centre** *(enter from the riverside)*. The items on show illustrate the history of the town and the law courts.

Église St-Pierre ⊘ – The main features of this former collegiate church are the 16C-17C stone bell-tower, the 18C brick nave and chancel faced with stone, and the 18C apsidal chapel surmounted by a graceful bulb. Stand to left of the church for the best view.

Armes (Pl. d')	**BY** 2	Dubois (R. P.)	**BX** 18	Orchies (R. d')	**BX** 34
Bellain (R. de)	**BY** 3	Faidherbe (Bd)	**BY** 19	Paris (R. de)	**BZ**
Bellegambe (R. J.)	**BY** 4	Foulons (R. des)	**AZ** 20	Phalempin (Bd Paul)	**BY** 35
Boutique (R. A.)	**BX** 7	Gouvernement (R. du)	**BY** 23	Pont St-Vaast (R. du)	**BX** 36
Brebières (R. de)	**AZ** 8	Leclerc (Av. Mar.)	**BY** 24	Raches (R. de)	**BX** 37
Canteleu (R. du)	**BY** 9	Madeleine (R. de la)	**BY** 25	St-Christophe (R.)	**BY** 39
Carnot (Pl.)	**BY**	Mairie (R. de la)	**BY** 26	St-Jacques (R.)	**BY** 40
Chartreux (R. des)	**AX** 10	Malvaux (R. des)	**BX** 27	St-Michel (R.)	**BX** 41
Cloche (R. de la)	**AY** 13	Marceline (R.)	**BX** 28	St-Samson (R.)	**AY** 44
Clocher-St-Pierre (R. du)	**BY** 14	Massue (R. de la)	**AY** 29	St-Sulpice (R.)	**BX** 45
Cloris (R. de la)	**AY** 15	Merlin-de-Douai (R.)	**BY** 30	Université (R. de l')	**BZ** 46
Comédie (R. de la)	**AZ** 17	Ocre (R. d')	**AX** 33	Valenciennes (R. de)	**BZ** 49
				Victor-Hugo (R.)	**BY** 50

Beffroi	**BY D**	Hôtel de la Tramerie	**AZ F³**	Palais de justice	**AY J**
Église Notre-Dame	**BZ**	Hôtel de ville	**BY H**	Parc Ch. Bertin	**BZ**
Église St-Pierre	**BY**	Hôtel du Dauphin	**BZ K¹**	Porte	
Hôpital général	**BY F¹**	Mont-de-piété	**BZ K²**	de Valenciennes	**BZ**
Hôtel d'Aoust	**ABZ F²**	Musée de la Chartreuse	**AX**	Théâtre	**BZ T**

Inside, the chancel is as long as the nave; it was reserved for canons and members of the Parliament. Note the 18C organ case originally from Anchin Abbey, and the three 18C paintings in the right transept arm. They were the work of Deshayes and Ménageot.

The Modern Style boutique in rue Bellegambe *(opposite the church)* features a shop front decorated with sunflowers. Slightly further on *(no 5)* is the birthplace of painter Henri-Edmond Cross (1856-1910).

Porte de Valenciennes – This monumental gateway today stands alone, 15C Gothic on one side and late-17C Classical on the other. Nearby stands the general hospital (18C), built during the reign of Louis XV. One of the four refectories houses temporary exhibitions.

Église Notre-Dame ⓥ – The church, formerly abutting the ramparts, has always been part of Douai's history. The sandstone and brick nave was built in the early 13C. The 14C Gothic chancel has five bays; the ribs of the pointed vaults are stone, the cells brick. The five-sided apse is pierced by tall lancet windows. The church has been restored since the damage of 1944. Note the statue of the local poetess, Marceline Desbordes-Valmore by the local artist A Bouquillon.

EXCURSIONS

Flines-les-Raches – *11km/7mi north by exit ①, on D 917 and D 938.*
The village has a curious **church**, which is entered through a very old brick and sandstone belfry-porch (some say dating back to AD 800). The narrow nave opens onto chapels from various periods. In the first two chapels on the right, the roof beams are decorated with historiated corbels; they bear the arms of Philippine Torck, Abbess of Flines from 1561 to 1571.

★★Centre historique minier de Lewarde – *See Centre historique minier de LEWARDE.*

DUNKERQUE
DUNKIRK – Conurbation 192 852
Michelin map 51 folds 3, 4 or 236 fold 4

The "heroic town" of Dunkirk (Dunkerque) was 80% destroyed during the Second World War. Since its rebuilding it has expanded rapidly, both commercially and industrially, owing to the enormous growth of its port. The town centre, renovated and extended through the Neptune project, now offers visitors three fine museums and the carnival brings in its fair share of popular rejoicing.

Church of the Dunes – Until the 7C the site on which Dunkirk stands was covered by sea. Its name, which means "church of the dunes", did not appear until 1067. Until the end of the 17C, possession of this poorly defended fishermen's town was fought over by Spanish, French, English and Dutch alike. In 1658 it was taken by Turenne after the Battle of the Dunes and fortified shortly after by Vauban.

Evacuation of Dunkirk (May-June 1940) – From 25 May to 4 June Dunkirk was the scene of a bloody battle at the time of the evacuation of Allied forces who were cut off from their bases after the German breakthrough at Sedan and the subsequent push towards the coast. The boats in Dunkirk's port and on the beaches from Malo to Bray-Dunes made the journey back and forth between the French coast and England. Despite the limpet mines, torpedoes, bombs and the pounding of heavy German shells, almost 350 000 men were rescued, about two-thirds of them British.

Dunkirk Carnival

The carnival began at the end of the 19C. Before leaving town for several months to go fishing for cod in the frozen Islandic waters, the *visscherbende* (groups of fishermen, in Flemish) would organise a lively feast at the shipowners' expense. Afterwards they said goodbye and left. Today the Dunkirk Carnival is one of the most popular in the north of France. It means five weeks of mass hysteria: processions of overexcited people, accompanied by fifes and drums, winding through the streets, dancing side by side and a long succession of popular balls (Bal des Corsaires, Nuit des Acharnés,...) with plenty to drink of course!

★★THE PORT

Dunkirk's harbour traffic is largely dependent on the importance of the town's industrial complex founded on steel, petroleum and petrochemical products. The shipyards closed down in 1987 after turning out more than 300 ships.

Since then, the eastern and western ports have been linked by a **deep-water canal** to the Nord-Pas-de-Calais region of France, Belgium and the Paris Basin. The port installations extend along 15km/9mi of coastline.

Jean Bart, the "king's official privateer"

During the wars fought by Louis XIV, the privateers of Dunkirk destroyed and captured 3 000 ships, took 30 000 prisoners and wiped out Dutch trade. The most intrepid of all the privateers was **Jean Bart** (1650-1702).

He was as famous as the privateers from St-Malo, Duguay-Trouin and Sur-couf, and was a virtuoso of the North Sea trade routes.

Unlike pirates, who were outlaws attacking any and every passing ship and, in many cases, murdering the crews, privateers were granted "letters patent" from the sovereign entitling them to hound warships and merchant vessels. In 1694, Jean Bart saved the kingdom from famine by capturing 130 ships loaded with wheat. His success owed much to the existence of an ultra-modern arsenal and the constant presence of a royal fleet. He was a simple, plain-spoken man but his exploits were many and varied. As a result, he was raised to the nobility in 1694 then, three years later, was given the rank of Commodore. It is said that Louis XIV announced the appointment personally. "Jean Bart, I have appointed you to the rank of Commodore". The brave seafarer is said to have replied, "Sire, you were right to do so". The following year he avoided a combat with nine large ships while taking the Prince de Conti to Poland. Once the danger was past, the prince said to him, "Had we been attacked, we should have been captured". "Never," replied Jean Bart, "We should all have been blown sky high for my son was in the munitions hold and he had orders to set light to a powder keg as soon as I gave the command".

B.N. Paris /HARLINGUE-VIOLLET

Jean Bart

Port-Est

The eastern port is serviced by an outer harbour (80ha/198 acres) and three locks, the largest of which, the Charles-de-Gaulle Lock (365_50m/400_55yd) can receive 115 000t vessels. The **harbour basin** (6km/4mi long) is divided into six open basins and specialised industrial basins, in addition to storage installations. Well equipped for ship repairs, the port has four dry docks and one floating dock. The quays, extending from the northern end of open basin no 6 to the entrance of the deep-water canal, handle heavy cargo ships.

① **Tour on foot** – *About 1hr.*

◪ *Start from place du Minck (fish market) between the Bassin du Commerce and the Cale aux Pêcheurs and cross the old citadel district, where the customs forwarding agents are established today. The channel and the marina are on the right. Cross Trystam Lock and turn right towards the lighthouse.*

Built between 1838 and 1843, the **lighthouse** ⊘ is 59m/194ft tall and its 6 000 watts produce beams which can be seen 48km/30mi away. From the top the **view** extends to the impressive harbour installations, the beach at Malo-les-Bains and the surrounding area.

Beyond the floating docks is Watier Lock. The eastern port's control tower stands at its entrance, to the right on the bunker; there is a good **view** of the port and harbour entrance from the terrace. The view also includes the long jetty where the French troops embarked in 1940.

In the basin opposite the **Musée portuaire** are a three-master, the *Duchesse Anne*, once a sailing school ship (1902), a light vessel, the *Sandettie* (1949), and an old barge, the *Guilde* (1929), which houses an exhibition on inland navigation in its hold.

② **Boat trips** ⊘ – Boats leave from the Bassin du Commerce, the largest of the three old basins, and cruise the entire length of the port. The trip takes visitors past the tug basin, the workshops (dry docks), the various locks, the wet docks and storage areas, the sugar terminal (Transterminal Sucrier), the BP refinery and the petroleum wharves, the EDF power station etc.

Eating out

MODERATE

Le Tormore – *11 place Charles-Valentin* – ☎ *03 28 63 15 95 – 69/119F*. A pub on the ground floor and a sparsely decorated restaurant upstairs. Brasserie-type fare and Flemish cuisine are served in a smoky and convivial atmosphere. Try out their "Welsh", a toasted sandwich of regional inspiration.

Soubise – *49 route de Bergues, 59210 Coudekerque-Branche – 4km/2.5mi south of Dunkerque by D 916* – ☎ *03 28 64 66 00 – closed 22 Apr-3 May, 28 July-23 Aug, Sat lunchtime and Sun evening – 95/218F*. A former 18C post house built in local brick, this restaurant is set up along the canal. The dining room with wainscoting and light wall hangings is decorated with paintings. Regional cuisine at reasonable prices.

Where to stay

MODERATE

Chambre d'Hôte Le Withof – *Chemin du Château, 59630 Bourbourg – 14km/8.7mi southwest of Dunkerque by A 16 heading towards Calais (exit 23)* – ☎ *03 28 62 32 50 – 5 rooms 250/300F – meal 100F*. Get away from the noise and bustle of the city and spend a few days at this peaceful hotel in the middle of the countryside. The 16C fortified farmhouse is circled by a moat teeming with fish. Quiet, comfortable rooms for non-smokers. Relax in the grounds or try a spot of angling in the moat.

MID-RANGE

Hôtel Borel – *6 rue L'Hermite* – ☎ *03 28 66 51 80 – 48 rooms 380/440F –* ☐ *57F*. If you are arriving by sea, you can moor the boat and reach the hotel on foot via the quays. Quiet, soundproofed rooms decorated with modern furniture. Wood panelled reception and adjoining bar-tobacconist's belonging to the hotel.

On the town

L'Estaminet – *6 rue des Fusiliers-Marins* – ☎ *03 28 66 98 35 – Tues-Fri 11am-3pm, 6pm-midnight, Sun 6pm-2am*. A genuine Flemish tavern with eye-catching decoration consisting of witches and other curiosities unearthed at flea markets. While sipping one of the numerous Belgian beers available (plain or flambéed), either by the old stove or in the pretty garden, you will discover some unusual board games such as *la grenouille* or Nicolas billiards, played with bellows. The right place to come to for a fun evening in friendly company.

Les 4 Écluses – **Café Musique** – *Rue de la Cunette* – ☎ *03 28 63 82 40 – rock-info.fr/4écluses – Thur-Sat 8pm-2am*. This café prides itself on being a melting-pot of different cultures, nationalities and musical genres, staging rock, jazz, blues, pop, rap, folk, hardcore, soul, songs... not to mention the jam sessions open to both amateurs and professionals. When the musicians are resting, the floor is taken over by a philosophy debate or by temporary exhibitions that pay tribute to foreign, often unknown artists.

Molly Malone's Pub – *43 rue des Sœurs-Blanches* – ☎ *03 28 66 56 56 – Mon-Tues 7.30am-2am, Wed 7.30am-4am, Thur-Sat 7.30am-4am, Sun 4pm-2am*. The prime quality of this rambling pub is that it remains open when all other night spots are closed. The ambience is real hot and the theme evenings are conducted by a DJ. Two good reasons to rally round and pledge allegiance to the Irish flag hanging from the ceiling!

Showtime

Le Bateau Feu-Scène Nationale – *Place du Général-de-Gaulle* – ☎ *03 28 51 40 40 – lebateaufeu@nordnet.fr - consult the of events – bookings Tues-Sat 2-7pm – closed Aug*. The policy of this state-subsidised theatre is to favour all performing arts stage, dance, ballet, music, opera... Its programming, which cleverly associates culture and entertainment, has proved a resounding success. The theatre consists of two rooms, with seating capacities of 764 and 158.

Sport

Dunkerque Yachting Club – *Base de la Licorne* – ☎ *03 28 26 27 55 – Dyc@nordnet.fr – June-Sept Sat-Sun and public holidays, daily during school holidays*. The Dunkerque Yachting Club, locally known as DYC, is run by an energetic team that organises a great many water sports activities (windsurf, sailing dinghies, catamaran, kayak, speed sailing). It also holds unusual events like flysurf competitions, in which a surfboard is dragged along by a kite.

DUNKERQUE

Port-Ouest

The western port has the advantage of a very deep (20.50m/67ft) outer harbour with a wharf which can receive oil tankers.

It contains a rapid-transit port to which ships gain access without having to pass through any locks and 2km/1.5mi of quays. In order to receive the largest container vessels, this rapid-transit port has a series of quays equipped with storehouses and powerful hoisting equipment.

TOUR OF THE TOWN

Belfry ⊘ – Built in the 13C and heightened in 1440, it served as the bell-tower to **Église St-Éloi** which burnt down in 1558. This high tower (58m/190ft) contains a peal of 48 bells which play "Jean Bart's tune" on the hours and other popular tunes on the quarter hours. The tourist office is housed on the ground floor. A war memorial has been erected under the arch opposite Église St-Éloi.

Église St-Éloi – The church was built in the 16C and remodelled in the 18C and 19C. It has a neo-Gothic west front and a pyramid roofline along the side aisles and apse. The proportions appear odd since the suppression of the transept; the church is 68m/221ft long and 53m/172ft wide.

Note the size of the five aisles with quadripartite vaulting supported by elegant piers, and its apse with radiating chapels. The restored pointed windows feature stained glass by the master glassworker Gaudin. On the north side of the chancel, a white marble slab marks the tomb of **Jean Bart** *(see box above)*.

Place Jean-Bart – On this square at the centre of the town stands a statue of the famous corsair, Jean Bart, by David d'Angers (1848).

Hôtel de ville – Built in 1900 by Louis Cordonnier, who designed the Peace Palace in the Hague, it includes a 75m/246ft central belfry. Inside, a stained-glass window by Félix Gaudin commemorates Jean Bart's return following his victory at Texel (off the Netherlands) in 1694.

Leughenaer – The liar's tower (Leughenaer is Flemish for a liar) is the only vestige of the Burgundian walls and 28 towers which encircled the city in the 14C. It owes its name to a watchman's mistake.

Chappelle Notre-Dame-des-Dunes ⊘ – The chapel was rebuilt in the 19C and contains a wooden statue of the Madonna which has been worshipped by sailors since 1405. Votive offerings.

SIGHTS

★**Musée portuaire** ⊘ – Laid out in a former tobacco warehouse dating from the 19C, this attractive museum gives an insight into the history and operating of the port of Dunkirk, Northern France's huge maritime gateway. Dunkirk used to specialise in fishing and trade but, from the 1960's onwards, it also became a major industrial port. The work of the pilots, access to the harbour, ship repairs, product handling, coastal fishing and Icelandic fishing are all described through dioramas, model ships, maps, paintings, engravings and the tools once used by dockers.

In the 17C, Dunkirk became the main privateering harbour, with Jean Bart to defend it. *The Battle of Texel* (a copy of a painting by Isabey kept in the Musée de la Marine in Paris), engravings, and models of privateers' boats illustrate his exploits.

Musée portuaire

Y. Tierny/MICHELIN

Every year exhibitions are organised around a specific topic linked to the sea or the harbour.

In the basin opposite the museum are several interesting ships *(see Tour of the Eastern Port)*.

★ **Musée des Beaux-Arts (Fine Arts Museum)** ⊘ – This museum (rebuilt 1973) houses beautiful collections of 16C to 20C paintings and documents tracing Dunkirk's history. One room is dedicated to the privateer Jean Bart. Note the strange 17C money box in the shape of a chained captive from the Église St-Eloi. The money placed in it was used to buy back slaves.

In the **modern art gallery** (1950-70) are works by César, Arman, Hartung, Mathieu, Pignon, Vasarely, Soulages, Appel...

The 16C and 17C **Flemish School** is well represented: Snyders, Jean de Reyn (several portraits), Van der Hoecke, Van Dyck etc.

Dutch and Italian schools: interesting portraits of women by Morelse, Aert de Gelder and Bylert, still-life paintings by Van der Poel and Claez; among the 18C Italian painters, note the work of Magnasco.

The **French School** from the 17C to the 20C contains canvases by Largillière, Vignon, Riguaud, Lesueur, Hubert Robert, Vernet, Corot, Boudin, and Carrier-Belleuse.

The natural history section in the basement includes reconstructions of the region's natural habitats (marshes, beaches etc).

★ **Musée d'Art contemporain** ⊘ – Architect Jean Willerval bore in mind the existing garden when he built his modern concrete building sheathed in white ceramic. This rather sober structure is preceded by a superb portico by Philippe Scrive; it is made of azobe, an African wood.

In 1994, the museum changed its original purpose and, as a result, its collection of paintings and sculpture was transferred to the Museum of Fine Arts. It is now devoted to contemporary earthenware and glassware. Working under the heading of **"Dialogues in ceramics"**, the museum aims to increase public awareness of this art form.

The Museum of Contemporary Art stands in the middle of a **sculpture park★** designed by landscape gardener Gilbert Samel. The paths climb outcrops and run down slopes, leading past great stone pieces by the sculptor Dodeigne, metal structures by Féraud and compositions by Viseux, Arman and Zvenijorovsky, all against the backdrop of the North Sea.

ADDITIONAL SIGHTS

⌂MALO-LES-BAINS

Founded before 1870 by a local shipowner named Malo, this seaside resort has become the residential district of Dunkirk. The large, gently sloping beach of fine sand extends east of the port; it is flanked by a promenade beside which stands the casino.

Musée aquariophile ⊘ – The aquarium's 21 tanks hold 150 species of fish of various origins, some of them from the North Sea.

Église St-Jean-Baptiste – This modern, brick-built church (1962), shaped like the prow of a ship, stands separately from its wooden belfry which rises like a mast. Inside there is a lovely Christ surrounded by four angels.

EXCURSIONS

La Côte des Dunes – *13km/8mi northeast by D 79 and D 60.*

Zuydcoote – The town found literary fame with the novel *Weekend in Zuydcoote* by Robert Merle, on which a film was based evoking the tragic episodes of the 1940 evacuation. The great sanatorium, transformed into a hospital, was at that time the setting of dramatic scenes, with an influx of wounded whose number reached 7 000.

Bray-Dunes – A promenade runs along the beach which stretches all the way to La Panne in Belgium; it is a popular spot for sand-sailing. On the promenade, a stele commemorates the soldiers who fought until 4 June 1940.

Gravelines – *13km/8mi west.*

The town is enclosed within classic, Vauban-style ramparts with brick bastions and stone courses; it was an important part of Dunkirk's defence in 1940. The 1742 powder magazine, now set within pleasant gardens, houses the **Musée du Dessin et de l'Estampe originale** ⊘ specialising in prints and engravings and temporary exhibitions. Another part of the museum is housed in the underground casemate (1693), a guard-room forming part of the fortifications. In the vaulted room with central pillar, temporary exhibitions are regularly organised.

The town also boasts a harbour full of yachts and sailing boats, a Flamboyant **church** with a Renaissance front portal, a **Maison du Patrimoine** ⊙ housing exhibitions of works by local artists and organising nature trails, and a **Maison de la Mer** ⊙ concerned with the history of shipbuilding, fishing and daily life on board ship. The **Maison du Sauvetage** ⊙ is a museum devoted to sea rescue.

FRESH OFF THE BOAT

Le Turbot – *26 rue de Dunkerque, Gravelines – ☎ 03 28 23 08 54 – closed 16 Aug-1 Sept, Sat lunchtime and Mon – booking essential – 128/195F.* If you have never tasted scallops, now's the time to start since it is the speciality of the house. A pleasing mix of regional and traditional fare is served at this unpretentious establishment.

Château d'ÉCOUEN ★★

Michelin map 101 fold 6, 106 fold 19 or 237 fold 18

Access is through the forest, on foot; cars must be parked at the entrance to the forest.

The Château d'Écouen, nestling in a park (17ha/42 acre), overlooking the plain was originally intended for Constable Anne de Montmorency *(see p 131)* and his wife Madeleine of Savoy, who lived here from 1538 to 1555.

When Constable Anne's grandson Henri II de Montmorency was beheaded in 1632, the château reverted to the Condé family but was later confiscated during the Revolution. Napoleon I salvaged the estate in 1806 by founding the first school for the daughters of members of the Légion d'Honneur there. In 1962 the château and its grounds were ceded to the Ministry of Culture, who undertook to turn it into a state museum devoted to Renaissance art.

TOUR *1hr*

Exterior – The Château d'Écouen reflects the transition of French art from the Early Renaissance period (Château of the Loire) to the High Renaissance during Henri II's reign.

Courtyard – The buildings feature pavilions at each corner and are surmounted by elaborate dormer windows with carved pediments. The beautiful east range was destroyed in the 18C and replaced by a low entrance wing.

Porticoes with Classical-style columns decorate the buildings. The most outstanding one is to the left, on the south wing (Anne de Montmorency's residence) built by Jean Bullant to house Michelangelo's famous *Slaves* in the niches on the ground floor. The statues (the originals are in the Louvre) were a gift to Anne de Montmorency from King Henri II.

North Terrace – Sweeping **view** of the surrounding cereal-growing countryside.

★★ Musée national de la Renaissance ⊙ – Some of the exhibits on display belonged to the Renaissance collections of the Cluny Museum in Paris. Écouen Museum presents a wide range of works dating from the 16C and early 17C, which introduce visitors to the various branches of the decorative arts: furniture, wainscots, tapestries and embroideries, ceramics, enamels etc.

Most of the exhibits were made in France, Italy or the Netherlands. They represent a small selection but the ambience they create is in keeping with the life of wealthy nobility during the Renaissance.

The original interior decoration consists mainly of grotesques, painted on the friezes below the ceiling and the embrasures of the windows. But it is for its **painted fireplaces** that Écouen is famed. Created during the reign of Henri II, these chimney-pieces are representative of the first Fontainebleau School: the central biblical scene is painted on an oval or rectangular medallion, surrounded by grotesques, garlands of fruit and motifs in leather; the hazy landscapes depicting antique ruins, fortresses and humble cottages are in imitation of Niccolo dell'Abbate.

Ground Floor – The monograms A and M (Anne de Montmorency and Madeleine of Savoy) have been included in the decoration of the chapel, built in 1544 and covered with painted vaulting resting on diagonal arches. This heraldic motif reappears in different places (musicians' gallery, panelling in the oratory, the vaulting in the sacristy). The Passion Altarpiece is adorned with enamelling and a copy of Leonardo da Vinci's *Last Supper*.

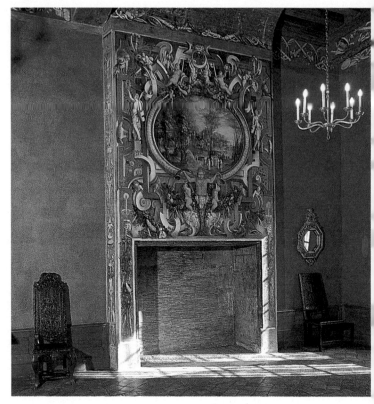

Painted fireplace in the Château d'Écouen

Several rooms are devoted to a particular trade or technique and illustrate various aspects of Renaissance life; note a clock of German origin in the shape of a ship known as Charles V's clock, now shown incorporated into a 16C collector's cabinet and, in the reconstruction of a 16C goldsmith's workshop, a goldsmith's work bench set in an inlaid chest. It comes from the Kunstkammer of Augustus I in Dresden. The northwest pavilion was formerly occupied by Catherine de' Medici.

First Floor – In the south wing, visitors are shown round the constable's bedroom and Madeleine of Savoy's suite, both interesting on account of the period furniture. The west wing is almost exclusively taken up by the **Tapestry of David and Bathsheba**★★★ (1510-20) which runs from the Abigail pavilion to the king's bedchamber, along the Psyche Gallery. The 75m/246ft hanging divided into 10 sections tells of the romance between King David and Bathsheba. The outstanding quality of the tapestry – woven with wool and silk threads, as well as silver braid – is equalled only by that of *The Hunts of Maximilian* in the Louvre, without doubt the two most precious examples of 16C Brussels tapestry work existing in France.

The hanging ends in the King's Apartment, situated in the northwest pavilion. *For explanations of the monograms read the paragraph entitled "Henri II's Château" in the chapter on Fontainebleau.*

The king's suite occupied the northern wing. One of the rooms contains the floor tiles made specially for the château in 1542 by the Rouen potter Masseot Abaquesne. The winged victory on the central panel of the monumental fireplace was taken from a similar design in the François I Gallery at Fontainebleau.

The two tapestries are part of the famous *Fructus Belli* made in Brussels to cartoons by Jules Romains.

Second Floor – In the northeast pavilion, many pieces of Isnik pottery (mid-16C to early 17C) are exhibited in glass cabinets, illustrating the exotic tastes of 16C collectors. The first room in the north wing presents religious stained glass painted in *grisaille*; admire the Virgin and Child, dated 1544.

The second hall deals entirely with French ceramics (Bernard Palissy, Saint-Parchaira, and Masséat Abaquesne's work, *The Flood*) and there is a reconstruction of another floor designed specially for the château, showing the arms of the Constable, those of his wife, of Henri II and Catherine de' Medici.

The 15 marriage chests *(cassoni)* on show in the northwest pavilion form a remarkable ensemble; these painted panels are taken from wooden chests that were presented to newly-weds in sets of two.

The cabinets in the west gallery contain enamels (pieces by Léonard Limosin including portraits of Claude of Lorraine and Antoinette de Bourbon), tin-glazed pottery or majolica from Deruta in Italy and glasses (goblets belonging to Anne de Bretagne and Catherine de' Medici).

The southwest pavilion concentrates on silverware (cutlery, jewellery), mainly of German origin. There is an extraordinary Daphne by the great Nuremberg goldsmith, Wenzel Jammitzer (1508-85). Above the chapel is the former library of Constable Anne which still has some of the original gilded wainscoting. It is representative of the world of books during the Renaissance period.

ADDITIONAL SIGHT

Église St-Acceul ⊘ – The chancel by Jean Bullant is the most interesting part of the building. The complex rib patterns of the vaulting *(temporarily concealed by supporting timber)* date it to the 16C.

St Acceul features several Renaissance **stained-glass windows**★; those in the north aisle are dated 1544: Dormition and Assumption of the Virgin, Annunciation and Visitation, Nativity and Adoration of the Magi.

Château de FERRIÈRES★

Michelin map 101 fold 30, 106 folds 21, 22 or 237 fold 19

The shooting parties on Ferrières estate, the luxurious furnishings of the château and the precious collections gathered by the members of the Rothschild dynasty were the talk of the town for over 100 years.

The landscape park – created at the same time as the Bois de Boulogne – is extremely attractive, especially in the vicinity of the lake.

The nearby town got its name from iron ore *(fer)* extracted in great quantities during the 16C and 17C.

A Challenge to Tradition – In 1829 James de Rothschild, founder of the French line of the family, acquired 7 500 acres of hunting grounds formerly belonging to Fouché, with a view to building a villa which would accommodate his invaluable collections and satisfy his taste for splendour. The baron did not choose a professional architect; he broke with tradition and hired **Joseph Paxton**, the English glasshouse and garden designer with a penchant for modern materials such as iron and glass. Already famed for the Crystal Palace in London (destroyed in 1936), Paxton erected a rectangular building flanked by square towers, with a central hall equipped with zenithal lighting. Construction work was completed in 1859. The decoration, left in the hands of the baroness, was entrusted to the French specialist Eugène Lami.

On 16 December 1862 Napoleon III paid an official visit to the Rothschilds in their new residence. Delighted by the splendid apartments and the 800 head of game for his day's shoot, the Emperor planted a sequoia tree as a commemorative gesture.

Less than 10 years later, Jules Favre – in charge of Foreign Affairs in the new National Defence government – turned up at the gates of the château on 19 September 1870. In his capacity as Minister, Favre came to see Chancellor Bismarck, who was staying at Ferrières with Kaiser Wilhelm I of Prussia, to ask him to agree to an armistice.

Castle

The chancellor however made this conditional on the surrender of Strasbourg, Toul and Bitche, and further implied that the cession of Alsace and part of Lorraine was inevitable. Jules Favre left the premises the following morning. On 28 January 1871, Paris fell to the hands of the enemy.

In 1977 Baron Guy de Rothschild and his wife Marie-Hélène donated their château and part of the estate to the Confederation of Paris Universities.

TOUR ⊘ 2hr

Exterior – Its architecture reflects the various styles of the Renaissance period, including the odd eccentricity that was acceptable in the 19C. Although balusters, galleries and colonnades reigned supreme, the façades were each different. The most striking and the most typically English is the main front overlooking the lake, with its centrepiece flanked by turrets and its display of superimposed galleries. Step back to take in the tall decorative stone chimneys, reminiscent of the Château de Chambord.

Interior – A pavilion sporting a large clock is fronted by the main entrance porch which bears the baron's monogram (JR) and the family coat of arms (the five Rothschild arrows).

The main staircase leads to the central hall – 40m/130ft wide and 12m/40ft high under the glass ceiling – now stripped of its paintings and tapestries. Above the main door, a row of telamones and caryatids in bronze and black marble support a musicians' gallery. The use of such statues was a popular decorative feature in the mid 19C. The Salon Bleu, overlooking the park, has busts of the Empress Eugénie and Bettina de Rothschild, the first proprietress of the château. The Louis XVI salon is the most typical example of Eugène Lami's work: it features off-white wainscoting with pinkish hues, a painted ceiling inspired by Boucher and reproduction Louis XVI furniture. Opposite is the Salon Rouge, in which the 1870 negotiations took place. It now presents an exhibition on the history of the estate.

Musée de l'Imaginaire ⊘ – This small museum housed on the second floor showcases a changing collection of paintings and sculptures by an international group of contemporary artists who express their extravagant visions in the style known as Fantastic Realism. The works are shown here before being offered for public sale.

★**Park** ⊘ – The park designed by Paxton boasts a number of superb compositions, mainly consisting of ornamental coniferous trees: cedars of Lebanon, numerous Atlas cedars – including the highly decorative blue form – and sequoias, introduced into France around 1850.

Several individual trees also deserve a mention: a Lebanese cedar with unusually long, spread-eagled branches, swamp cypresses, with twigs which turn deep russet and drop off in winter, copper beeches, groves of plane trees and, on the far side of the lake, feathery weeping species, adding an autumnal touch to the tableau.

Outside the park, the allée des Lions presents an imposing driveway of stately sequoias.

THE LAP OF LUXURY

St-Rémy – *24 rue Jean-Jaurès, 77164 Ferrières-en-Brie – ☎ 01 64 76 74 00 – www.hotel.st.remy.fr – 25 rooms from 650F – �) 70F – restaurant 135/195F.* Located right behind the church, this late-19C house has kept its old-fashioned features and charm despite its recent renovation. Note the upstairs village hall that was originally inaugurated by the Rothschild family. The rooms are comfortable and the restaurant is charmingly appointed with modern wooden furniture.

Forêt de Ferrières – In 1973, the Île-de-France region acquired the forest surrounding the castle and covering 2 800ha/6 919 acres. It now includes parking and picnic areas as well as numerous footpaths and cycle paths accessible all year round. The Étang de la Planchette is an angler's paradise *(fishing permits delivered on the spot)*.

FOLLEVILLE

Population 63
Michelin map 52 fold 13 or 236 fold 34

The modest village of Folleville, located on a hill at the end of the Noye Valley, was once the seat of an important fief. The ruins of a castle (13C-16C), once owned by the illustrious Lannoy and Gondi families, stand as testimony to the town's former importance.

A Valiant Knight – Raoul de Lannoy, the son of a Flemish family, was Chamberlain and Counsellor to Louis XI, Charles VIII and Louis XII. He achieved great glory in 1477 at the siege of Le Quesnoy, and Louis XI presented him with a gold chain saying: "Because, my friend, you are too furious in combat you must be chained to contain your ardour, as I do not want to lose you". This chain is exhibited in Folleville Church. During the Italian campaign Lannoy was named Governor of Genoa by Louis XII, and died there in 1513.

Monsieur Vincent's First "Mission" – In January 1617 a humble, wise old priest – Vincent de Paul – travelled through the lands of Françoise de Gondi, heiress of the fief of Folleville through her mother Marie de Lannoy. The region was in an advanced state of secularisation. Horrified, the priest entered the pulpit and preached such an eloquent sermon that a general confession ensued. Following this experience, in 1625 Vincent founded the Congregation of the Priests of the Mission, later known as Lazarists.

CHURCH ⊙ *1hr 30min*

The exterior of this early-16C church is decorated with remarkable carvings: 16C statue of St James on the corner of the west front and a Virgin and Child in the niche of a buttress.

Nave – A Renaissance font stands near the entrance; the white Carrara marble basin is carved with the symbolic chain and the coat of arms of the Lannoy family. In the south aisle the pulpit from which Vincent de Paul preached still stands.

★**Chancel** – The chancel is constructed in a largely Flamboyant architectural style but also features numerous Renaissance decorative elements. Note the finely carved ribbed vault.

The first **tomb**★★ on the left is that of Raoul de Lannoy and his wife Jeanne de Poix. The white marble sarcophagus was made in Genoa in 1507, when Raoul de Lannoy was still alive, by the Milanese sculptor Antonio Della Porta and his nephew Pace Gaggini; the recumbent effigy of Lannoy is portrayed wearing the gold chain he was given by Louis XI. The base is adorned with graceful weeping children, the family coat of arms and an epitaph. The recess in which the tomb lies is a masterpiece of French art with its delicate sculptures and carvings. The background is garlanded with sweet peas *(fleurs de pois)*, a reference to Lannoy's wife. It is crowned by a double ogee framing a graceful Virgin and Child emerging from a fleur-de-lis and surmounted by a tent-shaped canopy; a trellised enclosure, a daisy chain, cherubs and the symbols of the Evangelists complete the composition.

The second **tomb**★ shows the progress of funerary art, moving in 50 years from recumbent effigies to kneeling stone figures. Among those kneeling are François de Lannoy, Raoul's son who died in 1548, and his wife Marie de Hangest. The base of the white marble surround is decorated with figures of the Cardinal Virtues (Prudence, Temperance, Fortitude and Justice).

Recess and piscina – A pointed arch beyond the altar opens on to a large festooned recess revealing a sculpted Christ appearing to Mary Magdalene; on either side angels carry the instruments of the Passion. On the right of the altar, a pretty piscina is decorated with statuettes of St Francis and John the Baptist, the patron saints of François de Lannoy and Jeanne de Poix.

FONTAINEBLEAU★★★

Population 15 714
Michelin map 106 folds 45, 46 or 237 fold 31

Access from Paris: *SNCF rail link from Gare de Lyon*

It was not until the 19C that Fontainebleau started to develop, owing to the growing popularity of country residences and the general appreciation of its unspoilt forest. The area owes its name to a spring at the heart of a forest abounding in game, which was known as the "Fontaine de Bliaut" or "Blaut", probably after a former owner. However, Fontainebleau essentially owes its fame to the castle and the park named on UNESCO's World Heritage list. Visitors are attracted by the Renaissance features of the castle, its famous horseshoe staircase and striking historic associations, in particular Napoleon's farewell to his guards.

In addition, the town is the ideal starting point of excursions to Vaux-le-Vicomte, Barbizon or Courances.

Castle

Military and equestrian traditions – Throughout French history, whether under monarchic or republican rule, independent units have been posted to Fontainebleau. Tradition, it seems, favoured the cavalry, present in the 17C with the king's body-guard. A number of racecourses and riding schools were created under Napoleon III; the Centre National des Sports Équestres perpetuates this tradition *(see Calendar of events)*, while the forest caters for riding enthusiasts.

The history of the town has been marked by several military organisations, notably the École Spéciale Militaire (1803 to 1808, before St-Cyr), the polygon-shaped École d'Application d'Artillerie et du Génie (1871 to 1914) and the SHAPE (Supreme Headquarters, Allied Powers, Europe) headquarters of NATO, which gave the town a cosmopolitan touch from 1947 to 1967.

★★★ PALACE ⏱

The Palais de Fontainebleau owes its origins to royalty's passion for hunting; it owes its development and decoration to the kings' delight in amassing works of art and displaying them in their "family home". This palace has an extremely dis-tinguished past; from the last of the Capetians up to Napoleon III, it was designed for and occupied by French rulers.

A hunting lodge – A spring – called Bliaud or Blaut fountain in the middle of a forest abounding in game – prompted the kings of France to build a mansion here. The exact date is not known but it was probably before 1137 as a charter exists issued under Louis VII from Fontainebleau, dating from that year. Philip Augustus celebrated the return of the Third Crusade here during the Christmas festivities of

1191 and St Louis founded a Trinitarian convent, whose members were called Mathurins; Philip the Fair was born here in 1268: unfortunately he also died here following a serious riding accident.

The Renaissance – Under François I almost all the medieval buildings were pulled down and replaced by two main edifices, erected under the supervision of Gilles Le Breton. The oval-shaped east pavilion – built on the former foundations – was linked to the west block by a long gallery. To decorate the palace, François I hired many artists; he dreamed of creating a "New Rome" furnished with replicas of Classical statues.

The actual building consisted of rubble-work as the sandstone taken from the forest was too difficult to work into regular freestones. The harled façades are enlivened by string-courses of brick or massive sandstone blocks.

The Fontainebleau School – **16C** – The teams of painters and stucco workers were supervised by Rosso, one of Michelangelo's pupils and a native of Florence, and by Primaticcio, a follower of Giulio Romano who came from Bologna. They developed a decorative technique strongly inspired by enigmatic allegories. Attention to detail, which typified Late Gothic architecture, was no longer in vogue beyond the Loire Valley as it had been during the Early Renaissance. The Fontainebleau artists were more intent on depicting a dreamy form of elegance, characterised by the representation of human bodies arched into arabesques.

These painters formed the First Fontainebleau School, which blossomed during the reign of François I. The school created a style of decoration incorporating both stucco and paintings – exemplified by the François I Gallery – in semi-miniature works referred to as "French style" by the Italians.

Rosso died in 1540. Primaticcio was sent to Rome to make moulds of famous Antique statues – the *Laocoon*, the *Belvedere Apollo* – which were brought back to Fontainebleau and cast in bronze.

In his private suite *(Appartement des Bains)*, the king could feast his eyes on masterpieces by Raphael and Leonardo da Vinci *(The Mona Lisa)*, while the Pavillon des Armes housed the gold and silver plate, jewellery and miscellaneous curios that delighted contemporary royalty.

Henri II's château – Henri II pursued the efforts undertaken by his father. He gave orders to complete and decorate the ballroom, which remains one of the splendours of Fontainebleau Palace. The monograms – consisting of the royal H and the two intertwined Cs of Catherine de' Medici – were legion. In a form of ambiguity that was generally accepted in its day, the two C's placed immediately beside the H form a double D, the monogram of the King's mistress Diane de Poitiers.

When Henri II was killed in a tournament, his widow Catherine de' Medici sent her rival to Chaumont-sur-Loire *(see The Green Guide Châteaux of the Loire)* and dismissed the architect in charge of the building work Philibert Delorme, who was Diane's protégé. He was replaced by the Italian Primaticcio; those working under him, including Niccolo dell'Abbate, favoured light, cheerful colours.

Henri IV's palace – **17C** – Henri IV, who adored Fontainebleau, had the palace enlarged quite significantly. The irregular contours of the Oval Court were corrected and he gave orders to build the Kitchen Court and the Real Tennis Court *(Jeu de Paume)*. These he had decorated by a new group of artists of largely Flemish, and not Italian, inspiration: frescoes were replaced by oil paintings on plaster or canvas. In the same way, the plain wood panelling highlighted with gilding gave way to painted wainscot. This was the Second Fontainebleau School, whose representatives moved in Parisian circles.

The House of Eternity – Louis XIV, XV and XVI undertook numerous renovations aimed at embellishing their apartments. The Revolution spared the château but emptied it of its precious furniture. Napoleon, who became consul, then emperor, thoroughly enjoyed staying at the palace. He preferred Fontainebleau to Versailles, where he felt haunted by a phantom rival. He called the palace "The House of Eternity" and left his mark by commissioning further refurbishments. The last rulers of France also took up residence in this historic palace. It was eventually turned into a museum under the Republic.

Exterior *1hr*

★★**Cour du Cheval Blanc** or **des Adieux** – This former bailey was used only by domestics but its generous size soon earmarked it for official parades and tournaments. It was sometimes called the White Horse Court after the day Charles IX set up a plaster cast of the equestrian statue of Marcus Aurelius in Rome; a small slab in the central alley marks its former location.

The golden eagles seemingly hovering above the pillars of the main gate remind visitors that the Emperor had this made into his main courtyard. He gave orders to raze the Renaissance buildings that lay to the west of the court but kept the end pavilions. It is clear, walking between the two long wings, that only the one on the left with its brick courses has retained the elegance that characterised the work of Gilles Le Breton, François I's favourite architect. The right wing – which boasted the Ulysses Gallery decorated under the supervision of Primaticcio – was dismantled by Louis XV and rebuilt by Jacques-Ange Gabriel.

At the far end of the court the main block, fronted by a balustrade marking the site of the former moat, was completed in several stages from the reign of François I to that of Louis XV. Nonetheless the façades show a certain unity of style. The large horizontal planes of the blue slating are broken by the white façades, the trapezoidal roofs and the tall chimneys of the five pavilions. The celebrated horse-shoe staircase executed by Jean Du Cerceau during the reign of Louis XIII is a harmoniously curved, extravagant composition showing clearly royalty's taste for splendour. The staircase served as a majestic backdrop on many occasions. St Simon described the arrival of the 11-year-old Princess Marie Adélaïde of Savoy at Fontainebleau on 5 November 1696 for her betrothal to the Duke of Burgundy. "The entire Court was assembled waiting to receive them on the horseshoe stair-case, with the crowd standing below, a magnificent sight. The King led in the princess, so small that she seemed to be emerging from his pocket, walked very slowly along the terrace and then to the Queen Mother's apartments which were to become hers..."

The Farewell

On 20 April 1814 the Emperor Napoleon appeared at the top of the horse-shoe staircase; it was 1pm. The foreign army commissioners in charge of escorting him away were waiting in their carriages at the foot of the steps. Napoleon started to walk down the staircase with great dignity, his hand resting on the stone balustrade, his face white with contained emotion. He stopped for a moment while contemplating his guards standing to atten-tion, then moved forward to the group of officers surrounding the Eagle, led by General Petit. His farewell speech, deeply moving, was both an appeal to the spirit of patriotism and a parting tribute to those who had followed him throughout his career. After embracing the general, Bonaparte kissed the flag, threw himself into one of the carriages and was whisked away amid the tearful shouts of his soldiers.

★**Cour de la Fontaine** – The fountain at the edge of the pond *(Étang des Carpes)* used to yield remarkably clear water. This was kept exclusively for the king's use and to that end the spring was guarded by two sentinels night and day.

The present fountain dates back to 1812 and is crowned by a statue of Ulysses. The surrounding buildings feature stone masonry and the whole ensemble forms a pleasant courtyard. At the far end, the Galerie François I is fronted by a terrace; it rests on a row of arches which once opened onto the king's bathroom suite. The **Aile de la Belle cheminée** on the right was built by Primaticcio around 1565. The name originated from the fireplace that adorned the vast first-floor hall until the 18C. At that point in history Louis XV – who had turned the room into a theatre and rechristened it Aile de l'Ancienne Comédie – dismantled the fireplace, and the low-relief carvings were scattered. The monumental external steps consist of a dog-legged staircase with two straight flights in the Italian style.

On the left the Queen Mothers' and Pope's wing ends in the Grand Pavillion built by Gabriel.

★**Étang des Carpes (Carp Pond)** – In the centre of the pond – alive with carp – stands a small pavilion built under Henri IV, renovated under Louis XIV and restored by Napoleon. It was used for refreshments and light meals.

★**Porte Dorée** – Dated 1528, this gatehouse is part of an imposing pavilion. It was the official entrance to the palace until Henri IV built the Ponte du Baptistère. The paintings by Primaticcio have all been restored and the tympanum sports a stylised salamander, François I's emblem. On the two upper levels are Italian-style loggias. The first floor – its loggia sealed off by large bay windows – used to house Mme De Maintenon's suite.

The ballroom is flanked by an avenue of lime trees. The view from the bay windows is splendid and it is regrettable that the initial plans to build an open-air loggia were changed on account of the climate. The east end of the two-storeyed chapel dedicated to St Saturnin can be seen in the distance.

★**Porte du Baptistère** – The gateway opens onto the Oval Court. The base of the gateway is the rustic entrance with decorative sandstone that once held the draw-bridge across the old moat. It opened onto the Cour du Cheval-Blanc and was designed by Primaticcio. It is crowned by a wide arch surmounted by a dome. The door is named after the christening of Louis XIII and his two sisters, Élisabeth and Chrétienne, celebrated with great pomp on a dais on 14 September 1606.

The pavilion of the Étang des Carpes

★**Cour Ovale** – This is by far the most ancient and the most interesting courtyard of Fontainebleau Palace. The site was the bailey of the original stronghold; of the latter there remains only the keep, named after St Louis, although it was probably built prior to his reign. François I incorporated it into the structure he had erected on the foundations of the old castle, shaped like an oval or rather a polygon with rounded corners. Under Henri IV, the courtyard lost its shape, although not its name; the east side was enlarged, the wings were aligned and squared by two new pavilions framing the new Porte du Baptistère. The general layout of the palace was preserved.

Cour des Offices – Its entrance faces the Porte du Baptistère and is guarded by two arresting sandstone heads depicting Hermes, sculpted by Gilles Guérin in 1640. The Cour des Offices was built by Henri IV in 1609; it is a huge oblong, sealed off on three sides by austere buildings alternating with low pavilions. With its imposing porch executed in the style of city gates, it bears a strong resemblance to a square. Walk through the gate and admire its architecture from place d'Armes; the sandstone front presents rusticated work and has a large niche as its centrepiece.

Continue the tour of the palace exterior. The east and north wings of the Cour des Princes are two functional buildings designed or redesigned under Louis XV to provide further accommodation for members of the court.

1) Horseshoe staircase
2) Aile des Reines-Mères et du Pape
3) Galerie François 1er
4) Aile de la Belle Cheminée
5) Ballroom
6) Real Tennis Court

★**Jardin de Diane** – The queen's formal garden created by Catherine de' Medici was designed by Henri IV and bordered by an orangery on its northern side. In the 19C the orangery was torn down and the park turned into a landscape garden. Diana's fountain, an elegant display of stonework dated 1603, has survived in the middle of the grounds. It has now resumed its original appearance; the four bronze dogs formerly exhibited in the Louvre Museum sit obediently at the feet of their mistress, the hunting goddess.

Grands Appartements ⓘ

The main apartments are reached by the stucco staircase (**a**), the Galerie des Fastes (**b**) and the Galerie des Assiettes (**c**) which features 128 beautifully decorated pieces of Sèvres porcelain.

★**Chapelle de la Trinité** – The chapel takes its name from the Trinitarian church set up on the premises by St Louis. Henri IV had the sanctuary reinforced by vaulting and then decorated. Martin Fréminet (1567-1619), one of the lesser-known followers of Michelangelo, painted the arches with strong, vigorous scenes characterised by perspective and a daring use of foreshortening. The scenes represent the mystery of the Redemption and a number of figures from the Old Testament.

It was in this chapel that Louis XV was wedded to Marie Leszczynska in 1725 and that Louis Napoleon, later to be Napoleon III, was christened in 1810.

★★★**Galerie de François I** – This gallery was built from 1528 to 1530 and was originally open on both sides, resembling a covered passageway. When Louis XVI enlarged it in 1786, he filled in the windows looking over Diana's garden. A set of false French windows was fitted for reasons of symmetry. The greater part of the decoration – closely combining fresco and stucco work – was supervised by Rosso, while the wood panelling was entrusted to an Italian master carpenter. François I's monogram and his emblem the salamander were widely represented. The scenes are difficult to interpret, but they seem to split into two groups, one on either side of the central bay which is adorned with an oval painting depicting two figures: Danaë by Primaticcio and the Nymph of Fontainebleau (1860) after Rosso.

The east side, near a bust of François I, features mostly violent scenes, perhaps referring to the recent misfortunes of the French king (the defeat of Pavia, the king's captivity in Madrid), the inescapable nature of war and death (the battle between the Centaurs and the Lapiths, Youth and Old Age, the Destruction of the Greek fleet). Beneath the vignette depicting Venus and Love at the edge of a pond, note the miniature picture set in a tablet, representing the château around 1540 with both the gallery and the Porte Dorée clearly visible.

On the west side, near the entrance, the decor exemplifies the sacred qualities of the royal function – Sacrifice, the Unity of the State – and the concept of filial piety in the old-fashioned sense of the word (the twins Cleobis and Biton): the king, his mother Louise of Savoy and his sister Marguerite d'Angoulême were devoted to one another.

The most striking scene is the portrait of an elephant whose caparison bears the royal monogram; the pachyderm no doubt symbolises the perennity of the monarchy.

Ballroom

GRANDS APPARTEMENTS
1st FLOOR
0   50 m

Jardin
de
Diane

Jeu
de
Paume

Cour du
Cheval-Blanc

Galerie de Diane

Cour
des
Princes

★Chapelle de la Trinité

★ APPARTEMENT INTÉRIEUR DE L'EMPEREUR

Cour Ovale

C B A

Galerie François 1er ★★★

★★APPARTEMENTS ROYAUX

★★Escalier du Roi

Chapelle St-Saturnin

Appartements des Reines Mères et du Pape

Ballroom ★★★

★MUSÉE NAPOLÉON 1er

Cour de la Fontaine

APPARTEMENTS DE Mme DE MAINTENON

★★ Escalier du Roi – The staircase was built in 1749, under Louis XV, in what was once the bedchamber of the Duchess of Étampes, François I's favourite. The murals – the history of Alexander the Great – were by Primaticcio (note Alexander taming Bucephalus above the door) and dell'Abbate (Alexander placing Homer's books in a chest, on the far wall). Primaticcio's stucco work is highly original; the upper frieze is punctuated by caryatids with elongated bodies.

★★★ Salle de Bal (Ballroom) – This room (30m/100ft long and 10m/33ft wide) was traditionally reserved for banquets and formal receptions. It was begun under François I and completed by Philibert Delorme under Henri II. A thorough restoration programme has revived the dazzling frescoes and paintings by Primaticcio and his pupil dell'Abbate. The marquetry of the parquet floor, completed under Louis-Philippe, echoes the splendid coffered ceiling, richly highlighted with silver and gold. The monumental fireplace features two telamones, cast after Antique statues in the Capitol Museum in Rome.

Appartements de Mme de Maintenon – Note the delicate wainscoting in the Grand Salon, most of which was executed in the 17C.

★★ Appartements royaux – At the time of François I, Fontainebleau featured a single suite of apartments laid out around the Oval Court. Towards 1565, the regent Catherine de' Medici gave orders to double the curved building between the Oval Court and Diana's Garden. Subsequently, the royal bedrooms, closets and private salons overlooked Diana's Garden. The original suite now houses antechambers, guard-rooms and reception rooms where the king used to entertain his guests.

Salle des Gardes (1) – Late-16C ceiling and frieze.

A wide arch leads from the **Salle du Buffet (2)** to a chamber in the oldest tower of the castle.

Salle du Donjon (3) – Until the reign of Henri IV this sombre room was occupied by French kings, who used it as a bedroom hence its other name, the St Louis Bedroom. The equestrian low-relief sculpture (c 1600) portraying Henri IV on the fireplace came from the "Belle Cheminée". It was carved by Mathieu Jacquet.

Salon Louis XIII (4) – It was here that Louis XIII was born on 27 September 1601. His birth is evoked by the coffered ceiling which depicts Cupid riding a dolphin (the word *dauphin* means both dolphin and heir to the throne). The panel with painted wainscoting is crowned by a set of 11 pictures by Ambroise Dubois; the Romance between Theagenes and Chariclea, works dating from c 1610.

Salon François I (5) – Of Primaticcio's work there remains only the fireplace.

Salon des Tapisseries (6) – This room, having been the queen's chamber, the guard-room and the queen's first antechamber, became the empress's principal drawing room in 1804, the guard-room once more in 1814 and finally the Tapestry Salon in 1837. The fireplace dates from 1731 and the Renaissance ceiling in pine wood is the work of Poncet (1835). The furniture was made during the Second Empire (mid 19C). The tapestries telling the story of Psyche were manufactured in Paris in the first half of the 17C.

Antichambre de l'impératrice (7) – Formerly the queen's guard-room, this chamber was built on the site of the old royal staircase; the ceiling and panelling are both dated 1835. The Gobelins tapestries, executed after cartoons by Le Brun, illustrate the four seasons. The Second Empire furniture features a console, a carved-oak writing desk (Fourdinois, 1865) and a set of armchairs of English inspiration. Note the two Indian-style enamel vases produced by the Sèvres factory.

Galerie de Diane – This long gilt passageway (80m/263ft) was decorated during the Restoration and turned into a library under the Second Empire.

Salon blanc. Petit salon de la reine (8) – In 1835 the room was decorated with furnishings from an earlier period: Louis XV wainscoting, Louis XVI fireplace inlaid with bronze etc. The furniture is Empire: chairs in gilt wood by Jacob Frères, settee, armchairs and chairs from St-Cloud, mahogany console and heads of fantastic animals in bronzed, gilt wood (Jacob Desmalter).

Grand Salon de l'Impératrice (9) – This drawing room, formerly the queen's gaming room, features a ceiling painted by Berthélemy; the scene is Minerva crowning the Muses. The furniture dates from the reign of Louis XVI (chests by Stöckel and Beneman, seats upholstered with painted satin, a carpet made by the Savonnerie works) or from the First Empire (seats and chests by Jacob-Desmalters, the so-called "Seasons Table" made of Sèvres porcelain and painted by Georget in 1806-7, and a carpet rewoven to an old design). The two sets of furniture are displayed in turn.

Chambre de l'Impératrice (10) – This used to be the queen's bedroom. The greater part of the ceiling was designed for Anne of Austria in 1644; the wood panelling, the fireplace and the top of the alcove were created for Marie Leszczynska in 1747 and the doors with arabesque motifs were installed for Marie-Antoinette in 1787. The brocaded silk was rewoven according to the original pattern in Lyon at the end of Louis XVI's reign. Among the furniture note Marie-Antoinette's bed, designed in 1787 by Hauré, Séné and Laurent, a set of armchairs attributed to Jacob Frères and several commodes by Stöckel and Beneman (1786). The vases are Sèvres porcelain.

Boudoir de la Reine (11) – This delightful room was designed by Marie-Antoinette. The wainscoting was painted by Bourgois and Touzé after sketches by the architect Rousseau. The ceiling – representing sunrise – is the work of Berthélemy. The roll-top writing desk and the work table were made by Riesener in 1786.

Throne room

Ph. Gajic/MICHELIN

Salle du Trône (**12**) – This was the king's bedroom from Henri IV to Louis XVI; Napoleon converted it into the throne room. The ornate mural paintings, dating from several periods, were harmonised in the 18C. Above the fireplace is a full-length portrait of Louis XIII, painted in Philippe de Champaigne's studio.

Salle du Conseil (**13**) – This room was given a semicircular extension in 1773. The ceiling and panelling are splendid examples of Louis XV decoration.

Five pictures by Boucher adorn the ceiling, representing the four seasons and Apollo, conqueror of Night. The wainscoting presents an alternation of allegorical figures painted in blue or pink monochrome by Van Loo and Jean-Baptiste Pierre.

★ **Appartement Intérieur de l'Empereur** ⊘ – **Napoleon** had his suite installed in the wing built by Louis XVI, on the garden side running parallel with the François I Gallery.

Chambre de Napoléon (**A**) – Most of the decoration – dating from the Louis XVI period – has survived. The furniture is typically Empire.

Petite chambre à coucher (**B**) – A little private study which Bonaparte furnished with a day bed in gilded iron.

Salon de l'Abdication (**C**) – According to tradition, this is the room in which the famous abdication document was signed on 6 April 1814. The Empire furniture in this red drawing room dates back to that momentous time.

The François I Gallery leads to the Vestibule du Fer-à-cheval, at the top of the curved steps of the same name. This was the official entrance to the palace from the late 17C onwards. Both the gallery of the chapel and the Appartements des Reines-Mères give onto this hall.

★ **Musée chinois** ⊘ – This small museum, commissioned by Empress Eugénie on the ground floor of the Gros Pavillon, comes as a surprise because of the contrast between the comfortable, heavy furniture and the slender elegance of the objects on show. The collection was originally the booty captured during the Franco-British conflict with China in 1860, especially as a result of the ransacking of the imperial palace. The following year, a delegation of Siamese ambassadors completed the collection with a number of opulent presents, an event which was faithfully recorded in a painting by Gérôme.

The tour begins in the **antechamber** decorated with two luxurious Siamese palanquins. The "**nouveaux salons**" beyond are decorated with crimson wall hangings, padded armchairs, ebony furniture and objects from China and Siam. Most of the collection, however, is to be seen in the **cabinet de laque** decorated with 15 panels from an 18C Chinese fan. Note the four large tapestries on the ceiling and the huge glass-fronted cabinet filled to the brim with objects, including a copy of the Siamese royal crown.

★Musée Napoléon-Ier

The **museum** ⊘ is dedicated to the Emperor and his family; it occupies 15 rooms on the ground level and first floor of the Louis XV wing. Exhibits include portraits (paintings and sculptures), silverware, arms, medals, ceramics (Imperial service), clothing (coronation robes, uniforms) and personal memorabilia. Thanks to the numerous works of art and furniture adorning their interior, these apartments have kept their princely character.

The rooms on the first floor evoke the Coronation (paintings by François Gérard), the Emperor's various military campaigns, his daily life (remarkable folding desk by Jacob Desmalter), the Empress Marie-Louise in formal attire or painting the Emperor's portrait (picture by Alexandre Menjaud) and the birth of Napoleon's son, the future King of Rome (cradles).

The ground floor presents the Emperor's close relations. Each of the seven rooms is devoted to a member of the family: Napoleon's mother, his brothers Joseph, Louis, Jérôme and sisters Elisa, Pauline and Caroline.

Petits Appartements et galerie des Cerfs ⊘

These rooms are located on the ground floor below the François I Gallery and the Royal Suite overlooking the Jardin de Diane.

Petits Appartements de Napoléon Ier – This suite comprises François I's former bathroom suite (located beneath the gallery and converted into private rooms under Louis XV for the king, Mme De Pompadour and Mme Du Barry), and the ground floor of the new Louis XVI wing, situated under the Imperial Suite. The rooms opening onto the garden have been decorated with Louis XV wainscoting and Empire furniture.

★ **Appartements de l'Impératrice Joséphine** – This suite of rooms adorned with Louis XV panelling was designed for Joséphine in 1808. It lies beneath the grand royal suite.

The study, with its large rotunda, is located beneath the Council Chamber *(first floor)*. The Empire furniture here has a feminine touch: Marie-Louise's tambour frame, her easel etc. The Salon Jaune constitutes one of the palace's most perfect examples of Empire decoration. The gold-coloured wall hangings provide an elegant setting for Jacob-Desmalter's choice furniture set off by a large Aubusson carpet with a white background.

★**Galerie des Cerfs** – The gallery is decorated with numerous deer heads (only the antlers are genuine). The mural paintings were renovated under Napoleon III; they show palatial residences at the time of Henri IV, seen in perspective. It was in this gallery that Queen Christina of Sweden had her favourite, Monaldeschi, assassinated in 1657. The original casts used to make Primaticcio's 1540 replicas of Antique statues are on display in the gallery.

★GARDENS

These consist of the Jardin de Diane *(see above)*, the Landscape Garden, the parterre and the park.
Follow the route indicated on the map below.

★**Grotte du Jardin des Pins** – This rare ornamental composition carved in sandstone reveals the popular taste, copied from the Italians, for ponds, man-made features and bucolic landscapes in vogue towards the end of François I's reign. The rusticated arches are supported by giant telamones. The frescoes have disappeared.

★**Jardin Anglais** – The garden was created in 1812 on the site of former gardens – featuring a pine grove – redesigned under Louis XIV and abandoned during the Revolution. The Bliaud or Blaut fountain – which gave its name to the palace – plays in a small octagonal basin in the middle of the garden.

Parterre – This formal garden was laid out under François I, reviewed under Henri IV and eventually redesigned by Le Nôtre. The Tiber and Romulus basins take their name from a Classical-style sculpture which adorned them in the 16C and then the 17C. The Tiber – melted down during the Revolution – was cast after the original *(in the Louvre)* a second time and is now back in the place Louis XIV had assigned it. Skirt the Canal du Bréau to get a broad view of the palace.
Until the 18C, a series of cascades marked the end of this first group of tiered fountains. At present there remains only a basin of the same name, its ornate niches adorned with marble statues.

Park – The park was created by Henri IV, who filled the canal (in 1609) and had the grounds planted with elms, pines and fruit trees. Sixty years before the installation of the Grand Canal at Versailles, this dazzling sight was a great novelty for the *Ancien Régime*, as were the aquatic displays.

ADDITIONAL SIGHT

Musée Napoléonien d'Art et d'Histoire Militaires ⊘ – The museum contains around 100 figures, complete with full equipment and weaponry: swordsmen and veterans from the Imperial Grand Army, soldiers who fought for the conquest of Algeria and the Second Empire.
The first floor houses a **collection** of statutory **swords and sabres**★ dating from the 19C.

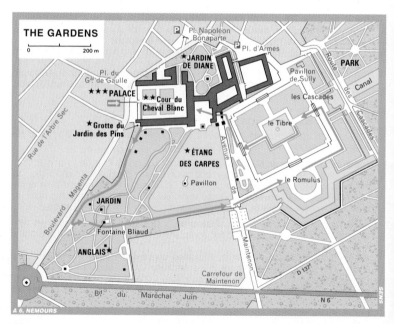

Eating out

MODERATE

Le Wooden Horse – *10 rue de Montebello* – ☎ *01 60 72 04 05* – *closed Tues lunchtime and Mon* – *booking recommended* – *79/250F*. This restaurant in the town centre is the perfect place to satisfy your appetite and quench your thirst after a long, tiring walk in the woods... Diners can choose between the elegant dining hall or the small courtyard beneath its glass cupola. For a cocktail, settle in one of the comfortable armchairs in the pub-style bar.

MID-RANGE

Croquembouche – *43 rue de France* – ☎ *01 64 22 01 57* – *closed Aug, over Christmas, Thur lunchtime and Wed* – *130/210F*. A modest, unpretentious establishment downtown patronised by many locals. Warm welcome and cosy, low-key decoration. Traditional fare made with fresh regional produce.

Where to stay

MODERATE

Hôtel de la Chancellerie – *1 rue de la Chancellerie* – ☎ *01 64 22 21 70* – *hotel.chancellerie@gofornet.com* – *25 rooms 220/320F* – ☐ *35F*. This small hotel is housed on the former premises of the Chancellerie, in the city centre. Small, light rooms and a friendly welcome. Suitable for tight budgets.

LUXURY

Hôtel de Londres – *1 place du Général-de-Gaulle* – ☎ *01 64 22 20 21* – *closed 13-18 Aug and 23 Dec-8 Jan* – ☐ *11 rooms from 650F* – ☐ *60F*. This stately hotel built opposite the château in 1850 is a pretty sight to behold, with its white rooms decorated with period furniture and hunting engravings. The rooms giving onto the street afford lovely views of the town. Not to be missed.

L'Aigle Noir – *27 place Napoléon* – ☎ *01 60 74 60 00* – ☐ – *49 rooms from 990F* – ☐ *110F* – *restaurant 195/450F*. A stone's throw from the château, this former private residence embellished by a lovely gate is a model of sophistication. The personalised rooms are elegant and appointed with Napoleonic furniture. Its restaurant, Le Beauharnais, serves delicious food in a cosy dining room adorned with frescoes.

On the town

Le Montijo – *27 place Napoléon-Bonaparte* – ☎ *01 60 74 60 00* – *daily 6pm-1am* – *closed 23-30 Dec*. This piano bar is housed in the Aigle Noir, one of Fontainebleau's two four-star hotels. Warm, cosy ambience. Live guitar and piano music Wed to Sat evenings.

Sport

Jeu de Paume de Fontainebleau – *Château de Fontainebleau* – ☎ *01 64 22 47 67* – *daily 11am-7pm* – *closed July*. The sport known as *jeu de paume*, from which both tennis and squash derived, has been practised here since 1601, in a chamber of Fontainebleau Château boasting 18C tiling. Visitors can watch a game or sign up to play.

EXCURSIONS

Croix du Calvaire – *5km/3mi from the palace. Leave by boulevard du Maréchal-Leclerc (direction ② on the map above). Just before the swimming pool, take the second turning on the left and proceed along route de la Reine Amélie.*

Almost 1.5km/1mi after the road starts to rise, turn left to reach the esplanade and calvary; admire the fine **view** of the town nestling amid woodlands.

Avon – *Leave Fontainebleau by boulevard du Maréchal-Juin and at the junction, carrefour de Maintenon, fork left to D 137ᴱ.*

Église St-Pierre – Built in the 11C, this church features a Romanesque nave surmounted by diagonal arches. The bell-tower was erected in the 13C and the Renaissance door dates from the 15C. The Gothic chancel, the work of architect Jean du Montceau, was completed in 1555. Note, among the tombstones, that of the Marquess of Monaldeschi, the favourite of Queen Christina of Sweden who had him assassinated at Fontainebleau in 1657. The recently restored porch was erected in the 18C.

Leave Avon and proceed along D 137 then turn right on entering By-Thomery.

By-Thomery, Atelier de Rosa Bonheur ⊙ – Rosa Bonheur (1822-99), an animal painter widely acclaimed by her contemporaries, bought the Château de By in 1859 to satisfy her need for space (she had numerous pets) and quiet. Empress Eugénie paid her a visit when she was awarded the French order of merit, the Légion d'Honneur. Another famous visitor, Buffalo Bill, gave her one of his outfits, which is still exhibited in the corridor.

The tour includes the study (portrait of the artist by Achille Fould, banker and government minister to Napoleon III), the studio (stuffed animals, deer antlers, her last, uncompleted picture) and a closet furnished with her bed, her wardrobe and a glass cabinet of memorabilia.

Vulaines-sur-Seine, Musée départemental Stéphane-Mallarmé ⊙ – *Leave Fontainebleau on the Avon road then take the first turning on the left after the Valvins bridge.* Housed in **Stéphane Mallarmé**'s former home on the banks of the Seine, this little museum gives an insight into the life of the poet who was so fond of this picturesque spot. "The water, light and greenery all play music..." On the upper floor, the apartments have been restored and reflect his lifestyle quite accurately. They contain personal memorabilia and the original furniture. Visitors can also see his small garden, which has been carefully restored.

Château de Bourron ⊙ – *7km/4.5mi south. Michelin map 237 fold 37. Leave Fontainebleau by ④ the N 7 and turn left at Bourron-Marlotte.* Built on the remains of a medieval stronghold in the late 16C, the château consists of an austere central block flanked by two perpendicular pavilions; these are fronted by two low wings (stables). The stone and brick patterns of the façades and the horseshoe staircase are reminiscent of the Cour du Cheval-Blanc at Fontainebleau. On the northern side, a swivel bridge spanning the moat leads to another horseshoe staircase. The parterre to the south affords a good view of the stately and harmonious proportions of the château. Note the delightful Ste-Sévère spring, which flows into the Grand Canal to the north of the park. Louis XV came to the Château de Bourron to meet his father-in-law Stanislas Leszczynski, the dethroned King of Poland, who was staying on the estate.

Château de Fleury-en-Bière – *13km/8mi northwest.* The château *(private)* dates from the 16C and was designed for Cosme Clausse *(see above).* The stately proportions of the courtyard, sealed off from the street by a stout wall, can be glimpsed from the entrance. At the far end, surrounded by a moat, stands the brick and stone château, flanked on its right side by a large stone tower. Several huge outbuildings stand on either side of the building. The gracious Romanesque chapel *(set back to the right)* serves as a parish church.

Forêt de FONTAINEBLEAU★★★
FONTAINEBLEAU FOREST
Michelin map 106 folds 44, 45, 46 or 237 folds 30, 31

This lovely (25 000ha/62 000 acres) forest surrounding Fontainebleau is largely State-owned and has always provided magnificent hunting grounds. It is immensely popular with ramblers and climbing enthusiasts. The forest was damaged in several places by the violent storm of December 1999.

GENERAL APPEARANCE OF THE FOREST

Geological formation – The relief of the forested area comprises a series of parallel sandstone ridges running in an east-west direction. These ridges are thought to be the result of a tropical spell during the Tertiary Era, when strong winds gradually accumulated sand deposits in this part of the Paris Basin. The sand dunes subsequently solidified into a hard sandstone matrix and were then buried beneath deposits of Beauce limestone, which resulted in the preservation of the area's rolling landscape. Where the upper layer of Beauce limestone was spared by erosion, the valley sides culminate in small **hillocks**. They reach a maximum height of 144m/475ft and bear some of the forest's most charming groves.

Where the limestone has eroded revealing the sandstone, the resultant rocky areas are known locally as **platières**.

These **moorlands** covered with heather and other shrubs are often cracked and dotted with ponds. When the sandstone layer has many crevices and holes, water seeps through and starts to wash away the underlying sands. The upper sandstone strata is no longer supported and crumbles as a result, producing picturesque rocky clusters, the famous Fontainebleau **rochers**. **Vales** or **plains** averaging 40-80m/130-260ft in height are found where the sandstone layer has been eroded away, exposing the sand or the Brie marl and limestone beneath. The planting of conifers fertilises the soil, making it possible to grow beeches. These produce humus and are eventually replaced by oaks, the ideal tree species for a forest.

Eating out

MID-RANGE

Auberge de la Treille – *5 rue Grande, 77210 Samoureau – 6km/3.7mi east of Fontainebleau by D 210 –* ☎ *01 64 23 71 22 – closed 1-7 Jan, 15-30 Aug, spring school holidays, Wed and Sun evenings and Mon – 120/200F.* A village inn featuring a terrace and a small back garden. The restaurant serves traditional fare at affordable prices.

La Marine – *52 quai O.-Metra, at the Écluse, 77590 Bois-le-Roi – 10km/6.2mi north of Fontainebleau by N 6, D 116 then D 137 –* ☎ *01 60 69 61 38 – closed Feb, Oct, Mon and Tues – 135/220F.* This congenial establishment is situated next to a lock on the banks of the River Seine. Settle down on the terrace, resembling the prow of a barge, or inside the dining room with its visible beams. Traditional French cuisine.

La Maison de Champgosier – *In Samois-le-Haut, 77920 Samois-sur-Seine –* ☎ *01 64 24 60 71 – closed 2-6 Jan, 21-24 Aug, 13-28 Nov, Sun evening, Mon and Tues – 200/290F.* This Briard-style house in the heart of the village is overflowing with charm. Passing through the small inner courtyard, you will glimpse the pretty patio under its wooden frame that is used as a terrace in summer. Large radiant dining room exuding a warm, cosy atmosphere.

Where to stay

MODERATE

Camping Les Courtilles du Lido – *77250 Veneux-les-Sablons – 8km/5mi southeast of Fontainebleau by D 148, route de Sens –* ☎ *01 60 70 46 05 – open 22 Apr-1 Sept–*✇ *– booking recommended – 196 plots 85F.* This carefully kept camp site with shaded plots is the perfect starting point for excursions to Fontainebleau Forest and the surrounding area. Swimming pool.

MID-RANGE

Hôtel du Pavillon Royal – *40 avenue Gallieni, 77590 Bois-le-Roi – 10km/6.2mi north of Fontainebleau by N 6, D 116 then D 137 –* ☎ *01 64 10 41 00 –* ▣ *– 26 rooms 350F –* ☲ *40F.* Conveniently located next to the Hydraulic Institute, this modern hotel welcomes many foreign visitors. Large, soundproofed rooms. Take a stroll in the charming garden or have a dip in the outdoor pool.

The Fontainebleau Forest

Forest layout – The forest is divided into 747 plots maintained in such a way as to provide the finest possible trees.

Most of the forest (9/10ths) consists of copses and thickets; the remainder is moorland and rock. Sessile oaks cover 8 000ha/19 768 acres, Norway pines 7 500ha/18 532 acres, and beeches 1 500ha/3 706 acres. The other species (hornbeam, birches, maritime and Corsican pines, larches, chestnuts, acacias, and service trees) are reminders of older attempts at acclimatisation or the remains of lightly wooded moorland. Some 416ha/1 028 acres constitute a biological reserve.

Denecourt-Colinet footpaths – Footpaths laid out by the "two Sylvains" (Denecourt and Colinet) take tourists to the most famous spots in the forest. Sylvain Denecourt served with Napoleon's Grande Armée. He removed rocks and boulders from caves, cleared the finest beauty spots, and laid out 150km/93mi of waymarked footpaths. On carefully selected trees (see the guide book entitled *Remarkable trees of the Fontainebleau Forest*) or rocks, discreet blue lines topped by numbers (1 to 16) indicate the main paths. Blue letters (also explained in the guide edited by the Amis de la Forêt) and stars are also used as markings on specific sights. Colinet, once a civil servant with the Ponts et Chaussées (Ministry of Public Buildings and Works) continued where his predecessor had left off. The markings were completed, after 1975, by the inclusion of white enamelled signposts bordered in green at all the main junctions.

"Bleau" and "Bleausards" – By 1910, a few climbing enthusiasts from the Club Alpin Français had already begun to train at Le Cuvier-Châtillon, La Dame-Jeanne, L'Éléphant etc camping overnight near their favourite rock if necessary.

In the inter-war years, the idea of a rock climbing school became commonplace among climbers in France. Fontainebleau was the ideal spot for climbers living in Paris, especially for the members of the Groupe de Haute Montagne.

Described by one of the great mountain guides of Chamonix as "rocks ideal for scouring pots and pans", the compact sandstone in the forest provides a challenge and a few valuable examples of potential difficulties: overhanging ledges, and slabs of rocks which, if there are many in succession, are a good preparation for climbs in the Alps, Himalayas or Andes. Many a well-known climber has come here to train.

Since then, the "Bleausards" have continued to practise their sport in the forest. There are more than 100 climbs marked out with arrows on the rocks.

Each of them is a succession of climbs, descents and, in some cases, jumps; there are never any walks along paths.

HIKES AND TOURS

Because of heavy traffic on N 6, N 7 and route Ronde between the Table du Roi and Grand-Veneur crossroads, it is not advisable to include these roads or sections of road in sightseeing tours. In many cases, it is forbidden to turn left onto minor forest roads.

★★GORGES DE FRANCHARD

1 Round tour starting from La Croix de Franchard

🚶 *30min to 2hr on foot there and back.*
From the Croix de Franchard crossroads, drive to the spacious shady esplanade at the Ermitage de Franchard, a very popular spot at weekends.

Ancien ermitage de Franchard – A hermitage developed here in the 12C, and in the 13C a community moved in to look after the pilgrims. By the 19C, the pilgrimage had become a country fête held on the Tuesday after Whitsun. Today only the chapel walls remain, incorporated into the forest warden's house.

★**Grand Point de vue** – 🚶 *30min on foot there and back.* Beyond the warden's garden skirt the sandy track on the left and climb towards the rocks without changing direction. This leads to a very sandy road (route de Tavannes); after

300m/330yd a mushroom-shaped rock will appear ahead. At the plateau turn right and on reaching the rock bear left to a bench overlooking the ravine. The view of the gorge is breathtaking.

To return to the hermitage, walk down three steps and bear left. This path returns to the route de Tavannes.

★★Circuit des Druides –

2hr – Beyond the Grand Point de Vue shown on the map, go down three steps and turn right. Follow the blue markings indicating Denecourt-Colinet path 7 which wends its way through a labyrinth of half-splintered boulders, some of them forming overhangs. At the bottom of the "gorge", cross a sandy road beside an isolated oak tree and climb back up among the rocks (follow the "♣" signs) to the "second belvedere" marked by a star.

Remain on the edge of the plateau. There is a wonderful view of the gorge and across the **Belvédère des Druides** (marked "P"). Go down to the easterly footpath and, at the bottom of the gorge, join the "route Amédée". Turn right. At the first crossroads, turn left onto the route de la Roche-qui-Pleure which climbs back up the hill and through a gap in the side of the plateau to the hermitage. *(Do not follow the path with the blue signs; it zigzags its way up through the rocks on the left.)*

★GORGES D'APREMONT

2 Round tour starting from Barbizon

10km/6mi – about 3hr 30min on foot

Leave Barbizon by allée aux Vaches, the continuation of Grande Rue, a magnificent tree-lined avenue that was so well known to artists. This road leads to the **carrefour du Bas-Bréau**, an intersection near a cluster of trees now protected by a preservation order spearheaded by a group of artists.

★Chaos d'Apremont – *45min on foot there and back from the crossroads.*
Follow the path marked in blue left of the refreshment chalet *(buvette)* and continue up amid the rocks; at the top bear right and follow the edge of the plateau. Views are over the wooded slopes of the gorge and the Bière plain. The path veers left: a clump of acacia and pine trees marks the entrance to the **Caverne des Brigands** *(take a torch)*.

Return to the car.

Take the Sully road up through the woods to the bare plateau high above the distant ravines.

★Grand Belvédère d'Apremont – *15min on foot.* About 1 700m/1mi from the crossroads called Le Bas-Bréau, park at the junction with the "road" to Le Cul-de-Chaudron. Progress along the plateau and turn left onto the path with blue markings. At a crossroads with a Denecourt-Colinet sign, turn right.

The path runs downhill past boulders and rocks. Bear left, remaining above the rocks. Below is the "gorge", its slopes strewn with blocks of stone. To the west is the Plaine de Bière.

Return to the car and to carrefour du Bas-Bréau.

★★Circuit du Désert – *3hr 30min on foot.* This part of the forest is famous for its barren and desert-like appearance that was so well known to artists and, later, to film directors.

Take the old road from Barbizon to Fontainebleau; after 1.6km/1mi turn south onto the road to Le Clair Bois. Take the first lane on the right, route de la Chouette, over a pass and down to the Désert d'Apremont, a valley dotted with oddly shaped boulders. Bear left onto path no 6 marked in blue. On reaching the rock resembling an animal with two snouts (reference N), bear right. At the carrefour du Désert take the blue-marked path which lies between route du Clair-Bois and route de Milan; it leads to a ravine framed by boulders, then along a rocky ledge.

Immediately after the Grotte des Dryades, marked with a star, bear left and walk down path "6-6" and up the far side of the valley to the raised platform; the pond called Mare aux Sangliers lies to the left. The prominent part of the plateau offers a good **view** of the Désert d'Apremont and the Bière plain.

Return to the car via carrefour du Désert and route du Clair-Bois.

LE LONG ROCHER

⑤ Round tour starting from carrefour de Marlotte

1.5km/1mi – then 2hr on foot there and back. From route Ronde branch off towards Marlotte.

After 1km/0.6mi, before reaching a steep slope, turn left onto route du Long Rocher, a sandy forest lane (ONF board: "Zone de Silence de la Malmontagne").

Park at the next crossroads (barrier). Take route des Étroitures (first turning on the right). After 90m/100yd, turn right onto path no 11, marked in blue.

Belvédère des Étroitures – *Trail marker U.* Admire the view of Marlotte and the Loing Valley.

Turn round and follow the blue-marked path which soon begins to wend its way between the boulders in the shade of the pine trees. It then winds here and there along a seemingly aimless route until it reaches the top of the plateau, the "Restant du Long-Rocher".

★★Restant du Long Rocher – The edge of the plateau, strewn with boulders, offers several good views of the southern and northern areas of the forest through the pine trees. Return to the blue path and continue in an easterly direction. Leave the plateau via the steep slope which includes Grotte Béatrix. Walk past a series of boulders

used for exercise by mountaineering schools *(red arrows)*.

Further along, the path rises slightly; branch off left and take the steep, clearly marked track down. This leads back to route du Long Rocher; bear left to return to the starting point.

★LES TROIS PIGNONS

7 Round tour starting from Arbonne

2.5km/1.5mi – then 3hr on foot there and back

Leave from the southern end of Arbonne (junction of the Fontainebleau-Milly road). Take the Milly road but immediately turn left onto the Achères-la-Forêt road (D 64). After 1.6km/1mi the road veers towards the motorway; turn right under it. Park the car.

Les Trois Pignons massif is an unusual extension of Fontainebleau Forest: it is a stony, barren site, unique in Île-de-France, with dry valleys, eroded peaks and other peculiarities which are common to sandstone landscapes.

From the car park go straight ahead and follow the road past two houses on the right. At the corner of the fencing, bear right and walk to the edge of a sandy depression, to the starting point of the Denecourt-Colinet path (no 16).

On the other side of the depression, directly opposite the plaque, is the first blue mark. The path crosses a flat stretch of land dotted with boulders and leads past the platform of the old Noisy telegraph transmitter to the plateau. An hour's walk will bring you to a chestnut grove. The path follows the recesses of the impressive Gorge aux Chats and continues south-east and then south, crossing a sandy, rocky area cleared of trees.

★★Point de vue de la Vallée Close – The edge of the plateau offers a good **view★★** of the uplands. In the foreground, a monument crowned by a cross of Lorraine honours the local Resistance network.

The blue path then turns north and descends eastwards, avoiding the wide sandy track previously explored to lead through oak coppices and heathers back to the starting point.

Suggestions for additional tours:

– north of Fontainebleau 3 Hauteurs de la Solle★ along **route Louis-Philippe★** and **route du Gros-Fouteau★** through ancient groves and then to the **Rochers du Mont Ussy★** where a pleasant path leads through pine trees;

– a round trip north-east of the town 4 taking in **Tour Dénecourt**, a 19C tower offering **panoramic views★**, and **Samois-sur-Seine,** an attractive and once-important town on the banks of the river;

– to the south-west 6, pleasant rambles through the Cirque des Demoiselles and to the **Rocher des Demoiselles★**.

FOURMIES

Population 14 505

Michelin map 53 fold 16 or 236 fold 29 – Local map see AVESNES-SUR-HELPE

Fourmies is a busy town which developed an important textile industry in the 19C; it is surrounded by huge forests and a series of lakes. The lakes were created by monks from Liessies and it is from them that the best-known of these, the **Étangs des Moines** with fishing, boating and swimming facilities, derive their name.

Écomusée ⊘ – The museum's aim is to preserve and promote the different economic and cultural aspects of life, past and present, in the region. Established with the help of the local population, the museum has branches specialising in different areas. *Marked itineraries starting from place de l'Église. Leaflet available at the museum.*

★**Musée du Textile et de la Vie sociale** ⊘ – The museum, which is housed in an old spinning mill, displays a collection of textile machines from the late 19C to the present day, all in working order.

Photographic records, reconstructions – of a textile laboratory, a hosiery workshop, and a street with a bar and shops – evoke the life of the locals over a century and retraces the events which marked their history (the strike of 1 May 1891 during which soldiers opened fire killing nine people in the crowd).

> **A QUIET NIGHT**
>
> **Hôtel Ibis** – *2km/1mi east of Fourmies by D 964 then a minor road –* ☎ *0327602154 – 31 rooms 300F –* ⌲ *37F.* Nature lovers will enjoy strolling down the shaded lanes skirting the small ponds scattered close to the hotel. You are guaranteed to sleep peacefully, lulled by the soft swaying of the trees beneath your windows. Comfortable but impersonal rooms belonging to the Ibis chain.

FRANCE MINIATURE★

Michelin map 106 folds 28, 29 or 237 fold 16

Access from Paris: *A 13 then A 12 to St-Quentin. Rejoin N 10 and head for Rambouillet. In Trappes, take D 23 to Élancourt.*

This theme park, laid out in Élancourt on a 5ha/12-acre site, is, as its name suggests, shaped like a gigantic relief map of France, bordered by lakes forming the coastline. In it are almost 2 000 models of the main sights and historic buildings in France, built to a scale of 1:30.

TOUR ⊘

Like Gulliver setting foot in Lilliput, visitors begin by climbing to the top of the Alps (altitude 9m/29ft!) for a panoramic view of France Miniature. In the middle of the mountains, plains and rivers is a network of footpaths that take visitors through all the French provinces and show them the most outstanding architectural sights and the most representative industrial developments. The Roman arena in Arles, the Pont du Gard, the Château de Chambord, the railway bridge at Gabarit (16m/52ft long), the Futuroscope in Poitiers, the Hospice de Beaune and the 10m/32ft high Eiffel Tower are as enthralling and interesting as Versailles. Also of interest are the dam at Bort-les-Orgues or the already famous Stade de France in St-Denis. Miniature trains, boats, planes and cars create a sense of movement amid the landscapes.

France Miniature

France Miniature

Palais de la Miniature – With his collection of more than 200 miniature works, Dan Ohlmann offers visitors a world tour.

GUÎNES

Population 5 105
Michelin map 51 fold 2 or 236 fold 2

Guînes, now a busy cereal market town, was the seat of a powerful count, a vassal of the English crown for more than 200 years, from 1352 to 1558. Surrounded by forests and marshland, the town is the pleasant starting point for tours of the Trois Pays area.

The Field of the Cloth of Gold

The famous encounter between **François I** of France and **Henry VIII** of England took place near Guînes, on the road to Ardres, in 1520. The 17-day meeting from 7 June now known as the Field of the Cloth of Gold *(Camp du Drap d'or)* was convened to discuss a possible Anglo-French alliance; however, it developed into a competition of one-upmanship.

François was staying in Ardres and Henry with the count at Guînes Castle; each was accompanied by his queen and a substantial court. The camp was arranged around jousting rails. On one side the English king occupied a "crystal palace" which sparkled in the sun, on the other François I sheltered under a tent of gold brocade; the surroundings had been arranged by the painter Jean Bourdichon.

This luxurious display proved fruitless however; Henry was irritated by the French King's extravagance, the crystal palace was damaged by the wind and he was toppled by his royal adversary during a contest.

Humiliated and angry, Henry returned to Gravelines and two weeks later made an alliance with the Emperor Charles V of Spain.

Musée municipal E.-Villez ⊘ – Numerous archeological remains, documents, objects, maps (Mercator atlas of 1609), engravings and paintings evoke the history of the town from its origins to the 20C.

FORÊT DE GUÎNES

▣ The road from Guînes enters this hilly area which is densely covered with varied species (oak, beech, hornbeam, birch) and extends (785ha/1 940 acres) to the northern edge of the Boulonnais region.

The road ends at the **Clairière du Ballon**. To the left and slightly set back, the **Colonne Blanchard** in marble marks the spot where, on 7 January 1785, the balloon flown by Jean-Pierre Blanchard (1753-1809) and the American physician John Jeffries landed, having achieved the first aerial crossing of the Channel.

A COUNTRY INN

Auberge du Colombier – Avenue de Verdun – ☎ 03 21 36 93 00 – closed 24 Dec-2 Jan – ▣ – 7 rooms 200/260F – ⌷ 30F. You will soon succumb to the charm of this handsome 18C manor house lost in the countryside. Arranged around a former dovecote, the spruce, peaceful rooms are housed in a modern outbuilding. The premises also accommodate a carefully laid-out camp site, a cluster of small chalets and a restaurant.

EXCURSIONS

Forteresse de Mimoyecques (Mimoyecques Fort) ⊘ – *10km/6mi south-west by D 231 and D 249 from Landrethun-le-Nord.*

Because of its position 8km/5mi from the coast and 150km/93mi from London, Mimoyecques was chosen as the launch site for the formidable V3 Howitzer, invented after the V1 and V2, to bombard London. To fire these shells the Germans had developed enormous, 130m/426ft long cannons. Work began in September 1943 when thousands of prisoners were forced to dig the 600m/1 968ft rail tunnel under 30m/98ft of chalk, and the trenches where the cannon were to be installed. The Allied forces bombed Mimoyecques from November 1943, and in July 1944 a Tallboy bomb pierced the concrete roof; this resulted in flooding which put an end to the works.

The huge scale of the project can still be seen, including the impressive tunnel where over 40 trains daily brought materials from Germany.

Ardres – *9km/5.5mi east on D 231.*

The Field of the Cloth of Gold by Bouterwek, Guînes

This pleasant and peaceful market town, where François I stayed during the **Field of the Cloth of Gold encounter**, was prosperous in Gallo-Roman times and later became a frontier town coveted by the English and the Spanish. The town lake *(swimming, fishing, sailboarding facilities)* was formed over the old peat bogs, out of which turfs were cut for fuel from Antiquity until the 19C.

The triangular, paved **main square** is bordered by picturesque old houses with pointed roofs. The old 17C Carmelite chapel stands opposite the east end of the 14C-15C church.

GUISE

Population 5 976
Michelin map 53 fold 15 or 236 fold 28

Guise (pronounced Gu-eez) lies in a pleasant setting at the bottom of the Oise Valley; despite its modern appearance the town has preserved an old district, near the church at the foot of the hill.

Elevated to a duchy by François I, Guise gave its name to an illustrious family – a junior branch of the House of Lorraine – whose most famous members were: **François de Guise** (1519-63) who defended Metz against Charles V of Spain and retook Calais from the English; and **Henri de Guise** (1550-88), head of the Catholic League during the Wars of Religion, who was assassinated in the castle in Blois on the orders of Henri III.

Guise was the birthplace of **Camille Desmoulins** (1760-94), the son of a lieutenant in the bailiff's court. The most famous French journalist at the time of the Revolution, Desmoulins publicly denounced the violence and injustices being committed in its name and was guillotined as a traitor for saying so.

In 1914 General de Lanzerac's army held back German troops attempting so cross the Oise, thereby allowing the French troops time to regroup for the Battle of the Marne.

SIGHTS

★**Château Fort des Ducs de Guise** ⊘ – *Access from the town, beyond Église St-Pierre.*

The castle was built in medieval times (11C) from Ardennes sandstone. Later, in the 16C, it was one of the first fortresses in France to have bastions added to it, at the instigation of the first dukes of Guise, Claude and François. Situated in the path of invaders of the Oise Valley, the castle was further reinforced by Vauban the following century. The buildings cover an area of 17ha/42 acres. After being subjected to artillery bombardments during the First World War, it was subsequently used as a quarry for materials and later as a rubbish tip.

In 1952 Maurice Duton, a local man, decided to save the castle with the help of young volunteers who were brought together under an organisation which they named the Club du Vieux Manoir.

Enter the castle through the restored 16C Porte Ducale which faces the town. From the Bastion de la Haute Ville cross the medieval passageway – which leads to the vaulted carriage entrance – to reach the prison and the large storeroom in which 3 000 men were garrisoned during sieges; continue along the vaulted passageway to the remains of the Palais du Gouverneur and the medieval keep. The foundations of the collegiate church, Église St-Gervais-St-Protais, are also visible. The guard-rooms in La Charbonnière and L'Allouette bastions have been turned into a museum exhibiting finds from excavations, including the coat of arms of François de Guise, the second Duke, and of his wife the Duchess of Este and Ferrara. Follow a series of underground passages to return to the Bastion de la Haute Ville and the Galerie des Lépreux.

Familistère Godin ⊘ – The creation of a workers' cooperative was the brainchild of Jean-Baptiste André Godin (1817-88), the founder of factories producing heating and cooking appliances.

The dwellings, built around courtyards with glazing supported on wooden or metal frameworks, can still be seen today. On each floor, walkways allow public access. The theatre is the venue of various events.

On the other side of the River Oise are the Godin factories which still operate.

A foresighted industrialist

Godin was a daring businessman who wished to put his ideas about the welfare of mankind into practice by building a "Social Palace" (1859-83), which included 500 modern homes, schools, swimming pool, theatre, wash-house, garden and general store. In 1880, Godin created a cooperative for capital and labour and ownership of the factory was gradually transferred to the workers.

Coupole d'HELFAUT-WIZERNES★★

Michelin map 51 fold 3 or 236 fold 4

This gigantic rocket-launching pad, built in 1943, is one of the most imposing relics of the Second World War. Symbolising Nazi madness, the site has now been turned into a **Centre d'histoire de la guerre et des fusées** (centre devoted to the history of war and rockets) which is both a memorial and an instructive place.

A project out of all proportion – Following the destruction in 1943 of the Éperlecques Bunker *(see p 329)*, Hitler decided to build a new one. The Todt organisation built a protective dome 72m/236ft in diameter and 5m/16ft thick, railway tunnels to convey the rockets, and miles of underground galleries to stock them.

Tallboy versus V2 – In spite of the heavy bombing which lasted from March to September 1944 and involved 5t Tallboy bombs, the dome was hardly damaged but the thrust forward of Allied forces in July 1944 forced the Germans to abandon the site before the launching pad was completed. V2 rockets were launched subsequently towards London and Antwerp from mobile bases, causing heavy casualties.

First rockets to reach the stratosphere – Adjusted in a top secret centre headed by Wernher von Braun in Peenemünde, on an island in the Baltic Sea, V2 rockets were built by the prisoners of the DoraNordhausen concentration camp who were made to work day and night. These formidable 14m/46ft-high weapons comprised 22 000 pieces; they could achieve a speed of 5 800kph/3 604mph and reach a target 300km/186mi away. They marked the beginning of man's venture into space.

Race to conquer space – At the end of the war, Von Braun joined the Americans and became one of the initiators of the Apollo space programme. This signalled the start of a race to conquer space between America and the Soviet Union.

TOUR ⊘

The tour starts in a tunnel through which travelled all trains arriving from Germany and continues along underground galleries intended for the storage of rockets. Visitors then proceed with the audio-guided tour by taking a lift up a 40m/131ft shaft which brings them beneath the huge dome weighing 55 000t. Two exhibitions, relying heavily on audio-visual techniques (documentaries lasting 7 to 20min including rare archive pictures, laser show) present German secret weapons (V1 flying bombs and V2 rockets) and the life of the local population in northern France from 1940 to 1944. One of the most moving sequences of the tour is focused on the last letter of a young member of the Resistance which shows up on a reconstruction of the Mur des Fusillés (execution wall) of the Lille citadel. An area is devoted to rockets and the conquest of space from 1945 to 1969 with models of Titan, Soyouz, Saturn, Ariane and a 20min film entitled *From the Earth to the Moon*.

A working model shows the firing site as it should have been; next to it, visitors can see a V1 flying bomb and an authentic V2 rocket, 14m/46ft high weighing 12t.

On the way back, the itinerary takes in the large octagonal hall, which remained unfinished, where rockets were prepared for launching (they were loaded with liquid oxygen and explosives) before being conveyed upright through two tunnels leading to two outside launching pads.

Schéma V2 supprimé.

HONDSCHOOTE

Population 3 654
Michelin map 51 fold 4 or 236 folds 4, 5

This Flemish-speaking town, which is bedecked with flowers in summer, has retained two windmills and several fine old houses, some of them gabled. Until the 17C Hondschoote produced a lightweight serge cloth *(sayes)* in 3 000 workshops, a prodigious number for a town with a population of only 28 000.

Hôtel de ville ⊘ – The building, which is dated 1558, was built on the main square in a Gothic-Renaissance style. The stone front is articulated by high mullioned windows linked by fine mouldings of curves and counter-curves. The rear façade is brick and stone, with a pointed tower crowned with an onion dome.

On the ground floor, a display of inscriptions by the writer Lamartine shows his affection for the local Coppens family, and a large painting portrays the 1793 Battle of Hondschoote in which the French triumphed over the English and the Austrians. On the first floor, an exhibition room displays ten 17C paintings showing nine noblewomen and Joan of Arc, together with works by Dutch painters. The inn beside the town hall dates from 1617.

Église – This hall-church type of building, with a tower at the west front and parallel aisles of equal height, is common in the maritime region of Flanders. The 16C tower (82m/269ft high) dominates the town; it was the only thing to survive the fire of Hondschoote in 1582. The aisles were rebuilt in the early 17C. Inside, the lyre-shaped organ case and the pulpit are 18C Flemish Baroque.

Hondschoote – The Noord-Meulen

The savings bank *(Caisse d'Épargne)* opposite is installed in the former manor house of the Coppens family, the lords of Hondschoote.

Moulin Spinnewijn ⊘ – The windmill bears the name of its former owner. It was rebuilt in 1993 for the bicentennial commemoration of the Battle of Hondschoote (8 September, 1793).

Moulin Noord-Meulen – *500m/550yd north of Hondschoote, near D 3.*
This windmill is thought to be the oldest windmill in Europe – its foundation dates back to 1127 – and was in use until 1959. The wooden cabin rests on a timber pivot and brick base.

LES MOËRES

The marshes – Extending as far as Furnes in Belgium, the marshes are below sea-level and were flooded over from 1645 to 1746 and again in 1940. Reclaimed from the sea in the 17C, using 20 windmills as water pumps, and protected by dykes, the marshes now provide fertile polders which are dotted with large farms and crisscrossed by canals full of tench, bream and pike. On the horizon stand the belfry, factories and cranes of Dunkirk.

Leave Hondschoote by D 947 and turn left onto D 3 towards Bergues, along the Canal de la Basse Calme; turn right onto D 79, then take the small road leading to the village of Les Moëres. Return to Hondschoote by D 947.

L'ISLE-ADAM
Population 9 979
Michelin map 106 fold 6 or 55 fold 20

Situated north of Paris along the Oise Valley, L'Isle-Adam has one of France's largest inland beaches, now a popular water sports centre: it features numerous facilities for yachting, sailing, rowing, canoeing etc. In 1014 a castle built on one of the islands in the River Oise was ceded to Adam de Villiers by Robert II the Pious, Hugh Capet's son. The former erected a priory on the estate.
Honoré de Balzac was a regular visitor to L'Isle-Adam and several of his novels are set in the area. In the 19C Villiers de L'Isle-Adam, the author of *Cruel Tales*, was to become one of the great names of French literature. L'Isle-Adam was also home to Henri Prosper Breuil (1877-1961), the renowned archeologist.
The old bridges – in particular Cabouillet Bridge, a 16C stone construction with three arches – command a pleasant view of the Oise, which is still frequented by traditional rowing boats *(boat hire office on the beach).*

SIGHTS

Église St-Martin – Like the Collégiale St Martin in Montmorency *(see MONT-MORENCY),* this church is typical of 16C architecture and presents highly intricate vaulting. It was consecrated on 1 October 1567, in the presence of Constable Anne. The tower erected in 1869 is a replica of the one adorning Église de la Trinité in Paris.
The interior offers a vast collection of well-preserved furnishings. The 1560 **pulpit★** – of German origin – features inlaid panels and portrays numerous statues, grouped in sets of four: Great Prophets, Evangelists, Doctors of the Church, Cardinal Virtues (also the three Theological Virtues).
On the northern side stands the funeral chapel of Louis-François de Bourbon (1717-76), the penultimate descendant of the Conti dynasty, Grand Prior of France of the Order of Malta. The remains of the original monument (1777), including the prince's medallion, have been reassembled.

Musée Louis-Senlecq – *46 Grande-Rue (between the post office and the church).*
Housed in a former 17C school, this art and history museum displays the town's collections gathered since 1939. The painting gallery is particularly interesting; if it contains the works of important groups of artists (Émile Boggio, Jules-Romain Joyant and Jules Dupré). Note the fine painting by Vlaminck entitled *Houses under snow.*

FRIENDLY AND INVITING

Le Relais Fleuri – *61 bis rue St-Lazare –* ☎ 01 34 69 01 85 – *closed 8-30 Aug, Feb school holidays, Mon evening and Tues –* 155F. This friendly inn with a provincial touch offers French specialities made with fresh market produce. If the weather is fair, you can sit out on the veranda or the small terrace backing onto the house.

L'Isle-Adam – The pagoda at Cassan

Centre d'Art Jacques-Henri-Lartigue – *31 Grande-Rue.*
Jacques-Henri Lartigue (1894-1986) was a famous photographer and a prolific painter: his foundation owns no fewer than 300 of his paintings exhibited in rotation. His style changed with time but his vigorous brushstrokes and his very bright colours are easily recognisable. The centre also organises temporary exhibitions featuring contemporary artists.

Pavillon chinois de Cassan – *To the north-east, along rue de Beaumont. Enter through the main gateway of the former park.*
This quaint pavilion overlooking a lake was built to adorn the landscaped park of Cassan. The estate used to belong to the financier Bergeret (1715-85), an enthusiastic art lover and patron of Fragonard; the rest of the estate has been turned into a residential area.
The pagoda, brightly decorated in red, green and saffron tones, stands on a stone base resting upon arches that house the spillway for the waters of the park (ponds and canals).
The pagoda-shaped roof is supported by a peristyle of eight wooden pillars. It conceals the elaborate network of imbricated domes which act as a lantern and crown the room, decorated with paintings. The mast at the top of the pavilion features several tiers of rings adorned with small bronze bells.

Forêt de L'Isle-Adam – This State-owned forest, which covers an area of 1 500 ha/3800 acres, is separated from the Forêt de Carnelle by the Presles Valley. Oak trees make up two-thirds of the thickets and copses; the remainder of the forest is beech, chestnut, hornbeam, birch and lime.
The forest was very carefully enclosed and maintained for hunting by the Princes de Conti until 1783 (the words *portes* and *grilles*, both meaning "gate", are frequently found in local place names). Nowadays, several major roads cut through it including D 64 to Paris and N 184, newly routed to avoid the banks of the River Oise.
The forest varies in altitude from 27m/88ft to 193m/627ft. The forest is in fact a series of copses. The area adjacent to L'Isle-Adam is fairly flat. The area near Maffliers is higher and more hilly. It is crossed by a network of roads fanning out from the remarkable star-shaped crossroads known as **Le Poteau La Tour**.

Abbaye de JOUARRE★

Michelin map 106 fold 24 or 237 fold 20

Jouarre stands on a hilltop high above the last loop of the River Petit Morin before it flows into the Marne.
The town already had two abbeys in the 7C. The monastery was short-lived but the convent adopted the Benedictine rule and survived. It soon acquired a prestigious reputation and the great ladies of France, among them Madeleine d'Orléans, François I's half-sister, were flattered to receive the title of abbess. In 1572, during the Wars of Religion, one of the abbesses, **Charlotte de Bourbon** was attracted by the new Calvinist ideas. She fled from Jouarre with several nuns and a handsome sum of money and renounced the Catholic religion. She later married William of Nassau, the founder of the Dutch Republic.

Badly damaged during the Hundred Years War, the abbey was rebuilt several times, particularly in the 18C. When the abbey was seized during the Revolution, it was the residence of a fervent, united religious community, close observers of monastic rules and widely praised by Jacques Bossuet. The monastery resumed its activity c 1837. The **principal offices** are celebrated according to Benedictine liturgy.

TOUR

Tower ⊘ – Only the tower remains from the old medieval sanctuary; it once served as bell-tower and porch to the 12C Romanesque church. The interior has been carefully restored: three vaulted rooms, furnished by Madeleine d'Orléans in the 16C, house abbey memorabilia (note the armorial bosses) and temporary exhibitions.

★ Crypt ⊘ – It lies behind the parish church, at the end of place St-Paul. This square presents an imposing 13C cross resting on a stone base with the Virgin and Child in the centre of a four-lobed medallion. The crypt consists of two formerly underground chapels which were linked in the 17C.

Crypte St-Paul, the mausoleum of the founding family, is considered to be one of the oldest religious monuments in France.

The crypt is divided into three aisles by two rows of three columns dating from Gallo-Roman times, made of marble, porphyry or limestone. It is believed that the capitals were made of white marble from the Pyrenees. The famous Merovingian wall near the entrance presents a primitive stone mosaic with geometric motifs (oblongs, squares, diamonds etc).

The most striking sarcophagus is the Tomb of St Agilbert, Bishop of Dorchester and later of Paris, the brother of Theodechilde; Christ sits enthroned, surrounded by the Chosen Few with upraised arms. One of the galleries affords a good view of the bas-relief at the head: Christ circled by the four Evangelists' symbols (man, lion, bull, eagle). The tomb of St Osanne – an Irish princess who allegedly died in Jouarre – presents a 13C recumbent figure. The most elaborate decoration is that of the sarcophagus of Theodechilde, the first abbess of Jouarre. A display of large cockleshells adorns a Latin inscription in honour of the wise Virgins.

Eating out

MODERATE

Auberge du Petit Morin – *77260 La Ferté-sous-Jouarre – 4.5km/2.8mi north of the abbey by D 402 then D 204 (route de Rebais) – ☎ 01 60 22 02 39 – closed 28 Aug-19 Sept and Feb school holidays – 98/230F.* A small restaurant lying on the outskirts of town. In high season, its terrace screened from the road by trees is extremely pleasant and its enclosed garden will delight children. The traditional French cuisine is served in two dining rooms, one of which features wood panelling and a welcoming fireplace.

Where to stay

MID-RANGE

Château des Bondons – *77260 La Ferté-sous-Jouarre – 5km/3.1mi north of the abbey by D 402 then D 70 (route de Montménard) – ☎ 01 60 22 00 98 – 🅿 – 14 rooms 500/1000F – ☕ 60F.* This attractive house surrounded by a park was once home to the 19C writer G Ohnet. The cosy, welcoming rooms are fitted with flowered fabrics and four-poster beds. The tastefully furnished salons have waxed parquet floors, wainscoting and old-fashioned fireplaces.

The **crypte St-Ébrégésile** is a small Romanesque church beyond the first crypt. An archeological dig carried out in 1989 revealed that it had been built between Merovingian walls. The capitals in the crypt are Merovingian, as is Bishop Ebrégésile's sarcophagus which was discovered in 1985 to the left of the altar. Recent excavations have revealed the nave of the modest St-Ébrégesile Church, along with several Merovingian sarcophagi.

Musée Briard ⊘ – Above these two crypts, a former chapel (17C) houses the museum which displays exhibits relating to regional folklore and history: costumes, tools, paintings etc.

Église Paroissiale ⊘ – *Enter by the south transept (see plan) at the end of the cul-de-sac.*
It was rebuilt after the Hundred Years War and completed in the early 16C.
The north arm of the transept features a 16C Entombment (studio of Michel Colombe), a 15C *Pietà* and two reliquaries (12C and 13C) covered in silver-gilt with enamels, cabochon and filigree work. The south aisle contains a 16C statue of Our Lady of Jouarre. The windows in the chancel and side aisles comprise many pieces of 16C stained glass.

EXCURSION

Doue – 10km/6.2mi south-west of Jouarre. The Doue hill (181m/594ft) offers a view of the Plateau de la Brie des Morins in the distance. The massive nave of the Église St-Martin contrasts with its lofty Gothic chancel and transept. Inside, note the luminosity of the chancel with its openwork design, characteristic of the Early Gothic style (13C).

JOUY-EN-JOSAS

Population 7 687
Michelin map 101 fold 23, 106 fold 30 or 237 fold 17 – Michelin plan 22
6km/3.5mi south-east of Versailles

This town has retained a noble aspect owing to the neat, tidy houses and the substantial estates, partly preserved after being ceded to various research and academic centres. The village was once a secluded spot favoured by memorable visits from Victor Hugo. In rue Victor-Hugo, a plaque indicates the small house rented by the poet for his mistress Juliette Drouet in 1835. His stay here inspired the writing of *Olympio.* The former French President Léon Blum and the bacteriologist Professor Albert Calmette, who discovered the vaccine against tuberculosis, are buried in Jouy cemetery.

A textile centre – In the 16C, printed cotton was imported from India, thus posing a serious threat to local manufacturers. In 1686, the king imposed a ban on printed material. The ban was lifted in 1759 and a year later, at the age of 22, **Christophe-Philippe Oberkampf** founded his first textile workshop, specialising in a type of printed calico known as *toile de Jouy*. In 1783 the factory became the Royal Works; business thrived. Oberkampf recruited his first skilled workers in Switzerland, and they in turn trained new apprentices. He showed a great interest in scientific advancement and modern machinery, and during the Continental Blockade he obtained permission from Napoleon to despatch several envoys to Switzerland, Alsace and even England. This gifted manufacturer employed up to 1 300 workers, a remarkably high number for the time.

The commercial losses sustained during the Napoleonic Wars, the foreign invasion (in which Oberkampf perished) and the advent of competition (over 300 firms in 1815) dealt a deathblow to the Royal Works. In 1843 the company was forced to file a petition for bankruptcy.

Musée de la Toile de Jouy

Toile de Jouy

SIGHTS

Musée de la toile de Jouy ⊘ – *54 rue Charles-de-Gaulle.*
The museum is housed in the 19C Château de l'Églantine, once the home of Maréchal de Canrobert who won fame

during the Crimean War. The rooms on the ground floor contain displays explaining the techniques used and the history of this famous product. Copper plates and cylinders or blocks of wood are used to print the pattern on the fabric. The Salon d'Oberkampf has been reconstructed with waxwork figures, some superb pieces of furniture stamped with the name of the cabinetmaker (Jacob), Jouy hangings and family portraits.

On the first floor are some fine show cases containing examples of the various motifs used in Jouy during the 18C and 19C. Note the various sets of bedclothes. Other French manufacturers (in Nantes, Rouen, Bordeaux, Alsace etc) are also represented.

Église ⊙ – *Place de la Division-Leclerc.*
The 13C base of the bell-tower is the oldest part of the building. Inside, at the far end of the single aisle, note the **Diège**★, a restored 12C painted wooden Virgin.

Musée de Jeanne et Léon Blum ⊙ – *4 rue Léon-Blum.*
The estate which the former French president acquired in 1945 and on which he lived until his death in 1950 provides an interesting insight into his life and political career. Several of the rooms contain documents relating to his early days, his literary works (essays, reviews) and his role in both the Socialist movement and French current affairs. The main room houses his writing desk and most of his private collection of books.

Léon Blum (1872-1950)

The young intellectual interrupted his brilliant studies in Paris to become a literary critic. Deeply affected by the Dreyfus affair, he joined the socialist party in 1902, following in the footsteps of Jaurès. He obtained his first government job during the First World War (1914-16) and became prime minister after the Front Populaire victory in the 1936 elections. He then passed several major social laws in a difficult economic climate: annual paid holidays, collective bargaing agreements, 40-hour work week, and launched an important rearmament plan. However he was soon abused for being Jewish and accused of having caused the flight of French capital abroad and the major strikes of June 1936. He resigned in June 1937. Handed over to the Germans by Laval in 1943, he was deported to Buchenwald where he narrowly escaped death. He served as prime minister once more in 1946-47 and died of a heart attack on 30 March 1950.

EXCURSION

Bièvres – The **Musée Français de la Photographie**★ ⊙ *(no 78 rue de Paris, in the direction of Le Petit Clamart)* presents a history of photography from technical and artistic viewpoints. The displays are being completely rearranged and the new museum is due to open in 2002. The many interesting exhibits range from Da Vinci's studies to the very latest apparatus, relying on sophisticated technology. The crucial discoveries of Nicéphore Niepce, who took the first photograph on 5 May 1816, are explained, as are Daguerre and his photographic process, the advent of amateur photography in 1888 (George Eastman-registered trademark "Kodak"), the invention of the miniature camera (Leica) in 1925 etc.

The museum highlights the continuous, sometimes naive quest for technical advancement, together with the craftsmanship involved; the large-format cameras are masterpieces of cabinetmaking and leatherwork. The first-floor collections are devoted to the bygone industry of amateur photography: plate cameras from the golden years (1910-45).

Some 15 000 apparatuses, including 300 Kodak cameras, and about a million photographs are on show.

LAON★★

Population 26 490
Michelin map 56 fold 5 or 236 fold 38

Laon occupies a splendid **site**★★, perched (over 100m/328ft high) like an acropolis on a rock, crowning a tall outcrop of land which overlooks the plain. The Carolingian town is a celebrated tourist destination on the borders of Picardy, the Paris Basin and Champagne incorporating a famous cathedral, interesting sights and houses in medieval streets overlooking a wide horizon.

There are two districts in the Ville Haute: the **Cité**, Laon's original heart around the cathedral; and the **Bourg**. An automatic cable railway, the **Poma**, links the old town to the railway station in the modern town at the base of the mount. The **Le Nain brothers** (17C), born here, evoked the life and people of Laon in their paintings and **Louis Cotte** (1740-1815), a native of Laon and a member of the Jesuit order, was one of the founders of modern weather forecasting.

LAON

HISTORICAL NOTES

Tertiary Age "Island" – At the north-eastern edge of the Paris Basin, following a line linking the towns of Monterau, Épernay, Reims, Corbeny and Bruyères, there is a sheer-sided chalky promontory; this is known by geologists as the "Île-de-France cliff". The rise on which Laon stands is a kind of island, set slightly apart from the other Tertiary Age formations and now strangely eroded. Once covered with grapevines, the land is still pitted with natural caves *(creuttes)*.

Carolingian Capital – Ancient Laudunum was the capital of France for a time during the Carolingian period (9C-10C). Berthe au Grand Pied, Charlemagne's mother, was born in Samoussy (north-east of Laon) and Charles the Bald, Charles the Simple, Louis IV d'Outremer, Lothar and Louis V all lived on "Mount Laon" in a palace near the Ardon Gate. The reign of the Carolingians finally came to an end with the arrival of Hugh Capet, who took Laon by treachery; Charlemagne's descendants were driven out and Capet established himself in Paris.

Cathedral City – St Remigius, who was born in Laon, founded the first bishopric in the 5C; under Hugh Capet the bishops became dukes and peers with the privilege of assisting the king during coronation ceremonies at Reims.
From the Carolingian period on, Laon became a renowned religious and intellectual centre, thanks to Jean Scot Erigène and Martin Scot in the 9C; to Anselm and Raoul of Laon in the 11C, under whose auspices the "Laon School", flourished; and to Bishop Gautier de Mortagne in the 12C, who had the cathedral built. In the 13C the town was surrounded with new ramparts and from the 16C Laon was a powerful military stronghold which was besieged on several occasions, once by Henri IV in 1594. In 1870 the munitions magazine exploded; over 500 people were killed or injured.

⬛ TOUR OF THE VILLE HAUTE *2hr 30min*

★★Cathédrale Notre-Dame – Laon boasts one of the oldest Gothic cathedrals in France; it was begun in the 12C and completed in about 1230. The cathedral's main feature is the traces of Romanesque architecture evident in its structure, in common with the cathedrals of Noyon and Soissons. These traces may be seen in the lantern tower and galleries, in the shape of some of the rounded arches and in the style of many capitals. There were originally seven towers: two on the west front, one over the transept crossing and four on the transept arms, two of which lost their spire during the Revolution.

The west front is one of the loveliest and most unusual in existence. The beautifully balanced appearance is due to the three deep porches decorated with majestic statuary (reworked in the 19C) and in particular to the famous towers (56m/184ft tall). The man thought to have designed them, **Villard de Honnécourt** said: "I have been in many lands but nowhere have I seen more beautiful towers than those of Laon". These towers, imposing yet light in appearance, are pierced by large bays and framed by slender turrets. They bear great oxen on their corners, recalling the legend of the ox which appeared miraculously to help a struggling team of yoked oxen working on repairs to the cathedral. The two towers of the transept arms are built in the same way (60m/196ft and 75m/246ft).

Interior – The interior is 110m/360ft in length, 30m/98ft in width and 24m/78ft in height (Notre-Dame de Paris: 130m/426ft, 45m/147ft, 35m/114ft). The **nave★★★**, roofed with sexpartite vaulting, rises to a magnificent height through four levels: great arches, galleries, a blind triforium and a clerestory. Beyond the nave, the wide chancel terminates in a flat east end, as in Cistercian churches. The chapter numbered 80 canons assisted by 50 chaplains.

The transept crossing offers a good view of the nave, chancel, transept arms and the Norman-style lantern tower (40m/131ft high). Beautiful 13C stained-glass windows grace the apse's lancet bays and rose-window, dedicated to the Glorification of the Church; the rose-window in the north transept also contains 13C stained glass representing the Liberal Arts.

The chancel railings and the organ date from the 17C. The south transept leads to the 13C **chapter-house** *(salle capitulaire)*; the bays look out onto a pretty cloister from the same period.

Leave the cathedral by the south transept and follow the outer wall of the cloister, which is decorated with a frieze of sculpted foliage; on the corner is an Angel with a sundial.

Hôtel-Dieu – In the past the bays and wide tierce-point arches of the 12C two-storey former hospital opened onto the street; today they are bricked up. The building has retained its great Gothic ward with three aisles which now houses the tourist office, and the room on the ground floor called the Passers-by Room.

Follow rue Châtelaine then one of the two lanes on the left leading to rue des Cordeliers. Cross place des Frères-Lenain and continue along rue G.-Ermant.

★Chapelle des Templiers ⊙ – The building recalls the Temple commandery founded here in the 12C which, after the order was suppressed, passed to the Knights of St John of Jerusalem. A peaceful flower garden has replaced the Knights Templar's

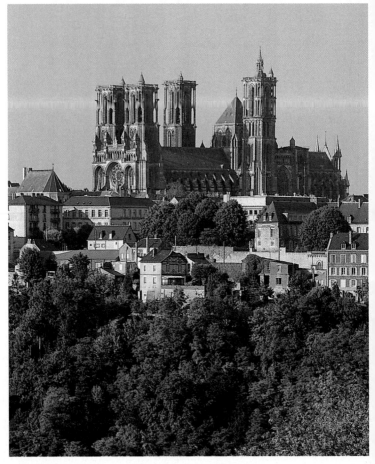

Laon – Notre-Dame Cathedral

cemetery but the Romanesque chapel has been preserved; it is octagonal with a gabled bell-tower and a small chancel with an semicircular apse. The porch and the gallery were added in the 13C and 14C. The interior houses two statue-columns of prophets from the west front of the cathedral and the 14C recumbent effigy of Guillaume de Harcigny, Charles VI's doctor and a forerunner of psychoanalysis in France.

On leaving, turn right onto rue G Ermant and round onto rue Vinchon.

The street is lined with old houses: no 44 was the 13C Val des Écoliers Priory (15C chapel and 18C portal) and no 40 the Val-St-Pierre Abbey refuge (15C-16C).

★**Rempart du Midi et porte d'Ardon** – The 13C Porte d'Ardon or Porte Royée (belonging to the *roi*, the king in French), stands at the end of the south ramparts, flanked by watchtowers with pepper-pot roofs; the gate overlooks a picturesque old public wash-house and drinking trough. The ramparts offer good **views**★ over St Vincent's plateau crowned by the Arsenal *(right)*, once St Vincent's Abbey, and the hills separating the Laon plain from the Ailette Valley *(ahead)*.

The south ramparts end in a **citadel** built for Henri IV by Jean Errard; walk round it along Promenade de la Citadelle which offers views of the plain dotted with other, small Tertiary Age hillocks.

Continue to the St Rémi rampart, turn left towards place du Général-Leclerc. Walk along rue du Bourg, rue St-Jean and rue St-Martin.

Hôtel du Petit St-Vincent – The building was constructed in the first half of the 16C as the town refuge for St Vincent's Abbey, which was outside the ramparts. The main body of the Gothic building by the road is surrounded by turrets and flanked with an entrance vault surmounted by a chapel. A later wing set at right angles overlooks the courtyard.

★**Abbaye St-Martin** ⊙ – This 12C-13C former Premonstratensian abbey church, restored after the fire in 1944, is a beautiful example of the Early Gothic style. The square offers a good general view; note the long, Romanesque-looking nave, the height (35m/114ft) and arrangement of the two towers at the corner of the nave and the transept (Rhenish influence), and the tall south transept with its rose-window and arcades.

The west front soars up, pierced by a great bay; its gable is decorated with a high-relief carving of St Martin sharing his cloak with a pauper. The tympana over the side doors depict the Decapitation of John the Baptist *(right)* and the Martyrdom of St Lawrence, who was roasted alive *(left)*.

Interior – The chancel and the transept chapels have flat east ends, following Cistercian custom. Recumbent figures lie near the entrance: Raoul de Coucy, a Laon Knight (late 12C) and Jeanne de Flandre, his sister-in-law, abbess of Sauvoir-sous-Laon (14C). The wooden panels in the nave are in the Louis XV style and those in the chancel Louis XIII. A 16C Christ of Compassion stands to the right of the Chapelle St-Eloi, separated from the church by a Renaissance stone screen.

Abbey buildings – The restored 18C section, visible from the cloister, houses the **library** (bibliothèque). A fine elliptical stone staircase leads to the first floor.

★**Porte de Soissons** – The gate was built in the 13C from quarried stone and rein-forced with round towers. It stands in a park containing a monument to Marquette (1637-75), a Jesuit from Laon who discovered the River Mississippi. A curtain wall links the gate to the great **Tour Penchée** or leaning tower, so-named following sub-sidence.

Rue Thibesard follows the sentry path along the ramparts, offering unusual **views**★ of the cathedral; its towers rise above the old slate roofs with their red-brick chimneys. Continue along the rampart and **rue des Chenizelles**, an old, cobbled street, to the 13C **Porte de Chenizelles**. The two towers create a narrow passageway through to rue du Bourg.

Eating out

MID-RANGE

La Rose des Sables – *2-4 rue Roger-Salengro* – ☎ *03 23 79 99 96* – *closed Aug and Mon – booking essential Sat-Sun – 102/162F.* If you long for a touch of exoticism, come here to sample succulent Northern African dishes such as couscous or tajines. Despite the simple decoration, the friendly ambience will not fail to move you.

Where to stay

MID-RANGE

Hôtel Les Chevaliers – *3 rue Sérurier* – ☎ *03 23 27 17 50* – *closed 16 Oct-14 May – 10 rooms 260/350F.* Originally built in the Middle Ages, this beautifully restored residence was given a new lease of life when it opened as a hotel. However, it has preserved its spirit and personality thanks to the old stones and brick, the visible beams, the cosy atmosphere and the generous welcome.

ADDITIONAL SIGHTS

Palais épiscopal – The palace, today used by the law courts, is preceded by a courtyard offering a view of the east end of the cathedral. The 13C building on the left rests on a gallery of pointed arches, its capitals decorated with plant motifs. Upstairs, the Grande Salle du Duché (over 30m/98ft long) today serves as the Assize Court.

The building at the far end was built in the 17C; it contained the bishop's apart-ments which lead directly to the two-storey 12C chapel. The lower chapel was reserved for servants and was used mainly for the Eucharist; the upper chapel, in the form of a Greek cross, served for religious ceremonies in the bishop's presence.

The **Maison des Arts**,⊘ opposite the palace, opened in 1971. It stands on the site of the third hospital founded in the 13C. The cultural centre comprises an exhibition hall, reading room, theatre, meeting rooms and a function or conference room. In rue Sérurier no 53 has a 15C entrance and no 33 bis incorporates the 18C door of the old town hall. The 16C-17C Dauphin Inn, at no 7-11 rue au Change, still has its beautiful wooden gallery.

★**Museum** ⊘ – The archeological collection is remarkable: Greek figure vases, baked clay figurines, 3C BC Greek head of Alexander the Great. There is also a prehis-tory section. Local finds are displayed on the mezzanine: bronzes and ceramics, Merovingian and Gallo-Roman jewellery.

Several rooms are devoted to painting: works by the Master of the Rohan Hours, the Le Nain brothers, Desportes and Berthélemy (18C).

Centre historique minier de LEWARDE ★★

The **Centre Historique Minier de Lewarde** ⊘ is housed in the converted buildings of the Delloye Colliery which operated from 1930 to 1971, producing up to 1 000t of coal per day. The museum's design has adapted the original structure to provide exhibition rooms, a restaurant, a conference, a film theatre etc.

REGIONAL CUISINE

Le Briquet – *In the Mining Centre, 59287 Lewarde – ☎ 03 27 95 82 82 – same admission times as for the Mining Centre – 89/139F*. Under the indulgent expression of St Barbe, the patron saint of miners, you can extend your tour of the mine by settling at a table in the former sawmill. The restaurant is named after the snack that miners used to take down with them in their lunchbox. Today, it offers more sophisticated fare inspired by regional tradition.

Tour

An exhibition describes life in and around the mine from the economic, technical, social and human point of view including the discovery of coal and the mining of the seams over a period of 300 years (animated model of mine working centre no 10 in Oignies), mining techniques (shafts, cutting) and their development, the miners' everyday life with its disasters and illnesses (firedamp explosions, silicosis, strikes).

P. Cheura/Centre Historique Minier

After touring the offices of the manager and accountant and the surveyors' room at their own speed, visitors are taken on a guided tour of the surface installations by an ex-miner (cloakroom, showers also known as the "hangman's room" because of the hooks on which the miners used to hang up their clothes, helmets and boots), and the lamp room, infirmary etc. A small train then takes visitors to shaft no 2 where they descend to the galleries by lift. A 450m/487yd walk through the galleries (audiovisual presentation and reconstruction of men working the coal face) gives a clear insight into changes in miners' lives from 1930 to the present day.

A tour of the processing building (extraction machines, coal-screening room) and the pit stables completes the visit. A vast collection of fossils is also on display, shown in the context of the formation of the mining basin 300 million years ago.

LILLE ★★

Lille, the lively capital of French Flanders, today enjoys a role as a regional and European metropolis owing to its location on major north-south and east-west routes. This lively convivial city seems to have acquired a new lease of life and successfully combines a definite high-tech appeal with its splendid Baroque style.

LIFE IN LILLE

The typical Lille citizen is reliable and hardworking but also a *bon vivant* who likes his food and appreciates a beer or two in one of the city's many brasseries. Place du Général-de-Gaulle, the pedestrianised place Rihour and nearby streets, particularly rue de Béthune with its numerous cinemas, are always lively.

Cultural Activity – Lille is now a major cultural centre following the establishment of a philharmonic orchestra, the opening of Opéra du Nord in Lille, the lyric workshop in Tourcoing, the Northern France Ballet Company and the institution of several

Lille — Grand'Place

B. Kaufmann/MICHELIN

theatre companies (including La Métaphore, the national company). Several cultural festivals take place here every year; the autumn festival includes concerts, fine arts, and theatre and dance performances.

Folklore – Folklore still plays an active part in the city, as it does in much of northern France; every district of Lille has its own feast day *(ducasse)*. Lille's **giants**, **Phinaert** and **Lydéric**, are paraded through the streets on holidays. According to legend, in about AD 600 a highwayman called Phinaert lived in a château where Lille stands today. One day the highwayman attacked the Prince of Dijon and his wife as they were on their way to England; the prince was killed but his wife was able to escape. Some time later she gave birth to a boy whom she put into hiding, before being caught herself by the highwayman. The baby was taken in by a hermit who baptised him Lydéric and had him suckled by a doe.

Once grown to manhood, Lydéric vowed to avenge the death of his parents; he challenged Phinaert to a fight and slew the highwayman. He then married the sister of King Dagobert and was entrusted with protecting the Flemish forests which had belonged to Phinaert.

LILLE TODAY

The town's new look – Successful efforts over several years to preserve and restore the lovely 17C and 18C buildings and monuments of the old district have turned Lille into an attractive artistic city; at the same time, much modernisation has taken place: the rebuilding of the district known as St-Sauveur and of the Forum; the creation of Villeneuve-d'Ascq and Euralille.

The "Dallas" of northern France – Owing to its location at the centre of a network of major routes and waterways, Lille has always been industrially and commercially important. The town is more than ever the economic centre of northern France. Business facilities (conference centre), traditional industries (textiles, mechanics), computer and technology giants, food production companies and research laboratories all co-exist here, side by side with the universities.

The urban area of Lille-Roubaix-Tourcoing is the centre of mail-order selling and also of business, with the Eurabille business centre, the Chamber of Commerce and Industry, and the Stock Exchange.

The metropolis of Lille is at the heart of a highly developed network of motorways leading to Paris, Brussels, Dunkirk and Antwerp; further, it has the third largest river port in France and an international airport at Lesquin.

The rail network, which has a large number of branch lines, uses the Lille-Europe station (1994), a fine example of contemporary architecture, built to cater to high-speed trains and the Eurostar service to London and Brussels; it is linked to the Lille-Flandre station by a viaduct built by Le Corbusier.

LILLE

The city boasts the world's most modern metro, the **VAL**, an entirely automatic system. One line links Lille to Roubaix-Tourcoing. Some of the stations are decorated with works of art:
– République: The Muses, a sculpture by Debeve, Spartacus by Foyatier, Autumn and Spring by Carrier-Belleuse, and reproductions of paintings displayed in the Musée des Beaux-Arts.
– Porte de Valenciennes: The Hand by César.
– Wazemmes: The Source of Life, a sculpture made of enamelled lavastone.
– Fives: frescoes by Dogand (The Cry and Graffiti).
– Pont de Bois: Bronze sculpture, Paternity, by Mme Leger.
The technology used for the VAL has attracted other cities in France (Bordeaux, Toulouse, Orly) and abroad (Taipei, Jacksonville, Chicago).
The famous Mongy that used to travel along the Grand Boulevard between Lille, Roubaix and Tourcoing, has been replaced by a more modern, elegantly designed tramway (its outline was drawn by Ferrari's designer).

A TURBULENT HISTORY

Lille has had a turbulent history having been sometimes Flemish, sometimes French, sometimes under Austrian or Spanish control. The city has faced 11 sieges and has been destroyed several times.

The Counts of Flanders – The name "l'Isle" (pronounced Lille) first appeared in 1066, in the charter of a donation to the collegiate church *(collégiale St-Pierre)* by Baudoin V, Count of Flanders, who owned a château on one of the islands in the River Deule. The town developed around this château and a port which existed on the site of the present avenue du Peuple-Belge.
In 1205 Count Baudoin IX, crowned Emperor of Constantinople during a crusade, died leaving two daughters, Jeanne and Marguerite. The young heiresses were raised by Philip Augustus; Jeanne, the elder daughter, was married to Ferrand of Portugal and the couple was then sent to Lille.
Although a French vassal, Flanders was linked, at least economically, with England and the Holy Roman Empire. Faced with Philip Augustus' claims on the northern regions, a coalition was formed which included the counts of Boulogne, Hainaut and Flanders, King John of England and the Holy Roman Emperor Otto IV. The **Battle of Bouvines**, the first great French victory, concluded this war on 27 July 1214. Ferrand was imprisoned in the Louvre, while Jeanne governed Lille.

The dukes of Burgundy and the Spanish – The marriage of Marguerite of Flanders to Philip the Bold in 1369 made Flanders part of the duchy of Burgundy. The presence of the dukes stimulated trade. **Philip the Good** (1419-67) had Rihour Palace built, where he made the "Pheasant Vow" in 1454 promising to leave for the crusades. His glittering court included the great painter Jan van Eyck.
The marriage of Marie of Burgundy, daughter of Charles the Bold, to Maximilian of Austria in 1477 brought the duchy of Burgundy, including Flanders, under Hapsburg control; the duchy later became Spanish when Charles V of Spain became emperor. After the Wars of Religion, owing to Spanish domination the situation deteriorated: gangs of peasants in revolt devastated the countryside and sacked the churches. Lille escaped the assault of the "Howlers" *(Hurlus)* thanks only to the inhabitants' energetic defence, led by the inn-keeper **Jeanne Maillotte**.

Traditional economy – During the Middle Ages Lille became famous for its cloth-making; later the high-warp weavers who had been forced out of Arras by Louis XIV came to establish their tapestry workshops here.
Lille devoted itself to cotton and linen milling in the 18C, whereas nearby Roubaix and Tourcoing specialised in wool. Large-scale industry came to Lille at the end of the 18C, creating an urban proletariat with its accompanying miseries: by 1846 the rate of infant mortality in the slums in St-Sauveur reached 75 % and the cellars where workers laboured achieved a notoriety which Victor Hugo evoked in tragic verse.

Médiathèque municipale Jean Lévy

Another of Lille's specialities was the milling of linseed, rapeseed and poppyseed to produce oil. Last but not least, the town was famous for the production of lace and ceramics.

Lille becomes French – Following his marriage to Maria-Theresa of Spain in 1663, Louis XIV laid claim to the Low Countries, taking advantage of the rights of his wife to a part of Spain's heritage. In 1667 he personally directed the siege of

Eating out

MODERATE

La Robe des Champs – *10 rue Faidherbe* – ☎ *03 20 55 13 74* – *74/150F*. This charming yellow and blue restaurant in the town centre gives pride of place to the potato, which is cooked and served in a great many ways. Whether you order a speciality from Lille, Paris or Normandy, your taste buds will be satisfied! .

La Taverne de l'Écu – *9 rue Esquermoise* – ☎ *03 20 57 55 66* – *85/120F*. At the end of a long corridor you will find a brasserie that has become one of the trendiest and busiest meeting places in Lille. Formerly a concert hall, this lively establishment has kept the same festive, noisy atmosphere, with waiters shuffling from table to table and beer flowing freely into the glasses... The menu presents regional cuisine.

Verzenay – *142 route Nationale, 59152 Chereng* – *6km/3.7mi north of Cysoing by D 90 then D 941* – ☎ *03 20 41 14 56* – *closed 15-30 Jan, 22 July-16 Aug, Sun evening and Mon* - *100/235F*. A welcoming façade just off the main road leading to Belgium reveals several dining rooms with contemporary decoration and a small mezzanine. The terrace backing onto the house is most pleasant in summer. Traditional cooking with a few regional eccentricities.

MID-RANGE

Aux Moules – *34 rue de Béthune* – ☎ *03 20 57 12 46* – *110/150F*. Mussels... mussels... and yet again mussels in this 1930-style brasserie set up in a pedestrian precinct. Along with a few other Flemish specialities.

La Tête de l'Art – *10 rue de l'Arc* – ☎ *03 20 54 68 89* – *closed 29 July-25 Aug, Sun and evenings except Fri and Sat* – *booking essential Sat-Sun* – *112/142F*. A charming pink façade fronts this wealthy mansion dating back to 1890. Inside, a narrow passage opens onto a welcoming dining room exuding conviviality. La Tête de l'Art is a favourite haunt for local diners, who enjoy discovering the different formulas proposed on the menu.

Le Passe-Porc – *155 rue de Solférino* – ☎ *03 20 42 83 93* – *closed 29 July-19 Aug and Sun* – *booking essential* – *120F*. This is exactly the sort of French bistro that foreign visitors dream of! A tiled floor, long padded seats and enamelled plaques on the wall acting as the backdrop to a remarkable collection of pigs... The friendly ambience and generous helpings are in perfect harmony with the amusing decor.

L'Écume des Mers – *10 rue du Pas* – ☎ *03 20 54 95 40* – *closed 30 July-22 Aug and Sun evening* – *130F*. The spread of seafood presented outside is truly mouth-watering. Venture inside the brasserie, where green is the dominant colour, and you will not be disappointed. The menu also offers some meat dishes.

Baan Thaï – *22 boulevard J.-B.-Lebas* – ☎ *03 20 86 06 01* – *closed 23 July-23 Aug, Mon lunchtime, Sat lunchtime and Sun evening* – *150/220F*. Thai restaurant housed on the first floor of an elegant residence. Exotica is the key word here, with refined decor, Oriental sculptures and ornaments, and sunshades lining the ceiling. The degree of spiciness of each Thai speciality is indicated on the menu.

Champlain – *13 rue N.-Leblanc* – ☎ *03 20 54 01 38* – *closed 1-21 Aug, Sat lunchtime and Sun evening* – *170/360F*. A 19C bourgeois house with lovely motifs painted on its windows. The two dining rooms have stucco ceilings and chandeliers embellished with glass pendants. Meals are served on the terrace in summer. Good selection of menus, including one for children.

La Cour des Grands – *61 rue de la Monnaie* – ☎ *03 20 06 83 61* – *closed Feb school holidays, 29 July-20 Aug, Sat lunchtime, Mon lunchtime, Sun and public holidays* – *booking essential* – *185/295F*. This building at the back of a small paved courtyard used to be the Mint, dating from the late 17C. The lofty dining hall adorned with wainscoting, gilding and mural motifs has retained its old-fashioned charm. Carefully prepared cuisine subject to daily variations.

Where to stay

MID-RANGE

Hôtel Flandre Angleterre – *13 place de la Gare* – ☎ *03 20 06 04 12* – *www.hotel-flandre-angleterre.fr* – *45 rooms 330/390F* – ☺ *28F*. Facing the station, near the pedestrian shopping area, this family business offers modern, comfortable and cosy rooms. Its location and reasonable rates make a good address to know.

Hôtel de la Paix – *46 bis rue de Paris* – ☎ *03 20 54 63 93* – *35 rooms 360/480F* – ☐ *50F*. Here you will be right next to the old city and the lively pedestrian quarter. The owners are enthusiastic art lovers who have enhanced their setting with copies of famous paintings. The rooms are appointed with solid cherry wood furniture and each one is devoted to a particular painter (Van Gogh, Matisse etc).

Lille Europe – *Avenue Le Corbusier, Euralille* – ☎ *03 28 36 76 76* – ▣ – *97 rooms 380F* – ☐ *40F*. A modern hotel located in the Euralille complex half-way between the two train stations. The rooms with contemporary furniture are soundproofed and well-equipped. The upstairs breakfast room is flanked by large bay windows.

LUXURY

Hôtel Alliance – *17 quai du Wault* – ☎ *03 20 30 62 62* – ▣ – *80 rooms from 1 050F* – ☐ *80F* – *restaurant 95/165F*. This former 17C convent in the heart of the city is perfect for a short retreat. The cloisters made with red brick and local stone are crowned by a glass pyramid.

On the town

El Sombrero – *10 rue de Rastibonne* – ☎ *03 20 40 27 65* – *Tues-Sat 9pm-4am*. This gigantic bar, which doubles as a night club, is undoubtedly the trendiest place in town. The clientele, consisting mainly of students in their twenties, meet up to listen to techno and house music. The speciality here, which is best consumed by a group of friends, is known as the "pyramid" – 100 glasses of beer balanced on top of each other like a house of cards.

L'Échiquier – **Bar de l'Hôtel Alliance** – *17 quai de Wault* – ☎ *03 20 30 62 62* – *www.goldentulip.com* – *Mon-Sat 9am-1am, Sun and public holidays 10am-11pm*. This bar, installed in the splendid 17C setting of a former Minim convent, is attached to the Alliance Hotel. A harp player performs Mon-Thur (7.30-9.30pm), followed by a piano player Mon-Thur (10-11.30pm), Fri-Sat (7.30-11.30pm), Sun (4-7pm). Impressive choice of champagne and cocktails.

L'Illustration – *18 rue Royale* – ☎ *03 20 12 00 90* – *Mon-Fri 12.30pm-2am, Sat 3pm-2am, Sun 10.30-2am*. Small friendly bar dating from the early 20C where writers and painters would gather to discuss their work. Literary debates and other theme evenings are organised for regulars. L'Illustration is renowned for its cocktails.

Opéra Night – *84 rue de Trévise* – ☎ *03 20 88 37 25* – *Tues-Sat 9pm-4am. Closed Mon, Sun*. This huge bar-night club is literally invaded by weekend crowds starting as early as Thursday. Trendy clientele in their twenties, avid techno fans.

Planet Bowling – *ZA du Grand-But* – ☎ *03 20 08 10 50* – *Mon-Thur 11am-2am, Fri-Sat 11am-4am, Sun 10am-2am*. American-style complex including bowling (32 alleys), billiards (20 American tables), a children's play area, facilities to link up with the Internet, shows (cabaret, comedy: Thur, Fri and Sat) and karaoke (Sun). Restaurant with a seating capacity of 250.

The Tudor Inn After Burn Café – *12 rue de la Vieille-Comédie (place Rihour)* – ☎ *03 20 54 53 35* – *Mon-Sat 11am-2am, Sun 3pm-3am* – *closed 24 and 31 Dec*. This pub has chosen to adopt a kitsch approach to the Excalibur legend and feudal society, to wit the imposing sword hanging behind the bar. Acoustic concerts (blues, rock 'n roll) on Sundays. Piano-bar on Mondays and Tuesdays. The Tudor Inn attracts both regular clients and passing trade. A special mention for beers and cocktails.

Showtime

Les Folies de Paris – *52 avenue du Peuple-Belge* – ☎ *03 20 06 62 64* – *www.foliesdeparis.com* – *Tues-Sat at 8pm (dinner), 10.30pm (show), Sun 1pm-1am* – *closed Aug*. This cabaret, where you can also have dinner, is the most popular in the area. It appeals to many people in Lille and nearby Belgium, particularly towards the end of the week.

Orchestre National de Lille – *30 place Mendès-France* – ☎ *03 20 12 82 40* – *Mon-Fri 9am-12.30pm, 2-6pm*. Since 1976, Jean-Claude Casadesus and the Orchestre National de Lille have been staging an average of 120 concerts every season. Venues are located in the Lille region, the north of France and abroad (30 foreign countries altogether). The programming is extremely varied as Jean-Claude Casadesus' artistic policy is to "spread music wherever it can go": classical, rare pieces, new productions, established composers and fresh talent...

Shopping

Place de la Nouvelle-aventure – On this square stands the massive covered market of Wazemmes built in red brick, a charming sight on Sunday mornings, when the flea market sets up its stalls.

Rue Basse – This is Lille's main street for antique dealers, although a few other unusual shops can be found, namely Le Bleu Natier, which sells furniture, decorative objects, artistic gifts and handcrafted jewellery.

Trogneux Chocolatier – *67 rue Nationale* – ☎ *03 20 54 74 42*. Chocolates galore: Fleur de Lille, Noir de Houille, flavoured with juniper berry, chocolates made with Jenlain beer and Réserve de Bacchus, filled with Alsatian or Burgundy wine.

Lille and triumphantly entered the city after only nine days of resistance, after which Lille became capital of the Northern Provinces. The Sun King hastened to have a citadel built by Vauban and enlarged the town, laying down regulations on the height and style of the houses.

Lille under Siege – In **September 1792**, 35 000 Austrians laid siege to Lille which was defended by only a small garrison. Cannon-balls rained down on the town and many buildings were destroyed; nevertheless, the courageous inhabitants held on and the Austrians eventually raised the siege. It is said that a barber who was shaving clients in the street used the fragment of a shell as a shaving dish.

In early **October 1914**, when six Bavarian regiments tried to breach the fortifications, Lille was very poorly defended. The town was obliged to submit after three days of bloody resistance during which time 900 buildings were destroyed. Prince Ruprecht of Bavaria, receiving the surrender, refused the sword of Captain de Pardieu "in recognition of the heroism of the French troops".

In **May 1940** during the Second World War, 40 000 French soldiers defending Lille held out for three days against seven German divisions and Rommel's tanks. The French troops finally capitulated on 1 June 1940.

★★★ PALAIS DES BEAUX-ARTS (FINE ARTS MUSEUM) ⊘

The art gallery was built between 1885 and 1892 to designs by architects Bérard and Delmas. The majestic building stands on place de la République, opposite the county offices *(préfecture)*. The architects Ibos and Vitard were responsible for the renovation and extension of the gallery (1992-97).

A narrow building 70m/228ft long and 6m/19.5ft. wide was built to the rear. It contains the café and restaurant on the ground floor, the drawings section and the gallery's offices.

Between the two buildings is the garden. The middle has been given a glass roof which lets light into the temporary exhibition halls below.

The vast entrance hall extending the whole length of the façade is lit by two large coloured-glass chandeliers by Gaetano Pesce. There is free access to the atrium where the bookshop, tearoom and café-cum-restaurant are situated *(garden entrance in rue de Valmy)*.

Basement

Stairs on the left in the atrium.

Archeology – Works from the Mediterranean basin: Egypt, Cyprus, Rome, Greece (three-legged toilet vase known as Exaleiptron, ceramics with black figures).

Middle Ages and Renaissance – The chased-bronze Lille incense-burner (12C Mosan art) is displayed in the centre of the first room. Next to it are a few ivory objets d'art from abbeys of northern France such as the *Old Man of the Apocalypse* (12C from St-Omer).

The vaulted galleries contain rare examples of Romanesque sculpture, including three fragments of a limestone high-relief carving representing the Deposition (c 1170). Gothic art is illustrated by various objects: a reliquary cross from Wasne-au-Bac said to have contained a piece of the True Cross (1200-20), *Herod's Feast*, a magnificent low-relief marble sculpture by Donatello, two panels from a triptych by Dirk Bouts *(Paradise* and *Hell)*, the *Virgin and Child from St-Sauveur*, in polychrome stone, the large *St George's altarpiece* from southern Tyrol and the *Mysterious Fountain* triptych by J Bellegambe.

Note, in the last room, the famous *Waxhead of a maiden* resting on a terracotta base (18C).

★ Relief maps – The large hall contains the plans of 15 towns situated on the northern borders of France at the time of Louis XIV.

PALAIS DES BEAUX-ARTS

1st Floor

0 _____ 20 m

↕ Lift

Closed or limited access

Flemish school 16C and 17C

Dutch school 17C

French school 17C

French school 18C and 19C

Italian and Spanish schools

Impressionists

Modern Art

Drawings

Ground floor

Ceramics – *To the left of the atrium.* A superb collection of 18C faience from Lille, Nevers, Strasbourg, Delft and Rouen, as well as German and Walloon sandstone exhibits and 18C porcelain from China and Japan.

Sculpture – *To the right of the atrium.* The collection gives an overview of 19C French sculpture with Frémiet *(The Knight Errant)*, Houdon (bust of *Le Fèvre de Caumartin)*, David d'Angers (original terracotta low-relief sculptures from the Gutenberg memorial on place Kléber in Strasbourg), Camille Claudel *(Giganti, Mme De Massary)*, and Bourdelle *(Penelope, c 1909)*.

First floor

The art collections are presented by schools around the atrium.

16C-17C Flemish School – Hermessan's *Vanity* (the museum's latest important acquisition) represents the 16C. Several characteristic canvases by Jordaens are displayed, ranging in themes from the religious *(The Temptation of Mary Magdalene)* to the mythological *(The Abduction of Europa)* or the rustic *(The Huntsman)*; his study of cows was later taken up by Van Gogh. There are important paintings by Rubens and from his workshop: *The Deposition* (1617), a variation of the one in Antwerp, and the original sketch; *The Ecstasy of Mary Magdalene; The Martyrdom of St Catherine; St Francis and the Virgin.* Other paintings include Van Dyck's moving *Christ on the Cross*, David Teniers II's beautifully coloured *Temptation of St Anthony*, *The Martyrdom of St Maurice* by Boeckhorst.

17C Dutch School – Dutch masterpieces by De Witte *(Nieuwe Kerk in Delft)* and Ruysdael *(The Wheat Field)* hang with still-life paintings by Van der Ast and Van Beyeren, Van Goyen's *The Skaters* and Pieter Codde's *Melancholy*.

17C French School - Works by Lille artists Wallerand Vaillant *(The Young Draughtsman)* and Monnoyer, Le Sueur, Philippe de Champaigne, La Hyre and Largillière *(Jean-Baptiste Forest)*.

18C and 19C French School - Remarkable works by Boilly (1761-1845), born at La Bassée near Lille, adorn the walls: *Le Jeu du Pied de Bœuf, Marat's Triumph* and numerous portraits, including Jules Boilly as a child and sketches of heads for Isabey's studio. Note Quentin de La Tour's portrait of Madame Pèlerin, the charming paintings by Louis Watteau, who adopted Lille as his permanent home *(Lille Shaving Dish, View of Lille)* and the work by his son François *(Alexander's Battle)*. Other great painters represented include David *(Belisarius Begging for Alms)*, Delacroix, Géricault, Corot and Courbet.

/Musée des Beaux-Arts, Lille

Musée des Beaux-Arts - *Belisarius Begging for Alms by David*

Italian and Spanish Schools – Italy is represented by Liss' *Moses Saved from the Waters*, Tintoretto's *Portrait of a Senator* and a sketch of *Heaven* by Veronese. The few Spanish paintings are of a rare quality: *Time or The Old Women* and *The Letter or The Young People* two **works★** by **Goya**, kind and cruel satirist of his period; and El Greco's *St Francis Praying*.

Impressionists – The end of the 19C is represented by works from the **Masson Bequest**. The pre-Impressionist paintings include canvases by Boudin *(The Port of Camaret)*, Jongkind *(The Skaters)* and Lépine. Impressionism itself is embraced in works by Sisley *(Port Marly, Winter: Snow Effects)*, Renoir *(Young Woman in a Black Hat)* and Monet *(The Disaster, The Houses of Parliament)*. Paintings by Vuillard, Carrière, Lebourg and several Rodin sculptures complete the collection.

Modern Artists – Figurative and abstract works on show are by Léger *(Women With a Blue Vase)*, Gromaire *(Landscape of the Coalmining Region)*, Poliakoff *(Composition no 2)*, Sonia Delaunay *(Colour Rhythm 1076)* and Picasso *(Portrait of Olga, 1923)*.

Drawings – This is one of the largest collections in France (about 4 000 works) especially as regards Italian drawings. The works are displayed on a rotating basis.

★★OLD LILLE 2hr

The real renewal of Lille's old district began in 1965, when a few architecture enthusiasts decided to do something to recover the beauty of the 17C and 18C façades, hidden under unsightly rough-rendering. The restorations progressed well and whole blocks of buildings changed completely in appearance. Luxury shops, interior decorators and antique dealers settled in the area which is today an attractive place to explore.

Lille style

The distinctiveness of the Lille style is due to the particular mix of bricks and carved stone. Façades decorated with quarry stones shaped into lozenges (place Louise-de-Bettignies) first appeared in the early 17C; then came the period of the Flemish Renaissance (Vieille Bourse, the Maison de Gilles de la Boé) where the wealth of ornamentation reached its limit. By the end of the 17C the French influence began to be felt in the decoration of the houses and in their arrangement in aligned rows. Ground floors consist of arcades in a close-grained sandstone which prevents humidity reaching the upper floors. The brick above alternates with limestone carved into cherubs, cupids, cornucopias, sheaves of wheat etc.

Façade, Vieille Bourse

Place Rihour – The main building on this square is the **Palais Rihour** which now houses the tourist office. This Gothic palace was built between 1454 and 1473 by Philip the Good, Duke of Burgundy. Outside, note the beautiful mullioned windows and the graceful octagonal brick turret. The guard-room, with its tall, pointed arches, still exists on the ground floor. The chapel, known as the Conclave Room, is upstairs; the chapel for the Duke's private worship, reached by an elegant stone staircase, has traceried vaults.

A monument to those who died during the two World Wars flanks the north-east side of the chapel.

To reach place du Général-de-Gaulle, take a very busy pedestrian precinct lined with pavement cafés. On the left, note the 17C houses built in a style that is a combination of Flemish and French. This form of architecture became commonplace in Lille after the town was taken over by Louis XIV.

★**Place du Général-de-Gaulle** – The Grand' Place or main square has always been the busy centre of Lille; as early as the Middle Ages it was a market place. The finest building in the square is the Vieille Bourse. *La Voix du Nord*, a daily newspaper, has its offices in the building (1936) with a stepped pediment beside the **Grand' Garde** (1717), which is surmounted with pediments and once housed the king's guard.

The Colonne de la Déesse (1845) rises in the middle of the square, a symbol of the city's heroic resistance during the siege of 1792 *(see above)*.

★★**Vieille Bourse** – The exchange was built in 1652-53 by Julien Destrée, at the request of the tradesmen of Lille who wanted an exchange to rival those of the great cities in the Low Countries. It consists of 24 mansard-roofed houses around a rectangular court which served in the past for commercial deals; today they house second-hand bookshops.

The profusion of decoration on the façade is due to the fact that Destrée was a wood sculptor. The caryatids and telamones on two storeys, the garlands and masks above the outer windows, the fruit and flowers carved on the inner court are all reminiscent of a Flemish chest Bronze busts, and medallions and tablets honouring learned figures and the sciences, can be seen under the arcades.

Place du Théâtre – The square is dominated by the imposing Nouvelle Bourse which houses the Chamber of Commerce (**C**) and its neo-Flemish bell-tower. Next to it stands the Louis XVI Opera.

These two buildings date from the beginning of the last century and are the work of architect Louis Cordonnier.

Opposite the Nouvelle Bourse stands the **"Rang de Beauregard"**, comprising houses adorned with pilasters surmounted by elegant cartouches. The terrace, built in 1687, is the most characteristic and most interesting example of late-17C architecture in Lille.

Rue de la Bourse – The street is lined with superb 18C house-fronts decorated with chubby cherubs and masks on the first floor.

Rue de la Grande-Chaussée – The old sandstone houses with their arcades have been renovated and now contain shops selling luxury goods. Some of the wrought-iron balconies and the upper part of the windows are very intricately worked. Note the first house on the right and nos 9, 23 (ship on the keystone of the window) and 29.

Rue des Chats-Bossus – The street acquired its curious name ("Street of the Humpback Cats") from an old tanner's sign.

"**L'Huître**", a famous seafood restaurant, has a typical Art-Deco front dating from the 1930s.

Place du Lion-d'Or – At no 15, the Olivier Desforges shop occupies the 18C Maison des Poissonniers.

Place Louise-de-Bettignies – The square bears the name of a First World War heroine. The **Demeure de Gilles de la Boé★**, at no 29 on a corner, was built in about 1636 and is a superb example of Flemish Baroque. The abundant ornamentation includes cornices and prominent pediments. In the past this building stood on the edge of the Basse-Deûle port, in the days when there was a great deal of river traffic. In 1936, the Basse-Deûle, a bustling harbour until the 18C, was filled in to make way for avenue du Peuple-Belge; the modern tower houses the law courts.

AN OYSTER-LOVER'S PARADISE

À L'Huître – *3 rue des Chats-Bossus* – ☎ *03 20 55 43 41 – closed 22 July-25 Aug, Sun evening and public holidays – 350/580F*. A first-rate establishment for fish and seafood lovers which has been duly acknowledged by the profession. The fishmonger's shop with its superb ceramic frescoes adjoins the dining room, decorated with light oak panelling, lamps and wall lights with pendants. The tables are ornamented with different varieties of fish and shellfish.

★**Rue de la Monnaie** – The Mint once stood in this street where the restored houses now attract antique dealers and interior decorators. On the left there is a row of 18C houses (note the apothecary's shop sign of a mortar and distilling equipment at no 3). The houses at nos 5 and 9 are decorated with dolphins, wheat-sheaves, palms etc.

At no 10 a statue of Notre-Dame-de-la-Treille adorns the front and at nos 12 and 14 the crow-stepped gable has been rebuilt. Neighbouring houses date from the first third of the 17C and flank the rusticated door (1649) of the Hospice Comtesse.

★**Hospice Comtesse** ○ – The hospital was built in 1237 by Jeanne de Constantinople, Countess of Flanders, to ask for divine intervention on behalf of her husband Ferrand de Portugal, taken prisoner at Bouvines *(see above)*. It was destroyed by fire in 1468 but was rebuilt and enlarged in the 17C and 18C. It became a hospice during the Revolution, then an orphanage. It changed again in 1939 and is today a museum of history and ethnography which also holds concerts and exhibitions.

The monumental 17C main entrance is built from beautiful rusticated sandstone.

Hospital ward – A long, sober building, rebuilt after 1470 on the old 13C foundations, flanks the main courtyard. Inside, the immense proportions of the interior and its panelled timber **vault★★** in the shape of an upturned boat are striking. It contains two beautiful tapestries, woven in Lille in 1704. One represents Baudouin of Flanders with his wife and two daughters; the other portrays Jeanne, the hospital's founder, flanked by her first and second husbands. The **chapel**, which extends the length of the interior, was enlarged and isolated by a rood screen after the fire of 1649. The old 15C window and traces of mural paintings have been revealed on the right wall. The vault is decorated with the heraldic arms of the hospital's benefactors.

Museum – Furniture and artworks evoking the atmosphere of a 17C religious establishment are displayed in the right wing, which was built by the community in the late 15C and heightened in the 17C: the kitchen features blue and white tiles from Holland and Lille; the Baroque overmantel in the dining room frames a 16C Nativity, the sombre Louis XIV panels of the parlour are decorated with a series of 17C votive offerings in the form of portraits of local children. The prayer room is lined with Louis XV wood panelling.

The last two chambers were used as the pharmacy and linen room.

The former dormitory on the first floor has carved ceiling beams. It contains 17C Flemish and Dutch paintings and a superb 16C wooden Crucifixion from Picardy. The cross-bar and main section of the Cross are decorated with medallions depicting the Evangelists. Two rooms flanking the dormitory are filled with exhibits relating to regional history: architectural features, objets d'art, and paintings by Louis and François Watteau representing Lille in the 18C.

Turn left onto rue Au-Pétérinck which still has some 18C houses. The street leads to the delightful little place aux Oignons. Continue along rue des Vieux-Murs then turn left onto rue des Trois-Mollettes.

On the left is the impressive **Cathédrale Notre-Dame-de-la-Treille**, a neo-Gothic construction that was never completed.

New Euralille district

Rue du Cirque leads to rue Basse.

Rue **Esquermoise** is lined with 17C and 18C houses. The **Pâtisserie Meert** shop at no 21 has a beautiful 19C interior, and lovely cakes to take away. At nos 6 and 4 cherubs are shown embracing or turning their backs on each other depending on whether or not they belong to the same house. Opposite is a superb restored house that belonged to a furrier (Gailliaerde).

WEST OF THE TOWN CENTRE

Euralille – Covering an area of almost 70ha/173 acres beyond Lille city centre is a whole new urban district designed by Dutch town planner Rem Koolhaas. Since May 1993, Lille's railway station, which was renamed **Lille-Flandres**, has catered for most of the high-speed trains from Paris. Linked by a viaduct with four arches, the new station, **Lille-Europe**, easily recognisable for its huge glass frontage, was built as part of the Paris-London and London-Brussels routes using the Channel Tunnel and for the high-speed train services between Lille and Lyon, Bordeaux, Nice, Montpellier etc. Two towers span the new stations, the **Tour Lille-Europe WTC** designed by architect Claude Vasconi and the L-shaped **Tour du Crédit Lyonnais★** designed by Christian de Portzampac.

The **Centre Euralille** was designed by the acclaimed French architect Jean Nouvel. Its spacious walkways and two floors contain more than 130 shops, a hypermarket, restaurants and a cultural centre called the Espace Croisé. It also has a theatre, private apartments, and a business school.

Euralille also includes the 8ha/20 acre **Parc Henri-Matisse**.

Porte de Roubaix (**EFY**) – This massive gate from the 1621 Spanish fortifications is composed of a sandstone base surmounted by a dripstone and a layer in brick. It was opened in 1875 to allow room for tramways and the moats have been turned into gardens. There is a similar gate 600m/656yd to the north, the **Porte de Gand**, reached via rue des Canonniers and rue de Courtrai.

Hôtel Bidé-de-Granville (**FY S**) – The industrialist AD Scrive Labbe established the first carding machine here in 1821. The building was constructed in 1773 and today houses the offices of the Regional Administration of Cultural Affairs.

QUARTIER ST-SAUVEUR *about 1hr30min*

This former working-class district was known for the misery of its slums which inspired Emile Desrousseaux, author of the famous French lullaby *Le P'tit Quinquin (statue in rue Nationale on the corner of avenue Foch)*. The area has today been completely remodelled into a business centre around the town hall. Relics of the past remain dotted among the modern buildings.

Hospice Ganthois – The hospice was founded in 1462 by Jean de la Cambe, known as Ganthois, and is still in use. The original ward has been preserved; its gable, on rue de Paris, is flanked on either side by 17C buildings. Note the sculpture on the door panels, dated 1664.

★**Porte de Paris** – This gate, built from 1685 to 1692 by Simon Vollant in honour of Louis XIV, is the only example of a town gate which also served as a triumphal arch; it was formerly part of the ramparts. It appears as an arch decorated with the arms of Lille (a lily) and of France (three lilies) on the outward side. Victory stands at the top, honoured by Fames, about to crown Louis XIV represented in a medallion. From the inner side the gate has the appearance of a lodge.

Hôtel de Ville ⊘ – The town hall was built from 1924 to 1927 by the Lille architect Émile Dubuisson and is overlooked by a tall belfry (104m/341ft). The two Lille giants, Lydéric and Phinaert *(see above)*, are sculpted at its base. The top of the **belfry** *(109 steps then lift)* offers a lovely **view**★ over the city and the surrounding area up to 50km/32mi away.

Pavillon St-Sauveur – This is the wing of an 18C cloister, preserved when a hospice was demolished in 1959. The brick and stone arches are surmounted by clerestory windows decorated with flowered medallions.

Noble Tour – This keep with its truncated appearance is the only relic of the 15C fortifications; it has become a Resistance memorial. There is a beautiful work by the sculptor Bizette-Lindet.

Chapelle du Réduit – This chapel is all that remains of Réduit Fort, built at the same time as the citadel to serve as its counterpart elsewhere in the city. The pretty Louis XIV front is decorated with the arms of France and Navarre. The chapel has been integrated into the engineering regiment's premises.

OTHER SIGHTS

★**Église St-Maurice** – This vast Gothic edifice was built from the 15C to the 19C. It is a beautiful example of a hall-church, with five aisles of equal height, five roofs and five gables. A 16C Christ of Compassion, often dressed in a long velvet mantle, stands in the chapel of the false left transept; it is venerated as "Jesus Scourged". South of the church stand two restored houses, the Croix de St-Maurice bakery (1729) and the Maison du Renard (1660). Opposite *(at no 74 rue de Paris)* is the Maison des Trois Grâces.

Follow rue de Paris then rue des Manneliers, which skirts the Vieille Bourse, and finally rue Esquermoise leading to rue Royale.

Rue Royale – This was the main route through the elegant district which was built during the 18C between the citadel and the old town. **Église Ste-Catherine**, with its austere 15C tower, stands on the left at the beginning of the street. **Église St-André**, a Carmelite chapel in the 18C, is an example of the Jesuit style. It was topped with a tower in 1890. Charles de Gaulle was baptised here on the day of his birth, 22 November 1890.

Rue Négrier *(on the right when you come from the town centre)*, running into rue du Pont-Neuf, leads to the **Église Ste-Marie-Madeleine**. Completed in 1715, it recalls the Église du Dôme at Les Invalides in Paris (centralised layout and 50m/164ft-high cupola). The west front was remodelled in 1884.

Musée Charles-de-Gaulle ⊘ – *9 rue Princesse.*

Charles de Gaulle was born on 22 November 1890 in this whitewashed brick house in Lille, where his grandfather had a lace works. The old workshop and the house have been turned into a small museum exhibiting photographs and memorabilia. On display are De Gaulle's christening robe and a

Lille – Porte de Paris

H. Gyssels/DIAF

LILLE

Château du Vert-Bois

replica of the car in which the General and his wife were travelling on the day of the attempt on their lives in Le Petit-Clamart. The original car was involved in a severe accident in 1971 and was only fit for scrap except the seats, steering wheel and dashboard which were used for the replica.

★**Citadelle (Citadel)** ⊘ – This citadel is the largest and best preserved in France. It was Louis XIV's first project after the conquest of Lille and is a fine example of Vauban's genius; it is still occupied by the army today. It took three years to build (1667-70) using 2 000 men. The result was this stone-faced brick construction comprising five bastions and five demilune fortifications, which protect the moats formerly fed by the River Deûle. These defences used to enclose a real town.

The **porte Royale**, which bears a Latin inscription praising Louis XIV, gives onto a vast pentagonal parade ground surrounded by buildings by Simon Vollant: the Classical chapel, the officer's quarters and a superb restored arsenal. These stone and brick buildings are representative of the French-Lille style which developed during this period. The citadel could be completely self-sufficient as it had its own wells, bakery, brewery, tailors, cobblers etc.

A zoo has been established in the **Bois de Boulogne**, near the Champ de Mars; there is also a tropical house and a playground. The **jardin Vauban** on the Deûle Canal bank is typical of mid-19C country gardens, with its clumps of trees, winding paths, flower beds and ponds. A statue of the Lille poet Albert Samain (1859-1906) stands within it.

During the last two World Wars many French patriots were executed by firing squad in the outer moats. The **Monument aux Fusillés** by Félix Desruelle stands in neighbouring square Daubenton; it dates from 1915 and commemorates the Lille citizens executed by firing squad. Its most striking feature is the nobility of the victims' bearing.

Musée des Canonniers ⊘ – Housed in the former Hôtel des Canonniers, once a convent. In 1804 the building was given by Napoleon to the corporation of gunners founded in 1483 and known as the Sainte-Barbe Brotherhood. The military museum illustrates the history of the various sieges Lille had to withstand and Faidherbe and Négrier's feats of arms. Some 3 000 objects are on display: rifles from 1777 to 1945, swords, sabres etc.

Maison Coilliot – *9 rue de Fleurus.*
Built in 1898 by Hector Guimard for Mr Coilliot, a local ceramics artist, this house illustrates the Art Nouveau style with its enamelled lavastone façade, curved lines and unusual double roof.

Musée d'Histoire naturelle et de Géologie ⊘ – The Natural History and Geology Museum was set up in 1822. Its collections were extended at the beginning of the 20C by two local geologists. Facing visitors as they enter the main hall are two impressive whale skeletons, the remains of mammals washed up on the coast.

The **zoology** collection on the left includes stuffed mammals and birds, reptiles, Batrachia, molluscs, fish, and insects. Dioramas are used to show French fauna in its natural habitat: huge boars, alert deer, beavers etc. The insect houses contain spiders, scorpions and cockroaches. The magnificent ornithological collection boasts more than 5 000 birds, including examples of species that are now extinct such as New Zealand huias or great auks.

The section on the right deals with **geology**. Fossils and rocks illustrate the history of Northern Europe from 600 million years BC to the Gallo-Roman period. Numerous plant fossils found in old mine workings are the remains of the dense forest that covered the region 300 million years ago. The work of miners is illustrated by a reconstruction of a coal seam, with its narrow gallery and heavy cart.

Jardin des Plantes ⊘ – *From boulevard J.-B.-Lebas take rue de Douai, rue Armand-Carrel and turn right after boulevard des Defenseurs-de-Lille.*
Among the 12ha/27 acres of lawns, trees and rare flowers stands a modern concrete and glass greenhouse containing tropical and equatorial plants.

EXCURSIONS

Marcq-en-Barœul: Fondation Prouvost-Septentrion ⊘ – *9km/5.6mi north. Leave Lille along N 17 then turn right onto D 952 and follow a road on the right which leads to the foundation.* An old farm not far from the Château du Vert-Bois holds temporary exhibitions of paintings, ceramics and objects representative of various civilizations. At the entrance, there is a fine collection of rare minerals gathered by Anne and Albert Prouvost during their travels.

Septentrion also consists of a gallery of contemporary art, a restaurant, a second-hand goods shop, a craft village, shops selling minerals etc.

★**Bondues**: **Château du Vert-Bois** ⊘ – *11km/7mi north. Leave on N 17 at Bondues turn right onto D 952, then right again to the château. The ticket office is located at the Fondation Prouvost.*
This charming 18C residence, surrounded by water-filled moats, contains splendid 18C furniture, old masters (J Vernet, Van Loo, Lallemant, Bonavia, Linnig), large tapestries and a collection of Persian plates from the 9C to the 13C.

LONGPONT★

Population 298
Michelin map 56 south-west of fold 4 or 237 fold 8

The village lies on the edge of Retz Forest and is overlooked by the ruins of the church and the buildings of the Cistercian abbey founded by St Bernard in the 12C. Longpont is a restful place to visit in summer.

Fortified gate – A picturesque 14C **fortified gate**, with four conical turrets, guarding the high street, is all that remains from the original fortifications.

★**Abbey** ⊘ – The large ensemble formed by the ruined abbey church and the buildings, restored in the 18C, is complemented by internal gardens opening onto a park. The abbey's former size is evoked in a model showing the 14C buildings.

Abbey church ruins – The pure Gothic church was consecrated in 1227 in the presence of the young Louis IX and Blanche of Castile. The abbey's possessions, deemed to be national property, were sold during the Revolution. The new owners of the church demolished it little by little, selling its stones until 1831 when it was bought by the Montesquiou family, which still owns it today. The west front remains but the tracery of the rose-window has disappeared. Inside, the ruined walls and pillars standing among the vegetation give a clear idea of the church's size: 105m/115yd long and 28m/ 92ft high (Notre-Dame de Paris: 130m/142yd by 35m/115ft high).

Abbey buildings – The great cloister's south gallery (rebuilt in the 17C) still exists and leads to the unique 13C **calefactory**, preserved intact with its central hooded fireplace. The west building was transformed in the 18C by the commendatory abbots, who had

Longpont – Abbey

S. Sauvignier/MICHELIN

tall windows with large wrought-iron balconies set into the façades, providing a Classical elegance. Inside, the vast entrance hall features a staircase with a beautiful 18C wrought-iron balustrade; the 13C monks' cellars with Gothic vaults have been turned into reception rooms.

Église paroissiale – *Entrance from the square.*
This church takes up four arches of the old undercroft. Two 13C reliquaries have been preserved; the one concerning Jean de Montmirail, councillor to Philippe Auguste, and the head of St Dionysius the Areopagite.

Other Cistercian abbeys in the region include Ourscamp, Vallones and Vaucelles. 1998 marked the ninth centenary of the foundation of the Cistercian Order by Robert de Molesmes. The order later spread throughout Europe under the leadership of St Bernard.

MAINTENON ★

Population 4 161
Michelin map 106 fold 26 or 237 fold 27

Access from Paris: *SNCF rail link from Gare Montparnasse*

This charming town on the banks of the River Eure is renowned for its château, irrevocably linked to the incredible destiny of **Françoise d'Aubigné**; she was born in 1635 to a family with Calvinist views, was orphaned at the age of 12, became the widow of the burlesque poet Paul Scarron at the age of 25, the clandestine governess of Mme De Montespan's children by the age of 34 and, in a secret ceremony, the wife of Louis XIV at the age of 48.

The corridors of power – When her clandestine charge, the Duc de Maine, was legitimised, Françoise Scarron made a public appearance at court. Thereafter Louis XIV, who was extremely fond of his son, used to see her every day. Initially, he found her a trifle pedantic but soon revised his opinion of "the Scarron widow" and succumbed to her charm, intelligence and strong temperament. In 1674 Françoise Scarron received the Maintenon estate from the King, who then publicly christened her "Madame De Maintenon".
After the Queen's death, Louis XIV secretly married Mme De Maintenon in the chapel at Versailles during the winter of 1683-84. The morganatic queen acceded to the rank of peer and marquise in 1688 - a privilege bestowed on her directly by the King - and from then on she became an extremely powerful figure in the country's political life. When the King died in 1715, she withdrew to St-Cyr, where she died in 1719.

A Herculean task – Between 1685 and 1688, the area around Maintenon saw one of the century's most ambitious projects: the diverting of the waters of the River Eure to the fountains of Versailles. François Louvois acted as supervisor; he left Sébastien Vauban in charge of the plans and entrusted him with the construction of an 80km/50mi long aqueduct linking Pontgouin *(Michelin map 60 fold 6)* to the Étang de la Tour, which was already linked with the Versailles reservoirs by rivulets from the Trappes plateau.
The Maintenon aqueduct was a colossal enterprise, involving a total length of 4 600m/15 000ft and three superimposed rows of arches, placed 72m/237ft above the level of the River Eure. In fact, it was only possible to fit in one row of arches. The link with the canals on the plateaux was to be implemented by pressurised pipes acting as a battery of pumps.
The operation was carried out like a military campaign; 20 000 soldiers took part in the excavation work, in addition to the 10 000 skilled workers summoned from remote villages and the local peasants who helped cart the materials. The River Voise and River Drouette were canalised and used to convey the freestones and sandstone rubble from the Gallardon and Épernon quarries. The shipments of Newcastle coal needed to work the lime and brick kilns, and the pipes and iron bars despatched from Champagne, Belgium and Pays d'Ouche were carried along the River Seine and River Eure.
In 1689, the wars triggered off by the Augsburg League interrupted the work. The French troops, in poor physical condition, were sent off to the borders to defend their country. The work was never resumed.
From then on, Mme De Maintenon ceased her visits to the château; she was offered the impressive but unfinished aqueduct to compensate for the damage to her estate.

SIGHTS

★**Château** ⊘ – The present château occupies the site of a former stronghold circled by the waters of the Eure. The construction work was undertaken by Jean Cottereau, Minister of Finance to Louis XII, François I and Henri II, and completed around 1509 in the Renaissance style.

The estate then came into the hands of the d'Angennes family. In 1674 Louis XIV bought the château from Françoise d'Angennes for 250 000 livres and gave it to the future Marquise de Maintenon. The Marquise left it to her niece, who was married to the Duke of Ayen, son of the first Maréchal de Noailles. The château has remained in this family ever since.

Exterior – The archway, flanked by two protruding turrets and bearing Jean Cottereau's arms (three lizards), leads to the inner court which is the starting-point for tours. The square 12C keep, now crowned with an elegant roof, is all that remains of the original stronghold.

The adjoining wing was built by Mme De Maintenon and the narrow

RELAX AND ENJOY

Le Relais des Remparts – *2 place du Marché-aux-Légumes, 28210 Nogent-le-Roi – 8km/5mi north of Maintenon by D 983 – ☎ 02 37 51 40 47 – closed 7-28 Aug, Feb school holidays, Sun and Tues evenings and Wed – 92/230F*. The family spirit prevails in this local village inn decorated with a light colour scheme. The homemade cooking is both tasty and reasonable and served with a beaming smile.

door set in the tower still sports the Marquise's emblem, a griffin's head. A door depicting St Michael and bearing the lizard emblem gives onto a staircase leading to Mme De Maintenon's suite. It consists of an antechamber, a bedroom - where Charles X spent the night on 3 August 1830 when he fled Rambouillet - and a small cabinet.

After leaving the main block, visitors are shown round the first floor of the Renaissance pavilion, redesigned to accommodate the apartments of Mme De Montespan and her royal charges.

The tour ends with the reception rooms furnished by the Noailles family in the 19C. The Grand Salon bears portraits of the two royal rivals, Mme De Montespan and Mme De Maintenon. In the Portrait Gallery, a collection of paintings represents the illustrious members of the family. The mortal remains of the Marquise lie in the chapel of St-Cyr Military Academy. A memorial was erected in her honour in 1980.

Parterre – The parterre is flanked by charming canals fed by the waters of the Eure. The bench at the far end offers an extensive view of the Grand Canal and three of the arches of Maintenon aqueduct. Turn round and enjoy the superb **vista**★ of the château with its elegant towers and grey and pink stone and brickwork.

★**Aqueduct** – The 50-odd arches that remain, many of which are crumbling and overgrown with plants and weeds, stretch from Maintenon station to the D 6 road, leading to St-Piat. On the way to Gallardon, the road runs under a curious arch of four ribs of archstones hanging suspended in mid-air.

Château de Maintenon

A. de Vairoger/MICHELIN

EXCURSION

Épernon – *8km/5mi east.* Built on a hillside, this old town has retained a remark-able architectural unity; the steep winding streets are lined with 15C half-timbered houses and porches with pointed arches. The **church** is characteristic of rural churches of the Chartres region: the chancel arch dates from the 13C and the painted wood-panelled vaulting (once concealed by a coat of plaster) of the 16C nave rests on octagonal pillars without capitals. The vaulting surmounting the side aisles has also been restored. Note the carved beams of the south aisle.

MAISONS-LAFFITTE★

Population 23 173
Michelin map 101 fold 13, 106 fold 18 or 237 fold 17
Michelin plan 18

Access from Paris: *SNCF rail link from Gare St-Lazare or RER line A 3/A 5*

Maisons-Laffitte, a residential town lying on the banks of the Seine and on the edge of St-Germain Forest, is famous for its castle and its racecourse.

Président Longueil – The château was built by the architect **François Mansart** between 1642 and 1651 for René de Longueil, President of the Parlement de Paris, appointed Governor of the royal châteaux at Versailles and St-Germain. The château was designed to receive royalty as it was one of the official places of residence assigned to French rulers. The palace was inaugurated during a brilliant reception celebrated in honour of Anne of Austria and Louis XIV, then aged 13. The Sun King subsequently took up residence at St-Germain and paid frequent visits to Maisons, as did his successors.

From Artois to Lannes – The Comte d'Artois, brother of Louis XVI, acquired the estate in 1777 and gave orders to build the famous racecourse. His extravagant parties were attended by everyone at court.
The estate was sequestered during the Revolution and sold to Marshal Jean Lannes, Duke of Montebello, in 1804. Napoleon I, who enjoyed the Marshal's company, was a regular visitor to the château.

Maisons-Laffitte – In 1818 the famous banker **Jacques Laffitte** (1767-1844) bought the estate, where he entertained the adversaries of the Restoration: General Foy, the Marquis de Lafayette, Casimir Périer, Benjamin Constant etc. Laffitte did much to secure Louis-Philippe d'Orléans' accession to the throne during the Revolution of July 1830 which overthrew Charles X. This shrewd financier was made Prime Minister to the new king in 1830 but proved unable to calm the disturbances that had broken out in the capital; mistrusted by both the Orleanists and the moderates, Laffitte was forced to resign in March 1831. Ruined, in debt to the tune of 50 million francs, he dismantled the imposing stables and used the stone to build houses in the Grand Parc. The stables had been two long, beautiful buildings designed by Mansart and erected on the avenue du Château (now avenue du Général-Leclerc). They provided a very impressive entrance to the Longueil's estate.
The château frequently changed hands and was bought by the State in 1905.

Château de Maisons-Lafitte

CHÂTEAU ⊙ 1hr

The château dates from the early part of Louis XIV's reign and has always been considered a model of French architecture. From the main driveway, formerly called the King's entrance – royal visitors generally approached from St-Germain Forest, to the west – there is a splendid view of the high-pitched roofs.

The façade facing the Seine is fronted by a dry moat, a terrace and the main staircase. The stone exterior presents Classical ornamentation: Doric on the ground floor, Ionic on the first floor and Corinthian on the attic storey level with the dormer windows. The alternating fluted columns and engaged pilasters form a pleasing, well-balanced composition.

Interior – Despite minor alterations during the ownership of the Comte d'Artois in the 18C, there are no major discrepancies between the austerity of Mansart's work, completed c 1650 and the cold formality of the neo-Classical features.

Salon des captifs – This drawing room, set in a corner of the château, is decorated with several fine paintings including H Robert's *Landscape with a Waterfall*. The room gets its name from the decoration on the monumental fireplace.

Vestibule d'honneur – Lying in the centre of the château, it constitutes a perfect entrance articulated by eight Doric columns. It was originally enclosed by two imposing wrought-iron gates. They were installed in 1650 and later moved to the Apollo Gallery in the Louvre. A group of mythological figures by Jacques Sarrazin symbolise the four Elements: Jupiter (fire), Juno (air), Neptune (water) and Cybele (Earth).

The eagles are not those associated with the emperor: their "long eye" *(long œil)* is merely a pun on the first proprietor's name.

Grand Escalier – The staircase, one of Mansart's major accomplishments at Maisons, is characteristic of the period with its square layout and straight flights of stairs. Groups of children sculpted by Philippe Buyster symbolise Music and Singing, Science and Art, War and Peace, Love and Marriage.

Appartement du Comte d'Artois – The corner dining room is an excellent example of carved neo-Classical decoration as commissioned by the Comte d'Artois. Two artists with a passionate interest in Antiquity, Bélanger and the sculptor Lhuillier, have left their mark on the room. It has a coffered ceiling, a group of Fames over the door, a fireplace flanked by bacchantes etc.

Appartement du Roi – First floor. A suite of rooms built in the Italian style, featuring domed or barrel-vaulted ceilings with no painted decoration. Walk down the **Grande Galerie** and enter the **Salon d'Hercule** (formerly the king's antechamber), which leads through to the **Chambre du roi**. Admire the domed ceiling, the original parquet floor and the ceremonial bed.

Cabinet des Miroirs – The parquet floor and panelling are masterpieces of marquetry inlaid with wood, bone and pewter.

Chambre Lannes – The passage leading to the bedroom houses a collection of figurines portraying various regiments of Napoleon's Grand Army. The queen's former bedchamber was redesigned to receive Marshal Jean Lannes. The furniture, chandelier and decoration are all Empire. In the centre stands a magnificent Restoration table inlaid with elm wood. The paintings include a scene which shows Napoleon's ashes being carried past Sartrouville Bridge in 1840.

In the basement, there is a small **racehorse museum**, recalling the major role played by the owners of the château in the history of horse racing.

DINING OUT

Rôtisserie Vieille Fontaine – *8 avenue Grétry* – ☎ *01 39 62 01 78 – closed 8-14 Aug, Sun evening and Mon – 177F*. This stately manor house with three dining rooms has specialised in grilled meat dishes prepared before your very eyes. The veranda opens onto a small park. Good value for money.

RACECOURSE AND PARK

The racecourse at Maisons-Laffitte, located on the banks of the River Seine, is well known to Paris racegoers.

The training stables and the tracks, second only to Chantilly in importance, lie to the north of the park, on the edge of the forest.

A walk in the park early in the morning (7am) will reveal the morning training of the various "charges"; mounted by stable hands, they will be walking or trotting along the sandy lanes. The most prestigious route, however, for exercising thoroughbreds is a circular ride known as the Cercle de la Gloire (Circle of Glory). The wider tracks used for galloping are not open to the public.

MANTES-LA-JOLIE

Conurbation 189 103
Michelin map 106 fold 15 or 237 folds 15, 16

Access from Paris: *SNCF rail link from Gare St-Lazare or Montparnasse*

This extremely active town has grown considerably with the industrial development of its suburbs. Fortunately Mantes-la-Jolie can still justify its name thanks to the collegiate church which has been towering over the Notre-Dame district for seven centuries.

Henri IV's Conversion – Henri IV, who had taken Mantes from the Catholic League in 1590, returned to the town on account of the ravishing Gabrielle d'Estrées. During one of his stays in May 1593 he decided to renounce Protestantism a second time (he had already done so once to escape the St Bartholomew's Day Massacre).

In view of the ceremony, a number of meetings took place between the king, supported by the Protestants Duplessis-Mornay and Sully, and Cardinal Duperron, the Abbot of St-Denis, as well as various other leading ecclesiastic figures. It was in Mantes, at the end of one of these meetings, that Henri IV replied to Duperron, "I place my soul in your hands. Please take care of it. From where you would have me enter, I shall leave only through death". Tears welled up in his eyes. Taking leave of his Huguenot adviser, he said, "What can I do? If I refused to renounce my faith, that would be the end of France". The famous words, "Paris is well worth a Mass" are said to be a somewhat free interpretation of this sentence. The abjuration ceremony took place in the Basilica of St-Denis on 25 July 1593.

★★ COLLÉGIALE NOTRE-DAME ⊘ *30min*

This church – which inspired Corot to paint one of his most beautiful works *(now in the Musée des Beaux-Arts, Reims)* – would compare favourably with many of France's cathedrals. It was built by the chapter of a collegiate church which owned large estates in the area. The funds for this ambitious project were provided by the municipality, William the Conqueror and several Capetian kings.

The construction of the church, started in 1170, ran into the 13C in the case of the nave and the chancel. The chapels were added in the 14C. The church stood within the fortified bailey that defended the old royal castle *(behind the east end, on the site now occupied by the public gardens)*.

Exterior – The west front is the oldest part of the church. The tower on the left and the narrow gallery linking it to the right tower were rebuilt in the 19C.

Three badly damaged doorways adorn the exterior. The one in the centre is dedicated to the Virgin Mary and was built between 1170 and 1195. Like the north doorway on the left, it features foliated scrolls on the jambs and bases of the colonnettes.

A walk round the right side leads to the protruding 14C Navarre Chapel. Note the unusual east end, with its gabled apses crowned by a gallery and backing onto a high wall circling the ambulatory. This open-work structure admitting large, round bays is supported by hefty buttresses. Above the fortified wall, the upper part of the chancel is supported by a series of sturdy flying buttresses.

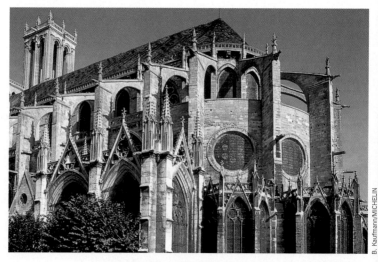

Collégiale Notre-Dame

B. Kaufmann/MICHELIN

Interior – The light, elegant nave (33m/108ft tall) is almost as high as that of Notre-Dame in Paris (35m/114ft). Its elevation of wide arches, brightly lit galleries and clerestory windows marks the transition from Romanesque to Early Gothic. The splendid rose-window (early 13C) in the west front depicts the last Judgement. Walking down the nave, note the arrangement of the sexpartite vaulting. The heavier supporting arches at each end rest on thick pillars, while the lighter ones end in round columns. The deep galleries above the aisles - a legacy from Romanesque architecture - open onto the nave by a series of bays with triple arcades.

The **Chapelle de Navarre**, built onto the south side of the chancel, forms a separate ensemble. It features early-14C windows with Radiant Gothic roundels. It is thought the name comes from the kings of Navarre, who belonged to the ruling house of Évreux (the counts of Évreux held the lordship of Mantes from 1328 to 1364). The entrance to the chapel is graced by four dainty statuettes dating from the 14C. The crowned women carrying a miniature model of the church are probably the founders of Notre-Dame: Jeanne de France, Comtesse d'Évreux (1312-49) and Jeanne d'Évreux, Queen of France by her marriage to Charles IV the Fair in 1324. The other two young women are probably Jeanne de France's daughters. Queen Blanche, who married Philip VI of Valois, and Agnès, wife of the famous Gaston Phoebus, Comte de Foix.

ADDITIONAL SIGHTS

Ancien Hôtel-Dieu ⊘ – *Close to the collegiate church*. Turned into a museum in 1996, the Hôtel-Dieu stages temporary exhibitions and houses the Musée Luce.

Musée Luce ⊘ – *Second floor*. The museum is exclusively devoted to the neo-Impressionist painter **Maximilien Luce** (1858-1941) and contains 100 of his works (lithographs, etchings, drawings and paintings). A friend of Seurat, Pissarro and of several anarchists, Luce often found his inspiration in the social context of his time: Foundry in Charleroi (1896), Varlin's Execution; he also painted landscapes of the Mantes region, in particular Rolleboise.

Vieux Pont de Limay – This humpback bridge resting on cutwater piers (only part of it remains) had mills and fisheries built on it until 1870. It has retained a house, the "Loge des Portiers", dating from 1750. The picturesque site inspired Corot to paint his famous *Bridge at Mantes*, now in the Louvre Museum.

Eating out

MID-RANGE

Auberge de la Truite – *78790 Rosay – 10km/6.2mi south of Mantes-la-Jolie by D 983 (route de Houdan) – ☎ 01 34 76 30 52 – closed Sun and Tues evenings and Mon – 145/340F*. This restaurant, set up in a spruce house over-grown with Virginia creeper and surrounded by blossoming flower beds in sum-mer, will win you over by its charm. Lovely terrace. The rustic dining hall features visible beams and a fireplace. Unusual dishes made with fresh local produce.

Port Maria – *35 rue Jean-Jaurès, 78520 Dennemont – 4km/2.5mi north of Mantes-la-Jolie by D 147 – ☎ 01 34 77 18 22 – 150F*. Fancy a Sunday outing at the water's edge? Settle down on this restaurant's terrace running along the banks of the Seine. Large crowds come here to enjoy the fair weather in sum-mer and to warm up in front of the fireplace in winter. A la carte fare comple-mented by daily specials made with fresh produce.

Where to stay

MODERATE

Camping Domaine d'Inchelin – *78980 St-Illiers-la-Ville – 16km/10mi east of Mantes-la-Jolie by N 13 then D 114 – ☎ 01 34 76 10 11 – open 1 Apr-15 Oct – booking recommended July-Aug – 150 plots 170F*. A haven of peace on the outskirts of the capital. Set up on the former premises of a half-timbered farmhouse, in a leafy park amid the rolling countryside, this camp site is both pleasant and well-kept. Its convenient location makes it an ideal base from which one can explore the region. Outdoor pool for the summer season.

MID-RANGE

Château de la Corniche – *78270 Rolleboise – 10km/6.2mi west of Mantes-la-Jolie by N 13 – ☎ 01 30 93 20 00 – closed 20 Dec-6 Jan, Mon except evening from Apr to Oct and Sun evening – 🖸 – 35 rooms 490/900F – ☕ 60F – restau-rant 220/360F*. This 19C manor house affords truly spectacular views of the nearby village and the Seine Valley. Some of the sparsely decorated rooms have been renovated. Outdoor swimming pool and tennis court.

Although a number of major property developments have spread across the Grandes Terres plateau since 1950, stretching towards Le Pecq, the name of Louis XIV remains firmly attached to this town.

Marly was the Sun King's favourite residence. Unfortunately, its golden age lasted barely 30 years. After the First Empire only the park remained, an impressive display of greenery bordering the old village, which has welcomed many writers and artists: the two Alexandre Dumas, Alfred Sisley, Camille Pissarro, the sculptor Maillol and the tragedienne Mlle Rachel, to name but a few.

The early stages – Marly's construction was due to Louis XIV's desire to retreat from the formal etiquette of Versailles. After the Treaty of Nijmegen in 1678, at the peak of his glory, tired of the continual entertaining at Versailles, the king dreamed of a peaceful country residence, far from the madding crowd. His barony at Marly offered a deep, lush valley which seemed to suit the purpose and he entrusted **Jules Hardouin-Mansart** with the plans.

Mansart came up with an ingenious idea: instead of designing one huge single pavilion which he knew the king would refuse he conceived a series of 13 separate units. The royal pavilion would stand on the upper terrace, while the other 12, smaller in size and all identical, would be arranged along a stretch of water. To promote his idea, Mansart explained that the decoration of the king's pavilion could symbolise the sun - Louis XIV's emblem - and that the surrounding buildings could represent the 12 signs of the zodiac. To cut down on costs, it was agreed to replace the carved bas-reliefs by trompe-l'œil frescoes. The King, delighted, gave orders to start building in 1679. It took nine years for the whole project to be completed. After working relentlessly all his life, Mansart died at the château in 1708.

Further embellishments – Right until the end of his reign, Louis XIV applied himself to the improvement of his Marly residence and kept a close watch on the various projects under way. He would even show gardeners how to trim the hedges properly. Behind the royal pavilion rose the steep, wooded slopes of the hillside. The Sun King gave orders to build the River, also called the Grande Cascade *(illustration above)*, the Wonder of Marly, which was served by the famous "Machine" *(see below)*: starting from the top of the hill, an impressive series of falls poured down a flight of 52 steps of pink marble set into the terraced slope. The whole ensemble - adorned with statues, porticoes and rockeries - was completed in 1699.

The same year, the King decided to clear the main perspective and raze the hillock that stood in the way, an enterprise that occupied 1 600 soldiers for a period of four years.

Life at Marly – Apart from his close relatives, Louis XIV brought very few guests to Marly; the facilities for accommodation were limited to 24 apartments. It is estimated that 500 lords and 300 ladies altogether were invited to the château over a period of 30 years. The King himself drew up a list of the guests and he personally determined where they should stay; the nearer they were to the royal pavilion, the greater

The Grande Cascade at Marly (18C gouache)

Archives Nationales, Paris/Revault/PIX

the honour. The "happy few" were not necessarily members of the aristocracy or high dignitaries, but lively, intelligent personalities whose wit and charm would enliven the King's stays.

The formal etiquette of Versailles was dropped at Marly. The King shared his meals with his guests, with whom he conversed in a free, casual manner. Hunts, forest walks, outdoor games, card games, games of chance, balls and concerts were a regular feature of life here. The standard of comfort at the place, however, left something to be desired; in summer the guests caught fever, in winter they shivered with cold or choked with smoke because it was too damp to start a fire. Louis XIV - who personally undertook to tackle the heating problem - introduced new systems every year, in vain.

The end of Marly – On 9 August 1715, the King suffered a bout of exhaustion after following the hunt in his carriage. He was taken to Versailles, where he died on 1 September, aged 77.

Louis XV and Louis XVI stayed in Marly from time to time. The costly Grande Cascade was abandoned in favour of the present "green carpet". The furniture was sold during the Revolution; in 1800, an industrialist bought the estate and set up a mill there. Having failed in business, he offered Napoleon the opportunity to buy Marly but he was turned down. He then proceeded to demolish the château and sell the building materials. One year later, Napoleon retrieved the estate which has since been the property of the French State.

★★MARLY PARK

Enter Marly Park by the Deux Portes. Take the first right turn through the woods to the car park near the presidential pavilion.

A large esplanade flanked by lime trees in the centre of the park marks the former site of the royal pavilion. A series of slabs defines the layout of the building; the large octagonal drawing room in the centre is surrounded by four corner rooms, separated by vestibules. The decoration in the King's rooms was red, the Dauphin's rooms were green (they were originally intended for the Queen but she never occupied them); the apartments for "Monsieur" (Louis XIV's brother) were yellow and those of "Madame", his second wife Elisabeth of Bavaria, were blue.

This is where the two perspectives of the park meet: across to the drive leading to the Royal Gates, and along the route running from St-Germain and the Seine Valley up to the Grand Mirror fountains and the green "carpet" of lawn.

The present grounds are suggestive of old Marly, with its terraces, fountains and hornbeam arbours. Further information can be obtained from the museum in the new outbuilding near the Grille Royale.

Grille Royale – Louis XIV would use this entrance when he arrived from Versailles. Admire the perspective of the steep road climbing up the hillside and its continuation on the opposite slope, slicing its way through the trees.

Musée-Promenade de Marly-le-Roi-Louveciennes ⊙ – The museum contains precious material on the 13 pavilions and the garden statues which no longer exist; the plans drawn up in 1753 and a miniature model of the whole project give a fair idea of what the king's country residence looked like. Note the interesting 18C approach to ornamental gardening.

The corner of the main pavilion houses the casts of the statues sculpted by Coustou and Lepautre, a painting of the château and its fountains by Martin the Younger (1723) and numerous line drawings of former copses and spinneys.

The room dedicated to Louveciennes displays a number of items concerning Mme Du Barry: Pajou's statue of *Loyalty*, a drawing by Moreau the younger portraying a banquet held in the Music Pavilion in honour of Louis XV in 1771. It also features the only religious work by Mme Vigée-Lebrun, as well as her two paintings *Summer* and *Autumn*, which were hung at Marly in 1755. Admire one of Desportes' hunting scenes and a *Lamentation* (1516) from St-Vigor Church.

Before leaving the museum, visit the small chamber presenting the "Marly Machine"; it contains drawings and plans, together with a model. The mural painting depicts the waterworks of Versailles.

Return to the car and leave the park by avenue des Combattants. Drive down to the Abreuvoir.

Abreuvoir (Horse-pond) – After a steep descent – known as Côte du Cœur-Volant – D 386 leads to the horse-pond, once used as a spillway for the waters of Marly park. From here, the water was conveyed back to the Seine by a system of pipes and drains. The terrace flanked by yew trees above the pond used to display Coysevox' *Winged Horses* and, at a later date, Guillaume Coustou's *Rearing Horses*. Two replicas stand in their place. The original statues once adorned place de la Concorde in Paris and have now been moved to the Louvre. Two reproductions have also been installed on the Parisian square.

EXCURSIONS

Port-Marly

★**Château de Monte-Cristo** ⊘ – *Entrance shared with the Clinique de l'Europe*. Built in 1846 on a hill overlooking the Seine Valley, this extravagant folly expressed the eccentricity of **Alexandre Dumas** through a wonderfully eclectic combination of Gothic, Renaissance and Moorish styles. After holding sumptuous receptions for the fashionable Paris set when his works *The Count of Monte-Cristo* and *The Three Musketeers* were enjoying great success, Dumas ran up enormous debts and was finally forced to sell up. The delightful building, which houses a library and information centre, is decorated with medallions representing the famous writer and those of his friends whom he was particularly fond of.

Some of the rooms contain portraits and documents. Visitors can also see the great man's study and the splendid **Moorish drawing room**★ in which the exuberance of the carvings and brilliant stained glass is equalled only by the furniture. The restoration of this room in 1985 was sponsored by Hassan II of Morocco, a great admirer of Dumas' works.

A few yards from the château is the little **Château d'If**, a pseudo-Gothic construction designed by Dumas as a place to which he could retire for peace and quiet. Note the titles of his works engraved on the freestone walls.

After being abandoned for many years, the **park** has now been exceptionally well preserved and again provides a charming setting with its grottoes and man-made features. The many natural springs have been skilfully channelled to form tiny waterfalls cascading into the basins and ponds. There is also an open-air theatre, a project planned by Dumas but never completed.

> ### DINNER IN TOWN
>
> **Le Village** – *3 Grande-rue* – ☎ *01 39 16 28 14 – closed Aug, Sat lunchtime, Sun evening and Mon – booking essential – 140/180F.* Le Village is located in the lively pedestrian area of the old city, where many restaurants are to be found. You will be delighted by the warm welcome of the owners and will relish the succulent, inventive dishes.

★LOUVECIENNES

This small residential town on the edge of Marly Forest still features several large estates. Many famous people, in particular artists, were attracted by this charming place: the portrait painter, Élisabeth Vigée-Lebrun (1755-1842), the poet André Chénier (1762-94), the sculptor Emmanuel Frémiet (1824-1910), a student of Rude, and, above all, several Impressionist painters.

🔲 Two itineraries lead visitors in the footsteps of the Impressionists, the "Chemin des Impressionnistes" *(4km/2.5mi starting from the town hall)* and the "Liaison Verte" *(6km/3.7mi starting from the Musée-promenade at Marly-le-Roi)*.

The **church** (12C-13C) on the village square retains a Romanesque look, but the polygonal bell-tower is 19C. The interior boasts an interesting collection of stone piscinae, resting against the east end.

The Moorish bedroom in the Château de Monte-Christo

F. Jalain/EXPLORER

Walk through the public gardens, along rue de l'Étang and down rue du Pont for a pleasant view of the 16C **Château du Pont** (private), the groves of trees and the rippling waters of the moat.

Follow rue du Général-Leclerc to the town hall, opposite which stand arches of the disused aqueduct that used to convey the waters of the Seine to Versailles thanks to the "Marly Machine".

Return to the church and walk along rue du Professeur-Tuffier, then follow the signposts to reach **Field Marshal Joffre's Tomb**. The Maréchal's estate can be seen on the corner of chemin des Gressets (plaque).

The rotunda-shaped temple seen from the chemin des Gressets was the last resting-place of the Victor of the Marne and his wife. Marshal Joffre, who died in 1931, was extremely fond of Louveciennes and insisted on being buried here rather than at Les Invalides in Paris.

★ BOUGIVAL

In the 19C Bougival was a centre of art, fêtes and bohemian life. Bizet, Corot, Meissonier and Renoir lived here. The "boaters" – fun-loving, young Parisian men and women – who flocked to the dances at La Grenouillère had their carefree lives evoked by Maupassant in his novels and short stories, and captured on canvas by Impressionists (Renoir, Berthe Morisot, Monet).

Musée Tourgueniev ⊘ – 16 rue Ivan-Tourgueniev. Access on foot via a small alleyway off N 13, level with the Forest Hill Hotel.

Built on the heights, the house where Turgenev lived during his exile was part of the property owned by his friends Louis Viardot and his wife Pauline, a singer like her sister La Malibran.

On the ground floor are some of the writer's documents, photographs of family and friends, engravings, and his piano. His works are evoked through extracts from novels and essays, among them the Récits d'un Chasseur published in 1852, in which he predicted the abolition of serfdom in Russia.

On the first floor, the writer's study and the room where he died on 3 September 1883 have been recreated. His body was taken to St Petersburg on 1 October: a photograph captures Ernest Renan giving a speech at the Gare du Nord in Paris (Adieu Paris); another shows the funeral procession in St Petersburg.

The Marly Machine – The Île de la Loge road bridge affords a good view of the 18C buildings (quai Rennequin-Sualem at Bougival) that contained the Marly Machine, and the pipes lining the hillside. At the top of the rise stands a white lodge by Ledoux: the **"pavillon de musique" de Madame du Barry** (closed to the public). It was inaugurated on 2 September 1771, during a sumptuous banquet attended by Louis XV.

A strange machine – It was decided to divert the waters of the Seine to supply the fountains of Marly and, subsequently, those of Versailles.

Colbert succeeded in finding a Belgian engineer, Arnold Deville, and a master carpenter, Rennequin Sualem, who agreed to take on the daring project of raising the water 150m/493ft above the level of the river. The work started in 1681, took three years and involved a considerable amount of equipment: 13 hydraulic wheels with a diameter of 12m/40ft operated 225 pumps ranged in three ranks, by which the waters were conveyed from the water tower - set at a height of 163m/535ft above the Seine - to the Louveciennes reservoirs via an aqueduct with a capacity of 5 000m³/176 575cu ft per day. From there they were channelled to Marly or Versailles. Since the 19C, several pumping devices have occupied the site; the last disappeared in 1967. For more information, read the explanations given on the panel located by the River Seine.

Forêt de Marly-le-Roi

The state forest – once royal hunting grounds, jealously guarded by high walls – covers a rough but picturesque plateau planted with oaks, beeches and chestnut trees. The total area is estimated at 2 000ha/5 000 acres.

The thicker groves, featuring some beautiful trees, lie west of the road from St-Germain to St-Nom-la-Bretèche, particularly between Étoile des Dames and Etoile de Joyenval.

Consult Michelin map 101 to see which lanes are closed to traffic (barriers). These may however be recommended as cycling paths.

Désert de Retz – Temporarily closed to the public. The park was created by Monsieur De Monvil, usher to the king's chamber, in the second half of the 18C. It lies on the edge of Marly Forest and is adorned with 17 buildings (Tartars' tent, Greek temple dedicated to Pan, Chinese house, ice-house in the shape of a pyramid etc), an Anglo-Chinese garden, two lakes, an open air theatre etc. Famous figures such as Marie-Antoinette and the King of Sweden visited the Desert.

Parc ornithologique du MARQUENTERRE★★

MARQUENTERRE RESERVE

Michelin map 51 fold 11 and 52 fold 6 or 236 fold 11

The Marquenterre area is an alluvial plain reclaimed from the sea which lies between the Authie and Somme estuaries and its name derives from *mer qui entre en terre* (sea which enters the land).

The stretches of land are made up of briny marshes, salt-pastures and sand dunes secured to the land by vegetation. Today these are home to 315 species of birds (the continent of Europe has 452 species in all), 350 species of plants, 40 species of mammals living both on land and in the water, including a large colony of seals; the most inquisitive of them are sometimes spotted at high tide near the quayside at St Valéry-en-Somme and Le Crotoy.

Reclaimed from the sea – The process of reclaiming the land was started in the 12C by monks from St-Riquier and Valloires who erected the first dikes and attempted to canalize the rivers. Many drainage canals were built. Perched on a hill, Rue, the future capital of the Marquenterre area, ceased to be an island in the 18C. However, the fragile dikes would easily be swept away by strong tides and torrential rain.

During the 19C, dikes and beaches were strengthened, which allowed the development of vegetable and cereal growing. In 1923, the industrialist H Jeanson bought an area of marshland along the coast, which his successors drained and diked using Dutch methods, so that it was eventually possible to grow bulbs on the land in the 1950s.

At the same time, trees were systematically planted. Unfortunately, the economic crisis which hit the horticultural sector put pay to these efforts and the idea of a bird sanctuary was then launched.

The birth of the bird sanctuary – The Marquenterre lands, particularly around the Baie de Somme where vast reaches of sand are uncovered twice a day at low tide, have always been an important stopover for migratory birds and a place of hibernation for many others. It was a paradise for hunters who, from hides, could fire on the hundreds of ducks, geese and sandpipers of all types, to the extent that many species disappeared.

As a result of the decimation, in 1968 the Hunting Commission *(Office de la Chasse)* created a reserve on the maritime land, to ensure the protection of the birds along 5km/3mi of coastline.

The owners of the Marquenterre estate next to the reserve decided in 1973 to set up a bird sanctuary within it to allow the general public to watch the extraordinary variety of birdlife in its natural habitat. Thirteen years later the site became the property of the Conservatoire du Littoral (Office of Coastal Preservation) and was granted in 1994 the status of "protected nature reserve".

★★ Parc Ornithologique (Bird Sanctuary) ⊙ – *It is advisable to visit on a rising tide when the birds leave the stretches of the Baie de Somme or during the spring and autumn migration periods.*

The Bird Sanctuary covers 250ha/627 acres at the edge of the Réserve de Marquenterre. Over 300 species of bird have been identified, among them many ducks including the red-beaked sheld-duck, geese, tern, waders such as the avocet with its delicately curved beak, seagulls, herons, sandpipers, spoonbills etc.

Two different trails are sign-posted:

Discovery trail – ◪ *1hr 30min, explanatory panels.* The tour of the lakes and aviaries at the foot of an old coastal dune, offering a close-up view of the birds which live here permanently: ducks, seagulls, geese and herons. Their calls attract wild birds of the same species.

A few familiar mammals can be seen on the way: Henson horses, weasels and hares, as well as amphibians such as toads and elegant insects such as dragonflies. The vegetation includes willows and sea buckthorns.

S. Maire/MICHELIN

Reserve

The Henson horse breed

This small robust horse is a cross between a French saddle horse and a Norwegian Fjord pony. Its coat varies from light yellow to brown, and its mane is a mixture of black and gold. This breed was developed in 1978 in a small village of the Baie de Somme area, thanks to the determination of Doctor Berquin. Hensons show remarkable endurance; they can remain out in the fields all year round and cover great distances without getting tired. Their docile and affectionate behaviour make them ideal companions for children and long-distance riders. They also fare very well in team competitions and horse shows generally.

A riding centre established next to the bird sanctuary organises excursions for beginners and experienced riders (Centre équestre Henson Marquenterre, Domaine du Marquenterre, 80120 St-Quentin-en-Tourmont, ☎ 03 22 25 03 06).

Observation trail – The 7km/4.3mi walk *(allow 3hr, binoculars recommended)* follows a path through the dunes to various observation hides, a heronry and a large aviary, from where the habits and movements of numerous species in their natural habitat can be studied.

An additional path (1.5km/1mi) shows the reserve from a completely different angle.

MEAUX★

Canurbation 63 006
Michelin map 106 folds 22, 23 or 237 fold 19

Access from Paris: *SNCF rail link from Gare de l'Est*

Nestling inside a deep bend of the River Marne, Meaux lies at the intersection of several main roads, in particular N 3 which runs through the town from east to west. In the summer months, a **son et lumière performance** featuring a cast of 2 100 re-enacts Meaux's moments of glory in the charming setting of the Episcopal Precinct *(see Calendar of events)*.

The Eagle of Meaux

Having completed his tutorial commitments towards the Dauphin, **Jacques Bossuet** was made Bishop of Meaux in 1682 at the age of 55.

The man later known as the "Eagle of Meaux" exercised his ecclesiastic duties with the utmost assiduity; he kept an attentive eye on catechism, was often seen preaching in his own cathedral and assumed full command of the religious communities in his diocese. For instance, despite his great esteem for Jouarre Abbey, he did not hesitate to have the place besieged when the abbess refused to dismiss two nuns whose presence he considered undesirable.

Bossuet enjoyed working in the huge library of the Episcopal Palace, or in his study at the end of the garden; it was there that he composed five of his most famous funeral orations including those dedicated to Louis XIV's wife Marie-Thérèse and the Great Condé. He also wrote a number of books defending Gallican orthodoxy.

He died in Paris in 1704, aged 77, at the height of his intellectual powens. As was his wish, he was buried in his cathedral in Meaux.

★EPISCOPAL PRECINCT *1hr 30min*

★**Cathédrale St-Étienne** – The construction of the church continued from the late 12C to the 16C, covering the entire gamut of Gothic architecture.

The façade (14C-16C) is pure Flamboyant. Only the left tower was completed. The one on the right – a plain bell-tower – is called the Black Tower on account of its dark-coloured shingles. The limestone used for the stonework has crumbled in several places and the exterior decoration is badly damaged. The Wars of Religion brought further destruction.

The south transept façade is an elegant example of Radiant Gothic. The south doorway – in poor condition – is dedicated to St Stephen.

Cathédrale St-Étienne

Enter the cathedral through this doorway.

The interior of the cathedral – last restored in the 18C – contrasts sharply with the badly weathered exterior. The lofty, well-lit nave is an impressive sight. The double side aisles are unusually high owing to the suppression of the upper galleries as in Notre-Dame in Paris. These were removed around the middle of the 13C, which had the effect of heightening the aisles.

The two bays of the nave next to the transept date from the early 13C; their austere appearance typifies Early Gothic. The west bays were completed in the 14C and the pillars redesigned in the 15C.

The transepts – in particular the south arm – are superb examples of 14C architecture; the elegant, generous proportions characterise the golden age of High Gothic. Below the huge stained-glass window runs an openwork triforium so fine that it allows a full view of the lancets. The chancel – also High Gothic – is a pleasing sight with its double aisles and its five apsidal chapels. Note the pretty 15C Maugarni doorway to the left.

A walk round the ambulatory leads to Bossuet's tomb, marked by a slab of black marble, visible through the parclose enclosing the chancel.

Vieux Chapitre – This is believed to have been the chapter's 13C tithe barn. The external staircase is roofed over and dates from the Renaissance period. The ground floor, linked to the cathedral by a wooden gallery, is used as a sacristy and a chapel annex.

Ancien Évêché ⊘ – The old palace houses a **museum** largely dedicated to Bossuet. The building was completed in the 12C and altered in the 17C. The main front overlooks the garden. The two magnificent Gothic rooms facing the park on the ground floor, the lower and the upper chapel are the oldest parts of the palace. The chapter-house holds temporary exhibitions. The amazing brick ramp was designed by Bishop Briçonnet in the 16C to enable the mules loaded with grain to reach the attics.

Enter the palace through the Salle du Synode which together with the western salons has been made into a Fine Arts Museum (15C to 19C). Among the many artists feature Boullogne, De Troy, Bouchardon, Millet, Courbet and Senelle. The donation made by Annie and Jean Pierre Changeux in 1983 has considerably enriched the collections of 17C and 18C French painting.

Bossuet's apartment, located in the east wing, has retained its original layout but the decoration was renewed in the Louis XV style. Admire Mignard's portrait of the bishop and a splendid Cressent commode (early 18C).

The former library contains an anonymous 17C portrait of Henrietta Maria of England, for whom Bossuet composed his famous funeral oration.

The chapel houses medieval sculptures, a fine reliquary illustrating **Christ's Lamentation** by Frans Floris.

The history of the town is also presented: 1738 plan by Monvoisin, pictures of the old bridge spanning the Marne with its picturesque mills (sadly disappeared), apothecary's shop of the former hospice, Moisan's electric oven (1892) for studying artificial diamonds.

Gardens – The gardens, shaped like a bishop's mitre, were designed by Le Nôtre in the tradition of French formal gardens.

Anciens remparts – *The ramparts are only accessible during the guided tours of the town.*

At the top of the steps stands the humble 17C pavilion which Bossuet used as a study. The bishop would retire here to collect his thoughts or to write in the peaceful hours of the night.

The centre of the terrace affords a good **view**★ of the gardens, the Episcopal Palace and the cathedral.

EXCURSION

Château de Montceaux

⏱ – *8.5km/5mi east. Leave Meaux by N 3 (east). Beyond Trilport, in Montceaux Forest, turn right onto D 19 (signposted Montceaux-les-Meaux). The lane to the château is on the right.*

Montceaux was known as the Château of the Queens. Catherine de' Medici had it built and Philibert Delorme almost certainly worked on it between 1547 and 1559. Henri IV later gave it to Gabrielle d'Estrées who had work continued by JA du Cerceau (1594-99). On the death of the one who was "almost Queen", the king gave the château to his bride Marie de Medici who entrusted the works to Salomon de Brosse before he started to build the Luxembourg Palace (1608-22 in Paris). The château then fell into disrepair and after 1650 became uninhabitable. Handsome ruins lurk among the trees and from the roofless entrance pavilion, there is an especially good view of a section of wall with gaping windows. The oblong-shaped moat has remained intact.

RIVERSIDE DINING

Le Moulin de Poincy – *77470 Poincy – 5km/3mi east of Meaux by N 3 then D 17a –* ☎ *01 60 23 06 80 – closed 4-24 Jan, 7-27 Sept, Tues and Wed – 170/345F.* This 17C mill nestling in the heart of the countryside along the banks of the River Marne features a beautiful garden. Whether you settle in the shade of lime trees or inside the cosy drawing room in winter, you will be enchanted by your stay here. Traditional cuisine with a few modern variations.

MEUDON★

Population 45 339
Michelin map 101 folds 23, 24 - Michelin plan 22

Access from Paris: *RER line C 5/C 7 or SNCF rail link from Gare Montparnasse*

This residential town is located south-west of Paris, on the slopes of the plateau covered by the Meudon Forest. The grave of the sculptor **Auguste Rodin** can be seen outside his former residence, now a museum.

In the mid 18C Mme De Pompadour acquired **Bellevue** estate and gave orders to build the château. Louis XV paid frequent visits to the estate and in 1757 he bought Bellevue from his mistress. He embellished the house, refurbished the grounds and installed a hot water heating system under the flooring. The last occupants were the two unmarried daughters of Louis XV, the aunts of Louis XVI. They added a botanical garden and a charming hamlet. The estate was pillaged during the Revolution and sold as State property. In the 19C it was parcelled out into building plots.

All that remains of the former estate is part of the terrace and its balustrade at the junction of rue Marcel-Allégot and avenue du 11-Novembre. The wonderful panorama of the past has been replaced by a view of modern Paris with, in the foreground, Boulogne-Billancourt and the Île Seguin.

On 8 May 1842, the small station on the left was the scene of a train crash in which the explorer Admiral **Dumont d'Urville** died (he had just discovered Adélie Land in the Antarctic), together with 40 other passengers who had been locked in the compartments according to regulations.

CHÂTEAU

The stately avenue du Château is lined with four rows of lime trees. Half way down the street, a plaque on the left marks the little house (no 27) where **Richard Wagner** composed the score for the *Flying Dutchman* in 1841.

Château of the House of Guise – In the 15C, the manor house belonging to the Duchess of Étampes became the property of the Cardinal de Lorraine, who belonged to the House of Guise. For 100 years Meudon remained in the hands of the Guise. The family later sold the estate to Abel Servien in 1654 owing to financial difficulties.

New owners – The wealthy Abel Servien, Marquis de Sablé and Minister of Finance, commissioned Le Vau to renovate the château at great expense and gave orders to build the terrace, a large-scale project. Servien led a life of luxury but his fortune soon ran out; when he died in 1659, his son sold the estate to Louvois, the lord of Chaville.

The new owner pursued the efforts of his predecessor, renewing the decoration and embellishing the park. He asked Trivaux to create the perspective and entrusted the plans of the gardens to Le Nôtre, then to Mansart. After Louvois' death, his widow agreed to give Louis XIV her domain in exchange for the Château de Choisy, which belonged to the King's son, the Grand Dauphin.

Royal property – An enthusiastic art lover, "Monseigneur" made considerable changes in the interior decoration and layout of the Old Château.

In 1706 he dismantled the grotto and replaced it with a new pavilion for his courtiers. This New Château was Mansart's last major accomplishment.

In 1711 Monseigneur died of smallpox and the following year his son the Duke of Burgundy succumbed to the disease. The château came into the hands of a two-year-old boy, who was to become Louis XV. His great-grandfather Louis XIV administered the estate up to 1715.

Military research centre – Until the Revolution, Meudon fell into disrepair. In 1793 the chemist Berthollet and Général Choderlos de Laclos - who wrote *Les Liaisons Dangeureuses*, adapted for the cinema by Stephen Frears as *Dangerous Liaisons* and by Milos Forman as *Valmont* - set up an artillery research centre in the Old Château. Unfortunately it was so badly damaged by a fire that the whole building had to be razed in 1804. Only the columns of pink marble still adorn the Luxembourg Palace and the Carrousel Arch, both in Paris.

The flames spared the New Château, which housed a workshop for military balloons. The famous aerostats which contributed to the victory of Fleurus (1794) were manufactured in Meudon. Napoleon I renewed the furniture in the New Château, which was occupied by Marie-Louise and the King of Rome during the Russian campaign.

In 1870 the terrace was turned into a redoubt for a Prussian battery intent on bombarding Paris. When the Germans withdrew the following year, Meudon was burned down along with St-Cloud. Only two small wings still stand. The central section of the building was restored and made into an observatory.

VISIT

★**Terrace** – The terrace (450m/1480ft long and 136m/447ft wide) is planted with handsome trees and sweeping lawns. It lies at an altitude of 153m/502ft and commands an extensive **view**★ of Meudon, the Seine Valley and Paris.

One of the forest's standing stones can be seen to the left of the gates. The pedestal-like pilasters adorning the breast wall of the upper terrace date from the 16C and 17C.

The far end of the esplanade rests on the foundations of the old orangeries of the château. From here, visitors may discover Le Nôtre's beautiful perspective with the modern complex of Meudon-la-Forêt in the far distance.

Observatoire ⊙ – *Temporarily closed*. On the right stands the observatory, housing the astrophysics section of the Paris Observatory. A large revolving dome with a diameter of 18.5m/60ft crowns the central block of the New Château. Note the astronomical telescope dating from 1893. Founded in 1876 by the astronomer Janssen, this observatory is considered the most important in France. It is also the leading aerospace research centre in France. A mushroom-shaped tower was added in 1965; its 35m/115ft shaft attracts the rays of the sun, which are then broken down and analysed under a spectroscope.

X. Desmier/RAPHO

Observatory

Musée d'Art et d'Histoire ⊙ – *11 rue des Pierres, at the foot of the terrace (drive there from the town centre).*

The museum, in the house which Molière's wife Armande Béjart bought in 1676, three years after the writer's death, centres on the history of the town, the celebrities who lived there and the châteaux of Bellevue and Meudon *(information centre)*. It also presents the municipal art collections: Dunoyer de Segonzac, Magnelli, Pape etc. The formal gardens are dotted with contemporary sculptures by Arp, Bourdelle and Stahly.

Musée Rodin, Villa des Brillants ⊘ – *19 avenue Auguste-Rodin.*
An indispensable complement to the Rodin Museum in Paris. The museum stands next to the Villa des Brillants, **Rodin**'s residence and studio from 1895. It contains moulds, drawings and rough sketches by the great sculptor, together with a number of original plaster casts *(The Gates of Hell, Balzac, The Burghers of Calais)*. The façade of the museum was taken from the old château at Issy-les-Moulineaux. Rodin died in 1917 and his grave was laid out in front of the museum. Sitting pensively on the tombstone is his famous statue *The Thinker*.

MILLY-LA-FORÊT★

Population 4 307
Michelin map 106 fold 44 or 237 fold 30

The locality of Milly-la-Forêt developed around the old covered market and it is now an important starting-point for many of the forest lanes crisscrossing the wooded uplands of Les Trois Pignous and Coquibus. Milly has been a long-standing centre for the growing of medicinal plants, including one variety still considered a local speciality: peppermint. Lily of the valley and a wide range of aromatic herbs for cooking purposes are also grown.

Halles – Located on the town square, the market building – made entirely of oak and chestnut wood – dates back to 1479.

Chapelle St-Blaise-des-Simples ⊘ – *On the way out of the village, along the road to Chapelle-la-Reine.*
In the 12C the chapel was part of the St Blaise leper house. More recently, **Jean Cocteau** decorated the walls in 1959; a huge line-drawing above the altar depicts Christ with a crown of thorns and a mural represents the Resurrection of Christ. The

FEAST IN THE FOREST

Auberge d'Auvers Galant – *77123 Auvers* – *4km/1.2mi south of Milly by D 948* – ☎ *01 64 24 51 02* – *closed 15 Feb-10 Mar and 21 Aug-1 Sept* – *130/280F.* This stone residence with quaint roof tiling offers delicious meals made with market produce, served by a blazing fire. In high season, sit down in the flowered courtyard and take in the intoxicating forest scents.

walls of the nave are adorned with illustrations of medicinal herbs or simples (mint, belladonna, valerian, buttercup and aconite).
The chapel houses a bust of Cocteau by the German sculptor Arno Breker, and the poet's grave. The epitaph on the tombstone simply reads: "I remain with you". The garden surrounding the chapel is planted with common medicinal herbs.

EXCURSIONS

Le Cyclop ⊘ – *Leave Milly on the Étampes road (D 837).*
This monumental sculpture was donated to the French government in 1987 by artists Jean Tinguely and Niki de Sainte-Phalle. It represents an enormous head 22.5m/73ft high made with 300t of steel. The sparkling face conceals a strange world of disorder and utopia. On the top of the piece is a vast water-filled basin dedicated to France's most innovative post-war artist Yves Klein (1928-62), noted for his use of a rich ultramarine commonly referred to as Yves Klein blue.

Château de Courances – *5km/3mi north.* Built around 1550 by Gilles le Breton for Cosme Clausse, Secretary of Finance to Henri II, the château acquired its present appearance in the 17C. It is a good example of the Louis XIII style: a brick building with sandstone bonding, pointed roofs and a sparsely decorated exterior. In the 19C the front was embellished with a replica of the horseshoe staircase at Fontainebleau. The château is still surrounded by a moat and a splendid avenue on the opposite side of the road completes this sweeping perspective.

★★**Park** – The approach to the château is very grand. Walk through the gate and cross the "forecourt", a vast stretch of lawn divided by a central path and flanked by two canals reflecting the plane trees.
The park, designed by Le Nôtre, extends behind the château and the rear façade overlooks a lush, green lawn. A path leads to the Grand Canal, which receives the waters of the École. Another path, set at right angles, skirts the small cascades and leads to the flower beds, offering a lovely view of the château mirrored in the crystal-clear water.

Château de Courances, garden façade

Before returning to the gate, turn right *(when level with the château)* towards the ruins of an old fuller's mill and its gushing stream. From the embankment on the left, admire the Japanese garden and, further back, the falls of an old mill.

Château ⊘ – From the south terrace, there is a view of the park. The tour includes a number of living rooms, low-ceilinged chambers and annexes. Note the corner dining room, tastefully decorated with walnut wainscot and ornamental plates, and the Monkeys' Gallery, named after three 16C tapestries with scenes of monkeys mimicking man.

MONTFORT-L'AMAURY★

Population 2 651
Michelin map 106 north of folds 27, 28

This old town is built on the side of a hill dominated by castle ruins. Before the French Revolution, Montfort was an important county town enjoying far more power than nearby Rambouillet. The composer Maurice Ravel and Jean Monnet, one of the founders of the European Union, were among the town's distinguished residents.
The district was founded and fortified in the 11C by the builder Amaury de Montfort. The most famous descendant of this illustrious family was Simon IV, the leader of the Albigensian Crusade, who waged a fierce war against the heretical Cathars of Languedoc. Simon de Montfort was killed by a stone in 1218, while besieging the town of Toulouse.

A Breton outpost in Île-de-France – In 1312 the marriage of the Breton Duke Arthur to one of the Montfort daughters made this citadel a part of Brittany.
Subsequently, when Anne of Brittany, Comtesse de Montfort married Charles VIII and then Louis XII, Montfort-l'Amaury became a French fief. The duchy became Crown property after the accession of Henri II, the son of François I and Claude de France – herself the daughter of Louis XII.

SIGHTS

★**Église St-Pierre** – The rebuilding of the church was commissioned by Anne of Brittany in the late 15C. The decoration work continued through the Renaissance and was completed in the early 17C; the nave was uniformly elevated and the bell tower and the façade were both remodelled.
Walk round the church, surrounded by quaint old houses. Observe the striking gargoyles that adorn the walls of the apse and the high flying buttresses supporting the chancel. The pretty doorway on the south front bears medallions portraying the benefactors whose generosity made it possible to carry out the renovation work in the Renaissance: André de Foix and his wife. The interior features a superb set of Renaissance **stained-glass windows**★ in the ambulatory and around the aisles *(read description in "Montfort-l'Amaury" booklet published by the Tourist Information Centre)*. The vaulting above the aisles features many hanging keystones. The historiated bosses in the nave include one bearing the emblem (ermine) of Anne of Brittany.

*★***Ancien charnier** – Admire the beautifully carved Flamboyant doorway. This old cemetery is enclosed within an arcaded gallery surmounted by splendid timbered roofing in the shape of an upturned ship. The left gallery is 16C, the other two date from the 17C. In accordance with medieval tradition, these galleries were intended to receive the bones of the dead when there was a lack of space in the graveyard.

Castle ruins – Take the narrow, twisting road to the top of the hill. Two sections of wall overgrown with ivy are all that remain of the 11C keep. The stone and brick turret belonged to the building commissioned by Anne of Brittany.
The summit offers a good **view★** of the town, the old-fashioned roofs and the edge of the forest.

> **A WARM WELCOME**
>
> **Chez Nous** – *22 rue de Paris –* ☎ *01 34 86 01 62 – closed a few days around 1 Nov, Sun evening and Mon except public holidays – 140/180F.* A homely establishment where quality and expertise are the key words, providing all the ingredients for a simple yet highly satisfactory meal.

Musée Maurice-Ravel ⊘ – In 1920 the French composer **Ravel** bought a tiny villa in Montfort-l'Amaury – called Le Belvédère – that he wrote most of his music: *L'Enfant et les Sortilèges*, *Boléro*, *Daphnis et Chloé* etc. The composer developed a brain tumour but stayed on in Montfort, despite doctor's orders to stop working in 1934. He was forced to move back to Paris in 1937, where he died soon afterwards.
The rooms are somewhat cramped and Ravel - who was a short man - had several of them made even smaller. The interior decoration has remained intact; much of the painting was done by Ravel himself and featured dark, sombre tones. The museum exhibits include the composer's piano, his gramophone and numerous mementoes reflecting his taste for refinement.

Maurice Ravel (1875-1937)

Ravel's relatively late admission to the Paris Conservatory in 1889 makes his precocious output as a composer even more surprising (*Habanera* dates from 1895) unless one is aware of the fact that his father, a music-loving engineer, took great care of his son's musical education. The principal of the Conservatory thought that Ravel made "terrible mistakes in his compositions". However, his composition teacher, Gabriel Fauré, was of another opinion: "a natural musician with new ideas and a disarming sincerity". In 1901, Ravel composed *Jeux d'eau* and won second prize in the coveted Prix de Rome competition with his cantata *Myrrha*. His name was beginning to be widely known. However, in spite of repeated attempts, he never won the Prix de Rome and the scandal that ensued prompted the principal of the Conservatory to resign and be replaced by Fauré. Ravel then produced some of his major works (*Rhapsodie espagnole*, 1907). In collaboration with Diaghilev's Russian Ballet, he created *Daphnis and Chloé* in 1912. After the war (during which he tried to enlist), his style became balder (*L'Enfant et les Sortilèges*, 1925; libretto by Colette). The *Boléro*, a ballet commissioned by Ida Rubinstein and created in 1928, was one of his major successes in symphonic writing.

EXCURSIONS

Vicq, Musée d'Art naïf de l'Île-de-France ⊘ – *4km/2.5mi north along D 76.* This museum devoted to the world of fantasy contains the Max-Fourny collection – more than 1 500 works displayed in rotation with temporary exhibitions.

La Queue-les-Yvelines, La Serre aux Papillons ⊘ – *4.5km/3mi north-west. Leave Montfort by D 155 and drive to La Queue-les-Yvelines.*
The butterfly house is part of the Jardinerie Poullain. More than 500 butterflies live in it, in tropical conditions.

Houjarray, Maison Jean-Monnet (Centre d'information sur l'Europe) ⊘ – *4.5km/3mi east. Leave Montfort by D 13 towards Tremblay-sur-Mauldre. Cross N 191 and turn right to Houjarray before Bazoches-sur-Guyonne. The centre is 1 500 m/1mi further on in Houarray.*
Jean Monnet (1888-1979), the political economist and diplomat, bought this country retreat in 1945; it has a thatched roof and a large, gently sloping garden which overlooks the surrounding countryside.

The text of the declaration regarding the Schuman Plan of 1950 (embodied in a treaty that same year) was conceived and written here; it led to the creation of the European Coal and Steel Community (ECSC).

Monnet would return to this haven of peace after his frequent trips around the world and had many famous figures and heads of State to stay. He retired here in 1975, writing his memoirs until his death.

Some of the original furnishings remain, together with various possessions: Monnet's *Memoirs*, letters from Schuman, Roosevelt, Adenauer and de Gaulle, various publications with Monnet on the cover, paintings by his wife Sylvia, a bust of Marianne (1945) by the sculptor Paul Belmondo. Display panels recount the important moments of his career.

One of the founders of the European Union

Jean Monnet (1888-1979) was an economist, a negotiator and a politician whose career was influenced by his relationship with the Anglo-Saxon countries. He was a member of the Allied maritime commission during the First World War. Between the wars he took part in the creation of an investment bank in New York and then played an important role as financial advisor in the co-ordination of the Franco-British war effort in 1939, negotiating the purchase of material in Washington on behalf of the British government. He was later sent to the United States by De Gaulle as a member of the French Committee of National Liberation. He once again showed his negotiating skills by obtaining a considerable reduction of the outstanding debt and new funding (Blum-Byrnes agreement). Thanks to his modernisation plan (Plan Monnet 1947) and to the Marshall Plan, France was able to straighten her economy. The Schuman Plan (9 may 1950) laid the foundations of the European Coal and Steel Community, of which he was the first president, thus becoming with Schuman one of the founders of the European Union. He also actively worked for the establishment of the United States of Europe. His memoirs were published in 1976; his ashes were transferred to the Pantheon in Paris on 9 November 1988.

Étang de la Porte Baudet ou des Maurus – *4km/2.5mi south-west then 45min on foot there and back. Leave Montfort by D 112 and D 138, towards St-Léger.* ◪ Go past the turning to Gambais *(right)* and turn left onto rue du Vert-Galant. Follow the plateau along the winding route which enters the wood *(the road surface rapidly deteriorates)*. Park the car at the *Zone de Silence de la Mare Ronde*. Certain forests in France have "silent areas" *(zones de silence)* where motor bikes, radios etc are prohibited.

Round tour in Rambouillet Forest – *21km/12mi then 30min on foot there and back.*

Château de la Mormaire – Built of stone and brick under Henri IV, this castle is reminiscent of the houses on place des Vosges in Paris.

Gambaiseuil – A former woodcutter's village that is now almost deserted. A few houses still exist in the old church quarter.

Étang Neuf – Situated in a remote corner of the forest, this pond is a popular fishing haunt. It lies in pleasant surroundings planted with beech trees.

Carrefour du Grand Baliveau – ◪ The road to the right of the sign "Route Forestière du Parc d'en Haut" offers a charming walk through a lovely green glade. One of the clearings affords a good **view**★ of a secluded valley.

MONTMORENCY★

Population 20 920
Michelin map 101 fold 5, 106 fold 19 or 237 folds 17, 18
Michelin plan 18

This charming town, set on hilly ground, consists of a town centre surrounded by wealthy residences. Its main claim to fame is to have been the home of the celebrated author and social theorist Jean-Jacques Rousseau (1712-78) for a period of his life. From the late 18C to the mid-19C, Montmorency and its forest were popular venues for writers, artists, politicians and young Parisian socialites.

The "First Christian Barons" – The Bouchard family, who held the lordship of Montmorency, had the reputation of being difficult vassals and it was only after the 12C that they served the French court loyally. Over a period of 500 years, the Montmorency family produced six constables, 12 marshals and four admirals.

Moreover, their land was made a duchy by Henri II. They had connections with every ruler in Europe and chose to call themselves the "first Christian barons". One of their most celebrated descendants was Constable Anne, companion-in-arms to François I, Henri II and Charles IX and builder of the Château de Chantilly.

The oldest branch of the family died out in 1632 when the constable's grandson Henri II de Montmorency, governor of Languedoc, was beheaded at the age of 37 for having plotted against Cardinal Richelieu. Despite the numerous appeals made to Louis XIII, the King refused to pardon the Duke and ordained that the execution take place. The duchy passed into the hands of Henri de Bourbon-Condé but the title was given to a member of the Montmorency-Boutteville family by Louis XIV.

During the Revolution, the town was called Émile in honour of Rousseau's famous treatise on education. It recovered its former name in 1832.

Jean-Jacques Rousseau's literary retreat – The author lived in Montmorency from 1756 to 1762. Invited by Mme d'Épinay, a society woman who moved in literary circles, Rousseau took up residence in the Hermitage, a small garden pavilion which has since been taken down. He was 44 years old. His short temper and quickness to take offence annoyed the other house guests. He was living with Thérèse Levasseur, a linen maid whom he later married, but fell passionately in love with his hostess' sister-in-law Mme d'Houdetot, who was nearly 20 years his junior.

His romantic involvements caused him to fall out with Mme d'Épinay in 1757, at which point he moved to Montlouis where he completed *The New Eloisa* and published *Emilius and Sophia* and *A Treatise on the Social Contract*. These were his three major works. The owners of Montlouis – the Maréchal de Luxembourg and his wife – took Rousseau under their wing. Their admiration for the writer, who would read them his latest chapters, helped them put up with his changing moods. The stately grounds of their estate have survived but the château has been replaced by a modern building.

In 1762 *Emilius and Sophia* was qualified as subversive literature by the Parlement de Paris and a warrant was issued for Rousseau's arrest. Fortunately, the author was forewarned; he fled Montlouis in the marshal's post-chaise and sought refuge in Switzerland.

SIGHTS

★**Collégiale St-Martin** – *Rue de l'Église*. Started in the 16C by Guillaume de Montmorency and completed by his son Constable Anne, St Martin's is characteristic of the Flamboyant Gothic style. It was originally designed to be the mausoleum of the Montmorency family.

Walk round the church to appreciate its **site** which dominates the new town of Montmorency, spread out in the valley. The view extends to the heights of Sannois and the Butte d'Orgemont *(tower)*.

The nave features complex ribbed vaulting in keeping with 16C architecture, except for the two ribs in the choir that present ornamental brackets at the point where they meet the pillars.

The chapel was specially designed to receive the remains of the Montmorency family and, in the 18C, the tombs of several members of the Condé family. The tombs were destroyed during the Revolution. Some were salvaged and moved to the Louvre, including those of Constable Anne and his wife Madeleine. The others have disappeared save for the funeral slab of Guillaume de Montmorency and his wife Anne Pot, of the famous Burgundian family; it has been placed at the top of the south aisle.

Montmorency — Detail of stained-glass window in the Collégiale St-Martin

D. Dorval/EXPLORER

★**Stained-glass windows** – *Explanatory panels are attached to the corresponding pillars.* The 14 windows that adorn the apse and the five nearest right-hand bays of the chancel provide a fine example of Renaissance decoration, tastefully restored in the 19C. The family connections of the Montmorency are illustrated by the effigies of their ancestors, the brightly coloured coats of arms and the saints they worshipped. Above the glass cage of the side doorway is a magnificent window representing the famous emblem of this illustrious family: alerions or eagles without beaks or feet painted in blue against a yellow background.

The other windows in the nave – executed in the 19C – harmonise well with the earlier Renaissance windows. They evoke the joys and sorrows of the dynasty up to the execution of Henri II de Montmorency in 1632, which heralded the start of a new era for the Condé.

The Polish heritage – Behind the west front are a number of busts, recumbent figures and plaques relating to the members of an aristocratic community from Poland who moved to Montmorency in the wake of the failed national insurrection (1831). They were attracted to the town by the fresh, vivifying countryside – reminiscent of their own homeland – and by the literary connections with Rousseau.

In the chancel is a copy of the painting, Our Lady of Czestochowa or the Black Madonna, the patron saint of Poland.

Musée Jean-Jacques-Rousseau ⊘ – *5 rue Jean-Jacques-Rousseau.*
This is the house where the French writer lived from 1757 to 1762 and where he wrote his major works. The museum evokes the daily life of Thérèse and Jean-Jacques. The old part of the house affords a good view of the valley. The arbour planted with lime trees leads through to the small garden pavilion Rousseau used as a study, which he sardonically called his "keep".

The exhibition hall and audio-visual room in the modern part of the museum present particular aspects of Rousseau's life and work. The 18C house at the edge of the grounds contains a library with numerous studies on Rousseau and the town's historic research centre.

EXCURSIONS

Montmorency Forest - *3km/2mi north.*
Extending over an area of 2 000ha/4 942 acres north of the River Seine, the Montmorency Forest covers the highest hill (195m/640ft) of the Paris region.

The area west of Domont and N 309 is the more interesting section of the forest, with deep wooded vales and patches of moist undergrowth. Oaks and chestnut trees are the dominant species, with the occasional birch. The forest boasts several footpaths (GR1, hiking trails), a cycle track which cuts through the forest (Route du Faîte), and the Caesar's Camp recreational area.

Château de la Chasse – *30min on foot from N 309 (green gate on the left, 2km/1.2mi beyond Montlignon Church).*
🔃 The oddly shaped castle, flanked with truncated towers, stands in a picturesque setting, on the edge of a pond.

"IN THE HEART OF THE FOREST"

Au Cœur de la Forêt – *Avenue du Repos de Diane, access by a forest lane* – ☎ *01 39 64 99 19 – closed 17-28 Feb, 8-31 Aug, Thur evening and Mon – 155/190F.* This modern pavilion in the woods has a lovely terrace for summer lunches and several fireplaces for the winter season. The tasty, unpretentious meals are made with fresh ingredients. A pleasant stopping place, away from the madding crowd.

Église St-Martin-de-Groslay – *2km/1.25mi east.* This 12C and 13C church which was altered and enlarged in the Renaissance features a lovely series of stained glass, among which note the **Tree of Jesse** inspired by the one in Beauvais Cathedral.

MONTREUIL ★

Population 2 450
Michelin map 51 fold 12 or 236 fold 12

Montreuil occupies a picturesque **site★** on the edge of the plateau overlooking the Canche Valley. This peaceful town preserves a slightly nostalgic charm in its old streets lined with 17C and 18C houses, its citadel and shaded ramparts commanding vast horizons. Montreuil's proximity to the coast and particularly to Le Touquet attracts numerous tourists in summer.

Royal patronage – Montreuil developed around two buildings: the monastery founded in the 7C by St Saulve, Bishop of Amiens, from which the town derived its name; and the fortress built in about 900 by Helgaud, Count of Ponthieu. From the 11C Montreuil became Crown property.

A "Storm in the Mind"

Montreuil's setting and surroundings have charmed many writers, among them Laurence Sterne (1713-68), the English writer and author of *A Sentimental Journey through France and Italy*, and also **Victor Hugo**. The latter visited Montreuil in 1837 and used the town as the setting for one of the main episodes in *Les Misérables*. The novel tells how the convict Jean Valjean, reformed by a life of generosity and sacrifice, becomes mayor of Montreuil; when, however, an innocent man is to be tried in his place, Valjean is subjected to a terrible moral dilemma, immortalised by Hugo under the heading "Storm in the Mind".

In 1537 Emperor Charles V's of Spain's troops forcibly seized the town, almost completely destroying it in the process. The ramparts were rebuilt by the engineers of François I, Henri IV and Louis XIII; and Montreuil included up to eight churches. In 1804, at the time of the Boulogne Camp, Napoleon stayed in Montreuil and in 1916 Douglas Haig, commander of the British troops, made his headquarters here.

Eating out

MODERATE

Auberge d'Inxent – *62170 Inxent – 9km/5.6mi north of Montreuil by D 127 –* ☎ *03 21 90 71 19 – closed Jan, Tues evening and Wed except in July-Aug – 85/225F.* This pretty 1765 house with its blue and white front, nestled at the heart of the village, has always been an inn. An agreeable stopping place if you are on a tour of the Course Valley. Large, comfortable rooms. The menu proposes specialities from the Artois region. The garden is well worth a visit.

MID-RANGE

Auberge La Grenouillère – *62170 Madelaine-sous-Montreuil – 2.5km/1.6mi west of Montreuil by D 139 then by a minor road –* ☎ *03 21 06 07 22 – closed Jan, Tues and Wed except in July-Aug – 200/400F.* In this charming country tavern the guest of honour is unquestionably the frog, whose presence can be seen everywhere: on walls, on 1930 paintings, on tables as ornaments and... on the menu! The delicious cuisine is served outside in summer. A few rooms are available.

Where to stay

MID-RANGE

Chambre d'Hôte La Haute Chambre – *124 route d'Hucqueliers, in the hamlet of Le Ménage, 62170 Beussent – 10km/6.2mi north of Montreuil by N 1 then D 127 –* ☎ *03 21 90 91 92 – closed 1-15 Sept and 15 Dec-15 Jan –* 🍽 *– 5 rooms 400/450F.* The house is a little difficult to find but you will be well rewarded for your efforts... The superbly restored 1858 manor house is surrounded by a charming park. The comfort of the rooms and the idyllic setting will make this a very special visit.

LUXURY

Château de Montreuil – *Chaussée des Capucins –* ☎ *03 21 81 53 04 – closed 17 Dec-3 Feb, Mon from Oct to Apr except public holidays and Thur lunchtime –* 🅿 *– 14 rooms from 860F –* ⊑ *80F – restaurant 300/400F.* In a luxuriant garden enclosed by walls, this fine residence has considerable charm. The carefully prepared meals have earned it a sound reputation and the large, comfortable and beautifully appointed rooms are each decorated in its own style. The ones in the main building tend to be cosier.

CITADEL AND RAMPARTS *1hr*

★**Citadelle** ☉ – Montreuil citadel was built in the second half of the 16C and was completely remodelled in the 17C by Errard and then by Vauban. Nevertheless, it still incorporates elements of the former castle (11C and 13C).
On the side facing the town, one of Vauban's demilunes protects the entrance. Having crossed this, the tour encompasses:
– the two 13C round towers which flank the royal château;
– Tour Berthe (14C), the tower which was the entrance to the town until 1594.

It is part of a 16C bastion and houses the emblems of the lords killed at Agincourt in 1415.

– the sentry walk, which offers attractive **views**★★ over the Canche Valley: the old charter house of Notre-Dame-des-Près and the opening of the Course Valley *(right)*, the wetlands of the Canche, the estuary and Le Touquet marked by its lighthouse *(left)*.

– the pillboxes built in 1840 and the 18C chapel.

★**Remparts (Ramparts)** – The red-brick and white-stone walls with bastions date largely from the 16C-17C, though some elements of the 13C walls have remained on the west front.

Leave the citadel by the bridge which crosses the ditch and turn right onto the small path which runs alongside the walls; continue for 300m/330yd towards the gate known as Porte de France.

From the sentry walk there is a lovely perspective of the curtain walls with their series of 13C towers incorporated into the 16C walls; one side offers a view over the roofs of Montreuil, the other of the Canche Valley and the plateau of the Montreuil region.

▮ For those with time to spare, it is possible to walk right round the ramparts *(1hr)* along a shaded path offering extensive views over the surrounding countryside.

ADDITIONAL SIGHTS

Chapelle de L'hôtel-Dieu – The chapel was rebuilt in 1874 by a follower of Viollet-le-Duc but retains its Flamboyant 15C doorway.

★**Église St-Saulve** ⊙ – This former Benedictine abbey church dates from the 11C (the north-easterly face of the belfry-porch in particular) but was altered in the 13C and again in the 16C following a fire which led to the collapse of the vaults. These were rebuilt lower than their original height, which accounts for the dim light in the church *(guided tours organised by the tourist office)*.

Inside, the frieze on the capitals to the right of the nave and two large 18C paintings are of particular note: on the main altar, *The Vision of St Dominic* by Jouvenet, and to the left, in the Lady Chapel (the old crossbowmen's chapel), *St Austreberthe taking the Veil* by Restout.

Rue du Clape-en-Bas – This charming cobbled street is lined with low, lime-washed houses with mossy tiled roofs. They are typical in the Canche Valley. Craftsmen work here during the season (weavers, potters etc).

MORET-SUR-LOING★

Population 4 174

Michelin map 106 fold 46 or 237 fold 31

Access from Paris: *SNCF rail link from Gare de Lyon*

Moret is a charming riverside town nestling on the banks of the Loing, at a comfortable distance from the busy motorways.

A fortified town and a royal residence – Situated near the Champagne border, Moret and its fortified castle defended the king's territory from the reign of Louis VII up to Philip the Fair's marriage to Jeanne of Navarre, the daughter of the Comte de Champagne (1284), which put an end to the feud between the two families. Its keep and curtain wall – the two gates still stand – lost their strategic value, and Fontainebleau became the official place of residence for French rulers. These fortifications remained until the mid-19C and the part of town traversed by the River Loing kept its quiet, secluded character.

The history of Moret was marked by a number of famous women, including Jacqueline de Bueil (1588-1651), one of the last loves of Henri IV, who founded the Notre-Dame-des-Anges hospital and convent. Marie Leszczynska was greeted in Moret by Louis XV on 4 September 1725; a commemorative obelisk marks the place where the betrothed met (at the top of the rise along N 5). The following day they were married in Fontainebleau.

SIGHTS

★**The site** – Branch off the road to St-Mammès and proceed towards the Pré de Pin which runs along the east bank of the Loing. Admire the **view** of the lake, the shaded islets, the fishermen, the church and the ancient keep. It provided inspiration for the Impressionist, Alfred Sisley.

Bridge over the Loing – One of the oldest bridges in the Île-de-France, it was probably built around the same time as the town fortifications but was frequently torn down and then widened. On the approach to the Porte de Bourgogne the ramparts and several houses with overhangs – one of which rises out of the Loing waters – come into view.

Eating out

La Palette – *Avenue Jean-Jaurès* – ☎ *01 60 70 50 72 – closed 6-21 Jan, 5-14 Apr, 16 Aug-8 Sept, Tues evening and Wed* – *110/280F*. After strolling along the river banks, settle down in this small restaurant tucked away from the city centre. You will be delighted by the warm, rustic decor featuring a fireplace and visible beams, and by the careful choice and preparation of regional dishes, made with tasty local produce.

Where to stay

Auberge de la Terrasse – *40 rue de la Pêcherie* – ☎ *01 60 70 51 03 – closed 22 Oct-4 Nov, Sun evening and Mon except public holidays – 17 rooms 195/390F – �'s 43F – restaurant 98/214F*. This pretty riverside restaurant has bay windows opening onto the peaceful waters of the Loing. Families are particularly welcome: free accommodation is provided for children under 10 years old and a kid's menu comes free with every two meals. Comfortable rooms with all necessary amenities.

Chambre d'Hôte M. et Mme Gicquel – *46 rue Renée-Montgermont, 77690 Montigny-sur-Loing – 7km/4.3mi southwest of Moret-sur-Loing by D 104* – ☎ *01 64 45 87 92 – ☞ – 3 rooms 230/260F*. As soon as you enter the paved courtyard of these former stables, you will be impressed by the prevailing peace and quiet. The rooms, with sloping ceilings, visible timbering and antique furniture, are quite charming. Breakfast is served in a fine dining hall opening onto the kitchen area.

Église Notre-Dame – The building is reminiscent of many great churches in the Île-de-France.

The **chancel** is believed to have been consecrated in 1166. The original elevation is visible in the apse and on the south side; the main arches resting on round columns are crowned by a gallery opening onto triple arching, surmounted by clerestory windows. The arches and the bays on the north side were walled up to offer greater support to the structurally unsound bell-tower erected in the 15C.

The elevation of the transept with its openwork design, and that of the nave with its tierce-point arches, were undertaken in the 13C and 14C. The Renaissance organ case presents a coffered front with delicate carvings and painted decoration.

Ancien hospice – The corner post at rue de Grez bears an effigy of St James. A few steps along rue de Grez a modern cartouche bears the foundation date of the hospital (1638). The place became famous for the Moret barley sugar sweets made by the nuns. This tradition was continued by the town's confectioners.

Maison de Sisley – **Alfred Sisley** (1839-99), the Impressionist painter of English parentage, spent the latter part of his life in Moret. His studio was at no 19 rue Montmartre *(private)*. He turned his back on a life in commerce to paint, and belonged to the Impressionist group but never achieved fame in his lifetime and was continually beset by financial difficulties. A pure landscape painter, Sisley delighted in the scenery of the Île-de-France and showed feeling for portraying water, light and air.

Rue Grande – At no 24 a commemorative plaque marks the house where Napoleon spent part of the night on his way back from Elba (19 to 20 March 1815).

Maison de François I – *Walk through the town hall porch and into the small courtyard.* Note the extravagant Renaissance decoration of the gallery, and the door crowned by a salamander.

Maison de François I

B. Kaufmann/MICHELIN

263

Porte de Samois – Also known as the Paris Gate. A statue of the Virgin Mary adorns the inner façade. Note the old-fashioned royal milestone that once marked out the highway leading from Lyon to Paris (now N 5).

La Grange Batelière ⊙ – *Take rue du Peintre Sisley east and then a private lane which leads off the towpath, on the right, just before the bridge spanning the Loing Canal.* Built in 1926, this was the residence of Michel Clemenceau (1873-1964), the son of Georges Clemenceau, known as "the Tiger", who personally supervised the finishing touches. Standing on the banks of the Loing, this charming cottage and its thatched roof was built in imitation of the traditional Vendée cottage. The house has been turned into a museum to the memory of the great statesman.

BOAT TRIPS ⊙

Embarcation du Vieux Pont. This is the best way to discover the River Loing as you glide along its still waters.

MORIENVAL★

Population 1 040
Michelin map 56 fold 2, 106 fold 11 (inset) or 237 fold 7

Beautifully set off by the trees and shrubs in the park of the former abbey and the greenery in the surrounding valley, Morienval is one of the earliest Gothic churches in France.

EGLISE NOTRE-DAME

Notre-Dame church depended on a nunnery said to have been founded by King Dagobert in the 7C. Little has changed since the 12C except for the reconstruction of the clerestory in the chancel. The narrow bays visible today date from the last restoration project (1878-1912).

Exterior – The abbey church has a typical silhouette with its three towers, one adjoining the west front and two flanking the chancel; the north tower is marginally shorter and slimmer than the south tower.
The base of the belfry-porch is the earliest part (11C), then the transept, the right bay in the chancel and the two east towers. Originally the belfry-porch stood apart from the Romanesque front and not attached to the extended aisles, an arrangement dating from only the 17C. The church's old porch has been reopened and the restored door reinstated.
Go northwards around the church to the apse; note the ambulatory which was squeezed onto the semicircle of the chancel at the beginning of the 12C, to give it extra strength.

Interior – The extremely narrow ambulatory is the most unusual part of the church. Its arches, dating from about 1125, are some of the oldest in France. Here for the first time ogee arches have been used in the curved part of a building; however, they are an integral part of the areas of vaulting that they support. The transition from groined vaulting to quadripartite vaulting can be seen.

Morienval - Notre-Dame Church

The nave and transept are not so old, having been vaulted in the 17C. The 11C capitals – with their spirals, stars, masks and animals, side by side – are the only certain remains of the Romanesque church.
A large number of memorial stones stand along the wall of the north aisle; one commemorates the great abbess Anne II Foucault (1596-1635). Farther along the same wall, past the northern arm of the transept, is a statue of Our Lady of Morienval (17C).
On the wall of the opposite aisle 19C engravings show the church as it was before the last restoration. In the southern arm of the transept stands a 16C Crucifixion group once mounted on a rood beam, and a large 17C terracotta St Christopher stand on the same side in the nave near the main doorway.

Grottes-refuges de NAOURS★

NAOURS CAVES

Michelin map 52 fold 8 or 236 fold 24 - 13km/8mi north of Amiens

The old village of Naours contains excellent examples of Picardy style cob houses. Below the surface of the plateau near Naours there exists the largest number of refuge-caves dug out of limestone; there are many in Picardy and parts of Artois, known as *creuttes*, *boves* or, in Naours, **muches**. During times of trouble the men of the village would hide there.

The story of the "Muches"

Human occupation of the caves of Naours is said to go back to the 9C and the Norman invasions, although they are mentioned in documents only from the 14C. They were much used during the Wars of Religion and the Thirty Years War. In the 18C salt-smugglers used them to avoid the collectors of the hated salt tax.

Forgotten for a while, they were rediscovered in 1887 by Abbot Danicourt, the local priest, who explored and cleared them with the help of the villagers. In 1905 treasure was found: 20 gold coins from the 15C, 16C and 17C. In 1942 the caves were occupied by the Germans.

Caves ⊙ – The underground passages form a town which could shelter 3 000 people in its 2km/1.25mi of streets and squares, its 300 rooms, three chapels, cattle sheds and stables, bakery with ovens, storerooms etc. Chimneys link the passages to the surface of the plateau, 30m/98ft above.

During the tour the different layers of the soil are revealed: chalk, clay in fissures and pockets, flint in parallel bands. The small **Musée du folklore** is housed in a few of the chambers; local crafts are presented in enormous dioramas.

It is also possible to climb to the top of the ridge, to the two reconstructed wooden Picardy post-mills; there were at one time up to seven windmills in Naours *(bird's-eye view over the town)*.

TIME FOR A BREAK

La Chèvrerie de Canaples – *172 rue de Fieffes, 80670 Canaples – 6km/3.7mi north of Naours by D 60 then D 933 –* ☎ *03 22 52 93 06 – closed Nov-Mar, Sun and public holidays –* ✉ *– booking essential – 40F.* An original way to round off your tour of the caves. This farmhouse can offer "high tea" or a cheese-tasting session (except between noon and 2pm). Ask to see the herds of goats and the shop selling freshly made regional produce.

Colline de NOTRE-DAME-DE-LORETTE★

NOTRE-DAME-DE-LORETTE HILL

Michelin map 51 fold 15 or 236 fold 15 - 11km/7mi south-west of Lens

In a dramatically bleak setting, under an often grey sky, the hill at Notre-Dame-de-Lorette (166m/544ft high) is the culminating point of the Artois hill range. It overlooks the battlefield and was the target of many attacks during the First World War. **General Pétain** had his command post at La Targette, 7km/4.3mi from Notre-Dame-de-Lorette hill, while the 33rd army corps pierced the German lines.

Sombre memories – Notre-Dame-de-Lorette is among many places, including Carency, Ablain St-Nazaire, Souchez (monument to General Barbot and the 1 500 "chasseurs alpins" killed in May 1915), Neuville St-Vaast, Vimy and La Targette (German cemetery) mentioned in dispatches during the First World War, especially during the first battle of Artois from May to September 1915.

Cemetery – A bronze viewing table is located to the left of the entrance. General Barbot's grave is the first on the left side of the main alley. The basilica in a Romanesque-Byzantine style, consecrated in 1937, is decorated with mosaics and marble.

Tour-lanterne ⊙ – The main ossuary with its lantern tower (52m/170ft high) and the seven other ossuaries house the remains of 20 000 unknown soldiers. From the top floor, there is a vast **panorama**★ of the mining basin *(north)*, the Vimy Memorial *(east)*, the ruined church of Ablain St-Nazaire, the towers of Mont-St-Éloi and Arras *(south)*.

Notre-Dame-de-Lorette

Musée vivant 1914-1918 ⊘ – Located 100m/109yd from the basilica, the museum houses many objects (photographs, uniforms, shells, helmets, stereoscopic plates), several reconstructions of underground shelters with laser effects, which recreate the environment of soldiers. Next to the museum, the Champ de bataille extends over an area of 3ha/7.4 acres with its maze of French and German trenches and its mementoes of the First World War (guns, machine-guns, turrets).

Musée de la Targette ⊘ – 7km south-east along D 937. The museum contains over 2 000 exhibits, including ancient weapons, but it is mainly devoted to the two World Wars and recreates fighting in the Artois region with the help of reconstructed scenes.

> **THE "RED CABARET"**
>
> **Ferme-Auberge Le Cabaret Rouge** – 1 rue Carnot, 62153 Souchez – 3km/2mi east of Notre-Dame-de-Lorette by D 58ᵉ then D 937 – ☎ 03 21 45 06 10 – open Sat all day and Sun lunchtime – ✍ – booking essential – 95/120F. Step inside this farmhouse and you will be amazed by the host of trinkets adorning the small yellow dining room. The menu focuses on home-grown vegetables and poultry reared on the premises. Before leaving, ask the owner to tell you the story of the "Cabaret Rouge".

NOYON ★

Population 14 426
Michelin map 56 fold 3 or 236 fold 36

Noyon is an ancient religious town with a rich history; its buildings are overshadowed by its imposing cathedral. It was the homeland of Calvin (1509-64) and the sculptor Sarazin (1592-1660).

The town lies at the heart of a picturesque area, known locally as the "Petite Suisse" (small Switzerland), which is today the main red-fruit producing region in France.

From St Médard to Hugh Capet - Originally Gallo-Roman, Noyon was elevated by St Medard to a bishopric linked to Tournai in 581. A century later, St Eligius was one of its bishops. The town has witnessed the splendour of two coronations, Charlemagne's in 768 as King of the Franks and Hugh Capet's in 987 as King of France. Noyon was one of the first French cities to obtain its own charter, in 1108.

Red-fruit festival – The local industrial activity is varied (smelting, printing works, food products). Agriculture, favoured by the presence of canning factories and storage businesses, is mainly centred on growing red fruit, 90% of the production being destined for the manufacture of sorbets. In July, when the red-fruit festival is on, the square in front of the cathedral is dotted with punnets of mouth-watering strawberries, redcurrants, cherries and blackcurrants. Popular activities include pastry tasting and competitions of fruit-stone throwing.

★★CATHEDRAL *30min*

Four buildings preceded the present cathedral, which was begun with the chancel in 1150 and finished in 1290 with the west front; this remarkable example of the Early Gothic style has a sober, solid Romanesque appearance combined with the breadth and harmony of the great masterpieces of the golden age of cathedral building. It was restored after 1918.

Place du Parvis – Edged with a semicircle of canons' residences, each entrance is surmounted by a representation of a canon's hat. The square has kept its old charm despite the fact that most of these buildings were rebuilt after 1918.

Exterior – The sparse front is preceded by an early-13C porch with three bays; it was reinforced in the 14C with two flying buttresses decorated with small gables. A gallery with tall, slender columns surmounts the great central bay, framed by two bell-towers with prominent corner buttresses. The more austere south tower is also the older; it was built in 1220. The north tower is one of the loveliest types of bell-towers built in northern France in the 14C; it is discreetly decorated with fine mouldings and twists of foliage on the gallery's arcades, and foliate friezes under the upper shoulders of the buttresses. The crowning of the two towers suggests that the original plan included spires which were never built.

The south transept ends in a beautiful semicircle. On the right are the ruins of the Episcopal chapel. The east end is surrounded by gardens; the arrangement of the radiating chapels, the ambulatory and the clerestory produces a lovely effect in spite of 18C additions.

To the north stands the old **chapter library** *(private)*, a fine 16C timbered building. It is known for housing the precious Gospel Book from Morienval which dates from the 9C. One of the library rooms containing blacklisted works was known as "Hell".

The north transept arm, surrounded by the canons' residences, is barely visible.

★★**Interior** – The proportions of the nave and chancel are extremely pleasing. The nave has five double bays. The elevation rises through four storeys: great arches, large and elegant galleries with double arcading which are particularly striking viewed from the transept crossing, shallow triforium and clerestory.

Among the side chapels, the Lady Chapel (Chapelle de Notre-Dame-du-Bon-Secours) in the south aisle contains stellar vaulting with hanging keystones representing sibyls.

The severity of the transept is accentuated by the absence of stained-glass windows. The transept arms, like the **chancel**, are rounded at the end. This feature, found also at the cathedrals of Soissons and Tournai, is thought to be the result of Rhenish influence.

The chancel vault is as high as the nave's. The eight ribs of the apse radiate from a central keystone and develop into a cluster of small columns. Nine chapels open onto the ambulatory.

Among the furnishings, the Louis XVI high altar shaped liked a temple is of particular interest, as are some largely 18C grilles which enclose the chancel and the chapels in the nave. Today only a single gallery remains of the **old cloister** *(north aisle)*; the bays with beautiful radiating tracery overlook the garden. The opposite wall is pierced with wide pointed arch windows and a door giving access to the 13C **chapter-house**. The pointed vaults rest on a series of columns.

Chapter library

B. Kaufmann/MICHELIN

ADDITIONAL SIGHTS

Musée du Noyonnais – This brick and stone Renaissance building (a remnant of the old bishop's palace), with a corner turret and a 17C wing which was rebuilt after the First World War, contains collections on local history. Many objects were discovered during excavations in Noyon and the surrounding area (Cuts, Béhéricourt): 12C chess pieces, a cache of Gallo-Roman coins, funeral objects, ceramics. Upstairs, 12C and 13C oak **chests** from the cathedral are exhibited.

Hôtel de Ville – Despite several alterations the façade of the town hall retains some 16C elements, among them the niches with traceried canopies which used to house statues. The lion-adorned pediment was added in the 17C.

LUNCHTIME

Dame Journe – *2 boulevard Mony* – ☎ *03 44 44 01 33* – *closed 2-7 Jan, 16-31 Aug, Sun, Mon, Tues and Wed evenings* – *115/290F*. The owner of this small restaurant near the town centre serves unpretentious food made with fresh market produce. Cosy dining room with a few tables beneath a veranda. Wide choice of menus.

Musée Jean-Calvin – The museum is installed in a house built in 1927 partly on the foundations, and following old plans, of the house where Calvin was born which was destroyed at the end of the 16C.

An audio-visual display *(10min)* presents Calvin and his time. The great reformer's room has been recreated and contains authentic portraits and engravings, together with a letter written by Calvin.

Among other exhibits are 16C French Bibles, including the famous Olivetan Bible and the Lefèvre d'Étaples Bible, models of a 16C printing works, of the round Paradise temple in Lyon (1564) and the galley ship *La Réale* and writings by Calvin and his contemporaries. The library holds 1 200 books dating from the 16C to the 20C.

Château d'OLHAIN★

Michelin map 51 fold 14 or 236 fold 15
6km/3.5mi south-east of Bruay-la-Buissière

Olhain Castle, set in a romantic lake at the bottom of a vale, is characteristic of fortified castles built in low-lying areas during the Middle Ages. It dates from the 13C-15C and boasts a large bailey from the Middle Ages which has been transformed for agricultural use.

Tour – The castle has retained its medieval structure. A drawbridge gives access to the bailey and from there to a watchtower *(staircase with 100 steps)*, a Gothic room known as the guard-room, cellars with 2-3m/6.5-10ft thick walls, and a chapel. Pleasant stroll along the edge of the moat.

Château d'Olhain

B. Brillion /MICHELIN

Parc départemental de Nature et de loisirs – *1km/0.5mi north on D 57*.
In this nest of greenery at the heart of the mining region, numerous facilities have been established: sports grounds, swimming pool, golf course, tennis, courts, playgrounds, picnic areas, footpaths etc.

Dolmen de Fresnicourt – *3km/2mi on D 57 and a little road to the right (signposted)*.
The "Fairies' Table" is situated on the edge of a small, once-sacred oakwood. It is an impressive sight, even though its capstone has slipped.
The crest of the hill on which the megalith stands, separating Flanders from Artois, provides extensive views.

Vallée de l'OURCQ

OURCQ VALLEY

Michelin map 106 folds 12, 23, 24 or 56 folds 12, 13

After La Ferté-Milon, the River Ourcq follows a winding course, which skirts the beds of hard coarse limestone of the Brie subsoil. Before the creation of the canal to divert its waters, the Ourcq used to flow into the Marne downstream from Mary-sur-Marne. **Canal cruises** along the Ourcq are available in season *(see Practical information)*. The poet Charles Péguy was one of the many French soldiers killed in the Battle of the Marne (1914).

The Canal de l'Ourcq

In 1802 Bonaparte decided to divert the course of the Ourcq by creating a canal-aqueduct to take the waters to La Villette north of Paris. The canal was inaugurated seven years later and permitted navigation between Paris and Claye-Souilly in 1813. By 1821 it had joined up with the canalised river running from Ourcq to Mareuil-sur-Ourcq. Five locks were built and those which already existed on the canalised watercourse were renewed. From 1920 to 1930 the canal was widened between La Villette and Les Pavillons-sous-Bois and a new lock built at Sevran.
The Canal de l'Ourcq supplies the locks of the St-Denis and St-Martin canals in Paris; it also provides water for factories in Paris. Commercial navigation between La Villette and Meaux ceased in 1960: it has been replaced by pleasure boating. The navigable section of the Ourcq is 110km/68mi long and may be divided into three parts. The canalised river (10km/6mi – 4 locks) starts upstream from La Ferté-Milon. The canal (90km/54mi – 6 locks), linking Mareuil-sur-Ourcq to Les Pavillons-sous-Bois, is 1.5m/5ft deep and 11m/37ft wide. Finally, a wide watercourse (no locks) flows into the "Rond-Point des Canaux" in Paris (La Villette).

BATTLE OF THE MARNE

The first Battle of the Marne originated with the Battle of the Ourcq, which in fact took place on the heights of the Multien plateau and not in the valley itself. The outcome of this battle did much to secure the success of the general offensive launched between Nanteuil-le-Haudouin, north of Meaux, and Révigny, north-west of Bar-le-Duc.
It is little known that this battle began – on both sides – with the engagement of large reserve units (55th and 56th French Divisions, 4th German Corps). Owing to the hazards of drafting and the movement of retreat, many of the French soldiers were in fact defending their native territory.

The retreat: 24 August to 4 September 1914 – After the invasion of Belgium (4 August) and the defeat at Charleroi (23 August), the Anglo-French armies suffered heavy enemy pressure and were forced to withdraw.
Joffre, who had been appointed commander-in-chief, ordered his men to withdraw in good order. His troops re-formed and he hoped to be able to launch another attack as soon as possible. On 27 August, the 6th Army led by General Maunoury was created to contain the German advance on the River Aisne. It was also to be used as a striking force against the left flank of the enemy pocket. Unfortunately, the retreat continued and by 1 September the armies had taken up position along a line running west of Beauvais, Verberie, Senlis and Meaux. On the right, it was continued by the 4th British Division led by Sir John French. At this point in the battle, the Germans – who were marching south-west towards Paris – wheeled their right flank south-east. Von Kluck's Army passed Paris. Gallieni, in charge of the Paris garrison and Maunoury's 6th Army, realised the reason for the manoeuvre; Von Kluck wanted to capture the British Army which was withdrawing to Le Grand Morin. After discussing the matter, Gallieni and Joffre decided to

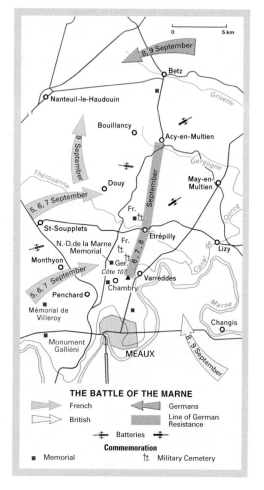

THE BATTLE OF THE MARNE

→ French
← Germans
⇨ British
▨ Line of German Resistance

✈ Batteries ✈

Commemoration

■ Memorial ⛪ Military Cemetery

attack the enemy's flank and crush the powerful right wing of their invaders. The offensive was scheduled for 6 September.

The check: 4 to 8 September – Gallieni and Maunoury's 6th Army prepared for combat on 4 September. The following day, they endeavoured to reach the position between Lizy-sur-Ourcq and May-en-Multien but ran up against the 4th German Corps. Despite their dominant position, the Germans were afraid of being outflanked and that night evacuated the wooded hills of Monthyon and the village of Penchard. Having suffered badly, the two French Divisions and the Moroccan Brigade - incorporating Lieutenant Juin, who was to rise to the rank of Maréchal – were withdrawn in order that they might re-form. Along the Grand Morin line, Sir John French's Army, exhausted by the retreat, swung slowly towards the north.

On 6 September, from his headquarters in Châtillon-sur-Seine, Joffre launched a moving appeal to all his men: "On the eve of the battle on which the future of our Country depends, it is important to remind all that there must be no looking back".

The French and British Armies advanced a further 200km/120mi; it was the start of a general attack. In the 6th Army sector, the French reached the Chambry-Douy-Bouillancy line.

The day of 7 September was marked by the bloody confrontation with the German front line. The toughest fighting took place in the villages of Étrépilly and Acy-en-Multien, the two bastions of the line, in the valleys of the Thérouanne and the Gergogne. A series of violent bayonet charges were delivered by d'Urbal's light infantry and the Zouaves of Colonel Dubujadoux. French's Army repulsed the German rearguard and took up position along the road from La Ferté-sous-Jouarre to Montmirail. On 8 September, the war of movement shifted north of Multien to the sector of Nanteuil-le-Haudouin. The previous night the town had received the 7th Division, dispatched by Gallieni and transported by the famous "Marne taxis". It was there that Maunoury and Von Kluck were desperately hoping for a definitive solution, relying on a strategy of encircling movements.

The victory: 9 to 13 September – Wednesday 9 was a turning-point in the Battle of the Marne. On the left, the French troops facing north in the Nanteuil-le-Haudouin sector suffered an assault of such violence that Maunoury began to fear for Paris. The British Army, however, succeeded in crossing the Marne.

In the centre, the French troops entered Étrépilly and Varreddes which had already been evacuated. Von Kluck's Army withdrew. The German commander-in-chief Von Moltke, astonished by the French recovery and afraid that his front line would not hold – an alarming gap separated Von Kluck's 1st Army from Von Bülow's 2nd Army, checked by Foch near the St-Gond marshes – gave orders for a general withdrawal following a line passing north of Soissons, Reims and Verdun.

This war of movement ended on 13 September. In October, the operations became bogged down and the battle developed into trench warfare.

The French offensive failed to fulfil its objective, ie to crush Von Kluck's Army but it halted the invasion at a critical moment. The official telegram sent by Joffre read: "The Battle of the Marne is an undeniable victory for us".

Eating out

MODERATE

L'Assiette du Marché – *1 place du Marché, 77840 Crouy-sur-Ourcq – 5km/3mi east of May-en-Multien by D 94 – ☎ 01 64 35 67 41 – closed 12 Feb-8 Mar, Thur and evenings except Fri and Sat – ⊡ – 75/105F*. This city residence on the market square houses a small yet delightful restaurant. The tiny dining room with its neat decoration, reminiscent of a tea shop, offers simple cuisine noted for its original flavours salads, daily specials and meat or fish dishes.

MID-RANGE

Auberge de l'Ourcq – *Rue Thury, 60890 Mareuil-sur-Ourcq – ☎ 03 44 87 24 14 – closed 22 Jan-12 Feb, 25 July-11 Aug, Mon and evenings except Fri and Sat – 140/215F*. Treat yourself to Sunday lunch at this country-style family inn in the heart of Mareuil village, where the Ourcq Canal commences its course. Warm welcome, traditional French cooking and reasonable prices.

THE BATTLEFIELD AND THE OURCQ VALLEY

Round tour starting from Meaux

96km/58mi – allow 4hr – local map see below

★**Meaux** – *See MEAUX.*

From Meaux take N 3 (west) towards Paris. After 6.5km/4mi, a memorial paying tribute to Gallieni stands on the left-hand side of the road. Turn right onto D 27, towards Iverny, then right again towards Chauconin-Neufmontiers.

Mémorial de Villeroy – It stands on the site of the early operations of 5 September 1914.

The funeral vault houses the remains of 133 officers and soldiers who died in the fields nearby. **Charles Péguy** (1873-1914) was buried with his comrades-in-arms belonging to the 276th Infantry Regiment (reserve). Their collective grave lies to the right of the vault. The cross celebrating the memory of the writer, philosopher and social reformer has been moved to the intersection of D 27 and D 129.

The 19th Company of the 276th Regiment was called in to relieve the Moroccan Brigade who accompanied them and who were dangerously engaged in battle near Penchard. It launched an attack towards Monthyon, under the fire of the enemy, sheltered in the valley around the Rutel brook. Péguy was the only surviving officer. He told his men to lie down and was inspecting the German positions when he was struck by a bullet.

At the next crossroads, turn left towards Chauconin-Neufmontiers. Drive through Penchard and follow directions to Chambry. Drive through the village.

The bell-tower of Barcy is visible to the left.

Cimetière National de Chambry – Most of the soldiers buried here died during the fighting that took place on 6, 7 and 8 September when they defended the village of Chambry, which was taken, lost and re-taken several times.

Along the road there is a view of the Chambry-Barcy Plateau covered in war graves that seem to mark out the progression of the Allied troops beneath the fire from the lines of German defence.

Located 500m/500yd east of the crossroads, the German military cemetery marks the place where the main German line – which roughly follows the dirt track – crossed the road to Varreddes.

Turn back, towards Barcy.

Monument Notre-Dame-de-la-Marne – This was erected in response to a vow made by Monseigneur Marbeau, Bishop of Meaux, in 1914 and dominates the whole battlefield.

Turn to the north for a good view of the Multien plateau in the far distance.

Proceed towards Puisieux. At the crossroads after the old factory, turn right to Étrépilly. In the centre of the village, 200m/220yd before reaching the church, turn left towards Vincy and Acy-en-Multien.

Étrépilly – The small national cemetery and the memorial evoke the fighting that took place during the night of 7-8 September, reaching a climax near the village graveyard.

Acy-en-Multien – This village nestling in the Gergogne Valley was the scene of intensive warfare on 7 September 1914. The winding alleys, the hillsides planted with small spinneys and the estate walls of the château provided many opportunities for close combat, often ending in tragic death.

Take the left-hand fork out of Acy, to Bas-Bouillancy.

Église de Bouillancy – Located in the lower part of the village. In the quiet valley – rural life is concentrated in the village on the plateau – lies an Early Gothic church (12C-13C) of harmonious proportions. Note the bell-tower flanked by buttresses featuring numerous projections.

Turn back to Acy and take D 18 up to the plateau.

Enjoy the view of **Acy** and the elegant village spire. Beyond Étavigny, the road moves away from the battlefield.

Just before Thury-en-Valois take D 922 to the right.

The road leads to **Mareuil-sur-Ourcq**, marking the start of the canal.

Cross Varinfroy to Crouy-sur-Ourcq.

Crouy-sur-Ourcq – Just after the level crossing, the road skirts the ruins of the **Château Fort de Houssoy**. In order to see the **keep**, which has remained separate, park the car in the station car park and walk to the courtyard gates. From the top of the tower, there is a fine view of the surrounding area.

Crouy Church features a Gothic interior with two 16C aisles. Admire the beautifully crafted panelling (1670) in the chancel. The colours are particularly harmonious. The patron saints of the church are represented above the altarpiece: St Cyricus, who was martyred at the age of 3, and his mother, St Julitta.

Turn back, and after the bridge turn left towards May.

The twisting, hilly road affords extensive **views** of the surrounding landscape.

May-en-Multien – The village is well situated 100m/330ft above the River Ourcq. It is visible from afar on account of its church tower, one of the highest landmarks in the area.

Drive down to Lizy. Do not cross the canal bridge but go up the hill on the north bank along the road to Congis (D 121).

View of the last loop of the Ourcq, overgrown with greenery.

Cross Congis and Varreddes and join D 405, south.

On the left stands the huge **American monument** that pays homage to the Marne combatants. The road dips and leads straight down to Meaux.

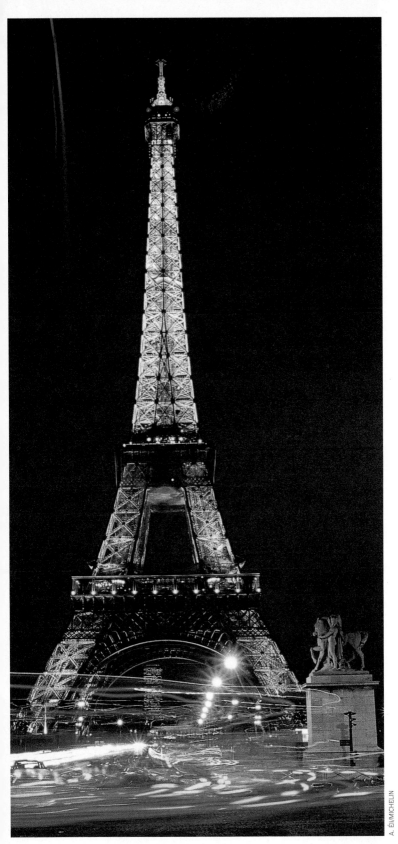

Eiffel tower by night

A. Éll/MICHELIN

PARIS★★★

Population 2 152 333 – Conurbation 9 060 257
Michelin plan 10 (single sheet) or 11 (atlas with street index)

Paris dominates France's intellectual, artistic, scientific and political life, and has done so since the 12C when the Capetian kings made it their capital. It is today a lively, beautiful city with considerable charm, boasting a wealth of attractions. The map and descriptions on the following pages give an outline of the most important sights in Paris, so that the visitor with just a day or two may become acquainted with the capital's landmarks and treasures. Like any city with a rich and varied history, however, Paris needs a little time to get to know; for longer stays in the French capital, consult **The Green Guide Paris**.

SIGHTSEEING

Civil Architecture

★★★**The Louvre** – The original Louvre was a fortress built in 1200 by Philippe Auguste on the banks of the Seine to protect the weakest point in his new city; it was used as treasure-house, arsenal and archive. In the 14C the fortress ceased its military functions with the erection of a new perimeter and Charles V converted it into a residence, installing his famous library in one of the towers. In 1527 François I took up residence in the Louvre. The keep was razed and defences knocked down but it was not until 1546 that a new royal palace was commissioned, on the site of the old keep, which was to become the residence of the kings of France. It was the architect Pierre Lescot who brought the Italian Renaissance style to the banks of the Seine; Jean Goujon added the sculpture. Over the following centuries, almost all the French monarchs added to and altered the evolving Louvre. The Florentine **Catherine de' Medici**, as Regent for Charles IX, ordered Philibert Delorme to build the Tuileries Palace nearby for her while work continued on the Louvre. Charles IX and Henri III both lived in and added to the Louvre, as did Henri IV and Louis XIII who both added pavilions. In 1662 the young King Louis XIV celebrated the birth of the Dauphin with lavish entertainment here.

The monumental, colonnaded façade facing the city was designed by Perrault, aided by Le Brun and Le Vau. It was begun in 1667 but completed only in 1811. Both Napoleon I and Napoleon III continued with additions, alterations and restorations. In 1871 the Communards set the Tuileries Palace and some of the wings of the Louvre ablaze, most of which were subsequently restored or rebuilt. The Tuileries Palace was finally demolished in 1883.

In 1984 President Mitterrand chose the glazed pyramid designed by the American IM Pei as the contemporary entrance to the Louvre Museum.

The **Louvre★★★** ⊙ is one of the largest and most famous museums in the world. It is divided into eight main sections: History of the Louvre and Medieval Louvre; Oriental Antiquities and Arts of Islam; Egyptian Antiquities; Greek, Etruscan and Roman Antiquities; Sculptures; Objets d'art; Paintings; Prints and Drawings. A ninth section, Arts of Africa, Asia, Oceania and the Americas, contains a selection of masterpieces from early civilisations, which will later move to a new museum on quai Branly, scheduled to open in 2004 *(recommended access via the Porte des Lions)*. Among its innumerable treasures are Mesopotamian statues; the Frieze of the Archers from Darius' Palace; the jewellery of Rameses II; the Winged Victory of Samothrace and the Venus de Milo; Michelangelo's *Slaves*; Renaissance master paintings by Giotto, Fra Angelico, Leonardo da Vinci *(Mona Lisa)*, through to Veronese, Caravaggio, Van Dyck, Rubens, Rembrandt, Watteau and many more. There are Classical and Romantic works by the great French painters David, Ingres, Delacroix and Géricault.

The objets d'art include the Crown Jewels of France; Brussels and Gobelins tapestries; fine furniture, clocks etc.

★★★**Hôtel des Invalides** – Guns captured at Vienna in 1805 line the Esplanade leading to the huge building (designed in 1671 to 1676 to house old soldiers invalided out of service) with a front (200m/650ft long) featuring dormer windows in the form of trophies. St Louis' Church within the precinct is the resting place of some of France's great soldiers; it also contains flags captured from the enemy. Berlioz' *Requiem* was first performed here.

The **Église du Dôme★★★** ⊙ was designed by Jules-Hardouin Mansart and begun in 1677; it is one of the great works of the Louis XIV style. The façade giving onto place Vauban has Doric and Corinthian orders, topped with a pediment carved by Coysevox. The soaring, gilded dome stands on a great columned drum supporting a balcony; an elegant lantern rises above.

The church took on its role as military necropolis when Napoleon had Maréchal de Turenne (d 1685) buried here. There is also a memorial to Vauban, the great military architect, and the tomb of Maréchal Foch. In an impressive crypt of green granite stands the unmarked red porphyry mausoleum, which is **Napoleon's Tomb★★★**.

Place de la Concorde

***Arc de Triomphe** ⊘ – The great triumphal arch is one of Paris' main focal points; it stands in place Charles-de-Gaulle - known as the Star (L'Étoile) owing to its 12 radiating avenues. The arch was designed in 1806 as one of the landmarks of Napoleon's imperial capital but was finished only in 1836, in the reign of Louis Philippe.

In 1920 the arch saw the burial of the Unknown Soldier; three years later the flame of remembrance was kindled for the first time. Sculpture on the arch includes Rude's 1836 masterpiece known as *La Marseillaise*, showing the departure of volunteers to fight the invading Prussians (1792).

***Place de la Concorde** – This perfect expression of the Louis XV style was designed by Jacques-Ange Gabriel in 1755 and completed over 20 years. In January 1793 the guillotine was set up here for the execution of Louis XVI and other victims of the Reign of Terror.

The square features colonnaded buildings to the north, massive pedestals, magnificent marble sculptures and the pink granite Luxor Obelisk, 3 300 years old and covered with hieroglyphics, which was brought back from Egypt in 1833.

***Tour Eiffel** ⊘ – The Eiffel Tower is Paris' most famous symbol. The first proposal for a tower was made in 1884; construction was completed in 26 months and the tower opened in March 1889.

In spite of its weight (7 000t) and height (320.75m/1 051ft) and the use of 2.5 million rivets, it is a masterpiece of lightness. The tower actually weighs less than the volume of the air surrounding it and the pressure it exerts on the ground is that of a man sitting on a chair.

*Palais de Justice** – This, the main seat of civil and judicial authority, has been the residence of Roman governors, Merovingian kings and the children of Clovis, Dagobert's mint, Duke Eudes' fortress and the royal palace of the rulers of medieval France. The Capetian kings gave it a chapel and a keep and its 1313 Gothic halls were widely admired. Later, Charles V built the Clock Tower *(Tour de l'Horloge)*, the first public clock in Paris.

The **Conciergerie** ⊘ served as antechamber to the guillotine during the Reign of Terror; it contains the Prisoners' Gallery, Marie-Antoinette's cell and the Girondins Chapel.

Palais-Royal – In 1632 Richelieu commissioned the huge building which became known as the Cardinal's Palace when it was extended in 1639. On his deathbed Richelieu bequeathed it to Louis XIII who renamed it the Palais-Royal. The formal gardens at the rear and the surrounding arcades were laid out in 1783; the adjoining Théâtre-Français was added four years later. The 260 columns in the outer courtyard were designed in 1986 by Daniel Buren.

*École Militaire** – Though lack of funds curtailed the original design, the military academy designed by Jacques-Ange Gabriel is an outstanding example of 18C French architecture.

It was begun in 1752, partly financed by Mme De Pompadour, and completed in 1773; various wings and buildings were added later. True to its original function, it houses the French Army's Staff College. The main front has a projecting central section with Corinthian columns rising through two storeys, crowned with a quadrangular dome and adorned with allegorical figures and military trophies.

The superb **main courtyard**★★ is lined by beautiful porticoes with paired columns.

275

★★Panthéon ⊘ – In 1744 Louis XV made a vow in Metz to replace the half-ruined church of St Genevieve's Abbey: in 1758 Soufflot began building on the highest point of the Left Bank. Despite predictions of collapse, it has stood firm over the years but has undergone extensive alteration. In 1791 it was closed to worshippers and turned into the last resting place of the "great men of the days of French liberty". The building, in the shape of a Greek Cross, is still crowned by Soufflot's dome; the pediment of the Corinthian portico was carved by David d'Angers in 1831. The crypt houses the tombs of the famous.

★★Opéra Garnier ⊘ – The National Academy of Music opened in 1875. The sumptuous interior is embellished with marble and a ceiling by Chagall.

★★Palais de Chaillot – These elegant buildings, constructed for the 1937 World fair, house the prestigious Théâtre national de Chaillot, the Musée de l'Homme (anthropology, ethnography), Musée de la Marine (naval museum) and Musée des Monuments Français. There is a **superb view★★★** over the Seine, the Eiffel Tower and the Champ-de-Mars.

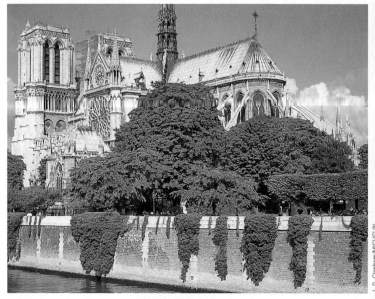

Cathédrale Notre-Dame

Religious Architecture

★★★ **Cathédrale Notre-Dame** – The metropolitan church of Paris is one of the triumphs of French architecture. People have worshipped here for 2 000 years and in many ways Notre-Dame is the cathedral of the nation. Work was begun by Maurice de Sully in 1163 on what turned out to be the last great galleried church and one of the first with flying buttresses.

The chancel was built during the reign of Louis VII and consecrated in 1182 in the reign of Philip Augustus. The double ambulatory and the tracery reinforcing the wide windows set new trends, and the extended spouts of the flying buttresses formed the first gargoyles. By 1210 the first bays of the nave had been built; within 10 years it was completed and the 28 statues of the Kings' Gallery were in place. By 1245 the bulk of the work was complete; St Louis held a ceremony for the knighting of his son and placed the Crown of Thorns here until the Sainte-Chapelle was ready to receive it. In 1250 the twin towers were finished and the nave given side chapels.

In 1430 the young Henry VI of England was crowned King of France in the cathedral; in 1455 a ceremony was conducted to rehabilitate Joan of Arc; in 1558 Mary Stuart was crowned here on becoming Queen of France by her marriage to François II, and in 1572 the Huguenot Henri IV married Marguerite de Valois here; the king converted to the Catholic faith in 1594.

Embedded in the cathedral square is a bronze disk, *kilomètre zéro*, the point from which distances along the main roads radiating from Paris are measured. Emmanuel, the famous bell weighing 13t, hangs in the south tower; its pure tone is said to be due to the gold and silver jewellery thrown by the ladies of Paris into the molten bronze when the bell was recast in the 17C. The great rose-window above the Kings' Gallery still contains medieval glass.

★★★ **Sainte-Chapelle** ⊘ – This masterpiece of High Gothic is strikingly different from Notre-Dame, though built only 80 years later it is lighter, with a greater clarity of structure.

The chapel was built for St Louis to house the recently acquired relics of the Passion; it was completed in a record 33 months. Like other royal chapels it is built on two storeys, the upper one for the monarch, the lower one for the palace staff. The upper chapel resembles a shrine with stained-glass walls; 720 of the 1 134 different scenes are still of original glass, some created by the masters who had worked on the windows at Chartres.

★★ **Église de St-Germain-des-Prés** – With the exception of Clovis, all the Merovingian kings were buried here. The church was subsequently destroyed by the Normans but restored in the 10C and 11C; the west tower has a fortress-like character. Around 1160 the nave was enlarged and the chancel rebuilt in the new Gothic style. From 1631 to 1789 the austere congregation of St Maur made the church a distinguished centre of learning and spirituality. "Improvements" in the 17C were followed in 1822 by an over-zealous restoration.

★★Église de St-Séverin – This Latin Quarter church consists of the portal's lower part and the first three bays of the nave in High Gothic, with the rest largely Flamboyant - note the famous spiral pillar in the ambulatory. In the 18C the pillars in the chancel were clad in wood and marble.

★★Église St-Eustache – St Eustache was once the richest church in Paris, with a layout modelled on Notre-Dame when building began in 1532, however, it took over 100 years to finish. Tastes changed and the Gothic frame was padded out with Renaissance touches such as Corinthian columns and semicircular arches; the chancel windows and Colbert's tomb, designed by Le Brun with Coysevox and Tuby, are Classical.

★★Église Val-de-Grâce – After many childless years, Anne of Austria commissioned François Mansart to design a magnificent church in thanksgiving for the birth of Louis XIV in 1638. The church recalls the Renaissance architecture of Rome; the ornate dome is obviously inspired by St Peter's. Inside, the Baroque spirit prevails: polychrome paving, highly sculptured vaults, massive crossing pillars and a huge canopy with six twisted columns. The **dome★★** has a fresco featuring 200 figures.

Urban Design

Since the sweeping away of much of medieval Paris in the 19C, three central districts have come to typify particular stages in the city's evolution.

★★★Le Marais – This smart shopping and residential area has Renaissance, Louis XIII and Louis XIV architecture. Charles V's move to the Marais district in the 14C led to the incorporation of a suburban area into Paris; the area soon became fashionable and rue St-Antoine the city's finest street. It was here that the characteristic French town house, the *hôtel*, took on its definitive form with the collaboration of architects and artists.

The **Hôtel Lamoignon★** (1584) is a typical example of a mansion in the Henri III style. It was the first time the Colossal order, with flattened pilasters, Corinthian capitals and a sculpted string-course, was seen in Paris. The Henri IV style appeared in the symmetrical **place des Vosges★★★** (completed 1612). The 36 two-storey houses of alternate brick and stone facings have steeply pitched slate roofs pierced with dormer windows.

Louis XIII's reign heralded the Classical style; in 1624 the **Hôtel de Béthune-Sully★** was built, with a gateway flanked by massive pavilions and a main courtyard with triangular and curved pediments and scrolled dormer windows. The early Louis XIV

A. ÉÚ/MICHELIN

Arc du Carrousel

style is seen in Mansart's fine **Hôtel Guénégaud**★★ (1648) with its simple lines, majestic staircase and small formal garden; in the **Hôtel de Beauvais**★ with its curved balcony on brackets; in the **Hôtel Carnavalet**★★ (now the Museum of Parisian History) built in 1655 by Mansart; and in Cottard's theatrical **Hôtel Amelot de Bisseuil**★ with its cornice and curved pediment decorated with allegorical figures. The Louis XIV style is seen in the **Hôtel de Rohan**★★ with its sculpture of the *Horses of Apollo* and the adjoining **Palais Soubise**★★ with its horseshoe-shaped courtyard and double colonnade; both have raised ground floors, massive windows, roof balustrades and sculpture on the projecting central sections.

★★★**La Voie Triomphale (From the Tuileries to the Arc de Triomphe)** – A great road leading from the courtyard of the Louvre to St Germain had been planned by Colbert but today's "Triumphal Way" was laid out under Louis XVI, Napoleon III and during the years of the Third Republic.

★**Arc du Carrousel** – This pastiche of a Roman arch is decorated with statues of Napoleonic military men. An impressive perspective runs from the Louvre through the arch to the obelisk in place de la Concorde, then on to the Arc de Triomphe.

★**Jardin des Tuileries** – The gardens were first laid out in the 1560s by Catherine de' Medici in the Italian style. A century later they were remodelled by Le Nôtre who created the archetypal formal French garden.

★★★**Place de la Concorde** – *See above.*

★★★**Champs-Élysées** – In 1667 Le Nôtre extended the road from the Tuileries to a new focal point, the Rond-Point. The avenue was a service road at the back of smart houses but when refreshment stalls were set up along it crowds began to cluster. In 1724 the Duke of Antin planted rows of elms to extend the "Elysian Fields" up to the Étoile. In 1729 street lanterns lit the evening scene. Finally, in 1836 the **Arc de Triomphe**★★★ *(see above)* was completed. The Champs-Élysées became fashionable during the reign of Louis-Napoleon, when high society flocked to its restaurants.

★★**La Défense** – This modern business centre with skyscrapers and pedestrian terraces descending towards the Seine was planned as an entire project, the individual buildings subordinated to the overall design.
The precincts are overlooked by the enormous cube of the marble-faced Grande Arche (1989) by Danish architect Johan Otto von Spreckelsen, which straddles the view along the Étoile and the Champs-Élysées. The area is also known for its public sculpture: works by Miró, Calder, Takis, Venet, Kowalski etc make it virtually an open-air museum.

THE POLITICAL CAPITAL

Palais de l'Élysée – This has been the Paris residence of the President of France since 1873. It was built in 1718 and was once the property of the Marquise de Pompadour. During the Revolution it housed a public dance hall, a gaming salon and a picture gallery. In Napoleon's time, Marie-Louise had a boudoir here and the young King of Rome, their son, a set of rooms.

Hôtel Matignon – The attractive town house (1721) has been the residence of the French Prime Minister since 1958.

★**Palais Bourbon** – This has been the seat of the Lower House of France's Parliament, the Assemblée Nationale, for over 150 years. The Assembly consists of directly elected members; it examines and where necessary amends all draft legislation.
The palace was built in 1722; during the Revolution it was the seat of the Council of Five Hundred. The decorative treatment of the façade (1804) which overlooks place de la Concorde was chosen by Napoleon.

★★**Palais du Luxembourg** – This is the seat of the Senate, the French Upper House. Its 283 members are elected for a period of 9 years but a staggered system ensures that a third of them face reselection every three years.
After the death of her husband the king, the regent Marie de Medici decided to move from the Louvre; in 1615 she commissioned a palace, something to remind her of the Pitti Palace in Florence, from Salomon de Brosse. The result has an exterior with ringed columns and rusticated stonework; a courtyard with columns, semicircular windows, curved pediments, balconies and roof balustrades; a south front with a quadrangular dome, a massive pediment and garden terraces.

★**Hôtel de Ville** – Central Paris is governed from city hall. Municipal government was introduced in the 13C under the direction of leading members of the powerful watermen's guild appointed by Louis IX. The place has long been the hub of uprising and revolt: during the Revolution it was held by the Commune, in 1848 it was the seat of the Provisional Government. The Republic was proclaimed from here in 1870 and, in March 1871, the Communards burnt it down. It was rebuilt from 1874.

THE INTELLECTUAL AND ARTISTIC CAPITAL

Intellectual Life

The city as a whole functions as the capital of the country's intellectual life, though there is a particular concentration on the Left Bank, in the Fifth and Sixth *arrondissements*. The capital's most venerable institutions stand in the area around Mont Ste-Geneviève, in the **Latin Quarter** (so-called because Latin was the language of instruction right up to the French Revolution).

★★**Institut de France** – The institute originated as the College of Four Nations founded by Mazarin for scholars from the provinces incorporated into France during his ministry (Piedmont, Alsace, Artois and Roussillon). Its building, which dates from 1662, was designed by Le Vau and stands over the river from the Louvre; it is famous for its dome, its semicircular flanking buildings and the tomb of Mazarin in the vestibule. The Institute is made up of five academies:

The **Académie Française**, the most prestigious of all, was founded in 1635 by Richelieu; its membership is limited to 40. The members, "Immortals", devote themselves to upholding the quality of the French language and enshrining it in the *Dictionnaire de la langue française*, the country's standard dictionary.

The **Académie des Beaux-Arts** dates from 1816. It has 50 members who cover painting, sculpture, architecture, engraving and music.

The **Académie des Inscriptions et Belles Lettres** was founded by Colbert in 1663. It deals with literary history and maintains an archive of original documents.

The **Académie des Sciences**, founded by Colbert in 1666, has 66 members working in astronomy, mathematics, medicine and natural sciences.

The **Académie des Sciences morales et politiques** was founded by the Convention in 1795. It has 40 members and is dedicated to philosophy, ethics, law, geography and history.

Collège de France – The college was founded in 1529 by François I under the name of the College of Three Languages (Latin, Greek, Hebrew) in order to combat the narrow scholasticism of the Sorbonne. The present buildings date from the time of Louis XIII, who renamed it the Royal College of France; it underwent major reconstruction in 1778. It was here, in 1948, that Frédéric Joliot-Curie formulated the laws controlling the process of nuclear fission and built a cyclotron to test his theories.

Sorbonne – This is the country's most illustrious university, the successor to the theological college founded in 1253 by Robert de Sorbon for 16 poor scholars. In 1469 France's first printing press was installed here by Louis XI. For many years, the university court constituted the highest ecclesiastical authority beneath the Pope.

The **Sorbonne Church★**, built by Lemercier from 1635, is a fine example of Jesuit architecture. **Richelieu's tomb★** (1694) by Girardon lies inside.

Pont des Arts and Institut de France

ENTERTAINMENT AND CULTURE

Paris remains a thriving cultural centre, with a large number of different shows, exhibitions and events on at any one time.

Entertainment – There are **about 60 theatres** and over **400 cinemas** in the capital. **Music hall**, **variety shows** and **reviews** take place at the Crazy Horse, the Folies Bergères, the Moulin Rouge... There are numerous **concert halls**, some with resident orchestras, as well as the Opera and the Comic Opera. There are also nightclubs, jazzclubs, cabarets, café theatres, circuses, concerts, recitals in churches etc. *The Green Guide Paris lists a selection of places to go for entertainment, as well as hotels and restaurants.*

Exhibitions – Paris boasts about 100 museums and 120 art galleries, plus about another 30 places for temporary shows. Museums include the world-famous Louvre, the **Musée d'Orsay★★★** ⊘ (1848-1914 art), the Centre Pompidou, the **Musée de Cluny ★★** ⊘ (Museum of the Middle Ages), the **Musée Rodin★★** ⊘ the Military Museum at the Invalides and the fascinating **Cité des Sciences et de l'Industrie★★★** ⊘ at La Villette.

Tourist Paris – Certain parts of the city have come to be identified in the visitor's mind with the very essence of Paris itself.

★★★**Montmartre** – The "Martyrs' Mound" became the haunt of artists and Bohemians in the late 19C; its steep and narrow lanes and precipitous stairways still evoke the picturesque village it once was. The mound rises abruptly above the city's roofs and at its centre is **place du Tertre★★** with its "art market".
The exotic outline of the **Sacré-Cœur Basilica★★**, a place of perpetual pilgrimage, rises nearby. The basilica offers an incomparable **panorama★★★** over the whole city.

★★★**Champs-Élysées** – *See above.*

★★★**Tour Eiffel** – *See above.*

★★★**Louvre** – *See above.*

★★**La Défense** – *See above.*

★★★**Notre-Dame** – See above.

★★★**Le Marais** – *See above.*

★★★**Centre Georges-Pompidou** ⊘ – The old Beaubourg district has been transformed by the construction of this cultural centre with its library, exhibitions and **Musée national d'art moderne** ⊘.

★★**Palais de Chaillot** – *See above.*

PÉRONNE

Population 8 497
Michelin map 53 fold 13 or 236 fold 26

At the confluence of the River Cologne and the Somme stands the old fortified town of Péronne, stretching between fish-filled lakes and "**hardines**", marshland vegetable gardens similar to the *hortillonages* of Amiens. This is an eel centre, which is reflected in the local gastronomy: eel pâté, smoked eels. Colvert is the local beer. The commercial port, on the north canal, is flanked by a marina.

The Meeting in Péronne – In 1468, a meeting was attended by **Charles the Bold** and **Louis XI**, who both wanted Picardy as part of their territory. Louis was a sly, wily man who had supported the uprising of the town of Liège against Charles; as a result he had been shut away in Péronne by his rival. Before he could recover his freedom, the King of France was forced to sign a humiliating treaty that went against the grain and his interests since it obliged him to take up arms against the people of Liège. He was to remember the insult in future years and tradition has it that his bitterness was kept alive by a parrot which kept repeating, "Péronne! Péronne!".

Miseries of War – In 1536 the town suffered a violent assault by the troops of Charles V of Spain; one heroic woman, however, saved the day: **Marie Fouré** managed to galvanise resistance and the assailants were forced to lift their siege. Each July a procession through the town and a fête commemorate the occasion.
In 1870 Péronne was besieged by the Prussians who bombarded the town for 13 days. During the Battle of the Somme in 1916 Péronne was occupied by the Germans. That year and the next saw the destruction of virtually the entire town.

SIGHTS

★**Historial de la Grande Guerre** ⊘ – The unusual and innovative Museum of the Great War is housed in a modern building standing on piles behind the 13C castle, on the banks of the Étang du Cam. Access to the museum is through an opening carved into the wall of the castle. Louis XI was held prisoner by Charles the Bold in one of the towers here.
The museum presents an insight into European society on the eve of the First World War and throughout hostilities.

Eating out

MODERATE

Hostellerie des Remparts – *23 rue Beaubois, 80200 Péronne* – ☎ *03 22 84 01 22 – 95/350F.* A large house with a colourful front bursting with geraniums, right by the ramparts. In the dining rooms appointed with regional furniture, we recommend that you choose the traditional bill of fare relying heavily on local produce, far more affordable than the à la carte formula.

Where to stay

MID-RANGE

Le Prieuré – *80360 Rancourt – 10km/6.2mi north of Péronne by N 17* – ☎ *03 22 85 04 43 – closed Sun evening –* ⊓ *– 25 rooms 295/335F –* ⊡ *42F – restaurant 78/260F.* This striking white house just off the main road stands out because of its recent architecture. A combination of brick and stonework serves as a setting for the drawing rooms, the bar and the dining room, enhanced by a set of Louis XVI chairs. The modern rooms are decorated with soft hues.

Maps, some of them illuminated, illustrate at regular intervals the development of various fronts. A large collection of objects, works of art, documents, letters and postcards reveal the thoughts and the pattern of daily life for those caught up in the conflict.

In shallow white-marble excavations representing the trenches are uniforms, arms and personal effects.

Clips from archive films are shown on videos dotted around the museum; a film by a British soldier shows the Battle of the Somme.

Hôtel de Ville – *Place du Cdt-Daudré.*

The town hall has a Renaissance façade flanked by turrets towards the square, and a Louis XVI front towards rue St-Sauveur.

Inside, the **Musée Danicourt** ⊘ contains a precious collection of ancient coins and Greco-Roman and Merovingian jewellery.

Porte de Bretagne – *Off rue St-Sauveur.*

This gateway dates from 1602 and was one of two entrances giving access through the town walls, which were destroyed before the First World War. It is now a free-standing brick pavilion with a slate roof, and is adorned with the emblem of Péronne. The wooden gates have been retained.

Beyond the moat, walk through the gate of the demilune and follow the old brick **ramparts** with stone courses (16C-17C) for an attractive view over the lakes and the "*hardines*".

EXCURSION

Athies – *10 km/6mi south along D 44, then D 937 towards Ham.*

Emperor Clovis' son, Clothar I, King of the Franks, had a palace here in which his future wife, Radegonde, was brought up. She later retired to Poitiers where she founded a convent and was canonised.

The church has a beautiful 13C portal with carved tympanum representing the Nativity and the Flight into Egypt.

Historial de la Grande Guerre, Péronne/D. Cry

Miniature aeroplane made from shrapnel and bullets

Château de PIERREFONDS★★

Michelin map 106 fold 11 (inset) or 237 fold 8 - Local map see Forêt de COMPIÈGNE

This famous castle, rising above a pretty town which, in its heyday, was a fashionable spa resort, has, since 1924, been the setting of many films. A small lake adds to the romantic image.

Louis of Orléans' Castle – A castle has stood on this site since the 12C. The Valois earldom – which was elevated to a duchy when Charles VI gave it to his brother, Louis of Orléans – consisted of the castellany of Pierrefonds together with Béthisy, Crépy and La Ferté Milon.

Louis of Orléans assumed the regency during the king's madness but was assassinated in 1407 by his cousin John the Fearless, Duke of Burgundy. Before his death he constructed a chain of fortresses on his Valois lands, of which Pierrefonds was the linchpin; to the south, barely 11km/7mi apart, stand the castles of Verberie, Béthisy, Crépy, Vez, Villers-Cotterêts and La Ferté-Milon forming a barrier from the River Oise to the Ourcq.

The Prince also had the medieval castle completely rebuilt by the King's architect, Jean le Noir, and Pierrefonds triumphantly withstood sieges by the English, the Burgundians and the royal troops. In the 16C the castle passed to Antoine d'Estrées, Marquess of Cœuvres and father of the beautiful Gabrielle. On the death of Henri IV the Marquess took sides with the Prince of Condé against the young Louis XIII; besieged once again by the royal forces, the castle was finally seized and dismantled.

Viollet-le-Duc's Castle – In 1813 Napoleon I bought the castle ruins for a little under 3 000 francs. Napoleon III, an enthusiastic archeologist and since his days in the army passionate about the art of siege warfare entrusted its restoration in 1857 to **Viollet-le-Duc**. It was only a matter of returning parts of it (the keep and annexes) to an inhabitable condition, leaving the curtain walls and towers as "picturesque ruins". At the end of 1861, however, the programme of works took on an altogether different, larger dimension; Pierrefonds was to be transformed into an Imperial residence. Work lasted until 1884 and cost 5 million francs, 4 million of which was deducted from the Emperor's civil list.

Fascinated by medieval life and Gothic architecture in particular, Viollet-le-Duc set about a complete reconstruction of the castle, following the basic shapes that were already outlined by the numerous walls and fragments remaining at the time.

Aiming at all times to "adapt the medieval architecture to modern needs" the architect nevertheless did not hesitate to invent parts of the building – encountering severe criticism from specialists in military architecture and purists when he did – and to give free rein to his ideas for the painted and carved decoration.

TOUR ⊙

Leave the car in place de l'Hôtel-de-Ville and approach the main entrance to the castle at the foot of the Arthus Tower. Walk round the castle along the route Charretière.

Eating out

MODERATE

Blés d'Or – *8 rue J.-Michelet* – ☎ *03 44 42 85 91* – *closed Jan and Wed* – *98/220F.* Situated half-way between the château and the lake, this inn is perfect for a friendly break. In summer, the terrace affords nice views of the château. There is an interesting selection of traditional French specialities. A few rooms are available upstairs.

Where to stay

MODERATE

Camping La Croix du Vieux Pont – *02290 Ressons-le-Long* – *19km/12mi north-east of Pierrefonds by D 335, D 81 then D 91* – ☎ *03 23 55 50 02* – ✉ – *booking recommended July-Aug* – *370 plots 110F* – *eating facilities.* With both a lake and a river, this is anglers' paradise! The well-designed camp site organises other activities such as pony rides for children, trips in pedal-boats or swimming in one of the pools...

MID-RANGE

Chambre d'Hôte Domaine du Bois d'Aucourt – *1.6km/1mi west of Pierrefonds by D 85* – ☎ *03 44 42 80 34* – *5 rooms 380/600F.* Each of the rooms in this 19C mansion is decorated around a particular theme: Scotland, Tuscany, Sevilla, Zen, the Tropics... Make your choice and enjoy the peace and quiet that prevail on this family estate in the heart of Compiègne Forest.

Château de Pierrefonds

Exterior – The quadrangular castle (103m/337ft long, 88m/288ft wide) has a large defensive tower at each corner and in the middle of the walls. On three sides it overlooks the village, almost vertically; to the south a deep moat separates the castle from the plateau.

The walls have two sentry walks, one above the other: the covered lower one is dressed with machicolations; the upper one only has merlons. The towers (38m/124ft high with 5-6m/16-20ft thick walls) are crowned with two storeys of defences; from the cart track *(route charretière)* they are a formidable sight. Eight statues of named military heroes *(preux)* adorn them, indicating the building's political significance: Arthus, Alexander, Godefroy, Joshua, Hector, Judas Maccabaeus, Charlemagne and Caesar.

On the chapel roof stands a copper statue of St Michael.

Having walked along the esplanade, cross the first moat to the forecourt known as Les Grandes Lices. A double drawbridge (**1**) – one lane for pedestrians, the other for vehicles – leads to the castle doorway which opens into the main courtyard.

Interior – A permanent exhibition in the barracks celebrates Viollet-le-Duc and his work (engravings, paintings, photographs of the ruins, history of the castle etc). Another exhibition, devoted to the **Monduit workshops**, displays a collection of works of art in lead, including the lion weathervane of the Arras belfry, the Cupid of Amiens Cathedral and some of the gargoyles decorating Notre-Dame Cathedral in Paris. The

exhibits are authentic since they were made in the Monduit workshops at the same time as the commissioned items. They were used to illustrate the workshops' skills on the occasion of world exhibitions.

The main front appears with its basket-handled arcading forming a covered shelter, surmounted by a gallery. Neither of these existed in the original castle, but were created by Viollet-le-Duc, freely inspired by the courtyard at the Château de Blois. The equestrian statue of Louis of Orléans (**2**) by Frémiet (1868) stands before the monumen-

CHÂTEAU
DE PIERREFONDS
1st FLOOR

tal stairway. The inside of the chapel, heightened by Viollet-le-Duc, presents a bold elevation with a vaulted gallery above the apse, which was another of the architect's inventions.

The doorway pier incorporates a figure of St James the Great with Viollet-le-Duc's features.

The keep, where the lord had his living quarters, stands between the chapel and the entrance. Viollet-le-Duc accentuated its residential function by giving it an elegant open stairway. It is flanked by three towers. The two on the outside are round whereas the one on the inside is square.

The provisions courtyard between the keep and the chapel communicates with the main courtyard by means of a postern gate and with the outside world by another postern, 10m/30ft above the foot of the castle walls. To introduce food and other supplies into the fortress, a steeply inclined wooden ramp was lowered; provisions were then dragged up.

Keep (Logis au donjon) – Reaching the first floor of the keep, the tour leads through the Imperial couple's rooms: the **salle des Blasons** or Grande Salle (**3**) with woodwork and a few, rare pieces of furniture designed by Viollet-le-Duc. Among the symbolic decorative motifs, notice the Napoleonic eagle, the thistle (Empress Eugénie's emblem) and on the chimney-piece the heraldic arms of Louis of Orléans (the "broken" arms of France) and another family emblem, a knotted staff. Beyond the Chambre de l'Empereur (**4**) – which enjoys a view down over the fortified entrance - the tour leads to the Salle des Preuses, leaving the keep.

Salle des "Preuses" – This timber-ceilinged hall (52_9m/170_29ft) was created by Viollet-le-Duc. The roof is shaped like an upturned ship. The mantelpiece of the double fireplace (**5**) is decorated with statues of nine women, heroines from tales of chivalry. The central figure of Semiramis, Queen of Assyria and legendarily of captivating beauty, has the features of the Empress whereas the others are portraits of ladies of the court.

Tour d'Alexandre et chemin de ronde Nord (Sentry walk) – The original walls on this side of the ruins still stand 22m/72ft high; note the different colour of the stones. Along the sentry walk Viollet-le-Duc highlighted the last step forward in defence systems before the arrival of the cannon: level walkways without steps or narrow doorways, which allowed the defenders (housed in nearby barracks) to muster quickly at critical points without blundering into obstacles. The view extends over Pierrefonds Valley.

Salle des Gardes ou des Mercenaires – A double spiral staircase (**6**) leads down to this guard-room which now houses beautiful lapidary fragments; remains of the original 15C statues of the heroic figures on each tower. The tour ends at the model of the castle.

Return to the town by the direct staircase (towards the car park).

POISSY

Population 36 745

Michelin map 101 folds 11, 12, 106 fold 17 or 237 folds 16, 17

Access from Paris: *RER line A 5 or SNCF rail link from Gare St-Lazare.*

The town of Poissy, situated on the banks of the Seine, was a royal residence as early as the 5C. St Louis was christened here in 1214; the king's private correspondence was even signed Louis de Poissy. The castle used to stand on place Meissonnier but it was demolished by Charles V.

Up to the middle of the last century, Poissy was the main Paris cattle market. Today, it is the site of a large automobile plant (Peugeot).

The Poissy Symposium

An Augustinian convent founded in the 11C was given to the Dominican order by Philip the Fair. From 9 September to 13 October 1561 the abbey refectory hosted the Poissy Symposium; Catholics and Protestants were invited to discuss their differences at the instigation of Chancellor Michel de l'Hôpital. The debate was attended by the papal legate, 16 cardinals, 40 bishops and the general of the Jesuit order on the one side, and by an important group of theologians led by Theodore Beza on the other. The symposium lasted 17 days, but these high-level talks proved vain for the divide between the two parties was even greater after the conference.

J.-L. Bohin/EXPLORER

16C Entombment, Collégiale Notre-Dame

SIGHTS

★**Collégiale Notre-Dame** ⊘ – The greater part of the collegiate church is Romanesque, dating from the 11C and 12C. Several chapels were added in the 15C and the whole church was restored by Viollet-le-Duc. The front tower, built in the Romanesque style, once served as a belfry-porch. The square base of the tower develops to an octagonal section on the highest level, ending in a stone spire. The central tower, also Romanesque, is eight-sided through two floors, and ends in a timberwork spire.

Interior – The vaulting of the nave now features ribbing. The capitals of the south columns in the first two bays were recarved in the 17C. The other capitals feature interlacing, monsters and foliage motifs. Some of them are thought to be older than this building and were probably taken from another church. The nave is very well lit owing to the installation of a triforium by Viollet-le-Duc in the three bays nearest to the chancel, which is circled by an ambulatory with groined vaulting. The side chapels – added in the 15C – pay homage to the various trade guilds: butchers, fishermen etc.

The first chapel to the right of the doorway contains fragments of the font used for St Louis' christening. For many centuries, the faithful would scrape the stone sides, dissolve the dust in a glass of water and drink the potion as a remedy for high fever. This explains why the font is in such bad condition.

The central Lady Chapel is the work of Viollet-le-Duc. The statue of the Virgin and Child is attributed to the Duchess of Uzès (c 1890).

The most impressive furnishings are in the first chapel on the right: majestic 15C statues of John the Baptist and St Barbara, and a superb 16C Entombment *(see below)* portraying Mary, John, Mary Magdalene, the Holy Women, Nicodemus and Joseph of Arimathea.

Musée d'Art et d'Histoire ⊘ – *12 rue St-Louis.*

The history of Poissy from Merovingian times (sarcophagi) up to the present day (automobile industry) is presented in a simple, pleasing manner. One of the glass cabinets displays numerous seals, some of which date back to the 12C, other exhibits include a painting by Meissonnier depicting summer bathing in the Seine, a splendid 16C painted wooden statue taken from the Church of Our Lady etc.

Musée du Jouet ⊘ – The toy museum is housed in the building flanked by two towers that used to mark the fortified entrance to the abbey. This was once a **Priory** dedicated to **St Louis** and it was here that a famous meeting was held in 1561. The toys and games exhibited in the museum date back to the days before the introduction of television. There is a large number of dolls showing the changes in production from porcelain and biscuit (Jumeau, 19C) to the celluloid used by French and German manufacturers in the 1930s. On the first floor, there is a display case full of clockwork toys, another filled with teddy bears and yet another with lead and paper soldiers dating from the 19C. On the top floor are collections of cars and trains, some clockwork, others powered by steam. An electric train track dating from the 1930's operates automatically as visitors approach.

The winding street in the old enclosure leads to Parc Meissonnier.

Eating out

MID-RANGE

Le Bon Vivant – *30 avenue Émile-Zola –* ☎ *01 39 65 02 14 – closed Aug, Feb school holidays, Sun evening and Mon – 200F.* This turn-of-the-century open-air café set up along an arm of the River Seine is the perfect destination for a country outing. Traditional French cuisine is served in two rooms, one of which boasts hunting trophies for the owner is a dedicated hunter. Pretty terrace in summer.

Where to stay

MID-RANGE

Les Romanciers – *Quai de Seine, 78670 Médan - 6km/3.7mi west of Poissy by D 153 then D 164 –* ☎ *01 39 75 82 22 – closed 27 Dec-15 Jan and Sun evening –* 🅿 *– 10 rooms 260/390F –* 🍽 *40F - restaurant 149/179F.* Situated opposite Medan-Villennes beach and close to Émile Zola's house, this hotel is a pleasant stopping place midway between land and sea... The large, well-appointed rooms all look onto the river and meals are served at the water's edge in high season.

Parc Meissonnier – The grounds once belonged to the Saint-Louis royal monastery and were already popular during the Middle Ages. Today, the 10ha/25-acre English-style park sloping towards the River Seine features a lake and a rich variety of tree species.

★**Villa Savoye** ⊙ – *82 rue de Villiers.*
This masterpiece of modern architecture was designed in 1929 by **Le Corbusier** and Pierre Jeanneret for the industrialist Savoye. The use of cylindrical piles made it possible to do away with load-bearing walls and introduce huge glass surfaces. The main rooms are located on the first floor, at a height of 3.5m/12ft. They are arranged around a large terrace which opens onto the countryside, as does the solarium occupying the top level of the house. The Villa Savoye features a ramp leading to the upper levels and a spiral staircase with vertical lines deliberately brought in to counter the horizontal configuration of the villa.
Nouveau texte

Centre de production Peugeot ⊙ – The Talbot trade mark has a long-standing, partly British tradition since it evolved from the association of the French industrialist Adolphe Clément with Lord Talbot, Earl of Shrewsbury. The French concern within the group was bought back in 1934; SIMCA was founded the same year. After the war, small car manufacturers were taken over by larger ones and, although Talbot-Iago won the 24 hours competition at Le Mans in 1950, it was taken over by the second largest French manufacturer in 1958. In 1960, SIMCA was split into two concerns controlled by Chrysler and Fiat. In 1978, Peugeot bought Chrysler's European subsidiaries, including Talbot. Just like the Renault factory in Flins, the Peugeot-Talbot factory in Poissy has contributed to shape the Seine Valley. Today, this ultra-modern car plant has a large number of industrial robots. It produces more than 1 200 cars every day.

Musée Caapy ⊙ – The museum contains some 45 veteran and vintage cars.

Abbaye de PORT-ROYAL-DES-CHAMPS★

Michelin map 101 fold 21, 106 fold 29 or 237 fold 16

Little remains of this famous abbey, which was the scene of a serious religious dispute for more than 100 years of French history.

An abbess aged eleven – In 1204 a Cistercian convent was founded in Porrois, a town later known as Port-Royal. Although this order was supposed to be strict, the rules grew extremely lax over a period of five centuries and by the turn of the 17C, the 10 nuns and six novices who resided at the abbey were leading a most unsaintly life; the cloister had become a promenade, fasting was a bygone practice and the vows of poverty were hardly compatible with the entertaining carried out at the abbey, including Carnival celebrations. In 1602 **Angélique Arnauld**, the 11-year-old daughter of an influential family of lawyers was passed off as 17 and appointed Abbess of Port-Royal.

A reformer without mercy – Recovering from a bout of ill health, Mother Angélique realised where her duty lay and set about reforming her nunnery. She reinstated the enclosure and would not receive her mother, nor her father, except in the parlour, despite their repeated supplications and threats (1609). She introduced the perpetual adoration of the Blessed Sacrament, and imposed observance of the Cistercian rule, meditation and manual labour. The abbey was transformed and greeted an increasing number of novices.

Mother Angélique chose Jean Duvergier de Hauranne, better known as the Abbot of St-Cyran, and Antoine Singlin to be the directors of Port-Royal-des-Champs. Like Angélique's parents and close relatives, many of whom were Calvinists, these austere confessors aspired to draw man away from earthly pleasures, make him see how corrupt he was and persuade him that divine grace alone could save him.

In 1618, the Cistercian order sent Mother Angélique to Maubuisson where she was to reform the abbey. While she was absent, one of her younger sisters, Mother Agnès, headed the Port-Royal community.

Angélique Arnauld by Philippe de Champaigne
(Musée de Versailles)

By 1625 when Mother Angélique returned to her abbey it became necessary to find new premises; the conventual buildings were too cramped and the surrounding marshes were ruining the nuns' health. The community moved to the capital, where it occupied new buildings and was renamed Port-Royal-de-Paris (now a maternity clinic).

The "Messieurs" of Port-Royal – One of Angélique's brothers was a theologian with great influence over his friends and relations, all of whom shared the pessimistic views propounded by the Abbot of St-Cyran. These men - known as the Solitaires or the Messieurs de Port-Royal - decided to withdraw from society in order to take up prayer and meditation. In 1637 they left Port-Royal-de-Paris and moved to Port-Royal-des-Champs, which had remained empty. There they applied themselves to the renovation of the abbey: they drained the land, raised the ground and enlarged the buildings. The following year, the Abbot of St-Cyran was incarcerated on the orders of Cardinal Richelieu, whom he had refused to serve. He died in 1643. Mother Angélique returned to Port-Royal-des-Champs in 1648 and from then on she and her flourishing community spent their time between this abbey and the one in Paris. The Solitaires were lodged in Les Granges perched on top of a hill overlooking the old town of Porrois. Influenced by St Cyran and haunted by the importance of early education, they set up the "Petites Ecoles" in the hope of achieving salvation. Here they provided an education that was widely acclaimed for its excellence and effectiveness. The "gentlemen of Port-Royal" included some of the greatest minds of the day, among them the Great Arnauld, Arnauld d'Andilly, their relatives the Lemaistres (including Lemaistre de Sacy who translated the Bible), Lancelot the Greek scholar, Nicole the philosopher and Hamon.

The Jansenist Movement – The growing influence that Port-Royal exerted over people at court and in Parliament, as well as over the younger generation, was resented by the Jesuits. They were especially indignant because Port-Royal published the works of Cornelius Jansen, the former Bishop of Ypres, who had been entrusted by Louvain University with the task of refuting the doctrine advocated by the Jesuit Luis de Molina. Molina maintained that man could attain self-improvement through his own will-power, overcome all the problems in this world if he genuinely wished to do so and expect God to come to his assistance in any circumstances, simply on account of his merits; quite the opposite of the Solitaires' belief.

Cornelius Jansen died in 1638, soon after having completed his treatise *Augustinus*, unaware of the dramatic developments that were to follow its publication.

Problems of conscience – The theologians connected with Port-Royal approved of *Augustinus* because it confirmed their views, many of which were close to the Calvinist theory. They circulated it in France. The Jesuits retaliated by accusing the Jansenists of holding heretical views and produced a text of heretical "quotes" by Jansen. The Church eventually took action with the result that, from 1653, nuns and priests were required to sign a document condemning these quotations taken out of context; the nuns at Port-Royal agreed that they could not sign the document without making a few reservations since the incriminating quote did not appear in the same form in Jansen's work. They nevertheless agreed that the actual quotes were heretical.

Abbaye de PORT-ROYAL-DES-CHAMPS

The theological war raged on. In 1656 the celebrated mathematician and religious philosopher **Blaise Pascal**, who was in retreat near Port-Royal-des-Champs, published a series of pamphlets – the **Provinciales** – which attacked Jesuit theory and staunchly defended the cause at Port-Royal.

From 1661 Jansenists were again persecuted (the Pope's death in 1655 had produced a brief lull) and in that year Mother Angélique died after a long illness during which each week brought new torment. For some 10 years from 1669 onwards, with new publications and religious studies, the Jansenist question seemed to fade into oblivion.

In 1679 Louis XIV decided to settle the whole affair once and for all; the noviciate was forbidden, the Solitaires were dispersed and some went into exile. The nuns at Port-Royal-de-Paris disowned their counterparts at Port-Royal-des-Champs, who were the object of continual persecution. By 1705 they numbered only 25, the youngest being 60 years old. On 20 October 1709 the remaining nuns were expelled by 300 musketeers. The mortal remains of Jean Racine, who had been buried in the northern cemetery, were moved to St-Étienne-du-Mont, in Paris, and he now rests beside Blaise Pascal.

In 1710 the monastery buildings were razed to the ground. The graveyard was desecrated and the bones of the nuns thrown into a communal grave in the cemetery of St-Lambert. The religious objects and furnishings went to a number of neighbouring parishes. The tombstone slabs which once paved the church at Magny-les-Hameaux have now been reassembled.

The Jansenist doctrine continued to arouse controversy during Louis XV's reign. The Parlement de Paris refused to ratify royal edicts and ordinances, and priests refused to distribute the Blessed Sacraments. Clandestine publications began to circulate. Jansenism became a religious sect and it was only after the Revolution that its influence over French society started to decline.

RUINS AND MUSEUMS *2hr*

The tour of Port-Royal estate comprises two parts. The pilgrimage to the abbey ruins is enhanced by a visit to the park (Porte de Longueville, canal, view of the ruins). The Little Schools building is situated on a plateau, surrounded by pleasant, shaded grounds. It now houses a national museum, containing a wide range of documents on the former teaching colleges. The farmhouse where the Solitaires used to stay is a farming concern (*closed to the public*).

Ruins and Abbey Museum ⊙ – The shaded path leading to the abbey branches off the Dampierre-Versailles road. *Park in the car park.*

The guided tour begins in a square area defined by avenues of lime trees, which was the site of the former cloister. The graveyard where the Cistercian nuns were buried after 1204 has been planted with grass. The church adjoined the cloister. Because the Solitaires had raised the floor level in an attempt to ward off the dampness, the building was razed down to the paving. When the original level was restored, the work uncovered the base of the pillars and the walls of the first building.

An oratory built in 1891 stands on the site of the chancel.

Next to the dovecote, a 17C barn houses a collection of paintings, engravings and memorabilia which illustrate and enliven the tour of the estate.

Les Granges, where the Solitaires lodged, lies above the valley on the north side screened by trees. Ascending and descending the steep slope daily to attend Mass in the abbey must have required great effort; it is said that the Hundred Steps were designed by the Messieurs themselves. The Hundred Steps are no longer open to the public.

Musée National des Granges de Port-Royal ⊙ – The building was specially designed for the Little Schools (established by the Messieurs to provide religious education) in 1651-52 and presents a suitably austere front. In the 19C a Louis XIII-style wing was added.

Most of the rooms have been restored to their former condition and contain books, engravings and drawings on the history of the abbey and the Jansenist movement, the Solitaires and the Little Schools. Other exhibits include a series of portraits by Philippe de Champaigne depicting the principal Jansenist leaders. Note the touchingly naive collection of 15 gouache paintings portraying the life of the Cistercian nuns.

Jean Racine lived at Port-Royal between the ages of 16 and 19, with a break at college in Paris. He was taught Greek and Latin and French versification, and was lectured on diction and rhetoric. The French poet learned much from his tutors and he soon became an outstanding reader. Louis XIV was spellbound by his beautiful voice and Racine's advice was sought by many an actor. The good Dr Hamon, of whom he was very fond, often used to take Racine with him when he went to treat poor patients, knitting clothes for them as he trotted along on an old donkey. Although the Jansenists were sceptical about the Arts, they accepted paintings inspired by authentic religious feeling. The exhibition hall dedicated to Philippe de Champaigne reminds visitors of the strong ties that linked this painter to the abbey: every day the nuns could admire his two works *Ecce Homo* and *Mater Dolorosa*. The museum building overlooking the farmyard was once home to Blaise Pascal, who wrote his *Mystery of Jesus* here in 1655. Tradition has it that his knowledge of mathematics came in handily during his stay at the abbey when he produced the calculations for a new winch for the well: this enabled the nuns to draw a huge bucket as big as nine ordinary buckets from a depth of 60m/197ft with no extra effort.

ADDITIONAL SIGHT

Église St-Lambert – This small picturesque country church is perched above the village. A granite pyramid erected in the church cemetery in the early 20C marks the communal grave that received the remains of the Cistercian nuns and the Solitaires. To the right of the drive stands a cross bearing the words "To the human race" *(À la personne humaine)*. It was set up in 1944 and celebrates the memory of those who suffered most during the Second World War, in particular in concentration camps, irrespective of race, nationality or creed.

> ### "THE BIRDSONG"
>
> **Au Chant des Oiseaux de Port-Royal** – *78114 Magny-les-Hameaux* – ☎ *01 30 43 73 16* – *chant.desoiseaux@wanadoo.fr* – *closed Sun evening and Mon* – *booking recommended Sat-Sun* – *155/195F.* This 1933 pavilion facing the abbey welcomes diners in its small, sober dining room or in the garden. Traditional fare. On Saturdays, however, there are live cabaret acts that are well worth a visit!

PROVINS★★

Population 11 608
Michelin map 61 fold 4 or 237 fold 33

Access from Paris: *SNCF rail link from Gare de l'Est*

Whether approaching Provins from the Brie plateau to the west or from Champagne and the Voulzie Valley, this medieval town presents the eye-catching and distinctive outlines of the Tour César and of the dome of St-Quiriace Church. The splendid ramparts contribute to the town's medieval atmosphere and the rose gardens add to its visual appeal.

The lower town, a lively shopping centre, sits at the foot of the promontory and extends along the River Voulzie and River Durteint.

The Provins fairs – In the 10C Provins became one of the economic capitals of the Champagne region, thanks to its two annual fairs which, with those of Troyes, were among the largest in the region. Traders from the north and from the Mediterranean came here to do business.

Linens, silks, spices from the Orient and wine were traded, attracting people from many walks of life: money agents and merchants among whom mingled the hard-working bourgeoisie of the region.

These fairs were prosperous until the early 14C, when the political and economic weight shifted to Paris, eclipsing the Champagne region.

Roses – According to tradition it was **Thibaud IV** the Troubadour who brought roses back from Syria and grew them successfully here in Provins. Edmund Lancaster (1245-96), brother of the King of England, married Blanche of Artois and was for a while suzerain of Provins, at which time he introduced the red rose into his coat of arms.

June is the best month to visit the rose beds at the **Pépinières et Roseraies Vizier** ⊘, rue des Prés.

Common Rose of Provins

★★UPPER TOWN

It is advisable to park in the car park near Porte St-Jean. This is the location of the tourist office and the departure point for the small tourist train which tours the Upper Town and then returns to the Lower Town.

Porte St-Jean – St John's Gateway was built in the 13C. This stocky construction is flanked by two projecting towers which are partially hidden by the buttresses which were added in the 14C to support the drawbridge.

Follow allée des Remparts which overlooks the old moat.

★★ **Remparts** – The town walls were built in the 12C and 13C along an existing line of defence, then altered on several occasions. They constitute a very fine example of medieval military architecture. A house straddling the curtain wall was the home of the Provins executioners. The last one to live here was Charles-Henri Sanson who executed Louis XVI. The most interesting part of the ramparts runs between Porte St-Jean and Porte de Jouy. The Tour aux Engins, on the corner, links the two curtain walls; it derives its name from a barn nearby in which engines of war were housed.

In summer, on a space behind this tower, within the ramparts, the falconers of the "Aigles de Provins" company put on a **show** of birds of prey; other birds of prey are displayed in shelters.

Beyond the 12C Porte de Jouy take rue de Jouy, which is lined by picturesque low houses with long tiled roofs or an overhanging upper storey. **Caveau St-Esprit** *(open during special events)* was once the store of an old hospital which was destroyed by fire in the 17C.

Place du Châtel – This vast, peaceful square, rectangular in shape, is bordered by attractive old houses: the 15C Maison des Quatre Pignons (south-west corner), the 13C Maison des Petits-Plaids (north-west corner), the Hôtel de la Coquille to the north. The remains of Église St-Thibault (12C) stand on the north-east corner.

In the centre, next to an old well with a wrought-iron cage, stands the Croix des Changes, where the edicts of the Counts of Champagne were posted.

Walk past the **Musée du Provinois**, housed in one of the town's oldest buildings, the "Maison Romane" (Romanesque house).

Église St-Quiriace – The church was begun in the 11C. The transept and nave date from the 13C, the dome from the 17C. On the square in front of the church stands a Cross on the site of the old bell-tower which collapsed in 1689.

★★Tour César – This superb 12C keep, 44m/144ft high and flanked by four turrets, is the emblem of the town. It was once part of the walls of the upper town. The pyramidal roof was built in the 16C.

The revetment wall which encloses the base of the keep was added by the English during the Hundred Years War, in order to house the artillery.

The guard-room on the first floor is octagonal and 11m/36ft high; it is topped by vaulting formed of four arcades of pointed arches ending in a dome and pierced by an orifice through which the soldiers on the floor above were passed supplies. The gallery

Tour César

encircling the keep at the height of the turrets was originally roofed over. One **view★** extends over the town and the surrounding countryside.

A very narrow stairway leads to the upper level. Under the fine 16C wooden roof are the bells of St-Quiriace, which have hung here since the church lost its bell-tower.

Return to Porte St-Jean via place du Châtel then rue St-Jean on the left.

Eating out

MODERATE

Petit Écu – *9 place du Châtel* – ☎ *01 64 08 95 00* – *closed Jan and evenings from Oct to Apr except Sat-Sun - 98/115F.* On a charming square in the old city of Provins stands this fine half-timbered house offering traditional French cuisine during the week. Alternatively, try the unusual weekend formula consisting of buffets based on a medieval theme...

Where to stay

MID-RANGE

Hôtel Aux Vieux Remparts – *3 rue Couverte* – ☎ *01 64 08 94 00* – ▣ – *25 rooms 420/750F* – ☱ *55F* – *restaurant 150/360F.* This modern building dating from the 1980s, located in the Cité des Roses, contains simple but comfortable rooms. French regional cooking. The peaceful, shaded terrace is especially popular in the summer months.

Chambre d'Hôte Clos Thibaud de Champagne – *1 rue du Souci, 77520 Cessoy-en-Montois* – *16km/10mi south-west of Provins by N 19 then D 75* – ☎ *01 60 67 32 10* – ☑ – *4 rooms 350/450F* – *meal 150F.* In a small village, this beautifully restored former Briard farmhouse has retained its authentic character. The garden commanding nice views of the surrounding landscape adds to the charm of the blissfully quiet bedrooms.

On the town

Auberge du Chatel – *2 rue Couverte* – ☎ *01 64 08 97 34* – *daily 9am-1am.* The slightly eccentric decoration of this bar lends it an old-fashioned touch with the odd reference to advertising. It is also an art gallery as the pictures and statuettes on display are for sale. Shaded courtyard with terrace.

Le Jardin Saint-Ayoul – *6 place St-Ayoul* – ☎ *01 64 00 38 75* – *www.tishase. aol.com - Tues-Sun 9.30am-1am.* This modest, unassuming café stages a number of interesting activities you can buy books at reduced prices, surf on the Internet or take part in weekend discussions centring on poetry or philosophical issues. If you have musical skills, why not settle at the piano and tease the keys while sipping your drink...

Showtime

À l'Assaut des Remparts – **Tournoi de Chevalerie** – 🎦 – *Office de Tourisme, chemin de Villecran* – ☎ *01 64 60 26 26* – *www.provins.net* – Near the Porte Saint-Jean, at the back of the moat, you will be plunged into the Dark Ages thanks to two remarkable shows of startling realism. First, there is a demonstration of military equipment and defensive weapons, then you will attend a jousting tournament in which competitors fight with swords or lances and sometimes even with their own feet.

Les Aigles des Remparts – 🎦 – *Rue de Jouy* – ☎ *01 64 60 26 26* – *www.provins.net* - One of the favourite pastimes of medieval lords was to observe the antics of birds of prey gliding through the skies. After the demonstration, the falconer takes those who wish around the aviary.

ADDITIONAL SIGHTS

★**Grange aux Dîmes** 🕐 – *Rue St-Jean.*
This massive 13C building belonged to the canons of St-Quiriace, who hired out the space to merchants during the major fairs. When the fairs went into decline the barn became a store for the tithes *(dîmes)* levied on the harvests of the peasants.
The atmosphere of the town's famous fairs is realistically recreated in a permanent exhibition entitled, **"Provins au temps des foires de Champagne"**.

Musée du Provinois 🕐 – This local museum is housed in one of the oldest buildings in the town, "The Romanesque House".
On the ground floor are displayed **the sculpture and ceramic collections★**, valuable works of local medieval and Renaissance art.
Exploiting the underground clay quarries enabled potters to produce pieces now noted for their remarkable variety and timelessness.

Église St-Ayoul – In 1048 Thibaud I, Count of Troyes and Meaux (and also Count of Blois under the name Thibaud III), grand protector of the abbeys, installed the monks from Montier-la-Celle in the St-Ayoul district in the Lower Town.
The three doorways project far beyond the line of the gable on the west front. Missing parts of the **central doorway** were replaced with new pieces by the sculptor Georges Jeanclos, who was responsible for the bronze **statues★** with antique patina which now harmonise well with the medieval reliefs.
Inside, in the north aisle, stand 16C **statues★★**: a graceful if rather affected Virgin Mary and two **musician angels** with wonderfully draped clothes.

Souterrains à graffiti 🕐 – *Entrance in rue St-Thibault, left of the doorway to the Ancien Hôtel-Dieu.* There is a substantial network of underground passages around Provins, some marked with ancient graffiti. The section which is open to the public runs through a layer of a tufa which lies parallel to the base of the spur on which the Upper Town stands. The entrance is through a low-roofed chamber with ribbed vaulting in the old hospice.

Le QUESNOY★

Population 4 890
Michelin map 53 fold 5 or 236 fold 18

This quiet town of low, white-washed houses lying in a lush, lake-filled setting close to Mormal Forest is a fine example of French military architecture.

★FORTIFICATIONS

The perfectly preserved fortifications still show clearly the unique qualities of the old stronghold. Built of coarse stone, flint and lime mortar covered with bricks, they form a polygon of defensive curtain walls with projecting bastions; despite apparently being in the style of Vauban these defences in fact date in part from the time of Emperor Charles V (16C); for example the bastions with projecting towers. Various all-season paths offer pleasant walks, enabling enthusiasts of military architecture to study the layout of the defences *(information panels)*.

🔳 *Leave from place du Général-Leclerc and head for the postern gate by avenue d'Honneur des Néo-Zélandais.*

The gateway gives access to the moat, to the spot where the men of the New Zealand Rifle Brigade scaled the walls in November 1918. The Monument des Néo-Zélandais commemorates their exploits.

Follow the moat around the south front of the ramparts.

From **Étang du Pont Rouge** continue to **Lac Vauban** which lies at the foot of the ramparts to each side of the Porte Fauroeulx.
The bridge provides a lovely view of the redbrick curtain walls and bastions and their reflection in the calm waters.

Étang du Fer à Cheval –
Lying north-west of the town, the lake was dug to a design by Vauban during Louis XIV's reign.
The calm and verdant setting is extremely peaceful.

A COUNTRY KITCHEN

La Flambée – *6 Les Quatre-Vents, 59530 Villers-Pol - 3km/2mi north of Le Quesnoy by D 934 heading towards Valenciennes –* ☎ *03 27 49 50 60 – laflambee@wanadoo.fr – closed Wed – booking recommended – 145/220F.* This restaurant occupying a former post house is fronted by a lovely brick façade. The charming garden and terrace at the back of the house come as a pleasant surprise. In the cosy, timberframed rustic dining room, the crackling fire is used for roasting and grilling meat.

Boutteaux (R. Gén.) .... **Z 3**	Leclerc (Pl. du Gén.) .... **Z 13**	Nouvelle-Zélande	
Fournier (R. Casimir) .... **Z 6**	Libération (Av de la) .... **Y 14**	(R. de) .... **Z 17**
Gambetta (R. Léon) .... **Z 7**	Lombards (R. des) .... **Z 15**	Tanis (R. Désiré) .... **Y 18**
Joffre (R. du Mar.) .... **Z 12**	Néo-Zélandais (Av. d'honneur des) **Z 16**	Weibel (R. Henri) .... **Z 24**

RAMBOUILLET ★

Population 24 343
Michelin map 106 fold 28 or 237 fold 28

Access from Paris: *SNCF rail link from Gare Montparnasse*

The combination of an attractive château, park and forest makes Rambouillet one of the main sights in the Île-de-France. Since 1897 it has been the official summer residence of the President of the French Republic. Distinguished guests include Hosni Moubarak (Egypt, August 1998), Nelson Mandela (South Africa, July 1996), Boris Eltsine (Russia, October 1995), George Bush (United States, July 1991) and Mikhaïl Gorbatchev (USSR, October 1990).

HISTORICAL NOTES

The death of François I – At the age of 52, François I fell ill and his health started to decline. He became restless and left his St-Germain residence in February 1547. He went to stay with his major-domo at Villepreux, paid a visit to his treasurer's widow in Dampierre, spent Shrove Tuesday in Limours with his mistress the Duchess of Étampes and indulged in a three-day hunt in Rochefort-en-Yvelines. On the way back, he dropped in to see the captain of his bodyguard Jacques d'Angennes at the Château de Rambouillet. The château was built in 1375 by Jean Bernier – a prominent court figure under Charles V – and had remained the property of the d'Angennes family since 1384. During his stay at Rambouillet François I's condition grew worse. Feeling that his end was drawing near, the King summoned his son Monseigneur le Dauphin and placed his servants and the French people in his hands. He died on 30 March 1547.

18C – In 1706 Louis XIV bought Rambouillet for the Comte de Toulouse, one of Mme Du Maintenon's legitimised sons. The Comte trebled the private apartments and added two perpendicular wings onto the main building.

Under Louis XVI the estate came into the hands of the Comte de Toulouse's son the **Duc de Penthièvre**. Like his father, he was a dedicated governor who applied himself to the improvement of his domain. He refurbished the grounds for his daughter-in-law the Princesse de Lamballe. A close friend of Marie-Antoinette, the princess was executed in the old La Force prison in Paris on 3 September 1792.

Louis XVI was an enthusiastic hunter who enjoyed staying at Rambouillet and he purchased the estate, and the opportunities it offered for hunting, in 1783. The Queen was bored by life at the château, which she referred to as a "Gothic toad hole". In an attempt to amuse her, the King gave orders to build the Dairy, a small pavilion reminiscent of the Trianon at Versailles. A landscape garden was started by Penthièvre and completed in accordance with plans by Hubert Robert.

A sense of destiny – In 1814 Marie-Louise met up with her father François II in Rambouillet; she decided to leave Napoleon and go to Vienna with the King of Rome. A year later, on 29 June 1815, Napoleon made an unexpected stop here on his way from Malmaison to St Helena, to spend a night of melancholy reflection on his time here with Marie-Louise after he had divorced Joséphine.

On 31 July 1830 at about 6pm Charles X arrived at Rambouillet, fleeing the insurrection at St-Cloud. For three days the ageing ruler debated what course of action to choose. The troops under his command disbanded and an army of citizens was approaching from Paris. He eventually abdicated and set sail for England.

It was in Rambouillet – where he stayed from 23 to 25 August 1944 – that General de Gaulle gave orders for the Leclerc Division to march on Paris.

International meetings in Rambouillet

Let to various persons after the abdication of Charles X, Rambouillet Château came back into State ownership at the fall of the Second Empire. In 1897, it became one of the official country residences of the presidents of the Republic. De Gaulle organised hunting parties on the estate. On the initiative of Valéry Giscard d'Estaing, the château was the venue of the first summit meeting of industrialised countries, which began as an informal get-together of six western heads of state. More recently, the Rambouillet conference of March 1999 attempted to find a solution to the Kosovo problem, unfortunately without success.

CHÂTEAU ⏱ *1hr*

Leave from place de la Libération, the site of the town hall *(if the car park is full, leave the car in the park – parking is tolerated in certain spots)*.

The château presents a triangular shape owing to the fact that Napoleon dismantled the left wing. The large François I tower belonged to the 14C fortress. It is difficult to distinguish because of the numerous additions made by the Comte de Toulouse.

Mezzanine – The reception rooms commissioned by the Comte de Toulouse are embellished with superb Rococo **wainscoting★**. Note the charming boudoir designed for the Comte's wife.

The corridor adjoining the François I tower leads through to the Imperial bathroom suite, adorned with Pompeian frescoes. This opens onto the Emperor's Bedchamber, where he spent the night of 29 June 1815, and the study. It was in the dining room – the former ballroom – that Charles X signed the abdication document. The view of the park is stunning.

Ground Floor – The Renaissance-style Marble Hall, dating from the time of Henri II, is entirely lined with marble tiles.

Rambouillet – Napoleon's bathroom

★PARK ⊙

Parterre – The château is set in a pleasant formal garden. On the right stands a quincunx, around several copses. The perspective ends with the Rondeau Basin and a sweeping avenue of swamp cypresses planted in 1805.

Jardin d'eau – These water gardens were remodelled by the Duc de Penthièvre. The central canal is continued by a green carpet of lawn. The other canals with their geometric lines enclose islets of greenery: Île des festins, Île des Roches etc.

★**Laiterie de la Reine** ⊙ – Louis XVI had the dairy built to amuse his wife Marie-Antoinette. The small sandstone pavilion resembling a neo-Classical temple consists of two rooms. The first – which houses the actual dairy – features marble paving and a marble table dating from the First Empire. The Sèvres porcelain bowls and jugs used for tasting have disappeared.

The room at the back was designed as an artificial grotto adorned with luxuriant vegetation. It includes a marble composition by Pierre Julien depicting a nymph and the she-goat Amalthea (1787).

Eating out

MID-RANGE

Le Cheval Rouge – *78 rue du Général-de-Gaulle –* ☎ *01 30 88 80 61 – closed 20 July-18 Aug, Tues evening and Wed – 135/185F.* This restaurant in the old quarter of Rambouillet offers traditional French cuisine served in a handsome dining room appointed with fine silverware and crockery. When the weather is fair, you can sit out on the veranda at the back of the house.

Where to stay

MODERATE

Camping Municipal l'Étang d'Or – *3km/2mi south of Rambouillet by a minor road skirting the lake –* ☎ *01 30 41 07 34 – booking recommended July-Aug – 220 plots 67F - eating facilities.* Half-way between Versailles and Chartres, this camp site features pleasantly shaded plots in the middle of a forest on the edge of a lake teeming with fish. A perfect location for walks and cycling tours. Many sights of historical interest in the vicinity.

MID-RANGE

Chambre d'Hôte Le Château – *2 rue de l'Église, 78125 Poigny-la-Forêt – 8km/5mi north-west of Rambouillet by D 936 then D 107 –* ☎ *01 34 84 73 42 – www.france-random.com/poigny –* ⊠ *– 7 rooms 325/395F.* The decoration of this hotel is an amusing kaleidoscope of historical periods and cultures. Each room has its own theme: Morocco, Coca-Cola, rural charm, Louis XIII, the 1950s... As for the garden, where dogs, ducks and horses run free, it could be likened to a miniature Noah's Ark!

LUXURY

Château d'Esclimont – *28700 St-Symphorien-le-Château – 14km/8.7mi south of Rambouillet by N 10, D 101 then D 122 –* ☎ *02 37 31 15 15 –* ☑ *– 47 rooms from 1 000F –* ⊒ *110F – restaurant 340/495F.* Turrets, stone bridges and a moat: this is your dream castle just outside Paris, surrounded by a superb leafy park with a pond, home to graceful white swans. Choosing one of the rooms can prove quite a challenge as they are all large and appointed with splendid furniture.

Shopping

Boutique Gourmande de la Bergerie Nationale – *Parc du Château –* ☎ *01 30 88 66 50 – Wed-Fri 1.30-6.30pm, Sat 10am-noon, 2-6.30pm, Sun 2-6.30pm.* The shop attached to the farmhouse sells fresh produce made by French farming schools. Specialities include poultry, foie gras, duck and goose conserve, salt meat and fish, honey, jam, wine and *bufflonnes* mozarella, a cheese sold in several Italian and French restaurants in Paris. Tourists can also buy scarves, ties, blankets and shirts made with the exceptional wool of the Merinos sheep, which have been reared at the Bergerie Nationale since 1786.

★**Chaumière des Coquillages** ⊘ – The landscape garden in the park features a charming cottage built by Penthièvre for the Princesse de Lamballe. The walls of the rooms are encrusted with a variety of sea shells, chips of marble and mother-of-pearl. A small boudoir with painted panelling adjoins the main room.

ADDITIONAL SIGHTS

★**Bergerie Nationale** ⊘ – In 1786, Louis XVI decided to add to his experimental farm the production of fine wool and so he purchased a flock of merinos from Spain. The sheep farm buildings were completed during the First Empire. Today it houses around 800 animals, including 120 merino sheep.

Musée Rambolitrain ⊘ – An astounding collection of more than 4 000 toy trains and models explains the history of the railway from its early beginnings to the present day. A large O-shaped circuit occupies the whole of the second floor.

★RAMBOUILLET FOREST

This vast forest has some delightful footpaths for those who enjoy walking. Some 20 or more lakes with picturesque banks, including the **Étangs de Hollande**, and a number of villages with old houses that are now holiday homes give it a very special charm. It was severely damaged by the violent storms which hit the Île-de-France region in December 1999.

Rambouillet is part of the ancient Yveline Forest that, stretched in Gallo-Roman times, as far as the outskirts of Nogent-le-Roi, Houdan, Cernay-la-Ville and Etampes.

Of the total 20 000ha/50 000 acres, 14 000ha/35 000 acres are State owned. They cover a clay plateau with an altitude of between 110m/358ft and 180m/585ft, crisscrossed by sandy valleys. In the Middle Ages, wide-scale deforestation took place and the vast clearances now divide it into three main areas of woodland: St-Léger and Rambouillet itself, the most popular areas with tourists situated north of Rambouillet, and Yvelines to the south which is rather more divided up into private estates.

Flora and fauna – At present the policy is to create copses. There is a predominance of oak (60 %) followed by pine (30 %) and other varieties (10 %) such as birch and beech. The forest round Rambouillet is damper and has more rivers, lakes and ponds than the one at Fontainebleau. From time immemorial it has been particularly well stocked with game such as deer, roe-deer and wild boar - and it remains so today.

Sights

Espace Rambouillet ⊙

Car park and visitors centre 500m/540yd to the south-west of the Rambouillet-Clairefontaine road (D 27).

This 250ha/625 acres wildlife park has been divided into three areas:
Forêt des Aigles, with more than 100 birds of prey in aviaries. Free flight shows.
Forêt des Cerfs, where observation hides provide a view of deer, stags, and wild oxen.
Forêt Sauvage, a 180ha/450 acres site in which the animals roam free.
Binoculars are recommended.

Étangs de Pourras et de St-Hubert ⊙ – 🏃 *30min on foot there and back. Leave from the large star-shaped St-Hubert crossroads. Follow the continuation of N 191, a rough track flanked by houses which leads to the road running between the two ponds.*
The ponds were part of one of Vauban's projects to create reservoirs for Versailles' water requirements. A series of six ponds separated by paths was laid out near the Étang de Hollande. Only the two end basins are filled with water. The two central ponds - known as Bourgneuf and Corbet - are now nothing more than by a rivulet overgrown with aquatic plants.
There are **cycle tracks** to be enjoyed by all *(see Michelin map 106).*

① The Guéville and Guesle valleys

41km/25mi – about 1hr then 1hr 30min on foot there and back

Leave Rambouillet by the Maintenon road. At Gazeran (5km/3mi) turn left onto D 62.

Réserve Zoologique de Sauvage ⊙ – This 40ha/100 acre park is surrounded by oak woods and dotted with boulders. It contains free-roaming antelopes, deer and kangaroos, and many aquatic birds including rare swans and ducks together with a colony of flamingoes.
The Tropical Aviary in which the temperature and humidity are kept at a constant level features many tropical bird species: toucans, eclectus parrots, gouras, hornbills etc.
Return to Gazeran.

Roches d'Angennes – *Leave from the parking area of the "Zone de Silence des Rabières". Walk 90m/100yd through the village up the steeper slope of the valley to find the right path leading to the summit. Go past an arena-shaped shelf circled by boulders to reach the crest:* **view** of Guesle Valley and Angennes Lake, bordered by bulrushes, reeds and other aquatic plants.

Carrefour du Haut Planet – *Leave your vehicle in the car park at La Croix Pater and walk back to this crossroads (shelter).* The ledge of the Haut-Planet plateau – planted with birches and conifers – commands a sweeping **view**★ northwards over the hills of St-Léger.

★**Balcon du Haut Planet** – 🏃 Bear right and take the straight path leading to Haut Planet, which crosses rough, hilly ground. After passing a spring fenced by wire netting on the right, the lane reaches a shaded terrace on the edge of the plateau *(shelter for ramblers).*
The path – offering beautiful vistas all the way – eventually leads to a rocky promontory. *Return to the car.*

② Round tour in Rambouillet Forest

See MONTFORT-L'AMAURY.

Château-fort de RAMBURES★

Michelin map 52 fold 6 or 236 fold 22 - 6km/4mi north-east of Blangy-sur-Bresle

Rambures Castle ⊙ is an interesting example of 15C military architecture; during the Hundred Years War it played an important role as a French enclave in the middle of the English-occupied territories, and it came to be called "the key to the Vimeu". The castle has remained in the same family since the 15C. Henri IV stayed in the castle.

Tour

Château-fort de Rambures

E. Baret

Exterior – The castle retains the look of a powerful fortress, with its enormous machicolated round towers and its rounded curtain walls (so that there were no level surfaces for the enemy to fire against), its deep moat and its tall watchtower. It was designed to resist the artillery of the time and its brick walls are 3-7m/10-23ft thick. In the 18C the castle was converted into a country residence and the courtyard façade was pierced with huge windows.

The English-style park is planted with ancient trees.

Interior – For many of the rooms the only source of daylight is still through loopholes, though the alterations begun in the 18C did provide reception rooms decorated with woodwork and marble chimney-pieces *(first floor)*.

After a glance over the 15C watch-path, the tour continues on the second floor, to the library-billiards room hung with a collection of portraits.

The kitchen is located in the old guard-room above the dungeons; the cellars were used to shelter the villagers during invasions.

La ROCHE-GUYON★

Population 561
Michelin map 106 fold 2 or 237 fold 15

This village lies between the River Seine and the Vexin plateau. It developed at the foot of an old stronghold; its crumbling keep still dominates the steep, rocky ledge. Life at La Roche-Guyon has resumed its peaceful character since the bombings of July 1944 and the Battle of Normandy, when Marshal Rommel established his headquarters in the castle. The village has retained some of its cave-dwellings and fine old houses.

The La Rochefoucauld estate – In the 13C, a residential château was erected at the foot of the cliff not far from the fortress; it was linked to the keep by a flight of steps carved in the rock. François I and his numerous retinue took up residence here in 1546. La Roche-Guyon was made a duchy peerage in 1621. Thirty-eight years later the title came into the hands of **François de La Rochefoucauld**, who wrote many of his famous *Maximes* at the château.

★**The banks of the Seine** – The quayside promenade commands a good **view**★ of the sleepy countryside and the meandering river. Behind, the two castles stand side by side. The abutment pier of the former suspension bridge (dismantled in the 19C) provides a good observation point.

The Duke and the young Romantic writers

In 1816 Louis-François Auguste, **Duc de Rohan-Chabot**, acquired the estate. He lost his wife in 1819 and took holy orders at the age of 31. On his return, he continued to entertain at the château, combining acts of charity with the fashionable manners of pre-Revolutionary France. Among the guests were fellow students at St-Sulpice Seminary and the young Romantic authors Victor Hugo, Alphonse de Lamartine, Hugues Lamennais, Henri Lacordaire and Father Dupanloup.

They delighted in the grand but respectful services celebrated in the underground chapel to the strains of a superb Italian organ. In 1829 the duke was appointed Archbishop of Besançon, and then Cardinal, and sold the château and its grounds to François de la Rochefoucauld-Liancourt. La Roche-Guyon has remained in this family ever since.

★Château ⓥ – The superb wrought-iron gates bearing the La Rochefoucauld crest open onto the courtyard and 18C stables which now house the reception desk and temporary exhibitions. The house still has some 13C features such as the towers flanking the main apartments. Built in the 16C, they stand on a terrace supported by arcaded foundations. The rooms are empty of furniture. The parapet walkway and "south-east" tower provide some wonderful panoramic views of the Seine Valley. A newly restored corridor leads to the three chapels. The main one is dedicated to Our Lady of the Snows. During the German occupation, numerous pillboxes were built into the cliffs. They now house a retrospective look at Rommel's stay at the château. The remainder of the buildings in the cliffs, including the orangery, are now used as the backcloth for a *son et lumière* show about regional art, entitled **"Parcours de lumière en Vallée de Seine"**.

La Roche-Guyon – The castle and the keep

A de Valroger/MICHELIN

Eating out

MID-RANGE

Auberge du Lapin Savant – *36 route de la Vallée Chantemesle, Haute Isle, 95780 La Roche-Guyon – 4km/2.5mi east of La Roche-Guyon by D 913 – ☎ 01 34 78 13 43 – closed Feb school holidays, Nov, Wed evening and Thur – booking essential – 135/165F.* This curious-looking half-timbered cottage with pointed roofs situated on the corniche houses a small country restaurant with a welcome fireplace in winter. Carefully prepared meals with market produce at decent prices.

Where to stay

MID-RANGE

Chambre d'Hôte Le Saint Denis – *1 rue des Cabarets, 95510 Chérence – 4km/2.5mi north-east of La Roche-Guyon by D 100 – ☎ 01 34 78 15 02 – ✉ – booking essential – 5 rooms 300F – ☕ 30F.* In the quaint medieval hamlet of Chérence, this former hotel-restaurant was converted into a bed and breakfast in 1996: the smallish rooms are unusual and slightly crooked. The most precious asset is the garden, where you will love to lounge around in summer. Warm, generous welcome.

EXCURSIONS

★Route des Crêtes – *Round tour of 4km/2.5mi.*
Take the road to Gasny which passes the entrance to the famous troglodyte caves or stables called **boves**, carved in the chalk. On reaching the pass, turn right onto D 100, also known as "Route des Crêtes". When the estates no longer conceal the view of the river, park the car on a belvedere near a spinney of pine trees.
View★★ of the meander of the Seine carpeted with the trees of the Forêt de Moisson and, further along the promontory, of the spurs of the Haute-Isle cliffs. Note, in the foreground, down below, the truncated **keep** ⓥ of the Château de La Roche-Guyon.

Continue along D 100. At the first junction, turn right onto Charrière des Bois, which leads back to the starting point. The road follows a steep downward slope and passes under the 18C aqueduct that supplies water to the village and the château.

Arboretum de La Roche – *On D 37 towards Amenucourt.*
The arboretum, which spreads over 12ha/29 acres, has been planted to reproduce the geography of the Île-de-France area. Each *département* is distinguished by a different species: oak for Seine-et-Marne, maple for Essonne, hornbeam for Val-de-Marne, ash for Val d'Oise, cherry for Seine Saint-Denis, lime for Les Hauts-de-Seine, and beech for Yvelines. The plane-trees in the middle represent Paris. They are all young trees, apart from the 20 year-old Lebanese cedar at the central roundabout. Among the plantations, snaking stretches of lawn evoke the valleys.

Vétheuil – *6km/3.7mi east along D 913.*
This former wine-growing village has a lovely riverside setting: it lies on the steep banks of one of the Seine's meanders. The village houses – built with a fine pale-yellow stone – are characteristic of the French Vexin region. The small town was made famous by the Impressionists, in particular Claude Monet who lived here for three years and whose wife Camille died in Vétheuil in 1879.

Church ⊘ – Perched right above the village the church makes a picturesque sight, but the Impressionist painters were more interested in the area around Lavacourt, on the south bank of the Seine.
From the main village crossroads take rue de l'Église which leads straight to the entrance steps. Although the chancel was first started in the late 12C the church was only completed under Henri II, when the last chapels were consecrated in 1580.
The west front dates from the mid-16C; the three levels of Renaissance galleries are flanked by two square turrets. The pier features a 16C statue of the Virgin and Child.
The south façade presents a doorway fronted by a Renaissance porch – note the 16C panels. Walk past the 16C nave to the late-12C chancel, which shows the transition from Romanesque to Gothic. A broad view of the elevation of the church reveals small round windows (oculi) on the first floor and a series of stepped buttresses around the east end. The bell-tower, built in the 13C, was the subject of many Impressionist paintings.
The church houses a number of **statues**★ (14C-16C), a few 16C and 17C paintings and several interesting carvings. The first chapel on the left – formerly dedicated to one of the brotherhoods of charity – is enclosed by a Renaissance parclose. In the third chapel stands a lively statue of St James (Burgundian School - 15C) and the north aisle bears a 16C Ecce Homo. Note the 14C Virgin and Child in the south transept crossing (Notre-Dame-de-Grâce de Vétheuil) and, in the adjacent chapel, St Veronica, a colourful stone statue dating from the 14C.

Domaine de Villarceaux – *10km/6.2mi north-east. From Chaussy, follow D 71 towards Magny-en-Vexin. Drive past the Louis XV-style castle and take the first road to the right (signposted "La Comté"). A little further on the right, a new access road leads to a vast parking area.*
Villarceaux estate is graced by a magnificent setting and two châteaux: a 15C-16C manor house which belonged to the celebrated beauty Ninon de Lenclos, and a Louis XV château.
Approaching the estate from the south, the road from Villers-en-Arthies offers a glimpse of a third edifice, the Château du Couvent surrounded by a golf course.
Prolonged by vast outbuildings forming a courtyard, the Manoir de Ninon replaced in the 16C a former fortified house now reduced to the Tour St-Nicolas. Ninon's pavilion ends with Ninon's tower which houses a charming Italian closet and an intriguing hideout dimly lit by a loophole.

Ninon de Lenclos

When Ninon (1620-1705) died at the age of 85, she had witnessed Louis XIII's reign and the absolute monarchy of Louis XIV. She was acquainted with all the leading personalities of her time and became a legendary figure of the 17C because of her charm and her wisdom; few of her contemporaries could claim to possess such an impressive collection of memories. It was at Villarceaux that she received the young Françoise d'Aubigné, the future Mme Scarron and Mme De Maintenon, who 32 years later was to marry Louis XIV. It was also here that she had a love affair with Louis de Mornay, the Marquis de Villarceaux. The youthful Voltaire was officially presented to her shortly before her death.

Villarceaux – Ninon's pavilion

★**Gardens** ⊙ – They illustrate the evolution of gardens through the centuries. The former Renaissance terraces on the left of the entrance are overlooked by the unusual St-Nicolas Tower, known as the "tower of the condemned" because witches were hanged there. The tour of the large pond leads past Ninon's pool, supplied by an Italian waterfall, and reveals a **view**★ of the south front of the Louis XV castle. The other façade of the 18C castle overlooks the open Vexin countryside.

Abbaye de ROYAUMONT★★

Michelin map 106 fold 7 or 237 folds 17, 18

Royaumont Abbey is an impressive symbol of the wealth that often accrued to the great French abbeys of the Middle Ages. A tour of this sanctuary is strongly recommended, particularly when a concert is scheduled there.

The abbey, founded in 1228 and completed in 1235, was occupied by members of the Cistercian order. It was richly endowed by the king and his successors, which explains the size and beauty of the buildings. Six of St Louis' relatives - three children, a brother and two grandsons - were buried in the abbey. Their remains have since been moved to St-Denis.

In 1793 Royaumont was sold as State property and the church dismantled. Since 1923 the abbot's palace and the grounds forming the estate have been separated from the abbey itself.

In 1964 the last owners Isabel and Henri Gouïn (1900-77) created the Royaumont Foundation for the Advancement of Human Science, to which they donated the estate.

A cultural mission

In 1978 the abbey was assigned a new cultural mission. The Centre Culturel de Rencontre set up on its premises ensures the preservation of the abbey; it also organises concerts, lectures, training seminars and exhibitions in its regional vocal arts centre, literary centre and ethnology centre.

TOUR ⊙

Church ruins – *See plan.* Royaumont Church was consecrated in 1235. The fragments of columns that remain mark the foundations of this unusually large building (101m/330ft long).

The chancel and its radiating chapels break with Cistercian tradition in that they do not feature a flat east end (eg Fontenay in Burgundy). A corner turret (**1**) belonging to the former north transept gives a fair idea of its elevation (the keystone was 28m/91ft above ground).

ABBAYE DE ROYAUMONT

CHANTILLY

★Abbot's residence
Abbey ★★

CHURCH

Ruelle des Convers
★ABBOT'S RESIDENCE

Cloisters

Sacristy
ABBEY ★★

Canal

Former kitchen quarters

Hostelry

Refectory

Latrines and machinery building

Canal

Non-existant parts

Cloisters – They surround a delightful garden. The west gallery (opposite the entry) is paralleled, at the back, by a narrow, uncovered passageway known as the "ruelle des Convers". It was built for the lay brothers in order that they might have access to their wing and to the church without passing through the cloisters, habitually reserved for the monks.

Refectory – This spacious dining hall – which consists of two aisles – is a masterpiece of Gothic architecture. It could accommodate 60 monks without difficulty (note the monolithic shafts of the columns).

St Louis would take his turn at serving the monks at table while they sat in silence listening to the reader who stood erect in a pulpit carved out of the thick stone wall.

Former kitchen quarters – The kitchens house a statue of the Virgin of Royaumont (**2**), carved in the 14C.

The strange building resting on 31 semicircular arches astride the canal is the **latrines and machinery building**. In former times, the water reached a higher level and activated the machinery in the workshops. One of the water wheels has remained intact.

★**Abbot's Residence (Palais Abbatial)** – Built on the eve of the Revolution for the last commendatory abbot of Royaumont, this white cubic construction is reminiscent of an Italian villa. In neo-Classical style, it is the work of Louis Le Masson. The façade facing the road to Chantilly is reflected in the waters of a charming pond.

Abbaye de Royaumont

B. Kaufmann/MICHELIN

Access from Paris: *RER line A 1*

The town of Rueil is famed for Malmaison, the delightful estate that remains firmly attached to the name of Napoleon Bonaparte.

Malmaison during the Consulate – Marie-Joseph-Rose Tascher de la Pagerie, born in Martinique in 1763, the widow of Général de Beauharnais, married General **Bonaparte** in 1796. Three years later, while Napoleon was away on campaign, she bought Malmaison and the 260ha/640 acres surrounding the château.
When Napoleon was First Consul he lived at the Tuileries, which he found "grand and boring". He decided to spend the end of each 10-day "week" at Malmaison. These were the happiest moments of his married life. Elegant, lively **Josephine** – she had 600 dresses and would change five or six times a day – was the spirit of the party at Malmaison. Life was carefree and formal protocol was dropped.

Malmaison in Imperial times – Crowned Emperor in 1804, **Napoleon** had no alternative but to stay at St-Cloud, Fontainebleau and the Tuileries, which were the official places of residence. Visits to Malmaison were too rare for the Empress' liking; she began to miss her splendid botanical and rose gardens, unparalleled in France. Josephine was a generous person with expensive tastes who spent money like water. When she ran into debt, her husband would complain bitterly but he invariably gave in, grumbling that this would be "the last time".

Malmaison after the divorce – Josephine returned here after her divorce in 1809. Napoleon had given her Malmaison, the Élysée and a château near Évreux. She fled the estate in 1814 but the Allied powers persuaded her to return. She behaved a little rashly by entertaining the Russian Csar and the King of Prussia at Malmaison. She caught cold while staying with her daughter Hortense at the Château de St Leu and died on 29 May 1814, at the age of 51. The debts she left behind were estimated at 3 million francs.

The farewell to Malmaison – Ten months after Josephine's death, Napoleon escaped from Elba and revisited Malmaison.
At the end of the Hundred Days he returned to the estate and stayed with Hortense, who had married Napoleon's brother, Louis, and was to give birth to Napoleon III. On 29 June 1815 the Emperor paid a last visit to the château and his family before leaving for Rochefort and St Helena.

SIGHTS

★★**Museum** ⊙ – After Josephine's death, the Château de Malmaison and its 726ha/1 800 acres of land passed to her son Prince Eugène, who died in 1824. The château was sold in 1828 and changed hands several times until it was bought by Napoleon III for the sum of one million francs. The Emperor undertook to restore the architecture and interior decoration to its former glory.

By 1877 the château was in a sorry state and the grounds reduced to a mere 60ha/148 acres. Malmaison was sold as State property and saw yet another succession of owners. The last proprietor, a Mr Osiris, acquired the estate – by now reduced to 6ha/15 acres – in 1896, restored the château and gave it to the State in 1904.

The site of the Mausoleum of the Imperial Prince was bequeathed to Malmaison by Prince Victor-Napoleon. Mr and Mrs Edward Tuck, an American couple who owned Bois-Préau Château, also gave their residence and its 19ha/47 acre park, formerly part of Josephine's private gardens.

The dining room at Malmaison

F. Jalain/EXPLORER

The entrance gate still sports its old-fashioned lanterns. The **château** was built around 1622 and when Josephine bought it in 1799 it featured only the central block; the square, jutting pavilions were added soon after and the conservatory in 1801-02. The museum was founded in 1906. It houses many exhibits which were purchased, donated or taken from either Malmaison, St-Cloud and the Tuileries, or from other national palaces connected with the Imperial family.

Ground Floor – Drawing room: beautiful furniture, including Marie-Louise's weaving loom; note the splendid fireplace, flanked by two paintings by Gérard and Girodet (based on the poems by Ossian).

Music Room: elegant furniture by the Jacob brothers; the Empress' harp; piano belonging to Queen Hortense.

Council Chamber: tent-shaped decor, embellished with military trophies; the armchairs were taken from the former château at St-Cloud.

Library: original decoration by Percier and Fontaine (note how mirrored panels cleverly conceal heating vents); furniture by the Jacob brothers; the books, furniture and military maps come from Malmaison and the Tuileries.

First Floor – The first rooms were occupied by the Emperor when he spent his last days in Paris (June 1815), between the Battle of Waterloo and his departure for St Helena.

Imperial Salon: several large portraits of the Imperial family, painted by Gérard.

Emperor's Bedroom: Prince Eugène's bed and a private collection of furniture, both taken from the Tuileries; the Victory standing on a pedestal table is the same one the Emperor was holding at the top of the Grand Army column on place Vendôme in Paris (it was torn down by the Commune in 1871); white hangings on the walls.

Marengo Room: paintings by David and Gros; ceremonial sabre and sword belonging to the First Consul.

Josephine's Room: portrait of the Empress; various personal items; porcelain dinner services manufactured in Sèvres and Paris; picture representing the Emperor surrounded by the marshals who took part in the Battle of Austerlitz.

Exhibition Gallery: frieze taken from the Paris mansion where the Imperial couple lived, located in rue Chanteraine, later renamed rue de la Victoire; Josephine's dressing table; bust of the Empress by Chinard.

Josephine's Suite (antechamber, State bedchamber, ordinary bedroom, bathroom, boudoir): portraits of the Empress by Gérard and Prud'hon.

Second Floor – One of the rooms contains glass-fronted cupboards containing a few of the Empress' clothes. In the next room is a display of ceremonial robes. Other rooms contain furniture and personal mementoes belonging to Queen Hortense as well as objects connected with Prince Eugène and others who frequented Malmaison.

The last room houses an exhibition relating to the history of the château and the estate.

Pavilions – The **Pavillon Osiris** contains all the collections that have been donated over the years: the works of art and Antique pieces belonging to Mr Osiris, a remarkable selection of snuff boxes, glass objects and caskets relating to the Napoleonic legend. The central area is dominated by Gérard's full-length portrait of Czar Alexander I. The **Pavillon des Voitures** displays several Imperial carriages, including the landau that Blücher captured at Waterloo in June 1815.

★Château de Bois-Préau ⊙ – This château, bought by Josephine in 1810 and rebuilt in 1855, and its park were bequeathed by Mr and Mrs Edward Tuck. The Malmaison museum housed in this château contains memorabilia of Napoleon's exile on St Helena and reminders of the return of his ashes. There is also an extensive display concerning the Napoleonic legend.

CHINESE CUISINE

Le Bonheur de Chine – *6 allée A.-Maillol -* ☎ *01 47 49 88 88 - closed Mon -160/230F.* The sculpted wooden façade and decorative fixtures shipped back from the Far East confirm that you are in China! Everything here is extravagant, ranging from the marble reception area and its giant fish-tank to the dining halls and even the menu...!

Musée d'Histoire locale ⊙ – This museum, housed in the old town hall, offers an interesting overview of Rueil's history (Cardinal Richelieu, barracks, Swiss guards etc) and of the town's main economic activities in the past: wine-growing, laundering (note the cast-iron oven used to heat irons). One room on the first floor is devoted to the Consulate and Empire periods (impressive collection of tin soldiers representing Napoleon's Grande Armée led by the Emperor himself). Another room illustrates the importance of Rueil at the beginning of the 20C (postcard-printing).

ADDITIONAL SIGHTS

Park – In the park (now limited to 6ha/15 acres) note the Marengo cedar tree planted soon after the victorious battle of 14 June 1800, the rose garden and a number of rare tree species. At the end of an avenue of stately lime trees stands the **Pavillon de Travail d'Été** that Napoleon used in conjunction with the library.

Leave the estate on foot and turn right to skirt the park along avenue Marmontel (gates).

On the left lies the Mausoleum of the Imperial Prince, the son of Napoleon III, who was killed by members of the Zulu tribe in 1879. The statue of the prince playing with his dog Nero is a replica of Jean-Baptiste Carpeaux' work (*the original is in the Louvre*).

Église St-Pierre-St-Paul – Built in the late 16C and completed under Richelieu, this church was restored thanks to the generosity of Napoleon III.

The interior is Renaissance. The **organ case★**, made in Florence in the late 15C, is among the most beautiful in France and was a present from Napoleon III.

To the right of the chancel lies the white marble tomb of the Empress Josephine. She is portrayed kneeling in formal attire, just as she was in David's painting of the coronation ceremony. Nearby stands a small mausoleum in memory of her uncle, governor of Martinique. The funeral monument to Queen Hortense – who died in 1837 – lies to the left of the chancel. The high altar features a beautiful 17C bronze low-relief sculpture representing the Embalming of Christ. It used to adorn the chapel in the Château de Malmaison.

Leave the church and bear left along D 39. Turn right onto rue Masséna to reach rue Charles-Floquet, which becomes chemin de Versailles. Enter the forest and continue to Étang de St-Cucufa. Park nearby.

Forêt de la Malmaison – This 200ha/500 acre forest is planted with oaks and chestnut trees; it is believed that a chapel was once built in the forest in honour of St Cucufa, who martyred in AD 304 during the rule of Diocletian.

In a small, wooded vale lies **Étang de St-Cucufa★**, a small lake which is covered with water-lilies during the summer months. Josephine gave orders to build a dairy at the water's edge which supplied the château with milk, butter and cheese. It has since disappeared. The wooden cottages lining the shores of the lake were built by Empress Eugénie.

Return to the car. On leaving the forest, take the first turning on the right.

Avenue de la Châtaigneraie and rue du Colonel-de-Rochebrune (D 180) cross the **Buzenval** district, where the heroes of the Paris Commune fought bravely in January 1871. A memorial has been erected on the top of the mound, which commands an extensive view of the northern lowlands.

ST-AMAND-LES-EAUX

Population 16 776
Michelin map 51 fold 17 or 236 fold 17, 18

The town is set on the west bank of the River Scarpe, which separates it from the vast Raismes-St-Amand-Wallers Forest; its name derives partly from St Amand, who was Bishop of Tongres in the 7C and founder of a Benedictine monastery here which became one of the most important abbeys in the north of France, and partly from its hot springs, used for the treatment of rheumatism and respiratory disorders. The four mineral springs produce water bottled by the Société des Eaux Minérales de St-Amand, the fifth largest producer in France. Culinary specialities include acorn tarts, hazelnut-flavoured flat cake and the local beer, known as "abbey beer".

SIGHTS

Abbey – The last reconstruction of these monastic buildings was undertaken c 1625 by Abbot Nicolas du Bois, with their solemn inauguration in 1673.

After the Revolution, only the impressive abbey tower and the magistrates' buildings remained.

★ Abbey Tower – Museum ⊙ – This is a colossal building (82m/269ft high) in a traditional Baroque style and was the narthex of a church with a nave (non-extant) which occupied much of what is now the public garden.

> ### Dumouriez changes sides
>
> In March 1793 **Dumouriez** established his headquarters in the Château de Fontaine-Bouillon (since demolished). It was here that the victor of the battles of Valmy and Jemmapes received the commissioners of the Convention who had come to arrest him; Dumouriez instead delivered them to the Austrian general Clairfayt. He then went over to the enemy with his staff, which included General Égalité, ex-duke of Chartres and future King Louis-Philippe.

The **façade** is divided into five levels, each using a Classical order: from the bottom to the top the orders run through Tuscan, Doric, Ionic, Corinthian and Composite. The Ionic level in particular features strange elaborately carved dragons. The columns and mouldings set the rhythm for the design which is unusual for the plethora of carvings. The damaged statues show God the Father, St Amand, St Benedict, St Martin and others. At the centre of the first level, a *trompe-l'œil* depiction of a church sheltered a now-faint scene of Christ expelling the money-lenders from the Temple.

The tower above the balustrade is crowned with a vast dome surmounted by a generously carved lantern turret and lantern; inside hangs the 17C Great Bell, weighing 4 560kg/nearly 5t.

Interior – The superb ground-floor chamber has carved stone vaulting around a central void to allow for the passage of the bells. Masks and scrolls, niches and stoups are reminiscent of the Antwerp Mannerist style. Temporary exhibitions are held here.

The first floor, with its lovely ribbed vault, houses a collection of 18C faiences from the two local potteries, Desmoutiers-Dorez and Fauquez; the collection includes over 300 pieces.

Climbing the tower *(362 steps)* gives a good **view** of the 17C timberwork. The workings of the 17C clock can be seen before reaching the bells themselves (48 of them), electrically operated each day between noon and 12.30pm.

An outside gallery offers a wide **panorama** over the Scarpe Valley and Raismes Forest as far as Valenciennes.

Échevinage ⊘ – The priory was designed by Nicolas du Bois as an entrance pavilion to the abbey, and was also used by the "magistracy" comprising the mayor and his aldermen.

The façade, flanked by towers with domes and a lantern, has a sandstone base and is in typically Flemish Baroque style: stone surrounds with vermiculated rustication, ringed columns, sculpted cartouches. The door is surmounted by a proclamations balcony or bartizan and the belfry houses the original "proclamations bell".

P	Parking	Picnic area		⋃	Sand pits
✖	Restaurant, inn, bar	Play area			Bird sanctuary
▲	Camping, caravaning	Horse riding			Discovery trail
◊	Recreation area	Watersports			Arboretum

Inside, on the first floor, the Salle de justice de Paix still has its original decor. On the second floor, two symmetrical rooms beneath the domes are covered by beautiful domed vaulting with radiating ribs. The Salle des Échevins reserved for the local council, has been entirely redecorated. The **Salon Watteau**, so-named because in 1782 Louis Watteau of Lille, great-nephew of the great painter, adorned it with religious and allegorical paintings, has kept its atmosphere.

Établissement thermal – *4km/2.5mi east by D 954 and D 151.*
Fontaine-Bouillon was known to the Romans for the curative powers of the spring water and was also a place of worship. When the exploitation of the waters began again in the 17C, under Vauban's direction, several ex-voto wooden statues left by those who had taken the waters in the past were found at the bottom of the basin. The waters and mud, bubbling up at a temperature of 26°C/82°F, are among the most radioactive in France; they are used mainly for the treatment of rheumatism and for physiotherapy.

The **établissement thermal**, which was rebuilt after the Second World War, also houses a hotel and a casino; its park (8ha/20 acres) extends into the forest along Drève du Prince which was marked out on the orders of Louis Bonaparte, who took the waters here in 1805.

★**Forêt de Raismes-St-Amand-Wallers** – This forest (4600ha/11370 acres), an important section of a larger Regional Nature Park (*parc naturel régional*), is however only a sliver of the great mantle which covered the Hainault region in the Middle Ages. The flat sand and clay soil, combined with the quarries of former mining works, has resulted in marshes and small lakes throughout the forest, which is made up of oak, beech, birch and poplar groves.

🔲 Amenities include trails, bridleways, picnic areas, a recreation area (*base de loisirs*), a water sports centre at the 100ha/247 acre **Amaury Lake** (*étang d'Amaury*) and the **Goriaux Pool** (*Mare à Goriaux*) bird sanctuary (*réserve ornithologique*) where numerous bird species such as the crested grebe, the common coot and the little ringed plover live. The Maison du Parc is on the edge of the forest, close to St-Amand-les-Eaux. The visitors' centre gives an insight into the beauty spots and natural environments contained within the regional park covering the Scarpe and Escaut plains.

ST-CLOUD★★

Population 28 597
Michelin map 101 folds 14, 24, 106 fold 18 or 237 fold 17
Michelin plan 22

Access from Paris: *Metro line 10 (station: Boulogne-Pont de St-Cloud)*

St-Cloud is situated on the west bank of the River Seine and belongs to the residential suburbs of the French capital. It is known mostly for its park, which once surrounded a splendid château.

Clodoald – Unlike his unfortunate brothers, Clodoald, the grandson of Clovis and Clotilda, escaped murder and became a disciple of the hermit Severin. He founded a monastery, where he died in 560; his tomb soon became a place of pilgrimage and the town of Nogent, which surrounded it, was subsequently renamed St-Cloud. The saint bequeathed his seignorial rights to the bishops of Paris who, until 1839, held the title of dukes of St-Cloud and peers of France.

The assassination of Henri III – In 1589 Henri III laid seige to Paris, which had fallen into the hands of the **Catholic League**: this religious alliance between members of the French nobility (led by the Guise and Montmorency families) and Spain had been formed in order to gain military and political power during a time of weak monarchy in France.
Following the King's alliance with his cousin, the Protestant Henri of Navarre, a vengeful young Jacobin friar called Jacques Clément gained admission to the King's presence and stabbed him in the abdomen. Henri III died two days later.

Monsieur's Castle – In 1658 the episcopal building became the property of Louis XIV's brother, known to all as "Monsieur". His first wife Henrietta of England died there in 1670. The Sun King's brother later married Charlotte-Elisabeth of Bavaria. He extended the grounds to 590ha/1 460 acres

---

St-Cloud porcelain

Founded by Pierre Chicaneau in 1677, the porcelain manufacture functioned for almost a century. The delicate, translucent porcelain objects are characterised by blue-monochrome lambrequin motifs enhanced by gold decorations. Some items are adorned with oriental motifs. The trade mark is a blue sun.

---

and asked Jules Hardouin-Mansart to draw up the plans for a series of beautiful buildings. The park and its impressive cascade were designed by **Le Nôtre**. Marie-Antoinette bought the estate in 1785 but it became State property during the Revolution.

The 18 Brumaire – When General Bonaparte returned from his campaign in Egypt, the army troops and the French people saw him as the leader who would restore peace and order. On 18 Brumaire of the year VIII in the new French calendar (9 November 1799), the seat of the Consulate was moved to St-Cloud.
The following day, the Five Hundred held a meeting at the orangery, presided over by Napoleon's brother Lucien Bonaparte. The General was greatly disconcerted by the hostile reception he got and was saved only by the swift intervention of his brother who had the assembly room cleared by Murat. The Directoire was abolished.

St-Cloud during the Empire – In 1802 Bonaparte was appointed consul for life and St-Cloud became his favourite official residence. He celebrated his civil wedding with Marie-Louise on the estate and followed it with a religious ceremony in the Square Salon of the Louvre (1810).
Later, in 1814, the Prussian Marshal Gebhard Blücher took up residence at the château. In an act of vengeance, he cut the silk hangings to ribbons, and wrecked both the bedroom and the library.
It was at St-Cloud that Charles X signed the Ordinances of July 1830, which abolished the charter and precipitated his downfall. It was also from St-Cloud that he went into exile.
On 1 December 1852 the Prince-President Louis-Napoleon was made Emperor. A meeting was held at the Château de St-Cloud on 15 July 1870, during which it was decided to declare war on Prussia. The building was badly damaged in a fire three months later; it was finally razed to the ground in 1891.

★★PARK

The 450ha/1 110 acre park which spreads from the slopes of the Seine Valley to the Garches plateau has retained most of the original layout designed by Le Nôtre. In the former Guards' Pavilion, a **Musée Historique** ⊙ tells the story of the estate and its château destroyed by fire in October 1870. Several thousand trees were brought down by the violent storms which swept through the Île-de-France region in December 1999.

★**Grande Cascade** – Designed in the 17C by Lepautre, these impressive falls were later enlarged by Jules Hardouin-Mansart. Dominated by allegorical statues of the River Seine and River Marne, the waters of the cascade flow into a series of basins and troughs before reaching the lower falls, from where they are channelled down to the edge of the park. The whole works are about 90m/296ft long. The **Grandes Eaux** ⊙ ★★ fountain display, staged every Sunday in June, is quite remarkable.

Grand Jet – Nestling in greenery near the Great Cascade, it is the most powerful fountain in the park and rises to a height of 42m/138ft.

Terrace – A cluster of yew trees and a marble layout mark the former site of the château, which was also the start of the lawns and their continuation, the allée de Marnes. The private gardens used to spread on either side of this avenue.

★**Jardin du Trocadéro** – These gardens were laid out on the site of the former château; they date from the Restoration period. This beautiful landscaped garden features a charming pond and an aviary.
The far end of the terrace commands a view of Paris. In the foreground, note the Pavillon d'Artois, part of which was built in the 17C.

Tapis vert – Running from the Grande Gerbe to Rond-Point des 24 Jets, these lawns command a lovely view of the flower beds and the city of Paris.

Rond-Point de la Balustrade – On this site Napoleon erected a monument surmounted by a lantern which was lit when the Emperor was staying at the château. It was based on a model from ancient Greece, which is why the Parisians called it Demosthene's lantern. It was blown up by the Prussians in 1870. The terrace offers a superb **panorama**★★ of Paris, stretching from the Bois de Boulogne to the woods at Clamart and Meudon.

Pavillon de Breteuil – This 18C pavilion – St-Cloud's former Trianon - houses the Bureau International des Poids et Mesures (World Centre for Scientific Measurement). The Bureau still has the old standard metre.

La Fayette Memorial – *West of the park, along boulevard Raymond-Poincaré.* The memorial was erected by an American foundation. It pays homage to the 209 pilots from the United States who volunteered to take part in the La Fayette Squadron during the First World War. The monument consists of an arch and a colonnade reflected in a small pond. The crypt beneath the terrace contains the mortal remains of the 67 pilots who perished, including the ace fighter Lufbery.

★**Institut Pasteur – Musée des Applications de la Recherche** – *3 avenue Pasteur and 3 boulevard Raymond-Poincaré*. In 1884 when **Louis Pasteur**, who had already done considerable research work, lacked space in Paris to pursue his studies on rabies, a decree ruled that he could move to the now State-owned Villeneuve-l'Étang estate; in 1885 he successfully invented the first vaccine for human use, crowning a lifelong career. The museum is housed in the Hundred Guards' Pavilion, occupied by Napoleon III's soldiers in the 19C. It presents the history of the struggle against infectious diseases through the accomplishments of Pasteur and his disciples: Pierre Roux, Yersin, Ramon, Calmette, Nicolle and Laveran, and concentrates on three major fields of research: serum therapy, vaccination and chemotherapy. The techniques used to overcome diseases such as diphtheria, tetanus, typhus, cholera, tuberculosis and polio are explained, together with the progress of modern research into hepatitis B, AIDS, immunology and artificial vaccines.

Louis Pasteur

EXPLORER

The room where Pasteur died in 1895 remains intact and features the family measuring rod bearing inscriptions made by Mme Pasteur. The study of Gaston Ramon, who discovered toxoids, has been reconstructed. The former drawing room houses a collection of 19C instruments from medical laboratories: Elie Metchnikoff's microscope, Chamberland's sterilizer and Doctor Roux' optical bench.

TOWN

Overlooked by the spire of the Église St-Clodoald (1865), the steep, narrow streets of the old town wind their way up the hillsides of the Seine Valley.

Pont de St-Cloud

In the 8C a bridge was built across the River Seine. According to tradition, no king was to set foot on it, or he would die a sudden death. Until the middle of the 16C, French rulers would cross the river in a boat.

However when François I died in Rambouillet, it was decided that the funeral procession would cross the famous bridge; no ill omens were feared as the King was already deceased. This put an end to the long-standing tradition. François' son Henri II replaced the old wooden bridge with a magnificent stone construction featuring 14 arches. The local people were astonished by such a massive display of stonework, which they claimed was the Devil's work, and the bridge had to be exorcised.

★**Église Stella-Matutina** ⊘ – *Place Henri-Chrétien along avenue du Maréchal-Foch*. The church was consecrated in 1965; it is shaped like a huge circular tent made of wood, metal and glass. It is fixed to a concrete base by nine pivots and fronted by a porch roof in the shape of a helm. The converging lines of the copper roofing and the pine timbering create an impression of loftiness and soaring height which is further emphasised by the concentric rows of fews round the altar.

Hippodrome de Saint-Cloud ⊘ – *1 rue du Camp Canadien*. The St-Cloud racecourse (which includes a golf course) extends over an area of 75ha/185 acres at the foot of Mont Valérien. It is well known for the quality of its flat-racing and events such as the Grand Prix de St-Cloud and the Journée de l'Élégance (fashion day).

ST-DENIS★★★

Population 89 988
Michelin map 101 fold 16, 106 folds 19, 20 or 237 folds 17, 18
Michelin plan 20

Access from Paris: *Metro line 13 (station: St-Denis-Basilique). By RER, line B, La Plaine-Voyageurs or line D, SNCF Gare Saint-Denis.*

St-Denis is an industrial and cultural town dating far back in history. For centuries, its destiny was directly linked to that of the abbey, then of the cathedral. In recent years, the **Stade de France**, inaugurated in January 1998, has given the town a boost, and stimulated the economy. The means of transport and the accommodation infrastructure were expanded for the France 98 Football World Cup. From the basilica to the stadium, an itinerary waymarked with informative panels illustrates the many facets of St-Denis: the historic and industrial town, the modern city and the privileged sports centre with a magnificent world-famous stadium.

"Monsieur St-Denis" – St Denis was a preacher, and the first Bishop of Lutetia. Legend has it that, after being beheaded in Montmartre, he picked up his head and walked away with it. He finally died in the country and was buried by a pious woman. An abbey was built over the grave of the man popularly known as "Monsieur (or Monsignor) St-Denis" and soon attracted large crowds of pilgrims. That, at least, is the legend. In fact, a Roman town stood on the site of St-Denis. It was called Catolacus and it had stood on the site since the 1C AD as it was possible to keep watch over the Paris-Beauvais road and the river from this spot. It was in a field outside this town that St Denis was said to have been buried in a secret ceremony, after his martyrdom. In AD 475, the first large church was built. Dagobert I had it rebuilt in AD 630 and set up a Benedictine community there with orders to take charge of the pilgrimage. The abbey was the wealthiest and most illustrious in France. The church was again rebuilt c 750 by Pepin the Short who included a "martyrium" under the chancel, a crypt in which people could pray at saints' tombs. The building we see today, however, dates mainly from the days of Suger in the 12C and Pierre de Montreuil in the 13C.

Abbot Suger – Suger is the outstanding figure in the history of St-Denis. He came from a poor family and was "given" to the abbey at the age of 10. His exceptional gifts gave him immense power over his fellow pupil, the son of Louis VI the Fat, who became a close friend of the young monk, summoned him to the royal court and consulted him on every possible subject. Suger was elected Abbot of St-Denis in 1122 and drew the plans of the present minster himself. As a minister during the reign of Louis VII, he was appointed Regent while the King was away fighting in the Second Crusade. His wisdom and his care for the public good were so great that, on his return, Louis VII called him the "Father of the Country".

Economic expansion – The Lendit fair was instigated by the abbey in 1109 and was held in the plain at St-Denis. For 600 years, it enjoyed fame throughout Europe. Twelve hundred wooden stalls were set up for the merchants. Every year, the University of Paris attended the fair in order to buy the parchment in the various faculties. Its proximity to Paris, however, brought it into the forefront of wars and epidemics. This may go some way towards explaining its active role in the French Revolution in 1789. It was then renamed Franciade, a name which it kept until 1800. Dyeing and printing works were set up. During the second half of the 19C, the town attracted heavy industries.

★★★BASILICA

The burial ground of kings – For 1 200 years from Dagobert to Louis XVIII, almost all the kings of France were buried here. In 1793, Barrère asked the Convention for permission to destroy the tombs. The bodies were thrown into communal graves. Alexandre Lenoir saved the most precious tombs by taking them to Paris, storing them in the Petits-Augustins which was to become the Musée des Monuments Français. In 1816, Louis XVIII returned the tombs to the basilica.

Construction – The structure is of prime importance in the history of architecture. It had the first large chancel and was a prototype, providing inspiration for the architects of countless late-12C cathedrals such as the ones in Chartres, Senlis and Meaux.

Ph. Gajic/MICHELIN

Window in the Basilica

Suger had the west front and first two bays built between 1136 and 1140, followed by the chancel and crypt from 1140 to 1144. The Carolingian nave was retained as a temporary measure but was refaced (1145-47).

Early in the 13C the left tower was topped with a magnificent stone spire. Then work began again on the chancel. The transept and the nave were totally rebuilt. St Louis commissioned Pierre de Montreuil to do the work. He was employed here from 1247 until his death in 1267.

Decline and Fall – In later years, the basilica was poorly maintained and the French Revolution brought with it further damage. In his work *Genius of Christianity*, Chateaubriand described the desolate atmosphere, "St-Denis is deserted. Birds fly through it and grass grows on the broken altars...". Napoleon had the most urgent repairs carried out and returned the basilica to the Church in 1806.

Restoration – The architect Debret took charge of the church in 1813 but he knew little or nothing about medieval architecture and his work raised public indignation. He began to work on the magnificent spire but used materials that were too heavy and the delicate balance was destroyed. In 1846, the spire threatened collapse and had to be removed.

Viollet-le-Duc – Replacing Debret in 1847, he gathered up documents that enabled him to restore the building to its original condition. From 1858 until his death in 1879, he undertook a considerable amount of work and the church we see today is due to his efforts.

Digs carried out in the crypt have revealed stretches of wall from the Carolingian martyrium and a Merovingian burial ground including the late-6C tomb of Princess Arégonde, Clothar I's wife, some magnificent sarcophagi, and several admirable pieces of jewellery. Foundations of earlier churches have also been uncovered.

Tour *1hr*

Exterior – The absence of the north tower mars the harmony of the west front. In the Middle Ages the building was fortified and some crenellations are still visible at the base of the towers. The tympanum on the central doorway represents the Last Judgment, that on the right doorway (it has been recarved) depicts the Last Communion of St Denis and on the left the Death of St Denis and his companions Rusticus and Eleutherus (also recarved). The door jambs feature the Wise and Foolish Virgins *(centre)*, the labours of the months *(right)* and the signs of the Zodiac *(left)*.

On the north side of the cathedral, the nave is supported by double flying buttresses. The transept, which presents a wonderful rose-window, was initially to have had two towers but work stopped after the first floor. If the original plans had been carried out, the church would have had six towers altogether.

The basilica has been floodlit every night since June 1998; the lighting by Yann Kersalé which illuminates the west front recreates the warm colours of stained glass.

Interior – The cathedral is 108m/354ft long, 39m/128ft wide in the transept and 29m/95ft high, making it slightly smaller than Notre-Dame in Paris.

The narthex is formed by the two bays beneath the towers. Part of its pointed vaulting, which rests on a series of sturdy pillars, was designed by Suger. The elegant nave is attributed to Pierre de Montreuil. The bays in the triforium open onto the exterior (one of the first examples of such arrangements). The stained-glass windows in the nave are modern.

★★★**The tombs** ○ – St-Denis houses the tombs of kings, queens and royal children, as well as those of leading personalities who served the French court, such as Bertrand

313

Effigies of Marie-Antoinette and Louis XVI

du Guesclin (**1**). The mausoleum may be seen as a museum of French funeral art through the Middle Ages and during the Renaissance period (79 recumbent figures). The tombs have been empty since the Revolution.

After the 14C it was customary to remove the heart and viscera from the bodies of French kings before embalming them. The inner organs, the heart and the body were all buried in different places. The bodies were taken to St-Denis.

Up to the Renaissance, the only sculpture adorning tombs were **recumbent figures**. Note the tombs of Clovis (**2**) and Fredegunde (**3**), featuring a copper cloisonné mosaic made in the 12C for St-Germain-des-Prés Church.

Around 1260 St Louis commissioned a series of effigies of all the rulers who had preceded him since the 7C. The figures were purely symbolic but they provide a telling example of how royalty was portrayed towards the mid-13C. They include the imposing tomb of Dagobert (**4**), with its lively, spirited scenes, the recumbent statues of Charles Martel (**5**) and Pepin the Short (**6**), and a female effigy carved in Tournai marble (**7**). The statue of Philippe III the Bold (**8**), who died in 1285, shows an early concern for accurate portraiture and bears a strong resemblance to the living character. Towards the middle of the 14C well-known people had their tomb built when they were still alive. The effigies of Charles V by Beauneveu (**9**), Charles VI and Isabella of Bavaria (**10**) are therefore extremely lifelike.

During the Renaissance, these **mausoleums** took on monumental proportions and were lavishly decorated. They were laid out on two levels, contrasting sharply with one another. The upper level featured the king and his wife, kneeling in full regalia. On the lower level, the deceased were pictured lying down as naked cadavers. Admire the twin monument built for Louis XII and Anne of Brittany (**11**), and that of François I and Claude de France (**12**), sculpted by Philibert Delorme and Pierre Bontemps.

Catherine de' Medici, who survived her husband Henri II by 30 years, gave orders to build the royal tomb. When she saw how she had been portrayed according to tradition, she fainted in horror and ordered a new effigy which substituted sleep for death. Both works are on display in the cathedral. Their making was supervised by Primaticcio (**13**), and Germain Pilon (**14**), respectively.

Chancel – The beautiful pre-Renaissance stalls (**15**), in the forward part of the chancel, were taken from the Norman Castle in Gaillon. On the right stands a splendid 12C Romanesque **Virgin Mary★** in painted wood (**16**), brought from St-Martin-des-Champs. The bishop's throne opposite (**17**) is a replica of Dagobert's royal throne (*the original is in the Medals and Antiquities Gallery at the Bibliothèque Nationale in Paris*). At the end, the modern reliquary of the saints Denis, Rusticus and Eleutherius (**18**) flanks Suger's **ambulatory★**, characterised by wide arches and slim columns.

The radiating chapels are decorated with several altarpieces and fragments of stained glass dating from the Gothic period.

★★ Crypt ⊙ – The lower ambulatory was built in the Romanesque style by Suger (12C) and restored by Viollet-le-Duc (capitals with plant motifs). In the centre stands a vaulted chapel known as Hilduin's Chapel (after the abbot who had it built in the 9C). Beneath the pavement lies the burial vault of the Bourbon family, which houses the remains of Louis XVI, Marie-Antoinette and Louis XVIII, among others. The communal grave in the north transept received in 1817 the bones of around 800 kings and queens, royal highnesses, princes of the blood, Merovingians, Capetians and members of the Orléans and Valois dynasties.

ADDITIONAL SIGHTS

Former Abbey ⊙ – It adjoins the cathedral that was once the abbey church. The present conventual buildings date from the 18C and are the work of Robert de Cotte. In 1809 Napoleon I made the abbey the seat of a college for the daughters of holders of the French order of merit, the **Légion d'Honneur**.

Musée d'Art et d'Histoire ⊙ – *22 bis rue Gabriel-Péri.*
The museum is set up in the former Carmelite convent, part of which has been restored. The convent was founded by Cardinal de Bérulle in 1625 and occupied by Louis XV's daughter Madame Louise de France between 1770 and 1787. The refectory and the kitchen contain archeological exhibits discovered in St-Denis (fragments of medieval pottery). Many of the items on display come from the old hospital, including a superb reconstruction of an apothecary's shop, that is of particular interest to ceramics enthusiasts (17C and 18C jars), and an apothecary's collection of ceramic phials and jars (17C and 18C).
The cells on the first floor contain many works of art, mementoes and paintings, including several by Guillot, evoking the daily life of the Carmelite nuns. Mystical adages have been inscribed on the walls.
On the second floor, once reserved for the king when he visited his daughter, there are numerous drawings, paintings and documents relating to the Paris Commune of 1871. One of the rooms contains works by the Impressionist painter Albert André. The former Louis XV pavilion, now renovated, houses an exhibition of the works of Paul Éluard, with a collection of personal memorabilia.
The **former Carmelite chapel** has a splendid Louis XVI dome. It was here that the prioress Louise de France died in 1787.

Musée Bouilhet-Christofle ⊙ – *112 rue Ambroise-Croizat.*
The famous gold and silverware manufacturing company – the first to apply the principle of electroplating - set up premises here in 1875. They became the official supplier to Napoleon III and their silver pieces still adorn the tables of many heads of State and rulers throughout the world. The museum presents a number of rare exhibits and some beautiful reproductions crafted in the St-Denis workshops in the late 19C. The history of the silverware industry covers Antiquity, the Gallo-Roman period (Hildesheim treasure), the Renaissance (Henri II's ceremonial armour), the 18C (Vinsac ewer), the Second Empire and the last century up to 1960 (objects by Gio Ponti Sabattini, Wirkkala etc). There is an annexe of this museum in Paris (9 rue Royale, 75008); it is also possible to visit the workshops on request.

Stade de France ⊙ – The France 98 Football World Cup was the force that generated it, and now it is the biggest multifunction Olympic-sized stadium in the world. The elliptic structure is 270m/295yd long, 230m/240yd wide, 35m/115ft high and covers an area of 17ha/42 acres. Thanks to its variable capacity, it can host all kinds of sporting and entertainment events. The circle of stands (25 000 seats) nearest the track can be reconfigured to accommodate athletics competitions. The middle stand has a capacity of 30 000 and the upper stand 25 000. When the field is used for concert fans, the total capacity reaches 105 000.

Parc de la Courneuve – *2.5km/1.5mi east along rue de Strasbourg and N 301 (on the right).*
This 440ha/1 090 acre stretch of greenery features a cycling track, bridlepath, a ski jump, a little train, sports facilities, and playgrounds for children. Rowing boats and pedaloes may be hired to explore the 12ha/30 acre lake *(bathing prohibited).*

France 98

In 1998, France won the coveted World Football Cup for the first time since its inauguration in 1928, by defeating the legendary Brazilian team 3 goals to nil. The French people had been waiting for this moment for a long time! Hopes were raised as far back as 1938 when France, as the host country, staged the final in Colombes, a northern suburb of Paris. Sixty years later, another northern suburb, this time St-Denis, the burial ground of French kings, was chosen as the site of a huge stadium, in keeping with this gigantic event.

Population 39 926
Michelin map 101 fold 12, 106 folds 17, 18 or 237 fold 17
Michelin plan 18

Access from Paris: *RER line A 1*

St-Germain is both a residential district and a popular resort, with many tourists attracted by its château, its huge terrace and its forest. The town owes its name to St Germain, a Paris bishop, and *laye* which probably means "forest path".

Annual event

The Fête des Loges, which goes back to St Louis, takes place every year in the St-Germain Forest on a site known as "Les Loges". This convivial funfair lasts for seven weeks from the end of June to the Sunday following the 15 August. The numerous attractions and stands appeal to around 3 million visitors who also enjoy the roast chickens, sauerkraut and beer on offer...

HISTORICAL NOTES

The old castle – In the 12C Louis VI, the Fat, eager to exploit the strategic position of the St-Germain hillside, built a fortified stronghold on the site of the present château. In 1230 St Louis added a charming little chapel which still stands today. The fortress was destroyed during the Hundred Years War and restored by Charles V around 1368.

In 1514 Louis XII married his daughter Claude de France to the Duc d'Angoulême, who became François I the following year. The young ruler was acquainted with Italian culture and the ancient citadel was hardly suited to his taste for palatial comfort and luxury. In 1539 he had the whole building razed with the exception of Charles V's keep and the chapel built by St Louis. The reconstruction was entrusted to Pierre Chambiges, who produced the present château.

New Château – Even the new building presented itself as a fortified structure equipped with machicolations and defended by a garrison numbering 3 000. Henri II, who wanted a real country house, commissioned Philibert Delorme to draw up plans for a new château on the edge of the plateau. The construction work was completed under Henri IV. The château became famous on account of its fantastic location and the terraces built along the slopes overlooking the River Seine.

The area beneath the foundation arches has been arranged into artificial grottoes where hydraulically propelled automatons re-enact mythological scenes: Orpheus playing the viola and attracting animals who come to listen, Neptune's chariot in full motion etc. This wonderful mechanism was the work of the Francine, a family of Italian engineers, to whom Louis XIV later entrusted the waterworks of Versailles.

Chronology of court events – The court occupied both the new château and the old castle which were used as a palatial residence, or a safe retreat when riots broke out in Paris. Henri II, Charles IX and Louis XIV were all born at St-Germain. Louis XIII died here. Mary Queen of Scots lived here between the ages of 6 and 16. In 1558 she married the Dauphin François, aged only 15, and was crowned Queen of France the following year. Her husband died after a year, however, and she was forced to return to Scotland, where her tragic destiny led her to die on the scaffold.

Many poets and writers took part in the royal festivities organised in St-Germain: Malherbe, then Benserade and Molière who wrote some brilliant court ballets at the beginning of Louis XIV's reign.

Mansart's improvements – Louis XIV – who was born, christened and brought up at St-Germain – grew fond of the château. As king, he paid frequent visits to the estate. The apartments of the old castle had become too cramped for Louis' liking and he commissioned **Jules Hardouin-Mansart** to build five large pavilions as a replacement for the five corner turrets adjoining the outer walls. Le Nôtre drew up the plans for the park, the terrace and the forest; in 1665 the grounds were replanted with five and a half million trees. In 1682 the court moved from St-Germain to Versailles. In 1689 the deposed King of England James II came to stay at the old castle, where he died, in great financial straits in 1701, a well-loved figure (funeral monument in St-Germain Church, facing the château).

Maréchal Louis de Noailles (1713-93) subsequently became the important figure at St-Germain as governor of the château and its estate, which was divided up and acquired the reputation of being the most fashionable residential area in town.

Final developments – In 1776 the badly dilapidated new château was ceded to the Comte d'Artois by his brother Louis XVI. The future king Charles X had the building demolished, except for the Henri IV pavilion on the terrace and the Sully Pavilion, in

Le Pecq. He originally intended to reconstruct the building according to new plans but he dropped the work at St-Germain when he purchased the château at Maisons-Laffitte. The remains, together with the park, were sold during the Revolution.

The old castle was stripped of its furniture. Under Napoleon I it was the seat of a cavalry college, under Louis-Philippe it housed a military penitentiary but Napoleon III ordered its closure in 1855. It was then entirely restored under the guidance of the architect Millet, succeeded by Daumet.

The five pavilions added by Mansart were demolished and the building regained the appearance it had during the reign of François I.

In 1867 Napoleon III inaugurated the National Museum of French Antiquities which he had set up on the premises. The signing of the 1919 peace treaty with Austria took place in the château at St-Germain.

THE CHÂTEAU AND ITS NEIGHBOURHOOD

The most striking approach to the château is from the north, along the road from Les Loges. The tour starts from the square beside the château, place Charles-de-Gaulle. The express RER line (which runs underground at St-Germain and has an exit opening onto the square) has replaced the famous railway track between Paris and St-Germain; its inauguration between Le Pecq and the French capital on 26 August 1837 was an unprecedented landmark in the history of French railway services.

*__Château__ – The château is the shape of an imperfect pentagon; its moats were originally filled with water. The feudal foundations are distinguishable together with the covered watch-path and a series of machicolations restored by Daumet. The roof, laid out as a terrace edged with vases and a balustrade and dominated by tall chimneys, was an innovative idea.

At the northern end of the façade overlooking place Charles-de-Gaulle stands the quadrilateral keep built by Charles V, to which a bell-tower was added under François I.

Senior officers were housed on the ground floor while the mezzanine apartments were occupied by princes of the blood, ladies-in-waiting, mistresses and ministers, among them Mazarin, Colbert and Louvois.

The royal suites were on the first floor; the king and the dauphin lived in the wing facing the parterres, the queen's suite looked towards Paris and the children's rooms were in the wing which now faces rue Thiers. Under Henri IV 12 of the 14 royal infants, born to five different mothers, romped noisily in these quarters.

*__Ste-Chapelle__ – Built by St Louis from 1230 to 1238, this chapel precedes the Ste-Chapelle in Paris by some 10 years. It was probably designed by the same architect, Pierre de Montreuil, but its tall windows do not have the stained glass that gives such dazzling splendour to its counterpart in Paris. The fine rose-window in the west front was blocked off by other buildings.

Within the thickness of the keystones are carvings of figures thought to represent St Louis, his mother Blanche of Castille, his wife, and other people close to him. If this is true, it would make these precious images the oldest pictures of royal families in existence.

J. Bénazet/PIX

Château de St-Germain-en-Laye, main courtyard

RMN

Lady of Brassempouy, Musée des
Antiquités Nationales

★★ Musée des Antiquités Nationales ⊘ – The museum contains many rare archeological exhibits relating to France's early history, ranging from the first signs of man's existence (Paleolithic Age) to the Middle Ages.

Prehistory and protohistory (Mezzanine) – The Paleolithic or early Stone Age goes back one million years before our era.

The glass cabinets on the right provide general information on materials such as stone (flint), quartz, bone and antlers, and displays toolmaking techniques of that period. Note the traces of man's existence in prehistoric times: photographs of the handprints at Gargas, mould of the footprints found in a cave at Aldène. The left-hand cabinets displaying the results of the excavations are in chronological order. The major works of art dating from the Paleolithic Age are surprisingly small: the **Lady of Brassempouy** (3.6cm/1.44in high), the oldest human face found to date (c 20000 BC), a bison licking itself (Magdalenian - c 16000 BC), the Bruniquel baton in the shape of a jumping horse (c 13000 BC), the Mas-d'Azil head of a neighing horse (c 10000 BC) etc. During the Neolithic Age, man developed farming and cattle rearing, community life in huts and the use of ceramics. He produced arms and tools by polishing very hard stones (jadeite).

The discovery of an alloy combining copper and tin led to the early stages of metallurgy (Bronze Age). Gold too was widely used and the museum displays several objects and pieces of jewellery made of solid gold or gold leaf. Note the numerous weapons (daggers, axes with curved blades) and the metal necklaces and other decorative objects (open bracelets) which give these particular collections the sparkle that characterised some of the so-called "primitive" civilizations of the modern world.

The large iron sword is typical of the items from princely burial sites dating from the early Iron Age (the period known as Hallstatt). It was found together with clasps, ceramics, pieces of furniture (Magny-Lambert cist), horses' tack and even four-wheel funeral carriages.

The La Tène period that followed benefited from the contributions made by foreign civilizations and especially the increasingly important trade relations with the Mediterranean world. Most of the objects exhibited here come from excavation sites in Champagne and Burgundy (jewellery, vases). Gallic tribes still buried funeral chariots in their tombs, worked gold (jewellery) and minted coins. The fall of Alésia (52 BC) put an end to their own culture.

Gallo-Roman and Merovingian Antiquities (First floor) – The lengthy period of Roman peace *(Pax Romana)*, the indulgence of the victors and the deeply rooted religious feeling for indigenous gods gave rise to a flourishing industry of mythological and funeral sculpture (until then the Celts had shown little interest in statuary art). Note the large collection of gravestones.

Ceramic pieces played an important role in domestic life; one of the cabinets offers a fairly comprehensive presentation of "sigillate" ceramics, decorated with stamped motifs, made in workshops at Lezoux, La Graufesenque, Banassac etc (1C-4C AD). Little is known about the following period (3C-8C AD), though its heritage consists mostly of Merovingian burial places rich in arms – swords with damascene blades – and items of finery: heavy flat buckles for belts, S-shaped clasps etc.

The large ballroom in the château – also called the Salle de Mars - is a beautiful vaulted room with ornate stone ribbing and a fireplace bearing François I's emblem, the salamander. It is dedicated to comparative archeology; a superb selection of objects from all five continents makes it possible to draw parallels between techniques and lifestyles belonging to geographically distant civilizations, from very different historical periods.

The displays are carefully arranged according to two thematic approaches; the transition from one continent to another is evident if the visit runs from one end of the room to the other, while the chronological evolution of technology is clear when visiting one side and the other in succession.

Observe the splendid Egyptian collections dating from pre-Dynastic times, a set of bronze sculptures from Kodan and Armenian Talysh (Asia), **Mérida's Chariot** (6C BC), a masterpiece of Iberian workmanship (28cm/11in long and 12cm/5in high), which depicts a rider and his dog chasing a wild boar.

ST-GERMAIN EN-LAYE

Bonnenfant (R. A.) .... **AZ** 3
Coches (R. des) .... **AZ** 4

Denis (R. M.) .... **AZ** 5	Pain (R. au) .... **AZ** 20
Detaille (Pl.) .... **AY** 6	Paris (R. de) .... **AZ**
Giraud-Teulon (R.) .... **BZ** 9	Poissy (R. de) .... **AZ** 22
Gde-fontaine (R.) .... **AZ** 10	Pologne (R. de) .... **AY** 23
Loges (Av. des) .... **AY** 14	Surintendance (R. de la) **AY** 28
Malraux (Pl. A.) .... **BZ** 16	Victoire (Pl. de la) .... **AY** 30
Marché-Neuf (Pl. du) .... **AZ**	Vieil-Abreuvoir (R. du) ... **AZ** 32
Mareil (Pl.) .... **AZ** 19	Vieux-Marché (R. du) ... **AZ** 33

Exterior

Parterres – Enter the gardens through the gate on place Charles-de-Gaulle and skirt the château. Built into the façade is the loggia opening onto the inner main staircase. The moat contains restored megalithic monuments and replicas of Roman statues. The east esplanade – now the site of a pillbox - was the scene of the last judicial duel during which the will of God was invoked. The duel between Jarnac and La Châtaigneraie was attended by Henri II, accompanied by his retinue of courtiers. La Châtaigneraie, one of the finest swordsmen in Europe, was confident about the outcome of the battle. Jarnac, however, had learnt a new tactic: he severed the left hamstring of his adversary, who collapsed and slowly died.

Pavillon Henri-IV – The brick pavilion was built on the very edge of the escarpment; it is crowned by a dome, and, together with the **Sully Pavilion** set lower down on the hillside at Le Pecq, is all that remains of the new château. It contains the Louis XIII oratory where Louis XIV was baptised on 5 September 1638, the day he was born.
The hotel which opened in this historic building in 1836 became an important meeting place for 19C writers, artists and politicians. Alexandre Dumas wrote *The Three Musketeers* and *The Count of Monte Cristo* while he was staying here, Offenbach composed *The Drum Major's Daughter* and Léo Delibes produced the ballet *Sylvia*. The statesman and president Thiers died here in 1877.

★★**Terrace** – The Small Terrace starts beside the hotel and extends to the Rosarium roundabout. There, a worn Touring Club of France viewing table is a reminder of past views towards the western suburbs of Paris.

The Grand Terrace extends beyond the roundabout. It is one of Le Nôtre's finest accomplishments and was completed in 1673 after four years of large-scale construction work. Lined with stately lime trees, it is 2400m/8000ft long and is one of the most famous promenades around Paris.

The vista from the terrace being the same all the way along, visitors pressed for time may return to their car through the lovely **landscape garden★**.

ADDITIONAL SIGHTS

★**Musée départemental du Prieuré** ○ – The Priory was founded in 1678 by Mme De Montespan and was originally designed as a royal hospital. In 1915 it became the property of the painter **Maurice Denis** (1870-1943), who moved there with his large family and freely entertained his friends of the Nabis movement.

The rooms are former dorters and attics joined by double spiral staircases featuring surbased groined vaulting.

The museum explains the origins of the **Nabis** group – founded by Paul Sérusier in 1888 – and illustrates their passion for various forms of pictorial and decorative expression: painting, posters, stained glass etc. The works assembled in the priory testify to the considerable influence the symbolic movement – the "search for the

Eating out

MID-RANGE

Feuillantine – 10 rue des Louviers – ☎ 01 34 51 04 24 – 148F. Located in a lively pedestrian area of the city, Feuillantine offers traditional fare with seasonal variations in a dining room with visible beams and wall seats that make for a congenial, friendly ambience.

Clémentine – 24 rue St-Pierre – ☎ 01 34 51 77 78 – closed 15-31 Aug, Sun and Mon - 169/250F. This appealing restaurant in the heart of St-Germain-en-Laye has a delightfully sunlit dining room decorated with brightly coloured lithographs and furnished in contemporary style. The menu of Provençal specialities is frequently renewed and Iranian caviar is available for the wealthy...

Where to stay

MID-RANGE

Havre Hôtel – 92 rue Léon-Desoyer – ☎ 01 34 51 41 05 – 10 rooms 280/340F – ☲ 38F. Near the administrative centre, tucked away from the historical quarter, this little hotel is a colourful sight indeed. The simple, lively and spruce rooms are all you will need. The three bedrooms facing the cemetery are more peaceful.

LUXURY

Hôtel de l'Ermitage des Loges – 11 avenue des Loges – ☎ 01 39 21 50 90 – ▣ – 56 rooms from 580F – ☲ 60F – restaurant 98/175F. Conveniently situated near the château, this hotel, whose soundproofed rooms are tastefully furnished, presents an artful combination of colour and texture, comfort and aesthetics. Note the delightful bar and drawing rooms.

On the town

Couleur Café – 18 rue de la Salle – ☎ 01 39 10 07 70 – daily 8am-8pm. A curious-looking Italianate café made with chrome metal and blue wood. The interior can accommodate only 20 people, so the terrace looking onto a pedestrian street is heated in winter. A highly popular and trendy meeting place for locals, who drop in here for a cup of tea, chocolate or coffee (eight varieties to choose from). If you're feeling peckish, why not try their cookies or bilberry muffins while browsing through the magazines dotted around the room. Light meals.

Showtime

La Clef – 46 rue de Mareil – ☎ 01 39 21 54 90 – http://www.rockinfo.fr/laclef consult the Calendar of events. Tickets can be bought beforehand from La Clef, O'Sullivans and FNAC. Zebda (one of the biggest summer hits in 1999), Miossec, Louise Attaque and even the Cuban singer Compay Segundo came to this concert hall to perform on stage and many of them went on to achieve international acclaim.

invisible" – had on the art world at large: literature, decorative arts, sculpture, painting and music. Rejecting Realism and Naturalism, this movement claimed the necessity to put feeling at the centre of every work of art. The Pont-Aven School is represented by Gauguin, Émile Bernard, Filiger, Moret, Slewinsky, Seguin etc; the Nabi group by Sérusier, Ranson, Bonnard, Vuillard, Maurice Denis, Cazalis, Lacombe, Rousseli, Valloton and Verkade. The

Dessert in the Garden, Maurice Denis

museum also displays works by Toulouse-Lautrec, Anquetin, Mondrian, Lalique etc.

Chapelle – The chapel was entirely decorated by Maurice Denis between 1915 and 1928: stained glass, frescoes, liturgical furnishings...

Atelier – Maurice Denis had this studio built by his friend Auguste Perret in 1912 when he was working on the decoration for the ceiling of the Théâtre des Champs-Élysées. Vast profane and religious projects are on display.

Park – A series of terraced flower beds are pleasantly dotted with statues by Antoine Bourdelle. The park offers a charming vista of the priory façade and its elegant severity.

Maison Debussy ⊙ – *38 rue au Pain.* This house was the birthplace of the composer Claude Debussy on 22 August 1862. The restored building contains the tourist office on the ground floor and mementoes of the composer on the first floor.

Forêt de St-Germain

Circled by one of the Seine's loops, the forest was once part of the Forest of Laye. It is planted with oaks, beeches and hornbeams, and with conifers on the poorer soil of the northern massif. Reduced to 3 500ha/8 650 acres, it nevertheless features 120km/74mi of footpaths and 60km/37mi of bridleways, hunting lodges, wayside crosses, old gates and clearings.

Forêt de ST-GOBAIN★★
ST-GOBAIN FOREST
Michelin map 56 fold 4 or 236 fold 37

This beautiful forest (6 000ha/14 000 acres) between the River Oise and River Ailette covers a plateau pitted with quarries and furrowed with vales which are dotted with lakes. Tree species include oak and beech, with ash on the clay, birch in the sandy areas and poplar in the valleys.

The region is rich in deer and used to be the home of wolves and wild boar. Deer-hunting, a tradition here since the time of Louis XV, still continues today.

Signposted trails lead through the forest; in season, the area provides a rich crop of mushrooms and lily of the valley.

FORÊT DE ST-GOBAIN ⊙
23km/14mi round tour – about 2hr 45min.

St-Gobain – The town was established as a consequence of pilgrims visiting the Irish hermit Gobain, who settled in the forest and lived there for 20 years until he was beheaded by the Vandals. St-Gobain lies on the edge of a limestone ridge which reaches a height of 200m/656ft in parts.

St-Gobain is best-known for its **Mirror Factory** *(manufacture de glaces)* founded by Louis XIV at Colbert's request, and established in 1692 in the ruins of the castle that had belonged to the lords of Coucy. It was the first to use a method of casting which allowed the production of very large mirrors. The factory entrance has a monumental 18C gateway. This manufacture preceded the St-Gobain Company now part of the St-Gobain-Pont-à-Mousson group, one of the top producers of glazes in the world.

Eating out

MODERATE

Auberge de Bernagousse – *02700 Barisis-aux-Bois – 5km/3mi south-west of St-Gobain by D 534 –* ☎ *03 23 39 56 05 – closed 19-26 Feb, 3-10 Sept, Sun evening and Mon – booking essential Sat-Sat – 59/180F.* Take some time off and retreat to this sparsely decorated restaurant in the heart of the forest. Their Sunday afternoon brunch, complete with pies and cider, is famous throughout the area and will give you strength to resume your long walks in the country.

Le Parc – *8 rue Luce-de-Lancival, 02410 St-Gobain –* ☎ *03 23 52 80 58 – closed 14 July-14 Aug, Sun evening and Mon – 100/180F.* This is yet another appealing stopover... A 19C bourgeois residence in a small garden where a warm welcome will be extended to you. Handsome stone fireplace and parquet flooring. Meals are served outdoors during the tourist season.

Take D 7 (Laon road) east for 3km/2mi; at the crossroads (La Croix-des-Tables) turn left onto D 730.

The **Roches de l'Ermitage** *(15min on foot there and back)* are very picturesque. There are three hiking trails: the pond (2hr, blue markings); the abbeys (4hr, red markings) and the rocks (20min, white markings).

D 730 joins D 55.

Turn right onto D 55 and first left onto D 556.

★**Le Tortoir** – The walls of Le Tortoir, a 14C fortified priory which was a daughter-house of the abbey of St-Nicolas-aux-Bois, appear in a clearing surrounded by lakes where teal and moorhen are to be found.

Around the courtyard of the priory (now a farm) stand the guesthouse (28m/91ft long) and the prior's residence with its elegant mullioned windows; the chapel dates from the early 14C.

Return to D 55 and continue south.

Soon after the village of St-Nicolas-aux-Bois, the ruins of the abbey become visible *(right)*.

★**Abbaye St-Nicolas-aux-Bois** – The Benedictine abbey, the remains of which have been incorporated into a private property, occupied a delightful setting here on the floor of a valley. The road first skirts the moat which protected the abbey walls and then two ponds encircled by greenery, beyond which the 15C abbey buildings appear.

Croix Seizine – *400m/440yd from D 55.* This expiatory monument was erected by Enguerrand IV, Lord of Coucy, who was condemned in 1256 by St Louis for having executed four students from St-Nicolas-aux-Bois who were caught hunting on his land.

Continue along D 55. At the picturesque village of **Suzy** *turn right onto D 552.*

★**Abbaye de Prémontré** ⊘ – This former abbey nestling in a wooded valley was founded by **St Norbert**, who was born at the end of the 11C near the Rhine in the Duchy of Cleves. He lived a worldly life until one stormy day he was thrown from his horse like St Paul and a voice reproached him for his dissolute living. Touched by grace, Norbert sold all his possessions and retreated to Prémontré where he founded the abbey and the order which took its name.

Former Priory of Le Tortoir

The **Premonstratensian order**, which adopted St Augustin's rule, was recognised by the Pope from 1126 and prospered – numbering 1 500 houses for men and women. The fathers wore the biretta (cap) and white habits.

The abbey was rebuilt in the 18C, converted to a glassworks in 1802 and is now a psychiatric hospital. Three buildings stand around the flower beds; they feature remarkable "colossal Ionic" pilasters which set the rhythm for the façade. The main body has a round outer porch with an unusual curved triangular pediment, with a cardinal's shield above. Note the wrought-iron balcony with the cardinal's arms and the finely carved keystones of the windows.

The wings are simpler; their porches are topped with a shell framed by monumental urns. The left-hand building contains a stairway of advanced design, entirely supported by the walls of the oval well.

The abbey church was never built; an adjacent building housed the canons' chapel.

Follow D 14 to Septvaux.

Septvaux – The Romanesque church with its two belfries stands on a mound overlooking the lovely 12C wash-house *(on the road to Coucy).*

D 13 returns to St-Gobain.

ST-LEU-D'ESSERENT★

Population 4 288
Michelin map 106 folds 7, 8 or 237 folds 6, 18
North-west of Chantilly

The Archbishop of Sens, St Leu, who died in 623, gave his name to several French localities. St-Leu-d'Esserent, located on the banks of the River Oise, boasts a magnificent church which the philosopher and historian Ernest Renan once compared to a Greek temple on account of its pure, harmonious lines.

★CHURCH *30min*

Leave Chantilly and proceed towards St-Leu along D 44. The bridge over the Oise affords the best **general view** of the church from a distance. Nearby quarries produced the lovely stone which was used for the construction of many other churches and cathedrals as well as the palace at Versailles.

The Germans converted these quarries into workshops for their V1 missiles. As a result, the town was repeatedly bombed and the church wrecked in 1944.

Exterior – The façade has been significantly restored since the 19C – in particular the sculpted decoration – and is separate from the nave. It forms a Romanesque block (first half of the 12C) presenting a porch and, on the upper level, a gallery, each consisting of three bays.

Skirt the right side of the church, walking past the entrance to the former priory.

The chancel is dominated by two square towers with saddleback roofs. It is surrounded by the ambulatory and five radiating chapels which date back to the second half of the 12C. The flying buttresses were added to consolidate the buttresses which supported the transept crossing.

★**Interior** – The nave offers a superb perspective. It is filled with a golden light filtering through modern stained glass (1960). The chancel and the first two bays of the nave are Romanesque (12C) whereas the rest of the nave is 13C.

Originally the chancel was to include galleries, as is usual with Romanesque buildings. In the 13C, however, when the flying buttresses were added to support the east end, the architects realised that the counter-thrust provided by galleries was no longer necessary and so replaced them with a single triforium. They decided to apply this principle to the whole building.

Before returning to the car, stroll to the nearby promontory

View of the upper part of the church.

ST-OMER★★

Conurbation 53 062
Michelin map 51 fold 3 or 236 fold 4

St-Omer is an aristocratic, wealthy and religious town which has largely retained its ancient appearance. It is characterised by quiet streets lined with 17C and 18C pilastered mansions and houses with sculpted bays. The cathedral is said to have some of the finest furniture in France. This refined atmosphere is in contrast to the simpler nature of the northern suburbs, where low Flemish houses line the quays of the River Aa. Flat-bottomed boats, known as *bacôves*, take visitors round the Marais Audomarois which specialises in market gardening.

Clerics Take Action – In the 7C Benedictines from Luxeuil evangelised the Morini region, a marshy land with Thérouanne as its capital. They were led by the future **St Omer**, joined by Bertin and Mommolin who founded a monastery on the island of Sithieu in the Aa marshes; it was named after St Bertin. Omer, for his part, had been named Bishop of Thérouanne and in 662 had a chapel built on the hill overlooking Sithieu island; a small market town quickly formed around it.

St-Omer developed from the joining of the monastery and the chapel, by then a collegiate; the link between the two religious establishments is reflected in the town's layout.

★★CATHEDRAL DISTRICT

★★**Cathédrale Notre-Dame** – The cathedral is the most beautiful religious building in the region and is surprisingly large and majestic. It stands at the heart of a peaceful area which was formerly the canons' "Notre-Dame cloister". The **chancel** dates from 1200, the transept from the 13C, the nave from the 14C and 15C; the powerful west front tower (50m/164ft) with its network of vertical, English-style blind arcades is crowned by 15C watch-turrets. The pier of the large south door is ornamented with a 14C Virgin Mary and the tympanum bears a Last Judgement in which the chosen are very few. In a corner of the chancel stands an octagonal Romanesque tower.

CATHÉDRALE NOTRE-DAME

0   20 m

Astronomical clock
Octagonal Tower
Ambulatory
4
CHANCEL
5
3
TRANSEPT
Grand Dieu de Thérouanne
NAVE
1   2
Carved alabasters
Enclos Notre-Dame
Organ case
Descent from the Cross by Rubens
N

The complex arrangement of the vast interior (100m/110yd long, 30m/33yd wide, 23m/75ft high) consists of a three-storey nave (arcades, a tall, blind triforium and clerestory) flanked by side aisles, a **transept** with aisles, and a chancel with ambulatory and radiating chapels. The chapels off the side aisle, formerly reserved for the canons, are screened by richly traceried and painted marble.

★★Works of Art – Among the numerous interesting pieces, note in particular:

– the 13C cenotaph (**1**) of St-Omer *(left of the nave)*;

– the 16C mausoleum (**2**) of Eustache de Croy, Provost of the St-Omer Chapter and Bishop of Arras. This striking work by the Mons artist Jacques Du Broeucq presents the deceased kneeling in his episcopal robes and also lying nude in the Antique manner *(right of the nave)*.

– 15C engraved gravestones and a *Descent from the Cross* by Rubens *(first bay of the south aisle)*;

– 15C funerary monuments and

Base of the St-Bertin Cross, Hôtel Sandelin

16C and 17C carved alabasters with a charming Madonna with a Cat *(south aisle)*;

– the 13C statue of Notre-Dame-des-Miracles (**3**), a highly venerated object of pilgrimage *(south transept)*;

– a 13C low-relief Nativity (**4**); the 8C tomb of St Erkembode (**5**), Abbot of St Bertin's *(ambulatory)*;

– the Astronomical Clock with a mechanism dating from 1558 *(north transept)* and the Flamboyant rose-window above;

– the "Great God of Thérouanne", a famous 13C carved group which stood at a height of 20m/65ft. over the portal of Thérouanne Cathedral which was destroyed by Emperor Charles V. The shapes, which seem deformed, were foreshortened by the artist to take into account the distorting effect of perspective *(north transept)*.

Take rue des Tribunaux.

The street runs behind the east end of Notre-Dame and in front of the **palais épiscopal**, which dates from the 17C and now houses the law courts, leading to place Victor-Hugo. The square is the busy centre of St-Omer and features a fountain placed there to celebrate the birth of the Count of Artois, the future Charles X.

★Hôtel Sandelin ⊘ – The house was built in 1777 for the Viscountess of Fruges. It is set between a courtyard and a garden, with access through a monumental portal with an elegant Louis XV gate.

Ground Floor – The drawing rooms overlooking the gardens form a charmingly old-fashioned suite of rooms with light-coloured, finely carved wainscoting and 18C fireplaces that form a beautiful setting for the Louis XV furniture and the paintings from the bequest of Mme Du Teil-Chaix d'Est-Ange. Among the paintings are Lépicié's *Rising of Fanchon* in the style of Chardin, the portrait of *Mme De Pompadour as Diana the Huntress* by Nattier and four lively works by Boilly *(The Visit, The Improvised Concert, The Quenching of the Flame of Love, The Jealous Lover)*.

The woodcarving room (religious sculptures and medieval tapestries) and the Salle Henri Dupuis containing ebony cabinets made in Antwerp lead to the **Salle du Trésor** where exhibits include the famous **base of the St Bertin Cross★** (12C), a masterpiece of Mosan art made of gilt and enamel. It is decorated with the Evangelists and enamelled scenes from the Old Testament and comes from the abbey of St Bertin, as does the beautiful ivory representing one of the old men of the Apocalypse. Note, too, the **cross reliquary** with its double crossbar (1210-20) from the abbey in Claimarais. The rear has fine filigree work and is encrusted with gemstones.

The small wall cabinets in the chapel corridor (so-called because of the impressive altar made of ebony, tortoiseshell and gilded bronze) contain various pieces of gold and silverware and ivories.

The rooms overlooking the courtyard have an interesting collection of works by Flemish Primitives: *St Crispin and St Crispinian* altarpiece (c 1415), *The Holy Family and an Angel* by Gérard David's School, a triptych of *The Adoration of the Magi* by the Master of the Adoration, Khanenko, *The Flemish Feast* by Hell Brueghel, and several works by lesser-known 17C Flemish and Dutch masters including *The Smoker* by Abraham Diapram, *Lizard and Shells* by Balthasar Van der Ast, *Portrait of a Woman* by Cornelis de Vos, and *The Bawdy Woman* by Jan Steen.

First and Second Floors – Collection of ceramics including some produced in St-Omer. Also an outstanding series of **Delft** (750 items). *Closed for restructuring.*

Église St-Denis ⊘ – This church, restored in the 18C, still has its proud 13C tower and the 15C chancel hidden by 18C wainscot (rich canopy with a gilded coffered ceiling). A chapel left of the chancel houses an alabaster Christ attributed to Du Broeucq.

★**Ancienne chapelle des Jésuites** – This chapel, now the chapel of a secondary school *(lycée)*, is an example of the early Jesuit style. Gothic influences can be seen in the shape of the bays and the layout of the ambulatory. The chapel was designed by Du Blocq, a Jesuit from Mons, and completed in 1629. Its height is striking, as are the alignment of the scrolling in the nave and the narrow square towers enclosing the chancel in the Tournai tradition. The most beautiful part of the building, however, is the monumental brick-and-white-stone **façade**, five storeys high and adorned with sculptures.

Bibliothèque ⊘ – The library contains 350 000 volumes including over 1 600 manuscripts (11C Life of St Omer) and nearly 200 early printed books or "incunabula" (famous Gutenberg Bible). They are presented in bookcases from St Bertin's Abbey.

Musée Henri-Dupuis ⊘ – The museum is housed in an 18C mansion with a beautiful period Flemish kitchen. The ground floor houses a large collection of **birds** from the Arctic to Indonesia in their natural habitat (dioramas, information panels). On the first floor, an impressive collection of **shells**★ is on display, reminding visitors of an 18C natural history room.

TOWN WALK

★**Jardin public** – This vast park (20ha/48 acres) is located on part of the old 17C ramparts. The moat has been turned into a formal French garden; on the slope is an English garden with winding paths shaded by beautiful trees. There are lovely views of the bastion, the roofs and the cathedral tower. The large moat south of the garden now contains a swimming pool.

Place du Maréchal-Foch – The town hall was built between 1834 and 1841 using stones from the former abbey church dedicated to St Bertin. An amphitheatre was set in the centre of the building. At 42 bis, the **Hôtel du Baillage** (now the Caisse d'Épargne or savings bank) was originally the royal courthouse which challenged the authority of the town's aldermen. It is an elegant Louis XVI building decorated with pilasters, Doric capitals, wrought-iron work, and garlands of flowers. The four statues on the balustrade represent the Virtues.

Follow rue L.-Martel, walk across place Victor-Hugo and take rue des Epeers and rue St-Bertin.

Ancien Collège des Jésuites – The school was built in 1593 and became a military hospital. Altered in 1726, it features a beautiful front decorated with garlands and pilasters surmounted by composite capitals.

Ruines de St-Bertin and Faubourg Nord – All that remains of the abbey are a few arches and the lower part of the tower (1460). The square in which the ruins lie contains a marble statue of Suger, who was a benefactor to the abbey. Rue St Bertin provides a lovely view of the ruins surrounded by great trees.

Via place du Vanquai, stroll through the Faubourg Nord (north suburb), along quai des Salines and quai du Commerce lined with low Flemish houses reflected in the still waters of the canalised River Aa.

At the end of quai des Salines, turn left on rue de Dunkerque then right on rue St-Sépulcre.

Église St-Sépulchre – This hall-church (the three aisles are of the same width and height) was consecrated in 1387 and used to be the seat of the largest parish in the town. It has a spire 52m/169ft high. The name of the church is uncommon; there are only seven churches named after the Holy Sepulchre in France. It comes from the involvement of three local lords in the Crusades. The

Ancien palais épiscopal (Palais de justice)   X J

church inherited a doorway from the abbey dedicated to St Bertin, a masterpiece of joinery. It also has two Baroque statues of St John the Evangelist and St John the Baptist. The chancel contains fine 19C stained-glass windows connected with the Holy Sepulchre.

Rue de Dunkerque leads back to place du Maréchal-Foch.

L'AUDOMAROIS

This region gets its name from the Latin word *Audomarus* meaning "Omer" and it covers the area around St-Omer. It is an important part of the Regional Nature Park. The area known as the Marais Audomarois, or Omer Marshes, is one of the most unusual parts of the park.

Bacôve in the Audomarois

Y. Tierny/MICHELIN

Grange-Nature ⊘ – This is the visitor centre for the Audomarois section of the **Parc naturel régional Nord-Pas-de-Calais**; it contains exhibitions and audio-visual presentations on nature and wildlife. The centre is also the starting-point for footpaths, some within the Romelaere Nature Reserve (observation and study trails).

Marais audomarois – *4km/2.5mi north-east on D 209.*
The marshes sit in a vast depression (3 400ha/8 401 acres) stretching from Watten in the north to Arques just south of St-Omer, and from Clairmarais Forest (northeast) to the Tilques watercress beds (north-west). They are the result of painstaking efforts begun in the 9C by the monks of St. Bertin's to transform the area.
Today the marshes encompass a series of small plots of land linked by **waterways** *(watergangs)*, which are used by large flat-bottomed boats known as *bacôves*. A large number of the plots are devoted to market gardening; their most famous vegetable is the St-Omer cauliflower. The marshes also provide good fishing: pike, eel, sauger, perch, roach... and bird-watching as they are a stopover for migratory birds (heronry). From D 209 beside Neuffossé Canal the circulation and drainage canals can be seen here and there, crossed by culverts and lift bridges; but for a proper **tour of the marshes** ⊘ it is necessary to hire a boat or join one of the tours in a *bâcove* or other vessel.

EXCURSIONS

Forêt de Rihoult-Clairmarais – *4.5km/2.5mi north-east on D 209.*
◩ When he stayed at St-Omer, Charlemagne hunted here in the oak groves; in the 12C it was the property of Cistercian monks.
The forest (1 167ha/2 884 acres) is now managed with tourists in mind *(picnic tables)*, especially around **étang d'Harchelles**, the last of seven ponds dug by the Cistercians for peat or for fish.

Arques – *4km/2.5mi south-east. Leave St-Omer by N 42.*
Arques, which is an industrial town known chiefly for its crystal glassware, is also an important port at the junction of the canalised Aa and the Neuffossé Canal, linking the River Aa to the River Lys.

Verrerie Cristallerie d'Arques ⊘ – Founded in 1825, this undertaking is now a world leader in fine tableware production. Every day, six million items in glass, opal and crystal are manufactured. A tour of the premises provides a close look at the magical materials used to make so many lovely things (cooking utensils, tableware, decoration). Glass is made from a mixture of sand, soda, lime and cullet (ground glass).

Maison du parc de l'Audomarois ⊘ – Le Grand Vannage houses the Maison du parc de l'Audomarois, a white-stone and pink-brick building spanning the Aa. The sluice gate room where the river level is regulated can be visited.

In Arques, take N 42 east towards Hazebrouck; about 1km/0.5mi beyond the bridge over the Aa, turn right onto a small road marked "Ascenseur des Fontinettes" which ends near a factory.

Eating out

MODERATE

La Charrette – *32 place Foch –* ☎ *03 21 98 28 29 – closed 1-15 Aug and Sun –* 🍽 *– booking essential Sat-Sun - 60/95F.* This restaurant in the lively town centre has a long, narrow dining room where tasty traditional fare is served at extremely reasonable prices. Fresh local produce and the authentic personality of the owner have made La Charrette one of the town's most popular establishments.

MID-RANGE

Hostellerie St-Hubert – *62570 Hallines – 6km/4mi south-west of St-Omer by D 928 then D 211 –* ☎ *03 21 39 77 77 – closed 8-15 Jan, Sun evening and Mon – 185/300F.* Tucked away behind the century-old trees gracing its park, the 19C hostelry has retained the elegance and luxury of its early days. There are two dining rooms with sculpted panelling adorning the walls and ceilings. A few large, cosy bedrooms are available.

Where to stay

MID-RANGE

Hôtel Les Frangins – *5 rue Carnot –* ☎ *03 21 38 12 47 – http://www. frangins.fr – 26 rooms 290/350F –* ☲ *40F.* In the old quarter of St-Omer, near the museums and high street, this hotel offers refurbished, functional and quiet rooms.

Moulin de Mombreux – *62380 Lumbres – 11km/6.8mi south-west of St-Omer by D 208ᴱ then D 211 –* ☎ *03 21 39 13 13 – closed 20-29 Dec –* 🅿 *– 24 rooms 500/720F –* ☲ *60F – restaurant 220F.* The soft burbling of the waterfall, the shaded park along the banks of a river and an old brick and stone mill all make for a delightful setting... The huge wheel that once operated the mill can be admired next to the fireplace in the living room.

LUXURY

Château Tilques – *62500 Tilques – 6km/3.7mi north-west of St-Omer heading towards Calais by N 43 then by a minor road –* ☎ *03 21 88 99 99 –* 🅿 *– 53 rooms from 700F –* ☲ *70F – restaurant 210/350F.* A 19C red-brick château surrounded by a lush expanse of green, ideal for your early morning run or your constitutional walk before dinner. The rooms in the château are furnished with English antiques, whereas those in the annex are more modern. The restaurant is housed in the former stables.

On the town

Le Map' Monde – *12 rue du Lion-d'Or –* ☎ *03 21 12 27 77 – daily 9am-1am (bar), 11am-3pm, 6-11pm (brasserie).* The walls here are covered with newspapers recounting long sea voyages or presenting unusual cocktails and coffee beans from all around the world... However, this is hardly an incentive to travel once you have sunk down into the deep leather armchairs of the café.

Le Queen Victoria – *15 place Foch –* ☎ *03 21 88 51 17 – Sun-Thur 9am-1am, Fri-Sat 9am-2am.* Worn parquet flooring and brick walls are the backdrop to this cosy pub exuding a friendly atmosphere. High seats are arranged around the bar and the small back room boasts a stunning fireplace to warm up the long winter months. Large terrace on the square.

Boat trips

Le Haut Pont – *92 rue des Faiseurs-de-Bâteaux –* ☎ *03 21 38 12 43 – reception area open Tues-Sun 10am-9pm – daily July-Aug – closed Sept-May.* Boat trips of the marshes and the many small bridges around St-Omer. The tour is punctuated by remarks on local fauna and flora, as well as the history and economy of the marshes. Meeting point outside the Café du Haut-Pont.

Isnor Clairmarais – *3 rue du Marais, 62500 Clairmarais –* ☎ *03 21 39 15 15 – www.isnor.fr – daily in summer 9am-6pm, Sat-Sun and public holidays only in winter.* Several types of boat are at your disposal for exploring the surrounding marshes passenger boats, rowing boats, motorboats and canoes.

★ **Ascenseur à bateaux des Fontinettes** (Fontinettes Barge Lift, Arques) ⊘ – The barge lift, which was in use from 1888 to 1967, is an interesting remnant of 19C technology. It was built on the Neuffossé Canal to replace the five locks needed to negotiate the 13.13m/43ft drop in the canal. The principle is simple: the barges took their place in one of two water-filled basins, attached to two enormous pistons which were a kind of hydraulic balance; one went up while the other simultaneously went down.

A visit to the engine room and a working model explain how it functioned.

The lift was replaced by an impressive **giant lock**, 500m/550yd upriver. This can contain six barges and requires 20min to operate.

Abbaye St-Paul-de-Wisques ⊘ – *7km/4mi west. Leave St-Omer by N 42.*

Benedictine monks occupy the château which consists of both old buildings (15C tower, 18C house and portal) and modern buildings (chapel, cloister, refectory and bell-tower). The bell-tower houses Bertine, the bell from St Bertin's abbey church, which dates from 1470 and weighs 2 600kg/over 2.5t.

The road *(D 212)* continues past the Petit Château (1770) and climbs to a summit where the Abbaye Notre-Dame, the Benedictine monastery, stands.

Return to St-Omer by D 208.

The route offers pretty **views** over the town, dominated by the basilica church (Notre-Dame) and the Jesuit chapel.

Esquerdes – *8km/5mi south-west.* This village lies in the Aa Valley and has been famous for papermaking since 1473. It still has several paper mills.

The **Maison du papier** ⊘ was built on the ruins of the old Confosse mill. The exhibition explains papermaking techniques from the earliest used in China to the most modern. Visitors can try making their own sheet of paper in the workshop, an unusual souvenir to take home.

★ **Blockhaus d'Eperlecques** ⊘ – *15km/9mi north-west. Leave St-Omer by D 928 and turn left at Watten.*

This 22m/72ft concrete mountain rising out of the forest is the largest concrete bunker ever built; V2 bombs loaded with explosives with which to bombard London were to be launched from here. Its construction – in fact only a third of its planned size – involved over 35 000 French, Belgian, Dutch, Polish, Russian and other prisoners during 1943 and 1944. On 27 August 1943, 185 British "flying fortresses" bombed the bunker, disabling it at the cost of numerous lives of detainees working there. After this episode the bunker was enlarged to become a factory making liquid oxygen; a film inside evokes these tragic events.

ST-QUENTIN

Conurbation 69 188
Michelin map 53 fold 14 or 236 fold 27

St-Quentin is perched on a limestone hill riddled with caves and underground passages, and overlooks the canalised River Somme which crosses the Isle marshlands. St-Quentin's waterways and railways link it to the north European capitals and the Ruhr, making it a transportation centre between Paris, the English Channel, the countries north of France and the Champagne region. It suffered terribly during the First World War but has since strengthened its industrial position. Its art deco heritage dates from the town's rebuilding period.

St-Quentin Canal

Before the Canal du Nord was built, this was the busiest canal in France. It links the basins of the River Somme and River Oise to the River Escaut (Scheldt), flowing for about 100km/62mi between Chauny and Cambrai. Napoleon considered it one of the period's greatest achievements.

It is made up of two sections: the Crozat Canal, running between the River Oise and River Somme, which was named after the financier who had it constructed, and the St-Quentin Canal proper, which crosses the plateau between the River Somme and River Escaut partly through tunnels at Tronquoy (1km/0.5mi long) and Riqueval. It is the St-Quentin Canal which is used for regular shipments of sand, gravel and especially grain to the Paris region. The enlargement of the canal, which is part of a long-term project, will improve the town's links with Dunkirk.

Béguinages

Beguine convents were founded in the Middle Ages for pious women who did not take their final vows. In St-Quentin, the tradition dates back to the 13C. The population explosion that occurred in the 19C led to a need for accommodation for single or elderly people and the name *béguinage* was extended to cover such housing. Only six large enclosures have survived, grouping some 40 houses around a communal garden. There are also six small enclosures. The most interesting ones are to be seen in rue Quentin-Barré (crow-stepped gables), rue de Bellevue and rue du Moulin.

TOWN WALK

The Art Deco Trail – ⊠ St-Quentin suffered extensive damage during the First World War and was partially rebuilt during the 1920s to designs by the architect Guindez. A walk through the town's streets reveals numerous house fronts decorated with bow windows, projecting balconies, floral or geometric motifs, coloured mosaics, wrought-iron work etc.

Among the most outstanding buildings are the post office *(rue de Lyon)*, the council chamber in the Hôtel de Ville (town hall), the Carillon cinema *(rue des Toiles)*, the music school *(47 rue d'Isle)*, the buffet in the railway station and, next to it, the bridge flanked by lantern towers.

Rue des Canonniers – The 18C **Hôtel Joly de Bammeville** has a fine staircase with wrought-iron banisters. It houses the town library (a major venue during the *Festival de la Nouvelle*). The entrance to the old **Hôtel des Canonniers** *(no 21)* has military trophies carved in low relief.

Go to place de l'Hôtel-de-Ville and follow rue des Toiles. Walk round the basilica, cross rue du Gouvernement near the east end of the basilica. Rue E.-Ovres leads to the Champs-Élysées gardens.

Champs-Élysées – The site of the original fortification was turned during the Restoration into a pleasant park (10ha/24 acres): playgrounds, sports field, flower garden.

The Marais de l'Isle is accessible via boulevard Gambetta and place du 8-Octobre leading to the quai Gayant bridge; turn left after crossing the bridge.

Marais d'Isle – This zone covering over 100ha/247 acres has been provided with fishing and water sports facilities, and it also includes a **nature reserve** ⊘ which lies along the route taken by migratory birds from Northern and Eastern Europe.

The flora of wetlands is very varied and includes rare species like water hemlock (also known as dropwort or cowbane) or strange ones like bladderwort, a carnivorous plant. Among the numerous birds here there are nest-building species (crested grebes) and overwintering species (ducks).

The **Maison de la nature**, a small visitors centre in Rouvray presents an audio-visual show and documents relating to the ecosystem of the lake. A path around the reserve allows one to spot some of the birds.

SIGHTS

★**Hôtel de Ville** ⊘ – This is a gem of Late Gothic architecture (early 16C). The vigorous design of the façade includes ogival arches topped with pinnacles, mullioned windows and a traceried gallery beneath three gables. It is decorated with picturesque carvings in the Flamboyant Gothic style. The campanile was rebuilt in the 18C. It houses a peal of 37 bells.

Interior – The gables on the façade correspond to the vaulting of three aisles in the shape of an upturned ship. The **Salle des Mariages** still has its old rafter and a huge Renaissance fireplace. Note the carvings representing the town's main celebrities: the treasurer, the executioner etc. The **Salle du Conseil** has an Art Deco interior (lamps made of wrought iron and glass paste, Brazilian rosewood wainscoting with medallions representing various trades).

Espace St-Jacques – *14 rue de la Sellerie.*

This neo-Gothic building was erected on the site of Église St-Jacques and was formerly the seat of the Chamber of Commerce. Today it houses temporary exhibitions on the ground floor, with an entomological museum on the first floor.

Musée des Papillons ⊘ – This collection of butterflies and other insects is the largest in Europe. It includes about 600 000 specimens, of which about a fifth are exhibited at any given time.

There are many different forms and colours in the butterflies, especially the ones from tropical countries. They include the metallic blue Morpho, the Thysania from Guyana (the world's largest butterfly), leaf miners, and a yellow and black species found locally.

Eating out

MID-RANGE

Restaurant Le Riche – *10 rue des Toiles* – ☎ *03 23 62 33 53* – *closed Sun evening* – *booking essential Sat-Sun* – *130/190F*. This Art Deco brasserie, where the legendary singer Édith Piaf used to spend her evenings, has succeeded in creating a subtle jazzy ambience that immediately puts you at ease. As for the cuisine, there are many different suggestions, served in a warm setting with yellow walls and long seats in imitation leather...

Ferme-Auberge du Vieux Puits – *5 rue de l'Abbaye, 02420 Bony* – *15km/9.3mi north of St-Quentin by N 44* – ☎ *03 23 66 22 33* – *closed 25 Dec-1 Jan and Thur lunchtime* – *booking essential at lunchtime* – *125F*. Comfortable rooms with simple furniture are available to you in this farmhouse. If you are feeling hungry, take a seat at the inn and sample the delicious dishes made with fresh farm produce. Heated pool, tennis court and mountain bikes on the premises.

Where to stay

MID-RANGE

Hôtel du Château – *02100 Neuville-St-Amand* – *3km/2mi south-west of St-Quentin by N 44 then D 12* – ☎ *03 23 68 41 82* – *closed 31 July-20 Aug, 24-31 Dec, Sat lunchtime and Sun evening* – 🅿 – *15 rooms 330/390F* – ☕ *48F* – *restaurant 125/295F*. At the heart of leafy woodland stands this early-20C manor house with cosy, comfortable rooms. The dining hall looks onto the grounds in this haven of peace.

★**Basilica** ⊘ – The basilica of St-Quentin is a mainly Gothic building which could rival many of the great cathedrals. It began as a collegiate church dedicated to St Quentin, who worked as a missionary in the region and was martyred at the end of the 3C; it became a basilica in 1876.

After the famous 1557 siege, a fire in 1669 and bombing in 1917, the basilica came close to total destruction in October 1918.

Exterior – The west front incorporates a massive belfry-porch; its lower part dates from the late 12C whereas the upper storeys were rebuilt in the 17C and the top after 1918. The spire dates from 1976 and reaches the height of the original one (82m/269ft).

Left of the church, Square Winston Churchill (wrought-iron well) offers a good **view**★ over the large and small transepts and the east end; note the soaring, triple flying buttresses.

A walk around the church continues to offer interesting **views** of this remarkable building. At the south arm of the small transept stands the St Fursy Chapel, which was tacked on in the late 15C. The pretty, Flamboyant Lamoureux porch can be seen on the left.

Interior – The impressively large 13C **chancel** consists of a double transept, double aisles, an ambulatory and radiating chapels. The vaulting of the chapels right of the ambulatory rests on two columns, following the elegant arrangement of the Champagne region. The Lady Chapel contains old stained-glass windows depicting the Life of the Virgin Mary; a 13C statue of St Michael stands left of the chapel entrance.

The chancel screen, reworked in the 19C, portrays scenes from the life of St Quentin; on the left sits the stone chest *(sacrarium)* (1409) in which church plate was kept. Note the great hieratic figures of the stained glass adorning the clerestory in the centre, and the 16C glass in the north arm of the small transept, portraying the Martyrdom of St Catherine and that of St Barbara.

The bold, 15C nave (34m/111ft high) has a long maze (260m/284yd) traced on its floor, which the faithful followed on their knees. The superb organ case (1690-1703) was designed by Bérain; the instrument itself, by Clicquot, was destroyed in 1917; it was replaced by a modern organ with 74 stops.

The sculpted Tree of Jesse, at the start of the south aisle, dates from the early 16C; the second chapel bears 16C mural paintings.

During the summer, a tour of the upper section provides a view of the pinnacles, piers and surrounding countryside as far as Laon.

Musée Antoine-Lécuyer ⊘ – The pride of the museum is the splendid **portrait collection**★★ by the pastel artist **Quentin de La Tour** (1704-88), who was born and died in St-Quentin. La Tour, who painted all the important 18C society figures, is representative of an age marked by the importance of individuality. His works, both sensitive and honest, are "incomparable illustrations of moral anatomy": each smile has its own personality, whether spontaneous, ironic, mischievous, benevolent, embittered etc.

Wiii/TOP

Self-portrait by Quentin de la Tour, Musée
Antoine-Lécuyer

The main room is devoted to the 17C
and 18C French schools. The next
three rooms are set aside for La Tour
and contain 78 remarkable portraits:
princes and princesses, great lords,
financiers, clerics, men of letters
(Jean-Jacques Rousseau) and
artists. The greatest are perhaps of
Father Huber reading; of Marie Fel
a friend of the artist; and a self-portrait, which is an exceptional study,
both introspective and penetrating.
A bust of the artist by JB Lemoyne
stands in the second room.
Downstairs is an exhibition of 18C
faience.
A room upstairs displays 19C painting,
illustrating various artistic movements: works by Lebourg, Corot, Fantin-Latour and Renoir (pastel portrait
of Mlle Dieterle). Another room presents 20C painting with works by Gromaire, Ozenfant and Lebasque.
There are also interesting collections
of ivories, enamels, furniture and
busts of Voltaire.

EXCURSION

North of St-Quentin *Round trip of 30km/18mi*
Take N 44 north for 15km/9mi.

Mémorial américain de Bellicourt – The memorial stands north of the village
over the Riqueval tunnels. It consists of a white stone cenotaph which commemorates the 1918 attack by the US Army's 2nd Division against Hindenburg's line.
From the surrounding area there is a **panoramic view** of the plateau bearing traces
of the German trenches (American cemetery at Bony).
Continue on N 44 and turn first right to Mont St Martin.

Mont St-Martin – The ruins of an old Premonstratensian abbey may be seen here.
North of the village, a path gives access to the **source of the River Escaut** (**Scheldt**)
which is hidden in a quiet and mysterious spot, once a place of pilgrimage. The
clear water flows between rows of aspens and ash trees which form a leafy vault
in summer: this is the beginning of the river's 400km/250mi course through
France, Belgium and Holland.
Drive north along D 71 to Gouy and turn right (D 28) to Beaurevoir.

Beaurevoir – This village has preserved a tower of the château where Joan of Arc
was a prisoner from August to November of 1430. She was held by the Count of
Luxembourg, who handed her over to the English.

ST-RIQUIER★

Population 1 166
Michelin map 52 fold 7 or 236 folds 22, 23 - 9km/5.5mi north-east of Abbeville

This ancient fortified town boasts an imposing Gothic church to rival many cathedrals
and a picturesque turreted belfry with look-out posts. St-Riquier grew around an
ancient Benedictine abbey which is the setting, in July, of a renowned classical music
festival. Visitors arriving from Abbeville are greeted by the Maison Petit, a house built
for a soldier of Napoleon's Grande Armée with an oddly shaped gable recalling the
Emperor's famous hat.

A hermit and a son-in-law – The town was called Centule when, in 645, the hermit
Riquier died in Crécy Forest, near what is now the village of Forest-Moutiers. This ceno-
bite monk who came from a noble family had previously evangelised the Ponthieu
region; after his death his body was transported to Centule where it inspired many
pilgrimages.
A Benedictine monastery was founded as a result and prospered so much that in 790
Charlemagne gave it to his son-in-law, the poet **Angilbert**, the "Homer of the Palatine
Academy". Angilbert, to whom the Emperor paid several visits, gave a new lease of
life to the abbey and had the buildings rebuilt in the most precious materials: Italian
porphyry, marble and jasper. At that time the monastery also included a main church,
which housed the tomb of Riquier, and two secondary churches (St Benedict and
St Mary) with a triangular cloister in the middle.

SIGHTS

★Church ⓥ – *45min.*
Despite having been
destroyed and rebuilt several times, the present,
largely Flamboyant (15C-
16C) church has nevertheless retained some
13C architectural elements (lower parts of the
transept and chancel).
The ensemble was restored by Abbot Charles
d'Aligre (17C) who also had the furniture renewed, which is still in use today.

A NIGHT IN ST-RIQUIER

Hôtel Jean de Bruges – ☎ *03 22 28 30 30
– closed Jan –* 🅿 *– 8 rooms 500/700F –* ☖
60F. Facing the church, this handsome 17C
white stone residence is an obvious stopping
place in your tour of the medieval city. Converted into a hotel by a Belgian lawyer, its
rooms are a harmonious blend of antique and
modern furniture in a sober and remarkably
elegant setting. Pretty terrace-patio.

Exterior – The west front is essentially made up of a large square tower (50m/164ft
high) flanked by stair towers and covered in abundant, finely carved ornamentation. Above the central doorway, the gable bears a Holy Trinity surrounded by two
abbots and the Apostles. Higher still stands a Crowning of the Virgin Mary. Finally,
between the two windows of the belfry, a statue of St Michael can be seen. Above
the vaulting of the right doorway St Genevieve holds a candle which, according to
legend, the Devil used to blow out and an angel used to relight.

★★Interior – The beauty, size and simplicity of the architecture are worth admiring.
The two storeys of the large central nave (13m/42ft wide, 24m/78ft high,
96m/314ft long) are separated by a frieze and a balustrade. The chancel still has
its 17C decoration and furniture: wrought-iron **grilles★**, lectern and monks' stalls,
marble screen surmounted by a large wooden Crucifix by Girardon.
The south transept is unusual: its end is cut off by the sacristy and the treasury
above it which occupy three bays of the cloister gallery. The wall of the treasury
is decorated with fine sculptures and statues.
In the first of the ambulatory's radiating chapels, on the right after the staircase,
note the painting by Jouvenet *Louis XIV Touching Those Afflicted with the King's
Evil.* The lady chapel contains stellar vaulting with ribs running down to historiated corbels (Life of the Virgin Mary); at the entrance, *The Apparition of the Virgin
to St Philomena* (1847) is by Ducornet, an artist who painted with his feet as he
had no arms. In St Angilbert's Chapel the five polychrome statues of saints are
typical of 16C Picardy sculpture: they show *(left to right)* Veronica, Helen,
Benedict, Vigor and Riquier.
The north transept contains a Renaissance font, its base carved with low-relief
sculptures showing the Life of the Virgin Mary and the Baptism of Christ.

Treasury ⓥ – This was the abbot's private chapel. The walls of the beautiful early-
16C vaulted chamber are decorated with murals from the same period; the best
of them depicts the Meeting of the Three Dead and the Three Living, which symbolises the brevity of life.
The treasury contains a 12C Byzantine Crucifix, 13C reliquaries, a 15C alabaster
altarpiece and a curious 16C hand-warmer.

Abbey buildings – Rebuilt in the 17C during the d'Aligre abbacy, they now house
the **Centre culturel départemental de l'abbaye de St-Riquier** that includes a **museum** ⓥ of
rural life and crafts and a **conference centre** with seminar rooms and accommodation.
The rooms used for temporary exhibitions also host concerts and conferences.

Hôtel-Dieu ⓥ – The hospital dates from the early 18C. It stands to the left behind
the belfry. The chapel has some attractive wrought-iron grilles. The altarpiece is
decorated with a painting by Joseph-François Parrocel. The two angels and the
statues of St Nicholas and St Augustin are by Pfaffenhoffen who lived in St-Riquier
for many years.

St-Valery (pronounced Val'ry), the capital of the Vimeu region, occupies a lush setting overlooking the peaceful countryside of the Somme Bay. It consists of a walled upper town with half-timbered houses and a lower town beside the port used by coasters, yachts and fishing boats known as *sauterelliers* (a *sauterelle* is a grey shrimp). Every year the coast around St Valery becomes the playground of an important colony of seals. Salt-meadow lamb is a local speciality.

St-Valery began as an abbey founded by a monk called Valery from Luxeuil in Lorraine. In 1066 William the Conqueror stopped here before invading England; Joan of Arc passed through the town in 1430 as prisoner of the English, on the way from Le Crotoy. The town prospered in the 18C through the import of salt from the Vendée region.

VILLE BASSE

The lower town extends for almost 2km/1.25mi, to the mouth of the River Somme where the port is located.

A QUIET PLACE TO STAY

Relais Guillaume de Normandy – *Quai Romerel* – ☎ *03 22 60 82 36 – closed 15 Dec-15 Jan and Tues except from 14 July to 31 Aug* – 🅿 – *14 rooms 240/350F* – ☕ *42F – restaurant 85/210F*. Right in the medieval quarter, the tower of this small red-brick manor house dominates the River Somme and the peaceful embankment lined with plane trees and lime trees. Your nights will not be troubled at the Relais Guillaume. The sunlit dining room has tall bay windows opening onto a terrace where meals are served in summer.

★**Digue-promenade** – The promenade, which is shaded in summer by plane and lime trees, leads to a sheltered beach and offers lovely **views** over the Somme Bay to Le Crotoy and the headland at Le Hourdel. Pleasant villas set in gardens stand inland; beyond the Relais de Normandie are the ramparts of the upper town, overlooked by St Martin's church.

Calvaire des Marins – Access from rue Violette and sentier du Calvaire, through the sailors' district which is full of charming painted cottages. **View** over the lower town and the estuary.

★**Écomusée Picarvie** ⊘ – This appealing little museum faithfully recreates regional life before the industrial age. Reconstructions of workshops and stalls show the work of basket weavers, cobblers, locksmiths, coopers, blacksmiths, joiners etc and there is also a village with a school, café and barber's shop. An entire period farm has been recreated on the first floor, with the bedroom, kitchen, cowshed, stable, cider-press and the barn where flax, grown in the surrounding villages, was beaten to make linen.

VILLE HAUTE

Part of the fortifications have been preserved.

Porte de Nevers – The name of this 14C gate, which was heightened in the 16C, harks back to the dukes of Nevers who owned St-Valery in the 17C.

Église St-Martin – The exterior of this Gothic building bordering the ramparts is of flint and sandstone laid in a chequered pattern. In the north aisle, a Renaissance triptych portrays the Crucifixion, the Baptism of Christ and the Martyrdom of John the Baptist.

Porte Guillaume – The 12C gate stands between two majestic towers and offers an extensive view over the Somme Bay.

Ecomusée Picarvie

Chapelle St-Valery or Chapelle des Marins – Take rue de l'Abbaye beyond the Porte Guillaume: **St Valery's Abbey** used to lie in the vale to the left. The abbey's brick and stone château survives, with a carved 18C pediment.

From place de l'Ermitage take the path up to the chapel (30min there and back).

The chequered sandstone and flint chapel houses the tomb of St Valery. Overlooking the Somme Bay, the chapel offers an extensive **view★** of the salt meadows and the estuary as far as the Marquenterre reserve in the distance.

SCEAUX★★

Population 18 052
Michelin map 101 fold 25, 106 fold 31 or 237 fold 17
Michelin plan 22

Access from Paris: *RER line B 2 (town centre), B 4 (park)*

The town of Sceaux, a suburb of Paris, boasts one of the finest parks for which the Île-de-France region is famous.

Colbert's Sceaux – In 1670 Louis XIV's superintendent of buildings **Colbert** commissioned Claude Perrault, Le Brun, Girardon and Coysevox to build a superb residence in Sceaux. The two groups of sculptures flanking the entrance pavilion were created by Coysevox: the dog and the unicorn, representing loyalty and honesty, were Colbert's emblems. The grounds were laid out by Le Nôtre, who succeeded admirably in spite of the rough, uneven terrain. The canal, basins and fountains were supplied by the waters diverted from the hillsides of Le Plessis-Robinson. The château was inaugurated in 1677 at a lavish reception attended by the Sun King in person; one of the many attractions that night was the performance of Jean Racine's famous tragedy *Phaedra*.

In 1685 Colbert's son Seignelay entertained Louis XIV and Mme De Maintenon at the château, an occasion for which Racine and Lulli composed their *Ode to Sceaux*.

Sceaux in the hands of the Duc du Maine – In 1700 the estate became the property of the Duc du Maine, the legitimated son of Louis XIV and Mme De Montespan. The King often came to stay with his favourite son.

The Duchesse du Maine, the Great Condé's grand-daughter, surrounded herself with a large court of brillant personalities. She entertained on a grand scale, providing opera, ballet, comedy and tragedy for her many guests. The dazzling "Nights of Sceaux", enhanced by superb displays of fireworks and twinkling lights, were the talk of all Paris and Versailles.

On the eve of the Revolution, the estate of Sceaux belonged to the Duc de Penthièvre, the Duc du Maine's nephew, for whom the fabulist Florian acted as librarian. The domain was confiscated and subsequently sold to a tradesman who had the château razed to the ground and the park turned into arable land.

Sceaux today – In 1856 the Duc de Trévise, who inherited the estate through his wife's family, built the château that stands today. The grounds gradually slipped into a state of neglect; Alain-Fournier found inspiration there for his novel *Le Grand Meaulnes*. In 1923 the château was bought by the Seine *département*, which undertook to restore both the building and its park. The Île-de-France Museum was installed in 1936. The estate now belongs to the Hauts-de-Seine département.

The famous physicists **Pierre** (1859-1906) and **Marie** (1867-1934) **Curie** and their daughter **Irène Joliot-Curie** (1897-1956) lived in Sceaux. Their remains were transferred to the Panthéon in Paris in 1995.

★★CHÂTEAU AND PARK ⊙

Main Entrance – Designed for Colbert, the two entrance pavilions with sculpted pediments are flanked by two small lodges surmounted by Coysevox's groups of statues.

Orangerie ⊙ – This conservatory (60m/196ft long) was designed by Jules Hardouin-Mansart in 1685. It is decorated with a series of carved pediments. In summer it was used as the ballroom - note the interior decoration - and in winter it sheltered the 300 orange trees of Sceaux Park.

Today the orangery is a venue for conferences, exhibitions and concerts *(see Calendar of events)*.

★**Musée de l'Île-de-France** ⊙ – The museum is housed in the château that once belonged to the Duc de Trévise. It was refurbished in 1994 and is laid out on the basis of four themes: Sceaux, the estate and its owners; ceramics from the Paris Basin; royal and princely residences; and scenery in the Paris Basin from the 18C to 20C.

The estate in Sceaux has a long history which is illustrated in the small drawing room where the main architectural feature is the superb marquetry floor. The reception rooms contain numerous portraits of successive owners, among them Colbert (French School, 17C) and the Duc de Penthièvre painted by JB Charpentier. The oval room is given over to Sceaux faience and boasts the largest existing collection of this local production. The "japanned faience" *(see Introduction, Faience and porcelain)* by J Chapelle make renewed use of the Rococo style. Two other rooms are part of this section of the museum. The library has 18C porcelain (Vincennes, Sèvres, St-Cloud etc) and the Millet room on the first floor includes fine 19C faience recognisable for its unusual background colouring and decoration (ropework for Montereau, flowers for Creil).

The luxurious residences built in the vicinity, some of which have since been demolished, are illustrated at length. There are etchings by Rigaud, oils including the *Château de St-Cloud* by C Troyon, furniture such as the elegant bureau made by Riesenburg (Château de St-Hubert) and Caroline Murat's bed produced by the Jacob brothers (Château de Neuilly).

The variety of landscapes in the Paris Basin has provided much inspiration for artists such as A-H Dunoy, G Michel, Lebourg, Utrillo, Luce etc. The museum has a large collection of works by Paul Huet, André Dunoyer de Ségonzac and Jean Fautrier.

Painted wainscoting from the folly built by the famous 18C dancer "La Guimard" in Pantin decorates a small drawing room.

The **Centre de Documentation** ⊘ houses several million written documents about and illustrations of the Île-de-France area.

★Grandes Cascades ⊘ – The waters are approached from allée de la Duchesse; they spring out of carved masks by Rodin and tumble down a series of 10 terraces before flowing into the Octagonal Basin. The sight of these various fountains and cascades is particularly spectacular when all the fountains are playing during the **Grandes Eaux★**. This perspective is continued by a green lawn.

L'Octogone – The basin has kept its original design by Le Nôtre. Of ample proportions, circled by a row of plane trees, it exudes a majestic, peaceful atmosphere. The jets of water reach a height of 10m/32ft.

Pavillon de Hanovre – The pavilion was built by the architect Chevotet in 1760 and moved from boulevard des Italiens in Paris to Sceaux in 1930.

★Grand Canal – It is as long as the Petit Canal at Versailles (1 030m/3 380ft) and flanked by a double row of Lombardy poplars.

Terrasse des Pintades – From the canal, two ramps lead up to a terrace which is the starting point for the park's two sweeping perspectives: one extends towards the château while the other follows the line of the Grand Canal.

Petit Château – An elegant early-17C building which was incorporated into the estate by Colbert. The children of the Duchesse du Maine were brought up here.

The Grandes Cascades at Sceaux

G. Dubois/PIX

Pavillon de l'Aurore 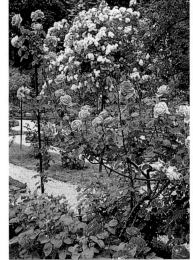 – This charming pavilion crowned by a dome is attributed to Claude Perrault. It is approached by a series of staircases featuring dainty, neatly arranged balusters. The interior decoration forms a harmonious ensemble: wainscot, flooring, ceilings and a superb dome by Le Brun, reproducing the delicate tints of sunrise. It was here that Colbert received the French Academy in 1677. For this momentous occasion the poet Quinault composed a poem of 900 lines on the subject of Le Brun's fresco. He read it out to the members of that prestigious assembly, who spent most of the evening craning their necks towards the ceiling to follow Quinault's detailed explanations.

Intendance – This is a splendid Louis XVI building, and was formerly the residence of the intendant of Sceaux.

The rose garden at L'Haÿ-les-Roses

Anciennes Écuries – The stables were built under Colbert, after studies made by Le Pautre. Facing the stables stands a horse-pond *(visible from the esplanade)*.

TOWN

Jardin des Félibres – Florian, the celebrated fabulist from the Cévennes, died in 1794 and was buried at Sceaux. Since the 19C this garden has been a place of pilgrimage for Provençal poets and writers - known locally as *Félibres* - who come and pay their respects once a year (on a Sunday in June). The garden contains several busts of Provençal poets, including one of Frédéric Mistral.

Église St-Jean-Baptiste – The church was rebuilt in the 16C and was given a façade and a spire under Louis-Philippe. The 17C *Baptism of Christ* by Tuby behind the high altar was taken from the chapel of the former château. The altar in the north aisle is adorned with a medallion of the Virgin Mary by Coysevox (18C).

Jardin de la Ménagerie – This menagerie used to belong to the Duchesse du Maine and to the burial place of her canaries (beneath the columns) and her favourite cat (in a funeral urn). It was used to host popular dances during the Revolution; the famous *Bal de Sceaux*, attended by the *Muscadins* and the *Merveilleuses*, was very much in vogue at the time and gave its name to one of Honoré de Balzac's novels. Subsequently it went out of fashion and was replaced by dancing at Robinson.

Ancienne manufacture de céramique – The old works were founded by the Duchesse du Maine and lie at the corner of rue des Imbergères. The ceramics production is on display at the Île-de-France Museum.

EXCURSION

L'Haÿ-les-Roses – This town, located in the suburbs just south of Paris, is famed for its spectacular rose garden, occupying a corner of a pleasant **park**.

★★**Roseraie** (Rose Garden) ⊘ – The garden was created in 1892 and subsequently embellished by Jules Gravereaux, a man passionately fond of roses who was also one of the founders of the famous Parisian department store Le Bon Marché.
The flower beds are planted with thousands of wild and grafted roses from all over the world. The gardens also feature a display of arches, trellises and colonnades for the climbing varieties to the delight of visitors. The selection of roses is extended every year.
This impressive collection of roses, regrouped typologically, allows the visitor to trace the evolution of this noble flower from the prickly rose *(Rosa acicularis)* to the most recent award-winning hybrids.

SENLIS★★

Population 14 432
Michelin map 56 fold 11, 106 folds 8, 9 or 237 folds 6, 18

Access from Paris: *SNCF rail link from Gare du Nord to Chantilly; bus link to Senlis.*

Senlis derives its romantic charm from its picturesque old streets, its connections with Frankish rulers, enterprising bishops and abbots, the rich cornfields of Valois and the wooded horizons.

The election of Hugh Capet – The conquerors of Senlis built a massive strong-hold over the first Gallo-Roman ramparts of the town. The kings of the first two Frankish dynasties would often take up residence here, lured by the game in the nearby forests. The Carolingian line died out when Louis V suffered a fatal hunting accident. In 987 the Archbishop of Reims called a meeting at Senlis Castle in which he and the local lords decided that Hugh Capet - the Duc des Francs - would be the next king.
Senlis went out of fashion as a royal place of residence and was gradually replaced by Compiègne and Fontainebleau. The last French ruler to have stayed at the castle was Henri IV.

Eating out

MODERATE

Les Jardins de Séraphine – *18 rue de Beauvais* – ☎ *03 44 60 04 00* – *closed 13-29 Aug, Sun evening and Mon* – *booking essential Sat-Sun* – *60/150F.* This *crêperie* in Senlis town centre offers salads, daily specials and of course... sweet and savoury pancakes! Warm welcome and affordable prices. Although the decor is somewhat plain, the terrace is always popular in summer. Tea room on Sundays.

MID-RANGE

Le Bourgeois Gentilhomme – *3 place de la Halle* – ☎ *03 44 53 13 22* – *closed 14-28 Aug, Sun evening and Mon* – *145/405F.* Named after a famous play by France's celebrated author Molière, this restaurant pays tribute to the great man, a fact reflected in both the decoration and the succulent food. The owner will enjoy showing you round his splendid 12C cellar for a pre-lunch apéritif.

Where to stay

MID-RANGE

Hostellerie de la Porte Bellon – *51 rue Bellon* – ☎ *03 44 53 03 05* – *closed 20 Dec-6 Jan* – *18 rooms 290/420F* – ☕ *35F* – *restaurant 125/189F.* Situated in the vicinity of the bustling town centre, this imposing residence, formerly a post house, features pleasing bedrooms with all the necessary amenities. The charming paved courtyard, basking in the shade of century old trees, opens onto the garden. Meals are served here whenever the weather permits.

A carriage ride through town

Horse-drawn carriages leave from in front of the cathedral daily at 10.30am, noon, 2.30 and 5.30pm. The trip (there is a recorded commentary in French) takes you through the old streets of Senlis. The cost is 180F for one to three passengers and 50F for each extra rider.

★★CATHÉDRALE NOTRE-DAME

Its construction was started in 1153 – 16 years after St-Denis and 10 years before Notre-Dame in Paris – but progressed at a slow pace owing to insufficient funds. The cathedral was consecrated in 1191. In about 1240 a transept, which had not originally been planned, and a spire were added. The building was struck by lightning in June 1504; as a result, the clerestory and the transept walls needed to be rebuilt. A set of new side aisles was also added, giving the cathedral its present appearance. Initially, the two towers were identical. It was only towards the mid-13C that the right tower was crowned with the magnificent **spire★★** which was to have such a strong influence over religious architecture in the Valois area *(see below)*. The spire reaches a height of 78m/256ft.

The **main doorway★★** – dedicated to the Virgin Mary and celebrating her Assumption – is strongly reminiscent of the doorways at Chartres, Notre-Dame in Paris, Amiens and Reims. The lintel features two famous low-relief carvings representing the Dormition of the Virgin Mary and the Assumption. The realism and freedom of expression of the sculpture were unusual for the 12C; note the touching swiftness with which the angels raise Mary off the ground and remove her to the celestial skies.

Main doorway of Notre-Dame cathedral

Ph. Gajic/MICHELIN

The embrasures are adorned with eight figures from the Old Testament, depicted in a lively manner. The heads were smashed during the Revolution and remodelled in the 19C. On the left, Abraham is about to sacrifice his son Isaac, while an angel holds the sword in an attempt to stop him. The statues rest on square bases presenting a series of light-hearted panels sculpted into the labours of the months. The calendar starts with January, on the right-hand side near the door.

South front – Constructed by Pierre Chambiges in the 16C, the **transept crossing**★★ contrasts sharply with the west front. It is interesting to follow the evolution of Gothic architecture from the austere 12C to the 16C, when Late Flamboyant already showed signs of Renaissance influence, introduced after the Italian wars. The clerestory and its huge Flamboyant windows were also completed in the 16C. The lower part (12C) of the east end and the radiating chapels are intact. The axial chapel was replaced by a larger structure in the 19C. The galleries - dating from Romanesque times - support the nave and chancel with the help of Gothic flying buttresses.

Interior – Enter through the south doorway. The church interior is 70m/230ft long, 9.2m/30ft wide and measures 24m/79ft to the keystone. Above the organ, the 12C vaulting which escaped the ravages of the fire in 1504 marks the original height of the church: 17m/56ft. The nave and the chancel, comparatively narrow in spite of their height, are graced with an airy lightness. The triforium galleries above the aisles are among the finest in France.

The first chapel to the right of the south doorway features superb vaulting with pendant keystones, a 14C stone Virgin and a lovely set of stained-glass windows. These are the only original panes to have remained intact. A statue of St Louis from the 14C is placed in the south aisle of the ambulatory. The north transept chapel houses a 16C Christ made of larch. The left-hand aisle features an elegant statue of St Barbara dating back to the 16C.

Leave through the north door.

North doorway – The north side is similar to the southern façade but less ornate. The gable surmounting the doorway bears François I's salamander and the capital F as a reminder of the 16C reconstruction campaign, financed by the generous contributions of the French king.

North side – The cathedral's setting on this side is much less solemn; it features several patches of greenery and is extremely picturesque. Skirt the little garden that follows the east façade of what was once the bishop's palace. The building rests on the ruins of the old Gallo-Roman ramparts; the base of one tower remains. Lovely view of the cathedral's east end.

OLD TOWN *1hr*

Jardin du Roy – These gardens occupy the former moat of the Gallo-Roman ramparts which, at their widest point, measured 312m/1 024ft across and at their narrowest 242m/794ft. Twenty-eight towers (7m/23ft high and 4m/14ft thick) defended the city walls; 16 remain today, some still intact, others badly damaged. There is a lovely **view**★ of the ramparts and the towers, the cathedral and the scattered buildings that once formed the castle.

Return to rue de Villevert and proceed towards place du Parvis.

SENLIS

★Place du Parvis – A charming little square beside the cathedral.

Église St-Pierre ⊘ – The church was started in the 12C and underwent extensive alteration in the 17C. The small left tower and its stone spire are both Romanesque, while the heavier tower on the right dates from Renaissance times (1596). The badly damaged but very elaborate façade is characteristic of Flamboyant Gothic. The church was abandoned during the Revolution. It is now used as a venue for a variety of cultural activities.

The itinerary takes you past the Art and Archeology Museum housed in the old bishop's palace, which is made up of a series of buildings dating from the 13C to the 18C *(see SIGHTS below)*.

Ancien Château royal ⊘ – Before entering the castle courtyard, start to walk up rue du Châtel to see the original fortified entrance to the stronghold now walled up. Adjoining the old doorway, the 16C Hôtel des Trois Pots proudly sports its old-fashioned sign.

The fortified site was occupied at least as early as the reign of the Emperor Claudius (AD 41-54). Throughout its history, up to the time of Henri II, it featured a charming collection of ruins.

The sturdy square "praetorium" tower is the most striking piece of architecture that still stands today; the 4.5m/15ft thick walls are further supported by a set of hefty buttresses. Although apparently dating from the Middle Ages, the castle's history is not entirely clear. It now houses the Musée de la Vénerie *(see SIGHTS below)*.

S. Sauvignier/MICHELIN

Senlis

★Old Streets – Rue du Châtel used to be the main street through Senlis for those travelling from Paris to Flanders. In 1753 it was succeeded by rue Neuve de Paris, now called rue de la République. Its southern continuation, named "rue Vieille de Paris", thus refers to the ancient thoroughfare.

Take the charming **rue de la Treille** and walk to the "Fausse Porte", which was the postern of the former Gallo-Roman ramparts. On the left stands the Chancellerie, flanked by two towers.

The **town hall** (Hôtel de Ville) on place Henri-IV was rebuilt in 1495. The front bears a bust of Henri IV and an inscription conveying his affection for the town of Senlis. These date back to a visit by Charles X on his way back from his coronation in Reims Cathedral (1825).

Walk back along rue du Châtel to place du Parvis.

SIGHTS

★**Musée d'Art et d'Archéologie** ⊘ – The Gallo-Roman collections are exhibited on the ground floor: glass, merovingian jewellery, small bronze statues, strange votive offerings carved in stone from a small sanctuary in Halatte Forest *(see below)*, a **bronze base**★ dating from AD 48 and engraved with a dedication to Emperor Claudius.

In the crypt there are traces of a house built on this site in the early 2C; the foundations of the Gallo-Roman wall (3C) are also visible, made up of fragments of columns, pilasters and carved stonework from buildings of the earlier town which stood here.

In the Gothic Room (late 14C) there are striking medieval sculptures including the **Head of a Bearded Man**★ (early 13C) and a majestic marble **Virgin and Child** (late 14C). Note also the entertaining series of small figures of painted and gilded wood which came originally from a depiction of the Passion on a late-15C altarpiece made in Antwerp.

At the bottom of the stairs the mid-12C stained-glass windows recount the creation of Eve and the Temptation of Adam and Eve.

Paintings dating from the 17C to 20C are on display in the four rooms on the first floor: Philippe de Champaigne, Luca Giordano, Francesco Solimena, Corot, Boudin, Sérusier, Thomas Couture (1815-79) who was born in Senlis. Centring on works by Séraphine Louis, nicknamed Séraphine de Senlis, is a collection of works by 20C naive artists.

Musée des Spahis ⊘ – *By the entrance to the old Royal Castle.*
This museum retraces 150 years of history of the North African cavalry, which held a special place in the French Army from 1780 to 1814 and from 1830 to 1964. It largely concentrates on the old Spahis (native Algerian horsemen), Goumiers (indigenous horsemen and foot soldiers), Meharists (dromedary riders) and Saharans (cameleers).

Musée de la Vénerie (Hunting Museum) ⊘ – In the 13C St Louis founded St-Maurice priory next to the Royal Castle. The relics of St Maurice of Agaune were kept here by the monks until the Revolution. A new building was built in the early 18C which now houses the Hunting Museum.

The works presented here were chosen from among the many illustrations of stag hunts which have enriched French culture. Desportes (1661-1743) and Oudry (1688-1755) represent the Ancien Régime, while later animal painters include Carle Vernet, Rosa Bonheur, Charles Hallo (the founder of the museum) etc. The walls are hung with numerous trophies and stags' heads.

The display of historical hunting gear renders the exhibition particularly interesting. The hunting costume of the Condé - fawn and amaranth-purple - can be seen on a figure representing a Chantilly forest warden, and in the painting depicting the young Duc d'Enghien (1787). Note the famous collection of hunting "buttons", which were the most highly prized trappings of a hunting outfit, chased hunting knives, horns (including a beautiful silver hunting horn made in 1817) etc.

Musée de l'Hôtel de Vermandois ⊘ – This small museum installed in a 12C mansion – a lovely example of Romanesque vernacular architecture – illustrates the history of the town and its cathedral through an audio-visual presentation. Sculpture plays a large part: a 12C head of an angel from one of the doorways of Notre-Dame; carved capitals and consoles from the cathedral and from the priory chapel. One of the brackets is decorated with a carving of "The Wrestlers" (1260). The original spire of the cathedral has been placed in one of the two rooms.

Chapelle Royale St-Frambourg ⊘ – Hugh Capet's wife the pious Queen Adelaide founded this chapel before 990 to house the relics of a recluse from the Bas-Maine, known as St Frambourg or St Fraimbault. The chapel was rebuilt by Louis VII after 1177 but abandoned during the Revolution.

The chapel was restored as the Franz Liszt Auditorium in 1977, through the efforts of the pianist Georges Cziffra. The Cziffra Foundation organises concerts and exhibitions for lovers of classical music.

The **church** and its single Gothic nave have been restored to their former grandeur. Descend to the archeological **crypt**. Excavations have revealed the floor of a sanctuary dating from about AD 1000 featuring fragments of columns. Two fragments of pilasters belonging to the flat east end of this church still bear the mural paintings of bishops. At the east end the crypt comes to rest on a sturdy round tower of fine brickwork and on the inner ramparts of the town, which follow the old Gallo-Roman wall.

Ancienne Abbaye St-Vincent ⊘ – *South-west of the town, via rue l'Apport-au-Pain and rue de Meaux.*
St Vincent's Abbey was founded in 1060 by Henri I's wife Anne of Kiev, following the birth of their son Philippe, heir to the throne, possibly owing to a vow. The child's christening marked the introduction into France of the Byzantine name Philippe.

A 12C open-work bell-tower – one of the finest and the most delicate in Ile-de-France – dominates the church, the silhouette of which has been marred by successive building and reconstruction campaigns.

The former abbey buildings, rebuilt in the 17C, house a cloister with classical features: slender columns with Doric capitals and stone vaulting with coffering.

EXCURSIONS

★**Forêt d'Halatte** – This large forest north of Senlis includes beech groves, cherished by the Capetians, and oaks, hornbeams, pine trees etc to the south.

Aumont-en-Halatte – This charming village houses a museum on the activist author Henri Barbusse (1873-1935), best-known for his wartime novel *Under Fire* (1917) recounting life as a French soldier in the trenches.

★**Butte d'Aumont** – ◪ *30min on foot there and back from Aumont Church: towards Apremont take the first public lane on the left (chain), a sandy track flanked by wire fences.* The hillock offers a superb **panorama**★ over the wooded horizon and the towns. Follow the itinerary leading past the old **St-Christophe priory** (now housing offices of the French National Health Service); fine view over Fleurines and the forest.

Mont Pagnotte – *North-east of the forest.* ◪ One of the heights of the Paris region, Mont Pagnotte reaches an altitude of 221m/727ft (television transmitter). A footpath runs along the edge of the plateau at its summit.

Pont-Ste-Maxence – *11km/7mi north by N 17.* Because of its old bridge spanning the River Oise, the town has always been an important staging post. It owes the second part of its name to an Irish saint who was martyred here in the 5C. East of the town stands **Abbaye du Moncel** ⊘★ which Philip the Fair had built next to a royal castle, two towers of which still remain. The abbey, dedicated to the St Clare order, found favour with Philippe VI, the first ruler of the Valois dynasty (1328-50). In 1347 the abbey received the mortal remains of his wife Jeanne of Burgundy, and after Philippe's death, his second wife Blanche of Navarre retired there.

The main façade still looks medieval and offers two imposing chimneys. The **courtyard**★ is surrounded by three wings crowned with tall roofs of brown tiles (restored). Other elements of note include one of the galleries from the 16C cloister, the storeroom and its pointed vaulting, the Gothic chapter-house and the amazing 14C **timberwork**★ above the nuns' dorter, made with oak from Halatte Forest.

Château de Raray – *13km/8mi north-east by D 932ᴬ. At Villeneuve-sous-Verberie, turn right.*

Standing on the edge of a charming hamlet, the château (now part of a golf club) is famous for the striking decoration of its main courtyard, used in Jean Cocteau's film *Beauty and the Beast.* Its game enclosures consist of an alternating series of arcades, recesses and niches housing busts of the gods of Antiquity and 17C historical figures. These are crowned by two lively hunting scenes carved in stone, a stag hunt and a boar hunt.

St-Vaast-de-Longmont – *16km/10mi north-east by D 932A.*
Seen from the village cemetery, the Romanesque bell-tower and its stone spire appear to be extremely ornate: cornices with billet moulding, arcades resting on colonnettes decorated variously with spiralling, zigzag or torus motifs.

At **Rhuis** nearby *(west on D 123)*, the 11C Romanesque church has an elegant bell-tower with a double row of twinned windows. The tower is believed to be one of the oldest in Île-de-France. The interior features four bays and an apsidal chapel with no vaulting.

The bell-towers of the Valois area – *Tour of 48km/29mi. Allow 2hr 30min.* This tour leads across the arable plains which lie near the forest and through a string of small villages with charming 19C farmhouses. The route is dotted with bell-towers, the slender spires of which feature crockets.

Leave Senlis to the south-east, past the Abbaye St-Vincent - the first bell-tower of the tour - and then the Ponte de Meaux. Turn left soon afterwards and right onto D 330, towards Mont-l'Évêque. After passing over the motorway, take a right turning.

IN THE FORÊT D'HALATTE

Le Vieux Logis – *105 rue du Général-de-Gaulle, 60700 Fleurines – 5km/3mi north of Senlis by N 17 – ☎ 03 44 54 10 13 – closed 1-20 Aug, Sun evening and Mon – booking essential – 98/240F.* This charming place decorated like a country inn, with visible beams and stonework, is the perfect setting for tasty, original meals. In summer you can sit out on the garden terrace and admire the quaint brick oven.

Ph. Gajic/MICHELIN

Castle wall, Raray

Villemétrie – The bridge spanning the River Nonette offers a pleasant vista of the old mill, an ancient stone cross and the shady grounds of a park.

Turn round and proceed along D 330⁴.

Baron – Note the **church** ⊙ and its crocketed steeple (45m/148ft). The nave was rebuilt in the 16C and features many ornate embellishments on the exterior: stone buttresses round the roof, and rounded, pot-bellied piers at the east end. The 14C stone Virgin and the 18C **panelling★** inside were taken from the Abbaye de Chaalis.

Versigny – Presents a bell-tower typical of the Senlis style. Observe the strange **château** ⊙ on the opposite side of the road. This long, low, U-shaped building of Italian inspiration was first started in the 17C and subsequently remodelled under Louis-Philippe: the balustrades, curved pediments, steps and columns date from the Restoration period.

Proceed towards Nanteuil-le-Haudouin but on reaching the edge of the château grounds take a right turning at the next junction and follow directions to Montagny-Ste-Félicité. Drive up to the isolated church.

Montagny-Ste-Félicité – Superb open-work **bell-tower★**, rising 65m/213ft above the ground.

Turn round. At the crossroads north of Montagny, turn left to Baron and take the road to Senlis. Do not follow the direct route. Instead, at the Fontaine-Chaalis Junction, turn right towards Montépilloy.

Fourcheret – A former **barn** ⊙ belonging to the Abbaye de Chaalis still stands, supported by 18 pillars. Built in the 13C, this monastic structure (65m/213ft long and 18m/60ft wide) features an impressive display of timberwork.

Montépilloy – The ruins of the old stronghold - presently occupied by a farmhouse – are perched on top of the plateau that rises between the shallow valleys of the River Nonette and River Aunette. On 15 August 1429 Joan of Arc spent the night at Montépilloy, having fought the English troops of Bedford who occupied Senlis. A commemorative plaque has been affixed onto the church exterior. The 13C entrance gatehouse - itself a small castle - offers a view of the **farmhouse** *(not open to the public)* and, in the background, the ruins of the 14C keep which stand 40m/130ft high.

SÈVRES ★★

Population 21 990
Michelin map 101 fold 24, 106 fold 18 or 237 fold 17
Michelin plan 22

Access from Paris: *Metro line 9 (station: Pont de Sèvres)*

The **Manufacture Nationale de Porcelaine** (National Porcelain Factory) established here in the 18C has made the name of Sèvres famous throughout the world. The present buildings date back to 1876.

★★ MUSÉE NATIONAL DE LA CÉRAMIQUE ⊙

Founded in 1824 by Brongniart, the museum has an outstanding collection of pottery, faience, and porcelain classified by origin and by historical period *(see Introduction: Faience and porcelain)*.

On the **ground floor** are the collections of Islamic ceramics, some very old and very rare pottery (8C-18C) and a superb collection of Renaissance faience. Opposite is an exhibition and sale room presenting a range of pieces made in the pottery, some of them traditional models and others contemporary creations.

The collections on the **first floor** show changes in clay and decorative techniques in Sèvres, Europe and worldwide. In the central room, note the Chinese porcelain *(famille verte* and *famille rose)* and the decoration on the pieces of Meissen from Saxony (Kakiemon and Imari styles).

The rooms on the right focus on soft paste porcelain (18C-20C). French works are particularly well represented through Chantilly, St-Cloud, Vincennes and Sèvres. In the raised display cabinets, note the various background colours (green, purple, blue). The 19C collection includes the industrial arts service painted by Devely from 1823 onwards. It is representative of the Sèvres porcelain which, unlike others, must include gold.

A HILLTOP RESTAURANT

Auberge Garden – *24 route du Pavé des Gardes* – ☎ *01 46 26 50 50 – closed 7-29 Aug, 24 Dec-2 Jan, Sat lunchtime and Sun lunchtime – 178F.* This former inn perched on the heights of Sèvres is gradually being refurbished by its current owners. The menu is highly attractive and made with delicious produce. Traditional dining room with movable partitions and a piano. Terrace for the sunny days.

The rooms on the left have some splendid pieces of high-fired ceramics from French and European works. The decoration can be in a range of blues, like the porcelain from Rouen or Marseille (late 17C), but much of the high-fired porcelain has multicoloured decoration. This is shown in the magnificent pieces of regional porcelain dating from the 18C. The last rooms are given over to Nevers and Delft.

Sèvres pot-pourri vases (18C)

ADDITIONAL SIGHT

Maison des Jardies (Maison de Léon Gambetta) ⊘ – *14 avenue Gambetta.*
This modest gardener's lodge was once part of the Jardies estate, where Honoré de Balzac settled in 1838 and attempted to grow pineapples, unsuccessfully. Corot stayed here and Gambetta died here on 31 December 1882. Several of the politician's mementoes have been kept and are on show to the public. At the crossroads near the villa stands a memorial to Gambetta, by Bartholdi.

SOISSONS★

Population 29 829
Michelin map 56 fold 4 or 236 fold 37

Soissons rises in the midst of rich agricultural land which is overlooked by the tall spires of the town's abbey visible from far around. Although the town was largely rebuilt after the First World War, it retains many old monuments and boasts several parks and gardens.

The Frankish capital – The town played an important role at the time of the Frankish monarchy; it was at this town's gates that Clovis defeated the Romans, ruining them for his own benefit. The famous story of the **Soissons Vase** took place after this battle: Clovis demanded that his booty include a vase which had been stolen from a church in Reims. A soldier angrily opposed him, broke the vase and cried "You will have nothing, O King, but that which Destiny gives you"! The following year, while Clovis was reviewing his troops he stopped before the same soldier, raised his sword and split the soldier's skull saying, "Thus you did with the Soissons vase". This episode is illustrated in a low-relief carving on the war memorial.
Clotaire I, son of Clovis, made Soissons his capital as did Chilpéric, King of Neustria and husband of the notorious Frédégonde; the latter was famous for her rivalry with Brunhilda, whose sister she had had assassinated.
The election of Pepin the Short in the 8C, naming him successor to the fallen Merovingians, also took place in Soissons and in 923, following a battle outside the town walls, Charles the Simple gave up his throne in favour of the house of France.

★★ANCIENNE ABBAYE DE ST-JEAN-DES-VIGNES ⊘ *1hr*

The old Abbey of St John of the Vines, which was founded in 1076, was one of the richest monasteries of the Middle Ages. The generosity of the kings of France, bishops, great lords and burghers allowed the monks to build a great abbey church and large monastic buildings in the 13C and 14C. In 1805, however, an imperial decree approved by the Bishop of Soissons ordered the demolition of the church, so that its materials could be used to repair the cathedral; the resulting outcry led to the preservation of the west front.

West front – The cusped portals are delicately cut and surmounted with late-13C gables; the rest of the front dates from the 14C except for the bell-towers which were built in the 15C. An elegant openwork gallery separates the central portal from the great rose-window, which has lost its tracery. Statues of the Virgin Mary and the saints are placed in pairs beside the piers on the towers.
The two Flamboyant bell-towers are extremely graceful. The **north tower** is the larger, taller and more ornate; the platform of the buttresses is finely worked; the spires of the openwork turrets bear prominent groins and crockets; on the western side, against the mullion of the upper window, a Christ on the Cross stands with statues of the Virgin Mary and St John at his feet.
The back of the façade is much plainer, the north tower having been gutted from this side. The south portal contains a 13C door which linked the church and cloister.

St-Jean-des-Vignes

B. Kaufmann/MICHELIN

★**Réfectoire** – The **refectory** was built into the extension of the west front, at the back of the great cloister. The 13C construction has two naves with pointed vaulting. The transverse arches and ribs rest on seven slender columns with foliate capitals. Eight great lobed rose-windows pierce the east and south walls. The reader's pulpit still exists.

Cellier – This magnificent **undercroft**, located under the refectory and of the same shape, has pointed vaulting resting on solid octagonal pillars.
The building opposite was rebuilt in the 16C to serve as the abbot's residence.

Cloîtres – All that remains of the **great cloister**★ are two 14C galleries. The pointed arches separated by elaborate buttresses had a graceful blind arcade, remains of which can be seen in the south bays. The delicately worked capitals represent flora and fauna.
The **small cloister** nearby has two Renaissance bays.

★★CATHÉDRALE ST-GERVAIS-ET-ST-PROTAIS *1hr*

The pure lines and simple arrangement of St Gervase and St Protase Cathedral make it possibly one of the most beautiful examples of Gothic art.
Construction of the cathedral began in the 12C with the south transept; the chancel, nave and side aisles rose during the 13C; the north transept and the upper part of the façade were not completed until the early 14C. The Hundred Years War brought work to a halt before the north bell-tower was built; it was never to be finished.
After the First World War only the chancel and the transept remained intact.

Exterior – The asymmetrical front gives no hint of the beauty of the interior; some unfortunate 18C alterations, partly corrected in 1930, have disfigured the portals and today only their deep arching remains. The rose-window, surmounted by a graceful gallery, is set within a pointed arch. Rue de l'Évêché offers a good view over the south transept which ends in a semicircle; place Marquigny overlooks the solid and austere east end.
A portal with a soaring gable supported by two buttresses stands east of the north transept; the more ornate decorative art of the 14C may be seen here. The transept's façade is decorated with radiating blind arcades, also 14C, and is pierced by a great rose-window set within a pointed arch, topped by a gable flanked by two pinnacles.

★**Interior** – Excluding the transept arms, the cathedral (116m/380ft long, 25.6m/83ft wide and 30.33m/99ft high) is perfectly symmetrical; no superfluous detail breaks the perfect harmony of the vast nave. Cylindrical columns separate the bays of the nave and chancel. Their sparsely decorated capitals bear the weight of the great pointed arches. They also serve to support five shafts sustaining the vaulting, which are extended down to the base by an engaged column. The arcades are surmounted by a triforium and twinned clerestory windows.
The **south transept**★★ presents an extremely graceful arrangement, due largely to the ambulatory and the gallery above it. A two-storey chapel opens onto the ambulatory. A beautiful keystone adorns the intersection of the vaulting's ribs, which rest on fine columns framing the windows and on two huge columns at the entrance. The upper chapel, similar to the lower one, leads to the transept gallery.
The **chancel** is one of the earliest examples of the decorated Gothic style. The five lancet windows are embellished with beautiful 13C and 14C stained glass. The high altar is framed by two white marble statues representing the Annunciation. The pointed vaulting of the five radiating chapels links up with that of the ambulatory; the eight ribs of the vaulting intersect at the same keystone.
The **north transept** has the same arrangement as the nave; the rose-window containing old glass was a 14C addition. The *Adoration of the Shepherds* on the left was painted by Rubens for the Franciscans, to thank them for their care at Soissons.

ADDITIONAL SIGHTS

Musée municipal de l'ancienne abbaye de St-Léger ⊘ – St Leger's Abbey was founded in 1152 but devastated in 1567 by Protestants who also demolished the nave of the church.

Église – The 13C chancel and transept are lit by high and low windows. The chancel has a cant-walled east end. The west front and the nave with its double side aisles were rebuilt in the 17C. Note the tympanum and capitals from the old abbey at Braine.

Crypte – The crypt contains two galleries and two bays from the late 11C. The groined vaults are supported by pillars which are flanked by columns with square, foliate capitals. The nave leads into the 13C polygonal apse with pointed vaulting.

Eating out

MODERATE

Hostellerie du Lion d'Or – *1 place du Général-de-Gaulle, 02290 Vic-sur-Aisne – 12km/8mi east of Soissons by N 31 then D 13 –* ☎ *03 23 55 50 20 – closed 15-31 July, Sun and Tues evenings and Mon – booking essential Sat-Sun – 95/180F.* This is the place to aim for if you want to tuck into a proper meal in congenial company. Since it opened back in 1580, this restaurant has never disappointed its clientele and it continues to serve generous helpings of delicious food made with fresh ingredients. Before leaving, ask the owners to show you their "history album" (*album historique*).

Where to stay

MODERATE

Chambre d'Hôte Ferme de la Montagne – *02290 Ressons-le-Long – 8km/5mi west of Soissons by N 31 then D 1160 –* ☎ *03 23 74 23 71 –* 🖃 *– 5 rooms 200/300F.* The farmhouse attached to Notre-Dame-de-Soissons Abbey is perched on a plateau, commanding wonderful views of the Aisne Valley, especially from the drawing room. To ensure greater comfort and convenience, each room has its own private entrance.

Showtime

Le Cynodrome – *10 boulevard Branly –* ☎ *03 23 73 09 17 – every other Sun.* The ultimate venue for greyhound racing, where dogs from all over Europe come to compete on a 450m/1 477ft track. Dances and fairs are organised on important racing days. Do not miss this unusual sporting event. Members of the public are allowed to see the greyhounds being trained.

Salle capitulaire – The 13C chapter-house overlooks the cloister of the same date. The six quadripartite vaults rest on two columns.

Museum – The museum's various collections are housed in the old monastery buildings.

The prehistoric, Gallic and Gallo-Roman exhibits are on display on the ground floor. The first floor is devoted to 16C-19C painting: Northern School (note in particular the anonymous Flemish painting entitled *Allegory of Winter* c 1630-50, representing a bearded old man), Italian School and French School (Largillière, Courbet, Boudin and Daumier). The other room has maps, documents, paintings and models tracing the history of the town.

Avenue du Mail offers a view of both the east end of the church and the town hall which was the Intendancy under the Ancien Régime.

Abbaye de St-Médard ⊘ – This abbey was very well known during the Frankish period; today only the 9C pre-Romanesque crypt remains. It used to contain the tombs of St Médard and the founding Merovingian kings, Clotaire and Sigebert.

EXCURSION

Courmelles – *4km/2.5mi south; take D 1 for about 2km/1.5mi then take the small road on the right.*
The 12C church with its squat bell-tower has preserved its rounded Romanesque east end. Four buttresses of slender columns with finely carved capitals separate the rounded-arch windows, which are decorated with stars and surmounted by blind arcades of pointed arches. The projecting central window was formerly a recess for the altar.

La baie de SOMME★★
SOMME BAY
Michelin map 52 fold 6 or 236 folds 11, 21, 22

The Baie de Somme is the ideal area for visitors who wish to relax while watching seals sprawled on the sand and migratory wild ducks, or riding on the tourist train which merrily whistles away through the countryside. The bay offers its open spaces, its luminous landscapes and, at low tide, its endless stretches of sand and grass.

Slow silting-up process – Like all bays, the Somme experiences the flow of water and silt which settles and tends to widen the sandbanks; these become covered with grass, creating the **mollières** or salt-pastures where lambs now graze.

Discover the region aboard this train

The silting-up combined with a gradual increase in the size of boats in general has considerably affected the formerly active traffic here; the development of the Somme canal from 1786 to 1835 and the creation of a sheltered port at Le Hourdel merely slowed its decline. It is worth noting, however, that during the First World War the bay served as a British base: in 1919, traffic reached an exceptional 125 000t.

Hunting and fishing – The bay's three fishing ports (St-Valery, Le Crotoy and Le Hourdel) specialise in shellfish and squid fishing.

When the tide is out fish are also caught in the channels, pools and ruts on the shore: cockles, mullet, eels and flatfish, either speared or just picked up by hand. Wildfowl hunters lie in wait either in special boats or in hides formed in grassy mounds pierced with firing holes, using domestic or artificial ducks as decoys. The Marquenterre reserve and bird sanctuary, north-west of the Somme Bay, nevertheless serve as a stopping-off place for migratory birds; 315 of the 452 species found in Europe have been identified in the area (the Camargue region is host to 360 species).

AROUND THE BAY

It is possible, with a good pair of binoculars, to observe seals sprawled on the sand lining the estuary, ready to flee at the first sign of danger. A surveillance system has been set up by Picardie Nature to keep human interference to a minimum so that females can give birth without being disturbed; at the moment, two baby seals are born every year.

Chemin de fer de la baie de Somme ⊘ – A train comprising old carriages with viewing platforms pulled by steam or diesel engines runs between Le Crotoy, Noyelles, St Valery and Cayeux-sur-Mer providing a journey (16km/10mi) of discovery through this lush area bordered by the River Somme's grassy sandbanks.

★★ **Parc ornithologique du Marquenterre** – See p 250.

⌂ **Le Crotoy** – The resort is reached by a scenic route (D 940) which runs alongside grass-covered sandbanks *(mollières)*. The town was once a fortress, with a castle in which Joan of Arc was imprisoned in 1430 before being taken to St-Valery and then to Rouen. Today it is an attractive and popular seaside resort overlooking the Somme Bay. The **port**, close to place Jeanne d'Arc, the resort's lively centre, is used by small coastal fishing trawlers (which catch shrimps, flatfish and herrings); casting on the Somme's bed brings in plaice and eel.

Butte du Moulin – The hill is reached from the church by rue de la Mer and offers an extensive **view**★ from the terrace over the Somme Bay, St-Valery, Le Hourdel and the open sea.

★ **St-Valery-sur-Somme** – See ST-VALERY-SUR-SOMME.

★ **Maison de l'Oiseau** ⊘ – 🖾 A superb collection of stuffed birds assembled by an inhabitant of Cayeux was the basis for the Bird House, which is fittingly located in the ornithologically rich Somme Bay area. A building round a courtyard was especially constructed, following the layout of traditional farms. Inside, displays highlight local birds in their natural habitat: cliffs, sand and mudflats, dunes and gravel pits. In a room dedicated to ducks, a reconstructed hide looks out over a pond behind the house where wild duck, geese, waders etc live. Films, exhibitions and information for fledgling birdwatchers complete the presentation.

Eating out

MODERATE

La Clé des Champs – *80120 Favières – 5km/3mi north-west of Le Crotoy by D 940 then D 140 –* ☎ *03 22 27 88 00 – closed Feb school holidays, 28 Aug-11 Sept, Sun evening and Mon except public holidays – 88/240F.* A good address for gourmets in the heart of a tiny village. A rustic country inn with round tables decorated with painted plates and brass saucepans. Take time to relish the succulent fare lovingly prepared by the chef.

Where to stay

MID-RANGE

Chambre d'Hôte La Ferme du Château de la Motte – *36 route de la Froise, 80120 Monchaux – 11km/7mi north-east of Rue by D 940 then D 32 –* ☎ *03 22 23 94 48 – 5 rooms 300/360F –* ⊡ *40F.* Leave behind the seaside crowds and take a room in this peaceful bed and breakfast. You will be able to relax in the pretty park while at the same time indulging in the many activities organised locally: golf, sand-yachting, riding, water sports etc. Tennis court, outdoor pool and self-catering *gîtes* on the premises.

Le Hourdel – The typical Picardy houses of this small fishing harbour and yachting marina stand at the tip of an offshore bar which begins at Onival. The bar consists of pebbles which are crushed to make emery powders and filtering materials. Views over the bay.

Cayeux-sur-Mer – This resort is bordered by a promenade and an 1 800m/over 1mi long wooden path lined with more than 400 cabins. The long beach of hard sand extends from the Hâble d'Ault to the Pointe de Hourdel; footpaths crisscross the woods of Brighton-les-Pins.

Chinese cemetery in Noyelles

This is the largest Chinese cemetery in France. Situated along the road from Sailly-Flibeaucourt to the hamlet of Nolette, the cemetery includes more than 800 white tombstones engraved with Chinese characters. Following an agreement signed in 1916, thousands of Chinese nationals, most of them farmers from the north of China, undertook to serve the British army in exchange for a salary. The first contingent landed in April 1917; between 1917 and 1919, the camp welcomed 12 000 workers who worked in difficult conditions, were kept apart from the local population and could not come and go as they pleased. Some were killed in the fighting but most succumbed to the epidemic of Spanish influenza which hit the area in the autumn of 1918. At the end of 1919, most of the workers went back home, although a few chose to remain in France.

Vallée de la SOMME★

SOMME VALLEY

Michelin map 52 folds 6 to 10 or 236 folds 22 to 26

The slow-moving waters of the River Somme, "which made Picardy as the Nile made Egypt" (Mabille de Poncheville), often burst their banks to spill into silvery ponds or dark peat bogs and have formed a wide, lush valley in Picardy's chalky plateau.
As the Somme is a natural barrier and has long been a regional frontier, it has been the site of numerous encounters and has given its name to two battles, one in 1916, the other in 1940.

Meandering river – The source of the river is upstream of St-Quentin, at an altitude of 97m/318ft; from there it flows 245km/152mi westwards. The gentleness of this descent, together with the absorbent quality of the peat through which the river meanders, largely explains the lazy pace of the waters.
The regular flow of the river is, however, assured by the uninterrupted seeping from the chalk plateau, which produces numerous springs along the sides of the valley. This moisture is the reason for the fresh, green countryside.
Along the river bed, edged with willows and poplars, the waters are separated in places by small islands.
During their journey, the waters wind past peat bogs hidden under tall grasses, and meadows where laundry used to be spread out to bleach in the sun; past farmed fields and slopes pitted with quarries; past woods revealing shaded springs... In places, the bogs have been drained and turned into vegetable plots *(hortillonnages)*.

Peat — The deep-looking, rectangular ponds were formerly peat bogs. In the past the dense, black **peat** *(tourbe)* was used as a household fuel in modest Picardy homes. It formed in the swamps when vegetation decomposed, producing 60% carbon. The peat was cut out in bars with special shovels *(louchets)* and sliced up into blocks; these were then dried in the meadows or in small barns *(hallettes)*.

Navigation — Navigation on the river has always been limited owing to the fords and the shallowness of the water, but the River Somme nevertheless once carried **gribannes** between Amiens and St-Valery. these heavy skiffs transported wheat from Santerre and wool from Ponthieu downstream; salt and wine were brought upstream. In the 19C a few steamboats joined this traffic.

The **Somme Canal** which was finally completed in the 19C links St-Quentin and St-Valery. Sometimes it follows the course of the river, at other times it runs alongside it or takes shortcuts across the meanders. The canal was hardly used, however, as there was never a true maritime port at the end.

Hunting and Fishing — Hunting chiefly consists of lying in wait for wildfowl, in either a boat or the shelter of a hide *(see ST-VALERY)*. A great quantity of duck and snipe provide the game here; hunting wild swans, however, has not been allowed since the early 18C.

The river, ditches and ponds teem with fish, although the salmon and sturgeon which were so numerous in the 18C are rarely seen. Excellent pâté is made from the abundant swarms of eels which share the waters with pike, carp, perch, tench etc.

PERONNE TO AMIENS *63km/38mi – about 1hr 30min*

Leave Péronne on D 938 (north-west).

The road crosses the Canal du Nord, passing the Étangs de la Haute-Somme near Cléry, then crosses the motorway. As you drive along the plateau, you can see the valley below.

At the entrance to the town of Maricourt, turn left on D 197 then left again on the chemin de Vaux.

★**Belvédère de Vaux** — This spot is a good place to enjoy the panorama over the meanders of the River Curlu and the red rooftops of the hamlet of Vaux. Péronne is in the distance, visible on a clear day.

The road goes down to Vaux and crosses the River Somme.

Take the road to Cappy, which runs along the canal. In Cappy, cross the river and follow D 1 to Bray.

Bray-sur-Somme — This old port town has a lovely **church** ⊘ with a big square bell-tower and a Romanesque chancel.

Froissy — This town on the canal has a little train museum in the old covered market; in the summer months visitors can ride in an old train which was used to supply the trenches during the First World War.

Return to Bray and take D 1.

The drive takes you through the middle of two landscapes: lakes and ponds, sometimes hidden in the fronds of forest ferns, on one side, and steep cliffs on the other. You can see the towers of **Corbie** on the horizon at certain bends in the road.

Corbie and La Neuville — *See CORBIE.*

After La Neuville, the road passes through an area where watercress is grown and rises up a hill. Drive through Daours, continue along D 1; about 11km/7mi beyond the town, you may have your first glimpses of Amiens and its cathedral.

AMIENS TO ABBEVILLE *58km/36mi – about 3hr*

★★★**Amiens** — *See AMIENS*

Leave Amiens on N 235 (west) towards Picquigny; follow the road parallel to the Paris-Calais railway line.

Ailly-sur-Somme — The market town is overlooked by the sober lines of the modern church: its unusual design comprises a great slanting roof like the sail of a boat, which on one side rests on a stone wall and on the other, the ground.

Cross to the north bank of the Somme and turn left towards La Chaussée Tirancourt.

★**Parc Samara** ⊘ — This park (25ha/62 acres) lies at the foot of a Celtic settlement overlooking the River Somme (known as the Samara in the days of the Gauls). Footpaths lead to an **arboretum** (110 species), a botanical garden with quite a few rare plants, the marshes at the bottom of the valley and reconstructions of

Parc Samara - Reconstructed Prehistoric dwellings

dwellings from the Neolithic, Bronze and Iron Ages. The working of flint, wood and pottery is brought to life by demonstrations of prehistoric techniques. Various ecosystems are cultivated and explained in this educational park, including the peat bog, where peat is extracted using techniques which were once common and have almost completely gone out of use..

Daily life in Picardy from the Paleolithic era to the Gallo-Roman period is evoked in the **exhibition pavilion**: a reindeer hunter's house, a bronzesmith's and an Iron Age ironsmith's workshop, a Gallic village street, Gallo-Roman kitchen etc.

Ⓒ Visitors can have a look at the whole park from a tethered hot air balloon, which carries 30 passengers at a time, aloft at 150m/500ft.

Picquigny – In 1475 Trève Island in the middle of the Somme was the setting for the Peace Treaty of Picquigny signed by **Louis XI** and **Edward IV** of England.

The town itself defends a passage across the Somme and is crowned by the ruins of a **castle** ⊙ : its 14C fortifications include a massive keep with walls 4m/13ft thick. A beautiful Renaissance kitchen, a great chamber, underground passages and prisons may all be seen. The château is early 17C. The church contains a 13C nave with 15C apse and tower.

Take D 3 (north-west) out of Picquigny.

Abbaye du Gard – This abbey was founded in 1137 by the Cistercians; in the 17C Mazarin was its commendatory abbot. After the Revolution the buildings were used by the Trappists, the Fathers of the Order of the Holy Spirit and Carthusian reclusive nuns; they were then abandoned and fell into ruin.

In 1967 the abbey was bought by the monks of St-Riquier *(see ST-RIQUIER)* who restored the beautiful 18C main building and gave the abbey back its role as a place of prayer and meeting.

Hangest-sur-Somme – The village specialises in growing watercress. The 12C-16C **church** contains 18C furniture from the Abbaye du Gard.

In 1940 the German 7th Tank Division commanded by **Rommel** crossed the River Somme between Hangest and Condé-Folie using the only railway bridge that had not been blown up. There is a large French military cemetery at **Condé-Folie**.

Beyond Hangest, the road climbs a hill, affording fine views of the valley.

Longpré-les-Corps-Saints – The town derives its name from the relics which the church founder, Aléaume de Fontaine, sent from Constantinople during the Crusades.

The **church** features a portal with a tympanum depicting the Death and Resurrection of the Virgin Mary. The reliquaries are on display at the end of the chancel.

1km/0.5mi beyond Longpré, turn right at Le Catelet onto D 32 towards Long.

The road crosses the floor of the valley, here dotted with ponds, offering a lovely view of the Château de Long.

Long – The great church in this pretty hillside village was rebuilt in the 19C, in the Gothic style, but retained its 16C spire; Cavaillé-Coll organ.

The elegant Louis XV **château** has a slate mansard roof and red brick and white stone. Note the unusual, rounded wings and the graceful openings surmounted by keystones carved with masks and other ornamentation. It resembles the Château de Bagatelle *(see ABBEVILLE)* apart from a few characteristic details. Inside there is an interesting collection of 18C clocks and automata.

Cross the Somme again and return to D 3.

Église de Liercourt – The charming Flamboyant **church** with its gable tower stands just before the village. The fine basket-handled doorway is surmounted by the arms of France and a recess containing a statue of St Riquier.

Turn right onto D 901, crossing the Paris-Calais railway line.

Château de Pont-Remy – This château was built on an island near Pont-Remy in the 15C but was rebuilt in 1837 in the "Gothic Troubadour" style.

Return to D 3.

The road runs along the bottom of the hillside, skirting ponds and meadows, and approaches the Monts de Caubert.

Turn right to Abbeville.

Abbeville – *See ABBEVILLE.*

La THIÉRACHE★

Michelin map 53 folds 15, 16 or 236 folds 28, 29, 39

The Thiérache region forms a green patch in the bare, chalky plains of Picardy and Champagne. The high altitude (250m/820ft in the east) provides greater rainfall which, combined with the terrain's lack of porousness, creates a well-watered area, devoted to forestry and especially grazing. The main lines of communication follow the deep valleys of the River Oise and River Serre and their tributaries. The area between Guise and Hirson is ideal country for hikers and the whole region is the paradise of history buffs.

The woodland is interspersed with meadows, cider-apple orchards and a scattering of farms. For eight months of the year black and white Friesian cows graze in the pastures. Their milk is dispatched throughout the region and to Paris; some of it is used to make butter, milk powder or the French Maroilles and Edam cheeses; the whey is kept for the pigs. Basket-making is a speciality around **Origny**, which is not surprising, in light of the many graceful basket willows growing there.

★FORTIFIED CHURCHES

Until the reign of Louis XIV the Thiérache region was a frontier and so repeatedly invaded – by 14C mercenaries led by Du Guesclin, by German foot soldiers – particularly during the Hundred Years War, the Wars of Religion and the conflicts between France and Spain under Louis XIII and Louis XIV. From the late 16C and during the 17C, local inhabitants, lacking fortresses and ramparts, fortified their churches. This accounts for the watch-turrets, round towers and square keeps pierced with arrow slits found on most of the 12C and 13C buildings, resulting in an uncomfortable architectural mix of brick and stone. Other fortress-churches, such as that at Plomion, date entirely from the turn of the 17C.

1 Round Trip starting from Vervins
65km/40mi – about 3hr

Natives of Vervins

Marc Lescarbot (1570-1634), a lawyer, writer and traveller, was one of the founders of Port-Royal in Acadia. He wrote the first *History of Nouvelle-France* (1609), now a classic of Canadian literature.

In the 16C, **Nicole Obry**, known as "the devil of Vervins", lured all the exorcists to the region. Charles IX insisted on meeting her and the Pope himself inquired after her.

Vervins – The charm of the town, which is the region's capital, lies in its ramparts, its cobbled and winding streets and its squares bordered by houses with steeply pitched slate roofs and brick chimneys. The **church** features a 13C chancel, 16C nave and imposing brick tower (34m/111ft tall) with stone string courses (note the double buttresses on the corners). Inside, 16C mural paintings adorn the piers and a huge, brightly coloured composition by Jouvenet (1699) portrays *Supper in the House of Simon*; 18C organ case and pulpit.

Leave Vervins by D 372 (south-east); at Harcigny take D 37 east.

Plomion – The 16C church features a fine west front flanked by two towers; note the square keep with its great hall leading up to the garret.

A large covered market in front of the church testifies to Plomion's commercial activities.

Take D 747 east towards Bancigny and Jeantes.

Jeantes – The façade of the **church** is flanked by two towers. Expressionist frescoes on the walls of the interior, representing scenes from the Life of Christ, are the work of painter Charles Van Eyck (1962). Note the 12C font.

Dagny – This old village has preserved its cob houses and half-timbered houses with brick courses.

Morgny-en-Thiérache – The chancel and nave of the church date from the 13C. Fortification mainly affected the chancel, which was raised by a storey to create an extra room for those seeking a safe refuge.

Dohis – There are many half-timbered and cob houses here. The church (12C nave) is particularly interesting because of its porch-keep, added in the 17C.

Turn around from the church and take the first road on the left (south); fork left to Parfondeval.

Parfondeval – This lovely village stands perched on a hill, its warm-toned brick houses clustering around a broad green. The 16C **church** rises at the end of the square, an indisputable fortress behind a fortification of neighbouring houses. The white stone portal is in the Renaissance style. On the walls, glazed bricks form a crisscross design.

Back at the entrance to the village take D 520 (west) to Archon.

The road offers a good view over Archon and the undulating countryside dotted with copses.

Archon – Cob-walled and brick houses encircle the church, which is guarded by two great towers; a footbridge between the towers also served as a look-out point. Follow D 110 west through **Renneval** (stone church with fortified chancel) to Vigneux.

At Vigneux take D 966 north-west to Hary.

Hary – A 16C brick keep rises above the chancel and nave of this 12C, white stone, Romanesque church.

D 61 follows the Brune Valley.

Église de Burelles – The 16C and 17C village **church** has a number of defences: arrow slits; a reinforced keep with watch-turrets; barbicans and watch-turrets above the months transept; the chancel flanked by a turret. The upper floor of the transept has been turned into a vast fortified room.

Église de Prisces – *Restoration work in progress.* The 12C chancel and nave of the **church** ⓥ were given an enormous, square brick keep (25m/82ft tall) with two turrets on diagonally opposing corners. The four floors inside allowed about 100 soldiers to take shelter with their arms and provisions.

Cross the River Brune and follow D 613 to Gronard.

Gronard – The façade of the church is almost hidden behind lime trees. The keep is flanked by two round towers.

Return to Vervins along D 613 and D 966.

The route offers a picturesque view of Vervins and its surrounding area.

② From Vervins to Guise

51km/32mi - about 2hr

This tour largely follows the Oise Valley which also features many fortified churches.

Vervins – *See above.*

From Vervins take D 963 to La Bouteille.

La Bouteille – The church has thick walls (over 1m/3ft) and is flanked by four turrets. It was built by Cistercians from the nearby **Abbaye de Foigny**, now in ruins.

D 751 and D 382 lead to Foigny. Cross D 38 and take the little road which runs beside the abbey ruins, to Wimy.

Wimy – The enormous keep of the fortified church is flanked by two large, cylindrical towers. Two fireplaces, a well and a bread oven were added inside. The first floor has a vast room for those seeking refuge.

D 31 crosses Etréaupont and continues through **Autreppes**, a village of brick buildings. The road runs in front of the fortified church and continues past the village of **St Algis** which is overlooked by its church keep.

Marly – The 13C and 14C sandstone church has a beautiful, pointed arch portal to which two great watch-turrets were added. The large arrow slits near the base allowed crossbows to be used.

Take D 774 north to Englancourt.

HOME STAY

Chambre d'Hôte Mme Piette – *7 place des Marronniers, 02120 Chigny – 15km/9.3mi east of Guise by N 29 then D 26 –* ☎ *03 23 60 22 04 – ✉ – 5 rooms 190/ 270F – meal 90F.* Nothing beats old-fashioned charm, as you soon realise when you step inside Madame Piette's quaint abode where time seems to stand still. Your kind, considerate hostess will make sure that your stay here is a pleasant one. Three of the rooms do not have a private bathroom.

Englancourt – The fortified **church**, in a pretty location overlooking the River Oise, has a west front flanked by watch-turrets, a square keep in brick and a chancel with a flat east end reinforced by two round towers.

Return to D 31 via D 26.

Beaurain – The **church** stands isolated on a hill which rises from lush surroundings. The beautiful fortress dates entirely from the same period. The great square keep is flanked by towers, as is the chancel. A Romanesque font stands by the entrance.

Follow D 960 to Guise.

Guise – *See GUISE.*

THOIRY★★

Population 835
Michelin map 106 folds 15, 16 or 237 fold 16

Access from Paris: *By car, take A 13 then A 12 to St-Quentin-en-Yvelines. Leave the motorway at the Bois d'Arcy exit towards Dreux and follow N 12 to Pontchartrain, then turn onto D 11 to Thoiry.*

Thoiry is a vast estate comprising a large Renaissance château and 250ha/625 acres of gardens and park. The family who has owned it for the past 400 years or more has undertaken a considerable amount of work to turn it into a magical spot where history and nature merge.

Château ⊘ – Raoul Moreau, Treasurer to Henri II, was passionately interested in alchemy and esoterics. It was he who had this "solar house" built on a magnetic fault, to designs using the Golden Section. This outstanding position on a hilltop enables the château to act as a solar instrument, with spectacular sights such as the sunrise or sunset in line with the façade at the solstices.

The house is also a "time machine" which has come down to us through the centuries and now gives an insight into an eventful history. The ancestors conversing from their picture frames in the portrait gallery (no, you are not dreaming!) and the spicy tales uncovered in the 50 trunks full of family archives are all rather unconventional means of taking a look at history.

Zoological and botanical park ⊘ – The area of park adjacent to the château has been laid out as a zoo, with numerous special events. The most impressive section is the tiger enclosure which visitors cross on a concrete footbridge among the

Eating out

MID-RANGE

La Licorne – *Place du 8-Mai-1945, 78770 Beynes – 6km/3.7mi east of Thoiry by D 119 – ☎ 01 34 89 96 17 – closed 12 Aug-3 Sept, Sun evening and Mon – booking essential Sat-Sun – 118/160F.* A good address barely a few miles from the African park. The rustic setting and fresh, inventive cuisine will win you over. Good service and warm welcome.

Where to stay

LUXURY

Château de Villiers le Mahieu – *78770 Villiers-le-Mahieu – 2km/1mi south-west of Thoiry by D 45 – ☎ 01 34 87 44 25 – closed 24 Dec-31 Jan – ▯ – 36 rooms from 610F – ⌂ 78F.* You will succumb to the charm of the rooms in this former 13C stronghold surrounded by turrets and a moat, nestling in an 11ha/27-acre park. Once home to the painter Bernard Buffet, the castle currently hosts seminars and banquets. Treat yourself to a royal weekend in a truly historic setting!

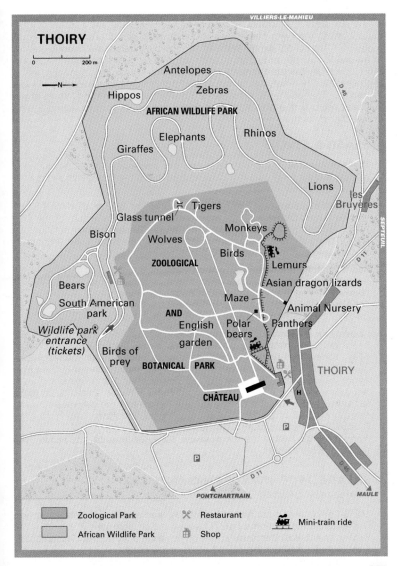

trees. It is also possible to see the animals from the glass tunnel in which only the armoured glass separates visitors from the claws and teeth of these wild beasts. Various trails pass the elegant but fearsome black panthers, the emus and cassowaries, the mandrill island, and a tribe of lemurs running free. There are demonstrations of birds of prey in flight. The trees, too, speak to visitors about the natural environment. Do not miss the impressive Asian dragons (5m/16ft long) and become familiar with the ecosystem of European rivers (otters).

The park is also appreciated for its varied vegetation: an audio-guided trail makes it easy to discover its diversity.

African wildlife park ⊘ – The park is visited by car (all windows closed) since the animals roam free. For your own safety, please comply with the rules.

The park is so vast that many different species of African wildlife can live together quite happily. The road covers a distance of 10km/6mi and visitors can see antelopes with strangely shaped horns, bison, giraffes, zebras, elephants, rhinos, and hippos. A drive through two high-security enclosures provides a close-up view of lions and bears.

Le TOUQUET-PARIS-PLAGE ♨♨♨

Population 5 596
Michelin map 51 fold 11 or 236 fold 11

Le Touquet lies between the sea and the forest, its parallel streets intersected by access roads to the beach. Villas and establishments with a certain old-world charm nestle among pine trees in a picturesque clash of architectural styles and a splash of bright colours: white walls with blue edging, red tiles, lawns and flower beds impeccably hedged in... The holiday spirit is in the air all-year-round in this vast "seaside garden". At the end of the 19C, an English business man saw the tourist potential of the place and founded the Touquet Syndicate Ltd and the first seaside residences appeared as early as 1882. The resort was almost immediately adopted by the English and took the name Le Touquet Paris-Plage in 1912. Since then it has developed into an all-year European resort with a substantial hotel trade, year-round sporting activities and a thalassotherapy centre.

SEASIDE STROLL

Digue-promenade – Along the seafront, the **promenade** is edged by numerous gardens and car parks. The south end leads to the sand-yachting club and the thalassotherapy centre.

The beach and port – The gently sloping beach of fine, hard sand, which is uncovered for 1km/0.5mi at low tide and stretches as far as the mouth of the River Authie (12km/7.5mi), attracts many sand yachts. The **coast road** which follows the line of the dunes leads to the marina and the water sports club, well sheltered by the headland known as Pointe du Touquet.

Sports and leisure activities – Near the attractive shopping galleries of the Hermitage district are the **Sports Centre**, the select **Casino du Palais** and the **Palais de l'Europe** where conferences and cultural exchanges take place.

The **Museum** ⊘ displays works by the Étaples School (1880-1914). It also includes paintings by Le Sidaner and a section devoted to modern art.

"Jardins de la Manche" – The forest (800ha/1 900 acres) was planted in 1855; its maritime pine, birch, alder, poplar and acacia trees protect about 2 000 luxury villas - either Anglo-Norman in style or resolutely modern - from the wind. Some 45km/28mi of bridlepaths and 50km/31mi of forest tracks reserved for hikers run across the woods and the residential districts with their neat gardens.

Four walks start from place de l'Hermitage: **La Pomme de Pin** for "amateurs", **Le Daphné** for serious hikers, **La Feuille de chêne** for keen "explorers" and **L'Argousier** for really "experienced" hikers (leaflets available from the tourist office).

Three golf courses extend south of the forest.

Along the River Canche are the **racecourse**, the **equestrian centre**, the **shooting range** (archery) and the **airport**.

BALADE 1900 (TURN-OF-THE-CENTURY WALK)

From place de l'Hermitage, take avenue du Verger.

This is Le Touquet's most fashionable avenue, lined on the right with flower beds and white-painted boutiques (1927) recalling the art deco style.

Further on the **Hôtel Westminster** is one of the resort's most prestigious establishments with its red-brick façade and protruding windows.

LE TOUQUET-PARIS-PLAGE

Aboudaram (Av. L.)	**BZ** 2	Genets (Av. des)	**ABZ** 27	Pins (Av. des)	**BZ** 40
Atlantique (Av. de l')	**ABZ** 4	Grande Rue	**AZ** 28	Pouget (Bd J.)	**AYZ** 41
Bardol (R. E.)	**BY** 6	Hubert (Av. L.)	**ABY** 29	Recoussine (Av. F.)	**BZ** 42
Bourdonnais		Londres (R. de)	**AYZ** 31	Reine May (Av. de la)	**ABZ** 43
(Av. de la)	**ABY** 10	Metz (R. de)	**AYZ** 33	St-Amand (R.)	**AZ** 45
Bruxelles (R. de)	**AYZ** 12	Monnet (R. J.)	**AYZ** 35	St-Jean (R.)	**ABZ** 46
Calais (R. de)	**BY** 15	Moscou (R. de)	**AYZ** 35	St-Louis (R.)	**AZ** 47
Desvres (R. de)	**AZ** 18	Oyats		Tourville (Av. de l'Amiral)	**ABY** 50
Dorothée (R.)	**AZ** 21	(Av. et R. des)	**ABZ** 37	Troènes (Av. des)	**BZ** 52
Duboc (Av. et R. J.)	**ABY** 23	Paix (Av. et R. de la)	**ABZ** 38	Verger (Av. du)	**BZ** 54
Garet (Av. et R. L.)	**ABY** 26	Paris (R. de)	**AYZ** 39	Whitley (Av. J.)	**BZ** 56

Aqualud	**AY**	Digue promenade	**AYZ**	Marché couvert	**AZ K**
Base nautique	**BY**	Église Ste-Jeanne-d'Arc	**AZ**	Musée	**BZ M**
Base nautique		Hôtel de ville	**AZ H**	Palais de l'Europe	**BZ**
de char à voile	**AZ**	Hôtel Westminster	**BZ**	Phare	**BY**
Casino du Palais	**BZ**	Institut		Plage	**AY**
Centre sportif	**BZ**	de Thalassothérapie	**AZ**	Village Suisse	**BZ**

Bear left and walk along rue St-Jean.

The **Village Suisse** (1905) on the left is in mock medieval style with turrets and crenels. The shopping arcades have terraces upstairs.

Return to the hotel and follow avenue des Phares.

Situated on the right, behind the hotel, the red-brick **lighthouse** was rebuilt by Quételart in 1949. Its hexagonal column, resembling a Doric column, is crowned with two white balconies.

Cross avenue des Phares and follow rue J.-Duboc leading to boulevard Daloz.

Villa Cendrillon (1923) on the corner of the boulevard boasts a lovely loggia and an unusual overlapping roof. At no 44 along the same boulevard, **Villa La Wallonne** stands at the beginning of the lively shopping centre. Note the façade of **Villa des Mutins** (1925) at no 78 with its two gables overlooking rue de Lens; it was the home of Louis Quételart. **Villa Le Roy d'Ys** at no 45 looks like a traditional house from Normandy with its timber-framed stone walls.

Eating out

MODERATE

Pérard – *67 rue de Metz* – ☎ *03 21 05 13 33* – *closed Jan* – ✉ – *98/145F*. The restaurant prides itself on making the best bouillabaisse in the area... The other dishes are prepared with freshly caught produce sold in the adjoining shop... which also belongs to the owner! 1970s decor.

Le Nemo – *Boulevard de la Mer, Aqualud* – ☎ *03 21 06 20 66* – *www.aqualud. com* – *closed Jan* – *100/150F*. This restaurant will plunge you into the aquatic world imagined by Jules Verne in his novel *Twenty Thousand Leagues Under the Sea*! It's all there, from deep-sea diving suits to mariner's charts... arranged in a wood and brass setting. If you want a sweeping view and a breath of fresh air, choose the terrace giving onto the beach. The menu, predictably, is mainly devoted to fish and seafood.

MID-RANGE

Flavio – *Avenue du Verger* – ☎ *03 21 05 10 22* – *closed 10 Jan-10 Feb and Mon (except during July-Aug and public holidays)* – *195/720F*. This restaurant close to the Westminster Hotel has become an institution. Despite its somewhat unremarkable exterior, it has succeeded in creating a warm, cosy atmosphere in the dining room, where local gourmets come to appreciate the chef's speciality – lobster – at deservedly high prices.

Where to stay

MODERATE

Hôtel de la Forêt – *73 rue Moscou* – ☎ *03 21 05 09 88* – *closed over Christmas* – *10 rooms 250/280F* – ⌥ *31F*. Small family business in the town centre, a stone's throw from the beach. The smallish rooms, well-kept and soundproofed, are gradually being renovated.

LUXURY

Manoir Hôtel – *At the golf course* – *2.5km/1.6mi south of Le Touquet* – ☎ *03 21 06 28 28* – *closed Jan* – 🅿 – *42 rooms from 635F* – *restaurant 150F*. Charming manor house overgrown with ivy lying on the edge of a golf course. Enjoy the peace and quiet of the handsome rooms and the cosy ambience reigning in the bar and drawing room. A popular destination among golfers. A few less luxurious rooms are housed in the annex.

Hôtel Westminster – *Avenue du Verger* – ☎ *03 21 05 48 48* – *closed Feb* – 🅿 *-115 rooms from 650F* – ⌥ *95F* – *2 restaurants*. The splendid façade and the lavish interior decoration suggestive of a bygone era reminds one of the days when Parisian families would come to northern France to go bathing... Guests can choose between two restaurants the Coffee-Shop for light snacks and the Pavillon for dinner.

On the town

Le Perroquet Bleu – *60 rue de Metz* – ☎ *03 21 05 69 79* – *Sun-Thur 5pm-4am, Fri-Sat 5pm-5am* – *closed Jan and Mon in low season*. Cane chairs out on the terrace, a padded bar at the entrance, wall seats and pouffes in the larger room, and glass tables in a small colourful chamber beneath a glass dome... whatever your tastes, this karaoke bar is bound to suit you!

Le Philae Café – *28 rue St-Jean* – ☎ *03 21 05 98 63* – *daily 11am-3am (eve of public holidays until 4am)*. The decoration of this luxurious establishment faithfully reproduces the Egyptian frescoes and colourful columns adorning the Temple of Philae. The coffee tables are engraved with hieroglyphs and some walls are ornamented with low-relief sculptures. Every Friday, there are karaoke concerts relayed onto a huge screen and you can sip exotic cocktails to the strains of rock 'n roll or jazz. The café livens up around 10pm. While you are waiting, why not try to spot a mistake in the hieroglyphs?

Sport

Aéroport du Touquet – ☎ *03 21 05 03 99* – *hélicobage@wanadoo.fr* – *airport open daily 9am-8pm*. Enjoy your very first flight in a plane or a helicopter.

Centre de Char à Voile – *Base Nautique Sud* – ☎ *03 21 05 33 51* – *charavoile@letouquet.com* – *reception area open daily 10am-noon, 2-5pm*. This beach extending for over 15km/9.3mi is the ideal place for practising sand-yachting. Moreover, you will be given invaluable advice by Bertrand Lambert, the record-holder for speed (151.55kph/94.12mph!) and already four times world champion.

Centre Équestre Régional du Touquet – *Avenue de la Dune-aux-Loups –* ☎ *03 21 05 15 25 – reception area open daily 9am-noon, 2-6pm*. This equestrian centre spread out over 50ha/125 acres of woodland is devoted to the raising of 150 horses, most of whom have been entrusted by their owners. However, the 40 horses and ponies belonging to the club are at your disposal for long or short rides, depending on your ability and experience.

Theme parks, zoos

Aqualud – *Boulevard de la Mer –* ☎ *03 21 05 90 96 – www.aqualud.com – daily 10am-6pm (July-Aug Sun-Thur 10am-7pm, Fri-Sat 10am-midnight) – closed Nov-Jan*. Aquatic theme park with a capacity of 9 600sq yd (plus 4 800sq yd in summer). Both the water and air in the covered section enjoy a temperature of 27°C all year round.. The attractions include giant toboggans, surprise rivers, pools with waves, jacuzzi, Black Hole and Twister… but parents need not fear for their children's safety as there are almost as many lifeguards…

The **Église Ste-Jeanne-d'Arc**, built in 1912 and restored in 1955, features decorative stained glass and ironwork. Nearby, the **Hôtel de Ville** was built from local stone in 1931 in Anglo-Norman style with cimented timber-framing; it is flanked by a belfry (38m/125ft tall).

Follow rue Jean-Monnet towards the beach.

Villa Le Castel (1904) at no 50 combines the neo-Gothic and Art Nouveau styles. Rue Jean-Monnet continues through the arch of the **covered market** (1927-32), a half-moon-shaped ensemble, and leads to boulevard Pouget on the seafront lined with other holiday houses.

Rejoin avenue du Verger which leads back to place de l'Hermitage.

EXCURSIONS

Stella-Plage – *8km/5mi. Leave Le Touquet along avenue F.-Godin and after 5km/3mi, turn right onto D 144.*
Behind the dunes which extend along the beach are villas dotted across the woods forming a continuation of the woods in Le Touquet.

St-Josse – *10km/6mi south-east on N 39, D 143 and D 144* (views of Étaples). St-Josse, which stands on a hill, was once the home of an abbey founded by Charlemagne in memory of St Josse, a 7C pilgrim and hermit whose reliquary is venerated in the church's early-16C chancel.
About 500m/550yd east, in the middle of a wooded close, stand St Josse's Chapel, which is a place of pilgrimage, and St Josse's fountain.

VALENCIENNES

Conurbation 33 6481
Michelin map 51 fold 17 or 236 folds 17, 18

This busy commercial town, located on the River Escaut (Scheldt), is surrounded by boulevards which replaced the former ramparts. Only the 15C Tour de la Dedenne has survived. The architectural variety in Valenciennes is a result of the damage inflicted on the town during the two World Wars; the bombings of 1940 and 1944 completely destroyed the old, wood-built centre.

Valenciennes was once the capital of the steel industry and metallurgy in the north, while the coal basin nearby was fully active. Today these industries have decreased markedly but have been replaced by others: rolling stock, car manufacturing, paints, pharmaceutical laboratories, mechanical engineering, electronics etc. Toyota has recently established a car manufacturing plant in Onnaing, near Valenciennes.

The presence of a science faculty has contributed to the development of the town which is today an important cultural centre with fine collections of paintings by Watteau and sculpture by Carpeaux.

Among the culinary specialities of Valenciennes is *langue Lucullus*, smoked ox tongue cut into slices and covered in foie gras

Athens of the North – Valenciennes earned this nickname because of the town's long-standing interest in the arts and the many artists who were born here.

VALENCIENNES

Native sculptors include André Beauneveu (14C) – the "image-maker" of Charles V – who was also a painter; Antoine Pater (1670-1747); Saly (1717-76) who went to work for the court of Denmark and in particular **Carpeaux** (1827-75), who brought new life to French sculpture.

Famous local painters are also numerous: in the 18C, the great **Antoine Watteau** (1684-1721) and Jean-Baptiste Pater (1695-1736) who both specialised in genre painting in the *fête galante* style, Louis and François Watteau, grand-nephew and great-nephew of Antoine, and in the 19C, the landscape painter Henri Harpignies (1819-1916).

In the 18C the citizens of Valenciennes, wishing to encourage the arts, founded an Academy, a Salon and a School of Fine Art. The granting of scholarships was also established with the same aim.

Jean-Baptiste Carpeaux

Jean-Baptiste Carpeaux (Valenciennes 1827-Courbevoie 1875) was a sculptor, painter and draughtsman. He won the Grand Prix de Rome in 1854.

Having become an official sculptor, he produced a large number of elegant busts of celebrities during the Second Empire and was also involved in the decoration of public buildings:

– *Triumph of Flora*, a low relief for the pediment of the Louvre's Flora pavilion in Paris;
– *Dance*, a group sculpture for the front of the Paris Opera House, now in the Musée d'Orsay;
– *The Four Quarters of the Globe*, for the fountain at the Observatoire in Paris;
– A statue of Watteau in Valenciennes.

A commemorative statue by Félix Desruelles was erected in memory of the great man in avenue du Sénateur-Girard in Valenciennes.

Other works, plaster casts or earthenware models can be seen in the Musée d'Orsay and the Musée du Petit Palais in Paris, the Musée Roybet-Fould in Courbevoie and the Musée des Beaux-Arts in Valenciennes.

SIGHTS

Maison espagnole – This 16C half-timbered, corbelled house was built during the Spanish occupation. It has been restored and is today the home of the tourist office.

Église St-Géry ⊘ – This old Recollect church was built in the 13C and altered in the 19C. Restoration has reinstated the original Gothic purity to the nave and chancel.

The fountain in nearby **square Watteau** is overlooked by a statue by Carpeaux of Antoine Watteau, who was born at 39 rue de Paris.

The **Église St-Nicolas**, once the Jesuit chapel, has a delightful 18C west front. It is no longer consecrated and has been turned into the Auditorium St-Nicolas. The **Maison du Prévôt Notre-Dame**, at the corner of rue Notre-Dame, is one of the oldest buildings (15C) in the town, constructed in brick and stone. The mullioned windows, crow-stepped gable, and turret with bell-cote give it a certain elegance.

★**Musée des Beaux-Arts** ⊘ – This vast museum, which was built at the beginning of the century, has a particularly large collection of works from the 15C-17C Flemish School (Rubens), 18C French works and 19C sculptures (Carpeaux). It has been renovated throughout and now has a bookshop and gift shop, café, lecture hall etc.

15C-17C Flemish School – The first room contains a double panel by Hieronymus Bosch, *St James and Hermogenes the Magician*, next to Van Leyden's triptych of *The Last Judgement* and Marinus Van Reymerswaele's *Tax Collector*.

The next three rooms cover the 17C with major works from the Dutch, French, Italian and, more particularly, Flemish schools.

In the Rubens room, works by the great artist from Antwerp include the triptych depicting the *Martyrdom of St Stephen* that used to hang in the abbey in St-Amand, and two large paintings entitled *Elija and the Angel* and *The Triumph of the Eucharist*. The vast gallery deals with Flemish religious painting from Mannerism until the Baroque period. It contains *The Adoration of the Magi* (16C triptych by Coecke van Aelst), the *Holy Family* by Martin de Vos, *The Calvary* by Janssens, *Christ's Lamentation* by Pieter van Mol, *St Augustin's Ecstasy* by Crayer, and *St Paul* and *St Matthew*, two heads by Van Dyck. The other two rooms show changes in genres such as portraits (*Elisabeth of France* by Pourbus), still-life painting (Snyders' *Store*

Eating out

MID-RANGE

Les Forges – *58 rue Émile-Drue, 59770 Marly – 2km/1mi east of Valenciennes by avenue de Verdun (D 934) – ☎ 03 27 41 31 22 – closed 1-15 Aug, Sun evening and Mon – 108/190F.* This family business, in a brick and beam setting, extends a warm welcome to its guests. The owner and the chef serve an inventive cuisine made with fresh produce.

Where to stay

MID-RANGE

Hôtel Notre Dame – *1 place Abbé-Thellier-de-Poncheville – ☎ 03 27 42 30 00 – 35 rooms 300/400F – ☙ 40F.* In a quiet district of town, this hotel features functional rooms located in the two wings of the building, connected by the reception hall. Most of them give onto a small garden.

Cupboard, Beuckelaer's *Vegetable Carrier*), genre painting (*The Young Chatter like the Old Sing* by Jordaens), and landscapes (Soens and Rubens).

18C French School – The French School is divided between two rooms. The first one contains two works by Watteau, a portrait of the sculptor Antoine Pater and a work painted in his youth. Note, too, the *Portrait of Jean de Jullienne*, a friend and patron of the artist by François de Troy; the *Rustic Concert* and the *Joys of Country Life* by JB Pater who worked with Watteau. The second room displays a set of works by Louis and François Watteau, the latter being better known as Watteau of Lille (*The Four Hours of the Day* - a series of four paintings).

Carpeaux – In the centre of the museum, in a vast hall filled with light, is a set of sculptures that reveal the changes in Carpeaux' artistry. There are huge works, numerous busts and sketches of women and children showing the artist's fascinating ability to suggest movement and life. A few paintings illustrate the artist's social life and his skills as a portraitist (series of self-portraits) or as a visionary artist. Next to his works are others by contemporary artists such as Crauk and Desruelles.

19C-20C French School – The huge size of the canvases show the popularity of historical paintings at this time. They include *The Death of Maréchal Lannes* by Guérin, *The Youth of Peter the Great* by Steuben, *The Execution of Mary Queen of Scots* by Abel de Pujol, or *The Sword of Damocles* by Félix Auvray. Landscapes are well represented with Charlet, Boudin, Rousseau, Lépine, Zicau and Harpignies.

The small 20C section illustrates the search for line and colour by artists such as Herbin or Félix Delmarle.

Archeological crypt – From the centre of the museum, steps lead down to the regional archeological collections. There are murals from Famars, bronzes and a silver platter from the Gallo-Roman period, cloisonné enamel jewellery, funerary paintings (Abbaye de Beaumont) and medieval tombs (Jean d'Avesnes, 14C).

Bibliothèque municipale – The library is housed in the buildings of the old **Jesuit school**. It was founded in the early 17C. The pleasing brick and stone façade has Louis XVI garlands and bull's-eye windows on the ground floor. On the first floor is the **Bibliothèque des Jésuites** ☺ with painted decoration

Detail of a statue by Carpeaux

H. Gyssels/DIAF

361

dating from the 18C. This library contains 350 000 works. They include the manuscript of St Eulalie's famous *Cantilene*, the oldest known poem in French written in the language of northern France c 880 AD, very old books (incunabula), rare or valuable printed books dating from the 17C to 20C etc.

EXCURSIONS

St-Saulve – *2km/1.25mi north-east. Leave Valenciennes by avenue de Liège, N 30.*
Chapelle du Carmel – *1 rue Barbusse.* This Carmelite chapel, which was completed in 1966, was inspired by a model created by the sculptor Szekely and then built to plans prepared by the architect Guislain who favoured effects of mass and the use of simple materials. The chapel stands back from the road and is flanked by an asymmetrical bell-tower. The interior is bathed in a gentle light which filters in above the altar through stained-glass windows featuring geometric designs.

Sebourg – *9km/5.5mi east. Leave Valenciennes by D 934 towards Maubeuge, turn left at Saultain on D 59; beyond Estreux turn right onto D 350.*
This little market town attracts people from Valenciennes owing to its rural aspect and stretches over the verdant slopes of the Aunelle Valley.
The 12C-16C **church** ⊘ is the destination for pilgrimages to St Druon; the 12C shepherd-hermit is invoked to cure hernias. In the south aisle lie 14C recumbent effigies of Henri of Hainault, Lord of Sebourg, and his wife.

Bruay-sur-l'Escaut – *5km/3mi north by D 935.*
The **church** ⊘ contains the **cenotaph** of St Pharaïlde, the sister of St Gudule; the 13C block of white stone depicts a graceful woman's form.

Denain – *10km/6mi south-west by N 30.*
Denain is famous for Maréchal de Villars' defeat of the army led by Prince Eugène on 24 July 1712.
After the discovery of coal in 1828, this rural village became a major industrial centre. The town had up to 15 mine shafts at one time (the last one, the Puits du Renard, was closed in 1948 but its slag heap still dominates the town). It was in this town and in the countryside nearby that Zola came to seek inspiration for his work *Germinal*. Traces of the town's heyday are still visible. One large building (1852) remains of the mining community in avenue Villars; it is now the Academy of Music. It was here that the poet-miner Jules Mousseron (1868-1943) lived.
The **Cité Ernestine** *(park your car and take the alleyway between 138 and 140 rue Ludovic-Trarieux)* has retained its working-class atmosphere. It consists of 20 or more semi-detached miners' houses (known locally as *corons*). The **Cité Bellevue** to the north consists of a fine group of foremen's houses, some of them built to each side of the bread oven.

Abbaye et jardins de VALLOIRES★

Michelin map 51 fold 12 or 236 fold 12

The old Cistercian abbey is located on a remote site in the Authie Valley, surrounded by woods and orchards; it is a rare and beautiful example of 18C architecture. The Jardin des "Îles" forms an ocean of greenery dotted with colourful islands and the rose garden offers thousands of sweet-smelling roses.

War and peace – The abbey was founded in the 12C by a count of Ponthieu and became a burial place for his family. In 1346 the bodies of knights killed at Crécy were transported here.
In the 17C the abbey was ravaged by several fires, but the monks were wealthy and in 1730 the abbot ordered that huge amounts of wood be cut in order to begin rebuilding. Reconstruction, following plans by Coignard, took place from 1741 to 1756. The decoration is the work of Baron **Pfaff de Pfaffenhoffen** (1715-84) from Vienna who was forced to leave his city after a duel; he settled in St-Riquier in 1750.
From 1817 to 1880 the **Basiliens**, members of a lay congregation founded in Mons in 1800, lived in Valloires. All members of the community exercised their profession, scrupulously fulfilled their religious duties and wore an all-blue outfit: a cotton cap, loose shirt and leggings. The monastery is today a child-care centre.

ABBEY ⊘

A 16C dovecote stands in front of the long building which is extended to the left and rear by the east front of the **abbey lodgings**; these in turn are surrounded by smaller buildings. The chapter-house is no longer near the church as in the Middle Ages, but is in the main building itself; Pfaffenhoffen's elegant decoration has given it the look of a drawing room.

The simple cloister gallery has groined vaulting. The refectory is located on the ground floor of the east wing; the abbot's rooms and the monk's cells are upstairs. The vestry is decorated with wood panels by Pfaffenhoffen and paintings by Parrocel.

★**Church** – "It would delight Mme De Pompadour yet St Bernard would see nothing to take exception to." This comment by an English traveller illustrates the balance between the building's architectural restraint and the elegant ornamentation of its decor.

Inside, the **organ** (**1**) is supported by a gallery carved by Pfaffenhoffen with musical instruments; the statues at each side symbolise religion. The balustrade and small organ case are decorated with *putti* and cherub musicians. Caryatids support the great organ case, which is crowned by a statue of King David accompanied by angel musicians.

The beautiful **grilles★** (**2**) are of a graceful and light design: the central part is surmounted by the Valloires arms and Moses' brazen serpent (prefiguration of the Crucifixion), framed by baskets of flowers. The creator of the grilles, Jean Veyren, was also responsible for those in the cathedral in Amiens.

Two adoring angels in gilded lead by Pfaffenhoffen are located around the high altar (**3**), dominated by a curious and rare eucharistic monstrance in the form of an abbot's crook, another masterpiece of ironwork by Jean Veyren. Two white papier mâché angels seem to be flying over the altar.

Carved religious emblems adorn the stalls (**4**); those reserved for the abbot and the prior stand on either side of the entrance to the apsidal chapel, which is decorated with wood panels by Pfaff.

The south transept houses recumbent effigies of a count and countess of Ponthieu (**5**). In the north transept is the window through which sick monks could follow services.

GARDENS⊘

This 7ha/17 acre park, landscaped in 1987 by Gilles Clément, contains 4 000 species of plants and trees. Part of it is laid out in the formal French style with a magnificent rose-garden containing 100 varieties, including the Valloires rose created in 1992 and the Delarle Cistercians' rose created in 1998 for the 900th anniversary of the Cistercian order. The roses grow among aromatic plants and medicinal herbs, such as would have been found in the monks' garden.

The English-style park is laid out on high ground and includes an Island Garden whose colours change with the seasons.

The Garden of the Five Senses contains a selection of plants and trees connected with the different senses: strawberries and apples (taste), thorny plants (touch), aspens with leaves that rustle with the slightest breeze (hearing), colourful petunias (sight), jasmine, lily and mint (smell).

Lower down lies the wilder Marsh Garden with its artificial canal reminiscent of the arm of the River Authie which used to flow across the estate.

Eating out

MODERATE

Le Moulin de Maintenay – *62870 Maintenay – 3km/2mi from Valloires Abbey by D 192* – ☎ *03 21 90 43 74 – closed 1 Jan-15 Feb – booking essential – 60/100F.* Treat yourself to a magic moment on the banks of the Authie! This tastefully restored 12C mill, where culture goes hand in hand with a hearty appetite, will amuse visitors of all ages and the pancakes and "miller's slices" prepared on the premises will delight the appetite...

Where to stay

MID-RANGE

Chambre d'Hôte de l'Association de Valloires – *In Valloires Abbey –* ☎ *03 22 29 62 33 – 6 rooms 370/460F – meal 90F.* These bed and breakfast rooms enjoy a privileged location above the cloisters, in this truly majestic setting of a former abbey. Large and comfortable, they all look onto the splendid grounds.

EXCURSION

Buire-le-Sec – *4km/2.5mi north. Cross the bridge; in Maintenay, take D 139.*

★**Musée des Marionnettes du monde** ⊘ – This journey through the world's various cultures enables you to discover Guignol from Lyon and Jacques from Lille as well as Asian, Indian, Greek, Czech and African puppets, not forgetting Cabotans from Picardy or Lafleur and Sandrine from Amiens.

🔾 Don't miss the splendid **puppet theatre from Java**, dating from the 1920s, which includes 80 charming characters.

Château de VAUX-LE-VICOMTE★★★

Michelin map 106 folds 45, 46 or 237 fold 31 – 6km/4mi north-east of Melun

This château, built by Fouquet, foreshadowed the splendour of Versailles and remains one of the greatest masterpieces of the 17C. A walk through the gardens laid out by Le Nôtre offers an unforgettable experience.

The rise of Nicolas Fouquet – Born to a family of magistrates, Fouquet became a member of the Parlement de Paris by the age of 20. He was made Procureur Général of this respectable assembly and was appointed Superintendent of Finances under Mazarin. Owing to the customs of the time and the example of Cardinal Mazarin, he acquired the dangerous habit of confusing the finances of the State with his own. He was forever surrounded by a large retinue of senior personalities whose services cost vast sums of money. Intoxicated with success Fouquet chose a squirrel as his emblem - in Anjou patois *fouquet* means a squirrel - and decreed his motto would be *Quo non ascendam* (How high shall I not climb?).

Château et parc de Vaux-le-Vicomte

In 1656 Fouquet decided to grace his own seignory of Vaux with a château worthy of his social standing. He showed excellent taste when it came to choosing his future "collaborators": the architect **Louis Le Vau**, the decorator **Charles Le Brun** and the landscape gardener **André Le Nôtre**. He was equally discerning in other matters; the famous chef Vatel was hired as his major-domo and La Fontaine as close adviser.

The builders were given carte blanche. A total of 18 000 workers took part in the project, which involved the demolition of three villages.

Le Brun created a tapestry works at Maincy to fulfil his commission. After Fouquet's fall it was moved to Paris, where it became the Manufacture Royale des Gobelins. The whole operation took five years to complete and the result was a masterpiece that Louis XIV wished to surpass with the construction of Versailles.

An invitation to royal vexation – On 17 August 1661 Fouquet organised a fête for the King and his court, who were staying at Fontainebleau. The reception was one of dazzling splendour. The King's table featured a service in solid gold; this detail annoyed him intensely as his own tableware had been sent back to the smelting works to meet the expenses incurred by the Thirty Years War.

After a banquet at which Vatel had surpassed himself, the guests could feast their eyes on the garden entertainments, enhanced by 1 200 fountains and cascades. The programme included country ballets, concerts, aquatic tournaments and lottery games in which all the tickets won prizes. It also included the première of *Les Fâcheux*, a comedy ballet by Molière, performed by the author and his troupe against a delightful backdrop of greenery.

The King was vexed by such an extravagant display of pomp and luxury, unparalleled at his own royal court. His first impulse was to have Fouquet arrested immediately but Anne of Austria managed to dissuade him.

The fall of Nicolas Fouquet – Nineteen days later, the Superintendent of Finances was sent to jail and all his belongings sequestrated. The artists who had designed and built Vaux entered the King's service and were later to produce the Palace of Versailles. At the end of a three-year trial, Fouquet was banished from court but this sentence was altered by the King to perpetual imprisonment. Only a few close friends remained loyal to the fallen minister: Mme De Sévigné and La Fontaine, who composed *Elegy to the Nymphs of Vaux*.

On account of her dowry, Fouquet's wife was entitled to recover the ownership of the château. After the death of her son, the estate was bought by the Maréchal de Villars in 1705, when it was made a duchy peerage. It was sold in 1764 to one of Louis XV's ministers, the Duc de Choiseul-Praslin, and survived the Revolution without suffering too much damage.

In 1875 Vaux was bought by a wealthy industrialist Mr Sommier, who applied himself to restoring and refurnishing the château, as well as refurbishing its grounds. This task has been continued by his heirs.

TOUR

Available to visitors: L'Écureuil Restaurant, a boutique, 4-seater electric cars and "nautils" (animal-shaped boats to glide along the canal).

★★Château ⊘ – The château stands on a terrace surrounded by a moat. The impressive approach leads towards the château's imposing northern front, with its tall windows indicating the *piano nobile* on a raised ground floor. The

SPENDING THE NIGHT NEARBY

Chambre d'Hôte Labordière – *16 rue Grande, Hameau de la Borde, 77820 Châtillon-la-Borde - 12km/7.5mi south-east of Vaux-le-Vicomte by D 215, D 47 (via Blandy) then D 47ᴱ –* ☎ *01 60 66 60 54 – closed Nov –* ✉ *– 3 rooms 230/260F – meal 130F.* This former 1850 farmhouse adjoins the local town hall. Relax in the large leafy garden, a haven of peace, and enjoy the table d'hôte meals while discovering new local flavours. The bedrooms, enhanced by pretty wainscoting, all have sloping roofs. Simple, unpretentious atmosphere.

building is characteristic of the first period of Louis XIV architecture.

The glass doors in the entrance hall – presently covered up by tapestries – opened onto the Grand Salon and the perspective of the formal gardens. This vestibule leads up to the first floor, occupied by the **suites of Mr and Mme Fouquet**.

Visitors are shown the superintendent's antechamber (large ebony desk inlaid with gilt copper), his study and his bedroom (superb ceiling attributed to Jean Cotelle), followed by Mme Fouquet's boudoir (*Beauty cutting the wings of Love* by Le Brun), the Louis XV study and bedroom embellished with contemporary furniture (large tester bed attributed to F Leroy) and the Praslin bedchamber.

It is possible to climb another 80 steps to see the timberwork of the roof and the lantern of the dome which offers a super panoramic **view★★** of the park.

Back on the ground floor, enter the **Grande chambre carrée**, a square chamber that has the only Louis XIII interior in the château, with a French-style ceiling.

Six reception rooms looking onto the gardens are laid out on either side of the Grand Salon. The ceilings were decorated by Le Brun, who conferred a sense of unity to the ensemble. Admire his rendering of *The Nine Muses* in the **Chambre des Muses★★**, *Sleep* in the **Cabinet des Jeux** and *Hercules Entering Mount Olympus* in the **Antichambre d'Hercule**. The latter houses an equestrian statue of Louis XIV by François Girardon. It is a miniature bronze of the monument set up on place Vendôme in 1699 and destroyed during the Revolution.

★**Grand Salon** – This room, crowned by the central dome, was left unfinished after Fouquet's arrest and suffers from the absence of decoration (the various studies made by Le Brun are on display). The 16 caryatids supporting the dome symbolise the 12 months and the four seasons of the year. The only remains of the original furnishings are two marble tables, as well as six statues and six paintings discovered by Mr Sommier when he moved in.

★★**Chambre du Roi** – The King's bedchamber communicates with the former antechamber (now a library beautifully furnished in the Regency style).
Its decoration is characteristic of the Louis XIV style that was to leave its mark on the State Apartments at Versailles. The ceiling features stuccowork by Girardon and Legendre, and a central painting by Le Brun representing *Time Taking Away Truth from the Skies*. Below the cornice is a frieze of palmette motifs alternating with tiny squirrels.

★**Appartements de la duchesse et du maréchal de Villars** – The Duchesse de Villars' boudoir formed part of the king's apartments; note the allegorical portrait of the duchess by Coypel and *Queen Marie Leszczynska's visit to Vaux in 1728*. After the Maréchal's study, which houses archives of his campaigns, comes his bedroom with a splendid **baldaquined bed★★**, decorated with embroidered draperies.

Salle à manger – The Salle des Buffets probably served as a dining room in Fouquet's time. It gives onto a wood-panelled passageway hung with paintings, where a long row of dressers would receive the bowls of fruit and other dishes brought from the distant kitchens.
A tour of the basement shows a number of rooms (Salle des Plans, Salle des Archives) and the kitchen quarters, which were used up to 1956. Note the servant's dining hall, complete with a fully laid table.

Outbuildings – The **Musée des Équipages★** ⊙ lies in the western outbuildings, next to the visitors' entrance. It presents harnessing and saddlery, an old-fashioned smithy and fully equipped carriages.

★★★**Gardens** ⊙ – Mr Sommier carefully restored Le Nôtre's masterpiece, of which the most striking feature is its sweeping perspective. The grounds offer several "optical illusions", including the discovery of basins which are not visible from the château. Walk to the far end of the upper terrace to get a good view of the southern façade. The central dome and its surmounting lantern turret, the corner pavilions, heavier than on the north side, and the decoration of the forepart, crowned by statues form an impressive, if somewhat heavy, composition.
Starting from the château, walk past the *boulingrin* or former bowling green, two areas of garden laid out like a piece of lacework.
The three main water perspectives – the moat, the two rectangular canals and the Grand Canal – suddenly come into view in a most impressive manner. Owing to the prevailing customs of that period, the artificial grottoes appear to have been arranged around the edge of the very last square basin, as the Grand Canal is optically hidden from view.
The Grand Canal – known as the *"poêle"* (frying pan) on account of its rounded

extremity – is approached by a steep flight of steps level with the Petites Cascades located opposite the grottoes. The niches at each end house two statues of river gods, some of the most important examples of 17C sculpture at Vaux; these Mlle De Scudéry fondly imagined to be the Tiber and the Anqueuil (local name given to the Almont stream).
Skirt the Grand Canal and walk up to the foot of the Farnese Hercules which ends the great perspective. The very last basin called the spray – *La Gerbe* – affords an extensive **view★** of the château and its stately grounds.

D. Thierry/DIAF

Salle des Buffets

Château de VERSAILLES★★★

Michelin map 101 folds 22, j23, 106 folds 17, 18 or 237 folds 16, 17
Michelin plan 22

Access from Paris by car: A 13 motorway towards Rouen, exit Versailles, Vaucresson.

Versailles, created by the Sun King, epitomises the golden age of French royalty and, except under the Regency, it remained the seat of government and the political centre of France from 1682 to 1789. The outstanding royal residence consists of the palace, its grounds and the Trianons. For an unforgettable and "royal" experience, make a point of visiting Versailles when the fountains are in operation throughout the gardens. The prestigious domain is now protected as one of UNESCO's World Heritage sites.

Louis XIII's Château – In the 17C the locality of Versailles was the seat of a medieval castle perched on a hillock. At the foot lay the village, surrounded by marshes and woodland abounding in game. Louis XIII used to come hunting here fairly often and in 1624 he bought part of the land and gave orders to build a small country residence. In 1631 the Archbishop of Paris, Monseigneur Gondi, granted him the lordship of Versailles, and he commissioned Philibert Le Roy to replace the manor with a small château built of brick, stone and slate.

Louis XIV's artistic taste

Louis XIV, whose education was neglected owing to the rebellion known as the "Fronde", inherited from his mother, Anne of Austria, an inclination for politeness and refinement and acquired from Mazarin a collector's passion. The festivities organised at Vaux-le-Vicomte showed him how splendid garden entertainment and fountains could be. The King, who spoke Italian and Spanish fluently made his court the melting pot of his own aesthetic values reflected by festivities, balls, games and fashion. Until 1671, the King performed on stage (dressed as the Sun in the Ballet de la Nuit in 1653), playing the roles of gods or mythological heroes, of Roman emperors, even of Alexander the Great. He particularly liked music and had a good ear. He often played the guitar, "better than a master" according to Palatine, and learned to play the harpsichord which he appreciated at the end of his life thanks to Couperin; he kept himself informed of Delalande's compositions and Lully's operas, attended rehearsals and sang arias. Evolved from a hunting lodge, Versailles was thus designed for music with the chapel as its temple.

The glorious task of taming nature – 1661 marked the year of Louis XIV's accession to the throne. The King hired the various artists, builders, designers and landscape architects who had produced Vaux-le-Vicomte and entrusted them with an even more challenging task. Louis was wary of settling in Paris following the Fronde uprisings and so searched for a site on the outskirts of the capital. He chose Versailles as he had spent many happy days there as a boy and, moreover, he was fond of hunting. It was by no means an ideal site; the mound was too narrow to allow Louis XIII's château to be enlarged. Although the surrounding land was swampy, and therefore unsuitable for growing ornamental plants, it did not yield enough water to supply the many fountains and canals that were an essential part of 17C gardens. The King ruled that nature be tamed and gave orders to divert the waters of nearby rivers, drain the land and bring in heavy loads of earth to consolidate the site.

The problem of water supply was of great concern to Colbert, and later Louvois. The waters of Clagny Pond – located near the present Rive Droite railway station – proved insufficient and the builders were forced to divert the course of the Bièvre and drain the Saclay plateau. The Marly Machine conveyed the waters pumped from the River Seine but the diversion of the Eure *(see Maintenon)* was a fiasco.

An ambitious project – In the early stages, **Louis Le Vau** built a stone construction around the small château in 1668; it was reminiscent of Italian architecture and was aptly named the "Envelope". André Le Nôtre designed the new gardens and created his celebrated perspectives. The first receptions were held at the new château in 1664. In 1678 **Jules Hardouin-Mansart**, aged only 31, was appointed head architect, a position he kept until he died in 1708. From 1661 to 1683 **Charles Le Brun** supervised a team of accomplished painters, sculptors, carvers and interior decorators. **Le Nôtre** applied himself to the embellishment of the grounds. When designing the waterworks, he joined forces with the Francines, a family of Italian engineers.

It was necessary to build a hill to accommodate the entire length of the château (680m/2230ft). Whole forests were transplanted and the King's gardeners produced 150 000 new flowering plants every year. The orangery housed around 1 080 rare species: orange and pomegranate trees, oleanders...

It took 50 years to complete the structural work on the palace at Versailles, allowing for the interruptions and slack periods attributed to contemporary wars.

Palace gates, Versailles

Ph. Gajic/MICHELIN

Life at Court – When the King and his entourage moved to Versailles, the palace and the adjacent outbuildings were required to lodge at least 3 000 people.

The Fronde movement had been a humiliating experience for the King, who had witnessed many intrigues involving men in high places. Consequently, his main concern was to keep the aristocracy with him at court, in an attempt to stifle opposition that might threaten the stability of the throne. The lavish entertainments suited his extravagant tastes and served to keep the nobility under his thumb. For the first time in French history, the royal suites in the palace were given fixed, permanent furnishings.

TOUR OF THE STATE APARTMENTS, CHAPEL CRUSADES GALLERY, 17C GALLERIES

TOUR OF THE "KING'S BEDCHAMBER" THE KINGS PRIVATE SUITE, THE ROYAL OPERA

THE QUEEN'S PRIVATE SUITE MME DE MAINTENON'S APARTMENT

THE KING'S PRIVATE APARTMENTS

MUSEUM OF FRENCH HISTORY

Permanent exhibit: "Les Grandes Heures du Parlement"

Closed to the public

Revolution, Consultate and Empire Galleries

★★★ STATE

HALL

★ Salon de la Paix

h

3

18

17

2

★ The Queen's Private Suite

k

m

16

1

★★ The QUEEN'S SUITE

n

★★★

PRIV

Coronation Room

1830 Room

19

Mme de Mainten Apartment

★ Battle Gallery

p

Galerie   de   Pierre

5

★★★ 1 8

Dauphin's Apartment

28   29   Lowe

27

25

33

24

26

23

Dauphine's Apartment

22

21

6

SOUTH WING

P

Revolution, Consultate and Empire Rooms

South Arcade —

C

Galerie   de   Pierre

5

Princes'

ROYAL

Court

Hemicycle

370

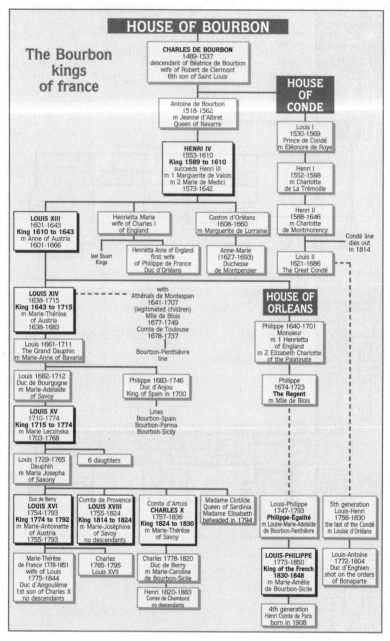

HOUSE OF BOURBON

The Bourbon kings of france

CHARLES DE BOURBON
1489-1537
descendant of Béatrice de Bourbon
wife of Robert de Clermont
6th son of Saint Louis

HOUSE OF CONDE

Antoine de Bourbon
1518-1562
m Jeanne d'Albret
Queen of Navarre

Louis I
1530-1569
Prince de Condé
m Eléonore de Roye

HENRI IV
1553-1610
King 1589 to 1610
succeeds Henri III
m 1 Marguerite de Valois
m 2 Marie de Medici
1573-1642

Henri I
1552-1588
m Charlotte
de La Trémoille

LOUIS XIII
1601-1643
King 1610 to 1643
m Anne of Austria
1601-1666

Henrietta Maria
wife of Charles I
of England

Gaston d'Orléans
1608-1660
m Marguerite de Lorraine

Henri II
1588-1646
m Charlotte
de Montmorency

last Stuart
Kings

Henrietta Anne of England
first wife
of Philippe de France
Duc d'Orléans

Anne-Marie
(1627-1693)
Duchesse
de Montpensier

Condé line
dies out
in 1814

Louis II
1621-1686
The Great Condé

LOUIS XIV
1638-1715
King 1643 to 1715
m Marie-Thérèse
of Austria
1638-1683

with
Athénaïs de Montespan
1641-1707
(legitimated children)
Mlle de Blois
1677-1749
Comte de Toulouse
1678-1737

HOUSE OF ORLEANS

Philippe 1640-1701
Monsieur
m 1 Henrietta
of England
m 2 Elizabeth Charlotte
of the Palatinate

Louis 1661-1711
The Grand Dauphin
m Marie-Anne of Bavaria

Bourbon-Penthièvre
line

Louis 1682-1712
Duc de Bourgogne
m Marie-Adélaïde
of Savoy

Philippe 1683-1746
Duc d'Anjou
King of Spain in 1700

Philippe
1674-1723
The Regent
m Mlle de Blois

LOUIS XV
1710-1774
King 1715 to 1774
m Marie Leczinska
1703-1768

Lines
Bourbon-Spain
Bourbon-Parma
Bourbon-Sicily

Louis 1729-1765
Dauphin
m Maria Josepha
of Saxony

6 daughters

| Duc de Berry **LOUIS XVI** 1754-1793 **King 1774 to 1792** m Marie-Antoinette of Austria 1755-1793 | Comte de Provence **LOUIS XVIII** 1755-1824 **King 1814 to 1824** m Marie-Joséphine of Savoy no descendants | Comte d'Artois **CHARLES X** 1757-1836 **King 1824 to 1830** m Marie-Thérèse of Savoy | Madame Clotilde Queen of Sardinia Madame Elisabeth beheaded in 1794 | Louis-Philippe 1747-1793 **Philippe-Égalité** m Louise-Marie-Adélaïde de Bourbon-Penthièvre | 5th generation Louis-Henri 1756-1830 the last of the Condé m Louise d'Orléans |

Marie-Thérèse
de France 1778-1851
wife of Louis
1775-1844
Duc d'Angoulême
1st son of Charles X
no descendants

Charles
1785-1795
Louis XVII

Charles 1778-1820
Duc de Berry
m Marie-Caroline
de Bourbon-Sicile

LOUIS-PHILIPPE
1773-1850
**King of the French
1830-1848**
m Marie-Amélie
de Bourbon-Sicile

Louis-Antoine
1772-1804
Duc d'Enghien
shot on the orders
of Bonaparte

Henri 1820-1883
Comte de Chambord
no descendants

4th generation
Henri Comte de Paris
born in 1908

Thanks to Colbert's efforts to encourage the production of luxury goods (tapestries, furniture, lace etc) on a national scale, the palace – which remained open to the public – offered a standing exhibition of arts and crafts in France.

Strict etiquette governed the visits that the French people would pay to Versailles. The famous chronicler Saint-Simon described a day at court as a "clockwork ceremony" consisting of a series of banquets, audiences and entertainments. After 1684, the pious Mme De Maintenon put an end to these large-scale festivities; the court had to find other ways to overcome its boredom.

When Louis XIV died in 1715 his successor was still a young boy. The Regent Philippe d'Orléans administered the King's affairs from the Palais-Royal, his Paris residence. During this time, the court left Versailles and moved to the Tuileries.

Louis XV – In 1722 Louis XV, aged 12, decided to settle at Versailles. In order that royal etiquette might not interfere with his private life, he gave orders to convert several of the private apartments. He dreamed of having the front of the palace remodelled, a task he entrusted to Jacques-Anges Gabriel. Unfortunately, no major alterations could be carried out owing to insufficient funds, but the Petit Trianon was built.

Louis XVI – Louis XVI and Marie-Antoinette commissioned no further works. The Queen was perfectly happy to stay in the Petit Trianon; it was for her that the hamlet and the present grounds were designed in 1774. On 6 October 1789, the national insurrection forced the royal family to return to Paris. After that date, Versailles ceased to be a place of residence for the kings of France.

To the glory of France – After the storming of the Tuileries and the fall of the monarchy on 10 August 1792, most of the furniture was removed and auctioned. The major works of art – paintings, carpets, tapestries and a few items of furniture – were kept for the art museum which opened in the Louvre in August 1793. After the renovation work undertaken by Napoleon and Louis XVIII, Versailles was threatened once more; it was spared demolition by Louis-Philippe, who contributed a large part of his personal fortune to turn it into a museum of French history in 1837.

More recently, Versailles was restored following the First World War, thanks to the generosity of the Academy of Fine Arts and the handsome contributions made by a number of wealthy patrons, including the American JD Rockefeller.

A major **restoration** campaign was launched in the early 1950s, permitting the renovation of the Royal Opera, the installation of central heating and electric lighting, and the completion of various refurnishing and maintenance projects. The King's Bedroom and the Hall of Mirrors, in particular, were both restored to their 18C splendour.

Phases of construction and other historical events

Louis XIV kept a close watch on the various works under way, except when he marched to war. He was a critical overseer who made numerous comments aimed at altering, rectifying and improving the plans of his new residence. During the 18C, Louis XV and Louis XVI had the apartments redecorated in keeping with current fashion. Work was continually in progress at the château. This explains why very few rooms have retained their Louis XIV decoration. The greater part of the château is decorated in the rocaille style in fashion during the reign of Louis XV.

1631	Completion of Louis XIII's château.
1643	Death of Louis XIII. Five-year-old **Louis XIV accedes to the throne**. France is ruled by the Regent Anne of Austria and Cardinal Jules Mazarin.
1661	Louis XIV comes of age. After Mazarin's death, he decides to reign without the assistance of a Prime Minister.
1664	The first sumptuous receptions are held.
1666	The Versailles fountains play for the first time.
1668	Louis Le Vau starts work on the château.
1671	Charles Le Brun and his team of artists begin the interior decoration.
1674	Louis XIV's first major stay at Versailles.
1682	The court and government officials take up residence at the palace.
1683	Death of Marie-Thérèse of Austria. Louis XIV is secretly married to Mme De Maintenon.
1684	The Hall of Mirrors is completed.
1687	The Porcelain Trianon is replaced by the Marble Trianon.
1710	Birth of Louis XV, great-grandson of the Sun King.
1715	Death of Louis XIV. Five-year-old Louis XV accedes to the throne. France is ruled by the Regent Philippe d'Orléans. The court leaves Versailles.
1722	The court returns to Versailles.
1729	Birth of the Dauphin, later father to Louis XVI, Louis XVIII and Charles X.
1745	Mme De Pompadour becomes Louis XV's mistress. Her "reign" lasts 15 years.
1754	Birth of Louis XVI.
1770	Marriage of Louis XVI to the Austrian Archduchess Marie-Antoinette.
1774	Death of Louis XV. **Louis XVI accedes to the throne**.
1783	The Treaty of Versailles is signed, granting independence to 13 American States.
1789	The States-General meet in the town. The royal family leaves Versailles.

Château de VERSAILLES

THE CHÂTEAU AND ITS SURROUNDINGS
★★Place d'Armes

This huge square was the junction of the three wide avenues leading to Paris, St-Cloud and Sceaux, separated by the **Écuries royales★**, the stables built by Jules Hardouin-Mansart. Identical in size, the Grande and the Petite Écuries were so named for reasons of convenience.

Grande Écurie – Formerly used for saddle horses, it now houses the **Musée des Carrosses** ⊘ where various sedan chairs and carriages can be seen, (carriages used for Napoleon's wedding, Charles X's coronation, presidential elections under the 3rd Republic etc).

Petite Écurie – It was used for carriages, and carriage-horses.

★★★Courtyards

The wrought-iron railings date from the reign of Louis XVIII. Beyond them stretches a series of three courtyards.

The forecourt or **Cour des Ministres** is flanked by two long wings linking the four pavilions in which the King's ministers were accommodated.

An equestrian statue of Louis XIV, commissioned by Louis-Philippe, stands in the middle of the drive. The **Cour royale** was separated from the outer courtyard by railings through which only persons of high rank (peers, princes of the blood, noblemen etc) might pass in carriages. The two wings lining this court were originally separate from the palace and used as outbuildings. They were joined to the main building and fronted by a set of colonnades under Louis XV and Louis XVIII. Beyond the North Arcade – leading through to the park – and the South Arcade stand three gilded gates marking the entrance to the State Apartments. On the left rises the Queen's Staircase.

The **Cour de Marbre★★** (Marble Court) – paved with slabs of black and white marble – has been raised to its original level. It is surrounded by Louis XIII's old

Versailles, garden façade

château, the façades of which were altered and greatly improved by Louis Le Vau and Jules Hardouin-Mansart: balustrades, busts, statues, vases etc. On the first floor of the central pavilion, the three arched windows belonging to the king's bedroom are fronted by a gilded balcony resting upon eight marble columns.

★★★Garden Façade

Walk under the North Arcade, skirt the main part of the palace and step back to get a good view.

The huge building occupies a total length of 680m/2230ft and yet its general appearance is not monotonous; the central body stands proud from the wings, and the length of the façade is articulated with intermittent rows of sculpted columns and pillars to break the rigidity of the horizontal lines. The flat roof, built in the Italian style, is concealed by a balustrade bearing ornamental trophies and vases. The statues of Apollo and Diana, surrounded by the Months of the Year, surmount the central body which housed the Royal Suite. Certain members of the royal family, including several of the King's children, stayed in the South Wing.

The terrace extending in front of the château commands an extensive view of the park and its many perspectives. It bears two **giant vases★**, one at each end; the one to the north was executed by Coysevox and symbolises War, while the south vase, attributed to Tuby, is a representation of Peace. They are appropriately placed outside the bay windows of the Salon de la Guerre and the Salon de la Paix respectively.

At the foot of the main building lies a row of four sculptures, the very first to be cast by the Keller brothers who drew inspiration from a classical model: Bacchus, Apollo, Antinoüs and Silenus.

The terrace offers a general view of the grounds and their distinctive features *(description below)*: in the foreground the Water Gardens *(Parterres d'Eau)*, with a sweeping perspective as far as the Grand Canal: on the left the South Parterre *(Parterre du Midi)*; on the right the North Parterre *(Parterre du Nord)* and groves *(Bosquets du Nord)*, cut across by another canal leading to the Neptune Basin.

Return to the Cour de Marbre through the South Arcade in the south wing.

D. Hée/MICHELIN

TOUR OF THE GRANDS APPARTEMENTS ⏱

The visitors' entrance (Entrance **A**) leads through to a vestibule which houses the ticket office. From there, go to the Salles des Croisades.

★SALLES DES CROISADES

The five rooms, decorated in a neo-Gothic style, illustrate events which took place during the crusades and contain a collection of paintings commissioned by Louis-Philippe, including a copy of *The Crusaders Enter Constantinople* by Delacroix (the original is in the Louvre), *The Defence of Rhodes* by the Belgian painter G Wappers and the colourful *Capitulation of Ptolemais* by MJ Blondel. The emblems of the families who took part in the crusades decorate the pillars, coffered ceilings and part of the walls.

17C GALLERIES

These small rooms – occupying the greater part of the north wing – feature a charming selection of paintings and portraits, also busts and console tables.

Ground Floor – *Guided tours only.* The vestibule by the chapel leads to this suite of 11 rooms. The first six were once occupied by the Duc de Maine, the son of Louis XIV and Mme De Montespan, while the last four housed the apartments of the Princes of Bourbon-Conti.

The series of portraits includes Henri IV, who enjoyed visiting the site of Versailles, and Louis XIII, the founder of the original château.

First Floor – Portraits of the royal family, Mme De Maintenon, Louis XIV's legitimised children and the celebrated figures of the King's reign, painted by Le Brun, Mignard Van der Meulen, Coypel, Rigaud Largillière etc, bring these rooms to life. Note the set of portraits of famous men (Colbert, Racine, Molière, La Fontaine, Le Nôtre and Couperin) and the vast battle scenes by Van der Meulen, characterised by attention to detail and a true love of nature.

The galleries offer a lovely view of the gardens.

One reaches the level of the chapel's gallery.

★★★CHAPEL

Guided tours combined with a visit of the Appartement du Roi.

It was only in 1710 that the chapel was finished. By that time, Louis XIV had reached the age of 72.

Dedicated to St Louis (Louis IX), the chapel at Versailles is an elegant display of stonework decorated in white and gold tones. This masterpiece is the work of Mansart and was completed by his brother-in-law Robert de Cotte in 1710.

Grands Appartements (State Apartments) ⏱

These consist of the various reception rooms – the Salon d'Hercule and a suite of six rooms known as the Grands Appartements – together with the famous Hall of Mirrors *(Galerie des Glaces)* and the living quarters where the king and queen would appear in public.

While visiting the palace, it is helpful to remember a few facts concerning the layout of great châteaux of Classical and Baroque inspiration.

Generally speaking, French rulers would spend their day between the ornate reception rooms of the State Apartments – their official, semi-public quarters – and the private apartments which afforded a certain amount of privacy. In the 18C, Louis XV and later Louis XVI enjoyed a greater degree of intimacy in the Petits Appartements.

A standard example of State Apartments – The two suites belonging to the king and the queen are placed symmetrically on either side of the central pavilion. Each suite consisted of at least one guard-room, several antechambers, the bedroom, the grand cabinet and a number of private drawing rooms (it was through these that the two royal suites communicated).

At Versailles, this symmetrical disposition was applied only between 1673 and 1682. When Marie-Thérèse died in 1683, there was no question of Mme De Maintenon occupying the apartments of the former queen. Louis XIV moved into new quarters was onto the Marble Court. His former suite opening transformed, at great cost, into a series of reception rooms.

Summer and winter furnishings – In the living quarters of the palace, the hangings were changed twice a year, at the beginning of summer and before the onset of winter. Thus the summer furnishings (silk) would alternate with the winter furnishings (velvet).

The fabric-dressed walls were then hung with paintings inspired by religious themes, by artists of the Italian School: Poussin, Veronese, Titian etc.

Daily life at Versailles

The court included some 4000 to 5000 people altogether, and up to 10000 on crowded days according to Madame de Sévigné. The Grand Maître de la maison du Roi (Grand Master of the King's Household), a post held since 1641 by the Prince de Condé, was in charge of food supplies. Suppliers were financiers who advanced the necessary funds and paid themselves back through advantages bestowed by the king. The remains of royal feasts were sold by all those who ordered, prepared and served the dishes. This was a very lucrative business. Meat and fish were sold to the town's shopkeepers through the Swiss guards; drinks, coffee, chocolate were sold from huts made of plaster or wood, located near the access ramps or the gates. Courtiers had no kitchens and had to be content with warming up dishes bought in this way. Improvised kitchens, dish-warmers and coal shops caused the upper and lower galleries to stink. If you add to this the continuous flow of visitors and lawyers who, provided they were properly dressed (men could hire swords at the entrance), mingled with the courtiers hoping to catch a glimpse of the king on his way to the chapel through the Grands Appartements, you can easily imagine the crowds.

The pillars and arches bear exquisite bas-reliefs by among others Van Clève, Le Lorrain, Coustou.

As the usual place for an organ is occupied by the royal gallery it stands instead at the east end in the gallery, a splendid piece of craftsmanship by Clicquot, enhanced by fine carvings based on studies by Robert de Cotte.

The marble altar is attributed to Van Clève. The altar front features a low-relief sculpture in gilded bronze representing the *Pietà*; it is the work of Vassé.

The painting in the apse is by La Fosse and depicts the Resurrection.

While the members of the royal family were seated in the gallery, the courtiers stood in the nave.

★★SALON D'HERCULE

This drawing room stands on the site formerly occupied by the fourth and penultimate chapel of the original château. Construction of the room was started in 1712, the year in which St Louis' Chapel was inaugurated; the decoration was completed by Robert de Cotte in 1736, during the reign of Louis XV.

The room boasts two splendid compositions by Veronese. **Christ at the House of Simon the Pharisee★** was a present to Louis XIV from the Venetian Republic. The room was in fact designed to house this huge painting, which has been returned to its precious gilt frame. The second work *Eliezer and Rebecca* hangs above the marble mantelpiece which is richly adorned with gilded bronze.

The ceiling – representing Hercules entering the Kingdom of the Gods – was painted by François Lemoyne, who spent three years on the 315m²/3 390sq ft fresco. His work met with widespread acclaim, but the following year the artist suffered a nervous breakdown and committed suicide (1737).

★★★LE GRAND APPARTEMENT

In former times, the apartment was approached from the Royal Court by means of the Ambassadors' Staircase (destroyed in 1752).

It provides a splendid example of early Louis XIV decoration. Note the use of noble materials such as multicoloured marble, bronze and copper, chased and gilded in the Italian Baroque style. Impressive rock crystal chandeliers hang from the ceiling and candelabra adorn the pedestal tables.

The suite of six salons was sparsely furnished with a few stools, folding chairs pedestal and console tables. The Grands Appartements – running from the Salon d'Hercule, dedicated to a man endowed with divine powers, to the Salon d'Apollon, built in honour of the son of Jupiter and Latona – symbolised the solar myth to which Louis XIV claimed to belong. The six rooms were all built by Le Vau in 1668 and decorated by Le Brun. The rooms are named after the subjects painted on the ceiling frescoes.

Three times a week, between 6 and 10pm on Mondays, Wednesdays and Thursdays, the King held court in the Grands Appartements. The ceremony was enhanced by dancing and gaming.

Salon de l'Abondance (b) – At the time of Louis XIV, on the days when the King held court, this reception room contained three buffets: one for hot drinks, two for cold drinks such as wine, eaux-de-vie, sorbets and fruit juice. The walls are hung with the winter furnishings, made of embossed velvet in deep emerald tones. Admire the four portraits of the royal family, painted by Rigaud and Van Loo: the Grand Dauphin, Philippe V, the Duke of Burgundy and Louis XV.

The next two rooms were originally vestibules leading to the Ambassadors' Staircase. The magnificent walls lined with marble are in keeping with the ornate decoration of the former main staircase.

Salon de Vénus (c) – The ceiling of this salon as well as those of the following rooms were painted by Houasse. It features decorated panels framed by heavy gilt stucco.

Salon de Diane (d) – This used to be the billiard room under Louis XIV. Observe the **bust of Louis XIV** by Bernini (1665), a remarkable piece of Baroque workmanship. The room displays several paintings by De Lafosse and Blanchard.

Salon de Mars (e) – The lavish decoration (wall hangings) is a reminder that this room once belonged to the royal suite (guard-room). Louis XIV subsequently used it for dances, games and concerts. The two galleries which housed the musicians were placed on either side of the fireplace. They were dismantled in 1750. The 18C paintings include *Darius' Tent* by Le Brun and *The Pilgrims on the Road to Emmaüs* after Veronese.

The side walls bear Rigaud's portrait of Louis XV and a painting of Marie Leczinska by Van Loo. The martial scenes on the ceiling are attributed to Audran, Jouvenet and Houasse. One of the Sun King's favourite paintings hangs above the fireplace: Domenichino's *King David*, in which he is portrayed playing the harp. It was originally displayed in the King's bedchamber.

Salon de Mercure (f) – A fire was lit in this former antechamber on the evenings when the King held court. It was here that Louis XIV lay in state for one week after his death in 1715. Seventy-two ecclesiastics took turns to watch over him, ensuring that four Masses could be said at the same time between 5am and midday. The ceiling was decorated by JB de Champaigne.

Salon d'Apollon (Throne Room) (g) – The former Throne Room. The throne was placed on a central platform covered by a large canopy. The three hooks to which the canopy was attached still remain.

The King received ambassadors in this chamber. When he held court, it was used for dances and concerts. The ceiling sports a fresco by De Lafosse: *Apollo in a Sun Chariot*. This room marks the end of the Grand Appartement. Set at a perpendicular angle, the Hall of Mirrors and the adjacent rooms dedicated to war and peace occupy the entire length of the main front giving onto the palace gardens.

★SALON DE LA GUERRE (WAR SALON)

This is a corner room joining the Hall of Mirrors and the Grands Appartements; it features a huge oval low-relief sculpture by Coysevox, representing the king defeating his enemies.

★★★GALERIE DES GLACES (HALL OF MIRRORS)

The Hall of Mirrors was completed by Mansart in 1686. It covered a short-lived terrace (1668-78) that Le Vau had built along the side overlooking the gardens. Together with the Salon de la Guerre and Salon de la Paix, it is the most brilliant achievement by Le Brun and his team of artists. The hall is 73m/240ft long, 10.5m/35ft wide and 12m/40ft high. The 17 large windows are echoed by 17 mirrors on the wall opposite. These are made up of 578 pieces of the largest size possible at the time. This hall was designed to catch the golden rays of sunset. The ceiling fresco – painted by Le Brun in amber, flame-coloured tones – pays tribute to the early reign of Louis XIV (from 1661 to 1678, up to the Treaty of Nijmegen).

The capitals of the pilasters bear an unusual ornamental feature: made of gilded bronze, they represent the "French order", which combines antique motifs with fleurs-de-lis and stylised cockerels (the emblem of French patriotism).

The Hall of Mirrors was used for court receptions, formal ceremonies and diplomatic encounters. On these occasions, the throne was placed under the arch leading into the Salon de la Paix. It is easier to picture the hall during court festivities, when it was thronged with elegant visitors in formal attire, brightly lit by the thousands of flickering candles reflected in the mirrors. The tubs bearing the orange trees, as well as the chandeliers and other furnishings, were made of solid silver under Louis XIV. For a period of 10 years, part of the country's monetary reserves was thus shaped into works of art.

In 1980 the Hall of Mirrors was restored to its former glory. With its crystal chandeliers and new set of candelabra – cast after the six surviving originals – it presents the same dazzling appearance as in 1770 when Marie-Antoinette was married to the Dauphin, the future King Louis XVI.

It was here that the German Empire was proclaimed on 18 January 1871, and that the Treaty of Versailles was signed on 28 June 1919.

The central windows offer a splendid **view**★★★ of the Grand Perspective.

★SALON DE LA PAIX (PEACE SALON)

Placed at the southern end of the Hall of Mirrors, this chamber counterbalances the Salon de la Guerre. Originally designed as an extension of the great gallery, it was made into an annexe of the Queen's Suite towards the end of Louis XIV's reign; it communicated with the Hall of Mirrors by means of a movable partition.

Above the mantelpiece hangs *Louis XV Bringing Peace to Europe*, a painting by François Lemoyne.

★★APPARTEMENT DE LA REINE (QUEEN'S SUITE)

This suite was created for Louis XIV's wife Marie-Thérèse, who died here in 1683.

Marie-Antoinette and her Children by Vigée-Lebrun

Chambre de la reine (h) – In 1975, after a restoration programme lasting 30 years, this room regained its summer furnishings of 1787. Originally designed for Maria-Theresa, the bedchamber was later occupied by the wife of the Grand Dauphin, Louis XIV's son; by the Duchesse de Bourgogne, wife of the Sun King's grandson, who gave birth to Louis XV here; by Marie Leszczynska, wife of Louis XV (for 43 years); and by Louis XVI's wife Marie-Antoinette. Nineteen children belonging to French royalty – among them Louis XV and Philippe V of Spain – were born in this bedroom.

A long-standing tradition ruled that the birth of royal infants should be a public event. Even the proud Marie-Antoinette had to comply with this French custom, surrounded by a crowd of curious onlookers.

The ornamental motifs on the wainscot and the ceiling were designed and made for Marie Leszczynska by the Gabriels, while the fireplace, imposing jewel chest, sphinx-shaped andirons, fire screen and bedspread were designed for Marie-Antoinette.

Note the magnificent silk hangings and furnishings decorated with flowers, ribbons and peacock tails, which were rewoven to the original pattern in Lyon.

Salon des Nobles de la Reine (k) – The official presentations to the Queen took place in this former antechamber. It was also here that the queens and dauphins of France used to lie in state prior to the burial ceremony. The original fresco on the ceiling, attributed to Michel Corneille, has been preserved. The rest of the decoration was considered staid and old-fashioned by Marie-Antoinette, who had it entirely refurbished by the architect Richard Mique (1785). Furnished with commodes and corner cupboards by Riesener and embellished with magnificent green silk hangings, the salon looks very much as it would have done on the eve of the French Revolution in 1789.

Antichambre du Grand Couvert (m) – This chamber was used as a guard-room under Marie-Theresa. It was here that Louis XV and Marie Leszczynska – and later Louis XVI and Marie-Antoinette – would dine in full view of the public. A family portrait of Marie-Antoinette and her children (1787) by Mme Vigée-Lebrun hangs here.

Salle des Gardes de la Reine (n) – The decoration was the work of Le Brun and N Coypel. It was moved from its original setting – the Salon de Jupiter – when the Hall of Mirrors was completed in 1687; the Salon de Jupiter was subsequently renamed the Salon de la Guerre. On 6 October 1789, several of the queen's guards were stabbed to death by a group of dedicated revolutionaries. The Louis XIV decor – featuring sumptuous marble-lined walls – has been beautifully preserved.

Salle du sacre (Coronation Room)

This room was initially used as a chapel between 1676 and 1682. The Parlement de Paris used to hold its sessions in this former guard-room. It was altered by Louis-Philippe in order to accommodate several huge paintings depicting the Emperor's coronation. David's second *Coronation of Napoleon* – painted between

1808 and 1822 – lies to the left of the entrance. The original is exhibited in the Louvre Museum (Salle Mollien). On the opposite wall hang David's *Distribution of Eagles on the Champ de Mars* and a painting by Gros representing *Murat at the Battle of Aboukir* (1806).

Salle de 1792 (p) – This large, unfurnished room lies at the junction of the south wing and the main central pavilion. The walls are hung with portraits of soldiers, paintings of famous battles and war scenes. Cogniet's work *The Paris National Guard* shows Louis-Philippe proudly sporting his Lieutenant-General's uniform.

★GALERIE DES BATAILLES

Created in 1836 on the site of the princes' suite in the south wing, the Galerie des Batailles caused quite a stir because of its huge dimensions (120m/394ft by 13m/43ft).

It was designed to house the 33 paintings of France's major victories under the Ancien Régime, the Empire and the Republic, from Tolbiac *(first on the left when entering)* to Wagram *(first on the right)* by Horace Vernet, Louis-Philippe's favourite painter (who also painted Iéna, Fontenoy, Bouvines and Friedland), and including works by Eugène Delacroix (Taillebourg) and Baron Gérard (Austerlitz).

Salle de 1830

Commissioned by Louis-Philippe, this room is devoted to the last king of France who was known as the "Citizen-king".

Take the Princes' Staircase ⑤ down to the Cour des Princes.

★★★TOUR OF THE "CHAMBRE DU ROI"

Audio-guided tour, Entrance C.

★★★APPARTEMENT DU ROI (LOUIS XIV'S SUITE) ⓘ

The king's quarters are arranged around the Cour de Marbre. They were designed by Jules Hardouin-Mansart and set up in Louis XIII's château between 1682 and 1701. The style shows a marked change in the Louis XIV period. The ceilings are no longer coffered but painted white, the marble tiling has been replaced by white and gold panelling, and large mirrors adorn the stately fireplaces.

Escalier de la Reine ⑥ – Towards the end of the Ancien Régime, the Queen's Staircase was the official entrance to the royal apartments. The decoration of the staircase is extremely ornate; from the top landing, admire the elegant display of multicoloured marble designed by Le Brun. The huge *trompe-l'œil* painting is jointly attributed to Meusnier, Poerson and Belin de Fontenay.

The guard-room (**1**) and a first antechamber (**2**) lead to the Salon de l'Œil-de-Bœuf.

Salon de l'Œil-de-Bœuf (second antechamber) (**3**) – The Bulls'-Eye Chamber was originally two rooms: the king's bedchamber between 1684 and 1701 – the part nearest to the two windows looking onto the Cour de Marbre – and a small study.

Versailles – Louis XIV's bedroom

The two were united under the supervision of Mansart and Robert de Cotte. Lightness and elegance are the principal characteristics of this charming drawing room, which contrasts sharply with the earlier achievements of Louis' reign. Level with the famous bull's-eye – echoed by a mirror on the opposite wall – runs a frieze depicting children at play. Note Coysevox' bust of Louis XIV.

The paintings by Veronese and Bassano have been replaced by a number of royal portraits, including an allegorical rendering of Louis XIV's family by Nocret.

It was in this antechamber that the courtiers assembled before witnessing the rising and retiring ceremonies of the king.

Chambre du Roi (**4**) – This became Louis XIV's state bedroom in 1701.

At the centre of the palace, this bedroom, facing the Cour de Marbre, looks out in the direction of the rising sun. Louis XIV, suffering from a gangrenous knee, died here on 1 September 1715.

The ritual rising and retiring ceremonies took place in this room from 1701 to 1789.

Daytime visitors were requested to make a small bow when passing in front of the bed, which symbolised the divine right of the monarchy.

The rising ceremony

The king was woken up at 7am by his first valet. The first visit he received was that of his doctor. Next came the "*grandes entrées*" (important guests including members of his family and those who held an office), then the "*secondes entrées*" (less important guests) and finally the nobility. Breakfast was followed by the dressing ceremony, then the king left his apartments to hear Mass in the chapel.

The King's bedroom is hung with its summer furnishings of 1722 – Louis XV's second year at the palace – and its decor has been scrupulously reconstructed. Beyond the beautifully restored gilded balustrade stands a raised four-poster bed, complete with canopy and curtains. The gold and silver embroidered brocade used for the bed and wall hangings, upholstery and door coverings has been entirely rewoven.

Six religious works – including Valentin de Boulogne's *Four Evangelists* – lie level with the attic. Above the doors hang *St Madeleine* by Domenichino, *John the Baptist* by Caracciolo and several portraits by Van Dyck.

Salle du Conseil (**5**) – Like the Salon de l'Œil-de-Bœuf, it originally consisted of two rooms: the Cabinet des Termes and the Cabinet du Conseil. The decoration of the present room – created under Louis XV – was entrusted to Gabriel. The mirrors dating from Louis XIV's reign were replaced with wainscoting by Rousseau, who produced a splendid Rococo interior.

Over a period of 100 years, many grave decisions affecting the destiny of France were taken in this council chamber, including that of France's involvement in the American War of Independence in 1775.

As you go by, admire the decoration of Louis XV's bedroom (via the open door on the right) before walking across the Hall of Mirrors and back to the Salon de l'Œil-de-Bœuf.

The king's valets

The Sun King had 28 valets who served and assisted him according to a very precise timetable. What were their privileges? They were close to him daily and could, if the need arose, request a favour from him. In addition, their office automatically made them members of the aristocracy, exempted them from paying the *taille*, a royal tax and provided them with a substantial income.

The best known of the king's valets was undoubtedly Marie Du Bois (a man in spite of his Christian name), who left a diary, and another famous valet was Alexandre Bontemps, an important member of the court for nearly 60 years, whom Louis XIV' trusted implicitly.

Appartement du Dauphin

From the Salon de l'Œil-de-Bœuf, go down a small staircase leading to the Dauphin's apartments.

These rooms have partially retained or regained their 18C ornamentation and have been redecorated and sometimes refurnished. All this contributes to combine artistic appeal and historic interest.

Access is through the first antechamber displaying portraits of the main "dauphins" (heirs to the throne).

The entrance was through the Salle des Gardes (on the right), which is now decorated with splendid Gobelins tapestries. The second antechamber completes the first by exhibiting portraits of Louis XV's daughters by Nattier.

Chambre du Dauphin (29) – Occupied from 1684, first of all by Louis XIV's son then by subsequent heirs to the throne until 1789 (the last occupant was Louis XVI's son), it has retained its original 1747 decor: wardrobe with lacquered panels (Bernard Van Rysenburgh – BVRB), commode by Boudin and an 18C embroidered canopied bed. The fireplace is one of the finest in the palace.

Grand Cabinet du Dauphin (28) – This room houses portraits of Mesdames Adélaïde, Louise, Sophie and Victoire by Nattier, as well as some beautiful pieces of furniture by Jacob, taken from Louis XVI's gaming room at St-Cloud. The amazing globe was commissioned by Louis XVI for his son's education.

Bibliothèque (27) – The library boasts magnificent wooden panelling in deep amber tones, enhanced by turquoise relief work. Admire Vernet's delicate seascapes above the doors. This room leads to the Dauphin's apartments which are visited in reverse order.

Appartement de la Dauphine

Cabinet Intérieur de la Dauphine (25) – This room features Vernis Martin wainscoting as in the Dauphin's library. Note Gaudreaux' commode and a writing desk by BVRB. The back rooms were refurbished under Louis XVIII for the Duchesse d'Angoulême, the daughter of Louis XVI: couch formerly belonging to the Comtesse de Provence, antechamber, study-library and servant's quarters.

Chambre de la Dauphine (24) – The bedroom contains a Polish-style bed and a magnificent set of six armchairs by Heurtaut. Note Nattier's two portraits of Mme Henriette and Mme Adélaïde, portrayed respectively as Flora and Diana.

Grand Cabinet de la Dauphine (23) – This room evokes the marriage of Marie Leszczynska to Louis XV. It also presents Lemaire's sculpted barometer, offered on the occasion of Marie-Antoinette's marriage to the Dauphin, and several corner cupboards by Bernard Van Risenburgh (BVRB). If one compares the Savonnerie tapestry with that of the next room, one notices that the fleur-de-lis motifs have been replaced by stars (Revolution).

Deuxième antichambre (22) – The fireplace is adorned with a bust of the Regent, which was taken from the Queen's Bedroom at the time of Marie Leszczynska. Savonnerie tapestry.

Première antichambre (21) – It houses a number of pictures representing the rulers who succeeded the Sun King: portrait of the five-year-old Louis XV by Alexis Belle (1723). *Cavalcade of the King (Louis XV) after His Coronation on 22 October 1722* by Pierre-Denis Martin.

★★★ APPARTEMENT PRIVÉ DU ROI (SUITE OF LOUIS XV) *Guided tour*

Appartement intérieur du Roi

This suite of rooms, with its superb wainscoting by Gabriel, provides a delightful feast for the eyes. The fine Rococo carvings are the work of Verberckt.

Chambre à coucher (6) – The absence of furniture makes it difficult to picture this room in its original state. Owing to the constraints of court etiquette, Louis XV (after 1738) and then Louis XVI (up to the end of the Ancien Régime) daily had to leave this room and slip away to the State bedroom, where they "performed" the rising and retiring ceremonies.
It was here that Louis XV died of smallpox on 10 May 1774.
The original paintings above the doors were taken down and replaced by portraits of the three daughters of Louis XV.

Cabinet de la Pendule (7) – This was a games room until 1769; a copper line running across the floor indicates the Versailles meridian.
In the centre of the room stands the equestrian statue of Louis XV by Vassé. It is a replica of Bouchardon's sculpture which initially adorned place Louis XV – now called place de la Concorde – in Paris and which was destroyed in 1792.

Antichambre des Chiens (8) – A charming passageway off the king's private staircase (known as *degré du Roi*). The decoration features Louis XIV panelling, in sharp contrast to the adjoining rooms.

Salle à manger dite des Retours de chasse (9) – Between 1750 and 1769 hunts were organised every other day in the forests surrounding Versailles. Louis XV and a few privileged fellow hunters would come here to sup after their exertions.

The King's desk

Cabinet intérieur du Roi (**10**) – This masterpiece of 18C French ornamental art was commissioned by Louis XV. Gabriel and the accomplished cabinetmaker Verberckt were responsible for the stunning Rococo decor.

The celebrated **roll-top desk★★★** by Oeben and Riesener (1769) was among the few prestigious works of art to be spared in 1792.

The **medal cabinet** attributed to the cabinetmaker Gaudreaux (1738) is heavily decorated with gilded bronze: it bears the 1785 candelabra commemorating the role played by France in the American War of Independence, flanked by two Sèvres vases (bronzes by Thomire). Two corner cupboards made by Joubert in 1755 to house Louis XV's ever-increasing collections, were added subsequently, as was a set of chairs attributed to Foliot (1774).

The room was originally private but under Louis XVI it took on a semi-official character. In 1785 it was the scene of a formal encounter attended by Marie-Antoinette, at which the King informed Cardinal de Rohan that he would shortly be arrested for his involvement in the Diamond Necklace Affair.

The Corner Room leads through to the study where Louis XV and Louis XVI kept all confidential documents relating to State affairs, and where they granted private audiences.

Cabinet de Madame Adélaïde (**12**) – This was one of the first "new rooms" laid out at the instigation of Louis XV. It overlooks the Royal Court and was designed by Louis XV for his favourite daughter Madame Adélaïde (1752). The ornate decoration features delightful Rococo wainscoting and gilded panelling embellished with musical instruments, as well as fishing and floral motifs: the room was used as a music room by the king's daughter. It is believed that the young Mozart performed on the harpsichord before the royal family in this very room, during the winter of 1763-64. Louis XVI later made the room his "jewel cabinet". Note the extraordinary medal cabinet attributed to Bennemann; each drawer is decorated with melted wax, delicately blended with feathers and butterfly wings and carefully poured onto thin glass plates.

Bibliothèque de Louis XVI (**13**) – Designed by the ageing Gabriel and executed by the wood carver Antoine Rousseau, this extremely refined library is a perfect example of the Louis XVI style (1774). The austere appearance of the bookcases, in which the door panels are concealed by a set of false decorative backs, is countered by the gay Chinese motifs on the upholstery and the curtains. Next to Riesener's flat-top desk stands the vast mahogany table where the King spent many enjoyable hours correcting geographical maps.

Salon des Porcelaines (**14**) – This room was used as the Hunters' Dining Hall under Louis XV, and from 1769 to 1789 under Louis XVI. It houses numerous exhibits of Sèvres porcelain, painted after drawings by Oudry. The whole collection was commissioned by Louis XVI.

Salon des Jeux de Louis XVI (**15**) – From the doorway admire the full effect of this perfect vignette of 18C furniture and ornamental art: corner cupboards by Riesener (1774), set of chairs by Boulard, curtains and upholstery in rich crimson and gold brocade.

Walk down the Louis-Philippe staircase ⑦ and leave by the North Arcade (a public passageway leading through to the park). The room on the ground floor houses a miniature replica of the Ambassador's Staircase (Escalier des Ambassadeurs) under the Louis-Philippe staircase.

★★OPÉRA ROYAL

Gabriel started work on the opera house in 1768 and completed it in time for the wedding ceremony of Marie-Antoinette and the future King Louis XVI in 1770. It was the first oval-shaped opera house in France and although it was built during the reign of Louis XV, its decoration was later to be termed Louis XVI. Pajou's work, inspired by the classical models of Antiquity, remains surprisingly modern looking. The court engineer Arnoult designed the sophisticated machinery required for the new opera house. For banquets and formal receptions, the floor of the stalls and of the circle could be raised level with the stage. This auditorium – its interior decoration made entirely of wood – enjoys excellent acoustics and can seat 700. The seating capacity could virtually be doubled by means of additional galleries set up on the stage.

In the middle of the circle lies the royal box, fronted by a mobile grid and surmounted by an elegant alcove. A number of other boxes, also enclosed by grilles, may be seen up above in the flies.

The low-relief sculptures adorning the boxes were executed by Pajou. They represent the gods of Mount Olympus (dress circle), groups of children and the signs of the Zodiac (upper circle).

Although initially reserved for members of the court, the opera house at Versailles was later used for lavish receptions organised on the occasion of official visits. A number of foreign rulers were received at the palace, including the King of Sweden (1784), Marie-Antoinette's brother the Emperor Joseph II (1777 and 1781) and Queen Victoria (1855). The sessions of the National Assembly were held in the Royal Opera between 1871 and 1875. It was here that the Wallon Amendment was voted on 30 January 1875, laying the foundation stone of the Third Republic. The latest restoration ended in 1957 and was marked by an official reception in honour of Queen Elizabeth II and Prince Philip.

LES GRANDES HEURES DU PARLEMENT ⊘

Audio-guided tour, Entrance P from the Jardins du parterre du Midi.

Versailles is a magnificent reminder of life during the days of the monarchy; it has also been the cradle of French democracy since 1789. Even now, the semicircular chamber in the south wing accommodates members of Parliament when changes are made to the Constitution. A permanent exhibition illustrates the history of French democracy and the parliamentary systems in various countries throughout the world. An audio-visual show (20min) sums up the main debates which have marked France's national and international politics.

★CABINETS INTÉRIEURS DE LA REINE (QUEEN'S PRIVATE SUITE)

These somewhat cramped apartments looking onto two inner courtyards were used as a daytime retreat by the queens of France. Unlike the king, the queen was not allowed to live anywhere but in her State Apartments. The 18C decoration and layout were designed by Marie-Antoinette, who gave the suite a delicate, feminine touch.

Cabinet doré (**16**) – The panelling by the Rousseau brothers marks the revival of Antique motifs: frieze with rosettes, sphinx, trivets, small censers… A lovely chandelier features among the magnificent bronze works. The commode was made by Riesener. Naderman's harp reminds visitors that the Queen was an enthusiastic musician in her spare time; she would often play with Grétry, Gluck or even his rival Piccinni. It was in this cabinet that Mme Vigée-Lebrun worked on her portrait of Marie-Antoinette.

Bibliothèque (**17**) – Note the drawer handles in the shape of a two-headed eagle, the emblem of the House of Hapsburg.

Méridienne (**18**) – This little octagonal boudoir was used for resting by Marie-Antoinette. It was designed in 1781 by the Queen's architect Mique in honour of the birth of the first dauphin. The decoration evokes romance and the period leading up to the dauphin's birth: lilies, hearts pierced with arrows and the famous dolphin.

The boudoir – embellished with blue silk hangings – is furnished with two arm-chairs by Georges Jacob and the original day couch.

Two of the many prestigious works of art given to the Queen are exhibited here: a clock presented by the City of Paris and a table on which the top is made of petrified wood (a present from one of Marie-Antoinette's sisters).

The second floor houses Marie-Antoinette's Apartment (open by prior arrangement).

APPARTEMENT DE MADAME DE MAINTENON

Inquire in advance.

This suite was located away from the throngs of courtiers but next to the King's apartments, reflecting a situation enforced by the King during the last 32 years of his reign, with a view to establishing an atmosphere of tact and mutual respect. The **Grand Cabinet** (**19**) was a private drawing room decorated with red hangings where Mme De Maintenon entertained members of the royal family – her favourite was the Duchess of Burgundy – and where Racine recited his famous plays *Esther* and *Athalie*.

★PETITS CABINETS DU ROI (KING'S PRIVATE APARTMENTS)

A tour of these apartments is recommended to visitors who are already acquainted with Versailles and who have a particular interest in 18C decorative art.

Louis XV did not share the taste for publicity which had been such a dominant trait of the Sun King's personality. Consequently he created a suite of private apartments to which he could retire and receive his mistresses, close friends and relatives. Some of the rooms overlooked the inner courts, others were located in the attics. They were approached by a series of narrow passages and staircases. In the privacy of these rooms the King would read, study, carve ivory and wooden pieces or eat on the tiny roof-top terrace, surrounded by tubs of flowers and several delightful aviaries. The decoration of these apartments was renewed at regular intervals – as were their occupants. Four of the rooms housed Mme De Pompadour's first suite. Louis XVI used the rooms overlooking the Cour des Cerfs when he wished to study or indulge in one of his favourite pastimes.

Appartement de Madame de Pompadour – This was the first suite occupied by Louis XV's mistress between 1745 and 1750. The Grand Cabinet features splendid carved woodwork by Verberckt.

Appartement de Madame du Barry – *2nd floor.*
The wooden panelling has been meticulously restored to its original colours. The suite looks out onto the Cour des Cerfs and the Cour au Marbre. It consists of a bathroom, a bedroom, a library and a **corner drawing room** (**20**) which was one of Louis XV's favourite haunts; he would enjoy sitting here and gazing out at the town of Versailles nestling among wooded slopes.

Appartements des ducs de Maurepas et Villequier – *2nd floor.*
These apartments were occupied by two ministers of Louis XVI. The decoration appears rather austere when compared to that of the royal suites. Most of the furniture was donated by the Duke and Duchess of Windsor.

The success which the château enjoys leads to overcrowding, which can be unpleasant. This problem already existed during the reign of the Sun King: courtiers in sedan chairs, tradesmen, footmen, musicians and workers cluttered the corridors of the palace and a great number of Swiss guards were required to keep this colourful crowd under control.

★★MUSEUM

The museum houses several thousand paintings and sculptures which present French history from the 17C to the 19C.

17C GALLERIES – *See the Tour of the Grands Appartements.*

★★★18C GALLERIES

Appartements du Dauphin et de la Dauphine – *See the Tour of the "Chambre du Roi".*

Galerie basse – Divided into apartments under Louis XVI and partly restored under Louis-Philippe, the gallery now stands as it did under Louis XIV. From 1782 to 1789 the rooms in this gallery were used by Marie-Antoinette and her children.

Appartement de Madame Victoire – The Sun King's former bathroom and its two marble piscinae underwent several alterations before being used as the antechamber to this suite, occupied by the fourth daughter of Louis XV.

Salle des Hocquetons

The **Grand Cabinet** (**30**) is an exquisite corner room with a delightful carved cornice and panelling by Verberckt. It has retained its original fireplace.

Mme Victoire's former **bedroom** (**31**) has been furnished with some outstanding pieces, set off by the newly restored summer hangings.

Appartement de Madame Adélaïde – These rooms housed the second suite of Mme De Pompadour, who died here in 1764. Five years later, Mme Adélaïde moved into the suite, which consisted of a private cabinet, a bedroom and a grand cabinet. The **Salle des Hocquetons** (**32**) was an annexe adjoining the former Ambassadors' Staircase, destroyed in 1752. The stately proportions of this room give an idea of how magnificent the flight of stairs once looked. Note the huge **clock**★ by Passement and Roque with bronze ornamentation by Germain; it dates from 1754 and illustrates the creation of the world.

The last rooms, overlooking the Cour de Marbre, housed the apartments of the Captain of the Guard.

The ground-floor suite of Marie-Antoinette, which she occupied during her last days at Versailles, has been partly recreated but as for the furniture in the bedroom and the bathroom (**33**) only the console table and the recently re-embroidered bedspread date from her period.

Revolution Consulate and Empire

South attic and Chimay attic on two floors (by appointment only)

A detailed exhibition of documents, drawings, engravings, watercolours and paintings, surrounded by wall-hangings of corresponding periods, brings to life the historic encounters, anecdotes, battles, ceremonies and the great figures of the Napoleonic period and the Bonaparte family who changed the course of French history.

19C GALLERIES

North attic on two floors (by appointment only)

Galleries dedicated to the Restoration, the July Monarchy, the Second Empire and the Third Republic – Numerous painting illustrate the major events which marked this period of French history: the *Entente Cordiale*, cemented with the official visits of Louis-Philippe and Queen Victoria; the conquest of Algeria; the Revolutions of 1830 and 1848; the Franco-Prussian War of 1870 and the Paris Commune; the signing of the Treaty of Versailles. Note the portraits of Louis XVIII, Charles X, Louis-Philippe and his family, Napoleon III and Eugénie.

Parc du château de VERSAILLES★★★

Michelin map 101 folds 22, 23, 106 folds 17, 18 or 237 folds 16, 17
Michelin plan 22

The park, for ever linked to the name of André Le Nôtre (1613-1700), can be visited on foot of course, but also in a barouche or even in a rowing boat along the Grand Canal. The gardens of the château and of the Trianons are extremely refined and best seen when the Grandes Eaux (fountains) are in operation.

Unfortunately the park was severely damaged by the storms which hit the Île-de-France region in December 1999, when thousands of trees were brought down.

The palace was built on top of a small hillock consolidated by vast loads of earth. The terrace rises above the Latona Basin by a height of 10.5m/35ft, the Apollo Basin by 30m/100ft, the Grand Canal by 32m/105ft and the Orangery by 17m/56ft.

The **gardens** cover an approximate area of 100ha/250 acres and the distance between the palace and their perimeter (the Apollo Basin) is about 950m/1 040yd.

Beyond the actual gardens of Versailles, the Versailles estate used to incorporate the **Petit Parc**, which already included the Grand Canal and the Trianon. Under the Second Empire its area gradually shrank from 1 700ha/4 200 acres to 600ha/2 000 acres; a large part of this land was used as a terrain for military training. The royal gates at the exit of the Petit Parc marked the entrance to the **Grand Parc**, a 6 000ha/15 000 acres hunting reserve surrounded by 43km/27mi of walls punctuated by a series of 25 "royal" gates. The Grand Parc was entirely divided up during the Revolution.

To ensure that all the **flower beds** would be in full bloom during the month of August, the gardeners had to supply 150 000 plants, including 32 000 for the North Parterre, 35 000 for the South Parterre and 35 000 for the Latona beds. During the reign of Louis XIV, the plants which were all in pots would be changed up to 15 times a year.

★★★GARDENS

Quick tour: allow 3hr

The terrace and parterres provide a perfect balance to the monumental front of the palace which screens the town of Versailles. Lower down, the lawns and the Grand Canal cut across the middle of the grounds, creating a sweeping perspective that extends into the far distance.

> **ENJOY A MEAL IN THE SPLENDOUR OF THE PARK**
>
> **La Flotille** – Parc du Château, Grand Canal – ☎ 01 39 51 41 58 – closed evenings – booking essential Sun – 135/190F. On the edge of the Grand Canal, in the château park, this small late-19C pavilion and its glass surround resembles an open-air café. It proposes two options, restaurant and brasserie, depending on your mood. The food is decent but the terrace makes all the difference in summer!

Numerous groves and straight paths are laid out on either side of this central axis. Their asymmetrical designs, basins and sculptures add a touch of variety to Le Nôtre's formal layout. The 300 sculptures which adorn the park make it one of the biggest open-air museums of classical sculpture.

The view towards the south extends to the heights of Satory.

Axe du Soleil

★★**Parterre d'eau** – The two huge basins that front the stately palace constitute a sort of aquatic esplanade where the three main perspectives meet: the central view, and the line along the North and South Parterres. The extremities of the basins bear allegorical statues of French rivers (portrayed as men) and their tributaries (portrayed as women). Along their sides are arranged groups of children at play, alternating with reclining water nymphs. These outstanding bronze sculptures were made by the Keller brothers.

Degré de Latone (Latona Staircase) – An imposing flight of steps and a double ramp flanked with yew trees and replicas of antique statues lead from the Parterres d'Eau down to the Bassin de Latone. From the top of the steps admire the wonderful **view**★★★ of the gardens and the Grande Perspective.

The two fountains – These stand to the left and the right of the steps. They were originally called the *Cabinets d'animaux* on account of the bronze works depicting dogs fighting wild beasts. They were named after the most striking statue of the three standing on the edge of the basins.

The Point du Jour (1) – Dawn – whose head is crowned by a star – is the work of Gaspard Marsy. The other two figures are Water and Spring.

★**Diane chasseresse (2)** – Le Hongre's statue, Air, is the one looking in the direction of Dawn. At its side stands the hunting goddess Diana, by Desjardins. The third statue was carved by Marsy and represents Venus, the goddess of love. These sculptures are among the finest works in the gardens.

ÉTOILE ROYALE

Gally

Allée

de

Allée

de

la

Ceinture

ravers

de

Bouillons

Av.

Allée

d

de

Gally

de

Fontenay

de

Avenue

de

Bailly

St-Cyr

Rond

d'Eau

du

Allée

du Rond

des

Étoile des
Ha!! Ha!!

Ha!!   Ha!!

Allée

Reine

Rendez-vous

Petite
Étoile

Allée

Grand
Carré

du

Grande
Étoile

Grand
Mail

la

Étoile de
la Reine

★ Gardens

21

22

20

GRAND
TRIANON ★★

Châteauneuf

de

Aée

de

du

Arboretum

National

de   Chèvreloup

Jardin
du Roi

Nursery
gardens

le Trèfle

Ice-houses

P

Salon Frais

Théâtre de
la Reine

Belvédère

Orangerie

Allée

Pavillon
Français ★

LES
RIANONS ★★

de   du Petit

Trianon

Trianons

PETIT TRIANON ★★

Farm

LE HAMEAU ★★

★★ Garden

Grand
Lac

Marlborough Memorial
and dairy

Temple de
l'Amour

Mill

Dovecote

Maison de
la Reine

Allée

St-Antoine

P

Porte St-Antoine

ST GERMAIN A 13

de

St-Antoine

le Chesnay

Petite

Avenue

St-Antoine

D 186

Boulevard

N

PARK

0   400 m

VERSAILLES

All these statues were part of the massive ensemble commissioned by Colbert in 1674: a total of 30 marble sculptures, including 24 statues divided into six themes. The four Elements, the four Times of Day, the four Poems, the four Seasons, the four Continents and the four Temperaments were to be installed on the terrace fronting the château. The initial plan was however never carried out; the court architects thought it a pity to break the classical lines of the esplanade with a row of great pale figures. Finally it was decided to adopt a more original approach: most of the bronze statues were cast as reclining figures and arranged around the basins while the others were set out in appropriate spots among the flower beds.

★**Bassin de Latone** (Latona Basin) – This vast composition by Marsy was the very first marble sculpture to grace the gardens of Versailles (1670). It tells the story of Latona (the statue is a mould of the original), the mother of Apollo and Diana, who was showered with insults by the peasants of Lycea and prevented from quenching her thirst. She appealed to Jupiter, the father of her children, who promptly avenged the offence by turning the culprits into aquatic animals. The Bassins des Lézards on the side picture the early stages of the metamorphosis... Originally the statue of Latona looked towards the palace, a clear indication of how the King viewed the public or private insults concerning his love life.

At the foot of the steps, to the right, lies the charming **Nymph with a Shell** (**3**), a modern replica of Coysevox' statue. The original work – inspired by the statues of Antiquity – has been moved to the Louvre.

★★**Tapis Vert** – The "Green Carpet" has been entirely replanted according to Le Nôtre's plans. From the foot of the Esplanade de Latone, admire the Axe du Soleil leading up to the palace and extending beyond the Tapis Vert, towards the Grand Canal.

This long stretch of lawn is lined with a superb collection of ornamental vases and statues, among them Cyparissus and his pet stag by Flamen and Poulletier's Dido. A stroll along the Allée du Midi leads to the **Richelieu Venus** (**4**), sculpted by Le Gros after an Antique bust that featured among the Cardinal's private collections.

Leave the Tapis Vert and enter the Bosquets du Midi.

Bosquets du Midi (South Groves)

★**Bosquet de la Salle de Bal** (**5**) – This elegant grove, also known as Bosquet des Rocailles, was part of Le Nôtre's original plans. Shaped as a circular stage, it is surrounded by gentle slopes, grassy banks and tiered rockeries where small cascades tumbled down. This outdoor theatre was used for performances given by members of the court or a corps de ballet.

Bassin de Bacchus (or Bassin de l'Automne) (**6**) – Attributed to Gaspard Marsy. The basins of the Four Seasons are laid out to plans by Le Brun in the form of a quadrangle flanked by the main paths. These groups of lead figures were recently regilded and decorated in "natural tones".

Bosquet de la Reine (**7**) – This grove lies on the site of a former maze and was created in 1775, at the time of the great replanting campaign.

In its centre stand a number of busts and bronze statues cast after Antique models: Aphrodite, a Fighting Gladiator etc. The maple groves are a magnificent sight in autumn.

Bassin du Miroir d'Eau (**8**) – Of the two basins circling the Royal Isle, the larger one began to silt up and Louis XVIII replaced it by a landscape garden, known as the Royal Garden. The only one to survive is the Bassin du Miroir d'Eau, handsomely adorned with statues.

★**Jardin du Roi** – A dazzling sight in summer, when all the flowers are in full bloom, this garden is a welcome change from the formal groves of Versailles. The wonderful central lawn is flanked by a charming selection of rare species of tree.

Bassin de Saturne (or Bassin de l'Hiver) (**9**) – This basin was designed by François Girardon.

★★**Colonnade** – *This grove is usually closed but can be seen quite clearly through the railings.*

Jules Hardouin-Mansart built this circular colonnade in 1684 with the help of 15 fellow sculptors. One of its most pleasing features is the elegant display of multicoloured marble: blue, red, lilac and white. Observe the carved masks on the keystones and, on the spandrels, the delightful groups of children playing musical instruments.

★Bassin d'Apollon (Apollo Basin)

The whole composition was made by Tuby. Apollo the Sun God is portrayed seated in his chariot, surrounded by marine monsters, rising from the ocean waters to bring Light to the Earth. This basin is continued by an esplanade leading to the Grand Canal. It is bordered by statues, parts of which are genuine antiquities (note the cracks where the different fragments join).

The Apollo Basin at Versailles

Bosquets du Nord (North Groves)

Bosquet des Dômes (10) – The grove was named after two pavilions crowned by domes which were designed by Mansart. They were demolished in 1820.
A series of low-relief sculptures adorns the edge of the basin, representing the weapons used in different countries. It has the unmistakably elegant touch of Girardon. Among the fine statues feature two works by Tuby, Acis and Galatea.

★★**Bosquet de l'Encelade (11)** – The stark realism of this recently restored Baroque composition by Marsy contrasts sharply with the other groups dotted around the gardens. A head and two arms is all that is visible of the Titan Enceladus, slowly being dragged down towards the bowels of the earth by the very rocks of Mount Olympus by which the Titan had hoped to reach the sky (a clear warning to Fouquet).

Bassin de l'Obélisque (12) – Designed by Mansart, this raised basin is surrounded by a flight of stone steps and several lawns. When the fountains are in operation, the central sculpture lets out a gigantic spray of water which resembles a liquid obelisk.

Bassin de Flore (or Bassin du Printemps) (13) – Another of the four seasons series by Tuby.

Bassin de Cérès (or Bassin de l'Été) (14) – Made by Regnaudin.

★★**Bosquet des Bains d'Apollon (15)** – *Open only during the fountain display (Grandes Eaux).* Designed by Hubert Robert in 1776, this grove heralded the Anglo-Chinese style which Marie-Antoinette later adopted for the Trianon park. On the edge of a small lake, a charming artificial grotto houses the **Apollo Group★**. Its lush, verdant setting is a far cry from the austere 17C Versailles. The Sun God, tired by the day's exertions, is portrayed resting, waited upon by a group of nymphs (Girardon and Regnaudin). The horses at his side are being groomed by tritons (Marsy and Guérin).

Carrefour des Philosophes (16) – Flanked by impressive statues. The "philosophers" crossroads offer an interesting sideways **view★★** of the palace (north-west corner). The sweeping perspective on the right is lined with a double row of yew trees and a set of bronze statues, including Girardon's Winter.

Bassins de Neptune, du Dragon, Allée d'Eau

★★**Bassin de Neptune** – *Stand in line with the basin, near the statue of Fame.*
This is by far the largest basin in Versailles. Its proportions are wildly extravagant by classical standards and it extends northwards beyond the rectangle formed by the gardens. It was designed by Le Nôtre but acquired its present appearance in 1741, during the reign of Louis XV, when it was enriched by a group of lead statues depicting Neptune and Amphitrite surrounded by various gods and sea monsters (by Adam, Lemoyne and Bouchardon).

Bassin du Dragon (17) – This allegorical sculpture evoking the victory over deep-sea monsters is a direct allusion to the crushing of the Fronde Revolt, symbolised by a wounded dragon. Though the dragon's body is the original, the remaining pieces were recast in 1889.

★**Allée d'Eau or des Marmousets** – A double row of 22 small white-marble basins bears delightful bronze groups of three children, each holding pink marble vessels.

The Parterres and Orangery

Parterre du Nord (North Parterre) – The very first royal suite looked out onto this "terrace of greenery".

Bassin des Nymphes de Diane (18) – The pond is surrounded by fine low-relief carvings by Girardon which inspired 18C and 19C painters such as Renoir.

★★**Parterre Bas** – Close to the groves, along its northern and western boundaries, the terrace is flanked by bronze statues representing the four Continents, four Poems, four Seasons and four Temperaments. The lead **Pyramid Fountain**★ (**19**), made by Girardon from a study by Le Brun, combines grace with originality: dolphins, crayfish and tritons.
At the top of the steps leading to the Parterres d'Eau note the **Knife-grinder**, a bronze replica of a classical statue. Coysevox' **Venus on a Tortoise** – called Venus as a Paragon of Modesty under Louis XIV – is a bronze cast, also inspired by Antique sculpture. The original is exhibited in the Louvre and is among the artist's finest works.

★**Parterres du Midi (South Parterres)** – These flower beds were laid out in front of the queen's apartments. With their vivid blossoms and their pretty boxwood patterns, they are a hymn to Nature. The terrace running along the orangery offers a good **view**★ of the 700m/2275ft long **Pièce d'Eau des Suisses** and, in the far distance, the wooded heights of Satory.

★★**Orangery** – One of Mansart's creations, the orangery forms the foundations of the South Parterre. It extends south by means of two corner pavilions set at right angles which support the colossal **Escalier des Cent-Marches**, a flight of 100 steps. At the time of Louis XIV, the orangery housed 3 000 rare trees in tubs; 2 000 of these were orange trees. Today it contains 1 080 bushes, some of which date back to before the French Revolution. The orangery looks splendid during the summer season, when the orange trees and palm trees (a recent introduction) are brought outside and arranged around the flower beds.

★★LE GRAND CANAL

The Grand Canal, which was completed in 1670, is shaped like a large cross: the long canal is 1 670m/5 480ft long by 62m/204ft wide; the shorter one measures 1 070m/3 500ft long by 80m/263ft wide.
The nearby buildings make up Petite Venise which housed the Venetian gondoliers in charge of the king's fleet (gondolas, models of battleships and merchant ships). Boat trips and the tourist train starting point nearby.

TRIANONS ⊘

★★GRAND TRIANON 1hr

Access on foot – *Avenue de Trianon (1km/0.5mi) starts at the Neptune Gate and leads directly to the Trianons. The avenue starting from the eastern extremity of the Grand Canal also leads there.*

Access by car – *See map above.*
A pavilion known as the Trianon de Porcelaine, faced with blue and white Delft tiling, used to be a quiet, secluded meeting place for Louis XIV and his favourite Mme De Montespan. It stood for 18 years, from 1670 to 1687. When Mme De Montespan fell from favour, the pavilion deteriorated and was eventually taken down. In just six months, Jules Hardouin-Mansart completed the Trianon de Marbre, a retreat built by Louis XIV exclusively for the royal family.
It was stripped of its furniture during the Revolution. Napoleon I commissioned major renovation work and refurnished the building on the occasion of his marriage to Marie-Louise. The Marble Trianon was restored under Louis-Philippe.
The latest renovation programme took place in 1962 at the instigation of General de Gaulle, who wished to use the Trianon for official receptions.

Marie-Antoinette's oak

Starting from La Flotille Restaurant, walk along allée de la Reine towards Grand Trianon then go down the stone steps to the grove and follow the path. The Queen loved to sit under this oak, the largest and oldest tree in Versailles Park.

★★ **Château** – Walk past the low railings and enter the semicircular courtyard to discover two buildings with a flat terrace roof, joined by an elegant peristyle. Note the delicate colours in the marble with pink overtones. Another wing called Trianon-sous-Bois stands at a right angle to the right-hand gallery, but it is not visible from the court.

The peristyle overlooks both the court and the gardens. It was designed by Robert de Cotte and adopted by Louis XIV despite Mansart's scepticism. It was used for banquets and formal receptions.

Apartments – The austere interior decoration has changed very little since the days of Louis XIV. The apartments were occupied by Napoleon and Louis-Philippe and their respective families. The furniture is either Empire, Restoration or Louis-Philippe and the paintings were by 17C French artists.

The Salon des Glaces in the left pavilion was used as a council chamber. Admire the splendid Empire furniture and the lavish silk hangings, rewoven according to the original pattern ordered by Marie-Antoinette (the four Continents of the World).

The bedroom contains the bed Napoleon commissioned for his apartments at the Tuileries: it was later altered for Louis-Philippe's use. The wall put in by Bonaparte level with the columns has been dismantled and the room has been restored to its original size. The reception rooms in the right wing were remodelled by Louis-Philippe, who gave them a more personal touch. These salons are enhanced by a collection of paintings by famous 17C French artists, dedicated to mythological subjects.

In Louis XIV's former Music Room, the musicians' loggias are enclosed by a series of shutters.

Louis-Philippe created a family drawing room, in which the two tables feature numbered drawers reserved for the princesses' needlework.

The Salon des Malachites was first the Sun King's Grand Cabinet and then the bedroom of the Duchess of Burgundy. It owes its name to the various objects encrusted with malachite given to Napoleon by Csar Alexander I following their talks in Tilsit (1807): basins, candelabra, bookcase etc. Malachite is a green semi-precious stone found in Siberia, and is easy to polish.

The north-facing drawing room houses four paintings representing the early days of Versailles, following the plans drawn up by Mansart (display of documents showing the palace and the grounds). The two filing cabinets (1810) and the console table (1806) were made by Jacob Desmalter from a drawing by Charles Percier.

The Salon des Sources – where Napoleon kept his various maps and plans – leads to the Imperial Suite *(open on request)*.

Placed at a right angle, the **Gallery**★ houses an extremely precious collection of 24 paintings by Cotelle. They conjure up a vivid picture of the palace and its stately grounds at the time of Louis XIV. The lovely Empire chandeliers were manufactured in the Montcenis glassworks in the Burgundian town of Le Creusot. At the end of the Gallery, the luminous Salon des Jardins features a fine set of chairs from the Château de Meudon.

★ **Gardens** – They derive their simple charm from the impressive displays of flower beds and the absence of allegorical meanings. Some of the flowers in fashion during the 17C and 18C, such as mayweeds... have now been reintroduced thanks to the research done by the gardeners in charge of the Trianon Gardens.

The terrace of the Lower Gardens *(Jardins Bas)* (**20**) commands a good view of the Lower Basin *(Bassin Bas)* (**21**), which is reached via a horse-shoe staircase, and of the Grand Canal beyond, seen from the side.

Beyond the parterres lies a charming wood featuring fine avenues, rows of stately trees and several small ponds *(best seen when the Trianon fountains are playing)*. The only sculpture with a mythological theme in the Trianon Gardens is Mansart's Buffet d'Eau (**22**), completed in 1703. It pictures the Sea God Neptune and Amphitrite, surrounded by a cluster of smaller statues.

Skirt Trianon-sous-Bois and walk through what was once the king's private garden. It is flanked by two square pavilions which housed the apartments of Mme De Maintenon and Louis XIV towards the end of the Sun King's reign.

To reach the Petit Trianon, cross the bridge erected by Napoleon I, known as Pont de Réunion.

★★ PETIT TRIANON *30min*

It was Louis XV's love of gardening and farming that prompted the construction of the Petit Trianon. The King gave orders to build a menagerie (experimental farm) and commissioned his "botanical expert" Claude Richard to design the greenhouses and botanical gardens. A College of Botanical Science was founded and entrusted to the famous botanist Bernard de Jussieu.

Gabriel finished the Petit Trianon in 1768, shortly before Louis XV's reign ended. Mme De Pompadour, the woman behind the initial project, never saw the château.

Louis XVI gave the Petit Trianon to his wife Marie-Antoinette. The Queen would often come here with her children and her sister-in-law Mme Elisabeth, relieved to get away from court intrigues and the formal etiquette that was expected from a woman of her rank. She insisted on a number of changes: the grounds were redesigned, a theatre was built and Jussieu's botanical gardens, complete with their experimental hothouses, were destroyed. On 5 October 1789 the Queen was resting in a grotto near the Belvedere when a messenger informed her that the mob was marching on Versailles. She left Trianon in great haste and was never to return.

Later, Empress Eugénie, who felt great sympathy for Marie-Antoinette, formed a collection of her personal mementoes and had the château refurnished in 1867.

★**Pavillon français** – This pavilion was built by Gabriel for Louis XV and Mme De Pompadour in 1750. It is surrounded by an enchanting formal garden. The cornice features a sculpted frieze representing the farm animals that were raised on the estate. Visitors can get a glimpse of the highly refined interior decoration through the large French windows.

The cool **Summer house** at the southern end of the gardens was rebuilt in 1982.

★★**Château** – The façade facing the courtyard is austere in the extreme. It overlooks the formal gardens and is a perfect example of Gabriel's talent as well as a masterpiece of Louis XVI's style; the four regularly spaced columns are crowned by a balustrade and two fine flights of steps lead from the terrace down to the gardens.

Enter the château and walk up the imposing flight of stone stairs lit by an old-fashioned lantern. The wrought-iron banisters are stamped with a decorative monogram, believed to be that of Marie-Antoinette.

First Floor Apartments – Guibert's craftsmanship is evident in the superb **panelling**★★ in the dining room and the drawing room. The decoration of the dining room presents fruit, flower and foliage motifs, set off against a pale green background, a welcome change from the "Trianon grey" prevalent throughout the 19C. The drawing room – partly refurnished by Empress Eugénie in the 19C (chairs, 1790 pianoforte) – houses one of Riesener's greatest achievements, the famous astronomical writing desk (1771).

The furniture in Marie-Antoinette's bedroom was designed by Jacob and adorned with ears of corn. Jacob also designed several pieces for the Comtesse de Balbi; they have been placed in a recently restored boudoir with unusual movable mirrors.

★★**Garden** – This charming Anglo-Chinese garden including a brook, several ornamental ponds, some fine trees and an interesting collection of manmade features was designed by an amateur, the Comte de Caraman, and built by the Queen's architect Mique who received advice from Hubert Robert.

Several of the trees are 150 to 200 years old and some were probably planted by Bernard de Jussieu in his botanical gardens. The oldest of all is a damaged pagoda tree (**23**) planted during the reign of Louis XV, which stands near the north-east corner of the château.

Belvedere or Salon de Musique – This delightful pavilion designed by Mique was also called the Music Room. It overlooks the Petit Lac and the interior decoration offers painted arabesques of the utmost refinement.

Le Petit Trianon

Off the winding paths of the landscape garden lies the Jardin Charpentier, planted with remarkable trees. Go on to the grounds of the Grand Trianon to have a look at the superb Lebanese cedar tree (**24**) near the Bassin au Trèfle, as well as the two entirely restored 17C ice houses standing in the background. Return to the Jardin Charpentier and note the two huge Wellingtonias (**25**) and single fastigiate oak (**26**). Bear left after the orangery to an ancient Siberian elm (**27**) with unusually deep striations. Start walking towards the Hamlet. Before the lake is a tulip tree from Virginia (**28**) and two spinneys of stately swamp cypresses (**29**).

★★**Le Hameau (Hamlet)** – The grounds around the lake (Grand Lac) are dotted with a dozen pretty cottages featuring cob walls and thatched or tiled roofs, inspired by the hamlet at Chantilly. Contrary to popular belief, the Queen was far too steeped in formal protocol to indulge in any farming activities.
The Memorial to Marlborough is a reminder of the popular nursery rhyme, "Chanson de Marlborough", introduced to Louis XVI's court by the Dauphin's nanny. On the way to the Temple de l'Amour, notice a remarkable plane tree (**30**) with thick spread-eagled roots.

Temple de l'Amour – One of Mique's creations (1778), the Temple of Love stands on a tiny islet. In the centre, Bouchardon's statue shows Cupid making his Bow from the Club of Hercules (*original in the Louvre*). The sculpture is fronted by a row of Corinthian columns resting on a circular flight of six steps.

Ville de VERSAILLES★★

Population 87 789
Michelin map 101 fold 23, 106 folds 17, 18 or 237 folds 16, 17 – Michelin plan 22

Access from Paris: *RER C from Invalides station to Versailles Rive-Gauche; SNCF rail link from Gare Montparnasse to Versailles-Chantiers and from Gare St-Lazare to Versailles Rive-Droite.*

The town was built as an annexe with a view to housing the numerous titled and untitled people who served the French court: dukes, ministers, craftsmen, civil servants etc. Owing to its former duties, the town has retained a certain austere charm with its private mansions, imposing churches and attractive collections which amply justify its title of Royal city.

Royal city – In 1671 Louis XIV decided that plots of land would be granted to those citizens who put in a request, in exchange for a levy of five sous for each arpent (3 194m²/3 833sq yd). The new buildings had to conform to the rules laid down by the Service des Bâtiments du Roi, a building commission answerable to the court. The purpose of these measures was to achieve architectural unity. Moreover, in order that the palace might continue to dominate the area, the roofs of the village houses were not to exceed the height of the Cour de Marbre. Today very little remains of these 17C buildings. Most of the old town was completed in the 18C, enlarged and renovated in the 19C.

Parliamentary town – France's defeat in the 1870-71 Franco-Prussian War enabled Versailles to regain its political role as the seat of the French government. The population rose from 40 000 to 50 000 in a matter of days. Senators and members of the National Assembly, who were unable to find lodgings in town, camped with government ministers at the château which also housed the Banque de France and other official institutions. The president and head of the government found room in the *préfecture*. This situation lasted until 1879, when Parliament returned to the capital. An amphitheatre was built to house it in the middle of the south wing. During the third and fourth republics, presidential elections were held there. Today the amphitheatre is only used for revising the constitution when both houses are required to sit together.

Versailles today – More than 200 years after the end of absolute monarchy in France, there are very few 17C houses left in Versailles: most of the old town dates from the 18C with 19C alterations. Having long suffered from being too close to Paris, Versailles has nevertheless managed to develop its own cultural programme and to enhance its exceptional site.

SIGHTS

Rue de l'Indépendance-Américaine – In the 18C this street housed many buildings occupied by ministries and public services, in particular the Grand Commun – now the Military Hospital – which lodged a total of 1 500 officials, cooks etc. At no 5 stands the former **Ministry of the Navy and Foreign Affairs**, fronted by a magnificent gate crowned by statues of Peace and War. It was here that an alliance was signed (1762) between France and the American "insurrectionaries", acting as a prelude to the 1783 treaties granting the independence of the United States. The mansion has been made into a public library (**bibliothèque municipale**) ⊙ .

Eating out

MID-RANGE

La Bodega – *4 bis rue de la Paroisse* – ☎ *01 30 21 01 73* – *closed Mon lunchtime and Sun* – *booking essential Sat-Sun* – *100/300F*. This is the place to come to if you are beginning to miss your last holiday in Spain. You will be able to sample tapas, caracoles and many other local specialities with exotic names. At weekends, night owls can stay up for longer by frequenting the Bagheera piano bar (see below).

Valmont – *20 rue au Pain* – ☎ *01 39 51 39 00* – *closed Sun evening and Mon* – *118/160F*. This prettily restored old house on place des Halles will undoubtedly catch your eye... Venture inside and you will soon be conquered by the excellent service, charming decoration, a clever blend of tradition and modernity, elegantly laid tables and succulent dishes. Definitely something to look forward to.

L'Annexe – *20 rue au Pain* – ☎ *01 39 50 33 00* – *closed Mon lunchtime and Sun* – *148F*. This restaurant set up on the market square specialises in fish and seafood, as illustrated by the mural paintings, the only touch of fantasy. A great meeting place among locals... for obvious reasons!

Au Chapeau Gris – *7 rue Hoche* – ☎ *01 39 50 10 81* – *chapeaugris@ wanadoo.fr* – *closed July, Tues evening and Wed* – *booking essential* – *160/200F*. Au Chapeau Gris is literally an institution, said to date back to the Age of Enlightenment. A grand ambience and decor fit for Versailles are the setting for traditional French cuisine which never goes out of fashion. One of Versailles' most sought-after restaurants...

Le Potager du Roy – *1 rue du Maréchal-Joffre* – ☎ *01 39 50 35 34* – *closed lunchtime, Sat, Sun evening and Mon* – *175/280F*. In this restaurant near the château, meals are lovingly prepared with fresh ingredients by the chef, whose expertise and initiative must be applauded. Excellent value for money.

LUXURY

Cuisine Bourgeoise – 10 boulevard du Roi – ☎ 01 39 53 11 38 – closed 5-28 Aug, Sat lunchtime, Sun and Mon – 250/310F. Feeling hungry in Versailles? Then walk into this brasserie-style restaurant, which provides unpretentious cuisine made with quality produce, presented by charming hosts. Three good reasons to stay. There are cheaper lunchtime menus for tight budgets.

Where to stay

MODERATE

Home St-Louis – 28 rue St-Louis – ☎ 01 39 50 23 55 – 25 rooms 220/350F – ☎ 35F. This hotel near the château has simply decorated, well-kept rooms at affordable prices. Who could ask for more?

LUXURY

Résidence du Berry – 14 rue d'Anjou – ☎ 01 39 49 07 07 – 38 rooms from 520F – ☎ 55F. This 18C building in the St-Louis district has been entirely renovated by Les Bâtiments de France. The comfortable bedrooms with antique beams have been refurbished and boast high-quality materials. In summer, breakfast is served on the veranda opening onto a patio.

Hôtel Versailles – *7 rue Ste-Anne (Petite place)* – ☎ *01 39 50 64 65* – ◘ – *46 rooms from 520F* – ☎ *57F*. In a quiet street, a short walk from the château, stands this restored hotel with large, sun-filled rooms decorated in a contemporary style with a slight Art Deco touch. Cosy bar and pretty terrace where breakfast is served in high season. On the whole, the prices are reasonable.

Sofitel Château de Versailles – *2 bis avenue de Paris* – ☎ *01 39 07 46 46* – ◘ – *146 rooms from 1 400F* – ☎ *115F* – *restaurant 175F*. Access to this modern hotel is through a listed 17C doorway opening onto the avenue leading to the château. The lofty rooms are well-appointed and efficiently soundproofed. Note the drawing room under its glass cupola and the cosy bar with live music every evening.

On the town

Bagheera – *4 bis rue de la Paroisse* – ☎ *01 30 21 01 73* – *Fri-Sat 10pm-2am*. This piano bar set up in a small cellar is frequented by music lovers who come here to listen to some jazz while they sample one of the many inventive cocktails prepared by the barman. The walls carry photographs of famous composers and musicians such as Miles, Chet and Dexter and the reputation of the place has been gained by word of mouth. Iberian restaurant with *tapas* on the ground floor.

Fenêtres sur Cour – *Passage de la Geôle – Quartier des Antiquaires – ☎ 01 39 51 97 77 – Mon-Wed 9.30am-4pm, Thur-Sun 9.30am-11pm – closed 3 weeks in Aug*. Installed beneath a huge glass roof, this restaurant, which also operates as a tea room, has chosen to take up residence in the area frequented by antique dealers. This choice is echoed in the somewhat eccentric and varied decoration: a profusion of lamps, carpets, tiles, plaster casts, statues, busts, paintings and other items picked up from markets. Note the excellent wine list. In summer, meals are served out doors on place de la Geôle.

Place du Marché – The four side streets running along the market square (where the best produce can be found in all seasons) form a pleasant itinerary dotted with bars (À la Gaieté, Le Franco-Belge, Le Ducis), pancake restaurants, pizzerias and restaurants. During the summer season, all these establishments set up chairs on their sunny terraces, to the delight of both tourists and local residents.

Pièce d'eau des Suisses – *Route de St-Cyr (D 10)*. Separated from the park by the road, this expanse of water prolongs the Orangery vista to the foot of the wooded Satory heights. At the end stands the equestrian statue of Louis XIV.

Parc Balbi – *12 rue du Maréchal-Joffre*. This small Anglo-Chinese garden was commissioned for the Countess of Balbi. Gradually restored, the park has regained the refined charm of a romantic garden so much appreciated in the 18C.

Quartier St-Louis – The St-Louis district south of avenue de Sceaux contains the official buildings of the former ministries, the 17C Real Tennis Court or **Jeu de Paume** ⊙ where the National Assembly took their famous oath on 20 June 1789, "old Versailles" built around the former village square and an 18C estate on the former Parc aux Cerfs, located close to Satory heights.

Carrés St-Louis – Louis XV gave orders to create a "shopping area" near St Louis' Church, along the streets presently named rue Royale and rue d'Anjou (1755). The shops – featuring mansard roofs – were arranged around four small squares known as *carrés*: Carré au Puits, Carré à l'Avoine, Carré à la Fontaine, Carré à la Terre. Some of these houses still exist and restoration work is in progress.

★**Cathédrale St-Louis** – St Louis' Cathedral was built in 1754 to serve the "old Versailles" and the Parc aux Cerfs, and lies close to the King's Vegetable Garden *(Potager du Roi)*. The west front with its two towers, and the dome above the transept crossing are reminiscent of the great classical churches.

The noble, austere nave still contains its organ and collection of 18C paintings, but the most interesting furnishings are the religious works dating from the 19C.

Quartier Notre-Dame – The Notre-Dame district features the oldest church in Versailles and a few houses built under Louis XIV, situated near the Notre-Dame market place which forms, with rue de la Paroisse, the town's main shopping centre.

Église Notre-Dame – The church built in rue Dauphine – renamed rue Hoche – by Jules Hardouin-Mansart in 1686 was the parish church of the king and his court. The king would attend Solemn Masses such as Corpus Christi here. The requirements of the Service des Bâtiments du Roi explain why the church presents a flattened front flanked by truncated towers.

A large open-work dome graces the church interior, characterised by Doric embellishments. The nave *(explanatory notices)* is surrounded by 12 carved medallions representing Apostles and figures from the New Testament; these were the works presented by the new entrants to the Académie Royale de Sculpture et de Peinture between 1657 and 1689. The axial chapel – the chapel of the Blessed Sacrament – houses the *Assumption*, a 16C painting by Michel Corneille.

★**Potager du Roi** – *6 rue Hardy, École nationale supérieure du paysage*. This "kitchen garden" was commissioned by Louis XIV from **JB Quintinie** (1624-88) to supply the king's table with a variety of fruit and vegetables many of which are now quite rare many of which are now quite rare. The result amounted to 29 separate gardens surrounding a large central square and protected by walls and terraces. The kitchen garden has survived and its produce is sold in a shop on the grounds.

★Musée Lambinet ⓒ – This museum is housed in the wood-panelled drawing rooms of the charming Hôtel Lambinet built in 1750 for Joseph-Barnabé Porchon, building contractor to the king, whose initials can be seen in the wrought iron-work on the balcony in the middle of the pleasing façade.

The atmosphere of an 18C town house is recreated by the period furniture, paintings and sculptures (Pajou, Houdon). At the same time, the museum illustrates the history of Versailles through numerous objects and documents, including a ceramics collection with a large number of pieces of Parisian porcelain from the last quarter of the 18C, engraved copper plates used to print the calico known as *toile de Jouy* and the reconstruction of actress Julie Bartet's "green drawing room". She was a member of the Comédie Française and was well known for her roles in Racine's works. Her skill in interpreting Victor Hugo's heroines placed her on a par with Sarah Bernhardt.

The first floor houses an extensive collection of items related to Revolutionary events and figures: the arrest of **Charlotte de Corday**, events in Versailles during 1789 with, in particular, the Declaration of Human Rights, Général Hoche, one of Versailles' most famous sons, and **Marat**.

On the second floor in the room devoted to **religious art★** (Room 23) there are two magnificent **abbesses' crooks** with rock crystal scrolls. They come from Maubuisson and Le Lys.

The museum also contains weaponry made by the famous manufacturer Boutet, the managing director of the little-known **Manufacture d'armes de Versailles**. The factory enjoyed an excellent reputation during the days of the Empire for the quality of the workmanship. This is evident in the collection of ceremonial arms (sabres, rifles) and the very fine boxed pistols with accessories said to have belonged to Général Scherer.

After this tour of 17C and 18C Versailles, the last rooms display 19C and 20C works of art: Boilly, Isabey, Carrière, Le Sidaner and Dunoyer de Segonzac.

EXCURSIONS

Arboretum National de Chèvreloup ⓒ – *Leave by D 186 north and turn left before entering Rocquencourt. Opposite the Parly II shopping centre.*
In 1927 a plot of land formerly belonging to the Grand Parc *(see Parc du château de Versailles)* was offered to the Natural History Museum of Paris so that the Botanical Gardens *(Jardin des Plantes)* could enrich their collection of tree species. The first steps were to set up a Tree Centre.
Visitors may tour only the south-east part of the park, planted with clusters and rows of conifers. Several types of horticultural species which do not grow locally are cultivated here: a row of Lawson cypresses, of unusual shapes and sizes; large groups of thujas next to yew trees and weeping conifers. The broad-leaved trees include birches and willow trees at the height of their development. The oldest species of all is one of the pagoda trees planted at the time of Louis XV and restored to life thanks to modern tree surgery.

Haras de Jardy – *2km/1.2mi north-east along N 182. Leave Versailles by avenue de St-Cloud towards Paris.* This huge stud farm, which is the paradise of horses, forms part of an important complex of leisure activities (tennis, golf, riding). The vast park offers fine walks and is the site of numerous showjumping competitions.

VILLENEUVE-D'ASCQ
Population 65 320
Michelin map 51 fold 16 or 236 fold 16 – 8km/5mi east of Lille

In 1970 the *communes* of **Annappes, Flers and Ascq** were grouped together to form Villeneuve-d'Ascq, one of nine new towns in France. The three centres of the old towns have remained hubs of activity.

From the 1960s universities have been located in the Annappes area. The Triolo, Cousinerie, Brigode and Pont de Bois residential and commercial districts developed around the science park (*cité scientifique*). Industries and research centres followed. Today most of the region's universities are located in Villeneuve-d'Ascq, which turns out 10 % of French engineers.

A stroll through the town reveals new concepts in urban living: overhead pedestrian walkways straddle the main roads; residential areas merge into commercial centres; numerous large civic amenities: a 35 000-seater stadium, a cultural centre, museums etc.

The town is linked to the remainder of the Lille conurbation by a network of motorways and an automatic *métro* system: the Val.

The town's name, Ascq, is a reminder of the tragic massacre of 86 patriots on 2 April 1944, which is commemorated by a monument and the **Musée du Souvenir**.

AROUND LAC DU HÉRON

Château de Flers ⊘ – This Flemish castle, built in 1661 is surrounded by a moat once spanned by a draw-bridge. The brick buildings with stone ties, surmounted by stepped gables, house the tourist office and an archeological museum (temporary exhibitions).

Parc et lac du Héron – *The park is accessible from the castle by following the meander of the lake or walking along avenue Champollion.*

🚶 A pleasant stroll beside the lake leads to the mills and the adjacent museum. Next to the traditional **flour mill** (1776) stands the **oil mill** (1743) which was used for processing linseed. In the 19C there were 200 of these oil presses around Lille; this is the last to have survived. Continue to the **Parc archéologique**. This 6ha/15 acre park contains reconstructions of regional dwellings from the Neolithic Era to the end of the Middle Ages: houses, barns, workshops.

Motherhood by Modigliani
(Musée d'Art moderne)

Routhier

SIGHTS

★★ **Musée d'Art moderne** ⊘ – *Leave N 227 at the "Château de Flers" exit.*
Lying by a lawn above Lac du Héron, the huge building by architect Rolland Simounet suggests a set of brick and glass cubes. The sculpture park displays contemporary works: a mobile and a stabile by Alexander Calder, *Southern Cross* (1969) and *Guillotine for Eight People* (1936). Note in particular the *Woman with Open Arms* (1962) by Picasso, an idol made of shingles and cement, which looks both colossal and fragile and seems to be as flexible as a sheet of paper. The foyer leads to the permanent and temporary exhibitions *(right)*, and to the reception and other services *(left)*: library, cafeteria, classrooms used for courses in the plastic arts.

The collection – Roger Dutilleul's collection, which contains over 230 works mainly from the first half of the 20C, was presented to the museum by Geneviève and Jean Masurel, Dutilleul's nephew. Dutilleul made his first acquisitions in 1907 and from the beginning recognised the talent of artists who were not then understood: one of the first paintings he bought was Braque's *Houses and Tree* which had just been refused at the Salon d'Automne.

The collection contains many Fauvist, Cubist, primitive and abstract works. The Fauvists include Rouault,

Derain and Van Dongen (*Pouting Woman* – 1909). Cubism is represented in paintings by **Braque** *(The Factories of Rio Tinto)* and **Picasso** *(Seated Nude, Head of a Woman)*; this section also contains collages: Picasso's *Head of a Man* and Braque's *The Little Scout*. Several works by **Fernand Léger** follow his development from a 1914 landscape to his sketch for a mural (1938), encompassing works such as *Woman with a Bunch of Flowers* and *Still-Life with Fruit Dish*. One room is devoted to **Modigliani**, paintings, drawings and the unique, white marble *Head of a Woman* (1913); this unfinished work denotes the influence of Khmer and African Art. His beguiling portraits reveal subtle plays of line and colour.

Works of abstract art featured are by **Kandinsky, Klee** and **De Staël**. De Staël knew Roger Dutilleul through the painter **Lanskoy**, who was the collector's protégé, and many examples of the latter's work are also on show. Other artists from the Paris School include **Charchoune, Buffet, Chapoval** and **Utrillo**.

Musée des Moulins ⊘ – After visiting the mills, it is interesting to tour the museum managed by a regionally based association Les Amis des Moulins. Exhibits describe the various mechanisms used in the mills, and include the tools used by carpenters, millers, woodcutters etc in the 18C and 19C. There are countless millstones, ranging from a hand-operated prehistoric stone to stones worked by an electric motor.

In June 1915, **Neuville-St-Vaast** further south was captured from the German troops by the 5th Infantry Division led by Général Mangin, after eight days of bloody fighting.

Écomusée du Patrimoine rural et des Métiers traditionnels: le Jardin des Patrimoines – This open-air museum is unique in northern France; it offers visitors the possibility of discovering rural life through the area's architectural heritage preserved in its original setting or reconstructed. Threatened buildings have been reconstructed on sites adapted to their original environment: meadow, orchard, vegetable garden, pond, field. Building sites are set up with the aim to teach and preserve traditional crafts. Every section of the museum schedules arts and crafts activities related to its original function.

Musée du Terroir ⊘ – *Access via rue du 8-Mai.* **Delporte Farm** in the old centre of Annappes is a typical local *cense*, built of Lezennes stone and brick; it now houses the folk museum. In the courtyard and buildings a collection of agricultural tools are displayed, along with traditional workshops: foundry, locksmith's, joinery, saddlery, dairy etc.

The national mill fair takes place every year on the 3rd Sunday in June.

Ferme D'en haut	**F1**	Ferme Verbecque-Courouble	**F6**
Ferme Descamps	**F2**	Forum des Sciences – Centre François Mitterrand	**F7**
Ferme Dupire	**F3**	Monument et musée du Souvenir	**M1**
Ferme Petitprez	**F4**	Musée des Moulins	**M2**
Ferme St-Sauveur	**F5**		

VILLERS-COTTERÊTS

Population 8 402
Michelin map 56 north of fold 13 and fold 3 or 237 fold 8

Villers-Cotterêts is a peaceful little town, almost entirely surrounded by Retz Forest; it was the homeland of the Orléans family until the Revolution and developed owing to the royal passion for hunting. It was the birthplace of Alexandre Dumas senior in 1802.

Birth of the State – In 1535 François I replaced the first 12C royal castle with a Renaissance building and added to the outbuildings which dealt with the management of the royal hunts.
It was here that the King announced the famous Statute of Villers-Cotterêts in 1539 prescribing the substitution of French for Latin in public registers and legal documents. Among its 192 articles it stated that parish priests should keep registers of the parishioners' dates of birth and death; here then, are the foundations of the modern registry system. Previously, except in noble families where records were kept, ordinary people had to rely on the memory of witnesses to prove identity. It was another 250 years (1792) before the keeping of State registers was entrusted to the local authorities.

A Child of the Islands – The first of the three generations – grandfather, father and son – of the famous Dumas family was the son of a Dominican settler, Marquess Davy de la Pailleterie, and Marie-Cessette Dumas, a coloured girl. Thomas-Alexandre assumed his mother's surname and pursued a career in the army where he later rose to become General, but his Republican opinions led to his being disgraced by Napoleon Bonaparte. He retired to Villers-Cotterêts which was his wife's homeland and lived a quiet life until his death, four years after the birth of his son Alexandre, the future novelist.

Alexandre Dumas' Youth – Many hard years passed for the widow and her son; Alexandre entered the study of one of the town's notaries and copied deeds there until he was 20. One day his mother told him that only 253 francs remained; Dumas took 53 francs as his share, left the rest for his mother and headed for Paris. He played billiards, gambling the cost of his fare to the capital, and won which allowed him to arrive in the capital with his nest egg intact. His beautiful handwriting landed him a job in the secretary's office of the Duc d'Orléans, the future King Louis-Philippe. His prodigious literary career was about to begin.

Dumas fils (Dumas junior) – Dumas senior married his neighbour who gave birth to a son in 1824. The child was named Alexandre after his father and, like his father, he became a famous writer. His novel, *La Dame aux camélias*, inspired Verdi's opera *Traviata*.

STROLL THROUGH THE TOWN

In the footsteps of the three Dumas – Place du Docteur-Mouflier, formerly place de la Fontaine, is mentioned in Dumas senior's memoirs. His grandfather's hotel stood on the square as did the lawyer's office where he was employed and Madame Dumas' tobacconist's shop. The writer's **birthplace**, indicated by a plaque, is at 46 rue A.-Dumas. The titles of his most famous works are written on either side of the garage door. Rue A.-Dumas leads to the square of the same name where a statue of the writer by Rodin used to stand; it was unfortunately melted down by the Germans during the First World War. Only his quill pen was saved and is now in the care of the museum. Rue de Bapaume leads from this square to the cemetery where the Dumas' family grave is located. The other statue of Dumas by Bourret stands in the small public garden on rue L.-Lagrange.

The town boasts three lovely fountains: Clapotis, a crouching young maiden by Ferenc Naguy, on place de la Madelon; Fontaine de Diane, a copy of the Louvre Museum's Artemis Agrotera (Diana the Huntress), on rue L'éveillé; and Fontaine de la Coquille on rue Pelet-Otto.

Musée Alexandre-Dumas ⊘ – Three small rooms are dedicated to the famous "Three Dumas": letters, novels paintings, satirical cartoons, busts and objects including the uniform Dumas junior wore as a member of the French Academy.

He was a friend of George Sand and defended the feminist cause. He was elected to the French Academy in 1875.

ALL FOR ONE AND ONE FOR ALL

Hôtel Régent – *26 rue du Général-Mangin* – ☎ *03 23 96 01 46* – *closed Sun from Nov to Mar except public holidays* – 🅿 – *18 rooms 230/410F* – 🛏 *48F*. This former 18C post house has kept its original decor, recalling the horse-drawn carriages that used to stop there. Enter through the porch and admire the paved courtyard and its trough. The large rooms fronting the building are appointed with antique furniture.

ADDITIONAL SIGHT

Château François I ⊘ – In 1806 Napoleon turned the empty château into a workhouse for the *département* of Seine; today it is a retirement home.

Within the courtyard, the east and west sides are bordered by buildings which retain Renaissance features: high attic windows in brick flanked by pillars crowned with urns. At the end stands the main front, with a shallow recessed loggia on the first floor, surmounted by a portrait of King François I.

The **main staircase★** alone is worth a visit; it is a Renaissance masterpiece, a double flight of stairs dating from the period of François I. The carvings on the coffered ceiling – crowned Fs, salamanders, fleurs-de-lis – are from the school of Jean Goujon. The same motifs are used in greater abundance in the State room, which was originally the chapel. The vaulting is concealed by a false ceiling. The stonework of the Renaissance altarpiece remains. At the end of the gallery *(display on local history)* the **King's staircase**, contemporary with the main staircase, has its original decoration of carved mythological scenes from The Dream of Polyphile.

Parc – All that remains of Le Nôtre's work are the outlines of the parterre and the perspective of the Allée Royale. In the middle of this splendid green expanse, one can still see the base of the circular pond. The white gate at the end of the Allée Royale and the Grandes Allées on the right side of the lawn all lead to the forest (footpaths).

EXCURSION

Montgobert – *10km/6mi north-east by N 2 and D 2 (left). Turn onto a small road towards Montgobert.*

Musée du Bois et de l'Outil (Wood and Tool Museum) ⊙ – The museum is housed in the **Château de Montgobert**, on the edge of Retz Forest. The 18C building was originally the property of Pauline Bonaparte and her husband, General Leclerc, who is buried in the park.

On the ground floor traditional woodworking tools used by cartwrights, sawyers, coopers, carpenters, joiners etc are displayed.

The first floor is dedicated to the life and management of the forest; exhibition on the role of the French Forestry Commission *(Office National des Forêts)*.

The second floor focuses on occupations related to wood within the forest (charcoal burning, woodcutting) together with reconstructions of workshops (joinery, spinning mill, dairy etc).

Château d'Oigny-en-Valois – *8km/5mi south-east along D 936 then left on D 1380.* The 15C castle, set in greenery has been in the care of the Pétrel family for the past 30 years.

Jardins – In addition to the arboretum, the rose-beds, the French-style garden, the rockeries, the aromatic park, aquatic and annual plants, the gardens include an astrological map of the sky as seen from the château, with the position of the planets on 1 January 2000 at midnight, as well as the "Églantine du Jardinier" (the gardener's wild rose), nine gardens on the theme of the five senses. A garden museum is housed in the former stables and there is a green boutique.

Mémorial canadien de VIMY★

Michelin map 51 fold 15 or 236 fold 15

Vimy Ridge, which overlooks the mining region, was captured in April 1917 by the four divisions of the Canadian Expeditionary Corps, which was part of the British Third Army under General Allenby.

The Ridge was the strongest defensive position in north-western France and of enormous importance: this 61m/200ft barrier on the plain safeguarded mines and factories which were in production for Germany, and covered the junction of the main Hindenburg Line and the defences stretching north to the coast. Despite the Canadians' great success, however, the German front was not penetrated.

The impressive white stone **memorial** ⊙, the most impressive Canadian memorial in Europe, was the result of a design competition won by a Toronto sculptor who said the idea came to him in a dream; it is made of "*trau*" stone from the Dalmatian coast; its construction began in 1925 and lasted 11 years. The monument rests on a reinforced concrete base weighing 11 000t and 6 000t of limestone were imported from an Italian quarry on the Adriatic in order to erect the shafts and statues. The two great

shafts symbolise the Canadian and French forces; various figures represent Canada, Peace, Justice, Truth, Knowledge... An inscription at the base of the memorial commemorates the Canadian soldiers (over 66 000 of them) who died during the First World War, and the ramparts bear the names of a further 11 000 men missing, presumed dead.

The foot of the memorial offers views over the old mining basin; the ossuary on Notre-Dame de Lorette Hill can be seen to the west.

To the south, on the slope of the hill, a network of Canadian and German trenches, dug-outs and tunnels have been restored. The **Grange Tunnel** was originally 750m/2 430ft long. The area is still littered with shell holes and mine craters.

To the south, **Neuville-St-Vaast** was retrieved from the Germans by the 5th infantry division of General Mangin in June 1915 at the end of eight days of fierce fighting.

G. Crépe/MICHELIN

The Canadian memorial at Vimy

Rolleboise – the Seine meanders through Île-de-France

Pratical information

Planning your trip

When to go

While the beaches of the Opal Coast are spectacular, stretching out for 1km/0.5mi at low tide, the relatively cool weather and the chilly waters of the Channel are generally more appealing for shell-seekers, horse riders, landsailers and kite-flyers than for swimmers. In the winter months, the coast is often buffeted by strong winds. Statistically, June is the sunniest month on the coast, August the warmest. It rains most in November, and least in April (for a total of 170 days per year). Peak summer temperatures usually hover around 25°C/77°F.

Inland, the winters are chilly and darkness falls early in the northern latitudes. As spring turns to summer, the days grow deliciously long and warm; in June the sun lingers until after 10pm.

Spring and autumn provide the opportunity to wander through the valleys of the Aa, Canche, Authie and Somme and the different regional nature parks. Spring in Île-de-France offers a glorious contrast between the vivid yellow of rapeseed fields against the green background of the copses and forests, while autumn in the oak and beech woods of Compiègne, Rambouillet, Sénart or St-Germain is accompanied by the warm colours of changing leaves.

FORMALITIES

Passport– Nationals of countries within the European Union entering France need only a national identity card. Nationals of other countries must be in possession of a valid national **passport**. In case of loss or theft, report to the embassy or consulate and the local police.

Visa – An **entry visa** is required for Canadian and US citizens (for a stay of more than three months) and for Australian and New Zealand citizens. Apply to the French Consulate (visa issued same day; delay if request submitted by mail).
US citizens should obtain the booklet *Safe Trip Abroad* (US$1), which provides useful information on visa requirements, customs regulations, medical care etc for international travellers. Published by the Government Printing Office, it can be ordered by phone – ☏ (202) 512-1800 – or consulted on-line (www. access.gpo.gov).

Customs – Apply to the Customs Office (UK) for a leaflet on customs regulations and the full range of «duty free» allowances; available from HM Customs and Excise, Dorset House, Stamford Street, London SE1 9PS, ☏ 0171 928 3344. The US Customs Service offers a publication *Know before you go* for US citizens: for the office nearest you, consult the phone book, Federal Government, US Treasury (www.customs.ustreas.gov).
There are no customs formalities for holidaymakers bringing their caravans into France for a stay of less than six months. No customs document is necessary for pleasure boats and outboard motors for a stay of less than six months but the registration certificate should be kept on board.
Americans can bring home, tax-free, up to US$400 worth of goods; Canadians up to CND$300; Australians up to AUS$400 and New Zealanders up to NZ$700.
Persons living in a Member State of the European Union are not restricted in regard to purchasing goods for private use, but the recommended allowances for alcoholic beverages and tobacco are as follows:

Spirits (whisky, gin, vodka etc)	10l	Cigarettes	800
Fortified wines (vermouth, ports etc)	20l	Cigarillos	400
Wine (not more than 60 sparkling)	90l	Cigars	200
Beer	110l	Smoking tobacco	1kg

EMBASSIES AND CONSULATES

Australia Embassy 4 rue Jean-Rey, 75015 Paris
 ☎ 01 40 59 33 00 – Fax 01 40 59 33 10.

Canada Embassy 35 avenue Montaigne, 75008 Paris
 ☎ 01 44 43 29 00 – Fax 01 44 43 29 99.

 Consulate 30 avenue Emile Zola, 59000 Lille
 ☎ 03 20 14 05 78

Eire Embassy 4 rue Rude, 75016 Paris
 ☎ 01 44 17 67 00 – Fax 01 44 17 67 50.

New Zealand Embassy 7 ter rue Léonard-de-Vinci, 75016 Paris
 ☎ 01 45 01 43 43 – Fax 01 45 01 43 44.

South Africa Embassy 59, quai d'Orsay, 75007 Paris
 ☎ 01 53 59 23 23 – Fax 01 53 59 23 33

UK Embassy 35 rue du Faubourg St-Honoré, 75008 Paris
 ☎ 01 44 51 31 00 – Fax 01 44 51 31 27.

 Consulate 16 rue d'Anjou, 75008 Paris
 ☎ 01 44 51 31 01 (visas).

 Consulate 11 square Dutilleul, 59800 Lille
 ☎ 03 20 12 82 72 – Fax 03 20 54 88 16

USA Embassy 2 avenue Gabriel, 75008 Paris
 ☎ 01 43 12 22 22 - Fax 01 42 66 97 83.

 Consulate 2 rue St-Florentin, 75001 Paris
 ☎ 01 42 96 14 88.

FRENCH TOURIST OFFICES ABROAD

For information, brochures, maps and assistance in planning a trip to France, travellers should apply to the official French Tourist Office in their own country:

Australia – New Zealand

Sydney – BNP Building, 12 Castlereagh Street
Sydney, New South Wales 2000
☎ (02) 9231 52 44 – Fax (02) 9221 86 82.

Canada

Montreal – 1981 avenue McGill College, Suite 490
Montreal PQ H3A 2W9
☎ (514) 288-4264 – Fax (514) 845 48 68.

Eire

Dublin – 10 Suffolk St, Dublin 2
☎ (01) 679 08 13 – Fax (01) 679 08 14.

South Africa

P.O. Box 41022, Craig Hall 2024
☎ (011) 880 8062

United Kingdom

London – 178 Piccadilly, London WIV OAL
☎ (0891) 244 123 – Fax (0171) 493 6594.

United States

East Coast: New York – 444 Madison Avenue, 16th Floor
NY 10022-6903
☎ (212) 838 7800 – Fax (212) 838 7855.

Mid west: Chicago – 676 North Michigan Avenue, Suite 3360
Chicago, IL 60611-2819
☎ (312) 751 7800 – Fax (312) 337 6339.

West Coast: Los Angeles – 9454 Wilshire Boulevard, Suite 715
Beverly Hills, CA 90212-2967.
☎ (310) 271 6665 – Fax (310) 276 2835.
Information can also be requested from **France on Call** at ☎ (202) 659 7779.

Cyberspace

www.info.france-usa.org
The French Embassy's Web site provides basic information (geography, demographics, history), a news digest and business-related information. It offers special pages for children, and pages devoted to culture, language study and travel, and you can reach other selected French sites (regions, cities, ministries) with a hypertext link.

www.fr-holidaystore.co.uk
The new Travel Centre in London has gone on-line with this service, providing information on all of the regions of France, including updated special travel offers and details on available accommodation.

www.ottowa.ambafrance.org
The Cultural Service of the French Embassy in Ottowa has a bright and varied site with many links to other sites for French literature, news updates and E-texts in both French and English.

www.visiteurope.com
The European Travel Commission provides useful information on travelling to and around 27 European countries, and includes links to some commercial booking services (ie vehicle hire), rail schedules, weather reports and more.

LOCAL TOURIST OFFICES

To find the addresses of local tourist offices throughout France, contact the **Fédération Nationale des Comités Départementaux de Tourisme**, 280 boulevard St-Germain, 75007 Paris. ☎ 01 44 11 10 30. Below, the addresses are given for each local tourist office by region and *département*. The index lists the *département* after each town and the *départements* are delimited on the Principal sights map in the introduction.

Île-de-France – Comité régional du tourisme, 91 avenue des Champs Elysées, 75008 Paris. ☎ 01 56 89 38 00 – Fax 01 56 89 38 39.

Nord-Pas-de-Calais – Comité régional du tourisme, 6 place Mendès-France, 59800 Lille. ☎ 03 20 14 57 57 – Fax 03 20 14 57 58.

Picardie – Comité régional du tourisme, 3 rue Vincent Auriol, 80011 Amiens Cedex 1. ☎ 03 22 22 33 66 – Fax 03 22 22 33 67.

Aisne – Comité départemental du tourisme, 24-28 avenue Charles-de-Gaulle, BP 116, 02005 Laon Cedex. ☎ 03 23 27 76 76.

S. Sauvignier/MICHELIN

Senlis

Essonne – Comité départemental du tourisme, 6 cours Monseigneur Roméro, 91025 Evry Cedex. ☎ 01 64 97 35 13.

Eure-et-Loir – Comité départemental du tourisme, 10 ruedu Docteur Maunoury, BP 67, 28002 Chartres Cedex. ☎ 02 37 84 01 00.

Hauts-de-Seine – Comité départemental du tourisme, 49 bis rue Paul-Vaillant-Couturier, 92140 Clamart. ☎ 01 46 42 80 52.

Nord – Comité départemental du tourisme, 6 rue Gauthier-de-Châtillon, BP 1232, 59013 Lille Cedex. ☎ 03 20 57 59 59. www.cdt-nord.fr.

Oise – Comité départemental du tourisme, 19 ruePierre-Jacoby, BP 80822, 60008 Beauvais Cedex. ☎ 03 44 45 82 12.

Pas-de-Calais – Comité départemental du tourisme, route La Trésorerie, 62126 Wimille. ☎ 03 21 10 34 60.

Seine-et-Marne – Comité départemental du tourisme, Hôtel d'Albe, 9-11 rue Royale, 77300 Fontainebleau. ☎ 01 60 39 60 39.

Seine-St-Denis – Comité départemental du tourisme, 21 avenue Karl-Marx, 93000 Bobigny. ☎ 01 41 60 06 03.

Somme – Comité départemental du tourisme, 21 rueErnest-Cauvin, 80000 Amiens. ☎ 03 22 71 22 71.

Val de Marne – Comité départemental du tourisme, Hôtel du Département, avenue du Général de Gaulle, 94011 Créteil Cedex. ☎ 01 49 56 87 97.

Val-d'Oise – Comité départemental du tourisme, Château de la Motte, 95270 Luzarches. ☎ 01 30 29 51 00.

Yvelines – Comité départemental du tourisme, 2 place André-Mignot, 78012 Versailles Cedex. ☎ 01 39 07 89 68.

The **Espace du tourisme d'Île-de-France**, Carrousel du Louvre, 99 rue de Rivoli, 75001 Paris, ☎ 08 03 81 80 00, **www.paris-ile-de-france.com**, is a handy tourist information bureau open daily, except Tuesday, 10am-7pm.
The **Espace du tourisme d'Île-de-France et Seine-et-Marne**, place des Passagers du Vent, 77700 Chessy-Marne-la-Vallée. ☎ 01 60 43 33 33, is a tourist information kiosk close to the RER station at Disneyland/Disney Village.
The **Maison du Nord-Pas-de-Calais**, 25 rue Bleue, 75009, Paris, ☎ 01 48 00 59 62, provides documents on the region, sells books and regional products and organises special events. It also has a useful web site (www.maison-nord-pas-de-calais.tm.fr).

Tourist offices – Further information can be obtained from the tourist offices or *syndicats d'initiative*, as they are called in smaller towns. The addresses and telephone numbers are listed after the symbol ⊞ in the Admission times and charges section.

Heritage trails – All over France, since 1975, *routes historiques* have been designated by the Caisse Nationale des Monuments Historiques et des Sites. See the section under Something Different *(page)* for details of these routes in the region covered by this guide.

Tourist Pass: 100 sights for 280F

This pass gives unrestricted access to more than 100 historic buildings managed by the *Centre des monuments nationaux*. It is valid for one year throughout France as of the date of purchase. It is for sale at the entrance to major historic buildings, monuments and museums.
The Paris Museum Pass allows free direct entry to the permanent collections of 70 museums and monuments **in and around Paris**. Valid for 1 day (80F), 3 consecutive days (160F) or 5 consecutive days (240F), it can be purchased in participating museums and monuments, at major Métro stations, the tourist information bureau at the Carrousel du Louvre, the National Tourist Bureau in the Champs Elysées or at the tourist information offices at the Montparnasse, Nord, Est, Lyon and Austerlitz railway stations, ☎ 01 44 61 96 60. Connect to www.intermusees.com for participating museums and monuments and hyperlinks.
The Passeport Intersites, obtainable free of charge, allows access at reduced rates to a number of monuments in the **Val-d'Oise** *département*, including the Château de La Roche-Guyon, Château d'Auvers, Château d'Écouen and Royaumont Abbey. ☎ 08 01 01 95 95.
Carte Intersites de Saint Denis. Three sights in St-Denis can be visited with this card – the basilica, the Musée d'Art et d'Histoire and the Stade de France (World Cup football stadium). The visit to the first sight is at the full rate, with a reduced rate for the following two sights. Further information can be obtained from the tourist office.
The Passeport pour Auvers-sur-Oise works on the same principal – the first sight is at full price, then subsequent visits to other sights in the town are at a reduced rate. The passport includes the Auberge Ravoux, Musée Daubigny, Château d'Auvers, Maison-atelier de Daubigny and the Musée de l'Absinthe.

Getting there

BY AIR

Various international and other independent airlines operate services to Paris (Charles-de-Gaulle/Roissy located 27km/14mi north of Paris or Orly located 16km/10mi south). There are also direct flights from London to Lille-Lesquin Airport, located 15min from the centre of Lille in northern France. Contact airlines and travel agents for information on package-tour flights with rail or coach link-ups or fly-drive schemes.

The major French carriers – Air Inter Europe, Air France, Air Liberté – offer frequent domestic flights between major French cities.

ARRIVING BY SEA FROM THE UK OR IRELAND

There are numerous **cross-Channel services** (passenger and car ferries, hovercraft) from the United Kingdom and Ireland, as well as the rail Shuttle through the Channel Tunnel (**Le Shuttle-Eurotunnel**, ☎ 0990 353-535). To choose the most suitable route between your port of arrival and your destination use the Michelin Tourist and Motoring Atlas France, Michelin map 911 (which gives travel times and mileages) or Michelin maps from the 1:200,000 series (with the yellow cover). For details apply to travel agencies or to:

P & O Stena Line Ferries	Channel House, Channel View Road, Dover CT17 9JT, ☎ 0990 980 980 or 01304 863 000 (Switchboard), www.p-and-o.com
Hoverspeed	International Hoverport, Marine Parade, Dover, Kent CT17 9TG, ☎ 0990 240 241, Fax 01304 240088, www.hoverspeed.co.uk
Brittany Ferries	Millbay Docks; Plymouth, Devon. PL1 3^{E}W, ☎ 0990 360 360, www.brittany-ferries.com
Portsmouth Commercial Port (and ferry information)	George Byng Way, Portsmouth, Hampshire PO2 8SP, ☎ 01705 297391, Fax 01705 861165
Irish Ferries	50 West Norland Street, Dublin 2, ☎ (353) 16 610 511, www.irishferries.com
Seafrance	Eastern Docks, Dover, Kent, CT16 1JA, ☎ 01304 212696, Fax 01304 240033, www.seafrance.fr

BY RAIL

Eurostar runs via the Channel Tunnel between **London** (Waterloo) and **Paris** (Gare du Nord) in 3hr, or **Lille** (Europe) in 2hr. There is a once daily service running directly from the UK to **Disneyland**, taking 3hr (bookings and information ☎ 0990 186 186 in the UK; ☎ 1-888-EUROSTAR in the US; www.eurostar.co.uk).

Eurailpass, Flexipass and **Saverpass** are travel passes which may be purchased in the US. Contact your travel agent or **Rail Europe** 2100 Central Ave. Boulder, CO, 80301, ☎ 1-800-4-EURAIL, or **Europrail International** ☎ 1-888-667-9731. They may also be purchased in person in the UK from 178 Piccadilly London W1V OBA, ☎ 08705 848 848. Information on schedules can be obtained on web sites for these agencies and the **SNCF**, respectively (www.raileurop.com.us, www.eurail.on.ca, www.sncf.fr).

For EU citizens, there are rail passes offering unlimited travel for a specified time. **Eurodomino** tickets are for unlimited rail travel within one European country over 3 to 8 days within any given month, while **Interail** passes allow a month's unlimited travel within a specified zone including several countries. Both are available in the UK, from Rail Europe at 178 Piccadilly, London WIV OBA, ☎ 08705 848 848. Tickets bought in France must be validated *(composter)* by using the orange automatic date-stamping machines at the platform entrance (failure to do so may result in a fine). Baggage trolleys (10F coin required – refundable) are available at mainline stations.

A good investment is the **Thomas Cook European Timetable**, which gives all the train schedules throughout France and Europe as well as useful information on travelling by train (US ☎ 1 800 367 7984).

The French railway company SNCF operates a telephone information, reservation and prepayment service in English from 7am to 10pm (French time). In France call ☎ 08 36 35 35 39 (when calling from outside France, drop the initial 0). Ask about discount rates if you are over 60, a student or travelling with your family.

BY COACH

Regular coach services operate from London to Paris and to large provincial towns:
Eurolines (London), 4 Cardiff Road, Luton, Bedfordshire, L41 1PP, ☎ 0990 143219, Fax 01582 400694, welcome@eurolinesuk.com and www.eurolines.co.uk
Eurolines (Paris), 28 avenue du Général-de-Gaulle, 93541 Bagnolet, ☎ 08 36 69 52 52

Getting around

The **Paris Visite** pass allows unlimited travel on the entire RATP network in the Paris and Île-de-France area and includes the metro, RER, bus, tram and suburban trains, depending on the geographical zone (1-3 for the inner zone and 1-5, 6, 7 or 8 for the outer suburbs of Île-de-France). Valid for 1, 2, 3 or 5 consecutive days, it can be purchased in main metro and all RER stations, or abroad (www.ratp.fr).

Other passes are also available on the RATP network, including the **carte orange hebdomadaire** for travel from Monday to Sunday in zones 1-8, or the **Mobilis** card, issued with a voucher valid for one day.

Métro lines are identified by a number. Some of them extend into the suburbs: St-Denis or Asnières on line 13, Créteil on line 8.

For **RER** lines A, B, C, D, E, which extend into the outer suburbs, cost depends on the distance travelled.

Six Parisian railway stations (Austerlitz, Est, Lyon, Montparnasse, Nord, St-Lazare) provide suburban train links to the towns of the Île-de-France region. Stations are open from 6am to 9pm. The cost of travelling on the *transilien SNCF* (Île-de-France regional network) varies according to length of journey, ☎ 01 53 90 20 20 (http://idf.sncf.fr).

There is a very frequent service to Lille by TGV (1hr) from the Gare du Nord. Arras is under an hour away from the capital, again by TGV. Journey times to Amiens take 1-2hr, depending on the number of stops made, whilst Beauvais takes a little over 1hr, ☎ 01 45 82 50 50 (information: 7am-11pm) or ☎ 01 45 65 60 60 (reservations: 8am-8pm).

TRAVELLERS WITH SPECIAL NEEDS

The sights described in this guide which are easily accessible to people of reduced mobility are indicated in the Admission times and charges section by the symbol ♿

Useful information on transportation, holidaymaking and sports associations for the disabled is available from the Comité National Français de Liaison pour la Réadaptation des Handicapés (CNRH), 236 bisrue de Tolbiac, 75013 Paris. Call their international information number ☎ 01 53 80 66 66, or write to request a catalogue of publications. Web-surfers can find information for slow walkers, mature travellers and others with special needs at www.access-able.com and www.handitel.org. For information on museum access for the disabled contact La Direction, Les Musées de France, Service Accueil des Publics Spécifiques, 6 ruedes Pyramides, 75041 Paris Cedex 1, ☎ 01 40 15 35 88.

The Red Guide France and the **Michelin Camping Caravaning France Guide** indicate hotels and camp sites with facilities suitable for physically handicapped people.

Motoring in France

Planning your route – The area covered in this guide is easily reached by main motorways and national routes. **Michelin map 911** indicates the main itineraries as well as alternate routes for avoiding heavy traffic during busy holiday periods, and gives estimated travel times. **Michelin map 914** is a detailed atlas of French motorways, indicating tolls, rest areas and services along the route; it includes a table for calculating distances and times. The latest Michelin route-planning service is available on Internet, **www.michelin-travel.com**. Travellers can calculate a precise route using such options as shortest route, route avoiding toll roads, Michelin-recommended route and gain access to tourist information (hotels, restaurants, attractions). The service is available on a pay-per-route basis or by subscription.

The roads are very busy during the holiday period (particularly weekends in July and August) and, to avoid traffic congestion it is advisable to follow the recommended secondary routes (signposted as *Bison Futé – itinéraires bis*). The motorway network includes rest areas *(aires)* and petrol stations, usually with restaurant and shopping complexes attached, about every 40km/25mi, so that long-distance drivers have no excuse not to stop for a rest every now and then.

Documents – Travellers from other European Union countries and North America can drive in France with a valid national or home-state **driving licence**. An **international driving licence** is useful because the information on it appears in nine languages (keep in mind that traffic officers are empowered to fine motorists). A permit is available (US$10) from the National Automobile Club, 1151 East Hillsdale Blvd., Foster City, CA 94404 ☎ 650-294-7000 or nationalautoclub.com; or contact your local branch of the American Automobile Association. For the vehicle, it is necessary to have the registration papers (logbook) and a nationality plate of the approved size.

Insurance – Certain motoring organisations (AAA, AA, RAC) offer accident insurance and breakdown service schemes for members. Check with your current insurance company in regard to coverage while abroad. If you plan to hire a car using your credit card, check with the company, which may provide liability insurance automatically (and thus save you having to pay the cost for optimum coverage).

Highway Code – The minimum driving age is 18. Traffic drives on the right. It is compulsory for the front-seat passengers to wear **seat belts** and it is also compulsory for the back-seat passengers when the car is fitted with them. Children under the age of 10 must travel on the back seat of the vehicle. Full or dipped headlights must be switched on in poor visibility and at night; use side-lights only when the vehicle is stationary. In the case of a **breakdown**, a red warning triangle or hazard warning lights are obligatory. In the absence of stop signs at intersections, cars must **yield to the right**. Traffic on main roads outside built-up areas (priority indicated by a yellow diamond sign) and on roundabouts has right of way. Vehicles must stop when the lights turn red at road junctions and may filter to the right only when indicated by an amber arrow.
The regulations on **drinking and driving** (limited to 0.50g/l) and **speeding** are strictly enforced – usually by an on-the-spot fine and/or confiscation of the vehicle.

Speed limits – Although liable to modification, these are as follows:
– toll motorways *(péage)* 130kph/80mph (110kph/68mph when raining);
– dual carriageways and motorways without tolls 110kph/68mph (100kph/62mph when raining);
– other roads 90kph/56mph (80kph/50mph when raining) and in towns 50kph/31mph;
– outside lane on motorways during daylight, on level ground and with good visibility – minimum speed limit of 80kph/50mph.

Parking Regulations – In town there are zones where parking is either restricted or subject to a fee; tickets should be obtained from the ticket machines (*horodateurs* – small change necessary) and displayed inside the windscreen on the driver's side; failure to display may result in a fine, or towing and impoundment. In some towns you may find blue parking zones *(zone bleue)* marked by a blue line on the pavement or road and a blue signpost with a P and a small square underneath. In this case you have to display a cardboard disc with various times indicated on it. This will enable you to stay for 1hr 30min (2hr 30min over lunch time) free. Discs are available in supermarkets or petrol stations (ask for a *disque de stationnement*); they are sometimes given away free.

Tolls – In France, most motorway sections are subject to a toll *(péage)*. You can pay in cash or with a credit card (Visa, Mastercard).

CAR RENTAL

There are car rental agencies at airports, railway stations and in all large towns throughout France. European cars have manual transmission; automatic cars are available in larger cities only if an advance reservation is made. Drivers must be over 21; between ages 21-25, drivers are required to pay an extra daily fee of 50-100F; some companies allow drivers under 23 only if the reservation has been made through a travel agent. It is relatively expensive to hire a car in France; Americans in particular will notice the difference and should make arrangements before leaving, take advantage of fly-drive offers, or seek advice from a travel agent, specifying requirements.

Central Reservation in France:

Avis: 08 02 05 05 05
Budget France: 08 00 10 00 01
SIXT-Eurorent: 01 44 38 55 55
Baron's Limousine and Driver: 01 45 30 21 21

Europcar: 08 03 352 352
Hertz France: 08 03 861 861
National-CITER: 01 44 38 61 61

Worldwide Motorhome Rentals offers fully equipped campervans for rent. You can view them on the company's web pages (mhrww.com) or call (US toll-free) US ☎ 888- 519-8969; outside the US ☎ 530-389-8316 or Fax 530-389-8316.
Overseas Motorhome Tours Inc. organises escorted tours and individual rental of recreational vehicles: in the US ☎ 800-322-2127; outside the US ☎ 1-310-543-2590; Internet www.omtinc.com

Petrol (US: gas) – French service stations dispense: *sans plomb 98* (super unleaded 98), *sans plomb 95* (super unleaded 95), *diesel/gazole* (diesel) and *GPL* (LPG). Petrol is considerably more expensive in France than in the USA. Prices are listed on signboards on the motorways; it is usually cheaper to fill up after leaving the motorway; check the large hypermarkets on the outskirts of town.

Accommodation

The **Places to stay map** *(see below)* indicates recommended places for overnight stops and can be used in conjunction with **The Red Guide France**, which lists a selection of hotels and restaurants.

Loisirs Accueil is a booking service that has offices in most French *départements*: contact the tourist offices listed above for further information, or Résérvation Loisirs Accueil, 280 boulevard St-Germain, 75007 Paris, ☎ 01 44 11 10 44 (www.resinfrance.com for internet booking).

HOTELS

A guide to good-value, family run hotels, **Logis et Auberges de France**, is available from the French Tourist Office, as are lists of other kinds of accommodation such as hotel-châteaux, bed and breakfasts etc. **Relais et châteaux** provides information on booking in luxury hotels with character: 15 rue Galvani, 75017 Paris, ☎ 01 45 72 90 00.

Economy Chain Hotels – If you need a place to stop en route, these can be useful, as they are inexpensive (under 200F for a double room) and generally located near the main road. While breakfast is available, there may not be a restaurant; rooms are small, with a television and bathroom. Central reservation numbers:
- **Akena** ☎ 01 69 84 85 17
- **B&B** ☎ 0 803 00 29 29
- **Etap Hôtel** ☎ 08 36 68 89 00 (2.23F per minute, from France)
- **Mister Bed** ☎ 01 46 14 38 00
- **Villages Hôtel** ☎ 03 80 60 92 70

The hotels listed below are slightly more expensive (from 300F), and offer a few more amenities and services. Central reservation numbers:
- **Campanile** ☎ 01 64 62 46 46
- **Climat de France** ☎ 01 64 46 01 23
- **Ibis** ☎ 0 803 88 22 22

RURAL ACCOMMODATION

The **Maison des Gîtes de France** is an information service on self-catering accommodation in the regions of France. *Gîtes* usually take the form of a cottage or apartment decorated in the local style, where visitors can make themselves at home.

Contact the Gîtes de France office in Paris: 59 rue St-Lazare, 75439 Paris Cedex 09, ☎ 01 49 70 75 75, or their representative, in the UK, **Brittany Ferries** *(address above)*. The web site is quite complete and has an excellent English version (www.gites-de-france.fr).

Gîtes de France, Springfield Books Ltd and FHG Publications/World Leisure Marketing all publish listings of *gîtes* in France with details of how to book. Try contacting the local tourist offices as they also pub-lish lists of available properties.

The Fédération Française des Stations Vertes de Vacances, 6 rue Ranfer de Bretenière, 21000 Dijon, ☎ 03 80 54 10 50 – Fax 03 80 54 10 55, is able to provide details of accommodation, leisure facilities and natural attractions in rural lo-cations selected for their tranquil-lity. Among the localities in northern France are **Bergues** in the Nord, **Montreuil-sur-Mer** in the Pas-de-Calais and **Poix-de-Picardie** in the Somme.

S. Sauvignier /MICHELIN

The guide **Bienvenue à la ferme** (Edi-tions Solar) includes the addresses of farmers providing guest facilities who have signed a charter drawn up by the Chambers of Agriculture. *Bi-envenue à la ferme* farms, vetted for quality and meeting official stan-dards, can be identified by the yel-low flower which serves as their logo. Information and brochures are also available from the following regional organisations:

Bienvenue à la ferme dans l'Aisne, Agriculture et tourisme 02, Maison de l'Agriculture, 38 boulevard de Lyon, 02007 Laon Cedex, ☎ 03 23 22 50 94.

Bienvenue dans les fermes du Pas-de-Calais, Relais départemental agriculture et tourisme, 56 avenue Roger-Salengro, BP 39, 62051 St-Laurent Blangy Cedex, ☎ 03 21 24 07 07.

Places to stay

Dover
Folkestone
Tunnel
Calais
Wissant
Wimereux
HARDELOT-PL.
Boulogne-sMer
LE TOUQUET
Stella-Plage
Montreuil
Berck-s-Mer
Fort-Mahon-Pl.
Quend-Plage-les-Pins
Rue
Le Crotoy
St-Valery-s-S.
Ault

BRUGGE
GENT
Malo-les-Bains
Bray-Dunes
Dunkerque
BELGIË
Bergues
Cassel
Kortrijk
Caps et Marais d'Opale
Tourcoing
St-Omer
BELGIQUE
Roubaix
LILLE
St-Amand-les-Eaux
Plaine de la Scarpe et de l'Escaut
Hesdin
Arras
Douai
Valenciennes
Le Quesnoy
Cambrai
Avesnois
Abbeville
AMIENS
Péronne
St-Quentin
Poix-de-Picardie
Somme
Noyon
Laon
Beauvais
COMPIÈGNE
Soissons
Senlis
Villers-Cotterêts
Chantilly
Vexin français
la Roche-Guyon
Mantes
Enghien-les-Bains
Meaux
PARIS
DISNEYLAND PARIS
Grand Morin
VERSAILLES
Rambouillet
Hte Vallée de Chevreuse
Provins
Maintenon
Melun
Chartres
Barbizon
Fontainebleau
Étampes
Moret-s-Loing
Nemours
Sens
Châteaudun
Montargis

Spas ⚓ and seaside resorts ⚓ are classified
according to the quality and range of facilities offered

● Seaside resort
● Spa

● Popular holiday destination
▢ Weekend destination
— Overnight stop
🏄 Beach sports

Bienvenue dans les fermes de l'Oise, Chambre d'Agriculture, Service Tourisme, rue Frère-Gagne, 60021 Beauvais Cedex, ☎ 03 44 11 44 50.

Ramblers can consult the guide entitled *Gîtes et refuges, France et frontières* by A and S Mouraret (Editions La Cadole, 74 rue Albert-Perdreaux, 78140 Vélizy, ☎ 01 34 65 10 40. This guide has been written mainly for those who enjoy rambling, cycling and canoeing-kayaking holidays.

BED AND BREAKFAST

Gîtes de France *(see above)* publishes a booklet on bed and breakfast accommodation *(chambres d'hôtes)* which include a room and breakfast at a reasonable price. You can also contact:

Bed & Breakfast (France), International reservations centre, PO Box 66, Henley-on-Thames, Oxon RG9 1XS, ☎ 1491 578 803, Fax 1491 410 806.

YOUTH HOSTELS

There are two main youth hostel *(auberge de jeunesse)* associations in France.
– **Ligue Française pour les Auberges de Jeunesse**, 67 rue Vergniaud, 75013 Paris, ☎ 01 44 16 78 78, Fax 01 44 16 78 80, www.auberges-de-jeunesse.com.
– **Fédération Unie des Auberges de Jeunesse**, 27 rue Pajol, 75018 Paris, ☎ 01 44 89 87 27, Fax 01 44 89 87 10, www.fuaj.org

Holders of an International Youth Hostel Federation card should contact Hostelling International in their own country for information and membership applications (US ☎ 202 783 6161 – hiayh.org; UK ☎ 1727 855215; Canada ☎ 613-237 7884; Australia ☎ 2-9565-1669; South Africa ☎ 21-424-2511).

CAMPING

There are numerous officially graded sites with varying standards of facilities throughout the region; the **Michelin Camping Caravaning France** guide lists a selection of the best camp sites. An International Camping Carnet for caravans is useful but not compulsory; it can be obtained from the motoring organisations or the Camping and Caravanning Club (Greenfield House, Westwood Way, Coventry CV4 8JH; England ☎ 2476 694-995).

Eating out

The Red Guide France – This guide book provides a very wide selection of restaurants serving the finest specialities in Flanders, Picardy, Paris and the Île-de-France region. When the word *repas* (meal) is printed in red, it refers to a high-quality but reasonably priced meal. Pictograms indicate places with a charming decor, a beautiful view or a quiet setting.

Fermes-auberges (Farm-inns) – These may or may not offer accommodation. They serve farm produce and local speciality dishes. They are open at weekends but advanced booking is required. Contact the Association des fermiers aubergistes de France, **Ferm'Auberge**, Les Perriaux, 89350 Champignelles, ☎ 03 85 45 13 22.

Brasseries in northern France – The best place to discover the friendliness of people in the north of France is in one of the many *brasseries* (the name derives from the French for «brewery»; hot and cold dishes are usually available all day long) often located on the main square, beside the belfry. This is also the best place to taste the traditional dish of mussels and French-fried potatoes, or a brown sugar tart washed down with a glass of beer. The ambience is lively well into the night.
In the Nord-Pas-de-Calais area, there are still several **traditional breweries** which produce beer in the old-fashioned way, even where ultra-modern equipment has been introduced. Some of them are open to the public:

B. Kaufmann/MICHELIN

Outdoor café in Lille

- **Brasserie d'Annoeullin**, 4 Grand'Place, BP 87, 59112 Annoeullin, ☎ 03 20 86 83 60.
- **Brasserie Castelain**, 13 ruePasteur, 62410 Bénifontaine, ☎ 03 21 08 68 68 (1hr guided tour by appointment).
- **Brasserie De Clerck**, 42 rue Georges Clémenceau, 80200 Péronne, ☎ 03 22 84 30 94.
- **Brasserie des Enfants de Gayant**, 63 faubourg de Paris, BP 89, 59550 Douai, ☎ 03 27 93 26 22.
- **Brasserie de Saint-Sylvestre**, route Nationale, St-Sylvestre Cappel, 59114 Steenvoorde, ☎ 03 28 40 15 49.
- **Brasserie Terken**, 3 quai d'Anvers, BP 409, 59057 Roubaix Cedex 1, ☎ 03 20 26 92 26.
- **Brasserie Thiriez**, 22 rue de Wormhout, 59470 Esquelbecq, ☎ 03 28 62 88 44.
- **Heineken**, rue du Général de Gaulle, ZI de la Pilaterie, 59370 Mons-en-Baroeul, ☎ 03 20 33 67 00.

Possibilities for eating:

- **LesBrasseurs**, 22 place de la Gare, 59800 Lille, ☎ 03 20 06 46 25.
- **Taverne de l'Écu**, 9 rue Esquermoise, 59800 Lille, ☎ 03 20 57 55 66.
- **Beck**, Eckelstraete, 59270 Bailleul, ☎ 03 28 49 03 90.
- **Au Baron**, 2 rue Piémont, 59570 Gussignies, ☎ 03 27 66 88 61.
- **Brasserie St-Poloise**, 2 rue de la Calandre, 62130 St-Pol-sur-Ternoise, ☎ 03 21 41 91 00.

To make one litre of beer, it takes:
- *200g (1 cup) of grain (mainly barley)*
- *2g (1/2 teaspoon) of hops*
- *1cl (0.33oz) of yeast*
- *pure water*

Estaminets – Food and drink are also served in the cafés known locally as *estaminets* (originally, a café where smoking was permitted). The warm, unpretentious atmosphere is typical of the region, as is the good beer served there.
- **De Vierpot**, 125 rue du Moulin, 59299 Boeschepe.
- **HetBlauwershof**, 9 rue d'Eecke, 59270 Godewaersvelde.
- **L'Estaminet flamand**, 6 rue des Fusilliers-Marins, 59140 Dunkerque.
- **Le St-Georges**, 5 rue de Caëstre, 59114 Ecke.
- **L'Haezepoel**, 3451 chemin de l'Haezepoel, 59122 Hondschoote.
- **'T Kasteelhof**, next to the mill, 59670 Cassel. Sharing premises with the *estaminet*, the **Maison du Pays** offers crafts and speciality foods from Flanders, Hainaut and Artois *(open from 10am to 7pm Wed-Sun; every day in June, July and August,* ☎ 03 28 40 59 29).

The coast – Those who enjoy fish will remember that Boulogne is France's leading fresh fish port. In addition to the gourmet restaurants serving fish soup, turbot with cream sauce, *sole meunière*, or a fish platter known as *la gainée* consisting of three different types of fish with a shrimp sauce, there are also fishmongers' stalls selling cod, herring and fresh eels.

Picardy – Soup has pride of place in this region and one of the best-known is the *soupe des hortillons*, made with fresh vegetables. Water fowl is used in many different ways, for example duck or snipe paté. The *ficelle picarde* is a ham pancake rolled up and filled with mushrooms then smothered in bechamel sauce and baked in the oven until the top is crisp and golden. Leek quiche also forms part of a simple but delicious meal.

You can obtain a copy of the *Guide des produits et de la gastronomie* for the Nord-Pas-de-Calais area and for Picardy by contacting:
- Chambre régionale d'agriculture Nord-Pas-de-Calais, 56 avenue Roger-Salengro, BP 39, 62051, St-Laurent-Blangy Cedex, ☎ 03 21 60 57 86.
- Terroirs de Picardie, comité de promotion, BP 2626, 80026 Amiens Cedex, ☎ 03 22 97 39 49.

Gourmet guide – The Picardy region boasts some spots which appeal to the gourmet tourist interested in discovering local specialities. Among the places which have been awarded the *Site remarquable du goût* (for «remarkable taste sensations») distinction are Houille, Loos and Wanbrechies, on the outskirts of Lille, known for *genièvre* (a juniper-flavoured eau-de-vie similar to gin); the port of Boulogne famous for its fish; the market gardens of the Marais Audomarois in St-Omer; and the *Hortillonnages* marshland in Amiens, for fruit and vegetables (traditional floating market on the 3rd Sunday in June, canal festival in September).

Basic information

MEDICAL TREATMENT

First aid, medical advice and chemists' night service rota are available from chemists (*pharmacie* – green cross sign). Prescription drugs should be clearly labelled and foreign visitors are advised to carry a copy of prescriptions.

It is advisable to take out comprehensive insurance cover as medical treatment in French hospitals or clinics must be paid for by the recipient. Nationals of non-EU countries should check with their insurance companies about policy limitations. Reimbursement can then be negotiated with the insurance company according to the terms of the policy held.

American Express offers a service, *Global Assist*, for any medical, legal or personal emergency.

British citizens should apply to the Department of Health and Social Security for **Form E 111**, which entitles the holder to urgent treatment for accident or unexpected illness in EU countries. A refund of part of the costs of treatment can be obtained on application in person or by post to the local Social Security Offices (Caisse Primaire d'Assurance Maladie).

The American Hospital of Paris is open 24hr for emergencies as well as consultations, with English-speaking staff, at 63 boulevard Victor-Hugo, 92200 Neuilly sur Seine, ☎ 01 46 41 25 25. Accredited by major insurance companies.

The British Hospital is just outside Paris in Levallois-Perret, 3 rue Barbès, ☎ 01 46 39 22 22.

CURRENCY

There are no restrictions on the amount of currency visitors can take into France, however, the amount of cash you may take out of France is subject to a limit, so visitors carrying a lot of cash should complete a currency declaration form on arrival.

French francs *(see illustration following)* are subdivided into 100 centimes. European currency units known as **euros** are being printed, and as of January 1999 the banking and finance industries began making the changeover. Euro banknotes and coins are scheduled to go into general circulation from 1 January 2002. Between 1 January and 17 February 2002, both currencies should circulate, but francs will gradually be withdrawn during that period. After 17 February, francs will normally no longer be accepted as a means of payment, although banks should continue to take them until 30 June 2002. In the meantime, both euro and franc values (1 euro is about 6 francs 50 centimes) are given in more and more instances (store and restaurant receipts, bank documents etc).

Tipping – Since a service charge is automatically included in the prices of meals and accommodation in France, it is not necessary to tip in restaurants and hotels. However if the service in a restaurant is especially good, or if you have enjoyed a fine meal, an extra tip (this is the *pourboire*, rather than the *service*) is a well-appreciated gesture. Usually 10 or 20F is enough, but if the bill is big (a large party or a luxury restaurant), it is not uncommon to leave 50F or more.

BANKS

Banks are usually open from 9am to noon and 2pm to 5pm and closed either on Monday or Saturday (except on market days); some branches open for limited transactions on Saturdays. Banks often close early on the day before a bank holiday.

A passport is necessary as identification when cashing cheques in banks. Commission charges vary and hotels usually charge more than banks for cashing cheques for non-residents.

Many banks and larger post offices have **cash dispensers** (ATM) which accept international credit or debit cards (have your PIN number handy), and are easily recognised by a CB logo and/or a hand holding a card. American Express cards can be used only in dispensers operated by the Crédit Lyonnais bank or by American Express.

Credit card purchases – Visa (Carte Bleue), Mastercard/Eurocard, American Express and Diners Club are widely accepted in shops,

A. ÉLI/MICHELIN

417

hotels, restaurants and petrol stations. If your card is lost or stolen, call one of the following 24-hour numbers:

American Express	01 47 77 72 00	**Visa**	08 36 69 08 80
Mastercard/Eurocard	01 45 67 84 84	**Diners Club**	01 49 06 17 50

You must report any loss or theft of credit cards or travellers' cheques to the local police, who will normally issue a certificate to show the credit card company.

PUBLIC HOLIDAYS

Public services, museums and other monuments may be closed or may vary their hours of admission on the following public holidays:

1	January	New Year's Day *(Jour de l'An)*
Easter Day and Easter Monday *(Pâques)*		
1	May	May Day
8	May	VE Day
40 days after Easter		Ascension Day *(Ascension)*
7th Sun-Mon after Easter		Whitsun *(Pentecôte)*
14	July	France's National Day (Bastille Day)
15	August	Assumption *(Assomption)*
1	November	All Saint's Day *(Toussaint)*
11	November	Armistice Day
25	December	Christmas Day *(Noël)*

National museums and art galleries are closed on Tuesdays; municipal museums are generally closed on Mondays. In addition to the usual school holidays at Christmas and in the spring and summer, there are long mid-term breaks (10 days to a fortnight) in February and early November.

POST AND TELEPHONE

Major post offices – These are open Monday to Friday 8am to 7pm and Saturday 8am to noon. Smaller branch post offices generally close at lunch time between noon and 2pm and in the afternoon at 4pm.

Postage via air mail to:

> UK letter (20g) – 3F
> North America letter (20g) – 4.40F
> North America postcard – 4.10F
> Australia and New Zealand letter (20g) – 5.20F
> South Africa letter (20g) – 3.90F

Stamps are also available from newsagents and tobacconists.
Stamp collectors should ask for *timbres de collection* in any post office.
Poste Restante (General Delivery) mail should be addressed as follows: Name, Poste Restante, Poste Centrale, postal code of the *département*, followed by town name, France. The Red Guide France gives local postal codes.

Public Telephones – Most public phones in France use pre-paid phone cards *(télécartes)*, rather than coins. Some telephone booths accept credit cards (Visa, Mastercard/Eurocard: minimum monthly charge 20F). *Télécartes* (50 or 120 units) can be bought in post offices, branches of France Télécom, *bureaux de tabac* (cafés that sell cigarettes) and newsagents and can be used to make calls in France and abroad. Calls can be received in phone boxes where the blue bell sign is shown; the phone will not ring, so keep your eye on the little message screen.

National calls – French telephone numbers have 10 digits. Paris and Paris region numbers begin with 01; 02 in northwest France; 03 in northeast France; 04 in southeast France and Corsica; 05 in southwest France.

International calls – To call France from abroad, dial the country code (33) + 9-digit number (omit the initial 0). When calling abroad from France dial 00, then dial the country code followed by the area code and the number of your correspondent.

International dialling codes (00 + code):

Australia	☎ 61	New Zealand	☎ 64
Canada	☎ 1	United Kingdom	☎ 44
Eire	☎ 353	United States	☎ 1
South Africa	☎ 27		

To use your **personal calling card** dial:

AT&T	☎ 0-800 99 00 11	Sprint	☎ 0-800 99 00 87
MCI..................	☎ 0-800 99 00 19	Canada Direct ..	☎ 0-800 99 00 16

International directory enquiries, all countries: 32 12
International operator: 32 12 or 31 23
Local directory assistance: 12
Toll-free numbers in France begin with 0 800.

Emergency numbers (free of charge):

Police:	17	**"SAMU"** *(Paramedics)*:	15
Fire *(Pompiers)*:	18		

Minitel – France Télécom operates a system offering directory enquiries, travel and entertainment reservations, and other services. These small computer-like terminals can be found in some post offices, hotels and France Télécom agencies and in many French homes. 3617 PAGES I is the code for **the International phone directory** (turn on the unit, dial 3617, hit the "connexion" button when you get the tone, type in "PAGES I", and follow the instructions on the screen). To find a number in France, the code is 36 11 (Pages Jaunes). The **French phone directory** can also be found in English on the Internet (www.annu.com).

Cellular phones – In France these have numbers which begin with 06. Two-watt (lighter, shorter reach) and eight-watt models are on the market, using the Itinéris (France Télécom), SFR or other network. "Mobicartes" are pre-paid phone cards that fit into mobile units. Cell phone rentals (delivery or airport pick-up provided):

Rent a Cell Express	☎ 01 53 93 78 00, Fax 01 53 93 78 09
A.L.T. Rent A Phone	☎ 01 48 00 06 60, e-mail altloc@jve.fr
Cell'Force	☎ 01 44 40 02 80, Fax 01 44 40 02 88

SHOPPING

The big stores and larger shops are open Mondays to Saturdays from 9am to 6.30 or 7pm. Smaller, individual shops often close for lunch from noon until 2pm and on Mondays. Food shops – grocers, wine merchants and bakeries – are generally open from 7am to 6.30 or 7pm; some open on Sunday mornings. Hypermarkets usually open until 9pm or even 10pm.

People travelling to the USA may not import plant products or fresh food, including fruit, cheeses and nuts, although there is no problem taking tinned products or preserves.

VAT refunds are available to visitors from outside the European Union only if purchases exceed US$200 per store, but repeat visits to a store can be combined. The value-added tax on goods varies between 5.5 and 19.6% of the sale price, so it can be worth your while to recover it. The system works in large stores which cater to tourists, in luxury stores and other shops advertising "Duty Free". Show your passport, and the store will complete a form which is to be stamped (at the airport) by a European customs agents. The sum due can be collected at the airport or by mailing the forms from home. In practice, the system works best in luxury stores or big department stores with special service desks for VAT recovery (they may offer an immediate discount): the amount can be credited directly to your bank card account.

ELECTRICITY

The electric current is 220 volts. Circular two-pin or three-pin plugs are the rule. Adapters are best bought before leaving home; they may also be bought at most international airports.

Conversion tables

Weights and measures

| 1 kilogram (kg) | 2.2 pounds (lb) | 2.2 pounds |
| 1 metric ton (tn) | 1.1 tons | 1.1 tons |

to convert kilograms to pounds, multiply by 2.2

| 1 litre (l) | 2.1 pints (pt) | 1.8 pints |
| 1 litre | 0.3 gallon (gal) | 0.2 gallon |

to convert litres to gallons, multiply by 0.26 (US) or 0.22 (UK)

| 1 hectare (ha) | 2.5 acres | 2.5 acres |
| 1 square kilometre (km²) | 0.4 square miles (sq mi) | 0.4 square miles |

to convert hectares to acres, multiply by 2.4

1 centimetre (cm)	0.4 inches (in)	0.4 inches
1 metre (m)	3.3 feet (ft) - 39.4 inches - 1.1 yards (yd)	
1 kilometre (km)	0.6 miles (mi)	0.6 miles

to convert metres to feet, multiply by 3.28. kilometres to miles, multiply by 0.6

Clothing

Women							Men
	35	4	2½	40	7½	7	
	36	5	3½	41	8½	8	
	37	6	4½	42	9½	9	
Shoes	38	7	5½	43	10½	10	**Shoes**
	39	8	6½	44	11½	11	
	40	9	7½	45	12½	12	
	41	10	8½	46	13½	13	
	36	4	8	46	36	36	
	38	6	10	48	38	38	
Dresses &	40	8	12	50	40	40	**Suits**
Suits	42	12	14	52	42	42	
	44	14	16	54	44	44	
	46	16	18	56	46	48	
	36	08	30	37	14½	14,5	
	38	10	32	38	15	15	
Blouses &	40	12	14	39	15½	15½	**Shirts**
sweaters	42	14	36	40	15¾	15¾	
	44	16	38	41	16	16	
	46	18	40	42	16½	16½	

Sizes often vary depending on the designer. These equivalents are given for guidance only.

Speed

kph	10	30	50	70	80	90	100	110	120	130
mph	6	19	31	43	50	56	62	68	75	81

Temperature

Celsius (°C)	0°	5°	10°	15°	20°	25°	30°	40°	60°	80°	100°
Fahrenheit (°F)	32°	41°	50°	59°	68°	77°	86°	104°	140°	176°	212°

To convert Celsius into Fahrenheit, multiply °C by 9, divide by 5, and add 32.
To convert Fahrenheit into Celsius, subtract 32 from °F, multiply by 5, and divide by 9.

Notes and coins

500 Francs featuring scientists
Pierre and Marie Curie
(1858-1906). (1867-1934)

200 Francs featuring engineer Gustave Eiffel
(1832-1923)

100 Francs featuring Post-Impressionist painter Paul Cézanne
(1839-1906)

50 Francs featuring pilot and writer Antoine de Saint-Exupéry
(1900-1944)

20 Francs

10 Francs

5 Francs

2 Francs

1 Franc

50 Centimes

20 Centimes

10 Centimes

5 Centimes

TIME

France is 1hr ahead of Greenwich Mean Time (GMT).

When it is **noon in France**, it is

3 am	in Los Angeles
6 am	in New York
11 am	in Dublin
11 am	in London
1 pm	in Pretoria
7 pm	in Perth
9 pm	in Sydney
11 pm	in Auckland

R. Corbel/MICHELIN

In France "am" and "pm" are not used but the 24-hour clock is widely applied.

Sport and recreation

WATER-BASED ACTIVITIES

Sailing and windsurfing

The Paris region boasts around 15 lakes and half a dozen locations on the River Seine and River Marne where sailing is available. There are a number of sports and recreation parks *(bases de loisirs)*, where windsurfing and dinghy or catamaran sailing are possible, occasionally combined with other activities such as tennis, swimming, horse riding, golf or water-skiing. Among others, they include St-Quentin-en-Yvelines, D 912, 78190 Trappes, ☎ 01 30 62 20 12; Moisson-Mousseaux, 78840 Moisson, ☎ 01 34 79 33 34; Jablines/Annet, 77450 Jablines, ☎ 01 60 26 04 31 and Cergy-Neuville, rue des Etangs, 95001 Cergy-Neuville, ☎ 01 30 30 21 55 .

There are sailing schools all along the coast of northern France from Bray-Dunes to Auly-Onival. Some of the inland lakes are also ideal for these sports, for example the Val-Joly recreation area in the Avesnois region *(see map under L'AVESNOIS)*, the Etangs de la Sensée and Escaut, and the Lac de Monampteuil near Soissons.

For information, contact the **Fédération française de voile**, 55 avenue Kléber, 75784 Paris Cedex 16, ☎ 01 45 53 68 00.

Canoeing and kayaking

There are numerous possibilities on both the sea and rivers. Just a few are mentioned below:

Sea kayaking – Centre Agora, esplanade Parmentier, 62601 Berck-sur-Mer, ☎ 03 21 09 01 81; Mer et Rencontre, 4 digue Nicolas II, 59242 Dunkirk, ☎ 03 28 29 13 80; 53 quai de Lejoille, 80230 St-Valery-sur-Somme, ☎ 03 21 09 01 81; Wissant – contact the tourist office, ☎ 03 21 85 15 62.

River kayaking – Canoë-kayak Club, base nautique du petit Bief, 80400 Ham, ☎ 03 23 36 53 84 or ☎ 03 23 81 08 42; Kayak centre (slalom), 4 rue des Moulins-des-Orphelins, 62170 Montreuil-sur-Mer, ☎ 03 21 06 20 16; Canoë-kayak Club, bassin de l'Aa, Ecluse St-Bertin, 62500 St-Omer, ☎ 03 21 38 08 47.

Cruising the waterways

The rivers and canals once plied by well-laden barges constitute over 1 000mi of navigable waterways providing holidaymakers with an opportunity to enjoy a cruise or hire their own boat; both excellent ways of visiting the region.

Voies Navigables de France, 175 rue Ludovic-Boutleux, 62408 Béthune Cedex, ☎ 03 21 63 24 24, can provide information on travelling the waterways. They also have offices in Calais, Douai, Dunkirk, Lille, Margny-lès-Compiègne, St-Quentin and Valenciennes.

Marne Loisirs – Quai Jacques-Prévert Prolongé, 77100 Meaux, ☎ 01 64 34 97 97. Live-aboard boat rentals (no permit required) for 2 to 12 people.

Continental Waterways – This operator has a fleet of luxury hotel-barges, offering all-inclusive 6-night cruises. One of them, the "Anacoluthe", cruises on the River Seine and River Yonne between Bougival and Joigny and includes a Paris cruise by night. In the US ☎ (800) 676-6613, Fax (212) 688-9467 (www.continentalwaterways.com).

Nogent-sur-Marne Marina – ☎ 01 48 71 41 65. Peddle boats and small motor boats for rent.

House boat on the Somme Canal

The **Comité régional de tourisme d'Île-de-France** has joined with the Paris Port Authority and Voies Navigables de France to publish a brochure on boating opportunities in Île-de-France, *Prenez le large en Île-de-France*. They can also provide the *Tourisme fluvial – Guide pratique*, which gives addresses of rental agencies and marina facilities.

Likewise, the **Comité regional de tourisme du Nord-Pas-de-Calais** *(address under Local tourist offices above)* publishes a brochure on the area's inland waterway network.

Boat trips

– in the Audomarois region *(see St-Omer)*.
– around the market garden district of Amiens *(see Amiens)*.

– **Paris Canal** – Bassin de La Villette, 19-21 quai de la Loire, 75019 Paris, ☎ 01 42 40 96 97. On the canals of Paris and along the meanders of the Marne (Paris-Chennevières-Paris).

– **Un canal, deux canaux** – 15 allée du Canal, 77440 Lizy-sur-Ourcq, b 01 60 01 13 65.

– **Compagnie Croisi-Seinoise** – 43 quai Aristide-Briand, 78510 Triel-sur-Seine, ☎ 01 39 65 82 05. Boat trips from May to September on Sundays and public holidays, in the afternoon from Conflans-Sainte-Honorine (30min) or Auvers-sur-Oise (1hr 45min).

– **Tourisme Accueil Val-d'Oise** – Château de la Motte, rue François-de-Ganay, 95270 Luzarches, ☎ 01 30 29 51 00. Boat trips, lunch or dinner cruises from La Roche-Guyon, Auvers and Pontoise.

Fishing

The area around Paris offers many lakes and rivers for anglers of all levels, moreover northern France is crossed by a myriad of rivers, waterways and lakes; a paradise for anglers, especially along the Somme, Course, Lys, Aisne, Oise, Aa rivers and in the seven-valleys region (Canche, Authie, Ternoise etc).

The map-brochure with commentary entitled *Pêche en France* can be obtained from the Conseil Supérieur de la Pêche, 134 avenue de Malakoff, 75116 Paris, (☎ 01 45 02 20 20) or from the Fédération de Pêche (angling union) in each *département*.

Obligatory fishing permits *(cartes de pêche)* are often for sale on site in cafés or sports shops located near popular spots. Between 1 June and 30 September, it is possible, in certain places, to obtain a special holiday fishing permit *(permis de pêche "vacances")*, valid for a fortnight.

Boat trips for anglers are organised in Berck (Les Sternes, ☎ 03 21 84 43 48), Boulogne (Les Arsouins, ☎ 03 21 87 55 99), Calais (Mr Guilbert, ☎ 03 21 34 65 07), Etaples (May to September: contact the tourist office, ☎ 03 21 09 56 94 or the Pavillon de la mer, ☎ 03 21 94 17 51 – boat trips for non-anglers can also be arranged here) and Le Touquet (La Gaule Touquettoise, information and permits available from the café "chez Élie", 60 rue de Calais, ☎ 03 21 05 19 63 or Mr Gillet, ☎ 03 21 05 00 41.

THE NATURAL ENVIRONMENT

Regional nature parks have brought a breath of fresh air to the landscapes of the Paris-Ile-de-France region and northern France. They are promoted as protected areas, not only in regard to the natural environment but also for traditional lifestyles, crafts and trades. Information can be obtained from the *Maison du Parc* associated with each one.

In the Paris region, the Château de Dampierre, the Château de Breteuil and the Abbaye de Port-Royal-des-Champs (see description in the Sights section) are within the **Parc naturel régional de la Haute Vallée de Chevreuse**, created in 1985 (Maison du Parc, ☎ 01 30 52 09 09). Woods and farmlands alternate on the plateau along with lush valleys. The park offers over 200km/125mi of blazed hiking trails.

In the northern area covered in this guide, the **Parc naturel régional Nord-Pas-de-Calais** is divided into several sectors (Audomarois, Boulonnais, Plaine de la Scarpe et de l'Escaut, Avesnois, Monts de Flandre, Littoral Nord), managed by the Espace naturel régional, 17 rueJean-Roisin, 59800 Lille, ☎ 03 20 12 89 12. Discover dunes, forests, bays and wetlands by following itineraries on foot, horseback or bike. The park also offers cultural and thematic programmes.

Conservation district – To protect coastal areas, the **Conservatoire du Littoral** (Corderie Royale, BP 137, 17300 Rochefort ☎ 05 46 84 72 50) was set up in 1975 to safeguard and maintain ecological balance. There are now 339 protected sites, including

Simple pleasures

the dunes at Garennes-de-Lornel in Pas-de-Calais, the first to be covered by preservation measures.

Wildlife reserves – These areas are protected by virtue of the rare or remarkable flora and fauna found there, exceptional geological characteristics, or their role as a way station for migratory species. Some reserves are vast while others are quite modest. Waymarked footpaths allow visitors to observe the natural habitat. These include:

– **le Platier d'Oye**, Pas-de-Calais. Information at the Espace Naturel Régional;
– **a Dune Marchand**, part of the Conservatoire du Littoral, guided tour, ☎ 03 28 26 50 20.
– **la Baie de Canche**, observation points along the trails. Information at the Musée du Clos St-Victor in Étaples.
– **l'Étang de St-Ladre**, Somme. Information from the Association de Gestion de l'Étang de St-Ladre, 22 rue Victor-Hugo, in Boves.
– **le Marais d'Isle**, Aisne, *see St-Quentin.*
– **la Baie de Somme** (the largest reserve in the region). Information at the Parc du Marquenterre.

WALKING, CYCLING, RIDING

Rambling

There is an extensive network of well-marked footpaths in France which make rambling *(la randonnée pédestre)* a breeze. Several **Grande Randonnée (GR)** trails, recognisable for the red and white horizontal marks on trees, rocks and in town on walls, signposts etc, go through the region. Along with the GR, there are also the **Petite Randonnée**

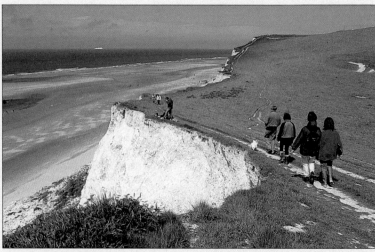

A brisk walk along the Côte d'Opale

(PR) paths, which are usually blazed with blue (2hr walk), yellow (2hr 15min-3hr 45min) or green (4-6hr) marks. Of course, with appropriate maps, you can combine walks to suit your desires.

To use these trails, obtain the *topoguide* for the area published by the **Fédération Française de la Randonnée Pédestre**. Their information centre is at 14 rue Riquet, 75019 Paris, ☎ 01 44 89 93 93, open Monday to Saturday from 10am to 6pm. Some English-language editions are available. Another source of maps and guides for excursions on foot is the **Institut National Géographique (IGN)**, which has a boutique in Paris at 107 rue de la Boétie (off the Champs-Elysées); to order from abroad, contact IGN-Sologne, Administration des Ventes, 41200 Romorantin-Lanthenay, ☎ 02 54 96 54 42, Fax 02 54 88 14 66, or visit the Web site (www.ign.fr) for addresses of wholesalers in your country. Among their publications, France 903 is a map showing all of the GR and PR in France (29F); the "Série Bleue" and "Top 25" maps, at a scale of 1:25 000 (1cm=250m), show all paths, whether waymarked or not, as well as refuges, camp sites, beaches etc (46-58F).

The **Conseil général du Nord** publishes, jointly with the **Association départementale de la randonnée**, itineraries covering various distances, with maps and information. Contact the **Comité départemental de tourisme du Nord** *(address under Local tourist offices above)*.

An association publishes a guide *(Guide des Sentiers de Promenade dans le Massif Forestier de Fontainebleau)*, on the famous forest southeast of Paris – a popular spot for ramblers, climbers, mushroom hunters and cyclists on day trips – ★nd provides guided tours that are open to all. For a programme, please send an international reply coupon to **Association des Amis de la Forêt de Fontainebleau**, 26 ruede la Cloche, BP 14, 77301 Fontainebleau, or call ☎ 01 64 23 46 45 (answering machine except Tuesdays 10am-midday and Fridays 2.30-4.30pm). To join up with fellow ramblers, try the **Randonneurs d'Ile-de-France** club, 92 rue du Moulin-Vert, 75014 Paris, ☎ 01 45 42 24 72, which organises walks in the region (small membership fee).

Cycling

The network of country roads is ideal for cycling. Lists of cycle hire shops are available from local tourist offices.

Bikes are carried free of charge on many regional trains and on the Paris-Amiens-Boulogne line. Cycle tours are easy to organise as there are cycle hire firms near or in train stations close to the main forests.

The **Fédération française de Cyclotourisme**, 8 rueJean-Marie-Jégo, 75013 Paris, ☎ 01 44 16 88 88, supplies itineraries covering most of France, outlining mileage, the level of difficulty of routes and sights to see.

Mountain biking *(VTT)*, or off-road cycling, has become very popular in France. There are many tracks laid out in the region, suitable for both new and experienced riders. The **Office National des Forêts** edits publications for mountain bike enthusiasts – *Guides VTT Evasion* (numbers 1 to 8). They include itineraries covering between 15km/9mi and 30km/18mi. In Île-de-France ☎ 01 40 19 58 82.

The **Fédération française de cyclisme** – 5 rue de Rome, 93561 Rosny-sous-Bois Cedex, ☎ 01 49 35 69 24 also publishes a guide with over 12 000mi of marked mountain biking tracks.

For the Somme, a *topoguide* published by the **Comité départemental du tourisme** in Amiens maps out a dozen itineraries of different lengths and levels of difficulty. Maps for other routes (Baie de Somme, Vallée de la Somme, Vallée du Scardon, Forêt de Crécy) are available from the **Syndicat intercommunal de développement économique et d'aménagement du Ponthieu-Marquenterre**, 3 rue de l'École-des-Filles, 80135 St-Riquier.

Horse-riding

The Nord-Pas-de-Calais and Ile-de-France regions have hundreds of miles of bridle paths running through forests or along the coast.

The **Délégation Nationale au Tourisme Équestre**, 9 boulevard Mac-Donald, 75019 Paris, ☎ 01 53 26 15 50, publishes an annual review called *Tourisme et loisirs équestres en France*. It lists all the possibilities for riding by region and *département*.

Addresses of riding stables and information on bridle paths are available from:

– **Association régionale de tourisme équestre Nord-Pas-de-Calais**, Le Paddock, 62223 St-Laurent-Blangy, ☎ 03 21 55 40 81.

– **Association régionale de tourisme équestre Picardie**, 8 rueFournier-Salovèze, B.P. 50354, 60203 Compiègne Cedex, ☎ 03 44 40 19 54.

– **Association régionale de Tourisme Équestre d'Île-de-France (ARTEIF)**, 1 rue Barbès, 95260 Beaumont-sur-Oise, ☎ 01 34 70 05 34. The brochure *Chevauchée en Île-de-France* lists the main centres in the region.

Horse racing

The Paris region has the largest number of race tracks anywhere in France, hosting all types of horse races. **France Galop** specialises in improving breeds of horses in France and manages the flat racing tracks in the Paris area: 46 place Abel-Gance, 92655 Boulogne Cedex, ☎ 01 49 10 20 30.

Track	Trotting	Flat course	Steeplechase	Main races
Chantilly		●		Prix Diane-Hermès (June) Prix du Jockey-Club (June)
Enghien	●	–	●	Prix de l'Atlantique (April) Prix d'Europe (July) Grand Steeple-Chase (October)
Longchamp		●		Grand Prix de Paris (June) Arc de Triomphe (October)
Maisons-Laffitte		●	Cross-country	Prix Robert Papin (July)
Saint-Cloud		●		Grand prix de St-Cloud (July) Critérium de St-Cloud (October)

The region also includes the Parisian race tracks of Auteuil (steeplechases) and Vincennes (trotting races).

Stud farm

It is possible to visit the **Haras national de Bréviaires**, a few miles north of Rambouillet. Visits daily except Sunday and public holidays; at 2.30pm and 4pm on Saturdays or by appointment during the week. Closed Sundays and public holidays. ☏ 01 34 84 92 07.

AND MORE...

Landsailing

Landsailers are a strange combination of three-wheeled go-kart and sailboat. Powered solely by the wind, they may exceed 100kph/62mph on the vast stretches of fine, hard sand along the coasts of northern France at low tide. In addition to landsailers, there are also speedsail boards which resemble windsurfing boards on wheels.
For information, contact the **Fédération française de char à voile**, Zone industrielle de la Vigogne, 62600 Berck-sur-Mer, ☏ 03 21 84 27 69.

Landsailing

Bird's-eye views

Tourist flights – In small planes from the Aérodrome de Cerny, 91590 Cerny, ☏ 01 64 57 55 85.
A 45min plane flight is one of the highlights of a weekend break (2 days and nights) in the Oise *département*: contact Loisirs Accueil at the **Comité Départementale du tourisme de l'Oise**, ☏ 03 44 45 82 12.

Hot-air ballooning – For individuals and groups from the Fontainebleau area. Flights with professional bilingual pilots from April to October, mornings and evenings, depending on the weather: France Montgolfières, 16 passage de la Main d'Or, 75011 Paris, ☎ 01 47 00 66 44 (www.franceballoons.com). This company is certified by the civil aviation authority. Flights also available in other areas of France.

Also available from La Roche-Guyon with Euro Montgolfières, ☎ 01 34 67 75 31 and in the Aisne *département* with Légend'Air, 10 rue du Village, 02600 Cutry, ☎ 03 23 55 50 50.

Tethered balloon rides – 150m/165yd above the château of Chantilly, from April to November. Contact Aérophile ☎ 01 44 57 35 35 *(see Chantilly)*.

Tethered rides are also organised outside the Parc préhistorique de Samara, near Amiens: Samara, 80310 La Chaussée-Tirancourt, ☎ 03 22 51 82 83.

Kite flying

This is another popular activity in northern France, particularly on the beaches. To obtain a good kite and learn how to fly it contact Atem, 110 rue de Metz in Le Touquet; for kite handling and building contact Centre Agora, Esplanade Parmentier in Berck-sur-Mer, ☎ 03 21 09 01 81.

Golf

Golfers can enjoy their favourite sport and take part in competitions in the region. Courses abound in the Nord-Pas-de-Calais region, in pleasantly rustic settings taking players up hill and over dale, on the edge of forests, or overlooking the sea. Contact the Comité Régional de Tourisme *(address under Local tourist offices above)* to obtain the brochure entitled *Golfs Nord-Pas-de-Calais*. Picardy has golf courses in Fort-Mahon, Quend-Plage, Grand-Laviers, Nampont-Saint-Martin, Salouel (3km/2mi from Amiens) and Querrien (7km/4mi from Amiens).

Rock climbing

The Île-de-France area offers climbers numerous possibilities for all levels at a number of natural sites – the most renowned and best equipped for bouldering, are to be found in and around **Fontainebleau Forest**. The highest rocks are at Larchant and the Dame Jouanne. The Massif des Trois-Pignons offers remarkable scenery and many different levels of difficulty. Bouldering may look easy, but requires good technique and adherence to safety procedures, and is thus best practised with a club or professional climbers.

Fédération française de la montagne et de l'escalade, 8 quai de la Marne, 75019 Paris, ☎ 01 40 18 75 50.

Club alpin Île-de-France, 24 rue Laumière, 75019 Paris, ☎ 01 53 72 88 00.

Health and fitness

Le Touquet is a well-known seaside resort with a sea therapy (thalassothérapie) centre offering a wide range of treatments (health, fitness, post-natal, dietetics, personalised programmes etc).

Institut Thalassa, sea front, 62520, ☎ 03 21 09 86 00; **Centre Thalgo** (Park Plaza hotel), 4 boulevard de la Canche, 62520, ☎ 03 21 06 88 84; **Centre Aquatique et Sportif de Remise en Forme** (Aqualud), the beach, 62520, ☎ 03 21 06 13 09.

Enghien-les-Bains has the only spa centre in Île-de-France. It specialises in throat ailments, skin diseases and rheumatism, but there are also programmes purely for relaxation lasting from 1 to 6 days. **Les Thermes**, 87 rue du Général-de-Gaulle, 95880, ☎ 01 39 34 12 00.

Something different ...

Dance halls

After the golden age of Impressionism in the late 19C, dance halls located along canals and rivers in the countryside around Paris, known as *guinguettes*, gradually disappeared from Île-de-France. These dance halls, serving drinks and meals, with music provided by a band, were reintroduced as part of regional policy and as a result of the enthusiasm of the *Culture Guinguette* association. They are now springing up again on the banks of the Marne and Seine, bringing back to life the picturesque atmosphere of the turn of the century.

You may prefer to be a casual spectator, enjoying simple fare at a riverside table. But if you have your dancing shoes on, dress with flair as the regulars do (men may need a tie to enter the ballroom). Brush up on your passo doble, tango and cha-cha-cha, and they'll be sure to take you for a native.

Association Culture Guinguette – 13 rue Jean-Guy-Labarbe, 94130 Nogent-sur-Marne, ☎ 01 48 73 44 11. This association for the promotion of these traditional gathering places can inform tourists of special events, and the dance styles – ranging from athletic rock to energetic polka by way of the classic waltz – practised in the member clubs:

- **Domaine Ste-Catherine**, 22-24 allée Centrale, Pont de Créteil, île de Brise-Pain, 94000 Créteil, ☎ 01 42 07 19 18.
- L'**Île du Martin-Pêcheur**, 41 quai Victor-Hugo, 94500 Champigny-sur-Marne, ☎ 01 49 83 03 02.
- **Le Moulin Vert**, 103 chemin du Contre-Halage, 94500 Champigny-sur-Marne, ☎ 01 47 06 00 91.
- **Quai 38**, 38 quai du Viaduc, 94500 Champigny-sur-Marne, ☎ 01 47 06 24 69.
- **La Goulue**, 17 quai Gabriel-Péri, 94340 Joinville-le-Pont, ☎ 01 48 83 21 77, www.la-goulue.com.
- **Le Petit Robinson**, 164 quai de Polangis, 94340 Joinville-le-Pont, ☎ 01 48 89 04 39, www.guinguette.com.
- **Chez Gégène**, 162 quai de Polangis, 94340 Joinville-le-Pont, ☎ 01 48 83 29 43.
- **La Grenouillère**, 68 avenue du 11-Novembre, 94210 La Varenne-St-Hilaire, ☎ 01 48 89 23 32.
- **Le Canotier**, 2 rue du Bac, 77410, Précy-sur-Marne, ☎ 01 60 01 62 12.
- **L'Auberge Charmante**, 20 quai de la Rive-Charmante, 93160 Noisy-le-Grand, ☎ 01 45 92 94 31.

HERITAGE TRAILS

These are itineraries based, for the most part, on architectural heritage presented in its historical context.

There are several historical routes in the area covered in this guide:
- Route du **Camp du Drap d'Or**: the "Cloth of Gold" route from Calais to Arras.
- Route des **Archers**: evoking the battle of Agincourt, when the French knights were defeated by the English archers during the Hundred Years War.
- Route des **Valois**: the Valois dynasty in the heart of the forests of Retz and Compiègne.
- Route du **Lys de France et de la Rose de Picardie**: "Lily of France and Rose of Picardy" route from Paris to Crécy-en-Ponthieu.
- Route de la **Vallée de l'Oise**: the Oise Valley route from Conflans-Ste-Honorine to Chimay (Belgium).
- Route des **Hauts Dignitaires**: from Breteuil to Fontainebleau: the châteaux of a number of the kingdom's important figures.
- Route des **Parcs et Jardins d'Île-de-France**: parks and gardens in Île-de-France.
- Route des **Peintres Impressionnistes**: Impressionist painters in the Val d'Oise.
- Route du **Roy Soleil**: châteaux occupied by the Sun King Louis XIV.

These and other special itineraries are the subject of brochures which can be found in most local tourist offices.

Route des villes fortifiées – This itinerary was set up by an association for the promotion of the **walled towns** of the Nord-Pas-de-Calais region. It includes 13 of the area's main citadels: Arras, Avesnes-sur-Helpe, Bergues, Boulogne-sur-Mer, Calais, Cambrai, Condé-sur-l'Escaut, Gravelines, Lille, Maubeuge, Montreuil-sur-Mer, Le Quesnoy, and St-Omer. The itinerary is 500km/310mi in length but is subdivided into shorter distances that provide many possibilities for excursions and tours. Each of the towns has a *Route des villes fortifiées* signpost at its entrance, accompanied by a logo. A map and brochure recounting the history of each town are available from the local tourist offices and from the **Comité régional de tourisme du Nord-Pas-de-Calais** (*address under Local tourist offices above*).

OTHER ITINERARIES

The **Route des Abbayes en Yvelines** is a tourist itinerary that passes via the Cistercian abbey of Les Vaux-de-Cernay and the abbey of Port-Royal-des-Champs, associated with the history of Jansenism.

The **Route des Maisons d'Ecrivains** opens the door to residences of famous authors in the Île-de-France, including Chateaubriand, Zola, Dumas.

TOURIST TRAINS

Le p'tit train de la Haute-Somme – South of Albert, 3km/2mi from Bray-sur-Somme, there is a narrow-gauge railway running from Froissy to Dompierre via the Cappy Tunnel (300m/325yd). The round trip covers a distance of 14km/9mi and takes about 1hr 30min. A visit to the railway museum rounds off the trip.

On Sundays and public holidays, the train is pulled by steam engine, with departures every hour from 2–5pm. From mid-July to the last week in August, it also runs during the week, except Mondays, at 2.30pm and 4pm and is pulled by a diesel engine. Adults 53F, children 33F.

For confirmation of dates and times and **bookings**, contact APPEVA, BP 106, 80001 Amiens Cedex 1, ☎ 03 22 44 55 40.

Baie de Somme – All aboard!

Le chemin de fer de la baie de Somme – A train of old carriages with platforms runs through fields and salt marshes from Noyelles to Le Crotoy, St-Valéry-sur-Mer and Cayeux-sur-Mer *(see Admission times and charges: Le CROTOY)*.

Chemin de fer touristique du Vermandois – From St-Quentin to Origny-Ste-Benoîte (44km/27mi round trip) via Ribemont. A steam train or an old-fashioned rail motor car crosses and then runs alongside the Canal de la Sambre in Oise.

For information, contact the tourist office in St-Quentin, ☎ 03 23 67 05 00 or C.F.T.V., BP 152, 02104 St-Quentin Cedex. For bookings, ☎ 03 23 07 88 02. The train runs from early June to the end of September on Sundays and public holidays.

Chemin de fer touristique de la vallée de l'Aa – The journey runs for 15km/9ml from Arques to Lumbres along the old branch of the St-Omer to Boulogne-sur-Mer line. It enables a visit to be made to the Fontinettes barge lift and stops at the Coupole d'Helfaut-Wizernes Second World War rocket-launching pad. Information can be obtained from Mr Chambelland at Longuenesse, ☎ 03 21 12 19 19.

Tramway touristique de la vallée de la Deûle – Trips by tram along a metre-gauge track over 2km/1.2mi between Marquette and Wambrechies in the suburbs of Lille. For information, contact AMITRAM, ☎ 03 28 42 44 58.

WINDMILLS

Once a common sight in the region, surviving examples of windmills have been taken under the wing of a local association which has begun to restore and develop them. The **Centre régional de molinogie**, 59650 Villeneuve-d'Ascq, ☎ 03 20 05 49 34, can provide brochures, maps and books on the subject. Most of the windmills cited in this guide are open to visitors. In addition, tourists are welcome at the Moulin de la Tourelle in Achicourt, south of Arras *(Friday 5-7pm and Sunday 3-6pm,* ☎ 03 21 71 68 68); the oil mill at St-Vaast-en-Cambrésis *(open to visitors May to September, Sunday from 2-7pm, contact Mr Bisiaux* ☎ 03 27 37 10 97 or Mr Leclercq ☎ 03 27 37 21 39).

On the plains of the Beauce and Brie, a few sails still catch the wind from time to time. Listed below are a few operating windmills whose owners accept visitors, at least for a look around the outside of the mill.

In the Beauce (Michelin map 60, folds 18, 19; A 10 "Allainville" exit or, from Orléans, the "Allaines-Chartres" exit):

– **Ouarville**: open 2-6pm, Sundays from Easter to 1 November, 10F. ☎ 02 37 22 13 87.
– **Levesville-la-Chenard**: Sunday afternoons, June to the end of August, or by appointment. ☎ 02 37 22 13 10.

In the Brie region (Michelin map 106, fold 36; 8km/5mi north of Nangis):

– **Gastins**: the Moulin Choix is open by appointment. ☎ 01 64 08 08 11.
– **Sannois**: on Mont Trouillet (near Enghien-les-Bains), open Sundays 1.30-6.30pm, 15F. Contact the Sannois town hall *(mairie)* ☎ 01 39 98 20 00.

The following windmills are described in the Sights section of this guide.
– Moulin de St-Maxent *(see ABBEVILLE)*.
– Moulin Den Leew à Pitgam *(see BERGUES)*.
– Moulin de CASSEL, Steenmeulen (at Terdeghem), Drievemeulen, Noordmeulen near Steenvoorde, Moulin de la Briarde at Wormhout *(see CASSEL)*.
– Noord-Meulen *(see HONDSCHOOTE)*.
– Moulin de Boeschepe *(see MONT DES CATS)*.
– VILLENEUVE D'ASCQ (windmill and museum)

The association's annual windmill festival is held around the region in June.

CARILLONS

Chiming bells are part of everyday life in many towns in northern France and particularly in Flanders. A carillon consists of several bells hung in a bell-tower or belfry. The bells ring out different refrains to indicate the hour, the quarter and the half hour. The word comes from a medieval term "quadrillon", a peal of four bells ringing in harmony. In the Middle Ages, clocks were mechanical; they included small bells which the bell-ringer struck using a mallet or hammer. After a gradual increase in the number of bells, the mallet was replaced by a keyboard. The automatic system with cylinders, used in some places, is progressively being replaced by an electrical system which is easier to maintain.

The main carillons in the Nord-Pas-de-Calais area are as follows:

Tourcoing – Eglise St-Christophe: 61 bells

Douai – Town hall: 62 bells

Bergues – Belfry: 50 bells

Avesnes-sur-Helpe – Collégiale St-Nicolas: 48 bells

Capelle-la-Grande – Belfry: 49 bells

Dunkirk – Tour St-Eloi: 48 bells

Le Quesnoy – Town hall: 48 bells

St-Amand-les-Eaux – Tower on the abbey church: 48 bells

Seclin – Collégiale St-Piat: 42 bells

Orchies – Church: 48 bells

Carillon concerts are held regularly in certain towns (for information, contact the tourist office).

FOR TRAVELLERS FROM OUTSIDE BRITAIN

A quick trip over the Channel to Kent or even London is possible if you have time to spare (passport required):

From Boulogne – 55min to Folkestone with the Hoverspeed Newcat. Five departures daily in the high season. ☎ 03 21 30 80 55.

From Calais – 75min by ferry or 35min by hovercraft to Dover. Seafrance offers day trips to Canterbury, by bus from Calais to Dover and train from Dover to Canterbury. ☎ 03 21 34 55 00.

Duo Line offers excursions to Folkestone or Canterbury from Calais in the high season. ☎ 03 21 91 57 58.

The **Eurotunnel** is situated at Coquelles (3km/2mi from the coast). For those travelling by car, the **Shuttle** links Calais with Folkestone, 24/24hr, 7 days a week. The journey lasts 35min, 28 of which are spent in the tunnel. ☎ 09 90 35 35 35.

From Paris or Lille – For those travelling by train, **Eurostar** takes 3hr for the journey from Paris-Gare du Nord to London-Waterloo, or 2hr from Lille-Europe *(see Getting there by rail above)*.

To obtain tourist information in Paris, contact the **Maison de la Grande Bretagne**, 19 rue des Mathurins, 75009 Paris, ☎ 01 44 51 56 20.

KID STUFF...

Below is a selection of some of the numerous theme parks and recreational areas in the regions covered in this guide.

Northern France

Aqualud, 62520 Le Touquet, ☎ 03 21 05 63 59/90 96 *(see le TOUQUET)*.

Bagatelle, 62155 Merlimont, ☎ 03 21 89 09 99 *(see Le TOUQUET: Excursions)*.

Bal Parc, 207 rue du Vieux-Château, 62890 Tournehem, ☎ 03 21 35 61 00.

Le Fleury, 5 rue de Bouchain, 59111 Wavrechain-sous-Faulx, ☎ 03 27 35 71 16.

Moulin de la Tour, 62560 Dennebrœucq, ☎ 03 21 95 11 39.

Olhain, 62150 Fresnicourt Le Dolmen, ☎ 03 21 27 91 79 *(see Château d'OLHAIN)*.

Prés du Hem, 7 avenue Marc-Sangnier, 59280 Armentières, ☎ 03 20 44 04 60.

Saint-Paul, 60650 St-Paul, ☎ 03 44 82 20 16.

Val Joly, 59132 Eppe-Sauvage, ☎ 03 27 61 83 76.

Loisinord, 62290 Nœux-les-Mines: water sports, ☎ 03 21 26 89 89; downhill skiing on an artificial slope (slag heap), ☎ 03 21 26 84 84.

Île-de-France

Parc Astérix, 60128 Plailly, ☎ 08 36 68 30 10 *(see Parc ASTÉRIX)*.

Disneyland Paris, 77777 Marne-la-Vallée, ☎ 01 64 74 30 00; advance booking, schedules and prices at www.disneylandparis.com *(see DISNEYLAND PARIS)*.

Mer de Sable, 60950 Ermenonville, ☎ 03 44 54 00 96 *(see Abbaye de CHAALIS)*.

France Miniature, 78990 Elancourt, ☎ 08 36 68 53 35 *(see FRANCE MINIATURE)*.

Thoiry, 78770 Thoiry, ☎ 01 34 87 40 67 *(see THOIRY)*.

Big Thunder Railroad at Disneyland Paris

PUPPETS

The north is an area traditionally known for its puppets *(marionnettes)* and a few theatres continue to give shows, to the great delight of children and adults alike:

Théâtre Le Grand Bleu, 36 avenue Max-Dormoy, Lille, ☎ 03 20 09 45 50.

Théâtre Louis Richard, 26 rue du Château, Roubaix, ☎ 03 20 73 10 10.

Théâtre du Broutteux, 11 bis place Ch.-Roussel, Tourcoing, ☎ 03 20 11 13 68.

Théâtre Mariska, 2 place de la Gare, Cysoing, ☎ 03 20 79 47 03.

Musée des Marionnettes du monde, Buire-le-Sec, ☎ 03 21 81 80 34.

Théâtre "Chès Cabotans d'Amiens", rue E.-David, Amiens, ☎ 03 22 92 42 06.

Souvenirs

Faience from Desvres

Les Artistes Faïenciers, 39 rue R.-Mingurt, 62240 Desvres, ☎ 03 21 92 39 94.

Fourmaintraux Dutertre, 114 rue Jean-Jaurès, 62240 Desvres, ☎ 03 21 91 65 55.

Desvres Tradition, 1 rue du Louvre, 62240 Desvres, ☎ 03 21 92 39 43.

Céramiques Modernes ANI-C, 108 chaussée Brunehaut, Longfosse, 62240 Desvres, ☎ 03 21 91 49 94.

Porcelain

From Arras – **Orfèvrerie-Porcelaine Caudron**, 15 place Vacquerie, 62000 Arras.
From Sèvres – on sale at the museum in Sèvres (☎ 01 45 34 34 00) or place André-Malraux, 75001 Paris, ☎ 01 47 03 40 20.

Glassware – **Verrerie-Cristallerie d'Arques**, 41 avenue du Général-de-Gaulle, 62510 Arques, ☎ 03 21 95 46 76.

Basketwork – **Vannerie la Belle Endormie**, 53-55 route Nationale, 80150 Le Boisle. Open Mon-Sat 9am-7pm and 2.30-7pm on Sundays and public holidays.

Lace – A tradition still present in three towns in northern France – Calais, Caudry-en-Cambrésis and Bailleul (there are lacework museums in each of these towns).

Puppets – From Buire-le-Sec or Amiens, in the Saint-Leu district, by the sculptor Jean-Pierre Facquier, 67 rue du Don, 80010 Amiens, ☎ 03 22 92 49 52.

Gastronomic specialities

Although it is unfortunately not always possible to take home fresh products, such as Brie or Coulommiers cheese, some foods are suitably packaged for transport and could include mustard from Meaux, Noyau de Poissy (an after-dinner drink made with brandy and an infusion of apricot kernels), Grand Marnier from Neauphle-le-Château (brandy and bitter orange), honey from the Gâtinais area or barley sugar candies from Moret-sur-Loing.

Further reading

Tourism, illustrated books

Cruising the French Waterways, Hugh McKnight *(London: A&C Black, 1991)*
France – the quiet way, John Liley *(London: Stanford Maritime, 1980)*
The Fair Face of Flanders, Patricia Carson, *(Tielt: Lannoo, 1991)*
Gothic Art, Andrew Martindale *(New York: Praeger, 1967)*
Impressions of the Seine, Carey More and Julian More *(New York: Rizzoli, 1991)*
Royal Palaces of France, Ian Dunlop *(London: Hamish Hamilton, 1985)*

History, commentary

Another World, Anthony Eden *(London: A Lane, 1976)*
Fatal Avenue: A Traveller's History of the Battlefields of Northern France and Flanders, 1346-1945, Richard Holmes *(London: Pimlico)*
Great Battles: Agincourt 1415, Christopher Hibbert *(Windrush Press)*
The Invention of Truth, Marta Morazzoni *(New York: AA Knopf, 1993)*
Our Fathers Have Told Us: The Bible of Amiens, John Ruskin *(London: George Allen, 1907)*
The Sands of Dunkirk, Richard Collier *(London: Collins, 1961)*

Fiction, literature

Complete Letters of Van Gogh, *(Boston: Bullfinch Press, 1991)*
Confessions, Jean-Jacques Rousseau
Germinal, Émile Zola
Letters of a Traveller, George Sand
The Middle Parts of Fortune: Somme and Ancre, 1916, Frederic Manning *(New York, St Martin's Press, 1977)*
The Snow Goose, Paul Gallico *(New York: AA Knopf, 1942)*
Ursule Mirouët, Honoré de Balzac

A few web sites

www.pas-de-calais.com is the regional tourist office site, with a complete English version. On it, you will find maps, useful addresses, scheduled events, information for booking *gîtes*, other furnished accommodation, and bed and breakfast establishments. There is a space for e-mailing your specific questions for reply.

www.chateauversailles.fr is a site as sumptuous as the palace, offering 360° views of the Hall of Mirrors and other highlights. The English version includes schedules of concerts and other special events.

www.francetourism.com is the official Web site for the French Government Tourist Office in the United States. It offers a very wide range of topics for perusal: history and culture, family activities, special interest events, news and general information.

www.franceway.com is an on-line magazine which focuses on culture and heritage. For each region, there are also suggestions for activities and practical information on where to stay and how to get there.

Calendar of events

FESTIVALS, FÊTES and FAIRS

Saturday throughout the year

Chartres .... "Les samedis musicaux de Chartres" (classical music, jazz, folk music). Information at the Office de tourisme, place de la Cathédrale. ☎ 02 37 27 18 52.

2nd half of February

Chambly .... "Bois-Hourdy" folk festival.

March-April

Seine-Saint-Denis .... Banlieues Bleues jazz festival. ☎ 01 43 85 66 00

Saturday March-July

Versailles .... Baroque music concert series. ☎ 01 39 20 78 78.

Y. Thierry/MICHELIN

Flying high at Berck-Plage

April

Abbeville et baie de Somme ...... Ornithology Film Festival (screenings, exhibits, nature walks, lectures). ☎ 03 22 24 02 02.

Valenciennes .... Action and Adventure film festival.

Palm Sunday weekend (Friday to Monday)

Coulommiers .... Cheese and wine fair. ☎ 01 64 03 88 09.

Last Sunday in April

Fortified towns .... Regional fortified towns festival. ☎ 03 27 49 50 05.
in the Nord-Pas-de-Calais

May

Amiens .... International jazz festival. ☎ 03 22 97 79 77.
Lille .... "Montgolfiades" balloon festival.
Laon .... Euromédiévales (banquet, displays, medieval markets).

3rd Sunday in May

Rambouillet .... Lily-of-the-Valley festival. ☎ 01 34 83 21 21.

Whitsun weekend

St-Quentin .... "Fêtes du Bouffon".

May-June

Auvers-sur-Oise .... Music Festival. ☎ 01 30 36 77 77.

3rd Sunday after Whitsun

Lille .... Fêtes de Lille: various events around the city.

June

Boulogne-sur-Mer..................... Music & Ramparts. ☎ 03 21 31 46 46.

Beginning of June

St-Valery-sur-Somme .... Festival of William the Conqueror. ☎ 03 22 60 93 50.

1st weekend in June

Bièvres..................................... Photo fair. ☎ 01 69 41 30 32.

Mid June (odd-numbered years)

Aérodrome du Bourget .... International Air and Space Show. ☎ 01 53 23 33 33).

2nd weekend in June

Provins..................................... Medieval festival. ☎ 01 64 60 26 26.

3rd Sunday in June

Gerberoy................................... "Fête des roses".

Windmills around the region ... National Windmill Day. Information: ARAM. ☎ 03 20 05 49 34.

23 June

Long .... "Feux de la Saint-Jean" mid-summer festival.

June-July

Saint-Denis .... Festival of classical music. ☎ 01 48 13 12 10.

Late June-mid August

St-Germain-en-Laye .... "Fête des Loges" fun fair. ☎ 01 30 87 21 70.

Saturday or Sunday June-September

Royaumont .... Concerts at the abbey. ☎ 01 34 68 05 50.

July

Côte d'Opale............................ Music Festival. ☎ 03 21 30 40 33.

St-Riquier .... Classical music festival.

1st Sunday in July

Noyon .... Red fruits market.

Around 14 July

Bray-Dunes .... World Folklore Festival.

July-August

Gravelines..................................... "Les Estivales" (outdoor theatre festival – night-time).

Hardelot.................................... Music Festival.

3rd Sunday in July

Buire-le-Sec .... Crafts and Trades Fair.

End July

St-Omer .... Procession of floats on the canal.

Tuesday, Thursday and Saturday at 9.15pm in July and August

Chartres .... "Soirées Estivales" (summer nights festival).

July-September

Sceaux .... "Festival de l'Orangerie". ☎ 01 46 60 07 79.

1st weekend in August

Calais.. Festival of the sea.

One week in mid August

Wimereux.................................. Wimereux during the Belle Epoque.

August

Le Touquet .... International music festival.

September

In Picardie .... "Festival des cathédrales". ☎ 03 22 97 37 49.

September-October

Throughout Île-de-France .... Festival: concerts. ☎ 01 44 94 28 50

1st Sunday in September

Arleux .... Garlic Fair.

1st weekend in September

Lille.. "Grande braderie" flea market and sale.

Garlic Festival

2nd Sunday in September
Armentières .... "Fête des Nieulles".

Last weekend in September (odd-numbered years)
Senlis .... "Rendez-vous de Septembre": car-free city, music festival in the streets on odd-numbered years, last weekend in the month. ☎ 03 44 53 06 40.

Late September-early October
Chatou .... "Grande foire nationale à la brocante et aux jambons" (flea market and ham fair). ☎ 01 47 70 88 78.

1st Sunday in October
Steenvoorde .... Hops festival.
Suresnes .... "Rues de Rêve" street theatre festival. ☎ 01 41 18 18 76.

October
Barbizon .... Painting awards.
Lille .... Festival de Lille. ☎ 03 20 52 47 23.

3rd Sunday in October
Sains-du-Nord .... Cider festival.

Mid October-mid November
Tourcoing .... Jazz Festival. ☎ 03 20 23 37 00.

November
St-Jean-de-Beauregard .... Fairs: "Fruits and vegetables from the past and present". ☎ 01 60 12 00 01.

3rd weekend in December
Licques .... Turkey festival.

24 December
Boulogne-sur-Mer .... "Fête des Guénels" (a *guénel* resembles a jack-o'-lantern, carved out of a beet!).

Les nieulles

The name of these little biscuits (pronounced *nee-uls*) comes from the Spanish *niola*, which means "crumb". In 1510, a banquet was held in the reception rooms of the Hôtel de Ville, presided by the Count of Luxembourg, Lord of Armentières. When the guests had finished feasting, the Count stepped out on the balcony. A crowd of children gathered below, holding their hands out for alms. The Count flung the crumbs from the cake at them, as if they were so many hungry birds.

PAGEANTS, "SON ET LUMIÈRE", FOUNTAINS

Easter-1 November

Provins..................................... Falconry show.

2nd and last Saturday of the month, April-October

Vaux-le-Vicomte......................... Fountains in the garden.

3rd Sunday of the month, May-September

Parc de Marly-le-Roi .... Grand fountain. ☎ 01 30 61 61 35.

Sunday May-September (3.30-5pm)

Versailles .... Fountains and music in the palace garden. ☎ 01 39 24 88 88.

Thursday and Saturday May-mid October between 8.00pm and midnight

Vaux-le-Vicomte......................... Candlelight tour of château and gardens. ☎ 01 64 14 41 90.

Sunday in June

St-Cloud.................................... Fountains. ☎ 01 41 12 02 90.

June-July

Coucy-le-Château .... "Coucy la Merveille" medieval "son et lumière".

Mid June-August

Provins..................................... Jousting tournament in the moat. ☎ 01 64 60 26 26.

Friday and Saturday mid June-mid July and early September

Meaux...................................... "Son et lumière" ("The Song of the Stones"). ☎ 01 64 33 95 15.

3rd weekend in June

Chantilly.................................... "Nuits de Feu" international fireworks competition, on even-numbered years. ☎ 03 44 45 82 12.

Saturday evening June-September

Moret-sur-Loing .... "Son et lumière" ("Reflections of History"). ☎ 01 60 70 41 66.

Certain Saturdays July-September

Versailles .... "Grandes Fêtes de Nuit au bassin de Neptune", fireworks, fountains and music in the palace garden. ☎ 01 30 83 78 88.

September

Évry-Courcouronnes .... "Son et lumière" on the lake, with fountains. ☎ 01 64 97 89 07.

Provins – Jousting tournament

SPORTS EVENTS

Mid February

Le Touquet .... "Enduro des sables" endurance race.
☎ 03 21 05 21 65.

Liévin .... International athletics meeting. ☎ 03 20 72 05 17.

End March-end November

Fontainebleau .... La Solle racetrack open. ☎ 01 60 74 99 99.

Landsailing competition

April

Berck-sur-Mer .... International kite festival.

2nd Sunday in April

Roubaix.................................... "Paris-Roubaix" cycle race.

Last Sunday in April

Bergues .... "Fête de la plume" (archery).

May

Dunkerque .... Cycle race.

Whitsun weekend

Aérodrome de Cerny................. Vintage aircraft show. ☎ 01 64 57 55 85.

1st Sunday in June

Chantilly.................................... "Prix du Jockey-Club" horse race.

2nd Sunday in June

Chantilly.................................... "Prix de Diane-Hermès" horse race.

June

La Courneuve............................ International Pétanque festival.

Mid August-mid September

Fontainebleau .... "Grande semaine du cheval", Sporting horse
breeders' week. Hippodrome du Grand Parquet.
☎ 01 60 74 99 99.

1st weekend in September

Boulogne .... The "route du poisson" (equestrian event).

Throughout September

Wimereux .... French funboard championships.

3rd weekend in September

Chantilly.................................... "Trophée de Polo", French championship.

October

Fontainebleau .... "Grande semaine du cheval" (French championship: jumping and dressage). Hippodrome du
Grand Parquet. ☎ 01 60 74 99 99.

Berck-sur-Mer .... Land sailing competition.

437

CARNIVALS AND GIANTS IN THE NORTH

Sunday before Mardi Gras and Mardi Gras Tuesday

Bailleul... Carnival with giant Gargantua.

Dunkerque................................. Carnival.

Equihen-Plage......................... Carnival.

Solesmes................................... Carnival warning: onlookers are hosed with water)

Sunday after Mardi Gras

Malo-les-Bains......................... Carnival.

Trélon... Carnival ("Fête de St-Pansar").

Sunday after mid Lent

Hazebrouck............................... Grand procession in traditional costumes, giants on parade. Carnival the following Sunday.

Easter Monday

Cassel.. Giants on parade: Reuze-Papa and Reuze-Maman.

Denain.. Carnival.

May

Amiens.. Carnival.

Carnival Giants

In the Picardy dialect, they are *gayants*; in the Flemish vernacular, *reuzes*; the French call them *géants.* The numerous (about 200) larger-than-life characters come out to play at carnival time and for other local festivities; in Hazebrouck they are displayed in the museum year round.

The first carnival giants appeared in Portugal in the 13C, and in the northern part of France in the 16C: 1530 in Douai, 1556 in Maubeuge, 1559 in Cambrai. Since the early 20C, the family has grown.

In recent years, they have held international family reunions, *Rondes de Géants* (1992 in Barcelona, 1993 in Steenvoorde, 1994 in Maastricht and Folkestone). The association **La ronde des géants**, 7 rue St-Bernard, 59000 Lille, ☎ 03 20 93 94 67, serves to promote and protect this age-old tradition.

One Sunday in June

Bourbourg................................. Giants on parade: Gédéon, Arthurine et Florentine.

map 51, fold 3St-Omer............ "Ronde des Géants".

July

Hazebrouck............................... Summer Carnival featuring giants – Roland, Tisje, Tasje, Toria and Babe Tisje.

Sunday following 5 July

Douai.. Grand parade featuring the Gayant (giant) family.

14 July

Arras.. Jousting and giants of Arras.

15 August

Cambrai...................................... Giants on parade: Martin and Martine.

2nd weekend of September

Valenciennes............................. "Les Folies de Binbin".

2nd Sunday in October

Comines..................................... "Fête des Louches" featuring giants – Grande Gueuloutte and P'tite Chorchine.

Admission times and charges

As times and charges for admission are liable to alteration, the information below is given for guidance only. Every sight for which there are times and charges is indicated by the symbol ⊙ *in the main part of the guide. Text in italics indicates that conditions are subject to change.*

Order: The information is listed in the same order as the entries in the alphabetical section of the guide.

Dates: Dates given are inclusive.

Last admission: Ticket offices usually shut 30min before closing time; exceptions only are mentioned below.

Charge: The charge is for an individual adult; where appropriate the charge for a child is given.

Disabled tourists: Sights which have comprehensive facilities for disabled tourists are indicated by the symbol &. *below.*

Guided tours: The departure time of the last tour of the morning or afternoon will be up to 1hr before the actual closing time. Most tours are conducted by French speaking guides but in some cases the term "guided tours» may cover group visiting with recorded commentaries; some of the larger and more frequented sights may offer guided tours in other languages. Enquire at the ticket office or bookstall. Other aids commonly available for the foreign tourist are notes, pamphlets or audio-guides.

Lecture tours: These are regularly organised during the tourist season in towns of special interest. The information is given under the appropriate heading. In towns labelled "Villes d'Art et d'Histoire" and "Villes d'Art" ▲, *tours are conducted by lecturers/guides approved by the "Caisse Nationale des Monuments Historiques et des Sites."*

Churches: Admission times are indicated if the interior is of special interest. Churches are usually closed from noon to 2pm. Visitors should refrain from walking about during services. Visitors to chapels are accompanied by the person who keeps the keys. A donation is welcome.

Tourist Information Centres: The addresses and telephone numbers are given for the local Tourist Information Centres, which provide information on local market days, early closing days etc.

A

ABBEVILLE 🖪 1 place Amiral-Courbet – 80100 – ☎ 03 22 24 27 92

Guided tours of the town – Contact the tourist office.

Collégiale St-Vulfran – Apr to Oct: 10am-noon, 2-6pm.

Église du St-Sépulcre – Summer: weekdays 2-6pm.

Musée Boucher de Perthes – Daily except Tues: 2-6pm. Closed 1 Jan, 1 May, 14 July, 1 Nov and 25 Dec. No charge. ☎ 03 22 24 08 49.

Excursions

Château de Bagatelle – July to end of Aug: guided tours (45min) daily except Tues 2-6pm. 50F. ☎ 03 22 24 02 69.

Friville-Escarbotin: Musée des Industries du Vimeu – Easter to end of Oct: guided tours (1hr) daily except Sat 2.30-5.30pm, Sun and public holidays 2.30-6.30pm. 15F. ☎ 03 22 26 42 37.

Huppy: Église St-Sulpice – 2-5pm

ALBERT

Musée des Abris – Mar to mid-Dec: 9.30am-noon, 2-6pm (July and Aug: 9.30am-6pm). 20F. ☎ 03 22 75 16 17.

AMIENS 🖪 6 bis rue Dusevel – 80000 – ☎ 03 22 71 60 50

Guided tours of the town ▲ – Amiens has been listed as a "Town of Art and History"; the guided tours (1hr 30min), organised by the tourist office, are conducted by guides approved by the Ministry of Culture. Sat at 2.30pm (daily July and Aug). 30F.

Cathédrale Notre-Dame – Guided tours available, contact the tourist office.

Towers – Apr to Sept: daily except Tues and Sun mornings 10.30-11.30am, 2-5pm; Oct to Mar: Mon-Fri 3-4pm. Closed 1 Jan, 1 May and 25 Dec. 15F. ☎ 03 22 80 03 41.

Stalls – 3.30-6.30pm. Closed 1 Jan and 25 Dec. No charge. ☎ 03 22 80 03 41.

Treasury – Contact the sales counter of the Centre des Monuments Nationaux (National Monuments Centre).

Théâtre de Marionnettes – **Chés Cabotans d'Amiens puppet theatre**: Tours – ♿ Guided tours by appointment (2 days in advance) daily except Mon and Tues 10am-noon, 2-6pm, unaccompanied tours Sun 2-6pm (mid-July to end Aug: unaccompanied tours). ☎ 03 22 22 30 90.

Hortillonnages – Apr to end of Oct: guided tours (1hr) by boat from 2pm onwards. Maison des hortillonnages, 54 boulevard Beauvillé. 30F (children 15F). ☎ 03 22 92 12 18.

Musée de Picardie – ♿ Daily except Mon 10am-12.30pm, 2-6pm. Closed 1 Jan, 1 May, 14 July, 11 Nov and 25 Dec. 20F, no charge 1st Sunday in the month. ☎ 03 22 97 14 00.

Musée d'Art local et d'Histoire régionale – Oct to Easter: Sun 2-6pm; Easter to Sept: Thur-Sun 2-6pm. Closed 1 Jan, 1 May, 14 July, 11 Nov and 25 Dec. 20F. ☎ 03 22 97 14 00.

Centre de documentation Jules Verne – ♿ Guided tours (1hr, last admission 1hr before closing time) 9am-noon, 2-6pm, Sat-Sun and public holidays 2-6pm. Closed 1 Jan, 1 May and 25 Dec. 20F. ☎ 03 22 45 37 84.

Jardin Archéologique de St-Acheul – ♿ June to Sept: 9am-1pm, 2-6pm; Oct to May: 9am-noon, 2-5pm (Mar to May and Oct: 9am-12.30pm, 2-5.30pm). Closed 1 Jan and 25 Dec. 30F. ☎ 03 22 47 82 57.

ARRAS

🅱 Hôtel de ville, place des Héros – 62000 – ☎ 03 21 51 26 95

Guided tours of the town 🅰 – Tours of the town centre (Grand'Place, town hall, St-Vaast Abbey, cathedral etc) last 2hr. End of June to mid-Sept: Wed, Sat-Sun at 3pm. 35F. Contact the tourist office.

Hôtel de ville – End of Sept to end of Apr: 9am-noon, 2-6pm, Sun 10am-12.30pm, 3-6.30pm; end of Apr to end of Sept: 9am-6pm, Sun 10am-1pm, 2.30-6.30pm. Closed 1 Jan and 25 Dec. 22F. ☎ 03 21 51 26 95.

Belfry – Closed for restoration work, reopening in 2001.

Tour of the subterranean passages – May to Sept: guided tours (45min) 9am-6.30pm, Sun and public holidays 10am-1pm, 2.30-6.30pm; Oct to Apr: 9am-noon, 2-6pm, Sun and public holidays 10am-12.30pm, 3-6.30pm. Closed 1 Jan and 25 Dec. 22F. ☎ 03 21 51 26 95.

Ancienne abbaye St-Vaast – 2.15-6pm.

Musée des Beaux-Arts – Oct to Mar: daily except Tues 10am-noon, 2-5pm, Thur 10am-5pm, Sat 10am-noon, 2-6pm, Sun 10am-noon, 3-6pm; Apr to Sept: daily except Tues 10am-noon, 2-6pm, Thur 10am-6pm. Closed 1 Jan, 1 and 8 May, 14 July, 1 and 11 Nov, 25 Dec. 20F, no charge 1st Wed and Sun in the month. ☎ 03 21 71 26 43.

Cathédrale St-Vaast – 2.15-5pm.

Parc ASTÉRIX

July and Aug: 9.30am-7pm; Apr: 10am-6pm; May to June: 10am-6pm, Sat-Sun and public holidays 9.30am-7pm; Sept: Wed 10am-6pm, Sat-Sun 9.30am-7pm; beginning of Oct to mid-Oct: Wed, Sat-Sun 10am-6pm. Closed mid-Oct to end of Mar. Opening days and times liable to modification, ask for information. 175F (children 125F, under 3's no charge). ☎ 08 36 68 30 10, 3615 Parc Astérix or Internet site: www.parcasterix.fr

AUVERS-SUR-OISE

Maison de Van Gogh – 10am-6pm. Closed between Christmas and beginning of Jan. 30F (children no charge). ☎ 01 30 36 60 60.

Musée de l'Absinthe – Sat-Sun and public holidays 11am-6pm (June to Sept: daily except Mon and Tues). 25F. ☎ 01 30 36 83 26.

Maison-Atelier de Daubigny – Easter to All Saints: Thur-Sun and public holidays: 2-6.30pm. 28F. ☎ 01 34 48 03 03.

Château d'Auvers – Voyage to the time of the Impressionists – Audio tours (2hr, last admission 1hr 30min before closing) daily except Mon 10.30am-4.30pm (Apr to Sept: 6pm). Closed 1 Jan and 25 Dec. 65F (children 40F). ☎ 01 34 48 48 48.

AVESNES-SUR-HELPE

Église St-Nicolas – Guided tours available, contact the tourist office.

Excursions

THE AVESNOIS REGION

Felleries: Moulin des Bois-Jolis – Apr to end of Oct: 2-6pm, Sat-Sun and public holidays: 2.30-6.30pm. 15F. ☎ 03 27 59 03 46.

Sars-Poteries: Musée-atelier du Verre – Daily except Tues 10am-6pm, Sat-Sun and public holidays 10am-7pm. Closed between Christmas and New Year's Day. 20F. ☎ 03 27 61 61 44.

Water mill – July and Aug: daily except Tues 3-7pm; Apr to June and Sept to Oct: Sun and public holidays 3-7pm. Closed Nov to Mar. 15F. ☎ 03 27 61 60 01.

Trélon: Atelier-musée du verre – ♿ Apr to end of Oct: 2-6pm, Sat-Sun and public holidays 2.30-6.30pm. 30F. ☎ 03 27 59 71 02.

Sains-du-nord: Maison du Bocage – Apr to end of Oct: 2-6pm, Sat-Sun and public holidays 2.30-6.30pm. 20F. ☎ 03 27 59 82 24.

AZINCOURT

Musée de Traditions populaires et d'Histoire locale – ♿ Apr to Oct: 9am-6pm; Nov to Mar: 10am-5pm. Closed 1 Jan and 25 Dec. 10F (40F from June 2001). ☎ 03 21 04 41 12.

B

Parc d'attractions de BAGATELLE

♿ Apr to Sept: 10am-7pm. 102F (3-7 years 82F). ☎ 03 21 89 09 99.

BAILLEUL

Beffroi – Guided tours (1hr) July and Aug: Tues, Wed and Fri at 4.30pm, Sat at 3pm, Sun at 11am; Apr to June and Sept: Sat at 3pm, Sun at 11am. 16F. ☎ 03 28 43 81 00.

Musée Benoît De Puydt – Daily except Tues 2-5.30pm. Closed during the carnival in Feb, 1 May and between Christmas and New Year's Day. 17F, no charge 1st Sunday in the month. ☎ 03 28 49 12 70.

Maison de la dentelle – Daily except Sun and public holidays 2-5pm. Closed between Christmas and New Year's Day. 10F. ☎ 03 28 43 81 00.

Excursions

Mont des Cats: Trappist Monastery – ♿ Mar to Sept: 9.45-11.45am, 2-6pm, Mon 2-5pm, Thur 9.45-11.45am, 2-5pm, Sun 2-6pm; Oct to Feb: 9.45-11.45am, 2.15-5pm, Mon and Sun 2.15-5pm. No charge. ☎ 03 28 42 52 50.

Centre d'accueil Charles Grimminck – Tues-Sat 10am-noon, 2.30-6pm, Sun and Mon 2.30-6pm. No charge. ☎ 03 28 43 83 70.

Boeshepe: Ondankmeulen – Apr to Oct: guided tours (45min) Sun and public holidays 1-6pm. Closed Oct to Mar. 10F. ☎ 03 28 42 50 24.

BARBIZON   🚹 55 Grande-Rue – 77630 – ☎ 01 60 66 41 87

Auberge du Père Ganne – School of Barbizon Museum – Daily except Tues 10am-12.30pm, 2-5pm (Apr to Sept: 6pm). Closed at Christmas. 25F. ☎ 01 60 66 22 27.

BAVAY

Musée archéologique – For times and prices, ☎ 03 27 63 13 95.

Excursion

Bellignies: Musée du Marbre et de la Pierre bleue – Mid-Feb to mid-Dec: 2-6pm. 12F. ☎ 03 27 66 89 90.

BEAUVAIS   🚹 1 rue Beauregard – 60000 – ☎ 03 44 45 08 18

Guided tours of the town 🅰 – Contact the tourist office.

Cathédrale St-Pierre: Astronomical clock – Sound and light show (30min) at 10.40am, 11.40am, 2.40pm, 3.40pm and 4.40pm (July and Aug: additional show at 12.40pm and 5.40pm). Closed 1st week in Jan and 1st week in Feb. 22F (children 5F). ☎ 03 44 48 11 60.

Musée départemental de l'Oise – July to mid-Oct: daily except Tues 10am-6pm; mid-Oct to end of June: daily except Tues 10am-noon, 2-6pm. Closed 1 Jan, Easter, Whitsun, 1 May, 1 Nov and 25 Dec. 10F, no charge on Wed. ☎ 03 44 11 43 83.

Galerie nationale de la tapisserie – Apr to Sept: daily except Mon 9.30am-noon, 2-6.30pm (last admission 30min before closing); Oct to Mar: daily except Mon 10am-noon, 2.30-5pm. Closed 1 Jan, 1 May and 25 Dec. 25F. ☎ 03 44 05 14 28.

Manufacture nationale de tapisserie – ☂ Guided tours (45min) Tues-Thur at 2.15pm and 3.30pm. Closed public holidays. 12F. ☎ 03 44 05 14 28.

Église de Marissel – Visits by appointment. ☎ 03 44 05 46 43.

Excursions

Château de Troissereux – Guided tours (1hr) 2-6pm (lecture-tours of the medieval clock 2.15pm). Closed 25 Dec. 45F (15F extra charge for the clock). ☎ 03 44 79 00 00.

Gerberoy: Museum – Apr to end of Sept: Sat-Sun and public holidays 2.30-6pm (July and Aug: daily except Tues). No charge. ☎ 03 44 82 26 17.

BERGUES
Place de la République – 59380 – ☎ 03 28 68 60 44

Belfry – 9.30am-12.30pm, 2-6pm, Sat-Sun and public holidays 9.30am-12.30pm, 2-6.30pm (low season: 9.30am-noon, 2-6pm, Sat-Sun and public holidays 10am-noon, 2-5.30pm). 10F. ☎ 03 28 68 71 06.

Bell concerts – Bell concert Mon at 11am, eve of public holidays at 5pm. Information available at the tourist office.

Musée municipal – Daily except Tues 10am-noon, 2-5pm. Closed in Jan. 15F. ☎ 03 28 68 13 30.

Excursions

Quaëdypre: Church – Guided tours available by request at the town hall. ☎ 03 28 68 66 03.

West-Cappel: Église St-Sylvestre – Guided tours 9am-noon, 2-6pm. Contact Mr Degrand, 122 rue du Sénateur-Vandaele.

Pitgam: Moulin "Den Leeuw" – End of Apr to end of Sept: guided tours (30min) 3rd Sun in the month 3-7pm. 10F. ☎ 03 28 62 10 90.

BLÉRANCOURT

Musée national de la coopération franco-américaine – ☂ Daily except Tues 10am-12.30pm, 2-5.30pm. Closed 1 Jan, 1 May and 25 Dec. 16F, no charge 1st Sunday in the month. ☎ 03 23 39 60 16.

Maison de St-Just – Tues-Thur 9am-noon, 2-5pm, Mon and Sat 2-5pm, Fri 9am-noon. Closed Sun (except June to Sept: 2.30-5.30pm) and public holidays. No charge.

BOULOGNE-SUR-MER
Quai de la Poste – 62200 – ☎ 03 21 80 56 78

Guided tours of the town Ⓐ – Contact the tourist office.

Belfry – Daily except Sun 8am-6pm, Sat 8am-noon. Closed public holidays. No charge. ☎ 03 21 87 80 80.

Basilique Notre-Dame:

Crypt and treasury – Sept to end of Apr: 2.30-5pm; May to end of June: 2-6pm, Sun and public holidays 2.30-6pm; July and Aug: 2-7pm, Sun and public holidays 2.30-7pm. 10F. ☎ 03 21 99 75 98.

Château-Musée – Daily except Tues 10am-12.30pm, 2-5pm (Sun 5.30pm). Closed 1 Jan, 1 May and 25 Dec. 20F. ☎ 03 21 10 02 20.

Nausicaa – ☂ 9.30am-6.30pm (July and Aug: 8pm, last admission 1hr before closing). Closed first 3 weeks in Jan and 25 Dec. 68F (3-12 years 48F). ☎ 03 21 30 98 98.

Musée San Martin – Guided tours (30min) daily except Wed and Thur 10am-noon, 2-6pm. Closed Jan and public holidays. No charge. ☎ 03 21 31 54 65.

Musée d'Histoire naturelle – ☂ 10-11.45am, 2-5.45pm, Sat-Sun by request 2-5.45pm. Closed 1 Jan, 1 May and 25 Dec. No charge. ☎ 03 21 80 09 80.

Excursions

Colonne de la Grande-Armée – Apr to Sept: 9am-noon, 2-6pm; Oct to Mar: daily except Tues 9am-noon, 2-5pm. Closed 1 Jan, 1 May, 1 and 11 Nov and 25 Dec. 15F. ☎ 03 21 80 43 69.

Le Wast: Church – July and Aug: Sat afternoon by request to Mme Bourdon. ☎ 03 21 33 32 05.

Manoir du Huisbois – May to Sept: Sun and public holidays 3-7pm. No charge. ☎ 03 21 83 38 79.

Hydrequent: Maison du marbre et de la géologie – ♿ July and Aug: 10am-12.30pm, 2-6.30pm, Sat-Sun 2.30-6.30pm; Apr to June and Sept to Oct: daily except Sat 9am-12.30pm, 1.30-6pm, Sun and public holidays 2.30-6.30pm. 25F. ☎ 03 21 83 19 10.

Aéroport du BOURGET

Musée de l'Air et de l'Espace du Bourget – ♿ Daily except Mon 10am-5pm (May to Oct: 6pm). 40F (children 30F). ☎ 01 49 92 70 62. Internet site: www.mae.org

Château de BRETEUIL

Guided tours (45min) 2.30-5.30pm, Sat 2.30-6pm, Sun and public holidays, zone C school holidays 11am-6.30pm; May to mid-Oct: costumed guides Sun and public holidays. Park opens at 10am. 58F (children 48F), park only 39F. ☎ 01 30 52 05 02. Internet site: www.castle-france.com

C

CALAIS
🄸 12 boulevard Clemenceau – 62100 – ☎ 03 21 96 62 40

Le phare – June to Sept: 2-6.30pm, Sat-Sun and public holidays 10am-noon, 2-6.30pm; Oct to May: Wed 2-5.30pm, Sat-Sun 10am-noon, 2-5.30pm. 14F (children 7F). ☎ 03 21 34 33 34.

Musée des Beaux-Arts et de la Dentelle – ♿ Daily except Tues 10am-noon, 2-5.30pm, Sat 10am-noon, 2-6.30pm, Sun 2-6.30pm. Closed public holidays. 20F, no charge on Wed. ☎ 03 21 46 48 40.

Musée de la Guerre – ♿ Feb to end of Nov: (last admission 45min before closing) daily except Tues 11am-5pm (Apr to Sept: daily 10am-6pm). 25F. ☎ 03 21 34 21 57.

CAMBRAI
🄸 48 rue de Noyon – 59400 – ☎ 03 27 78 36 15

Guided tours of the town 🄰 – The visits, the theme of which changes every year, last 2hr. June to Sept: Sun at 4pm. 25F. Contact the tourist office.

Cathédrale Notre-Dame – Guided tours available, contact the tourist office.

Église St-Géry – Visits on weekdays.

Musée des Beaux-Arts – ♿ Daily except Mon and Tues 10am-noon, 2-6pm. Closed 1 Jan, 1 May, 15 Aug and 25 Dec. 20F, no charge 1st Sat-Sun in the month. ☎ 03 27 82 27 90.

CASSEL
🄸 Grand-Place – 59670 – ☎ 03 28 40 52 55

Windmill – Apr to Sept: guided tours (30min) 10am-noon, 2-6pm; Oct to Mar: Sat-Sun and public holidays 10am-noon, 2-5.30pm (school holidays: daily). Closed 1 Jan and 25 Dec. 17F. ☎ 03 28 40 52 55.

Musée municipal – Closed for restoration until 2001.

Excursion

Steenvoorde: Steenmeulen – Mid-Apr to end of Sept: guided tours, preferably by request. 10F. ☎ 03 28 48 16 10.

Drievenmeulen – Guided tours (45min) by request (48hr in advance). 10F. Apply to the tourist office. ☎ 03 28 42 97 98.

Noordmeulen – Guided tours (45min) by request (48hr in advance). 10F. Apply to the tourist office. ☎ 03 28 42 97 98.

Wormhout: Moulin Deschodt – June to end of Aug: 1st and 3rd Sun in June, 2nd Sun in July, 1st and 2nd Sun in Aug. 11F. ☎ 03 28 62 81 23.

Musée Jeanne-Devos – Daily except Wed 10am-noon, 2-5pm, 1st two Sundays in the month 3-6pm. Closed public holidays. 11F. ☎ 03 28 62 81 23.

Abbaye de CHAALIS

Château-musée – Mar to mid-Nov: guided tours (1hr 15min, last admission 1hr before closing) 10.30am-12.30pm, 2-6pm, unaccompanied visits Sat-Sun and public holidays 10.30am-12.30pm, 2-6pm; Mid-Nov to end of Feb: tours of the park 10am-7pm, visits to the museum Sun and public holidays 10.30am-12.30pm, 1.30-5.30pm. Closed 25 Dec. 40F (15F park only). ☎ 03 44 54 04 02.

Excursions

Ermenonville: Parc J.-J.-Rousseau – Apr to Sept: daily except Tues 2-6.15pm, Sun 2-7.15pm; Oct to Mar: daily except Tues and Sun 2-6.15pm, winter 2pm to dusk. Closed between Christmas and New Year's Day. 12F. ☎ 03 44 54 01 58.

Mer de Sable – ዿ Apr to end Sept. Enquire for times. 90F (children 79F). ☎ 03 44 54 18 48. Internet site: www.mer-de-sable.com

Château de CHAMPS

Apr to Sept: daily except Tues 10am-noon, 1.30-5.30pm (Sat-Sun and public holidays 6pm); Oct to Mar: daily except Tues 10am-noon, 1.30-4.30pm (Sat-Sun and public holidays 5pm). Closed 1 Jan, 1 May, 1 and 11 Nov, and 25 Dec. 32F (under 12's no charge). ☎ 01 60 05 24 43.

Park – Daily except Tues 9.30am-4.30pm (May to Aug: 7.30pm; Sept: 7pm; end of Mar to end of Apr: 6.30pm; end of Feb to end of Mar and Oct: 5.30pm; Nov: 5pm). No charge. ☎ 01 60 05 24 43.

Château de CHANTILLY

Museum – Mar to Oct: guided tours (45min) daily except Tues 10am-6pm; Nov to Feb: daily except Tues 10.30am-12.45pm, 2-5pm, Sat-Sun and public holidays 10.30am-5pm. 42F (museum and park). ☎ 03 44 62 62 62.

Appartements des Princes – As for the museum.

Petits Appartements – Mar to Oct: guided tours (45min) daily except Tues at 11am, 2.45pm, 3.45pm and 4.45pm; Nov to Feb: at 11am, 2.30pm and 3.15pm. Closed some public holidays. 50F.

Park – ዿ As for the château. 17F.

Jardin Anglais – As for the park.

Musée vivant du Cheval et du Poney – Apr to Oct: daily except Tues 10.30am-5.30pm, Sat-Sun and public holidays 10.30am-6pm; Nov to Mar: 2-5pm, Sat-Sun and public holidays 10.30am-5.30pm. Closed 1 Jan and 25 Dec. 50F (children 35F). ☎ 03 44 57 13 13.

CHARTRES
🅱 Place de la Cathédrale – 28000 – ☎ 02 37 21 50 00

Guided tours of the town – Contact the tourist office.

Cathédrale Notre-Dame:

Ascent to New Bell-Tower – May to Aug: 9am-6pm, Sun and public holidays 1-6.30pm; Sept to Oct and Mar to Apr: daily except Sun 9.30-11.30am, 2-5pm, Sat 2-5pm (Sept: daily 1-6.30pm); Nov to Feb: 10-11.30am, 2-4pm. Closed 1 Jan, 1 May, Easter Monday (afternoon) and 25 Dec. 25F. ☎ 02 37 21 75 02.

Treasury – The treasury is not open to the public.

Crypt – Apr to Oct: guided tours (30min) at 11am (except Sun and public holidays), 2.15pm, 3.30pm, 4.30pm and 5.15pm (late June to mid-Sept); Nov to Mar: at 11am (daily except Sun and public holidays) and 4.15pm. Closed 1 Jan, 21 June and 25 Dec. 15F. ☎ 02 37 21 56 33.

Tourist train – Apr to mid-Nov: guided tours (45min) by train 10am-6pm. Leaves from place de la Cathédrale. 32F (children 18F). ☎ 01 42 62 24 00.

Église St André – 8am-8pm (during exhibitions 2-6pm). ☎ 02 37 21 03 69.

Grenier de Loëns: Centre International du Vitrail – ዿ 9.30am-12.30pm, 1.30-6pm, Sat-Sun and public holidays 10am-12.30pm, 2.30-6pm. Closed end of Sept and beginning of Oct, 1 Jan and 25 Dec. 20F. ☎ 02 37 21 65 72.

Musée des Beaux-Arts – Daily except Tues 10am-noon, 2-5pm, Sun 2-5pm (May to Oct: 6pm). Closed 1 Jan, 1 May, 1 and 8 May, 1 and 11 Nov, and 25 Dec. 15F. ☎ 02 37 36 41 39.

Le COMPA – ዿ Daily except Mon 9am-12.30pm, 1.30-6pm, Sat-Sun and public holidays 10am-12.30pm, 1.30-7pm. Closed 1 Jan, 1 May, 1 Nov and 25 Dec. 25F. ☎ 02 37 36 11 30.

Musée de l'École – ዿ Daily except Sat-Sun 10am-noon, 2-6pm (last admission 4.30pm). Closed public holidays. 18F. ☎ 02 37 30 07 69.

Maison Picassiette – Apr to end of Oct: daily except Tues 10am-noon, 2-6pm, Sun and public holidays 2-6pm. Closed 1 and 8 May. 15F. ☎ 02 37 36 41 39 or ☎ 02 37 34 10 78.

Le CHEMIN DES DAMES

Caverne du Dragon: Museum – ♿ July and Aug: guided tours (last departure at 4.30pm) 10am-7pm; Sept to June: daily except Mon 10am-6pm (guided tours at 4pm), Sat-Sun, public holidays and school holidays guided tours every 30min. Closed Jan. 30F. ☎ 03 23 25 14 18.

Excursion

Abbaye de Vauclair – ♿ 8am-8pm. No charge. ☎ 03 23 22 40 87.

COMPIÈGNE
🛈 Place de l'Hôtel-de-Ville – 60200 – ☎ 03 44 40 01 00

Guided tours of the town 🅰 – Tour (1hr 30min) of the streets of Compiègne and the town's monuments. Mid-May to mid-July and mid-Aug to mid-Oct: Sat-Sun and public holidays, departure from the tourist office at 3.30pm. 30F.

Palais:

Apartments – Guided tours (1hr, last admission 45min before closing) daily except Tues 10am-4.30pm (Mar to Oct: 6pm). Closed 1 Jan, 1 May, 1 Nov and 25 Dec. 35F (Sun 23F), no charge 1st Sunday in the month. ☎ 03 44 38 47 00/02.

Musée du Second Empire – Daily except Tues 10am-6pm (last admission: 5.15pm). Closed 1 Jan, 1 May, 1 Nov and 25 Dec. 35F (Sun 23F), no charge 1st Sunday in the month.

Musée national de la Voiture – Guided tours (1hr, last admission 5.15pm) daily except Tues 10am-6pm. Closed 1 Jan, 1 May, 1 Nov and 25 Dec. 25F (Sun 17F), no charge 1st Sunday in the month.

Musée de la Figurine historique – Daily except Mon 9am-noon, 2-5pm, Sun and public holidays 2-5pm (Mar to Oct: 6pm). Closed 1 Jan, 1 May, 14 July, 1 Nov and 25 Dec. 12F. ☎ 03 44 40 72 55.

Musée Vivenel – Daily except Mon 9am-noon, 2-5pm, Sun 2-5pm (Mar to Oct: 6pm). Closed 1 Jan, 1 May, 14 July, 1 Nov and 25 Dec. 12F. ☎ 03 44 20 26 04.

Wagon du maréchal Foch – Apr to mid-Oct: daily except Tues 9am-12.30pm, 2-6.30pm; mid-Oct to end of Mar: daily except Tues 9am-noon, 2-5.30pm. Closed 1 Jan and 25 Dec. 12F. ☎ 03 44 85 14 18.

Excursion

Rethondes: Church – 9am-5pm.

CORBIE

Museum – Daily except Mon 3-5.30pm, Sun and public holidays by request. No charge. ☎ 03 22 96 43 37.

Église St-Pierre – Contact the tourist office.

La CÔTE D'OPALE

Site des deux caps – July to end of Aug: guided tours of several natural sites (Platier d'Oye, Cap Blanc-Nez, Cap Gris-Nez, Dunes and the Slack estuary, Baie de Canche, Authie dunes). Eden 62, 3 square Bernard-Shaw, 62930 Wimereux, ☎ 03 21 32 13 74.

Ambleteuse: Fort d'Ambleteuse – July and Aug: Sat-Sun 3-7pm (last admission 6.30pm); Apr to June and Sept to Oct: Sun 3-7pm. 20F. ☎ 03 20 54 61 54.

Musée Historique de la Seconde Guerre mondiale – ♿ Apr to end of Sept: 9.30am-6pm, Sat-Sun and public holidays 10am-8pm (June to Sept: 7pm); Feb to Mar and Oct to Nov: Sun and public holidays 10am-6pm. Closed Dec and Jan. 33F. ☎ 03 21 87 33 01.

Cap Gris-Nez: Musée du mur de l'Atlantique – Feb to end of May: 9am-noon, 2-6pm; June to Sept: 9am-7pm; Oct and Nov: 9am-noon, 2-5pm. 30F. ☎ 03 21 32 97 33.

Wissant: Musée du Moulin – 2-6pm. 14F. ☎ 03 21 35 91 87.

Cap Blanc-Nez: Musée du Transmanche – Apr to end of Sept: daily except Mon 1.30-5.30pm, Sat-Sun and public holidays 1.30-6.30pm (July and Aug: daily 11am-7pm). 20F. ☎ 03 21 85 57 42.

COUCY-LE-CHÂTEAU-AUFFRIQUE

Château – May to Aug: 10am-noon, 2-6pm, Sat 10am-noon, 2-6.30pm, Sun 10am-6.30pm; Mar to Apr and Sept to Oct: 10am-noon, 2-5.30pm, Sat 10am-noon, 2-6pm, Sun 10am-6pm; Nov to Feb: 10am-noon, 2-4pm, Sat 10am-noon, 2-4.30pm, Sun 10am-4.30pm. Closed 1 Jan, 1 May, 1 and 11 Nov, and 25 Dec. 25F. ☎ 03 23 52 71 28.

Musée historique – May to Sept: 10.30am-12.30pm, 2.30-6pm; Oct to Apr: 2.30-5.30pm, Sat-Sun and public holidays 2.30-6pm. Closed between Christmas and New Year's Day. No charge. ☎ 03 23 52 44 55.

Église St-Sauveur – Open on certain Sundays.

CRÉPY-EN-VALOIS

Abbaye St-Arnoul – Apr to Oct Sun 3-7pm by prior request. ☎ 03 44 59 17 76.

Musée de l'Archerie – Daily except Tue 10am-noon, 2-6pm, Sun and holidays 10am-noon, 3-7pm. Closed mid-Nov to 3rd Sun in Mar. 20F. ☎ 03 44 59 21 97.

D

Château de DAMPIERRE

Apr to mid-Oct:. guided tours (45min) 2-6pm, Sun and public holidays 11am-noon, 2-6pm; unaccompanied tours of the park 11am-6pm. 52F (under 10's 15F). ☎ 01 30 52 53 24.

Les Vaux de Cernay: Abbey ruins and park – Apr to Oct: 9am-7pm, Sat-Sun and public holidays: 2-7pm; Nov to Mar: 9am-6pm, Sat-Sun and public holidays 2-6pm. 30F. ☎ 01 34 85 23 00.

DISNEYLAND PARIS

Mid-July to end of Aug: 9am-11pm; high season: 10am-6pm, Sat-Sun and public holidays 9am-8pm; low season: 10am-6pm, Sat 9am-8pm. ☎ 01 60 30 60 30. For guided tours, contact the City Hall on Town Square in Main Street, USA: 50F (children 30F). Parking: cars 40F, motorbikes 25F. Disneyland Passport in high season: 1 day 220F (children 3-11 years 170F); 2 days 425F (children 330F); 3 days 595F (children 460F). 2 and 3-day passports can be used non-consecutively. Readmission: to leave the park temporarily, visitors must have their hand stamped; visitors must keep passports and parking tickets.

DOUAI
🚹 70 place d'Armes – 59500 – ☎ 03 27 88 26 79

Guided tours of the town 🅰 – Douai has been nominated as a "Town of Art"; the guided tours (1hr 30min), organised by the tourist office, are conducted by guides approved by the Ministry of Culture. May to Oct: Sun at 3.30pm. 20F.

Boat trips on the Scarpe – July and Aug: Thur-Sun 2-8pm. Meeting point at the Palais de Justice landing-stage. 20F (children 10F). Agreeable trips on the Scarpe (30min) which is now no longer used by the "bélandres" (barges), running parallel to the quay-sides lined with numerous old dwellings.

Belfry – July and Aug: guided tours (1hr) at 10am, 11am, 2pm, 3pm, 4pm and 5pm; Sept to June: 2pm, 3pm, 4pm and 5pm; Sun and public holidays at 10am, 11am, 3pm, 4pm and 5pm. Closed 1 Jan and 25 Dec. 11F. ☎ 03 27 88 26 79.

Bell concerts – Sat 10.45-11.45am, public holidays at 11.30am (July and Aug: summer recitals Mon at 9pm).

Musée de la Chartreuse – Daily except Tues 10am-noon, 2-5pm, Sat 10am-noon, 2-6pm, Sun 10am-noon, 3-6pm. Closed public holidays. 20F, no charge 1st Sun of the month. ☎ 03 27 71 38 80.

Palais de Justice – May to end of Oct: possibility of guided tours (July and Aug: Sat-Sun and public holidays). Visit of the cells included in the boat trips. Information available at the tourist office. No charge.

Église St-Pierre – Daily except Mon 9-11.30am, 2-5pm, Sun and public holidays 2-6pm. Guided tours available. Contact the tourist office.

Église Notre-Dame – Daily except Mon.

DUNKERQUE
🚹 Beffroi, rue de l'Amiral-Ronarc'h – 59240 – ☎ 03 28 66 79 21

Boat tours of the harbour – On board *La Bazenne*. Mar to Dec (daily Mid-June to Aug). ☎ 03 28 59 11 14 (landing stage) or ☎ 03 28 66 79 21 (tourist office).

Belfry – July to end of Aug: guided tours (30min) daily except Sun and public holidays at 9.30am, 10.30am, 11.30am, 2pm, 3.30pm, 4.30pm and 5.30pm. 15F. ☎ 03 28 66 79 21.

Chapelle Notre-Dame-des-Dunes – Mon-Sat 10am-noon, 2.30-4.30pm.

Musée portuaire – 10am-12.45pm, 1.30-6pm (July and Aug: 10am-6pm). Closed 1 Jan, eve of Shrove Tuesday, 1 May and 25 Dec. 25F. ☎ 03 28 63 33 39.

Musée des Beaux-Arts – Daily except Tues 10am-12.15pm, 1.45-6pm. Closed 1 Jan, 1 May, 15 Aug, 1 Nov and 25 Dec. 20F, no charge 1st Sunday in the month. ☎ 03 28 59 21 65.

Musée d'Art contemporain – Closed for restoration ☎ 03 28 59 21 65.

Excursions

Malo-les-Bains: Musée aquariophile – ♿ Daily except Tues 10am-noon, 2-6pm. 12F, no charge on Sun (children no charge). ☎ 03 28 59 19 18.

Gravelines:

Musée du Dessin et de l'Estampe originale – Daily except Tues 2-5pm, Sat-Sun 3-6pm. Closed 1 Jan, 1 and 8 May, 14 July, and 25 Dec. 10F. ☎ 03 28 51 81 00.

Maison du Patrimoine – ♿ Mon-Fri 2-5pm, Sat-Sun and public holidays 3-6pm. Closed 1 Jan, 1 May and 25 Dec. ☎ 03 28 51 84 84.

Maison de la Mer – Easter to mid-Sept: daily except Tues 2-6pm, Sun and public holidays 3-6pm. 10F (includes access to the Maison du Sauvetage). ☎ 03 28 23 03 53.

Maison du Sauvetage – Easter to mid-Sept: daily except Tues 2-6pm, Sun and public holidays 3-6pm. 10F (includes access to the Maison de la Mer). ☎ 03 28 23 10 12.

E – F

Château d'ÉCOUEN

Musée national de la Renaissance – Daily except Tues 9.45am-12.30pm, 2-5.15pm. Closed 1 Jan, 1 May and 25 Dec. 25F. ☎ 01 34 38 38 50.

Église de St-Acceul – Contact the town hall. ☎ 01 3933 09 00.

Château de FERRIÈRES

Closed 1 Jan and 25 Dec. 35F (under 12's no charge). ☎ 01 64 66 31 25.

Musée de l'Imaginaire – May to Sept: Thur and Fri 2-6pm, Sat 3-6pm, Sun and public holidays 2-7pm; Oct to Apr: Sat 3-5pm, Sun and public holidays 2-5pm. Closed 1 Jan and 25 Dec. 16F. ☎ 01 64 66 31 25.

Park – ♿ Oct to end of Apr: 2-5pm; May to end of Sept: 2-7pm. Closed 1 Jan and 25 Dec. 16F (under 12's no charge). ☎ 01 64 66 31 25.

FOLLEVILLE

Church – Daily except Mon and Tues 10am-noon, 2-5pm, Sun 2-5pm (May to mid-Oct: 7pm). Closed mid-Dec to end of Jan. 15F. ☎ 03 22 41 49 52.

FONTAINEBLEAU

🅱 4 rue Royale – 77300 – ☎ 01 60 74 99 99

Palace:

Grands Appartements – ♿ Daily except Tues 9.30am-12.30pm, 2-5pm (May to June and Oct: 9.30am-5pm, July and Aug: 9.30am-6pm), last admission 45min before closing. Closed 1 Jan, 1 May and 25 Dec. 35F (children no charge), no charge 1st Sunday in the month. ☎ 01 60 71 50 60.

Appartements Intérieur de l'Empereur – Visit included in the tour of the Grands Appartements.

Musée Chinois – Visit on the theme of "Fontainebleau during the Second Empire" Wed, Fri and Sun morning or unaccompanied visits combined with the tour of the Grands Appartements. 16F (visit combined with the tour of the Grands Appartements 35F). ☎ 01 60 71 50 60.

Musée Napoléon-Ier – Guided tours (1hr) Mon, Thur and Sat morning. Telephone in the morning. 16F. ☎ 01 60 71 50 60.

Petits Appartements and **Galerie des Cerfs** – Guided tours (1hr) daily except Tues 2-5pm. Ask for information on the day. Closed 1 Jan, 1 May and 25 Dec. 16F. ☎ 01 60 71 50 60.

Musée napoléonien d'Art et d'Histoire militaires – Daily except Sun and Mon 2-5pm. Closed public holidays. 10F. ☎ 01 60 74 64 89.

Excursions

By-Thomery: Atelier Rosa-Bonheur – Guided tours (30min) Wed and Sat 2-5pm. 15F. ☎ 01 60 70 04 49.

Château de Bourron – Mid-Apr to end of Oct: unaccompanied visits Sat-Sun and public holidays 2-5.30pm. 10F. ☎ 01 64 78 39 39.

Park – Mid-Apr to end of Oct: Sat-Sun 2-6pm. 10F. ☎ 01 64 78 39 39.

FOURMIES

Ecomusée – For general information on various sites ☎ 03 27 60 66 11.

Musée du Textile et de la Vie sociale – ♿ July and Aug: guided tours (1hr 30min) 9am-6pm, Sat-Sun and public holidays 2.30-6.30pm; Sept to June: 9am-noon, 2-6pm, Sat-Sun and public holidays 2.30-6.30pm. Closed Jan and 25 Dec. 30F. ☎ 03 27 60 66 11.

FRANCE MINIATURE

♿ Apr to Aug: 10am-7pm, last admission 1hr before closing (July and Aug: Sat 10am-midnight, last admission 9pm); Sept to mid-Nov: 10am-6pm. 75F (children 50F). ☎ 08 36 68 53 35.

G

GUÎNES

Musée municipal E.-Villez – Tues and Thur 9am-noon, 2-5pm (July and Aug: Sun 3-6pm). 10F. ☎ 03 21 36 18 06.

Mimoyecques: Fortress – ♿ Apr to mid-Nov: 2-6pm, Sun and public holidays 10am-6pm (July and Aug: 10am-7pm). 30F. ☎ 03 21 87 10 34.

GUISE

Château fort des ducs de Guise – Guided tours (1hr) 10am-noon, 2-6pm (July and Aug: 7pm, winter: 5.30pm). Closed mid-Dec to beginning of Jan. 30F. ☎ 03 23 61 11 76.

Familistère Godin – Guided tours (1hr 30min) daily except Mon at 2.30pm and 4.30pm (Nov to Mar: daily except Mon at 2.30pm and 4.30pm, Sun at 3pm). Closed end of Dec to mid-Jan. 20F. ☎ 03 23 61 35 36.

H-I

Coupole d'HELFAUT-WIZERNES

♿ Apr to Sept: audio tours (3hr) 9am-7pm; Oct to Mar: 10am-6pm. Closed beginning of Jan to mid-Jan and 25 Dec. 55F. ☎ 03 21 12 27 27.

HONDSCHOOTE

Hôtel de ville – Daily except Sat-Sun 9am-noon, 2-5pm. Closed public holidays. 6F. ☎ 03 28 62 53 00.

Moulin Spinnewyn – Visits by appointment. 6F. ☎ 03 28 62 54 20.

J

JOUARRE

Tower – Closed for renovation until Aug 2000.

Crypt – Guided tours (30min) Nov to end of Mar: daily except Mon and Tues 10am-noon, 2-5pm; Apr to end of Oct: daily except Tues 9am-noon, 2-6pm. Closed 1 Jan, 1 May, 1 and 11 Nov and 25 Dec. 25F. ☎ 01 60 22 64 54.

Musée Briard – Guided tours (30min) Nov to end of Mar: daily except Mon and Tues 10am-noon, 2-5pm; Apr to end of Oct: daily except Tues 9am-noon, 2-6pm. Closed 1 Jan, 1 May, 1 and 11 Nov, and 25 Dec. 15F. ☎ 01 60 22 64 54.

Eglise Paroissiale – 9am-noon, 2-7pm.

JOUY-EN-JOSAS

Musée de la Toile de Jouy – ♿ Daily except Mon 11am-6pm. Closed 25 Dec. 25F. ☎ 01 39 56 48 64.

Church – July: 9am-6pm.

Maison de Jeanne et Léon Blum – May to June and Sept to Oct: Sun 2-5pm. Closed public holidays. 25F. ☎ 01 39 20 11 03.

Excursion

Bièvres: Musée français de la Photographie – Daily except Tues 10am-noon, 2-6pm. Closed public holidays. 20F. ☎ 01 69 35 16 50.

L

LAON

Guided tours of the town 🅰 – Laon has been listed as a "Town of Art and History"; guided tours (1hr 30min), organised by the tourist office, are conducted by guides approved by the Ministry of Culture. July and Aug: Sun at 10.30am. 35F. Book at the tourist office.

Chapelle des Templiers – Daily except Tues 9am-5pm (Apr to Sept: 6pm). Closed 1 Jan, 1 May, 14 July and 25 Dec. No charge. ☎ 03 23 20 19 87.

Abbaye St-Martin – July and Aug: 2-6pm; Sept to June: Fri 2pm, Sat 5.30pm. Guided tours available, contact the tourist office.

Maison des Arts – Daily except Sun and Mon (except during events) noon-7pm, Sat 1-6pm. Closed during Christmas school holidays and public holidays (except during events). No charge. ☎ 03 23 26 30 30.

Museum – Daily except Tues 10am-noon, 2-5pm (Apr to Sept: 6pm). Closed 1 Jan, 1 May, 14 July and 25 Dec. 20F. ☎ 03 23 20 19 87.

Centre historique minier de LEWARDE

Mar to Oct: guided tours (2hr) 9am-5.30pm; Nov to Feb: 1-5pm, Sun, school holidays and public holidays 10am-5pm. Closed Jan, 1 May, 1 Nov and 25 Dec. 66F, 58F in low season (children 33F/29F). ☎ 03 27 95 82 82.

LILLE

Guided tours of the town 🅰 – Tour of the old town of Lille: Sat at 3pm. 45F. Other theme tours (in July and Aug only): Îlot Comtesse, Wazemmes, Euralille or an evening tour which includes beer tasting. Contact the tourist office.

Palais des Beaux-Arts – Daily except Tues 10am-6pm, Mon 2-6pm, Fri 10am-7pm. Closed 1 Jan, 1 May, 14 July, 1st Sat-Sun in Sept, 1 Nov and 25 Dec. 30F. ☎ 03 20 06 78 00.

Palais Rihour – 9.30am-6.30pm, Sun and public holidays 10am-noon, 2-5pm. Closed 1 Jan, 1 May and 25 Dec. No charge. ☎ 03 20 21 94 21.

Hospice Comtesse – Mon 2-6pm, Wed, Thur, Sat-Sun and public holidays 10am-6pm, Fri 2-7pm. Closed 1 Jan, 1 May, 14 July, 1st Sat-Sun in Sept, 1 Nov and 25 Dec. 35F. ☎ 03 28 36 84 00.

Hôtel de ville: Belfry – Undergoing restoration work.

Musée Charles-de-Gaulle – Daily except Mon and Tues 10am-noon, 2-5pm. Closed public holidays. 15F. ☎ 03 28 38 12 05.

Citadelle – May to end of Aug: guided tours (2hr) Sun 3-5pm. 45F. ☎ 03 20 21 94 21.

Musée des Canonniers – Wed, Thur and Sat-Sun 2-5pm. Closed mid-Dec to mid-Feb and the first three weeks in Aug. 30F. ☎ 03 20 55 58 90.

Musée d'Histoire naturelle et de Géologie – Daily except Tues and Sat 9am-noon, 2-5pm, Sun 10am-5pm. Closed 1 Jan and 1 May. ☎ 03 28 55 30 80.

Jardin des plantes – May to Sept: 7.30am-9pm; Apr: 7.30am-6pm; Oct to Mar: 8.30am-6pm (greenhouses close at 4pm). No charge.

Excursion

Marcq-en-Baroeul: Prouvost Foundation-Septentrion – July to end of Aug: daily except Mon and Tues 2-6pm, Sat-Sun and public holidays 2.30-6.30pm. 40F. ☎ 03 20 46 26 37.

Bondues: Château – July to end of Aug: guided tours (1hr) daily except Mon and Tues at 3pm, 4pm and 5pm. 40F (under 10's no charge). ☎ 03 20 46 26 37.

Abbaye de LONGPONT

Abbey – ♿ Mid-Mar to end of Oct: guided tours (30min) Sat 2.30-6.30pm, Sun and public holidays 11am-noon, 2.30-6.30pm. 28F. ☎ 03 23 96 01 53.

M

MAINTENON

Château – Apr to Oct: daily except Tues 2-6pm, Sun and public holidays 10am-noon, 2-6pm; Nov to Mar: Sat-Sun and public holidays 2-5pm. Closed mid-Dec to end of Jan. 38F (children 23F). ☎ 02 37 23 00 09.

MAISONS-LAFFITTE

Château – Daily except Tues 10am-noon, 1.30-5pm (Apr to mid-Oct: 6pm, last admission 30min before closing). Closed 1 Jan, 1 May, 1 and 11 Nov and 25 Dec. 32F. ☎ 01 39 62 01 49.

MANTES-LA-JOLIE
🖩 Place Jean XXIII – 78200 – ☎ 01 34 77 10 30

Guided tours of the town – Contact the tourist office.

Collégiale Notre-Dame – Guided tours available, contact the tourist office. ☎ 01 34 77 10 30.

Ancien Hôtel-Dieu – &. Daily except Tues noon-8pm, Sat-Sun and public holidays noon-7pm. 30F (under 18's 15F). ☎ 01 34 78 86 60.

Ancien Hôtel-Dieu – **Musée Luce** – Same as for the Hôtel-Dieu.

MARLY-LE-ROI

Musée-promenade de Marly-le-Roi – Louveciennes – &. Daily except Mon and Tues 2-6pm. Closed public holidays. 20F. ☎ 01 39 69 06 26.

Excursions

Port-Marly: Château de Monte-Cristo – Apr to Nov: daily except Mon 10am-12.30pm, 2-6pm, Sat-Sun and public holidays 2-6pm, guided tours (45min) Sun afternoon; Nov to Mar: Sun and public holidays 2-5pm. Closed 1 Jan and 25 Dec. 30F, Sun 40F. ☎ 01 39 16 49 49.

Bougival: Musée Tourgueniev – Apr to Oct: Sun 10am-6pm. Closed public holidays. 25F. ☎ 01 45 77 87 12.

Domaine du MARQUENTERRE

Bird sanctuary – Apr to Sept: 9.30am-7pm (last admission 5pm); Oct to mid-Nov and mid-Mar to end of Mar: 10am-6pm. Closed mid-Nov to mid-Mar. 60F (children 45F). ☎ 08 36 68 80 21.

MEAUX
🖩 2 rue St-Rémy – 77100 – ☎ 01 64 33 02 26

Guided tours of the town 🅰 – Contact the Service du Patrimoine (Heritage Dept). ☎ 01 64 34 68 05.

Ancien Évêché (Musée Bossuet) – Apr to Sept: daily except Tues 10am-12.15pm, 2-6pm; Oct to Mar: daily except Mon and Tues 10am-noon, 2-5pm, Sun 2-5pm. Closed 1 Jan, 1 May and 25 Dec. 15F, no charge on Wed. ☎ 01 64 34 84 45.

MEUDON

Observatoire – Temporarily closed to the public. ☎ 01 45 07 75 30.

Musée d'Art et d'Histoire – Daily except Mon and Tues 2-6pm. Closed Aug and public holidays. 15F. ☎ 01 46 23 87 13.

Musée Rodin – Villa des Brillants – May to end of Oct: Fri-Sun 1.30-6pm (last admission 5.15pm). 10F, no charge 1st Sunday in the month. ☎ 01 41 18 61 10.

MILLY-LA-FORÊT

Chapelle St-Blaise-des-Simples – &. Daily except Tues 10am-noon, 2.30-6.30pm (Easter to All Saints: Sat-Sun and public holidays 10.15am-noon, 2.30-5pm). Closed last 2 weeks in Nov and mid-Jan to beginning of Feb. 12F. ☎ 01 64 98 84 94.

Excursions

Le Cyclop – May to end of Sept: guided tours (30min) Fri 10.15am-1pm, 2-4.45pm, Sat 11am-1pm, 2-5pm, Sun 11am-1pm, 2-5.45pm; Oct: last visit at 4.15pm, last visit Sun at 5pm. 35F. ☎ 01 64 98 83 17 or 01 64 23 10 48.

Château de Courances – Apr to All Saints: Sat-Sun and public holidays 2-6.30pm (Oct: 5.30pm). 40F (park only 26F). ☎ 01 40 62 07 62.

MONTFORT-L'AMAURY

Musée Maurice-Ravel – Daily except Mon-Tue Mar-Oct 10am, 11am, 2.30pm, 3.30pm, 4.30pm (and 5.30pm Apr to Sept). Closed between 25 Dec and 1 Jan. 6.10 €. ☎ 01 34 86 00 89.

Excursions

Vicq: Musée de Vicq en Île-de-France – 2-6pm. Closed 1 Jan. 36F (children 18F). ☎ 01 34 86 12 18.

La Queue-les-Yvelines: La Serre aux Papillons – &. End of Mar to mid-Nov: 9.30am-12.15pm, 2.30-6pm, Sat 9.30am-6pm (July and Aug: daily 9.30am-12.15pm, 2.30-6pm). 35F. ☎ 01 34 86 42 99.

Houjarray: Maison Jean-Monnet – 10am-5pm, Sat 1-6pm, Sun and public holidays 9am-6pm. Closed 25 Dec. No charge. ☎ 01 56 33 71 00.

MONTMORENCY

Musée J.-J.-Rousseau – Guided tours (30min) daily except Mon 2-6pm. Closed between Christmas and New Year's Day, and 1 May. 25F. ☎ 01 39 64 80 13.

MONTREUIL

🔲 place Darnétal – 62170 – ☎ 03 21 06 04 27

Citadelle – Mid-Mar to mid-Oct: 10am-noon, 2-6pm; Mid-Oct to mid-Mar: 10am-noon, 2-5pm. Closed mid-Dec to end of Dec and Feb. 15F. ☎ 03 21 06 10 83.

Église St-Saulve – Guided tours available, contact the tourist office.

MORET-SUR-LOING

🔲 place Samois – 77250 – ☎ 01 60 70 41 66

Guided tours of the town – Contact the tourist office.

La Grange Batelière – Guided tours (1hr 30min) Sun at 3pm (Sept to Oct: Sun 2.30pm). 30-50F. ☎ 01 60 70 51 21.

Boat trips – Large barge (5 adults + 1 child) or small (3 adults 1 child), 60F/hour, 180F/half day. Information at the Embaracdère du Vieux-Pont or ☎ 01 64 45 85 17.

N

NAOURS

Caves – Feb to mid-Nov: guided tours (1hr) 9am-noon, 2-6pm. 47F (children 37F). ☎ 03 22 93 71 78.

NOTRE-DAME-DE-LORETTE

Tour Lanterne – Apr to Sept: 9am-6pm (June to Aug: 7pm); Mar and Oct to Dec: 9am-5pm. No charge.

Musée vivant 1914-1918 – ♿ 9am-8pm. Closed 25 Dec. 20F (battlefield 5F). ☎ 03 21 45 15 80.

Musée de la Targette – ♿ 9am-8pm. Closed 1 Jan and 25 Dec. 20F. ☎ 03 21 45 15 80.

NOYON

🔲 Place de l'Hôtel-de-Ville – 60400 – ☎ 03 44 44 21 88

Guided tours of the town 🅰 – Contact the tourist office.

Musée du Noyonnais – Daily except Tues 10am-noon, 2-5pm (Apr to Oct: 6pm). Closed 1 Jan, 11 Nov and 25 Dec. 16F, ticket valid for the Musée Jean-Calvin, no charge 1st Sun in the month. ☎ 03 44 44 43 41.

Musée Jean-Calvin – As for the Musée du Noyonnais.

O – P

Château d'OLHAIN

Château – Apr to Oct: Sun and public holidays 3-6.30pm (summer school holidays: Sat 3-6pm). 25F. ☎ 03 21 27 94 76.

PARIS

🔲 127 avenue des Champs-Élysées – 75008 – ☎ 01 49 52 53 54

Île de France tourist centre – Place de la Pyramide-Inversée, Carrousel du Louvre, 99 rue de Rivoli, 1er, metro station – Palais-Royal-Musée-du-Louvre, ☎ 0 803 818 000. Internet site: www.paris-ile-de-france.com 10am-7pm. Tourist information on Paris and surrounding areas, hotel reservations, shows, bus-metro-regional express and train tickets.

PÉRONNE

🔲 1 rue Louis XI – 80200 – ☎ 03 22 84 42 38

Historial de la Grande Guerre – ♿ Daily except Mon 10am-6pm (Mar to Sept: daily). Closed mid-Dec to mid-Jan. 39F. ☎ 03 22 83 14 18.

Musée Danicourt – Daily except Sun and Mon 2.30-5.30pm, Sat 9am-noon, 2.30-4.30pm. ☎ 03 22 73 31 00.

PIERREFONDS

Château – Mar to Oct: 10am-12.30pm, 2-6pm, Sun 10am-6pm (May to Aug: 10am-6pm); Nov to Feb: 10am-12.30pm, 2-5pm, Sun 10am-5.30pm. Closed 1 Jan, 1 May, 1 and 11 Nov, and 25 Dec. 32F (Oct to May: no charge 1st Sunday in the month). ☎ 03 44 42 72 72.

Tourist train – Apr to mid-Nov: 4km/2.5mi round trip (30min) 1st departure at 2pm. Sat-Sun and public holidays 1st departure at 11am. 30F (under 10's 15F). Tourist train station, town centre car park.

POISSY

Collégiale Notre-Dame – Guided tours available by appointment with Mme Dieudonné. ☎ 01 39 65 08 03.

Musée d'Art et d'Histoire – Fri and Sat-Sun 2-5.30pm. Closed public holidays. No charge. ☎ 01 39 65 06 06.

Musée du Jouet – Daily except Mon 9.30am-noon, 2-5.30pm. Closed public holidays. 15F. ☎ 01 39 65 06 06.

Villa Savoye – Daily except Tues (last admission 20min before closing) 9.30am-12.30pm, 1.30-6pm (Nov to Mar: 4.30pm). Closed 1 Jan, 1 May, 1 and 11 Nov, and 25 Dec. 25F. ☎ 01 39 65 01 06.

Centre de production Peugeot – Guided tours (3hr) Mon-Thur at 8.30am and 1.30pm by appointment (2 months in advance). Closed Aug, mid-Dec to end of Dec and public holidays. Minimum age: 15 years. Peugeot-Poissy, Relations Extérieures, Visites d'usine, 45 rue J.-P.-Timbaud, 78307 Poissy Cedex, ☎ 01 30 19 30 50.

Musée Caapy – Guided tours (1hr 15min) Sat 10am-noon, 2-5pm. Closed Aug and public holidays. 15F. ☎ 01 30 19 41 15.

Abbaye de PORT-ROYAL-DES-CHAMPS

Ruines et musée de l'abbaye – Daily except Tues 2-5pm, Sat-Sun and public holidays 10am-noon, 2-5pm (summer: 6pm). Closed 1 Jan and 25 Dec. Price information not provided. ☎ 01 30 43 74 93.

Musée national des Granges de Port-Royal – Mid-Mar to early Nov: daily except Tues 10.30am-6.30pm; beginning of Nov to mid-Mar: Sat-Sun 10.30am-6pm. Closed between Christmas and New Year's Day. 16F. ☎ 01 39 30 72 72.

PROVINS
🛈 Chemin de Villecran – BP 44 – 77160 – ☎ 01 64 60 26 26

Guided tours of the town 🅐 – Classified as a "Town of Art", Provins offers visitors the services of guides approved by the Centre des Monuments Nationaux (National Monuments Centre). Beginning of June to end of Aug: Sat-Sun and public holidays at 3pm. 40F. Contact the tourist office.

Tour César – Apr to Oct: 10am-6pm; Nov to Mar: 2-5pm. Closed 25 Dec. 17F. ☎ 01 64 60 26 26.

Grange aux Dîmes – Apr to Aug: 10am-6pm; Sept to Nov: 2-6pm, Sat-Sun 10am-6pm; Nov to Mar: Sat-Sun, public and zone C school holidays 2-5pm. Closed 25 Dec. 22F. ☎ 01 64 60 26 26.

Musée du Provinois – Apr to Dec: 2-6pm (July and Aug: 2-7pm), last admission 30min before closing. Closed 25 Dec. 22F. ☎ 01 64 01 40 19.

Souterrains à graffiti – Apr to Nov: guided tours (45min) at 3pm and 4pm, Sat-Sun and public holidays 10.30am-6pm; Nov to Mar: Sat-Sun, public and zone C school holidays at 2pm, 3pm and 4pm. Closed 25 Dec. 22F. ☎ 01 64 60 26 26.

R

RAMBOUILLET
🛈 Hôtel de ville – 78120 – ☎ 01 34 83 21 21

Guided tours of the town – Contact the municipal tourist office.

Château – Guided tours (30min) daily except Tues 10-11.30am, 2-4.30pm (Apr to Sept: 5.30pm). Closed 1 Jan, 1 May, 1 and 11 Nov, 25 Dec and during presidential visits. 32F, no charge 1st Sun in the month from Oct to May. ☎ 01 34 94 28 79.

Park – ♿ May to Sept: 8am-7pm (June to Aug: 7.30pm); Oct to Apr: 8am-6pm (Nov to Jan: 5pm). No charge. ☎ 01 34 94 28 79.

Laiterie de la Reine and Chaumière des Coquillages – Guided tours (45min) daily except Tues 10-11.30am, 2-4.30pm (Apr to Sept: 5.30pm). Closed every other Sat-Sun, 1 Jan, 1 May, 1 and 11 Nov, and 25 Dec. 15F, no charge 1st Sun in the month from Oct to May. ☎ 01 34 94 28 79.

Bergerie nationale – Daily except Mon and Tues. 2-5.30pm. Closed between Christmas and New Year's Day. 25F (children 17F). ☎ 01 61 08 68 70.

Musée Rambolitrain – Daily except Mon and Tues 10am-noon, 2-5.30pm. Closed 1 Jan and 25 Dec. 22F. ☎ 01 34 83 15 93.

Forêt de RAMBOUILLET

Espace Rambouillet – Apr to Oct: 9am-6pm (Sat-Sun 6.30pm); Nov to Mar: daily except Mon 10am-5pm. 45F (children 35F). ☎ 01 34 83 05 00.

Étangs de Pourras et de St-Hubert – For information on regulations for fishing in the Étang de St-Hubert contact the Fédération des Yvelines pour la Pêche et la Protection du Milieu Aquatique, 19 rue du Docteur-Roux, 78520 Limay, ☎ 01 34 77 58 90.

The Guéville and Guesle Valleys: Réserve zoologique de Sauvage – 10am-6pm (earlier in winter). 40F (children 25F). ☎ 01 34 94 00 94.

Château fort de RAMBURES

Mar to Oct: guided tours (1hr) daily except Wed 10am-noon, 2-6pm (July and Aug: 10am-6pm); Nov to Feb: by request. 32F. ☎ 03 22 25 10 93.

La ROCHE-GUYON

Château – Mid-Mar to mid-Nov: 10am-6pm, Sat-Sun and public holidays 10am-7pm; mid-Nov to mid-Mar: 2-4pm, Sat-Sun and public holidays 10am-5pm. Closed during Christmas school holidays. 40F (children 25F). ☎ 01 34 79 74 42.

Excursions

Vétheuil: Church – Easter to All Saints: Sun and public holidays 3-6pm. Notre-Dame de Vétheuil Association. ☎ 01 34 78 27 49.

Domaine de Villarceaux: Gardens and manor tower – May to end of Oct: Sat-Sun and public holidays 2-6pm (last admission 1hr before closing). No charge. ☎ 01 34 67 74 33.

Abbaye de ROYAUMONT

♿ 10am-6pm (Nov to Feb: 10am-5.30pm), last admission 30min before closing. 28F (children 20F). ☎ 01 30 35 88 90.

RUEIL-MALMAISON

Museum – May to July: daily except Tues 10am-5.45pm, Sat-Sun and public holidays 10am-6pm; Apr, Aug and Sept: daily except Tues (last admission 45min before closing) 10am-12.30pm, 1.30-5.45pm, Sat-Sun 10am-6pm; Oct to Mar: daily except Tues 10am-12.30pm, 1.30-5.15pm, Sat-Sun 10am-5.45pm. Closed 1 Jan and 25 Dec. 30F (children no charge). ☎ 01 41 29 05 55.

Château de Bois-Préau – Summer: Thur-Sun 12.30-6.30pm (last admission 30min before closing); winter: Thur-Sun 12.30-6pm. 30F (ticket combined with the Château de Malmaison), no charge 1st Sun in the month. ☎ 01 41 29 05 55.

Musée d'histoire locale – Daily except Sun 2.30-6pm. Closed mid-July to end Aug and public holidays. ☎ 01 47 32 66 50.

S

ST-AMAND-LES-EAUX

Abbey Tower-Museum– Apr to Sept: daily except Tues 10am-noon, 2-5pm, Sat-Sun 10am-12.30pm, 3-6pm; Oct to Mar: daily except Tues 2-5pm, Sat-Sun 10am-12.30pm, 2-5pm. Closed 1-2 Jan, 14 July and 25-26 Dec. 10F, no charge on Wed. ☎ 03 27 22 24 55.

Échevinage – May to Sept: daily except Sat 9am-12.30pm, 2-6pm, Sun 2.30-6.30pm; Oct to Apr: daily except Sat-Sun 9am-12.30pm, 2-6pm.

ST-CLOUD

Musée Historique – Wed, Sat-Sun and public holidays 2-6pm. 15F. ☎ 01 41 12 02 90.

Grandes Eaux – See the Calendar of events section.

Église Stella Matutina – Tues and Thur 8.30am-6pm. Closed during school holidays.

Hippodrome de Saint-Cloud – St-Cloud racecourse is a favourite venue for flat racing enthusiasts. Situated at the foot of Mont Valérien it covers 185 acres and has the unusual distinction of having a golf course in the centre. The racecourse organises several well-known events such as the St-Cloud Grand Prix and Elegance day. 1 rue du Camp Canadien, 92210 St-Cloud. ☎ 01 47 71 69 26.
Mar to Oct: 7.30am-9pm (May to Aug: 7.30am-10pm); Nov to Feb: 7.30am-8pm. Cars: 20F, no charge for pedestrians. ☎ 01 41 12 02 90.

ST-DENIS

B 1 rue de la République – 93200 – ☎ 01 55 87 08 70

Guided tours of the town **A** – Contact the tourist office.

Basilica: **Royal Tombs** – 10am-5pm, Sun and public holidays noon-5pm (Apr to Sept: 7pm). Closed 1 Jan, 1 May, 1 and 11 Nov, and 25 Dec. 32F. ☎ 01 48 09 83 54.

Crypt – As for the tombs.

Former Abbey – Tours organised by the tourist office all year round for groups and during the summer for individual tourists.

Musée d'Art et d'Histoire – Daily except Tues 10am-5.30pm, Sun 2-6.30pm. Closed public holidays. 20F. ☎ 01 42 43 05 10.

Musée Bouilhet-Christofle – Daily except Sat-Sun 9am-6pm. Closed Aug and public holidays. Price information not provided. ☎ 01 49 22 40 40.

Stade de France – Unaccompanied visits **"Premiers Regards"** 10am-6pm. 38F (children 30F). Guided tours (1hr 30min) **"Les Coulisses du Stade"** at 10am, 2pm and 4pm. 90F (children 65F). It is advisable to enquire beforehand as visits are not allowed when shows are scheduled. ☎ 01 55 93 00 00.

ST-GERMAIN-EN-LAYE

B 38 rue au Pain – 78100 – ☎ 01 34 51 05 12

Guided tours of the town **A** – Contact the tourist office.

Musée des Antiquités nationales – 🔥 Daily except Tues 9am-5.15pm. Closed 1 Jan and 25 Dec. 25F (children no charge). ☎ 01 39 10 13 21.

Musée départemental du Prieuré – Daily except Mon and Tues 10am-5.30pm, Sat-Sun 10am-6.30pm. Closed 1 Jan, 1 May and 25 Dec. 25F. ☎ 01 39 73 77 87.

Maison Debussy – Daily except Sun and Mon 2-6pm. Closed public holidays. No charge. ☎ 01 34 51 05 12.

Forêt de ST-GOBAIN

Three footpath routes: the lake (2hr, follow the blue markers), the abbeys (4hr, follow the red markers) and the rocks (20min, follow the white markers).

Abbaye de Prémontré – By request at the hospital reception area (8 days in advance). ☎ 03 23 23 66 66.

ST-OMER

B Boulevard Pierre-Guillain – 62500 – ☎ 03 21 98 08 51

Guided tours of the town **A** – Contact the tourist office.

Hôtel Sandelin– Closed for renovation work. ☎ 03 21 38 00 94.

Église St-Denis – Open during religious services only; May to Sept: theme tour, Sun 3.30pm.

Bibliothèque – 🔥 Daily except Sun and Mon 9am-noon, 1-6pm. Closed public holidays, Easter and Whit Saturdays. No charge. ☎ 03 21 38 35 08.

Musée Henri-Dupuis – Daily except Mon, Tues and public holidays 10am-noon, 2-6pm. 16F. (02 31 38 00 94.

La Grange Nature – Easter and summer school holidays: 10am-12.30pm, 2.30-6.30pm; Apr to June and Sept to Oct: Sat 2.30-6.30pm (Oct: 5.30pm), Sun and public holidays 10am-12.30pm, 2.30-6.30pm (Oct: 5.30pm); Mar and Sat-Sun of the first fortnight in Nov: 2.30-5.30pm. ☎ 03 21 38 52 95.

Marais Audomarois – For a ride on a bacôve (flat bottomed boat) contact Mme Lalart, Pont de la Guillotine, Rivage de Tilques, 62500 Tilques, ☎ 03 21 95 10 19, Fax 03 21 95 10 19.

Excursions

Arcques: Verrerie Cristallerie d'Arques - 🔥 Guided tours (1hr 30min) daily except Sun at 9am, 10.30am, 2pm and 3.30pm. By appointment. 35F. Children under 8 years prohibited. ☎ 03 21 12 74 74.

Maison du Parc naturel régional de l'Audomarois – Daily except Sat-Sun 9am-noon, 2-6pm. Closed public holidays. "Le Grand Vannage", 62510 Arques. ☎ 03 21 87 90 90.

Les Fontinettes barge lift– Apr to end of Oct: (last departure 5.15pm) Sat-Sun and public holidays 3-6.30pm (mid-June to mid-Sept: daily). 25F. ☎ 03 21 12 62 30.

Abbaye St-Paul de Wisques – 11am-12.30pm, 1.30-5pm.

Esquerdes: Maison du Papier – 🔥 Mid-Feb to mid-Nov: daily except Sat 9am-noon, 2-6.30pm, Sun and public holidays 2-6.30pm. 25F. ☎ 03 21 95 45 25.

Blockhaus d'Éperlecques – June to Aug: 10am-7pm (last admission 6pm); Sept: 10am-noon, 2.15-7pm, Sun 10am-7pm; May: 10am-noon, 2.15-6pm, Sun 10am-7pm; Apr: 2.15-6pm; Oct and Nov: 2.15-5pm; Mar: Sun 2.15-5pm. Closed Dec to Feb. 41F (children 26F). ☎ 03 21 88 44 22.

Guided tours of the town 🄰 – Contact the tourist office.

Marais d'Isle nature reserve – 🔲 May to Sept: 8am-8pm; Oct to Apr: 9am-5pm. No charge. ☎ 03 23 05 06 50.

Hôtel de ville – June: guided tours (1hr 30min) by guides approved by the Ministry of Culture Sun at 3pm; June: Sat at 3pm. 35F. Meeting point in front of the basilica. Information at the tourist office.

Musée des papillons – Daily except Tues 2-6pm, Sun and public holidays 3-6pm. Closed 1 Jan, 1 May, Whitsun, 14 July, 1 Nov and 25 Dec. 15F. ☎ 03 23 06 30 92.

Basilica – As for visits to the town hall.

Musée Antoine Lécuyer – Daily except Tues 10am-noon, 2-5pm, Sat 10am-noon, 2-6pm, Sun 2-6pm. Closed 1 Jan, 1 May, 1 Nov and 25 Dec. 15F, no charge Wed. ☎ 03 23 64 06 66.

ST-RIQUIER

Church and treasury – 🔲 Apr to Oct: guided tours (1hr) daily except Wed afternoon and Sun morning 9.30-11.30am, 2-5pm; Nov to Mar: at 11am, noon, 2pm and 4pm. Closed mid-July to end of July. 10F. ☎ 03 22 28 20 20.

Centre culturel de l'abbaye de St-Riquier – Mar to Nov: 2-6pm, Sat-Sun and public holidays 10am-noon, 2-6pm (July and Aug: 10am-6pm; May, June and Sept: 10am-noon, 2-6pm). No charge. ☎ 03 22 68 20 20.

Classical music festival – In July, the abbey is the venue for a classical music festival. ☎ 03 22 28 82 82.

Hôtel-Dieu – 🔲 Guided tours (15min) daily except Sun and public holidays 9-11.30am, 2-4.30pm. No charge. ☎ 03 22 28 92 92.

ST-VALERY-SUR-SOMME

Écomusée Picarvie – Apr to mid-Oct: daily except Tues 2-6pm (June to Aug: daily). 25F. ☎ 03 22 26 94 90.

Parc de SCEAUX

🔲 From dawn to dusk. No charge. ☎ 01 46 61 44 85.

Orangerie: Chamber music concerts – For the programme, write to the "Saison Musicale d'été de Sceaux", BP 52, 92333 Sceaux Cedex. ☎ 01 46 60 07 79.

Musée de l'Île-de-France – 🔲 Daily except Tues 10am-6pm (Oct to Mar: 5pm). Closed some public holidays. 22F, no charge 1st Sun of the month. ☎ 01 41 13 70 41.

Centre de documentation – Daily by request except Sat-Sun 9am-5pm. Closed public holidays. ☎ 01 46 61 06 71.

Grandes Cascades – Wed, Sat-Sun and public holidays 11am-5pm (June and July: 9pm; Apr and May: 8pm; Aug and Sept: 7pm). No charge. ☎ 01 46 61 44 85.

Pavillon de l'Aurore – Daily except Tues 10am-6pm (Oct to Mar: 5pm). Closed some public holidays. 22F. ☎ 01 41 13 70 41.

Excursion

L'Haÿ-les-Roses: Roseraie du Val-de-Marne – 🔲 Mid-May to beginning of Sept: 10am-8pm; beginning of Sept to mid-Sept: tours by appointment. 20F. ☎ 01 43 99 82 80 or ☎ 01 47 40 14 14.

Guided tours of the town 🄰 – Contact the tourist office.

Calèche rides – Departure from place de la Cathédrale daily at 10.30am, noon, 2.30pm and 5.30pm for a trip through the old streets of the city with a commentary by Jean-Claude Brialy. Fixed price for 1 to 3 people 180F, 50F for each extra passenger. ☎ 03 44 53 83 11.

Église St-Pierre – Guided tours by appointment. Contact the tourist office.

Ancien Château royal – Guided tours (1hr) daily except Tues 10am-noon, 2-6pm, Wed 2-6pm (Nov to Jan: 5pm). Closed 1 Jan, 1 May and 25 Dec. 16F. ☎ 03 44 53 00 80 (ext 1315).

Musée d'Art et d'Archéologie – Daily except Tues and Wed mornings 10am-noon, 2-6pm (Nov to Jan: 5pm), last admission 1hr before closing. Closed 1 Jan, 1 May and 25 Dec. 16F (ticket combined with the Musée de l'hôtel de Vermandois). ☎ 03 44 53 00 80 (ext 1247).

Musée des Spahis – Daily except Tues and Wed mornings 10am-noon, 2-6pm (Nov to Jan: 5pm). Closed 1 Jan, 1 May and 25 Dec. 16F (ticket combined with the Musée de la Vénerie). ☎ 03 44 53 00 80 (ext 1315).

Musée de la Vénerie – Guided tours daily except Tue 1àam-noon, 2-6pm, Wed 2-6pm (Nov to Jan closes at 5pm). Closed 1 Jan, 1 May, 25 Dec. 16F. ☎ 03 44 53 00 80 (ext 1315).

Musée de l'hôtel de Vermandois – As for the Musée d'Art et d'Archéologie. ☎ 03 44 53 00 80 (ext 1219).

Chapelle Royale St-Frambourg – May to Oct: Sat-Sun and public holidays 3-6pm; Nov to Apr: Sun 3-5pm. 20F. ☎ 03 44 53 39 99.

Ancienne abbaye St-Vincent – Tour of the outside Sat-Sun and school holidays 9am-5pm.

Excursions

Pont-Ste-Maxence: Abbaye du Moncel – Guided tours (1hr) daily except Tues 10am-noon, 2-6pm. Closed mid-Dec to beginning of Jan. 35F (children 15F). ☎ 03 44 72 33 98.

Baron: Church – Guided tours by appointment with the presbytery, 3 rue du Cimetière, 60300 Baron. ☎ 03 44 54 25 48.

Versigny: Château – July and Sept: 2-6.30pm. No charge. ☎ 03 44 88 07 29.

Fourcheret: barn – Visits by appointment. Contact Mr Patria. ☎ 03 44 54 20 66.

SÈVRES

Musée National de Céramique – ♿ Daily except Tues 10am-5pm. Closed public holidays. 22F, no charge 1st Sun of the month. ☎ 01 41 14 04 20.

Maison des Jardies – Guided tours (45min) Thur and Fri at 2.30pm and 4.30pm. Closed 1 May, 25 Dec and public holidays. 25F. ☎ 01 45 34 61 22.

SOISSONS   🛈 16 place Fernand-Marquigny – 02200 – ☎ 03 23 53 17 37

Guided tours of the town 🅰 – Contact the tourist office.

Ancienne abbaye de St-Jean-des-Vignes – 8am-noon, 1.30-6pm, Sat-Sun and public holidays 9am-noon, 1.30-6pm. Closed 1 Jan, 1 May, 12 June, 14 July, 1 Nov and 25 Dec. No charge. ☎ 03 23 53 58 80.

Musée municipal de l'ancienne abbaye de St-Léger – July and Aug: daily except Tues 10am-6pm; Sept to June: daily except Tues 10am-noon, 2-5pm. Closed 1 Jan, 1 May, Whitsun, 14 July, 1 Nov, 25 Dec. No charge. ☎ 03 23 59 15 90.

Abbaye de St-Médard: Crypt – Daily by request at the municipal tourist office.

La baie de SOMME

Chemin de fer de la baie de Somme – Trains depart from Crotoy and St-Valery Apr to end of Sept: Wed, Sat-Sun and public holidays at 3.30pm (July and Aug: daily except Mon). Departure from St-Valery at 10.45am: Apr to end of Sept: Sun and public holidays (mid-July to mid-Aug: daily except Mon and Tues), from Crotoy at noon and from Cayeux at 3.30pm (July and Aug: Wed, Sat-Sun and public holidays). From 35F to 66F return according to the length of the trip and age. Diesel engine at Cayeux and steam engine at St-Valery and Crotoy. Bicycles are carried free of charge. ☎ 03 22 26 96 96.

Maison de l'Oiseau – ♿ End of Feb to mid-Nov: 10am-6pm (July and Aug: 7pm), last admission 1hr before closing. 59F, 39F low season (children 42F/28F). ☎ 03 22 26 93 93.

Birds of prey in flight – Apr to end of Aug: 3 shows (45min) at 11.30am, 2.30pm and 4.30pm; Sept to Oct: by request at 11.30am and 3.30pm.

La Vallée de la Somme

Bray-sur-Somme: Church – Guided tours available, contact Mr Vast. ☎ 03 22 76 04 79.

Parc Samara: Park – Mid-Mar to mid-Nov: 9.30am-5.30pm, Sat-Sun and public holidays 9.30am-6.30pm (July and Aug: 10am-7.30pm). 59F (children 45F). ☎ 03 22 51 82 83.

Hangest-sur-Somme: Church – Contact the town hall (daily except Wed and Sun 3-6pm, Sat 9am-noon). ☎ 03 22 51 12 37.

Picquigny: castle – July and Aug: guided tours (1hr 15min) daily except Mon at 11am, 3pm and 4.30pm; May to June and beginning of Sept to mid-Sept: Sat-Sun and public holidays at 3pm and 4.30pm. 20F. ☎ 03 22 51 46 85.

T

THOIRY

Château – ✆ Mayto beginning of Sept: 2-6pm; beginning of Sept to mid-Nov: 2-5pm; Feb to Apr: 2-5pm, Sun and public holidays: 2-5.30pm. 28F (children 22F). ☎ 01 34 87 40 67.

Zoo and botanical park – ♿ May to beginning of Sept: 10am-6pm; Feb to Apr: 10am-5pm; Nov to Dec: 11am-5pm. 105F (children 79F). ☎ 01 34 87 40 67.

African wildlife park – ♿ 10am-5pm. 105F (children 79F) including admission to the zoo. ☎ 01 34 87 40 67.

Le TOUQUET

Museum – Daily except Tues 10am-noon, 2-6pm, Sun and public holidays 10am-noon, 2.30-6pm. Closed public holidays. 20F. ☎ 03 21 05 62 62.

V

VALENCIENNES   🛈 1 rue Askievre – 59300 – ☎ 03 27 46 22 99

Église St-Géry – Guided tours. Ask at the presbytery. ☎ 03 27 46 22 04.

Musée des Beaux-Arts – ♿ Daily except Tues 10am-6pm, Thur 10am-8pm. Closed 1 Jan, 1 May, Mon following the 2nd Sun in Sept and 25 Dec. 20F, no charge 1st Sunday in the month. ☎ 03 27 22 57 20.

Bibliothèque des Jésuites – Tues and Thur 2-6.30pm, Wed and Sat 10am-noon, 2-6.30pm, Fri 10am-8pm. Guided tours by appointment Sat at 11am. ☎ 03 27 22 57 00.

Excursions

Sebourg: Church – Guided tours by request. ☎ 03 27 26 51 87 (Mr Heuclin) or ☎ 03 27 26 51 91 (Mr Dezobry).

Bruay-sur-l'Escaut: Church – By request at the presbytery. ☎ 03 27 47 60 89.

Abbaye de VALLOIRES

Apr to mid-Nov: guided tours (45min) 10am-noon, 2-6pm (Oct to mid-Nov: 5pm). 30F. ☎ 03 22 29 62 33.

Valloires gardens – Mid-Mar to early Nov: 10am-5pm (May to beginning of Sept: 6.30pm). 39F. ☎ 03 22 23 53 55.

Excursion

Buire-le-Sec: Musée des marionnettes du Monde – ♿ Summer school holidays: Wed-Fri 5-6.30pm, Sat-Sun and public holidays 2.30-6.30pm; zone B Easter school holidays: Wed-Sun 2.30-6.30pm; Apr to June: Sat-Sun and public holidays 2.30-6.30pm. No charge. Demonstrations (manipulation of puppets) and shows can be reserved (price information not provided). ☎ 03 21 81 80 34.

Château de VAUX-LE-VICOMTE

Mid-Mar to 11 Nov: 10am-1pm, 2-6pm, Sat-Sun and public holidays 10am-6pm; May to end Sept: candlelight visit Thur and Sat 8pm-midnight. 63F (château, garden and carriage museum), 80F (candlelight evening). ☎ 01 64 14 41 90. Internet site: www.vaux-le-vicomte.com

Musée des Équipages – As for the gardens.

Gardens – ♿ Mid-Mar to 11 Nov: 10am-6pm; May to end of Sept: candlelight visit Thur and Sat 8pm-midnight. 30F (garden and carriage museum). ☎ 01 64 14 41 90.

Château de VERSAILLES   🛈 7 rue des Réservoirs – 78000 – ☎ 01 39 50 36 22

Guided tours of the town 🅰 – Contact the tourist office.

Château:

The château and its surrounding areas – The courtyards and gardens of the château, the Trianon and the park (23F for cars) are open daily from dawn to dusk. An entrance fee is charged for visits to the château gardens during the Musical Fountain events (July and Aug: Sat 1-5pm; Apr to Oct: Sun 1-5pm).

Musée des Carrosses – Mar to end of Nov: Sat-Sun 2-5.30pm (May to Sept: 6.30pm). 12F (under 18's no charge). ☎ 01 30 83 77 88.

Château de VERSAILLES

Tour of the Grands Appartements – Daily except Mon 9am-6.30pm (Oct to Apr: 5.30pm), last admission 30min before closing. 45F (35F Tues to Sun from 3.30pm). ☎ 01 30 83 76 20.

Tour of the king's chamber – Audio tours (1hr) daily except Mon 9am-4.30pm (May to Sept: 5.30pm). 25F (there is also a variable entrance fee according to age, which gives access to the Grands Appartements). ☎ 01 30 83 78 00.

Lecture-tours – Daily except Mon, visitors must book on the day of the visit. Entrance D. Lecture-tours 1hr (25F – extra cost to be added to the 45F entrance fee) 1hr 30min (37F), 2hr (50F). ☎ 01 30 83 77 88.

Les Grandes Heures du Parlement – Daily except Sun and Mon 9am-6.30pm (Oct to Apr: 5.30pm), last admission 1hr before closing. Closed 1 Jan, 1 May and 25 Dec. 20F. ☎ 01 39 25 70 70.

Parc du château de VERSAILLES

Discovery tour of the wooded areas – Guided tours (1hr 15min) of the wooded areas daily, except Sat-Sun during the Musical Fountains event, 10.30am-3.30pm (summer: 5pm). 20F, take some small change (5F, 10F and 20F) for the automatic ticket machines. ☎ 01 30 83 77 80.

Tourist train – Tour of the park (40min) with a stop at the Trianon. Departure from the Parterre du Nord of the château. Mar to Apr: 10.30am-5pm; May to Aug: 10am-6.15pm; Sept: 10.30am-6.15pm; Nov: 11am-4.30pm; Dec to Feb: call for information. 33F (children 21F). ☎ 01 39 54 22 00.

Bicycle rental – There are three rental points in the park from Feb to end of Nov: near to the Grand Canal daily (except in rainy weather) 10am-6.30pm, 32F for 1hr; at the entrance to the Grille de la Reine and the Porte de St Antoine: Wed 1-6.30pm, Sat-Sun and public holidays 10.30am-6.30pm (July and Aug: 1-6.30pm, Sat-Sun and public holidays 10am-6.30pm), 27F for 1hr. ☎ 01 39 66 97 66.

Boat hire – Mar to end of Oct: 10am-6.30pm. 72F (1hr, boat for 4 people), 52F (30min) ☎ 01 39 66 97 66.

Grand and Petit Trianon – Apr to Oct: noon-6.30pm (last admission 30min before closing); Nov to Mar: noon-5.30pm. Grand Trianon 25F, Petit Trianon 15F, combined ticket 30F. ☎ 01 30 83 76 20.

Ville de VERSAILLES

Bibliothèque Municipale – Occasional lecture-tours of the rooms, contact the tourist office.

Salle du Jeu de Paume – May to end of Sept: Sat-Sun 2-5pm. No charge. ☎ 01 30 83 77 88.

Musée Lambinet – ♿ Tues and Thur 2-5.45pm, Wed 1-5.45pm, Fri 2-4.45pm, Sat-Sun 2-5.45pm. Closed public holidays. 30F. ☎ 01 39 50 30 32.

Excursion

Arboretum National de Chèvreloup: Apr to mid-Nov: Sat-Mon 10am-6pm (last admission 5pm). Closed 1 May. 15F. ☎ 01 39 55 53 80.

VILLENEUVE-D'ASCQ

Guided tours

On foot – Departure at 2.30pm;

By bicycle – Departure at 9.30am from the Château de Flers. Ask at the tourist office for prices and meeting times.

Château de Flers – Call for information. ☎ 03 20 43 55 56.

Musée d'Art moderne – ♿ Daily except Tues 10am-6pm. Closed 1 Jan, 1 May and 25 Dec. 43F, no charge 1st Sunday in the month 10am-2pm. ☎ 03 20 19 68 68.

Musée des moulins – Guided tours (45min to 2hr) daily except Sat and public holidays 2-5pm, Sun 3-6pm. Closed mid-Dec to mid-Jan. 30F. ☎ 03 20 05 49 34.

Musée du Terroir – June to Sept: daily except Mon 2.30-6pm, Sun 9.30am-1pm, 2.30-6pm; mid-Mar to end of May, Oct and Nov: Tues-Thur, 2nd and 4th Sun in the month, and public holidays 2.30-5.30pm, Sun 9.30am-1pm; beginning of Dec to mid-Mar: Sun 9.30am-1pm. 15F. ☎ 03 20 91 87 57.

VILLERS-COTTERÊTS

Musée Alexandre-Dumas – ♿ Daily except Tues 2.30-5pm (last admission 45min before closing). Closed public holidays and last Sun in the month. 20F. ☎ 03 23 96 23 30.

Château – Guided tours (45min) daily except Tues at 10.30am, 2.30pm and 4pm. Closed 1 Jan, 1 May and 25 Dec. 20F. ☎ 03 23 96 55 10.

Excursions

Montgobert: Musée du Bois et de l'Outil – Mar to end of Oct: Sat-Sun and public holidays 2-6pm (July and Aug: daily). 20F. ☎ 03 23 96 36 69.

Mémorial canadien de VIMY

Tunnel Storehouses – Apr to end of Nov: guided tours (30min) 10am-5.30pm; unaccompanied visits all year round of the historical interpretation centre, memorial and trenches. No charge. ☎ 03 21 48 72 29.

Useful French words and phrases

ARCHITECTURAL TERMS

See the ABC of Architecture in the Introduction

SIGHTS

abbaye	abbey
arc-boutant	flying buttress
beffroi	belfry
chapelle	chapel
cimetière	cemetery
cloître	cloisters
cour	courtyard
couvent	convent
écluse	lock (canal)
église	church
gothique	Gothic
halle	covered market
jardin	garden
mairie	town hall
maison	house
marché	market
monastère	monastery
moulin	windmill
musée	museum
place	square
pont	bridge
port	port/harbour
quai	quay
remparts	ramparts
romain	Roman
roman	Romanesque
tour	tower

NATURAL SITES

barrage	dam
belvédère	viewpoint
cascade	waterfall
corniche	ledge
côte	coast, hillside
étang	pond/mere
falaise	cliff
forêt	forest
grotte	cave
lac	lake
marais	marsh
plage	beach
rivière	river
ruisseau	stream
signal	beacon
source	spring
vallée	valley

ON THE ROAD

car park	parking
diesel	diesel/gazole
driving licence	permis de conduire
east	Est
garage (for repairs)	garage
left	gauche
LPG	GPL
motorway/highway	autoroute
north	Nord
parking meter	horodateur
petrol/gas	essence
petrol/gas station	station essence
right	droite
roundabout	rond-point
south	Sud
toll	péage
traffic lights	feu tricolore
tyre	pneu
unleaded	sans plomb
west	Ouest
wheel clamp	sabot
zebra crossing	passage clouté

TIME

today	aujourd'hui
tomorrow	demain
yesterday	hier
winter	hiver
spring	printemps
summer	été
autumn/fall	automne
week	semaine
Monday	lundi
Tuesday	mardi
Wednesday	mercredi
Thursday	jeudi
Friday	vendredi
Saturday	samedi
Sunday	dimanche

NUMBERS

0	zéro	10	dix	20	vingt
1	un	11	onze	30	trente
2	deux	12	douze	40	quarante
3	trois	13	treize	50	cinquante
4	quatre	14	quatorze	60	soixante
5	cinq	15	quinze	70	soixante-dix
6	six	16	seize	80	quatre-vingts
7	sept	17	dix-sept	90	quatre-vingt-dix
8	huit	18	dix-huit	100	cent
9	neuf	19	dix-neuf	1 000	mille

SHOPPING

antiseptic	antiseptique	newsagent, bookshop	librairie
bank	banque	open	ouvert
bakery	boulangerie	painkiller	analgésique
big	grand	plaster (adhesive)	pansement adhésif
butcher shop	boucherie	post office	poste
chemist's/drugstore	pharmacie	pound (half kilo)	livre
closed	fermé	push	pousser
cough mixture	sirop pour la toux	pull	tirer
entrance	entrée	shop	magasin
exit	sortie	small	petit
fishmonger's	poissonnerie	stamps	timbres
grocer's	épicerie		

FOOD AND DRINK

beef	bœuf	lunch	déjeuner
beer	bière	lettuce salad	salade
butter	beurre	meat	viande
bread	pain	mineral water	eau minérale
breakfast	petit-déjeuner	mixed salad	salade composée
cheese	fromage	mussels	moules
chicken	poulet	orange juice	jus d'orange
dessert	dessert	oysters	huîtres
dinner	diner	plate	assiette
duck	canard	pork	porc
eel	anguille	red wine	vin rouge
fish	poisson	salt	sel
fork	fourchette	sparkling water	eau gazeuse
fruit	fruits	spoon	cuillère
glass	verre	still water	eau plate
ham	jambon	sugar	sucre
ice cream	glace	tap water	eau du robinet
ice cubes	glaçons	turkey	dinde
jug of water	carafe d'eau	vegetables	légumes
jug of wine	pichet de vin	white wine	vin blanc
knife	couteau	yoghurt	yaourt
lamb	agneau		

PERSONAL DOCUMENTS AND TRAVEL

airport	aéroport	shuttle	navette
credit card	carte de crédit	the Shuttle	le Shuttle
customs	douane	suitcase	valise
passport	passeport	train/plane ticket	billet de train/d'avion
platform	voie	wallet	portefeuille
railway station	gare		

CLOTHING

coat	manteau	socks	chaussettes
jumper	pull	stockings	bas
raincoat	imperméable	suit	costume /tailleur
shirt	chemise	tights	collant
shoes	chaussures	trousers	pantalon

USEFUL PHRASES

goodbye	au revoir
hello/good morning	bonjour
excuse me	excusez-moi, pardon
thank you	merci
yes/no	oui/non
please	s'il vous plaît
Do you speak English?	Parlez-vous anglais?
I don't understand	Je ne comprends pas
Talk slowly	Parlez lentement
Where's...?	Où est...?
When does the ... leave?	A quelle heure part...?
When does the ... arrive?	A quelle heure arrive...?

When does the museum open?	A quelle heure ouvre le musée?
When is breakfast served?	A quelle heure sert-on le petit-déjeuner?
What does it cost?	Combien cela coûte?
Where is the nearest petrol/gas station?	Où se trouve la station essence la plus proche?
Where can I change traveller's cheques?	Où puis-je échanger des traveller's cheques?
Where are the toilets?	Où sont les toilettes?
Do you accept credit cards?	Acceptez-vous les cartes de crédit?
I need a receipt.	Je voudrais un reçu.

Index

Notes